COMPLETE

COMPUTERS
Information Technology in Perspective
TWELFTH EDITION

LARRY LONG • NANCY LONG

COMPUTERS

Information Technology in Perspective

TWELFTH EDITION

LARRY LONG • NANCY LONG

PEARSON

Prentice Hall

Pearson Education International

Vice President/Publisher: Natalie Anderson
Executive Acquisitions Editor: Jodi McPherson
Senior Marketing Manager: Emily Williams Knight
Marketing Assistant: Nicole Beaudry
Associate Director, IT Product Development: Melonie Salvati
Project Manager, Supplements: Melissa Edwards
Development Editors: Christine Wright and Jodi Bolognese
Senior Media Project Manager: Cathi Profitko
Editorial Assistants: Jodi Bolognese, Jasmine Slowik, and Alana Meyers
Production Manager: Gail Steier de Acevedo
Project Manager, Production: Tim Tate
Manufacturing Buyer: Tim Tate
Associate Director, Multimedia Production: Karen Goldsmith
Manager, Print Production: Christy Mahon
Design Manager: Maria Lange
Art Director: Pat Smythe
Cover Design: Kevin Kall, Bob Prokop
Cover Photo: Toshiba America Information Systems, Inc.
Interior Design: Lorraine Castellano
Interior Illustrator: Kenneth Batelman
Full Service Composition: Black Dot Group/An AGT Company
Printer/Binder: Courier Kendallville, Inc.
Cover Printer: Phoenix Color Corporation

Credits and acknowledgments borrowed from other sources and reproduced, with permission, in this textbook appear on appropriate page within text.

Pearson Education LTD.
Pearson Education Singapore, Pte. Ltd
Pearson Education, Canada, Ltd
Pearson Education–Japan
Pearson Education Australia PTY, Limited
Pearson Education North Asia Ltd
Pearson Educación de Mexico, S.A. de C.V.
Pearson Education Malaysia, Pte. Ltd
Pearson Education Upper Saddle River, New Jersey

10 9 8 7 6 5 4 3
ISBN 0-13-127314-0

To our children,

Troy and Brady,

The motivation for all we do.

IT Ethics and Issues, Personal Computing, and Crystal Ball Special Interest Items

ACKNOWLEDGMENTS

Any introductory book, especially this twelfth edition of *Computers* and its many mixed-media ancillaries, is a major undertaking involving many talented people. Each year, my friends and colleagues at Prentice Hall do an amazing job of articulating the focus of the book, supporting us during the writing process, and, ultimately, blending over a thousand separate elements of text and imagery into a beautiful and effective college textbook. These professionals should be very proud of *Computers,* for it is their book, too. Jodi McPherson, Jodi Bolognese, Natalie E. Anderson, Melissa Edwards, Cathi Profitko, and Jasmine Slowik comprise a committed team with unparalleled in-depth knowledge of the industry, in general, and in IT. "Jodi B." and development editor Christine Wright's intimate knowledge of the market, past editions, and the manuscript enabled them to provide critical, at times revolutionary, feedback at every stage of the writing and production process.

The quality of the production is evident and for that, we thank Tim Tate, Gail Steier de Acevedo, Melonie Salvati, and their colleagues. Karen Goldsmith, Christy Mahon and their colleagues do wonders with our Web and mixed-media supplements. The art and design is beautiful, thanks to Pat Smythe, Maria Lange, Kenneth Batelman, and Lorraine Castellano. Our book is made all the better with continuous feedback from Emily Knight and Nicole Beaudry in marketing. In addition, we would like to thank Sandy Reinhard, Kate Johnson, and Caryl Wenzel for diligence in the production process.

We would like to thank those who created key ancillaries for *Computers*: Tony Nowakowski of Buffalo State College (Interactive Study Guide and Test Item File), Stephanie Jones of South Plains College (Instructor's Resource Manual and content for WebCT and Blackboard online courses), and Steve St. John of Tulsa Community College (PowerPoint slides).

The feedback from numerous college professors has proven invaluable in refining this new edition to better serve their course needs. We would like to extend our heartfelt gratitude to these professors for their insight on this and previous editions of *Computers*.

11th and this Edition:
Dr. Nazih Abdallah, UCF-SEECS
Michael Carrington, Northern Virginia Community College
David Evans, Pasadena City College
Jonathan Gregory, Oklahoma Wesleyan University
Robert Heinrich, Richard Stockton College of New Jersey
Jeffrey M. Howard, Finger Lakes Community College
Jason Y. Huh, Pasadena City College
Rebecca A. Mundy, University of Southern California
Rob Murray, Ivy Tech State College
Jennifer Pickle, Amarillo College
Teresa Tegeler, Illinois Eastern Community College
Dr. Sam R. Thangiah, Slippery Rock University
Vahid Zardoost, Pasadena City College

9th and 10th Edition:

 Dr. David Bannon, Wake Technical Community College
 Cheryl Cunningham, Embry-Riddle Aeronautical University
 Dr. Charles Foltz, East Carolina University
 Dr. Homa Ghajar, Oklahoma State University
 Nancy Grant, Community College of Allegheny County
 Rob Murray, Ivy Tech State College
 Henry Wardak, Everett Community College
 Lynn Wermers, North Shore Community College

7th and 8th Editions:

 Home Ghajar, Oklahoma State University
 Nancy Grant, Community College of Allegheny County South Campus
 LindaLee Massoud, Mott Community College
 Gloria Melara, California State University at Northridge
 Behrooz Saghafi, Chicago State University
 Ruth Schmitz, University of Nebraska at Kearney
 Robert Spear, Prince George's Community College

6th Edition:

 Jeanann Boyce, University of Maryland
 Nancy Cosgrove, University of Central Florida
 Wendell Dillard, Arkansas State University
 Barbara Ellestad, Montana State University
 Dan Everett, University of Georgia
 Shirley Fedorovich, Embry-Riddle Aeronautical University
 Tom Gorecki, Charles County Community College
 Ken Griffin, University of Central Arkansas
 Cindy Hanchey, Oklahoma Baptist University
 Wayne Headrick, New Mexico State University
 Suzanne Konieczny, Marshall University
 Doug K. Lauffer, Community College of Beaver County
 Rajiv Malkan, Montgomery College
 Gary Mattison, Strayer College
 Dori McPherson, Schoolcraft College
 Carol Mull, Asheville-Buncombe Technical Community College
 Dr. Emmanuel Opara, Prairie View A&M University
 Rick Parker, College of Southern Idaho
 Judy Scholl, Austin Community College
 Marian Schwartz, North Central Technical College

5th Edition:

 Amir Afzal, Strayer College
 Gary R. Armstrong, Shippensburg University
 Shira L. Broschat, Washington State University
 James Frost, Idaho State University
 Jorge Gaytan, University of Texas, El Paso
 Helene Kershner, SUNY, Buffalo
 Ruth Malmstrom, Raritan Valley Community College
 Michael A. McNeece, Strayer College
 John F. Sharlow, Eastern Connecticut State University
 John Stocksen, Kansas City Kansas Community College

4th Edition:
Suzanne Baker, Lakeland Community College
Amanda Bounds, Florida Community College at Jacksonville
Don Cartlidge, New Mexico State University (emeritus)
Stephanie Chenault, The College of Charleston
Eli Cohen, Wichita State University
William Cornette, Southwest Missouri State University
Timothy Gottlebeir, North Lake College
Vernon Griffin, Austin Community College
Sandra Brown, Finger Lakes Community College
Mike Michaelson, Palomar College
Domingo Molina, Texas Southmost College
Joseph Morrell, Metropolitan State College of Denver
Patricia Nettnin, Finger Lakes Community College
Anthony Nowakowski, State University of New York College at Buffalo
Michael Padbury, Arapahoe Community College
Carl Ubelacker, Cincinnati State Technical and Community College

3rd Edition:
Amir Afzal, Strayer College
Carl Clavadetscher, California Polytechnic State University, Pomona
Ray Fanselau, American River College
Dr. Diane Fischer, Dowling College
Barry Floyd, California Polytechnic State University, San Luis Obispo
Fred Homeyer, Angelo State University
James Johnson, Valencia Community College
Peter Irwin, Richland College
Dr. Adolph Katz, Fairfield University
Constance Knapp, Pace University
Robert Keim, Arizona State University
Dr. John Sanford, Philadelphia College of Textiles and Science
Al Schroeder, Richland College
Dr. Diane Visor, University of Central Oklahoma

2nd Edition:
Michael J. Belgard, Bryant and Stratton College
Roy Bunch, Chemeketa Community College
Marvin Daugherty, Indiana Vocational Technical College
Joyce Derocher, Bay de Noc Community College
Kirk L. Gibson, City College of San Francisco
Randy Goldberg, Marist College
Don Hall, Manatee Community College
Seth Hock, Columbus State Community College
Dr. M. B. Kahn, California State University at Long Beach
Michael A. Kelly, City College of San Francisco
Constance K. Knapp, CSP, Pace University
Sandra Lehmann, Moraine Park Technical College
William McTammany, Florida Community College at Jacksonville
Margaret J. Moore, Coastal Carolina Community College
Thomas H. Miller, University of Idaho
Anne L. Olsen, Wingate College
Verale Phillips, Cincinnati Technical College
Mark Seagroves, Wingate College
Bari Siddique, Texas Southmost College
Dr. Joseph Williams, University of Texas at Austin
Larry B. Wintermeyer, Chemeketa Community College
Floyd Jay Winters, Manatee Community College

1st Edition:

Sally Anthony, San Diego State University
Harvey Blessing, Essex Community College
Wayne Bowen, Black Hawk Community College
Michael Brown, DeVry Institute of Technology, Chicago
J. Patrick Fenton, West Valley College
Ken Griffin, University of Central Arkansas
Nancy Harrington, Trident Technical College
Grace C. Hertlein, California State University
Shirley Hill, California State University
Cynthia Kachik, Santa Fe Community College
Sandra Lehmann, Morraine Park Technical Institute
Michael Lichtenstein, DeVry Institute of Technology, Chicago
Dennis Martin, Kennebec Valley Vocational Technical Institute
William McDaniel, Jr., Northern Virginia Community College at Alexandria
Edward Nock, DeVry Institute of Technology, Columbus
Lewis Noe, Ivy Technical Institute
Frank O'Brien, Milwaukee Technical College
Alvin Ollenburger, University of Minnesota
Beverly Oswalt, University of Central Arkansas
James Phillips, Lexington Community College
Nancy Roberts, Lesley College
Richardson Siebert, Morton College
Bob Spear, Prince George's Community College
Thomas Voight, Franklin University

Finally, we wish to thank the professionals from over 100 companies who have contributed resources (information, photos, software, and images) to this book and its supplements.

Larry and Nancy Long

LARRY AND NANCY LONG

For the past 25 years, **Larry and Nancy Long** have worked as a team to create innovative information technology learning resources for all types of media—textbook, software, video, and online. Larry, an engineer and scientist, and Nancy, a reading specialist, have collaborated to author numerous books for both the academic and professional markets on topics ranging from IT concepts to strategic planning.

Larry has served as an IT consultant to all levels of management in virtually every major type of industry. He has over 25 years of classroom experience at IBM, the University of Oklahoma, Lehigh University, and the University of Arkansas. He received his Ph.D., M.S., and B.S. degrees in Industrial Engineering at the University of Oklahoma and is a Professional Engineer.

Nancy has a decade of teaching and administrative experience at all levels of education: elementary, secondary, college, and continuing education. She received a Ph.D. in Reading Education and Educational Psychology, an M.S. in Personnel Services, and a B.S. in Elementary Education at the University of Oklahoma. Her wealth of knowledge in the areas of pedagogy and reading education is evident throughout the text.

Nancy, Larry, and their teenage sons, Troy and Brady, live in Fayetteville, Arkansas. Nancy is an active community volunteer. Larry enjoys coaching youth sports and is active with Rotary's international youth exchange program. In their spare time, they enjoy tennis, water sports, music, travel, and exploring the great outdoors.

PREFACE TO THE INSTRUCTOR

You, the teachers of introductory information technology courses, are scientists, historians, sociologists, psychologists, and more. In the same course you might toggle between lecture, lab, and, for some, distance learning via the Internet. You teach an ever-increasing body of IT knowledge to students with a wide range of career objectives and technical abilities. We understand and appreciate the challenges of the IT concepts course. Indeed, your challenges have been our motivation to create the text you need to provide a quality IT experience for your students. You have told us what you want and we have listened. Your requests and our responses are outlined below.

TELL THEM "WHY?"

Students want to know "Why?" They are motivated when they understand the relevance of a chapter or a specific topic and can relate that content to their personal experiences. *Why This Chapter Is Important to You* and *Why This Section Is Important to You* inspire commitment to learning.

KEEP IT CURRENT

Computers comes out in a new edition every year. Prentice Hall and we are committed to bringing you an IT concepts book that reflects the tempo of a rampaging technology. We are proud that your colleagues often point to *Computers* as the most up-to-date text.

MAKE IT INTERESTING

Computers and information technology can be fun topics. We generate interest by continually communicating the energy and excitement of IT to the student.

GIVE US FLEXIBILITY

Computers and its mixed-media teaching/learning system are organized to permit maximum flexibility in course design and in the selection, assignment, and presentation of material. Prentice Hall offers an extensive array of hands-on laboratory materials in support of *Computers*.

SELECT THE RIGHT CONTENT

We cover only that material which your colleagues have collectively deemed appropriate for modern IT competency.

MAKE THE LENGTH COMPATIBLE WITH THE ACADEMIC CALENDAR

Two versions, a brief version with seven chapters (one less than the last edition) and a full version with 10 chapters (two less than the last edition), are carefully designed to fit within the academic calendar.

BE CONSISTENT ON DEPTH OF COVERAGE

We present topics at depths consistent with introductory learning. Our focus is on information that will have an impact on the student's ability to flourish in our information society. We have been very careful to avoid information overkill.

GIVE US A WAY FOR OUR STUDENTS TO BEGIN CHAPTER 1 WITH CONFIDENCE

The students in an IT concepts course represent a broad spectrum of IT/computing knowledge. The very visual *Getting Started* section helps jumpstart the student's personal computing experience and enables leveling of IT understanding so that all students can read that first page with confidence.

COVER NET ISSUES ALONG WITH NET TECHNOLOGY

We are an interconnected society and it is our obligation to present the breadth of Internet applications, examine timely Internet issues, and gaze into the future of the Net.

COVER IT WITHIN THE CONTEXT OF SOCIETY

Just as IT is woven into the fabric of our society, IT ethics and issues are a continuing theme throughout *Computers*. Each chapter has a variety of IT Ethics and Issues scenarios and plenty of probing questions designed to spur lively in-class discussions.

MAKE IN-BOOK STUDY/REVIEW MATERIALS A PRIORITY

The comprehensive learning aids built into each chapter guide, complement, and assess learning. The extensive end-of-chapter material promotes student understanding and gives instructors plenty of assignment options.

PROVIDE AN ARRAY OF QUALITY SUPPLEMENTS

Computers is but one component of a comprehensive *mixed-media teaching/learning system* that is designed to give you maximum flexibility in course design and instruction.

STREAMLINE THE PRESENTATION

This edition of *Computers* is designed for faculty and students who want a book that presents important IT content in a straightforward manner without needless repetition and extraneous clutter. The result is a cleaner, more easily absorbed presentation.

GIVE US A BOOK THAT WORKS

In its 12th edition and its 20th year, you can be confident that *Computers* will work for your college, for you, and for your students.

WHAT'S NEW WITH THE TWELFTH EDITION OF *COMPUTERS*?

Computers, 12th edition, represents the most extensive revision of any Long and Long text. Information technology, curriculums, and student IT knowledge are in a dynamic swirl, so rather than "revise" *Computers* we decided to rebuild it. This 12th edition is our best attempt to reflect faculty consensus on *content, sequence,* and *depth of presentation*. Entire sections and chapters are cut, moved, added, and/or substantially revised to meet the needs of contemporary IT education. Moreover, the tenor of the book is changed to be more in tune with student expectations and interests. We think you will enjoy these and the many other progressive changes we've made to *Computers*.

FEWER BOLDFACE TERMS

Only terms that are relevant to introductory information technology are included. Our approach is to be realistic about the number of key terms we can expect a student to absorb and retain.

LESS VERBIAGE

In the rebuilt *Computers,* we have proven that concepts can be presented in an interesting and informative way, but with considerably fewer words.

EMPHASIS ON CRITICAL IT KNOWLEDGE

Our focus in this 12th edition is the everyday IT knowledge that students will need to thrive in our information society. For example, the "Personal Computing" sidebars offer many time- and money-saving hints that can enhance the student's personal computing experience.

PRESENTATIONS REVISED FOR EASE OF UNDERSTANDING

Every presentation, whether text or figure, was evaluated to determine if it could be presented in a more straightforward manner, without sacrifice to content.

QUICK START INTO CORE MATERIAL

The popular *Getting Started* section at the first of the book is restructured to get students up to speed and into the core material as quickly as possible.

EYE TO THE FUTURE

To help prepare students for the future, we have painted futuristic scenarios throughout the book in the running text and made intriguing predictions in the "Crystal Ball" sidebars. We feel that knowledge workers can be more effective if they have a good grasp of what to expect in the future.

STORAGE AND INPUT/OUTPUT IN A SINGLE CHAPTER

Today's college students are familiar with basic storage and I/O devices, so we decided to tighten the text and combine storage and input/output into one chapter.

CAREERS IN AN APPENDIX

"Careers" is an orphan topic that doesn't fit well into any traditional IT concepts chapter, so we placed the material that relates to careers and certifications in a convenient appendix. This gives instructors the flexibility to cover IT career options at any point in the course.

OFFICE SOFTWARE OVERVIEW ONLY

Recognizing that students already have been exposed to office productivity software and/or are learning these in a lab, we have reduced our coverage of this software to a cursory overview.

CONSOLIDATION OF TOPICS

We know when you begin a topic you want to finish it. We evaluated the entire book and consolidated like and/or orphan topics at the macro (input and output) and micro (buses and ports) levels.

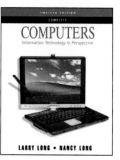

A *COMPUTERS* EDITION FOR EVERY COURSE

Computers comes in two editions.

The Brief Edition. Seven *core chapters,* plus a *Getting Started* section at the beginning of the book, introduce students to the world of information technology: concepts relating to interaction with computers; fundamental hardware, software, and communications concepts; going online (the Internet and its applications); and IT ethics, crime, and privacy. The brief book includes three colorful *IT Illustrated* modules: computer history, the making of integrated circuits, and a PC buyer's guide.

The Full Edition. The Full Edition is the Brief Edition plus three additional chapters and a "Careers" appendix. Chapter 8 introduces the student to e-commerce, database management, and IT security. A *two-chapter* sequence covers information systems concepts, programming, and emerging technologies, such as artificial intelligence and virtual reality.

THE COMPUTERS TEACHING/ LEARNING SYSTEM

Computers, 12th edition, continues the Long and Long tradition of having the most comprehensive, innovative, and effective support package on the market. The package includes a wealth of online learning tools that facilitate the teaching/learning process.

LONG AND LONG COMPANION WEBSITE *www.prenhall.com/long*

This text is accompanied by a Companion Website at **www.prenhall.com/long**. Features of this new site include an interactive study guide, downloadable supplements, online end-of-chapter materials, Internet Exercises, TechTV videos, Web resource links such as Careers in IT and crossword puzzles plus Technology Updates and Bonus Chapters on the latest trends and hottest topics in information technology. All links to Internet exercises are continuously updated to ensure accuracy for students.

The downloadable resources for faculty are dynamic, ever changing, and can also include supplementary PC exercises, supplementary images, applicable material contributed by colleagues, and other helpful teaching/learning aids.

ONLINE COURSE DEVELOPMENT AND MANAGEMENT

Prentice Hall provides the content and support you need to create and manage your own online course in *WebCT, Blackboard,* or Prentice Hall's own *CourseCompass*™. These online course development tools, along with embedded Long and Long content, offer you and your colleagues all the advantages of a custom-built program, but without the hassle. If you are considering offering all or part of your course via distance learning, then these tools can help you create, implement, and deliver a high-quality online course or course component with relative ease. If you already offer an online course, then these tools can assist you in formalizing your course.

These Web-course tools give you the flexibility to customize your online course by integrating your custom material with content from *Computers,* 12th edition. Content includes lecture material, interactive exercises, e-commerce case videos, additional testing questions and projects. Whether you are off and running or this is your first online course, these ready-to-go online course resources can save you countless hours of preparation and course administration time.

- *CourseCompass*™ *at* **www.coursecompass.com**. CourseCompass™ is a dynamic, interactive online course management tool powered by Blackboard. Best of all, Prentice Hall handles the hosting, the technical support, and the training so you can focus on your course by creating the best teaching and learning environment for both you and your students.

- *Blackboard at* **www.prenhall.com/blackboard**. Prentice Hall's abundant online content, combined with Blackboard's popular tools and interface, result in robust Web-based courses that are easy to implement, manage, and use—taking your courses to new heights in student interaction and learning.

- *WebCT at* **www.prenhall.com/webct**. Course-management tools within WebCT include page tracking, progress tracking, class and student management, gradebook, communication, calendar, reporting tools, and more.

INSTRUCTOR RESOURCES

The new and improved Prentice Hall Instructor's Resource CD-ROM includes the tools you expect from a Prentice Hall computer concepts text, like:

- The Instructor's Manual in Word and PDF formats
- Solutions to all questions and exercises from the book and Web site
- Multiple, customizable PowerPoint slide presentations for each chapter
- Computer concepts animations
- TechTV videos
- Image library of all of the figures from the text
- Test Bank with TestGen & Quizmaster Software

POWERPOINT SLIDES

This CD-ROM is an interactive library of assets and links. This CD writes custom "index" pages that can be used as the foundation of a class presentation or online lecture. By navigating through this CD, you can collect the materials that are most relevant to your interests, edit them to create powerful class lectures, copy them to your own computer's hard drive, and/or upload them to an online course management system.

TESTGEN SOFTWARE

TestGen Software: TestGen is a test generator that lets you view and easily edit test bank questions, transfer them to tests, and print in a variety of formats suitable to your teaching situation. The program also offers many options for organizing and displaying test banks and tests. A built-in random number and text generator makes it ideal for creating multiple versions of tests that involve calculations and provides more possible test items than test bank questions. Powerful search and sort functions let you easily locate questions and arrange them in the order you prefer.

QuizMaster, also included in this package, allows students to take tests created with TestGen on a local area network. The QuizMaster utility built into TestGen lets instructors view student records and print a variety of reports. Building tests is easy with TestGen, and exams can be easily uploaded into WebCT, Blackboard, and CourseCompass.

TRAINING AND ASSESSMENT *www2.phgenit.com/support*

Prentice Hall offers Performance Based Training and Assessment in one product—Train&Assess IT. The training component offers computer-based training that a student can use to preview, learn, and review Microsoft Office application skills. Web or CD-ROM delivered, Train IT offers interactive, multimedia, computer-based training to augment classroom learning. Built-in prescriptive testing suggests a study path based not only on student test results but also on the specific textbook chosen for the course.

TRAIN AND ASSESS IT

The Assessment component offers computer-based testing that shares the same user interface as Train IT and is used to evaluate a student's knowledge about specific topics in Word, Excel, Access, PowerPoint, Outlook, the Internet, Windows, Computer Concepts and much more. It does this in a task-oriented environment to demonstrate proficiency as well as comprehension of the topics by the students. More extensive than the testing in Train IT, Assess IT offers more administrative features for the instructor and additional questions for the student.

Assess IT also allows professors to test students out of a course, place students in appropriate courses, and evaluate skill sets.

TechTV VIDEOS

TechTV is the San Francisco-based cable network that showcases the smart, edgy and unexpected side of technology. By telling stories through the prism of technology, TechTV provides programming that celebrates its viewers' passion, creativity and lifestyle.

TechTV's programming falls into three categories:

1 **Help and Information**, with shows like *The Screen Savers*, TechTV's daily live variety show featuring everything from guest interviews and celebrities to product advice and demos, *Tech Live*, featuring the latest news on the industry's most important people, companies, products and issues, and *Call for Help*, a live help and how-to show providing computing tips and live viewer questions.

2 **Cool Docs**, with shows like *The Tech Of...*, a series that goes behind the scenes of modern life and shows you the technology that makes things tick, *Performance*, an investigation into

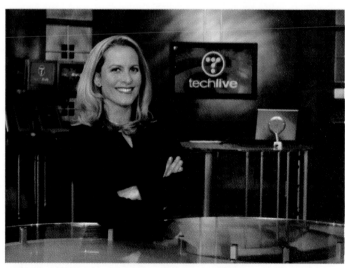

TECHTV VIDEOS TechLive reporter and computer security expert Becky Worley on the TechTV set

how technology and science are molding the perfect athlete, and *Future Fighting Machines*, a fascinating look at the technology and tactics of warfare.

3 Outrageous Fun, with shows like *X-Play*, exploring the latest and greatest in videogaming, and *Unscrewed with Martin Sargent*, a new late-night series showcasing the darker, funnier world of technology.

For more information, log onto **www.techtv.com** or contact your local cable or satellite provider to get TechTV in your area.

EXPLORE GENERATION IT
www.prenhall.com/exploreit

A Web and CD-ROM-based training program for computer competency, *EXPLORE IT,* includes a variety of interactive multimedia training modules, including Troubleshooting, Programming Logic, Mouse and Keyboard Basics, Databases, Building a Web Page, Hardware, Software, Operating Systems, Building a Network, and more.

EXPLORE Generation IT Lab

OTHER TEACHING/LEARNING RESOURCES

There is no slowdown to technological progress nor is there a slowdown between editions in Prentice Hall's commitment to providing timely teaching/learning resources. Prentice Hall is continually introducing new and updating existing teaching tools. For example, the handy *Compact Guide to Web Page Creation and Design*, a student favorite because it contains links to 250 interesting Web sites, is recently released in a new edition.

PREFACE TO THE STUDENT

Achieving information technology (IT) competency is the first step in a lifelong journey toward greater knowledge and interaction with more and better applications of IT. The material in this text and the accompanying course are designed to guide you toward IT competency so you can become:

- A participant in the information technology revolution.
- An intelligent consumer of PCs and related products.
- Better prepared to take advantage of Internet resources and services.
- Knowledgeable about a wide variety of software and services that can improve your productivity, give you much needed information, expand your intellectual horizons, and give you endless hours of enjoyment.

IT competency is your ticket to ride. Where you go, how fast you get there, and what you do when you arrive are up to you.

THE *COMPUTERS* LEARNING ASSISTANCE PACKAGE

Computers, 12th edition, is supported by a comprehensive mixed-media learning assistance package. The Long and Long Companion Website at **www.prenhall.com/long** includes *Online Exercises, Internet Links,* an *Interactive Study Guide,* and much more—all designed to help you learn about computers and information technology. Other online learning tools, videos, software, and so on are described in the Preface to the Instructor.

The following pages illustrate a variety of features and learning aids, which are built into each chapter. These can help you:

- Understand and retain information technology concepts and terminology
- Appreciate IT within the context of society
- Enhance your personal computing experience

BEFORE YOU BEGIN

Getting Started. This very visual Getting Started section at the beginning of the book helps to jumpstart your personal computing experience by introducing the essential information you need to get up and running.

AT THE BEGINNING OF THE CHAPTER

Learning Objectives. Provide a target for learning for each numbered section.

Why This Chapter Is Important to You. Offers compelling reasons why learning the material in this can help you achieve important life goals.

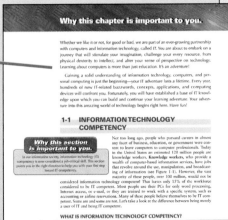

IN THE BODY OF THE CHAPTER

Section Self Check. Helps assess and reinforce your knowledge of the section's content (see the answers at the back of the book).

Numbered Section Heads. Numbered section heads provide an easy cross-reference to all related material in the book and in the supplements.

Why This Section Is Important to You. Answers the "Why this?" question for each numbered section.

TechTV Videos. Video clips you can view on the **www.prenhall.com/long** Web site that will enrich your understanding of chapter specific content.

Colorful Images. Images complement and illustrate IT concepts presented in the chapter text.

Personal Computing. Brief tips, hints, and recommendations to enliven your personal computing experience and make you a more effective user.

The Crystal Ball. Sidebar giving you to-the-point and timely predictions on information technology from 3 to 10 years into the future.

Memory Bits. These outlines of key points are positioned strategically to complement the running text.

Informative Illustrations. Figures and tables throughout the book help readers grasp and retain IT concepts.

THE END-OF-CHAPTER REVIEW MATERIAL

Chapter Summary. Overview of important points in the chapter.

Key Terms. Key terms with cross-references to the pages.

Matching. Match terms with concepts (see the answers at the back of the book).

Chapter Self-Check. More Self-Check questions for knowledge assessment (see the answers at the back of the book).

IT Ethics and Issues. Scenarios designed to encourage critical thinking and/or promote a lively in-class debate.

Focus on Personal Computing. Exercises designed to expand your personal computing horizons.

Online Exercises. Internet-based exercises at the Companion Website invite learning more about topics in this chapter and doing some just-for-fun surfing.

Discussion and Problem Solving. Questions that invite group discussion or individual/group problem solving.

IT ILLUSTRATED FEATURES

Colorful IT Illustrated Modules. IT Illustrated modules combine dynamic photos with in-depth discussions of interesting topics, such as the history of computing (left), how chips are made (bottom left), and a personal computing buyer's guide (bottom right).

GETTING STARTED

This Getting Started section is designed to give you a quick start on your adventure in computing and information technology. The emphasis here is on the essential concepts and terminology that you will need to know before you begin study of Chapter 1. Depending on your level of understanding and experience with computers and information technology, you may decide to carefully study this Getting Started section, skim it, or skip it altogether.

A COMPUTER SYSTEM
- The Personal Computer (PC): Desktop or Notebook?
- A Typical Computer System's Hardware

WORKING WITH WINDOWS
- The Boot Procedure
- The Shut Down Procedure
- Windows Wizards
- Running an Application from the Windows Desktop

SOFTWARE: POPULAR APPLICATIONS
- Word Processing
- Gaming

GOING ONLINE
- Networks
- The Internet and Internet Access
- Common Internet Applications

A Computer System

A computer system isn't as complex as you think. It has only four basic hardware components: *input*, *processor*, *output*, and *storage*. Each computer system can be outfitted with many different types of input and output (I/O), a variety of processors, and a wide array of storage devices. This section introduces the computer system plus its I/O, processing, and storage devices.

Desktop PC

Notebook PC

THE PERSONAL COMPUTER (PC): DESKTOP OR NOTEBOOK?

Most personal computers (PCs) are either a *desktop* PC or *notebook PC* (see Figure GS-1). The desktop PC can be found in every company and in most homes. The notebook PC, sometimes called a laptop PC, is a self-contained portable PC designed for use by mobile people.

Microphone

Speakers
(Stereo Sound)

Video Camera

Image Scanner

Multimedia Devices

Multimedia devices, which can be input and output, enable such applications as videophone, speech recognition, creating an electronic family photo album, and the playing of audio CDs. All personal computers are equipped with a *microphone* for audio input and *speakers* for audio output. The inexpensive *video camera* is a common multimedia input device. *Image scanners* work like copy machines except the scanning process produces a digitized image that can be manipulated by computers.

A TYPICAL COMPUTER SYSTEM'S HARDWARE

A wide range of input/output, processing, and storage devices can be attached to or installed inside a PC's system unit. Figure GS-2 shows devices commonly used with a computer system.

Common Input Devices

The most common input devices are the *mouse* and *keyboard*, which all PCs have for entering text and commands (for example, print document). The most commonly used is the *mouse;* however, other devices can aid you in navigating around the system. For example, many notebook PCs come with a touchpad.

FIGURE GS–2 COMPUTER SYSTEM DEVICES

Monitor   Printer

Keyboard   Mouse

Common Output Devices

A *monitor* displays temporary (soft copy) output, the result of some type of processing activity (for example, a report or an inquiry). A *printer* produces printed (hard copy) output.

The System Unit

Input and output devices are connected to a desktop PC's *system unit.* The system unit is the case plus the processing and permanent storage devices needed to operate the computer. The notebook PC is self-contained and houses the processing, storage, and several I/O functions. The *motherboard* is a single circuit board that includes the "chips"—the processor, temporary memory, and other *electronic components.* The *processor* is an electronic device that interprets instructions and performs the requested operations. The actual processor in a PC isn't much bigger than a postage stamp. Temporary memory holds instructions and data during processing operations. The *electronic bus* on the motherboard provides the electronic path through which the processor communicates with temporary memory, permanent storage components, and the various input/output devices.

Modem

Communications Devices

A *modem*, which may be internal (inside the system unit) or external (outside the system unit), provides a link to the Internet via a telephone line, digital TV cable, or satellite.

Hard disks   CD-ROM/DVD-ROM   DVD+RW/CD-RW Combination Drive   Floppy disk (diskette)

Storage Devices

The typical PC will have three types of permanent storage for data and software. The permanently installed *hard disk* is housed in the system unit. The typical system unit will also have a *floppy disk drive* and a *CD-ROM/ DVD+ROM drive* and/or a *DVD+RW/CD-RW combination* drive. Most commercial programs, such as Microsoft Office and music/audio CDs are distributed on CD-ROM discs. DVD movies are distributed on DVD discs. The *DVD+RW/CD-RW* drive enables "burning" of CDs and DVDs.

Software refers to a collective set of instructions, called *programs*, which can be interpreted by a computer. The programs cause the computer to perform desired functions and run *applications*, such as word processing or games. At the center of the software action is the *operating system*. It controls everything that happens in a computer. We interact with the PC via the operating system's user-friendly, "point-and-click" *graphical user interface (GUI)*. The operating system manages, maintains, and controls computer resources, such as processing and storage capabilities, and is, therefore, considered *system software*.

Microsoft Windows operating systems are installed on about 90% of the PCs in the world. Windows XP, the current version, is the basis for the examples used in this book. "Windows" is used as a collective reference to all Microsoft Windows operating systems.

FIGURE GS-3

BOOT PROCEDURE

1 Turn on the PC to begin the boot procedure.

2 A start-up program permanently stored in memory is run automatically. The start-up program performs a system check to verify that memory, electronic components, and I/O devices are operational. During the system check, the PC manufacturer's name, the name of the college/company, or other information is displayed on a "splash" screen.
If everything checks out, the program searches for the disk containing the operating system, usually the system's permanently installed hard disk. During the search process, you might hear the computer attempt to read from the floppy drive or the CD-ROM/DVD-ROM drive.

3 Upon finding the operating system, the start-up program loads it from disk storage to the computer's main memory, called *RAM*. Once loaded to RAM (random access memory), the operating system takes control of the system.

THE BOOT PROCEDURE

The *system startup* or *boot procedure* on almost any computer is straightforward—flip the power switch on the system unit to *on*. It is good practice to turn on needed input/output devices before turning on the computer. When you *power up* you also *boot* the system. See Figure GS-3.

4 Next, you are asked to choose a *user account* and enter a *password*. The *logon procedure* identifies you to the computer system and, possibly, a computer network and verifies that you are an authorized user.

5 In Windows, the boot procedure ends with the appearance of the Windows desktop, which is easily personalized with background images of your choice.

THE SHUT DOWN PROCEDURE

Unlike electrical appliances, computers are not simply turned off when you're finished using them. You must *shut down* your computer in an orderly manner before switching off the power. Shutting down involves an *exit routine,* exiting from all active applications before shutting off the power (click *File,* then *Exit* in the application program's menu). All programs have an *exit* routine that, if bypassed, can result in loss of user data and other problems (see Figure GS-4).

FIGURE GS-4

THE SHUT DOWN PROCEDURE

Choose Turn Off or Restart
The *Turn Off Computer* (or *Shut Down Windows*) dialog box appears on the desktop. A *dialog box* is a window that asks you to enter further information. Select *Turn Off* or *Restart* (to automatically reboot the system).

Start
Click the Start button to display the Start Menu

Select Turn Off Computer
Select *Turn Off Computer* (or *Shut Down*) from the Start Menu.

FIGURE GS-5   **THE ADD HARDWARE WIZARD**

WINDOWS WIZARDS

A *program* called a *wizard* is one of the most helpful features of the Windows operating system (see Figure GS-5). Windows provides wizards and many other *utility programs* that can help you with the day-to-day chores of maintaining a computer system. A wizard is a series of interactive dialog boxes that guide you through a variety of system-related processes, such as adding hardware or troubleshooting a problem. Wizards can also help you with other tasks, such as sending a fax (via your PC) or creating a Web site, resume, presentation, database, and so on. The wizard may ask you to choose from available options or enter specific information at each step.

RUNNING AN APPLICATION FROM THE WINDOWS DESKTOP

Any installed application can be launched (run, started, or opened) from the Windows desktop (see Figure GS-6).

Shortcut Icon
Click or double-click (tap left mouse button once or twice, respectively) on a shortcut icon (with embedded arrow) to run the application represented by the icon.

Desktop
The screen upon which Start button, icons, windows, and so on are displayed is known as the *desktop*.

Background
The desktop background can be a color or a user-selected image, such as this sunset image.

Paint
Select the desired application (Paint, in the example) and click on it to run the application.

Start
Click the *Start* button to display the *Start Menu*, run or open *Programs*, or find *Help and Support*.

Program Menu
Select a program or program group (the Accessories program group in the example).

Accessories Menu
This submenu lists the programs in the *Accessories submenu*.

Taskbar
The *taskbar* includes the Start button and shows what applications are running.

FIGURE GS-6

RUNNING AN APPLICATION

**Minimize Button, Maximize/
Restore Button, Close Button**
 Click the Minimize button to shrink the active window to a button in the taskbar.
or Click the Maximize/Restore button to fill the screen or restore the window to its previous size.
Click the Close button to close (exit) the application.

Menu Bar
The *menu bar* lists the menus available for that application. Select *File*, then *Open* to open and display a particular file, in this case "Horseshoe at Niagara Falls with rainbow.jpg."

Title Bar
The *title bar* at the top of each window shows the name of the application and current document.

Pull-Down Menu
A menu bar selection is pulled down.

Pop-Out Menu
Choosing a menu option with an arrow (◆) displays a pop-out menu.

Toolbar
Most applications have one or more toolbars that contain a group of buttons, each of which represents a frequently used menu option or command. Generally, toolbars display related user options (for example, formatting toolbar or drawing toolbar).

Application Window
Applications, such as Paint, are run in rectangular *application windows*.

Software: Popular Applications

Among the most popular types of applications software for personal computing are *word processing, gaming, e-mail, instant messaging,* and *Internet browsers.* It's quite possible that you will use all of these during your first or second time on a PC. E-mail, instant messaging, and Internet browsers will be discussed in the "Going Online" section. Word processing and gaming are the focus of this section.

Save
If you wish to work with the document later, you will need to give your document a name and save it to disk storage (*File, Save*).

Help
Click on *Help* to learn more about word processing and its features or get help with a task.

The Document
One or more word processing documents can be opened and displayed in the work area.

Format
Click *Format* to choose from a variety of options that you can use to make your document unique, including *Font* (typeface, size, and attribute) and *Paragraph* presentation.

Entering Text
Begin entering text from the keyboard at the text cursor position.

Text Cursor
The text cursor appears on the screen as a blinking vertical line and shows the location where you'll begin entering text.

Insert Images
You can insert images (*Insert, Picture, Clip Art,* or *From File*), such as the barn, and then resize and/or reposition them anywhere within the document.

Print Document
Click *File* then *Print* to print the document.

FIGURE GS-7

USING WORD PROCESSING

WORD PROCESSING

Word processing software, such as Microsoft Word (shown in Figure GS-7), lets you create, edit or revise, and format documents, which can be printed, displayed, posted to the Internet, e-mailed as attachments, faxed, and so on. *Document* refers to the information currently displayed in a software package's work area (the area in a window below the title bar or toolbar). When you create a document, you give it a name and save it to disk storage as a file, for example, "Newsletter.doc" (see the document name in the title bar). The three-letter extension to the right of the period denotes the type of file and/or associates the file with a particular program (for example, doc indicates a Microsoft Word file, and jpg indicates a specific type of image file).

GAMING

To put gaming software's popularity (see Figure GS-8) into perspective, the typical software retail outlet will devote up to 75% of their shelf space to PC-gaming software. Gaming can be you against the computer or you against others on the Internet, across town, or around the world. Computer games are given one of six ratings, ranging from "early childhood" to "adults only."

Action/Adventure
A large group of games place players in a fantasy world such as in *Jedi Knight II: Jedi Outcast* from Lucas Arts. In this genre, players run, leap, or climb to find entryways that let them progress to the next level. Along the way, they unlock mysteries so they can continue their journey and overcome evil people to reach an objective.

Edutainment
These games combine gaming and learning. In their quest to find the international sleuth, Carmen Sandiego, players learn about history, geography, and other topics.

Strategy
In strategy games, such as *Warcraft III-Reign of Chaos* from Blizzard, players become leaders who must collect and use their resources wisely to overcome their opponent, sometimes alien invaders.

RPG (Role Playing Game)
In RPG games, players take on a specific role, where they are at the epicenter of a fantasy that may involve war, betrayal, and faith, such as in *Neverwinter Nights* from BioWare. In their journey, players attain new skills and abilities by winning battles.

Racing
In racing games, such as *NASCAR 4* by Sierra, players "drive" cars, motorcycles, spaceships, jet skis, snowmobiles, and so on, to win races in a variety of venues.

Sports and Recreation
In this category of games, players play video versions of almost any type of sport or recreational game, from hockey (*NHL 2001* from EA Sports shown here) and baseball to darts and fishing. Players become batters, quarterbacks, and so on, and swing the bat or throw the ball.

Simulation
In simulation games, the game scenario allows players to operate in a simulated environment, such as piloting an airplane, or be a part of a life-like situation, such as living in and working in a simulated city.

Traditional
Many traditional board, card, and casino-type games are now available in video-game formats. Shown here is Bridge, one of many card games in *Hoyle Card Games* from Sierra.

Most existing computers are linked to a *network* of computers, often within an organization or a department, that share information and resources, such as printers, software, and Internet access. Home networks are becoming increasingly popular. Computer networks can be linked to one another, enabling the interchange of information between people in different companies or on different continents. Most personal computers are linked to a network and/or have ready access to the ultimate network, *the Internet,* which links millions of computers and networks and billions of people in every country in the world.

NETWORKS

Networks come in many different types and sizes. Networks can be as small as a home network or as large as one serving thousands of users. The most common type is a *local area network* (LAN). A LAN connects personal computers and other types of terminals and input/output devices in a suite of offices, a college laboratory, a home, or a building (see Figure GS-9).

LAN Server Computer Connected to Printer
In most computer networks, central computers, called *server computers,* manage the resources on a network. The printer is shared by all PCs/people on the network.

Wireless Connection
Frequently, LANs permit wireless links to the network.

Network Bus
A *network bus* is a cable that connects I/O devices and PCs.

FIGURE GS-9

LOCAL AREA NETWORKS AND THE LOGON PROCEDURE

Wiring Hub
Multiple PCs can be connected to a hub, which is connected to the network bus.

Client Computers
The server computers perform a variety of functions for the other computers on the network, called *client computers.*

Logon Procedure
Before you can "go online" and use network resources, you must log on to the network. You do this by opening the software that establishes the link to the Internet (see below) and entering a *user ID* and a *password.* The user ID is your electronic identifier and may be known by your friends and colleagues. The password, however, is yours alone to protect and use. The user ID identifies you for personal communications, such as e-mail, and it identifies you to the server computer. The password lets you gain access to a network and its resources. Typically, the user ID is your name in a standard format, often the first name, or its first initial, in combination with the last name (jansmith, jan_smith, jsmith). The password is any combination of contiguous characters (gowildcats, fyhi2005). To help protect the confidentiality of your password, a bullet or an asterisk is displayed for each character entered. It's a good idea to change your password frequently.

"Connect" Dialog Box
In Windows, use the "Connect" dialog box to logon to the Internet via a telephone dialup connection. Enter user name (user ID) and password. You will need a profile for the Internet access provider (ArkansasUSA in the example) with connection settings, including the telephone number.

THE INTERNET AND INTERNET ACCESS

The Internet is a worldwide collection of *inter*connected *net*works. The *Net* actually comprises millions of independent networks at academic institutions, military installations, government agencies, commercial enterprises, Internet support companies, and just about every other type of organization. Having access to the Internet means access to an amazing array of information and services on almost any conceivable topic.

Typically, people connect to the Internet via a *commercial information service*, an *Internet service provider (ISP)*, or a local area network with Internet access (see Figure GS-10).

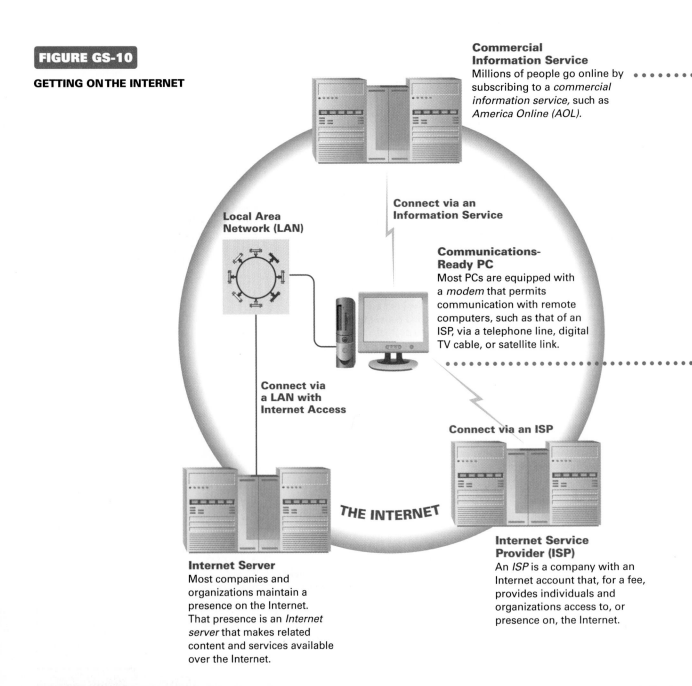

FIGURE GS-10

GETTING ON THE INTERNET

Commercial Information Service
Millions of people go online by subscribing to a *commercial information service,* such as *America Online (AOL).*

Connect via an Information Service

Local Area Network (LAN)

Communications-Ready PC
Most PCs are equipped with a *modem* that permits communication with remote computers, such as that of an ISP, via a telephone line, digital TV cable, or satellite link.

Connect via a LAN with Internet Access

Connect via an ISP

THE INTERNET

Internet Server
Most companies and organizations maintain a presence on the Internet. That presence is an *Internet server* that makes related content and services available over the Internet.

Internet Service Provider (ISP)
An *ISP* is a company with an Internet account that, for a fee, provides individuals and organizations access to, or presence on, the Internet.

America Online (AOL)

AOL, the largest of the commercial information services with about 30 million subscribers, offers a variety of online services via their own user interface software over their proprietary network. Also, AOL subscribers get access to the Internet. When you *sign on* to AOL, you enter a *screen name,* the AOL user ID, and your *password.* AOL's topical "channels" include music, travel, and news, plus myriad services such as real-time stock quotes.

CHANNEL	CAPACITY	
Regular telephone lines	POTS 56 K bps	DSL 256 K bps to 9 M bps downstream (receiving information) 256 K bps to 1.5 M bps upstream (sending information)
Cable modem (Over Cable TV lines)	400 K bps to 10 M bps	
Digital Satellite (Requires satellite dish)	400 K bps to 1.5 M bps downstream 56 K bps to 1.5 M bps upstream	

Communications Channel

A communications channel is the path or link through which information travels to get from one location on a computer network to the next. Communications channels offer a variety of *bandwidths,* the number of *bits* (on/off electrical signals) a channel can transmit per second. People link to the Internet via dialup access on telephone lines *(plain old telephone service* or *POTS)* at a maximum speed of 56 K bps (thousands of bits per second) or via high-speed *broadband access* (DSL, cable, or satellite), some measured in M bps (millions of bps).

Internet Browser

You tap the resources of the Internet via Internet browser software, such as *Netscape* (shown here) or *Internet Explorer.* This National Park Service Web site provides information for people planning a visit to the Mount Rushmore National Memorial, including a map of the park (inset).

COMMON INTERNET APPLICATIONS

Three of the most popular Internet applications are browsing and searching the *World Wide Web (the Web)* using an *Internet browser* and communicating with others via *e-mail* and *instant messaging*. The Web is the Internet's main application for delivery of information and services.

Internet Browser

Internet browsers let you retrieve and view the Internet's ever-growing resources as well as interact with Internet server computers. A browser runs on your PC and works with another program on an Internet server computer to let you "surf the Internet" (see Figure GS-11).

The Menu Bar
The menu bar in the user command area of the browser is used to select file options (print, save, and so on), to select edit options (including copy, cut, and paste), and to set and change a variety of options.

The Toolbar
Most of your interaction is with the buttons in the toolbar and the hyperlinks (see the Hyperlink annotation) in the Web pages. These navigation buttons are common to browsers:

- **Back.** Go to the last site visited.
- **Forward.** Go forward to the next site in the string of sites you have viewed.
- **Stop.** Stop the transfer of information.
- **Refresh.** Reload the current page from the server.
- **Home.** Go to your default home page, usually your college or company.
- **Search.** Go to your default search site, usually a major portal.
- **Favorites/bookmarks.** A list of sites you visit frequently.

Hyperlinks
Hyperlinks in a form of hypertext (a colored, underlined word or phrase), hot images, or hot icons permit navigation between Web pages on the Internet. Click on a hyperlink to jump (link) to another place in the same page or to another Web site. The cursor changes to a pointing hand 🖑 when positioned over a hyperlink.

Internet Portal
Often, browsing and searching the Web begins at a *portal,* such as Yahoo! (shown here). A *portal* is one of millions of Internet destinations, called a *Web site.* Your college has a Web site that has plenty of valuable information and useful services. A portal offers a broad array of information and services, including a *menu tree* of categories and a *search engine* that lets you do keyword searches for specific information on the Internet.

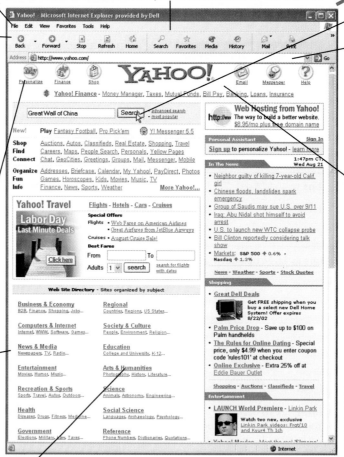

FIGURE GS-11

BROWSING AND SEARCHING THE WEB

Browsing the Net
Poking around the Internet with no particular destination in mind is called browsing. An Internet portal with its menu tree of categories (see example) is always a good place to start. You may navigate through several levels of categories before reaching the pages you want. For example, if you select "Arts & Humanities," Yahoo! lists 26 categories from which to choose (in alphabetical order). Selecting "Humanities" under "Arts & Humanities" presents 17 subcategories and links to several general humanities sites. Selecting "Literature" gives you another set of subcategories and appropriate links, including "Electronic Literature" and so on.

Search Results

The typical search results in a list of hyperlinks to Web sites that meet your search criteria ("Great Wall of China"). If you don't get results, try other search criteria and/or another search engine (Google, Lycos, HotBot, Ask Jeeves, MSN, and so on).

Searching the Net

There are two basic approaches to finding something on the Internet: *searching* and *browsing*. Each major portal has a search engine to help you find the information or service you need. Enter one or more keywords that describe what you want, such as "Great Wall of China" in the example.

URL Bar

The current URL is displayed in this box. The *URL* (Uniform Resource Locator) is the Internet equivalent of an address. We use browsers to go to and view content at a particular address on the Internet. The home page address for Yahoo! (shown here) is
http://www.yahoo.com/
and for the White House, the home page address is
http://www.whitehouse.gov/.
Each address begins with *http://* and is followed by a unique *domain name,* usually the name of the organization sponsoring the site. The domain name usually is prefaced by *www* to designate *World Wide Web.* What follows the domain name is a *folder* or *path* name containing the resources for a particular page. The White House tours URL is
http://www.whitehouse.gov/WH/Tours/visitors_center.html.

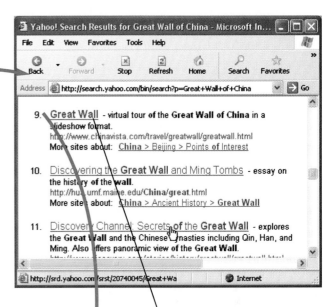

Click Hyperlink

Click on one or more of the resulting hyperlinks to go to a site (Discovery Channel, in the example).

Web Site Pages

Information on the Web is viewed in *pages.* The first page you will normally view is the site's *home page.*

E-Mail

E-mail lets you send electronic mail to and receive it from anyone with an e-mail address (see Figure GS-12). This is done with *e-mail client software,* such as Microsoft Outlook (shown here), or with *Web-based e-mail* via a browser.

E-Mail Client Software

The e-mail client software (Microsoft Outlook here) interacts with an e-mail server to enable sending and receiving of e-mail.

E-Mail Inbox

When you *logon* to the e-mail server, your messages are retrieved and placed in your *inbox* ready to be opened and read.

The E-mail Address

The e-mail address has two parts:

- *Username (jsmith@brassco.com).* On the left side of the @ separator is the username (usually your logon user ID).

- *Domain name for the Internet host/network (jsmith@brassco.com).* On the right side of the @ separator is the name of the *e-mail server,* usually Internet address for an ISP (earthlink.net), information service (aol.com), college (ou.edu), or company (wal-mart.com).

E-Mail Message

An e-mail message is opened and viewed. Click the *Reply* or *Forward* buttons to send a reply to the sender or forward the message to someone else.

Contacts List

Recipients can be selected from a contacts database.

Sending an E-Mail

To send an e-mail message, you select *New* message and enter the address(es) of the recipient(s) as *To, Cc* (copy to), *Bcc* (blind copy to), a subject, the message, and then click *Send* button.

Attachments

Any kind of file, such as a Word document or a digital image, can be "attached to" and sent with an e-mail.

The Internet

E-mail is routed over the Net to the destination e-mail server where it is stored in the recipient's electronic mailbox until opened.

Signature

The signature is optional "personal information" placed automatically at the end of each message.

Instant Messaging

Both instant messaging (IM) and e-mail enable personal communication but they have significant differences. Instant messaging allows messages to be sent and displayed in real-time (instantly), whereas e-mail is stored until retrieved by the recipient. Instant messaging allows text-based, voice, or video conversations with several friends. IM is used extensively in the business world, as well, because workers are informed immediately when their colleagues go online and are available.

The Windows Messenger software (shown in Figure GS-13) works with the .NET Messenger Service to deliver a variety of services, including file sharing, setting up online meetings or Internet games, sending text messages to cell phones, viewing programs simultaneously, and doing *whiteboarding* (a common online workspace for drawing and writing). To participate in instant messaging, you must sign up with one of the instant messaging services and install its software. Yahoo! and AOL offer popular messaging services. Instant messaging conversations can be between people on opposite ends of the world or between a father at the office and his son at home (illustrated here).

Status
The status area indicates whether you are online (signed in) or offline (signed out).

Sign In/Sign Out
Choose Sign In (in the *File* menu) to inform others who have you on their contact list that you are online. Choose Sign Out to end a session.

Online/Not Online
This area shows which of your contacts are online and which are not. Click on a contact to send a request to begin a conversation. A Windows Wizard guides you through the steps for adding contacts to your list.

Video Conversation
If your system is configured with a video camera, the person on the other end of the conversation can view the video in real-time. The picture-in-picture option lets you see both the send and receive images. Click *start/stop talking* or *start/stop camera* to add/end audio and/or video in the conversation.

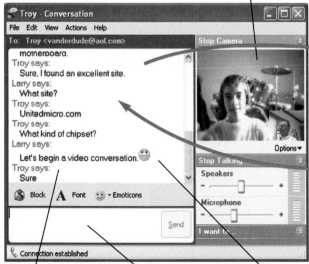

Conversation Window
All messages in a text-based conversation appear in this window immediately after they are sent.

Message Box
Key in your message in this box and click *Send*.

Emoticons
People add emoticons to express feelings.

FIGURE GS-13

COMMUNICATING VIA INSTANT MESSAGING

A COMPUTER SYSTEM

GS-1 Which is not one of the four basic hardware components of a PC: (a) input, (b) CD-ROM, (c) output, or (d) processor?

GS-2 The system unit houses all but which of the following: (a) ink-jet printer, (b) RAM, (c) processor, or (d) motherboard?

GS-3 Which of these is not a device for permanent storage: (a) hard disk, (b) RAM, (c) floppy disk, or (d) DVD+RW?

GS-4 The mouse is a(n): (a) draw-and-circle device, (b) point-and-draw device, (c) output device, or (d) small processor.

GS-5 The two most common input devices are the mouse and the: (a) keyboard, (b) microphone, (c) video camera, or (d) monitor.

GS-6 Which of these devices is not usually associated with multimedia: (a) image scanner, (b) microphone, (c) modem, or (d) video camera?

WORKING WITH WINDOWS

GS-7 We interact with the PC via the operating system's user-friendly: (a) glue, (b) GUI, (c) GIU, or (d) graphical screen.

GS-8 An interactive dialog box that guides you through system-related processes is a: (a) wizard, (b) magician, (c) juggler, or (d) power box.

GS-9 To begin the boot procedure, turn the PC: (a) off, (b) on, (c) to standby, or (d) around.

GS-10 The Start button is in the: (a) toolbar, (b) main menu, (c) status area, or (d) taskbar.

GS-11 Click which button to shrink the active window to a button in the taskbar: (a) Minimize, (b) Maximize, (c) Hide, or (d) Restore?

SOFTWARE: POPULAR APPLICATIONS

GS-12 You do what to a word processing document to recall it from disk storage: (a) hide it, (b) open it, (c) close it, or (d) unlock it.

GS-13 When selecting a font from the format menu in a word processing document, you are choosing a: (a) border, (b) typeface, (c) margin, or (d) document name.

GS-14 Which of these is not a gaming category: (a) simulation, (b) edutainment, (c) extreme XXX, or (d) RPG?

GOING ONLINE

GS-15 LAN stands for: (a) large active net, (b) local area network, (c) local access network, or (d) linear area network.

GS-16 On a network, multiple PCs can be connected to a: (a) bubba, (b) core unit, (c) focal point, or (d) hub.

GS-17 A company that provides individuals and organizations access to the Internet is a(n): (a) ISP, (b) Net provider, (c) PSI, or (d) ALO.

GS-18 Internet Explorer and Netscape are: (a) perusers, (b) surfers, (c) browsers, or (d) explorers.

GS-19 A browser is a: (a) customer program, (b) client program, (c) server program, or (d) logon procedure.

GS-20 What type of Internet Web site offers a broad array of information and services: (a) threshold, (b) gateway, (c) entry point, or (d) portal?

GS-21 Internet equivalent of an address is the: (a) Earl, (b) BOB, (c) URL, or (d) Yahoo.

GS-22 A good place to begin searching and browsing the Internet is a: (a) personal home page, (b) portal, (c) gateway, or (d) threshold.

GS-23 Internet users have electronic mailboxes to which what is sent: (a) e-mail, (b) e-correspondence, (c) e-letters, or (d) e-attachments.

GS-24 Instant messaging permits all but which of the following types of conversations: (a) text, (b) video, (c) voice, or (d) virtual?

COMPUTERS, INFORMATION TECHNOLOGY, AND YOU

LEARNING OBJECTIVES

Once you have read and studied this chapter, you will be able to:

- Explain what it means to achieve IT competency (Section 1-1).

- Place the Internet and its accompanying challenges into perspective (Section 1-2).

- Explain how information technology has influenced our lives and appreciate the impact it will have in the future (Section 1-3).

- Understand that we live in a global village linked by a worldwide Internet that has a vast array of information and services (Section 1-4).

- Talk about and understand the most popular categories of computers (Section 1-5).

- Describe the capabilities and limitations of computer systems (Section 1-6).

Whether we like it or not, for good or bad, we are part of an ever-growing partnership with computers and information technology, called *IT*. You are about to embark on a journey that will stimulate your imagination, challenge your every resource, from physical dexterity to intellect, and alter your sense of perspective on technology. Learning about computers is more than just education. It's an adventure!

Gaining a solid understanding of information technology, computers, and personal computing is just the beginning—your IT adventure lasts a lifetime. Every year, hundreds of new IT-related buzzwords, concepts, applications, and computing devices will confront you. Fortunately, you will have established a base of IT knowledge upon which you can build and continue your learning adventure. Your adventure into this amazing world of technology begins right here. Have fun!

1-1 INFORMATION TECHNOLOGY COMPETENCY

Why this section is important to you.

In our information society, information technology (IT) competency is now considered a job-critical skill. This section points you in the right direction to help you with your first step toward IT competency.

Not too long ago, people who pursued careers in almost any facet of business, education, or government were content to leave computers to computer professionals. Today in the United States an estimated 120 million people are knowledge workers. **Knowledge workers,** who provide a wealth of computer-based information services, have jobs that revolve around the use, manipulation, and broadcasting of information (see Figure 1-1). However, the vast majority of these people, over 100 million, would not be considered information technology competent! That leaves only 15% of the workforce considered to be IT competent. Most people use their PCs for only word processing, Internet access, or e-mail, or they are trained to work with a specific system, such as accounting or airline reservations. Many of these people believe themselves to be IT competent. Some are and some are not. Let's take a look at the difference between being merely a user of IT and being IT competent.

WHAT IS INFORMATION TECHNOLOGY COMPETENCY?

Information technology (IT) refers to the integration of computing technology and information processing. **IT competency** can be described as follows:

- Being conversant in the language of computers and information technology.
- Feeling comfortable using and operating a computer system.
- Being comfortable in cyberspace.
- Understanding the impact of computers on society, now and in the future.
- Being an intelligent consumer of computers, computer hardware, software, and other nonhardware-related computer products and services.

IT COMPETENCY ASSESSMENT

Some PC users are IT competent and some are not, mostly because their realm of exposure to IT is limited. Here is a simple test you can use to assess your level of IT competence. Can you describe five critical IT ethics issues facing our information society? Which port is

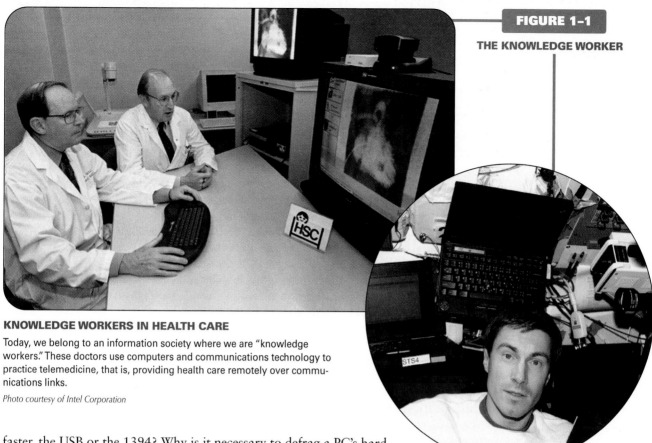

FIGURE 1-1

THE KNOWLEDGE WORKER

KNOWLEDGE WORKERS IN HEALTH CARE

Today, we belong to an information society where we are "knowledge workers." These doctors use computers and communications technology to practice telemedicine, that is, providing health care remotely over communications links.

Photo courtesy of Intel Corporation

faster, the USB or the 1394? Why is it necessary to defrag a PC's hard disk? What type of wiring is used in a typical home network? Name three top-level domain IDs other than .com and .edu. In cybertalk, BRB means what? What do TIF, PNG, and JPG files have in common? Describe five time- and/or money-saving personal computing applications for the home other than gaming, word processing, and Internet-based applications. Why would you filter information in an enterprise information system? How might an intelligent agent make your life a little easier? Given your circumstances, which broadband solution would be best for you?

KNOWLEDGE WORKERS IN SPACE

Astronauts, like this one, have ready access to onboard computers, which are linked to the NASA computers.

Courtesy NASA

These are just a few of the hundreds of points of knowledge that come with IT competency. If you fell short on a few of these, don't worry, because this book and course are about building and maintaining IT competency. There is one catch, however, in that your information technology competency is valid only for one point in time. The pursuit of IT competency is never-ending—IT is in constant motion.

1 To be IT competent, you must be able to write computer programs. (T/F)

2 A person whose job revolves around the use, manipulation, and dissemination of information is called: (a) an office wunderkind, (b) a knowledge worker, (c) a data expert, or (d) an info being.

3 Which of these is not one of the more common uses of PCs: (a) word processing, (b) computer-aided design, (c) e-mail, or (d) Internet access?

SELF-CHECK

SECTION

1-2 OUR CHALLENGE FOR THE TWENTY-FIRST CENTURY

The technology revolution is in its infancy. Only recently are we as an information society beginning to comprehend its potential and the array of challenges we must overcome to realize its possibilities.

THE VIRTUAL FRONTIER

We are living in and exploring a *virtual frontier*. This frontier extends to the electronic highways of the **Internet,** a worldwide network of computers, and beyond. The *virtual frontier* may be the last great frontier on Earth. Much of what lies beyond the virtual horizon is uncharted and potentially dangerous territory. Even so, pioneers set out each day to blaze new electronic trails. The virtual frontier is likened sometimes to America's "Wild West" because there are few rules and there is an endless string of pioneers seeking fame, fortune, and a new way of life in the cyberworld. Responsible pioneers accept and live by society's traditional rules of behavior, but the seedier elements of society are quick to observe that there is no virtual sheriff.

It's difficult to grasp the hardships endured by nineteenth-century pioneers who headed to the American West for a better life in their Conestoga wagons. The hardships along the electronic trails are not as physical or life-threatening, but they exist. We're still sloshing through the virtual mud in the virtual frontier. When we find a road, it's more like a trail or a roadway under construction than a highway. The highways that exist are narrow, filled with potholes, and have many detours.

The virtual frontier is growing in the same way the Wild West did. In the western frontier, cities grew from nothing overnight. In the virtual frontier, major services or capabilities unheard of a few years ago are becoming mainstream applications in the cyberworld. Just as it took many years for nineteenth-century ranchers and farmers to be friends, it might be some time before the various communications, hardware, and software industries can become friends and cooperate for the good of our information society.

Outlaws roamed the Wild West, creating havoc until law and order were established. At times, electronic outlaws may have had their way in the virtual frontier, but cybercops armed with stricter laws and electronic weaponry have served notice that Internet crimes will be enforced. Many cybercriminals now know that if they break the law in the virtual world they will do hard time in the real world.

The opportunity for a better life enticed early settlers in the American West to risk all and follow the setting sun. Eventually the Wild West was tamed and they realized their dreams, but only after enduring and overcoming major obstacles. The modern-day version of the Wild West presents us with the same opportunity. Bear in mind, though, that the *information superhighway* is truly a frontier that may not be tamed in the foreseeable future. The fact that it is a frontier, with all the associated risks, makes it even more exciting for you and other pioneers

YOUR CHALLENGE

The dynamics of rapidly advancing IT demands a constant updating of your skills and expertise. By their very nature, computers and IT bring about change. With the total amount of computing capacity in the world doubling every two years, we can expect change that is even more dramatic in the future. Someday in the not-too-distant future powerful, Internet-linked computers will be as commonplace on our person as wristwatches (see Figure 1-2).

The Internet, also known simply as **the Net,** and other related technologies have made it possible for us to communicate with someone on the other side of the world as easily as we would with someone down the street. International project teams work together via communications to create and support products from automobiles to video games and to create and support services from financial services to legal services. From now on, any country's national economy must be considered within the context of a world economy.

Many business traditions are vulnerable to IT: More people are *telecommuting* (working at home); company hierarchies are flattening out because the lines of communication are extended; the worker has greater visibility via the Internet and therefore greater mobility; methods of compensation are placing greater emphasis on innovation and productiv-

FIGURE 1-2

GETTING SMALLER

SMALLER, MORE POWERFUL CHIPS

The circuitry on this relatively recent network card is now contained in a single chip on the right. It's inevitable that we will have wristwatch-type computers that will listen and speak to us.

Photo courtesy of Hewlett-Packard Company

FASHIONABLY UNWIRED

This fashion show features runway models sporting wireless Internet technology products. The belt buckle on the model in the foreground is a wearable PC. Voice-recognition and a head-mounted display (over her right eye) enable communication with the PC. According to a recent national poll, more than half of American adults would, if given the choice, gladly carry around multiple wireless devices. The PC featured in this fashion show support digital cameras, GPS receivers, MP3 music files, and broadband streaming audio/video.

Courtesy of Charmed Technology

ity; the laws that govern commerce and intercompany relationships are under constant review; and the way we communicate is changing dramatically every few years.

So far, the cumulative effects of these changes have altered the basic constructs of society and the way we live, work, and play. PCs have replaced calculators and ledger books; e-mail and videoconferencing facilitate communication; word processing has eliminated typewriters; computer-aided design has rendered the drawing table obsolete; electronic commerce may eventually eliminate the need for money; online shopping is having a major impact on consumer buying habits; the Internet has opened the doors of many virtual universities … and the list goes on.

We as a society are, in effect, trading a certain level of computer and IT dependence for an improvement in the quality of life. However, this improvement in the way we live is not a foregone conclusion. Just as our highways play host to objectionable billboards, carjackings, and automobile accidents, the information highways are sure to have back roads lined with sleaze, scams, and cyberthiefs. It is our challenge to harness the immense power of information technology and our wired world so we can direct it toward the benefit of society.

Never before has such opportunity presented itself so vividly. This generation, *your generation,* has the technological foundation and capability of changing dreams into reality.

1 A decade ago, the virtual frontier was like the Wild West, but now it is tamed and tightly controlled by law. (T/F)

2 The laws that govern commerce and intercompany relationships are under constant review. (T/F)

3 A worldwide network of computers is known as: (a) the national e-highway, (b) the Internet, (c) the virtual frontier, or (d) the Wild West.

1-3   INFORMATION TECHNOLOGY IN OUR LIVES

Why this section is important to you.

We live in an information society. Your contribution to our information society is only enhanced when you appreciate the scope of the influence information technology has had and will have on your life. This section paints a picture of the past and present, but most of the canvas is devoted to where the technology is taking us during this first decade of the twenty-first century.

A stream of exciting new innovations in information technology continues to change what we do and how we think. Where will you be and what will you be doing in the year 2010? This is a tough question even for IT futurists, who are reluctant to speculate more than a year or so into the future. Things are changing too quickly.

IT IN OUR LIVES: YESTERDAY

To put the emerging information society into perspective, let's flash back a half century and look *briefly* at the evolution of computing (see Figure 1-3) and get a feel for how far we have come in this relatively short period of time.

- A little over 50 years ago, our parents and grandparents built ships, kept financial records, and performed surgery, all without the aid of computers. Indeed, everything they did was without computers. There were no computers!
- In the 1960s, mammoth multimillion-dollar computers processed data for those large companies that could afford them. These computers, the domain of highly specialized technical gurus, remained behind locked doors.
- In the mid-1970s, computers became smaller, less expensive, and more accessible to smaller companies and even individuals. This trend resulted in the introduction of personal computers.
- During the 1980s, millions of people from all lifestyles purchased computers. Suddenly, computers were for everyone!
- Today, most American families have at least one computer at home or work that is more powerful than those that processed data for multinational companies during the 1960s; moreover, their computers can reach around the world to interact with millions of other computers.

IT IN OUR LIVES: TODAY

The cornerstone of the technology revolution, the *computer,* is transforming the way we communicate, do business, and learn. Today, *personal computers,* or *PCs,* offer a vast array of *enabling technologies* that help us do all kinds of things at home, at play, at work, and at school/college.

At Home

Millions of people now depend on their PCs to help them with many everyday jobs around the house (see Figure 1-4): communicating with relatives, preparing the annual holiday newsletter, doing homework, managing the family investment portfolio, sending greeting cards, and much, much more. The home PC is a family's link to the Internet, with its remarkable resources and applications. People link to the Internet to learn which bank

A WORLD WITHOUT COMPUTERS

The industrial society evolved in a world without computers. The advent of computers and automation has changed and will continue to change the way we do our jobs.

GM Assembly Division, Warren, Michigan Courtesy of Ford Motor Company

offers the best mortgage rate, to order tickets to the theater, to learn about the Renaissance period, to get a good deal on a new car, or simply to browse the day away. Already, a third of the population is looking to the Internet first for their news.

A home may not only have several PCs, but it may have a variety of special-function computers. Many of these can be programmed by you to perform specific tasks, such as recording a movie on a VCR. We have small computers in VCRs, automobiles, air-conditioning systems, dishwashers, telephone answering systems, and in many more devices and appliances, including pet food dispensing devices. Computers are all around us at home.

At Play

Our leisure activities are changing almost as rapidly as the technology. Increasingly, we communicate with our friends and relatives via the Internet through *electronic mail* (*e-mail*) and

FIGURE 1–4

IT AT HOME

THE PERSONAL COMPUTING EXPERIENCE

Personal computing enriches life at home. After receiving a box of chocolates for Valentine's Day, this man immediately called his fiancée via a videophone Internet hookup to show his appreciation.

Photo courtesy of Intel Corporation

INTERNET APPLIANCES AROUND THE HOME

Internet appliances, such as this, are designed to provide easy access to the Internet for e-mail, online shopping, banking transactions, and so on.

Reprinted with permission of Compaq Computer Corporation. All Rights Reserved.

instant messaging (IM) (see "Getting Started" for an overview of both applications). Millions of people spend hours "chatting" with other people from around the globe on just about any subject from Elvis sightings to romance, often with people they don't know and may never hear from again.

Gaming is another major application of computers (see "Getting Started" for an overview). The software enables virtual worlds to be created within computers where gamers engage in mortal combat, immerse themselves in a virtual city, or work through a labyrinth for clues to save the world.

Today's personal computers have sophisticated audiovisual systems that allow you to listen to audio CDs or play the latest hit song directly off the Internet. If listening to the music isn't enough, you can view the music video, as well. People routinely watch DVD movies on their PCs.

Sports fanatics go to the Internet to view information and statistics on literally thousands of teams from junior soccer to major league baseball. Avid fans enjoy viewing real-time statistics and analysis on their PC while watching the game on television. No longer is the true fan cut off from the game because it's not televised or played on local radio stations. Most major radio stations are broadcasting over the Internet as well as the airwaves, making their signal available worldwide.

At Work

Knowledge workers in all areas of endeavor depend on their computers to do their jobs (see Figure 1-5). Millions of people can be "at work" wherever they are as long as they have their portable personal computers—at a client's office, in an airplane, or at home. The *mobile worker's* personal computer provides electronic links to timely and critical information and to clients and corporate colleagues, across town or across the country.

FIGURE 1–5

TECHNOLOGY IN OUR JOBS

Twenty-five years ago, college curricula in architecture, accounting, nursing, and, even, engineering included relatively little study in the area of computers and information technology. Today, knowledge workers in the office and on the shop floor rely on information technology for everything from product inspection to cost analysis.

Courtesy of Sun Microsystems, Inc.

Tasks that used to take hours, even days, now can be completed in minutes with the aid of IT. Rather than dictating to a machine for transcription by a secretary, managers can simply dictate messages *directly* to their computers. Marketing reps can prepare convincing presentations, complete with sound, video, and visual effects, in a tenth the time it took a generation ago. The managers' messages are timelier and the marketing reps' presentations are more effective.

At School or College

Information technology opens new doors for education. Millions of people now learn everything from agriculture to zoology via self-paced, interactive, computer-based courses. The computer is proving to be an effective teaching tool in enhancing traditional methods in kindergarten through higher education to continuing education for professionals. Many colleges now offer degrees whereby the student never sets foot on a physical college campus. This alternative to traditional education is blending well in our information society because it gives people the flexibility to pursue education at their own pace on their own schedule.

IT IN OUR LIVES: TOMORROW

Tomorrow, the next wave of technologies will continue to cause radical changes in our lives (see Figure 1-6). Each day new applications are being envisioned and created, many of which you may never have imagined or dreamed possible. A variety of these emerging technology-based applications is introduced in the remainder of this section.

Digital Convergence

We are going through a period of **digital convergence;** that is, we are converting whatever we can in the physical and communications worlds to binary on/off signals, called **bits,** which are compatible with computers. TVs, radios, PCs, telephones, movies, college textbooks, newspapers, and much, much more are converging toward digital compatibility. Digital convergence, combined with an ever-expanding worldwide network of computers,

techtv
EMERGING TECHNOLOGIES: ARCHITECTURE, COMPUTERS, AND CYBERSPACE

FIGURE 1-6

PORTABLE SHOPPING SYSTEM

Many retail establishments give customers access to a Portable Shopping System that lets shoppers save time by scanning the bar codes of goods as they shop rather than queuing at checkouts. After shopping, the customer puts the scanner in the rack and gets a bar-coded ticket detailing the items purchased.

Courtesy of Symbol Technologies, Inc.

is enabling our society to take giant leaps into the future. Already, digitized movies are being transmitted to theaters where they are shown via high-definition projection units. Most movies go to theaters as frames of cellulose, but these, too, are in the process of digital convergence. The 200,000 frames required for a full-length movie will converge to 16 billion bits. The printed pages of this book will converge to an 800 million bit electronic book, called an **e-book**. Millions of printed pages in the file cabinets of thousands of companies are being converted to more easily accessible digital images via *image processing*.

Digital convergence is more than a convergence of technologies. Information technology is the enabling technology for the convergence of industries, as well. For example, the financial industries—banking, insurance, and securities—are rapidly converging. Health care establishments—clinics, hospitals, medical insurers, medical schools—are converging. Government agencies, including the air traffic control agencies are consolidating their efforts through digital convergence.

With half the industrial world (and many governments) racing toward digital convergence, there is no question that our information society is going digital. This digital convergence is the foundation for the many exciting technology-based applications coming our way. Some of the applications that we can reasonably expect during this decade are discussed in the remainder of this section.

At Home in 2010

Let's fast forward to the year 2010. Computers are built into our environments at home and at work. Imagine this scenario: B. J. Rogers' invisible computer can be instructed to awaken him to whatever stimulates him to greet the new day. B. J.'s wake up call, which could just as well be yours, can be his favorite music, sports scores, a stock market report, the weather, or a to-do list.

Suppose B. J.'s wake up choice is a *to-do list* for the day. Besides listing the events of the day, his computer, which he calls Rex, might *verbally* emphasize important events, such as a dinner party (see Figure 1-7). Yes, the pace of the technology is on track to enable somewhat intelligent conversations between our computers and us by 2010. In response to B. J.'s request, the nearest video display (every room has at least one) is filled with a list of possible dishes for dinner. Just as B. J. notices that all dishes are meatless, Rex, the computer, reminds him of an important consideration (the guests are vegetarians). Rex might respond to his inquiry about ingredients by checking the home inventory and ordering as needed (all automatic).

Much of this futuristic scenario is within the grasp of today's technology. Even today, millions of people carry computers with them much of the day, many of which have a wireless link to the Internet. Many of these people routinely talk to their PCs via **speech-recognition technology,** which allows the user to enter spoken words into the system. Smart homes now are deemed an economically sound investment. So you see, we are well on our way to the day when this fictional scenario emerges as reality.

Entertainment Everywhere We Go, Whenever We Want It

Many of the initial commercial offerings on the Internet will be aimed at entertaining us. We'll have *video-on-demand;* that is, you will be able to choose what television program or movie you want to watch and when you want to watch it—even on your pocket or wrist PC. As you might expect, video stores and scheduled TV may become only memories in a few years.

Universal **broadband** (high-speed) access to the Internet is inevitable and will open the door for a more sophisticated form of entertainment. Already, major television networks are interweaving on-air and online statistics in broadcasts of sporting events. How long will it be before we have interactive soap operas? With the inevitable two-way communication capabilities of your future television/terminal, you can be an active participant in how a story unfolds. The soaps will be shot so they can be pieced together in a variety of ways. Imagine—you can decide whether Michelle marries Clifton or Patrick! You say this sounds far-fetched. Not really. Filmmakers are planning the production of interactive movies right now.

FIGURE 1-7   **AT HOME IN 2010**

"Rex," B. J. Rogers' computer, awakens him in the morning and is his ever-helpful assistant throughout the day.

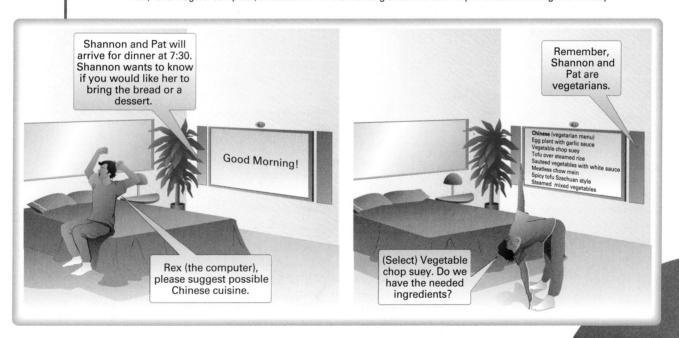

Your home entertainment center will become a video arcade, with immediate access to myriad of games and gaming options. You can hone your skills on an individual basis or test them, real time, against the best people in the land. Multiplayer games are already very popular on the Internet. The worldwide gamer community is in the hundreds of millions and it is conceivable that online gaming events featuring professional gamers could have more paying spectators than the Super Bowl or the World Cup.

The Cashless Society

The Internet may be the first step toward a *cashless society* because it provides the necessary link between individuals, businesses, and financial institutions. The question is not whether we move to a cashless society, but how quickly it happens. The reasons to become a cashless society are compelling. First, we are 99.9% there already. Each weekday, the financial institutions of the world transfer more than one trillion dollars electronically—that's $1,000,000,000,000 moving through cyberspace! On a more personal level, we use ATMs and we are beginning to use smart cards (see Figure 1-8). Millions of people now pay utility bills, mortgage payments, and many other bills through automatic electronic bank drafts. Many college students use prepaid debit cards to pay for sodas, photocopying, and concert tickets.

In a cashless society, the administrative work associated with handling money, checks, and credit transactions would be eliminated. We would no longer need to manufacture or carry money. Each purchase, no matter how small or large, would result in an immediate transfer of funds between buyer and seller. Think of it—rubber checks and counterfeit money would be eliminated.

A cashless society is not feasible until mechanisms are in place to accommodate small retail transactions. That's beginning to happen. A federal task force has been formed to plan for the transition to **electronic money,** or **e-money.** Financial institutions are establishing alliances to prepare for the cashless society. The major players in information tech-

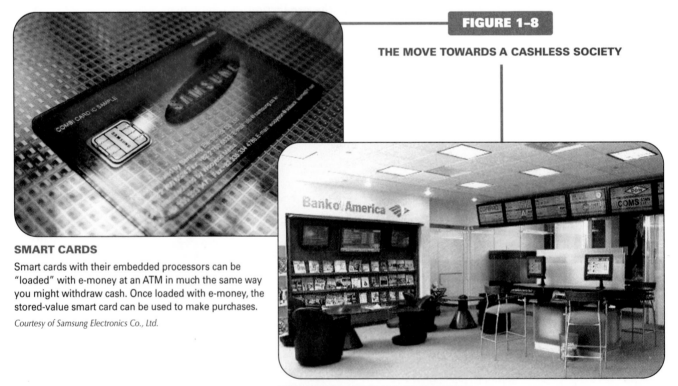

FIGURE 1-8

THE MOVE TOWARDS A CASHLESS SOCIETY

SMART CARDS

Smart cards with their embedded processors can be "loaded" with e-money at an ATM in much the same way you might withdraw cash. Once loaded with e-money, the stored-value smart card can be used to make purchases.

Courtesy of Samsung Electronics Co., Ltd.

THE FUTURE OF WALK-IN BANKING

This prototype Bank of America Financial Center is redesigned to accommodate the trend to greater use of e-money and with the latest in banking technology, such as Web-enabled ATMs and check imaging.

Courtesy of Bank of America

nology have agreed on a standard for the **electronic wallet,** an electronic version of the money, credit cards, and ID cards that we keep in our billfolds or purses.

The use of e-money opens new doors for barter. For example, when payment is entirely electronic, it is possible to pay for goods and services with very small amounts, called **micropayments.** If micropayments catch on, we might be charged automatically each time we play a song, watch a video, or search a database.

Shopping Anywhere, Anytime, for Anything

Each year online sales (see Figure 1-9) grow substantially at the expense of in-store sales because more and more people are opting for the convenience and value of electronic shopping. It's no longer necessary to drive from one bricks-and-mortar store to another seeking a particular style of sneaker in your size. You can go online and get the sneaker you want, often, at a price that is well below that of traditional stores. We can use our Internet-enabled personal computer, some of which have wireless access and are as small as a cellular phone, to select and purchase almost anything, from paper clips to pianos. Having a virtual mall will help speed the completion of routine activities, such as grocery shopping, and leave us more time for leisure, travel, and the things we enjoy.

The Internet offers great promise for the retail and wholesale industry, so we can anticipate a continuous string of "new and improved" online shopping services. Consider these advantages for the retailer: a corner bicycle shop in Pomona, California, has access to millions of customers; stores never have to be closed; transactions are handled electronically; and sales and distribution can be done more cost effectively. In the virtual marketplace, goods frequently are sent directly from the manufacturer to the customer, eliminating the extra stop (and expense) in traditional retailing.

Telemedicine: Networked Health Care

Telemedicine describes any type of health care administered remotely over communications links. Already, many states are practicing telemedicine (see Figure 1-10). Facilities, such as doctors' offices, nursing homes, and prisons, are networked to regional medical

FIGURE 1–9

INTERNET SHOPPING

Most people subscribe to an internet service provider (ISP) to get on the Internet. Once online, you can shop the electronic malls of the information superhighway to find exactly what you want, whether it's an 11-in-1 electronic survival kit or a home.

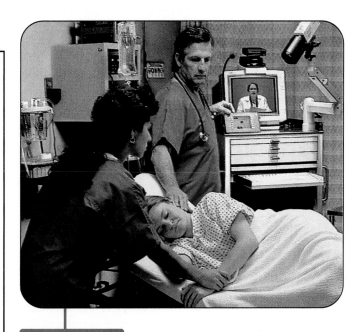

FIGURE 1–10

TELEMEDICINE

This workstation, called F.R.E.D.™ (Friendly Rollabout Engineered for Doctors), is designed for use in health-care facilities. F.R.E.D. provides a telemedicine solution for specialties such as cardiology that gives doctors virtual bedside access to their patients.

Photo courtesy of VTEL Corporation

centers. Sophisticated input/output hardware at remote sites, such as digital cameras and medical sensing devices, enable medical personnel and equipment to perform diagnostic procedures on patients.

Federal and state governments are optimistic that telemedicine has the potential to improve health care and reduce its spiraling cost. Recently a consortium of businesses and government agencies demonstrated telemedicine technology for members of Congress. The demonstration simulated a situation in which a car crash victim required doctors in different states to examine medical records, X-rays, and other images quickly. Congress was apparently impressed because millions of federal dollars are now being targeted to foster telemedicine.

Telemedicine is poised for rapid growth and is sure to have a major impact on the quality and scope of health care. For example, health-care capabilities can be delivered electronically to those rural areas currently without doctors. A group of doctors in every major specialty can travel with every ambulance—via telemedicine. By the time the ambulance arrives at the hospital, doctors may have run preliminary diagnostic procedures. The military uses similar systems in the battlefield. As telemedicine matures, look for it to play a major role in home care of the elderly, eliminating the need for costly hospitalization.

High-Tech Voting

Local, state, and federal elections might not require an army of volunteers. Politicians might not have to worry about low voter turnout on a rainy Election Day. In the not-too-distant future, we will record our votes over the *National Information Infrastructure*, or whatever our national network will be called. Such a system will reduce the costs of elections and encourage greater voter participation. Plus, we can avoid the confusion that surfaced in the 2000 election when the U.S. presidency hinged on legal opinions, voter recounts, butterfly ballots, and dimpled chads.

The state of Arizona's success with the Democratic presidential primary shows us that online voting by everyone in all elections may be only a matter of time. There was no confusion with the interface (the ballot), the accounting was computer accurate, and the number of people voting in the election was five times the number in the previous election, which did not permit online voting.

The Education Revolution

Our approach to education evolved with the industrial revolution—mass production with students (workers) in rows all doing the same thing at a pace dictated by the teacher (manager). Many educators are questioning the wisdom and effectiveness of traditional techniques in light of recent successes in technology-aided education. The computer has proven a marvelous tool for learning for people of all ages (see Figure 1-11). The advantages are too vivid to ignore.

- Learning is interactive.
- Students can work at their own pace.
- Learning can take place anywhere, anytime, via communications links to available resources.
- Learning materials are more sophisticated (animation, 3-D images, one-click links to related material, and so on).

Technology is rapidly changing the face of education at all levels. Many public school systems are accelerating their implementation of technology-aided education to improve the student/teacher ratio, raise test scores, and ease an ongoing budget crunch. Institutions of higher learning have introduced many ways to leverage information technology in education, including "networks on fly" where students bring their PCs to class so they can network with their classmates and professor. Already, the online university is here and growing. At some traditional colleges, online enrollment has surpassed enrollment in on-campus classes. The largest university in America is all online and has no classrooms. Curriculums are changing as universities opt to use technology to integrate the teaching of related topics. For example, rather than teach computers, finance, and ethics in separate courses, they are taught together in concert with applications.

FIGURE 1-11 TECHNOLOGY IN EDUCATION

THE VIRTUAL UNIVERSITY

The University of Phoenix exists mostly in cyberspace but it has approximately 150,000 students, more students than any other university in the United States. The barriers of time and place are eroding and opportunities to learn are everywhere.

THE TOOLS OF EDUCATION

High-tech tools, such as this tablet PC, may never replace paper and scissors in elementary schools; but each year, children spend more time interacting with technology-based learning tools.

Courtesy of Xybernaut

INTERNET CLASS

A broadcast technician (inset) controls the picture and sound for an innovative online botany class at Oregon State University. Students say the class provides a deeper level of understanding because of the interaction between students and professors at several universities.

Copyright 2001 Oregon State University

The National Database

The evolution of the Internet will provide the electronic infrastructure needed to maintain a national database. A **national database** will be a central repository for all personal data for citizens. The national database is among the most controversial information technology issues in that it offers tremendous benefits to society while posing opportunities for serious abuse. In the aftermath of the September 11, 2001, attack on America and the 2003 war in Iraq, the proposal for a more sophisticated national identification system is gaining momentum. Opponents of the national database claim it will lead to abuse and the erosion of personal privacy. However, recent polls have shown that people may be more willing to trade a certain level of their privacy for safety.

The creation of a national database would begin with each individual being assigned a unique identifier number at birth. This ID number or biometric identifier, perhaps a fingerprint or iris scan (eye), would replace the social security number, the driver's license number, the student identification number, and dozens of others. A national database would consolidate the personal data now stored on tens of thousands of manual and computer-based files. It could contain an individual's name, past and present addresses, dependent data, work history, medical history, marital history, tax data, criminal record, military history, credit rating and history, and so on.

A national database has certain advantages. It could monitor the activities of criminal suspects; eliminate welfare and food stamp fraud; identify illegal aliens; and make an individual's medical history available at any hospital in the country. The taking of the census would be done automatically each year (or even each month), rather than every 10 years. Governments at all levels would have access to up-to-date demographic information they could use to optimize the use of our tax dollars. Medical researchers could use the information to isolate geographical areas with inordinately high incidences of certain illnesses. The Bureau of Labor Statistics could monitor real, as opposed to reported, employment levels on a daily basis. The information possibilities are endless.

The Trend Toward Telecommuting

People who work at home have accounted for more than half of all new jobs since 1987. In 1990, 2 million Americans telecommuted to work. **Telecommuting** is "commuting" to work via data communications. In this new millennium, over 30 million telecommute to work at least part time (see Figure 1-12). Even if the soothsayers are half right, the telecommuting movement is on course to turn office tradition upside down.

Millions of people already work at home full time: stockbrokers, financial planners, writers, programmers, buyers, teachers (yes, some teachers and professors work exclusively with online students), salespeople, editors, manufacturer's representatives, project managers, and graphic artists, to mention a few. A larger group is working at home at least one day a week: engineers, lawyers, certified public accountants, company presidents, mayors, physicians, and plant managers, to mention some.

For many knowledge workers, work is really at a networked PC or over the telephone, whether at the office or at home. PCs and communications technology, such as instant messaging and videoconferencing, make it possible for these people to access needed information, communicate with their colleagues and clients, and even deliver their work (programs, stories, reports, or recommendations) in electronic or hard copy format. More and more people are asking: "Why travel to the office when I can telecommute?" Powerful PCs, broadband Internet access, home networks, personal and corporate economics, concerns about the environment, and other factors serve to fuel the growth of *cottage industries* where people work exclusively from their home offices.

We know that telecommuters are not only more productive, but they tend to work more hours. A Gartner Group study reported increases in productivity between 10% and 40% per telecommuter (as measured by employers). Various studies show that on average a telecommuter experiences a 2-hour increase in work time per day and saves the company about $6000 in annual facilities costs. Perhaps it is only a matter of time before all self-motivated knowledge workers at all levels and in a variety of disciplines are given the option of telecommuting at least part of the time.

FIGURE 1–12

THE ULTIMATE IN MOBILITY

This telecommuter can carry his IBM 10.5-ounce Wearable PC with him wherever he goes. This hands-free computer's headset provides audio output and a miniature eye-level display for viewing.

Courtesy of International Business Machines Corporation

SELF-CHECK

SECTION

1-4   OUR GLOBAL VILLAGE

At present, we live in a *global village* in which computers and people are linked within companies and between countries (see Figure 1-13). Virtually all classrooms and libraries in United States are linked to the Internet and, therefore, the world. The Internet has emerged as *the* enabling technology in our migration to a global village. It connects millions of computers in millions of networks in every country in the world. To put this in perspective, consider that it took decades for this kind of acceptance for the telephone.

The global village is an outgrowth of the **computer network,** which is a system of linked computers. Computer networks enable worldwide airline reservation data to be entered in the Bahamas and American insurance claims to be processed in Ireland. People in Hong Kong, Los Angeles, and Berlin can trade securities simultaneously on the New York Stock Exchange and other exchanges around the world. Computer networks can coordinate the purchases of Korean electronics, American steel, and Indonesian glass to make cars in Japan, and can then be used to track sales of those cars worldwide. Lotteries are no longer confined to a state, or even a nation. We can track every point in every match at the U.S. Open Tennis Tournament as the points are played.

Our global village created a global economy, in which businesses find partners, customers, suppliers, and competitors around the world. The advent of this global economy is changing society across the board, often in subtle ways. For example, customer service may continue to improve as companies realize how quickly a single irate customer can use the Internet to broadcast messages vilifying a company or a particular product to millions of potential customers. Computers, related hardware, and software products are especially vulnerable to such customer attacks. If a product does not stand up to advertised capabilities, the computing community in our global village will quickly expose its shortcomings to potential buyers. This same level of scrutiny will be applied ultimately to other products and services.

> ## Why this section is important to you.
>
> In 1967 Marshall McLuhan said, "The new electronic interdependence recreates the world in the image of a global village." His insightful declaration is now clearly a matter of fact, and going online is becoming an international pastime. It behooves us all to understand the scope and impact of our new wired world.

THE SPIRIT OF SHARING

The Internet emerged from a government-sponsored project to promote the interchange of scientific information. This spirit of sharing continues as the overriding theme over the Internet. For example, aspiring writers having difficulty being read or published can make their writing available to millions of readers, including agents and publishers, in a matter of minutes. Unknown musicians also use the Internet to gain recognition. *Surfers* on the Internet (Internet users) wanting to read a story or listen to a song, **download** the text or a digitized version of a song (like those on CDs) to their personal computer from an Internet computer, then read it or play it through their personal computer. Popular MP3 players can store and play digital music in *MP3 format*, a method of storing CD-quality music using relatively little memory (see Figure 1-14). Downloading is simply transmitting information from a remote computer (in this case, an Internet-based computer) to a local computer (in

FIGURE 1-13 THE GLOBAL VILLAGE

Computer-based communication is turning the world into a global village. We can communicate electronically with people on the other side of the world as easily as we might have a conversation with a neighbor.

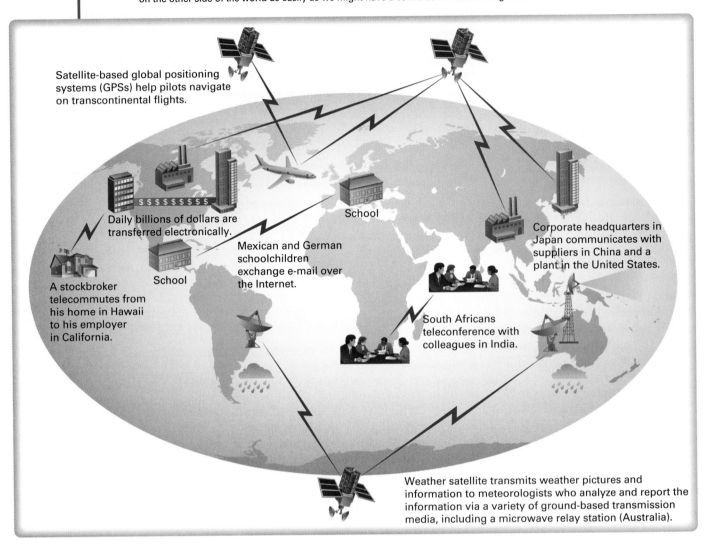

Satellite-based global positioning systems (GPSs) help pilots navigate on transcontinental flights.

Daily billions of dollars are transferred electronically.

School

Mexican and German schoolchildren exchange e-mail over the Internet.

School

A stockbroker telecommutes from his home in Hawaii to his employer in California.

Corporate headquarters in Japan communicates with suppliers in China and a plant in the United States.

South Africans teleconference with colleagues in India.

Weather satellite transmits weather pictures and information to meteorologists who analyze and report the information via a variety of ground-based transmission media, including a microwave relay station (Australia).

most cases, a PC). Information (perhaps a story or a song) going the other way, from a local computer to a remote computer, is said to be **uploaded.**

This spirit of sharing has prompted individuals and organizations all over the world to make available information and databases on a wide variety of topics. This wonderful distribution and information-sharing vehicle is, of course, a boon for businesses. Thousands of publishers, corporations, government agencies, colleges, and database services give Internet users access to their information—some provide information gratis and some charge a fee.

CRUISING THE NET

Vast, enormous, huge, immense, massive—none of these words is adequate to describe the scope of the Internet. Perhaps *the Internet* may someday emerge as a euphemism for anything that is almost unlimited in size and potential. There are at least as many applications on the Internet as there are streets in Moscow. To truly appreciate Moscow, you would need to learn a little of the Russian language and the layout of the city. Navigating the Internet also requires a little bit of knowledge. Gaining this knowledge takes time and a willingness to explore. In this book, we can hope to expose you to only some of the thoroughfares.

As you gain experience and confidence, you can veer off onto the Internet's side streets. For example, the Internet is a romance connection. Many married couples have met and courted over the Net. Of course, where there is marriage, there is divorce. Some couples

FIGURE 1-14

SHARING AND COMMUNICATING ON THE NET

MP3 PLAYER

There is a revolution under way in the way music is packaged, delivered, and played. Millions of MP3 songs are downloaded each day over the Internet and played on PCs or on portable MP3 players.

Photo courtesy of Intel Corporation

THE VIDEOPHONE NOW A REALITY

These schoolchildren in India are videoconferencing with children in the United States.

Photo courtesy of Intel Corporation

prefer to negotiate their divorce settlement over Internet e-mail. This written approach to arbitration allows parties to choose their words more carefully and to keep records of exactly what has been said.

Perhaps the most important Internet application is the *World Wide Web,* often called *the Web,* because it is this application that lets us view the information on the Internet. The information, which may be graphics, audio, video, animation, and text, is viewed in *Web pages.* Emotions of *newbies* (those new to the Internet) run high when they begin to visit *Web sites* and view Web pages. They simultaneously are shocked, amazed, overwhelmed, appalled, and enlightened. The Internet is so vast that seasoned users experience these same emotions. Figure 1-15 includes examples of a few of the millions of stops along the Internet.

FIGURE 1-15   CRUISING THE NET

The Internet makes a vast treasure trove of information and services available to people all over the world.

WEBCAMS

Webcams, which are cameras that capture a live image every few seconds or minutes, are strategically positioned in interesting locations, both inside and outside, in San Francisco (shown here) and all over the world.

INTERNET GREETING CARDS

It may be only a matter of time before online greeting cards overtake traditional greeting cards. Several Web sites let you create and send your own "greeting cards" (frogs singing "Happy Birthday" shown here).

FIGURE 1-15 continued

VIRTUAL TOURS OF THE WORLD'S GREAT MUSEUMS

Save the plane fare and enjoy virtual museums all over the world, including the Smithsonian's National Air and Space Museum (shown here) and the Louvre.

THE BEST OF THE WEB

Critics abound on the Internet. A select few make one of the "best" or "worst" lists. This "How Stuff Works" site is on many "Best of the Web" lists.

THE VISIBLE HUMAN

The Visible Human runs a Java applet that lets you interactively select and view two-dimensional slices of a human body.

VIRTUAL NEWS

You can listen to the news read by *Ananova,* a virtual news anchor, who reads the news in four different languages.

FIGURE 1-15   continued

SECURITIES ONLINE

Morgan Stanley's brokerage service offers customers quotes, charts, financial planning, online investing, securities research, and more.

LOOKING FOR A JOB?

The Net has many places that specialize in matching job applicants with employers. In the example, the user searches the 800,000-job Monster.com database for an "Information technology" position in "Florida-Miami."

1   The enabling technology in our migration to a global village is the: (a) Earthnet, (b) Internet, (c) cyberspace, or (d) Met.

2   A computer network is a system of: (a) linked computers, (b) HDTV hookups, (c) excess processor capabilities, or (d) Internet-based PCs.

3   The opposite of download is: (a) upstream, (b) downstream, (c) upload, or (d) upbeam.

SELF-CHECK

SECTION

1-5   PERSONAL COMPUTERS TO SUPERCOMPUTERS

Every day, more computers are sold than existed in the entire world 35 years ago. Back then, most medium to large companies had a computer, but they came in only one size—big. They filled large rooms, even buildings. Today, computers come in a variety of sizes. In this section we take a closer look at these popular categories of computers: personal computers (notebook PCs, desktop PCs, and wearable PCs), handheld computers, workstations, server computers, and supercomputers.

Why this section is important to you.

Computer systems come in many different shapes and sizes to meet a variety of computing needs. It's important that you understand the function and purpose of the different types of computers because it is likely you will be using and/or interacting with all of them at some time during the next few years.

COMPUTER SYSTEMS BASICS

General-purpose computers capable of handling a variety of tasks can be found in a range of shapes, from cube-shaped to U-shaped to cylindrical to notebook-shaped. However, the most distinguishing characteristic of any computer system is its *size*—not its physical size, but its *computing power*. Loosely speaking, size, or computing power, is the amount of processing that can be accomplished by a computer system in a certain amount of time, usually a second.

At one end of the power spectrum is the low-end personal computer that costs less than $500 and at the other is the powerful **supercomputer** that may cost more than an office building. There are several types of personal computers and each serves one person at a time. In contrast, computers designed to support businesses can handle the processing needs of many users at a time.

Over the past five decades, computers have taken on as many handles as there were niche needs. Terms like *mainframe computer* and *minicomputer* were popular in the 1970s and 1980s. Today, computers are generally grouped in these categories: notebook PCs, desktop PCs, wearable PCs, handheld computers, workstations, server computers, and supercomputers (see Figure 1-16). Give desktop PCs a slight edge in power over notebook PCs, but, generally, the two types offer similar computing capabilities. Wearable PCs are worn by the user, about the waist, head, or on the arm, providing the ultimate in mobile processing. The workstation is a notch above the top desktop PCs, offering individuals the performance they need for demanding scientific and graphics applications. In most computer networks, one or more central computers, called **server computers,** manage the resources on a network and perform a variety of functions for the other computers on the network, called **client computers,** which usually are PCs or workstations. PCs and workstations are linked to the server computer to form the network.

Any general-purpose computer, a notebook PC to a supercomputer, can be a server computer. But manufacturers build a special class of computers, called server computers, which are designed specifically for the server function. There are small ones for small businesses and larger ones to handle network needs for multinational companies. We should emphasize that these categories of computers are relative. What people call a personal computer system today may look like a workstation at some time in the future and be called by an entirely different name.

PCs, workstations, "servers," and supercomputers are computer systems. Each offers many **input/output,** or **I/O,** alternatives—ways to enter data into the system and to present information generated by the system. All computer systems, no matter how small or large, have the same fundamental capabilities—*input, processing, output,* and *storage.*

The differences in the various categories of computers are very much a matter of scale. Try thinking of a *supercomputer* as a *wide-body jet* and a *personal computer* as a *commuter plane.* Both types of airplanes have the same fundamental capability—they carry passengers from one location to another. Wide-bodies, which fly at close to the speed of sound, can carry hundreds of passengers. In contrast, commuter planes travel much slower and carry fewer than 50 passengers. Wide-bodies travel between large international airports, across countries, and between continents. Commuter planes travel short distances between regional airports. The commuter plane, with its small crew, can land, unload, load, and be on its way to another destination in 15 to 20 minutes. The wide-body may take 30 minutes just to unload. A PC is much like the commuter plane in that one person can get it up and running in just a few minutes. One person controls all aspects of the PC. The supercomputer is like the wide-body in that a number of specialists are needed to keep it operational. No matter what their size, airplanes fly and carry passengers and computers process data and produce information. Besides obvious differences in size, the various types of computers differ mostly in how they are used.

PERSONAL COMPUTERS: UP CLOSE AND PERSONAL

Most of today's personal computers (over 80%) are called **Wintel PCs** because they use one of the Microsoft *Windows* operating systems and an Intel Corporation or Intel-compatible processor. The Windows family of **operating systems** controls all hardware and software activities on Wintel PCs.

The Wintel PC represents the dominant PC platform. A **platform** defines a standard for which software is developed. Specifically, a platform is defined by two key elements:

- The processor (for example, Intel Pentium 4®, Intel Itanium™, Motorola® PowerPC®, AMD Athlon, and so on)
- The operating system (for example, Windows® XP, Mac® OS X, Unix®, Linux, and so on)

Generally, software created to run on one platform is not compatible with another platform. Most of the remaining personal computers are part of the Apple *Power Mac®, PowerBook®, iBook®, eMac™,* or *iMac™* line of computers. These systems use the *Mac® OS X* operating system and are powered by Motorola® *PowerPC®* processors.

The personal computer is actually a family of computers, some are small and portable and some are not meant to be moved (see Figure 1-17). The most common PCs, the notebook and desktop, have a full keyboard, a monitor, and can function as stand-alone systems.

Notebook PCs

Until recently, people in the business world often purchased two PCs, a self-contained **notebook PC** for its portability and a **desktop PC,** which is made up of several separate components, for its power and extended features. Now, modern notebook PCs offer desktop-level performance. These powerful notebook PCs let people take their "main" computer with them wherever they are, at work, at home, or on vacation. Each year, an increasing percentage of people choose to buy notebook PCs as their only PC. Today, close to half of all personal computers purchased for use in businesses are notebooks. That percentage continues to increase.

Notebook PCs, which also are called **laptop PCs,** are light (a few pounds up to about seven pounds), compact, and portable. They have batteries and can operate with or without an external power source, on an airplane or a wilderness trail. Some user conveniences must be sacrificed to achieve portability. For instance, input devices, such as keyboards and point-and-draw devices, are given less space in portable PCs and may be more cumbersome to use.

Many notebook PC buyers purchase a **port replicator,** too. The port replicator lets you enjoy the best of both worlds—portability plus the expanded features of a desktop PC. The port replicator provides a quick and easy way to connect a notebook PC to other input/output devices and to a network connection. The notebook PC, which supplies the processor and storage, is simply inserted into or removed from the port replicator, as needed. The process takes only a few seconds. The port replicator can be *configured* to give the "docked" notebook PC the look and feel of a desktop PC. Once inserted, the notebook PC can use whatever is connected to *ports* in the port replicator. **Ports** are electronic interfaces through which devices like the keyboard, monitor, mouse, printer, image scanner, and so on are connected.

Desktop PCs

The ubiquitous desktop PCs are to be stationary. The various input/output components of a desktop PC are connected to its **system unit,** a box which contains the processor, disk storage, and other electronic components. The system unit may be placed in any convenient location (on a nearby shelf, on the desk, or on the floor). The system unit for early desktop PCs was designed to lay flat on a desk to provide a platform for the monitor, thus the name "desktop" PC. Today's *tower* system unit with its smaller *footprint* (the surface space used by the unit) has made the early models obsolete. The desktop PC's footprint continues to dwindle as the tower shrinks and more users opt for the space-saving flat-panel monitors. By the end of this decade, the tower will approach the size of the laptop PC.

Personal Computer
(notebook PC and desktop PC)

Handheld
Computer

Wearable
PC

Workstation

Server Computer

Supercomputer

FIGURE 1-16

CATEGORIES OF COMPUTERS

FIGURE 1-17 **PERSONAL COMPUTERS: DESKTOPS AND NOTEBOOKS**

THE IMAC DESKTOP

This iMac, which has a 10.6-inch footprint, has a flat screen that "floats" in mid-air, allowing for ease of adjustment.

Courtesy of Apple Computer, Inc.

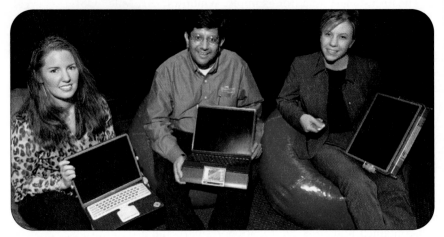

FUTURISTIC CONCEPT PCS

Intel Corporation is working with PC manufacturers to build better, simpler, and more effective personal computers. Shown here are several Intel Concept PCs that showcase the possibilities and benefits of drastically redesigned, easily upgradeable personal computers.

Photo courtesy of Intel Corporation

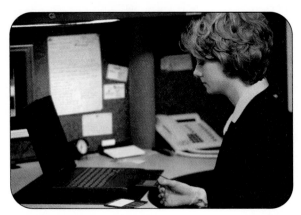

NOTEBOOK PC

When searching for a personal computer, this executive identified portability and flexibility as her primary criteria, so she chose a notebook PC.

Photo courtesy of Imation Corporation

DESKTOP PC

This home office desktop PC system is configured with a tower system unit, a large-screen monitor, an ink jet printer, a flatbed scanner, a digital video camera, and a satellite modem (atop the system unit) for high-speed Internet.

Long and Associates

Configuring a PC: Selecting the PC's Components

Typically, people who purchase PCs select, configure, and install their own systems. Virtually all PCs, both desktop and notebook, give you the flexibility to configure the system with a variety of storage and I/O peripheral devices. Of course, external I/O devices are disconnected when a notebook goes mobile. The typical PC includes the following components:

- System unit (this is self-contained in a notebook PC)
- Keyboard
- Point-and-draw device, such as a mouse
- Monitor

- Printer
- Hard disk (permanent storage of data and programs housed in the system unit)
- CD-RW and/or DVD+RW ("CD burner" and/or "DVD burner"; rewritable, interchangeable optical storage housed in the system unit)
- Microphone
- Speakers

Figure 1-18 shows the more common storage and I/O devices that can be configured with a PC. Many other peripherals can be linked to the "typical" PC, including video cameras, telephones, image scanners, other computers, security devices, and even a device that will enable you to watch your favorite television show on the PC's monitor.

Wearable PCs

Thousands of mobile workers could benefit from using a computer if only the computer were lighter, freed their hands, and didn't tether them to a desk or a power outlet. Now a new generation of wearable PCs promises to extend the trend begun by notebook and handheld computers.

Wearable PCs are worn by the user, about the waist, head, or on the arm, providing the ultimate in mobile processing. In an effort to create truly personal computers that meld a computer and its user, designers have divided the wearable PC's components into cable-connected modules that fit into headsets, drape across shoulders, hang around the neck, and fasten around the waist, forearm, or wrist. Lightweight (a pound or less), the components are covered in soft plastic and strapped on with Velcro.

Manufacturers of these wearable PCs combine existing or emerging technologies to create customized PCs for specific types of workers. The TLC (Tender Loving Care) PC for paramedics is a good example. At an accident scene, speech-recognition lets the paramedic dictate symptoms and vital signs into a microphone hanging from a headset. The computer, draped across the medic's shoulders, compares this data to a medical directory. The computer then projects possible diagnoses and suggested treatments onto the headset's miniature display. The TLC unit also helps administer telemedicine. Medics now use video camera and a body sensor strapped to their palm to *show* remote emergency-room doctors the patient's condition via a satellite link.

Certainly, the trend is toward increasingly smaller PCs. Some say that an emerging trend is toward increasingly wearable PCs. Perhaps within the decade, the PC will become as important to our wardrobe as it is as a business tool.

HANDHELD COMPUTERS: A COMPUTER IN HAND IS BETTER THAN . . .

Handheld computers are just that, computers that can be held in your hand. Handheld computers come in various form factors to address a variety of functions. The term **form factor** refers to a computer's physical shape and size. Computers, especially handheld computers and notebook PCs, continue to take on new form factors, often with unique features and capabilities. For example, one form factor integrates a cellular phone with a handheld computer. Another enables a notebook to be converted to a pen-based computer with handheld-like functionality.

Palmtop PC, personal digital assistant (PDA), connected organizer, personal communicator, mobile business center, and Web phone are just a few of the many names for handheld computers. Handheld computers weigh only a few ounces, can operate for days on their batteries, and can fit in a coat pocket or a handbag. As with notebooks, handheld computers must sacrifice some user convenience to achieve portability. The keyboards on those that have keyboards are miniaturized, making data entry and interaction with the computer difficult and slow.

The increase in the number of handheld computers in use is a by-product of our information society's transformation to a mobile, geographically dispersed workforce that needs fast, easy, remote access to networked resources, including e-mail. Some handheld computers have built-in wireless communications capabilities that give their users immediate access to the Internet, colleagues, and clients, and needed information, virtually anytime,

techtv
WEARABLE PCS

Digital camera

Wand scanner

Scanner

Video camera

Image processing
(input)

Data/video projector

Plotter   Desktop page printer

Hard-copy output

Modem (data communication
over telephone lines)

Facsimile
(fax) machine

Telephone

Microphone

Sound
(input and
output)

Monitor
(input/output)

Touch
screen
(input)

Keyboard
(input)

Uninterruptible power
supply (UPS) to enable
clean, steady power

**Point-and-
draw devices**
(input)

Mouse   Trackball

Digitizer tablet
and crosshair

Touchpad

Speakers (stereo
sound output)

Personal digital assistant
and laptop PC
(computer to computer)

Communications
(remote input/output)

Read/write optical
laser disk

CD-ROM/DVD

DVD±RW/CD-RW

Hard disk

3.5-inch diskette
and SuperDisk

Zip disk

Secondary storage

anywhere. Interaction with handheld computers can be via an electronic pen (handwritten text and graphics), by touching the keys on an on-screen keyboard, by keying on a reduced-key keyboard, or by speech (see Figure 1-19).

FIGURE 1–19   **HANDHELD COMPUTERS**

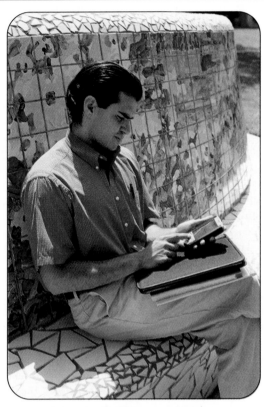

HANDHELD COMPUTER

The Compaq iPAQ Pocket PC and its accessories give people access to the Internet and important business and personal information at any given time, in any given place.

Reprinted with permission of Compaq Computer Corporation. All Rights Reserved.

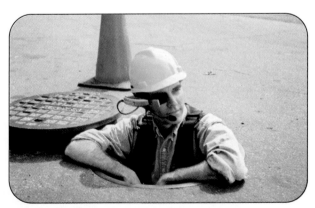

WEARABLE PC

This communications maintenance man uses a hands-free wearable PC, which is worn on a belt or shoulder strap and includes a display worn on the head like a headset. This man simply navigates to needed information by voice interface.

Courtesy of Xybernaut

POCKET PC WITH KEYBOARD

This HP Pocket PC, which can fit in a purse or a coat pocket, can run the same applications as its notebook and desktop cousins. This handheld computer is shown with the HP e-copier, which can be moved over any hard copy document to produce an electronic copy (image) of anything from a business card to a flip chart.

Photo courtesy of Hewlett-Packard Company

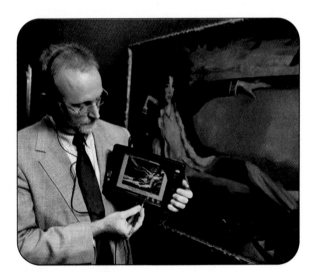

PCS IN MUSEUMS

People visiting the Whitney Museum of American Art can take a self-guided interactive gallery tour with the assistance of a handheld pen-based PC, which is loaded with multimedia information keyed to the artworks.

Photo courtesy of Intel Corporation

Mobile workers have found handheld computers that use an electronic pen, also called a **stylus,** in conjunction with a combination monitor/drawing pad to be very useful. These types of handheld computers, which are sometimes called **pen-based computers,** may or may not have a small keyboard. Users can select options, enter data via the on-screen keyboard, and draw with the pen. Pen-based computers often are designed for a particular application. For example, United Parcel Service (UPS) couriers use pen-based handhelds when they ask you to sign for packages on a touch-sensitive display screen with an electronic stylus.

Handwritten characters are interpreted by handwriting-recognition software and then entered into the system (see Figure 1-20). Insurance agents and claims adjusters who need to work at accident or disaster scenes have found handheld computers more suitable to their input needs, which may include entering both text and drawings. Speech-recognition is being integrated into high-end handheld computers. Speech recognition can be much faster than handwritten input, but it's impolite to talk to your computer during a meeting.

Generally, handheld computers support a variety of **personal information management (PIM)** systems. A PIM might include appointment scheduling and calendar, e-mail, fax, phone-number administration, to-do lists, and so on. Some handhelds can support a variety of PC-type applications, such as spreadsheets and personal financial management. Also, handhelds are designed to be easily connected to other computers and printers for data transfer, network access, and printing. Accessories for handhelds include a full-sized keyboard.

There are as many applications for handheld computers as there are organizations and functions. For example, a growing application for handhelds is emerging in the doctor's office, where the handheld may make the doctor's prescription pad a thing of the past. Thousands of doctors are using handheld computers to help them when they prescribe drugs. The doctor can ask the system to list applicable drugs for a particular medical condition. After selecting a drug, the system checks for possible drug interactions with other drugs the patient might be taking and it lists possible side effects. The system even makes recommendations relative to the patient's insurance coverage. Upon completion of process, the prescription is e-mailed directly to the druggist. The automation of the prescribing process is expected to give a boost to health-care quality considering that over 100,000 people die and 2 million people are hospitalized because of drug side effects and prescription errors.

Handhelds, though, are not all business. You can use them to play interactive games, chat with friends on the Internet, listen to downloaded MP3 music, or read a good e-book. Or, if you prefer, you can kick back, don your head set, and let the computer's **text-to-speech software** read the e-book to you!

FIGURE 1–20   **HANDWRITTEN INPUT**

These Graffiti characters, which are similar to capital letters, are the basis for entering handwritten data into Palm handheld computers. All characters are entered with a single stroke.

WORKSTATIONS: HOT RODS

What looks somewhat like a desktop PC but is not? It's a *workstation,* and it's very fast (see Figure 1-21). Speed is one of the characteristics that distinguish workstations from PCs. In fact, some people talk of workstations as "souped-up" PCs, the hot rods of computing. The workstation is for "power users"—engineers doing design work, scientists and researchers who do "number crunching," graphics designers, creators of special effects for movies, and so on. Although high-end desktop PCs may not perform as well as workstations, they are used for these applications, as well.

The workstation's input/output devices also set it apart from a PC. A typical workstation will sport at least one large-screen color monitor capable of displaying photo-like images. For pointing and drawing, the workstation user can call on a variety of specialized point-and-draw devices that combine the precision of a gun sight with the convenience of a mouse. Add-on keypads can expand the number of specialized *function keys* available to the user.

The capabilities of today's high-end PCs are very similar to those of low-end workstations. In a few years, the average PC will have the capabilities of today's workstation. Eventually the distinctions between the two will disappear, and we will be left with a computer category that is a cross between a PC and a workstation. Time will tell whether we call it a PC, a workstation, or something else.

SERVER COMPUTERS: CORPORATE WORKHORSES

Most computers, including PCs and workstations, exist as part of a network of computers. At the center of most networks are one or more server computers (see Figure 1-22). The *server computer* links and provides support of the *client computers* on the network. Typically, the client computer is a PC or a workstation.

Through the 1980s, huge mainframe computers performed most of the processing activity within a computer network. Back then, the shared use of a centralized mainframe offered the greatest return for the hardware/software dollar. Today, PCs and workstations offer more computing capacity per dollar than do mainframe computers. This reversal of hardware economics has resulted in a network model that as one or more server computers providing support for a number of networked client computers.

Server computers usually are associated with **enterprise systems**—that is, computer-based systems that service departments, plants, warehouses, and other entities throughout an organization. Many people using client computers share the server computer's processing capabilities and computing resources. For example, human resource management, accounting, and inventory management tasks may be enterprise systems handled by a central server computer. Depending on the size of the organization, a dozen people or 10,000 people can share system resources (for example, information, software, and access to the Internet) by interacting with the server computer via their PCs, workstations, handheld computers, and other communications devices.

SUPERCOMPUTERS: PROCESSING GIANTS

During the early 1970s, bankers, college administrators, and advertising executives were amazed by the blinding speed at which million-dollar mainframe computers processed their data. However,

FIGURE 1-22

SERVER COMPUTER

This Sun server computer system includes disk storage in the unit, a backup server, and several rack-mounted server computers. The system is capable of serving hundreds of client computers.

Courtesy of Sun Microsystems, Inc.

engineers and scientists were far from satisfied. They needed even more power to address truly complex problems. Automotive engineers could not create three-dimensional prototypes of automobiles inside a computer. Physicists could not explore the activities of an atom during a nuclear explosion. These types of scientific jobs involve the manipulation of a complex mathematical model and may require trillions of operations to resolve. In response to this need, computer designers began work on what are now known as supercomputers (see Figure 1-23).

Supercomputers are very fast computers that primarily address **processor-bound applications**, that is, applications which require little in the way of input or output. In processor-bound applications, the amount of work that can be done by the computer system is limited mostly by the speed of the computer. Such applications are highly complex, require a vast number of calculations (processor work), and very little input/output.

Supercomputers are known as much for their applications as they are for their speed or computing capacity, which may be 1000 times that of a typical corporate server computer. IBM's Blue Gene is a supercomputer with over a million processors that can perform 1 million billion (10^{15}) math operations per second. These are representative supercomputer applications:

- The simulation of airflow around an airplane at different speeds and altitudes
- The simulation of auto accidents by auto manufacturers (it is less expensive, more revealing, and safer than crashing the real thing)
- Studying how oceans and the atmosphere interact to produce weather phenomena, such as El Niño, so that meteorologists can make earlier and better forecasts concerning the paths of hurricanes and tornadoes
- Solving how the proteins are formed in the human body (IBM's Blue Gene is expected to take one year to calculate how a typical protein folds itself into a specific shape that determines its function in the body)
- Creating the advanced graphics used to create special effects for Hollywood movies such as *The Lord of the Rings Trilogy* and for TV commercials
- Sorting through and analyzing mountains of seismic data gathered during oil-seeking explorations
- The simulation of childbirth

FIGURE 1-23

SUPERCOMPUTERS AND THEIR APPLICATIONS

At Phillips Petroleum Company, this Cray Research supercomputer is used to analyze huge amounts of seismic/geological data gathered during oil-seeking explorations. The company uses the computer for many other processor-intensive applications.

Photo courtesy of Phillips Petroleum Company

Categories of Computer Systems
- Personal computer (PC)
  - Notebook PC
  - Desktop PC
  - Wearable PC
- Handheld computer
- Workstation
- Server computer
- Supercomputer

1. Supercomputers have greater computing capacity than personal computers. (T/F)
2. Workstation capabilities are similar to those of a low-end PC. (T/F)
3. A printer is an example of which of the four computer system capabilities: (a) input, (b) output, (c) processor, or (d) storage?
4. A notebook PC can be inserted into which of these to enable functionality similar to a desktop PC: (a) slate, (b) port hole, (c) runway, or (d) port replicator?
5. A platform is defined by an operating system and: (a) an I/O slot, (b) a processor, (c) a port, or (d) manufacture.
6. What would normally be associated with enterprise systems: (a) supercomputers, (b) server computers, (c) enterprise computers, or (d) neural computers?

Now that we know a little about the basic types of computer systems, let's examine what a computer can and cannot do. First, let's talk about one of the computer's most significant capabilities—processing data to produce information.

PROCESSING DATA AND PRODUCING INFORMATION

Information as we now know it is a relatively new concept. Just 50 short years ago, *information* was the telephone operator who provided directory assistance. Around 1950, people began to view information as something that could be collected, sorted, summarized, exchanged, and processed. But only during the last two decades have computers allowed us to begin tapping the potential of information (see Figure 1-24).

Computers are very good at digesting data and producing information. For example, when you order a cross-country bicycle from an Internet-based *e-tailer,* an online retailer, the data you enter to the system (name, address, product ID) are entered directly into the e-tailer's computer. When you run short of cash and stop at an automatic teller machine, all data you enter, including that on the magnetic stripe of your bankcard, are processed in *real time* (immediately) by the bank's computer system. A computer system eventually manipulates your data to produce information, such as a report showing bicycles sold in March. **Data,** the representation of facts, are the raw material for **information,** which is data that have been collected and processed into a meaningful form.

Traditionally, we have thought of data in terms of numbers (account balance) and letters (customer name), but information technology has opened the door to data in other formats, such as visual images. For example, dermatologists (physicians who specialize in skin disorders) use digital cameras to take close-up pictures of patients' skin conditions. These images become part of the patient's electronic file. During each visit, the dermatologist recalls the patient's information, which includes color images of the skin during previous visits. Data can also be a sound. For example, data collected during noise-level testing of

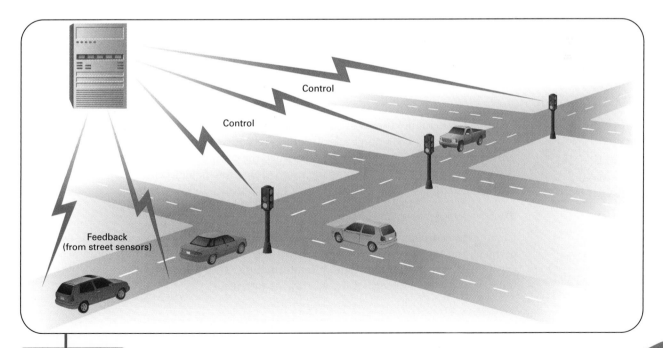

FIGURE 1–24

AN AUTOMATED TRAFFIC-CONTROL SYSTEM

In a continuous feedback loop, street sensors collect data that provide input to a computer system. The computer processes the data to produce the information (direction and volume of traffic flow) needed to control the lights.

automobiles include digitized versions of the actual sounds heard within the car.

The relationship of data to a computer system is much like the relationship of gasoline to an automobile. Data provide the fuel for a computer system. Your car won't get you anywhere without gas, and your computer won't produce any information without data. It's all about data.

THE COMPUTER'S STRENGTHS

In a nutshell, computers are fast, accurate, consistent, and reliable; plus, they aid in communications and can store huge amounts of data. They don't forget anything, and they don't complain.

Speed

Computers perform various activities by executing instructions, such as those discussed in the previous section. These operations are measured in **milliseconds** (one thousandth—*milli*), **microseconds** (one millionth—*micro*), **nanoseconds** (one billionth—*nano*), and **picoseconds** (one trillionth—*pico*). Understanding these time measures helps you to place computer speeds in perspective. For example, a beam of light travels down the length of this page in about one nanosecond. During that time, a server computer can perform the computations needed to complete a complex tax return.

Accuracy

Computers are amazingly accurate, and their accuracy reflects great *precision*. Computations are accurate within a penny (see Figure 1-25), a micron (a millionth of a meter), a picosecond, or whatever level of precision is required. Errors do occur in computer-based systems, but precious few can be attributed directly to the computer system itself. Most can be traced to a program logic error, a procedural error, or erroneous data—all of which are *human errors*.

Consistency

Baseball pitchers try to throw strikes, but often end up throwing balls. Computers always do what they are programmed to do—nothing more, nothing less. If we ask them to throw strikes, they throw nothing but strikes. This ability to produce the consistent results gives us the confidence we need to allow computers to process critical information.

Reliability

Computer systems are the most reliable workers in any company, especially when it comes to repetitive tasks. They don't take sick days or coffee breaks, and they seldom complain. Anything below 99.9% *uptime,* the time when the computer system is in operation, is usually unacceptable. For some companies, any *downtime* is unacceptable. These companies provide *backup computers* that take over automatically should the main computers fail.

Communications

Computers can communicate with other computers, and, by extension, with us. Using physical and wireless links, computers are able to share resources, including processing capabilities, and all forms of data and information. This communications capability is the force behind the emergence of the worldwide Internet.

Memory Capability

Computer systems have total and instant recall of data and an almost unlimited capacity to store these data, images, audio, video, or whatever can be digitized. A typical server computer system may have trillions of characters and millions of images stored and available for instant recall. A typical PC may have immediate access to billions of characters of data and thousands of images. To give you a benchmark for comparison, this book contains approximately 2 million characters and about 500 images.

MEMORY BITS

Computer Speed
- Millisecond = 0.001 second (one thousandth of a second)
- Microsecond = 0.000001 second (one millionth of a second)
- Nanosecond = 0.000000001 second (one billionth of a second)
- Picosecond = 0.000000000001 second (one trillionth of a second)

FIGURE 1-25

TRILLIONS OF DOLLARS TRADED WITHOUT ERROR

At the New York Stock Exchange, literally trillions of dollars' worth of securities are routinely bought and sold with nary a penny lost, a testament to the accuracy of computers.

Courtesy of the New York Stock Exchange

COMPARING COMPUTER AND HUMAN CAPABILITIES

The capabilities of computers and human beings are often compared because our information society is continually making decisions about whether a particular task is best done by a computer or a human. It's not always an obvious decision.

Human output (speech) is slow, maybe 120 words per minute for fast talkers, where computers talk in billions of bits per second. We recognize images (pattern recognition) more quickly than the fastest supercomputers. Computers struggle with pattern recognition. It's estimated that our memory capacity is comparable to the best supercomputers, but the computer is 100% accurate in recalling stored information This is seldom the case with humans. Computers can learn. So can we, but we do a much better job of applying what we learn to life situations.

The most significant difference between computers and humans is that we think. Computers don't—they do only what we tell them to do. For now and the foreseeable future, we will remain in control.

1 The raw material for information is: (a) records, (b) data, (c) statistics, or (d) manipulated figures.

2 A picosecond is what part of a second: (a) once thousandth, (b) one millionth, (c) one billionth, or (d) one trillionth?

3 When downtime is unacceptable, companies provide what type of computers: (a) secondary support, (b) assistive, (c) backup, or (d) auxiliary?

SELF-CHECK

SECTION

Chapter Review

1-1 INFORMATION TECHNOLOGY COMPETENCY

In an information society, knowledge workers focus their energies on providing myriad information services. The knowledge worker's job function revolves around the use, manipulation, and dissemination of information. Learning about computers is an adventure that will last a lifetime because information technology (IT), the integration of computing technology and information processing, is changing daily.

Information technology competency (IT competency) is emerging as a universal goal in our information society. The IT-competent person is also aware of the computer's impact on society and is conversant in the language of technology.

1-2 OUR CHALLENGE FOR THE TWENTY-FIRST CENTURY

The virtual frontier encompasses the electronic highways that comprise the Internet. It is likened sometimes to the Wild West because there are no rules. The opportunity for a better life is enticing pioneers to explore the virtual frontier.

The computer and IT offer you the opportunity to improve the quality of your life. It is your challenge to harness the power of the computer and direct it to the benefit of society.

1-3 INFORMATION TECHNOLOGY IN OUR LIVES

The computer revolution is transforming the way we communicate, do business, and learn. This technological revolution is having a profound impact on the business community and on our private and professional lives.

Through the 1970s, computer users related their information needs to computer professionals who would then work with the computer system to generate the necessary information. Today, users work directly with their PCs to obtain the information they need.

In this century, we can anticipate traveling an information superhighway that eventually will connect virtually every facet of our society. Today, millions of people have a personal computer (PC). This widespread availability has resulted in an explosion of applications for computers at home, at play, at work, and at school/college.

We are going through a period of digital convergence, converting whatever we can in the physical and communications worlds to bits so that are compatible with computers.

During the next decade, computers will be built into our domestic, working, and external environments. Eventually we will talk to our computers within our smart homes. They will help us perform many duties around the house.

A wide range of information and telecommunication services is now available for the Internet and many more are planned. These applications include video communication, video-on-demand, interactive television, the virtual mall, telemedicine, online voting, and a national database, to mention a few. Technology-aided education is being introduced rapidly at all levels of education.

Soon, we will be able to use our electronic wallet to purchase items electronically from retail stores. Micropayments will make it possible to pay for goods and services with very small amounts. The IT innovations bring the cashless society closer to reality.

Information technology and the Internet have fueled the trend toward telecommuting. This trend is rapidly changing not only the complexion of the workforce, but also where and how we work.

1-4 OUR GLOBAL VILLAGE

We now live in a global village in which computers and people are linked within companies and between countries. The global village is an outgrowth of the computer network, which is a system of linked computers.

This spirit of sharing continues as the overriding theme over the Internet. Surfers on the Internet are continually sharing information in every conceivable digital format.

The size and scope of Internet-base information and services is so enormous that they are difficult to comprehend. In an Internet session, you can be simultaneously shocked, amazed, overwhelmed, appalled, and enlightened.

1-5 PERSONAL COMPUTERS TO SUPERCOMPUTERS

The differences in the various categories of computers are a matter of computing power, not its physical size. Today, computers are generally grouped in these categories: notebook PCs, desktop PCs, handheld computers, workstations, server computers, and supercomputers. Server computers manage the resources on a network and perform a variety of functions for client computers. All computer systems, no matter how small or large, have the same fundamental capabilities—*input, processing, output,* and *storage.* Each offers many input/output, or I/O, alternatives.

Most PCs are called Wintel PCs because they use a Microsoft Windows operating systems and Intel (or compatible) processors. The Apple Computer line of computers defines the other major platform. Most personal computers are either notebook PCs (also called laptops) or desktop PCs. Many notebook PC buyers purchase a port replicator to enjoy the expanded features of a desktop PC. Ports are electronic interfaces through which devices like the keyboard, monitor, mouse, printer, image scanner, and so on are connected. The desktop PC's system unit contains the processor, disk storage, and other components. Many continuously in mobile knowledge workers use wearable PCs.

The typical off-the-shelf PC is configured with a keyboard, a point-and-draw device, a monitor, a printer, a hard-disk, a CD -RW and/or DVD+RW (CD or DVD burner), a microphone, and speakers.

Palmtop PC, personal digital assistant (PDA), connected organizer, personal communicator, mobile business center, and Web phone are just some of the names for handheld computers. A handheld can have a variety of physical shapes and sizes, referred to as its form factor. Pen-based computers which may or may not have small keyboards, make use of an electronic pen, call a stylus, to do such tasks as selecting options, entering data (via handwritten characters), and drawing. Speech-recognition technology, which allows the user to enter spoken words into the system, is being integrated into high-end handheld computers. Handheld computers support a variety of personal information management (PIM) systems, including appointment scheduling and to-do lists. You may also be using handhelds to read a good e-book via the computer's text-to-speech software.

The workstation's speed and variety of input/output devices set it apart from a PC. A common use of workstations is for engineering design.

The server computer performs a variety of functions for the other computers on the network, called client computers. Typically, the client computer is a PC or a workstation.

Supercomputers are very fast computers that primarily address processor-bound applications; that is applications which require little in the way of input or output.

1-6 COMPUTER SYSTEM CAPABILITIES

Computers are very good at producing information, which is data that have been collected and processed into a meaningful form.

The computer is fast, accurate, consistent, and reliable, and aids in communications and has an enormous memory capacity. Computer operations are measured in milliseconds, microseconds, nanoseconds, and picoseconds.

KEY TERMS

bit (p. 27)
broadband (p. 29)
client computer (p. 40)
computer network (p. 35)
data (p. 49)
desktop PC (p. 41)
digital convergence (p. 27)
download (p. 35)
e-book (p. 28)
electronic money (e-money) (p. 30)
electronic wallet (p. 31)
enterprise system (p. 47)
form factor (p. 43)
handheld computer (p. 43)
information (p. 49)
information technology (IT) (p. 20)

input/output (I/O) (p. 40)
Internet (the Net) (p. 22)
IT competency (p. 20)
knowledge worker (p. 20)
micropayment (p. 31)
microsecond (p. 50)
millisecond (p. 50)
nanosecond (p. 50)
national database (p. 34)
notebook PC (laptop PC) (p. 41)
operating system (p. 40)
pen-based computer (p. 46)
personal information management
  (PIM) (p. 46)
picosecond (p. 50)
platform (p. 40)

port (p. 41)
port replicator (p. 41)
processor-bound application (p. 48)
server computer (p. 40)
speech-recognition technology
  (p. 29)
stylus (p. 46)
supercomputer (p. 39)
system unit (p. 41)
telecommuting (p. 22)
telemedicine (p. 31)
text-to-speech software (p. 46)
uploaded (p. 36)
wearable PC (p. 43)
Wintel PC (p. 40)

MATCHING

_____ 1. Platform
_____ 2. Text-to-speech
_____ 3. Form factor
_____ 4. Internet
_____ 5. Server computer
_____ 6. Supercomputer
_____ 7. 1000 nanoseconds
_____ 8. MP3
_____ 9. Backup computers
_____ 10. Stylus

a electronic pen
b the Net
c reading e-books
d size and shape
e works with client computers
f music file
g takes over when computer fails
h processor-bound applications
i defined by operating system and processor
j 1 microsecond

TRUE/FALSE

1. IT competency, once gained, lasts a lifetime. (T/F)

2. Because of incompatible video formats, it is not yet possible to view DVD movies on a PC. (T/F)

3. The information highway is well-explored and would no longer be considered a frontier. (T/F)

4. The total computing capacity in the world is increasing at slightly less than 5% per year. (T/F)

5. A national database was approved by Congress and implemented in 1998. (T/F)

6. Internet gaming has begun its decline now that Generation Xers are entering the work force. (T/F)

7. The four size categories of conventional personal computers are miniature, portable, notebook, and business. (T/F)

8. The power of a PC is directly proportional to its physical size. (T/F)

9. A microsecond is 1000 times longer than a nanosecond. (T/F)

10. Supercomputers outperform humans when it comes to pattern recognition. (T/F)

MULTIPLE CHOICE

1. Information technology is the integration of computer technology and: (a) information processing, (b) societal trends, (c) PCs, or (d) knowledge workers.

2. Which of these is not a means of personal communication on the Internet: (a) electronic mail, (b) instant messaging, (c) instanotes, or (d) chat?

3. A metaphor frequently used as a reference to the wired world is: (a) cyberway, (b) virtual way, (c) information superhighway, or (d) NINI.

4. People talk to their PCs via: (a) voice typing, (b) voice overlay software, (c) speech acceptance technology, or (d) speech recognition technology.

5. High-speed access to the Internet is known as: (a) narrowband, (b) all-band, (c) megaband, or (d) broadband.

6. When health care is administered remotely over communications links, we call it: (a) telemedicine, (b) cybermedicine, (c) health-care magic, or (d) telehealth.

7. Money as we know it may soon be replaced by: (a) e-money, (b) electronic greenbacks, (c) cybercash, or (d) Eurodollars.

8. A national database has all but which of the following advantages: (a) virtual elimination of welfare fraud, (b) can monitor criminal suspect activities, (c) enables an annual census, or (d) elimination of all abuse of personal information?

9. PC users download a MP3 format song on the Net from an Internet computer to: (a) their PC, (b) another Internet computer, (c) to an upload site, or (d) an offline printer.

10. What Internet application lets us view Internet content: (a) World Wide Web, (b) Web World, (c) WW Net, or (d) World Web?

11. People new to the Internet are called: (a) dweebs, (b) webers, (c) novice surfers, or (d) newbies.

12. The Internet is also known as: (a) the Bucket, (b) the Global Interface, (c) the Net, or (d) Cybernet.

13. Supercomputers are oriented to what type of applications: (a) I/O-bound, (b) processor-bound, (c) inventory management, or (d) word processing?

14. Which of these is not a component of a typical PC: (a) printer, (b) hard disk, (c) wand scanner, or (d) keyboard?

15. Personal information management systems include all but which of the following: (a) appointment scheduling, (b) to-do list, (c) spreadsheet, or (d) calendar?

16. Components in a desktop PC are linked to ports in: (a) a system unit, (b) a desk, (c) a system entity, or (d) a white box.

17. A computer's physical shape and size are described by its: (a) beta specs, (b) form representation, (c) structure maps, or (d) form factor.

18. The drawing instrument associated with pen-based computers is the: (a) light pen, (b) stylus, (c) infrared marker, or (d) crosshair.

19. A client computer requests processing support or another type of service from one or more: (a) sister computers, (b) server computers, (c) customer computers, or (d) IT managers.

20. The most significant difference in the human/computer comparison is that: (a) humans think, (b) computers think, (c) humans can speak, or (d) computers have 100 percent recall of data.

IT ETHICS AND ISSUES

1. SHOULD PC OWNERSHIP BE AN ENTRANCE REQUIREMENT FOR COLLEGES?

As the job market tightens, colleges are looking to give their students a competitive edge. With computer knowledge becoming a job prerequisite for many positions, hundreds of colleges have made the purchase of a personal computer a prerequisite for admission (see Figure 1-26). Personal computers are versatile in that they can be used as stand-alone computers or they can be linked to the college's network, the Internet, or other personal computers in a class-

FIGURE 1-26

THE INTERACTIVE NETWORKED CLASSROOM

Owning a PC is a prerequisite for admission to the University of Oklahoma's College of Engineering. OU students shown here use PCs with wireless technology that lets them connect to the Internet anywhere within the engineering complex.

Courtesy of Sooner Magazine, University of Oklahoma

room. At these colleges, PCs are everywhere—in classrooms, lounges, libraries, and other common areas.

Wouldn't it be great to run a bibliographic search from your dorm room or home? Make changes to a report without retyping it? Run a case search for a law class? Use the computer for math homework calculations?

Instead of making hard copies of class assignments, some instructors key in their assignments, which are then "delivered" to each student's electronic mailbox. At some colleges, student PCs are networked during class, enabling immediate distribution of class materials. Students can cor-

respond with their instructors through their computer to get help with assignments. They can even "talk" to other students at connected colleges.

Discussion: If your college does not require PC ownership for admission, should it? If it does, should the policy be continued?

Discussion: What could students, professors, and college administrators do that they are not doing now (without a PC ownership requirement) if the entire campus were networked and every student were required to have a notebook PC?

2. HATE SITES ON THE INTERNET

How do some consumers voice grievances about companies, products, and services? How do some people voice their disgust over a rock group, a political organization, or even a university? They publish their thoughts, warts and all, on the Internet, usually on their own Web page. Just enter the keyword *hate* or *sucks* into an Internet search facility and see how many hits it gets. Anyone or anything is a potential target.

Some of this hate venom may be deserved, but perhaps it isn't. The Internet is a powerful voice that can be used to call attention to flaws in a company's products or services. It can also be used to vilify individuals who may simply be doing their jobs, effectively and legally.

Discussion: Some experts in the field of Internet monitoring say that the best response to hate site venom is no response. How would you respond if one or more Internet sites mounted an unjustified attack on your company's products? How would you respond to an unjustified personal attack?

Discussion: Visit a Web site that is dedicated to denouncing someone, something, an idea, or an organization. Is the content fair and is it appropriate for the Internet? Explain.

DISCUSSION AND PROBLEM SOLVING

1. What is your concept of information technology competency? In what ways do you think achieving information technology competency will affect your personal life? Your business life?

2. At what age should information technology competency education begin? Is society prepared to provide IT education at this age? If not, why?

3. What would be your number one reason to become IT competent?

4. Do you consider yourself IT competent? Why or why not?

5. List as many computer and information technology terms as you can (up to 30) that are used in everyday conversations at the office and at school.

6. Currently the Internet is open and all types of information flow freely, including pornographic text and images. A law enforcement official in Florida calls the Internet a "pedophile's playground."

One of the most important issues facing the information superhighway is censorship. Argue for or against censorship.

7. Information technology is touching all aspects of your life. Are you prepared for it? Explain.

8. Information technology has had far-reaching effects on our lives. How have the computer and IT affected your life?

9. Think back and discuss your earliest remembrances of computers. Compare those computers to today's.

10. The use of computers tends to stifle creativity. Argue for or against this statement.

11. Comment on how computers are changing our traditional patterns of recreation.

12. Discuss how the mix of jobs will change as we evolve from an industrial society into an information society. Give several examples.

13. Comment on how information technology is changing our traditional patterns of personal communication.

14. How has technology-based education influenced your personal quest for knowledge?

15. Will America eventually transition to a cashless society? If so, when? If not, why?

16. Speculate on how online voting in local, state, and national elections might affect the Democratic Party. The Republican Party.

17. Discuss why the percentage of online sales is experiencing such rapid growth.

18. If you are a current user of the Internet, describe four Internet services that have been of value to you. If not, in what ways do you think the Internet might be a benefit to you?

19. What might you want to download over the Internet?

20. Which types of Internet content and services are most appealing to you? Why?

21. List as many terms or phrases as you can that have been used to refer to our wired world.

22. The federal government is calling for "universal service" such that everyone has access to the Internet. Discuss the advantages of universal service to the Internet.

23. If you could purchase only one personal computer, which would you buy, a notebook PC or a desktop PC? Why?

24. Describe the circumstances that would prompt you to order a port replicator with a notebook PC.

25. Describe tasks or job functions where one of these professionals would use a handheld computer: a police officer, an insurance adjuster, a delivery person for a courier service, or a newspaper reporter.

26. Give at least two reasons why a regional bank might opt to buy six server computers rather than one supercomputer.

27. Lots of people wear their PCs. Speculate on why they wear them.

28. What would be your ideal form factor for a handheld computer?

29. Speculate on two supercomputer applications not mentioned in the book.

30. Discuss the relationship between the server computer and its client computers.

31. Give at least two examples in which you describe data, the source of the data, and any information that results from processing that data

32. Compare the information processing capabilities of human beings to those of computers with respect to speed, accuracy, reliability, consistency, communications, and memory capability.

FOCUS ON PERSONAL COMPUTING

1. *Exploring Windows Accessories Applications.* Go exploring and find out more about your PC (or the one in your college lab). Go to the "Accessories" group on the programs listing (click *Start, All Programs,* and highlight *Accessories*). Every Windows-based PC comes with some interesting and helpful programs. Open at least six Accessories group programs. Give a brief explanation of each and include your assessment of its applicability to your personal computing needs. The Accessories group includes a calculator, a graphics application, a sound recorder, and many more programs.

2. *Exploring Personal Computing Applications.* Continue your discovery adventure and run at least three more programs that are not in the Accessories group or are not a Microsoft Office program (Word, Excel, PowerPoint, and so on). Give a brief explanation of each program and include your assessment of its applicability to your personal computing needs.

ONLINE EXERCISES @ www.prenhall.com/long

1. The Online Study Guide (multiple choice, true/false, matching, and essay questions)

2. Internet Learning Activities
   • The Global Village
   • Personal Computers
   • Handheld Computers
   • Workstations
   • Server Computers
   • Supercomputers
   • Computer History

3. Serendipitous Internet Activities
   • At the Movies

IT ILLUSTRATED

The History of Computing

The history of computers and computing is of special significance to us, because many of its most important events have occurred within our lifetime. Historians divide the history of the modern computer into generations, beginning with the introduction of the UNIVAC I, the first commercially viable computer, in 1951. But the quest for a mechanical servant—one that could free people from the more boring aspects of thinking—is centuries old.

Why did it take so long to develop the computer? Some of the "credit" goes to human foibles. Too often brilliant insights were not recognized or given adequate support during an inventor's lifetime. Instead, these insights would lay dormant for as long as 100 years until someone else rediscovered—or reinvented—them. Some of the "credit" has to go to workers, too, who sabotaged labor-saving devices that threatened to put them out of work. The rest of the "credit" goes to technology; some insights were simply ahead of their time's technology. Figure 1-27 illustrates an abbreviated history of the stops and starts that have given us this marvel of the modern age, the computer. illustrates an abbreviated history of the stops and starts that have given us this marvel of the modern age, the computer.

FIGURE 1.27—JOURNEY THROUGH THE HISTORY OF COMPUTING

3000 B.C.: THE ABACUS

The abacus is probably considered the original mechanical counting device (it has been traced back 5000 years). It is still used in education to demonstrate the principles of counting and arithmetic and in business for speedy calculations.

Long and Associates

1623–1662: BLAISE PASCAL

Although inventor, painter, and sculptor Leonardo da Vinci (1425–1519) sketched ideas for a mechanical adding machine, it was another 150 years before French mathematician and philosopher Blaise Pascal (1623–1662) finally invented and built the "Pascaline" in 1642 to help his father, a tax collector. Although Pascal was praised throughout Europe, his invention was a financial failure. The hand-built machines were expensive and delicate; moreover, Pascal was the only person who could repair them. Because human labor was actually cheaper, the Pascaline was abandoned as impractical.

Courtesy of International Business Machines Corporation. Unauthorized use not permitted.

1642: THE PASCALINE

The Pascaline used a counting-wheel design: Numbers for each digit were arranged on wheels so that a single revolution of one wheel would engage gears that turned the wheel one tenth of a revolution to its immediate left. Although the Pascaline was abandoned as impractical, its counting-wheel design was used by all mechanical calculators until the mid-1960s, when they were made obsolete by electronic calculators.

Courtesy of International Business Machines Corporation. Unauthorized use not permitted.

3000 B.C. City of Troy first inhabited

1639 First North American printing press

1801: JACQUARD'S LOOM

A practicing weaver, Frenchman Joseph-Marie Jacquard (1753–1871) spent what little spare time he had trying to improve the lot of his fellow weavers. (They worked 16-hour days, with no days off!) His solution, the Jacquard loom, was created in 1801. Holes strategically punched in a card directed the movement of needles, thread, and fabric, creating the elaborate patterns still known as Jacquard weaves. Jacquard's weaving loom is considered the first significant use of binary automation. The loom was an immediate success with mill owners because they could hire cheaper and less skilled workers. But weavers, fearing unemployment, rioted and called Jacquard a traitor.

Courtesy of International Business Machines Corporation.
Unauthorized use not permitted.

1793–1871: CHARLES BABBAGE

Everyone, from bankers to navigators, depended on mathematical tables during the bustling Industrial Revolution. However, these hand-calculated tables were usually full of errors. After discovering that his own tables were riddled with mistakes, Charles Babbage (1793–1871) envisioned a steam-powered "difference engine" and then an "analytical engine" that would perform tedious calculations accurately. Although Babbage never perfected his devices, they introduced many of the concepts used in today's general-purpose computer.

Courtesy of International Business Machines Corporation.
Unauthorized use not permitted.

1842: BABBAGE'S DIFFERENCE ENGINE AND THE ANALYTICAL ENGINE

Convinced his machine would benefit England, Babbage applied for—and received—one of the first government grants to build the difference engine. Hampered by nineteenth-century machine technology, cost overruns, and the possibility his chief engineer was padding the bills, Babbage completed only a portion of the difference engine (shown here) before the government withdrew its support in 1842, deeming the project "worthless to science." Meanwhile, Babbage had conceived of the idea of a more advanced "analytical engine." In essence, this was a general-purpose computer that could add, subtract, multiply, and divide in automatic sequence at a rate of 60 additions per second. His 1833 design, which called for thousands of gears and drives, would cover the area of a football field and be powered by a locomotive engine. Babbage worked on this project until his death. In 1991 London's Science Museum spent $600,000 to build a working model of the difference engine, using Babbage's original plans. The result stands 6 feet high, 10 feet long, contains 4000 parts, and weighs 3 tons.

New York Public Library Picture Collection

1801 Thomas Jefferson elected Presiden

1838 Samuel F. B. Morse develops Morse Code

1816–1852: LADY ADA AUGUSTA LOVELACE

The daughter of poet Lord Byron, Lady Ada Augusta Lovelace (1816–1852) became a mentor to Babbage and translated his works, adding her own extensive footnotes. Her suggestion that punched cards could be prepared to instruct Babbage's engine to repeat certain operations has led some people to call her the first programmer. Ada, the programming language adopted by Department of Defense as a standard, is named for Lady Ada Lovelace.

The Bettmann Archive/BBC Hulton

1860–1929: HERMAN HOLLERITH

With the help of a professor, Herman Hollerith (1860–1929) got a job as a special agent helping the U.S. Bureau of the Census tabulate the head count for the 1880 census—a process that took almost eight years. To speed up the 1890 census, Hollerith devised a punched-card tabulating machine. When his machine outperformed two other systems, Hollerith won a contract to tabulate the 1890 census. Hollerith earned a handsome income leasing his machinery to the governments of the United States, Canada, Austria, Russia, and others; he charged 65 cents for every 1000 people counted. (During the 1890 U.S. census alone, he earned more than $40,000—a fortune in those days.) Hollerith may have earned even more selling the single-use punched cards. But the price was worth it. The bureau completed the census in just 22 years and saved more than $5 million.

Courtesy of International Business Machines Corporation.
Unauthorized use not permitted.

1890: HOLLERITH'S TABULATING MACHINE

Hollerith's *punched-card tabulating machine* had three parts. Clerks at the U.S. Bureau of the Census used a hand punch to enter data onto cards a little larger than a dollar bill. Cards were then read and sorted by a 24-bin sorter box (right) and summarized on numbered tabulating dials (left), which were connected electrically to the sorter box. Ironically, Hollerith's idea for the punched card came not from Jacquard or Babbage but from "punch photography." Railroads of the day issued tickets with physical descriptions of a passenger's hair and eye color. Conductors punched holes in the ticket to indicate that a passenger's hair and eye color matched those of the ticket owner. From this, Hollerith got the idea of making a punched "photograph" of every person to be tabulated.

Courtesy of International Business Machines Corporation.
Unauthorized use not permitted.

1924: IBM'S FIRST HEADQUARTERS BUILDING

In 1896 Herman Hollerith founded the Tabulating Machine Company, which merged in 1911 with several other companies to form the Computing-Tabulating-Recording Company. In 1924 the company's general manager, Thomas J. Watson, changed its name to International Business Machines Corporation and moved into this building. Watson ran IBM until a few months before his death at age 82 in 1956. His son, Thomas J. Watson, Jr., lead IBM into the age of computers.

Courtesy of International Business Machines Corporation.
Unauthorized use not permitted.

1883 Brooklyn Bridge completed in New York City

1923 Vladimir Zworykin patents first television transmission tube

1920s–1950s: THE EAM ERA

From the 1920s throughout the mid-1950s, punched-card technology improved with the addition of more punched-card devices and more sophisticated capabilities. The *electromechanical accounting machine (EAM)* family of punched-card devices includes the card punch, verifier, reproducer, summary punch, interpreter, sorter, collator, and accounting machine. Most of the devices in the 1940s machine room were "programmed" to perform a particular operation by the insertion of a prewired control panel. A machine-room operator in a punched-card installation had the physically challenging job of moving heavy boxes of punched cards and printed output from one device to the next on hand trucks.

Courtesy of International Business Machines Corporation. Unauthorized use not permitted.

1903–1995: DR. JOHN V. ATANASOFF AND HIS ABC COMPUTER

In 1939 Dr. John V. Atanasoff, a professor at Iowa State University, and graduate student Clifford E. Berry assembled a prototype of the ABC (for *Atanasoff Berry Computer*) to cut the time physics students spent making complicated calculations. A working model was finished in 1942. Atanasoff's decisions—to use an electronic medium with vacuum tubes, the base-2 numbering system, and memory and logic circuits—set the direction for the modern computer. Ironically, Iowa State failed to patent the device and IBM, when contacted about the ABC, airily responded, "IBM will never be interested in an electronic computing machine."

Courtesy of Iowa State University

1942: THE FIRST ELECTRONIC DIGITAL COMPUTER: THE ABC

A 1973 federal court ruling officially credited Atanasoff with the invention of the automatic electronic digital computer. The original ABC was dismantled decades ago. Ames Laboratory at Iowa State University used notes and drawings to reconstruct this working replica of Atanasoff and Berry's history-making invention.

Courtesy Ames Laboratory, Iowa State University

1944: THE ELECTROMECHANICAL MARK I COMPUTER

The first electromechanical computer, the *Mark I*, was completed by Harvard University professor Howard Aiken in 1944 under the sponsorship of IBM. A monstrous 51 feet long and 8 feet high, the Mark I was essentially a serial collection of electromechanical calculators and was in many ways similar to Babbage's analytical machine. (Aiken was unaware of Babbage's work, though.) The Mark I was a significant improvement, but IBM's management still felt electromechanical computers would never replace punched-card equipment.

Courtesy of International Business Machines Corporation.
Unauthorized use not permitted.

1946: THE ELECTRONIC ENIAC COMPUTER

Dr. John W. Mauchly (middle) collaborated with J. Presper Eckert, Jr. (foreground) at the University of Pennsylvania to develop a machine that would compute trajectory tables for the U.S. Army. (This was sorely needed; during World War II, only 20% of all bombs came within *1000 feet of their targets.*) The end product, the first fully operational electronic computer, was completed in 1946 and named the *ENIAC* (Electronic Numerical Integrator and Computer). A thousand times faster than its electromechanical predecessors, it occupied 15,000 square feet of floor space and weighed 30 tons. The ENIAC could do 5000 additions per minute and 500 multiplications per minute. Unlike computers of today that operate in binary, it operated in decimal and required 10 vacuum tubes to represent one decimal digit.

The ENIAC's use of vacuum tubes signaled a major breakthrough. (Legend has it that the ENIAC's 18,000 vacuum tubes dimmed the lights of Philadelphia whenever it was activated.) Even before the ENIAC was finished, it was used in the secret research that went into building the first atomic bomb at Los Alamos.

U.S. Army

1951: THE UNIVAC I AND THE FIRST GENERATION OF COMPUTERS

The first generation of computers (1951–1959), characterized by the use of vacuum tubes, is generally thought to have begun with the introduction of the first commercially viable electronic digital computer. The Universal Automatic Computer (*UNIVAC I* for short), developed by Mauchly and Eckert for the Remington-Rand Corporation, was installed in the U.S. Bureau of the Census in 1951. Later that year, CBS News gave the UNIVAC I national exposure when it correctly predicted Dwight Eisenhower's victory over Adlai Stevenson in the presidential election with only 5% of the votes counted. Mr. Eckert is shown here instructing news anchor Walter Cronkite in the use of the UNIVAC I.

The UNIVAC I just celebrated its golden anniversary (50 years). Forty-six companies and government agencies, including General Electric, DuPont, and the Internal Revenue Service, paid over $1 million for the UNIVAC I, a "walk-in" computer. The maintenance crew had to go inside the computer regularly to change burnt out vacuum tubes (the system had over 5000 of them). The 30-ton system's internal memory was a little more than 10Kb, less than a printed page worth of characters. *Courtesy of Unisys Corporation*

1954: THE IBM 650

Not until the success of the UNIVAC I did IBM make a commitment to develop and market computers. IBM's first entry into the commercial computer market was the IBM *701* in 1953. However, the *IBM 650* (shown here), introduced in 1954, is probably the reason IBM enjoys such a healthy share of today's computer market. Unlike some of its competitors, the IBM 650 was designed as a logical upgrade to existing punched-card machines. IBM management went out on a limb and estimated sales of 50—a figure greater than the number of installed computers in the entire nation at that time. IBM actually installed 1000. The rest is history.

Courtesy of International Business Machines Corporation.
Unauthorized use not permitted.

1947 **Chuck Yeager breaks sound barrier** | 1953 **Hillary and Norgay climb Mt. Everest**

1907–1992: "AMAZING" GRACE MURRAY HOPPER

Dubbed "Amazing Grace" by her many admirers, Dr. Grace Hopper was widely respected as the driving force behind COBOL, the most popular programming language, and a champion of standardized programming languages that are hardware-independent. In 1959, Dr. Hopper led an effort that laid the foundation for the development of COBOL. She also helped to create a compiler that enabled COBOL to run on many types of computers. Her reason: "Why start from scratch with every program you write when a computer could be developed to do a lot of the basic work for you over and over again?"

To Dr. Hopper's long list of honors, awards, and accomplishments, add the fact that she found the first "bug" in a computer—a real one. She repaired the Mark II by removing a moth that was caught in Relay Number II. From that day on, every programmer has *debugged* software by ferreting out its *bugs*, or errors, in programming syntax or logic.

The late Rear Admiral Hopper USN (ret) served the United States Navy and its computer and communications communities for many years. It's only fitting that a Navy destroyer is named in her honor.

Official U.S. Navy Photo

1958: THE FIRST INTEGRATED CIRCUIT

If you believe that great inventions revolutionize society by altering one's lifestyle or by changing the way people perceive themselves and their world, then the integrated circuit is a great invention. The integrated circuit is at the heart of all electronic equipment today. Shown here is the first integrated circuit, a phase-shift oscillator, invented in 1958 by Jack S. Kilby of Texas Instruments. Kilby (shown here in 1997 with his original notebook) can truly say to himself, "I changed how the world functions."

Texas Instruments Incorporated

1959: THE HONEYWELL 400 AND THE SECOND GENERATION OF COMPUTERS

The invention of the transistor signaled the start of the second generation of computers (1954–1964). Transistorized computers were more powerful, more reliable, less expensive, and cooler to operate than their vacuum-tubed predecessors. Honeywell (its *Honeywell 400* is shown here) established itself as a major player in the second generation of computers. Burroughs, UNIVAC, NCR, CDC, and Honeywell—IBM's biggest competitors during the 1960s and early 1970s—became known as the BUNCH (the first initial of each name).

Courtesy of Honeywell, Inc.

1957 *Sputnik* launched

1963: THE PDP-8 MINICOMPUTER

During the 1950s and early 1960s, only the largest companies could afford the six- and seven-digit price tags of *mainframe* computers. In 1963 Digital Equipment Corporation introduced the PDP-8 (shown here). It is generally considered the first successful *minicomputer* (a nod, some claim, to the playful spirit behind the 1960s miniskirt). At a mere $18,000, the transistor-based PDP-8 was an instant hit. It confirmed the tremendous demand for small computers for business and scientific applications. By 1971, more than 25 firms were manufacturing minicomputers, although Digital and Data General Corporation took an early lead in their sale and manufacture.

1964: THE IBM SYSTEM/360 AND THE THIRD GENERATION OF COMPUTERS

The third generation was characterized by computers built around integrated circuits. Of these, some historians consider IBM's *System/360* line of computers, introduced in 1964, the single most important innovation in the history of computers. System/360 was conceived as a family of computers with *upward compatibility;* when a company outgrew one model it could move up to the next model without worrying about converting its data. System/360 and other lines built around integrated circuits made all previous computers obsolete, but the advantages were so great that most users wrote the costs of conversion off as the price of progress.

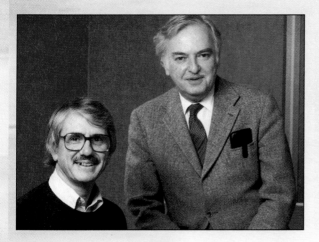

1964: BASIC—MORE THAN A BEGINNER'S PROGRAMMING LANGUAGE

In the early 1960s, Dr. Thomas Kurtz and Dr. John Kemeny of Dartmouth College began developing a programming language that a beginner could learn and use quickly. Their work culminated in 1964 with BASIC. Over the years, BASIC gained widespread popularity and evolved from a teaching language into a versatile and powerful language for both business and scientific applications. True BASIC is the commercial version created by Kemeny and Kurtz which now runs without change on nine popular operating systems.

1964 **Beatlemania develops in the U.S.**

1969: ARPANET AND THE UNBUNDLING OF HARDWARE AND SOFTWARE

The year 1969 was a big one for important technological achievements. Astronaut Neil A. Armstrong descended the ladder of the *Apollo 11* lunar module making the first step by man on another celestial body. Also in 1969, a U.S. Department of Defense's Advanced Research Project Agency (ARPA) sponsorship of a project, named ARPANET, was underway to unite a community of geographically dispersed scientists by technology. The first official demonstration linked UCLA with Stanford University, both in California. Unlike the moon landing, which had live TV coverage throughout the world, this birth of the Internet, had no reporters, no photographers, and no records. No one remembered the first message, only that it worked. By 1971, the ARPANET included more than 20 sites. Ten years later, the ARPANET had 200 sites. In 1990, ARPANET evolved into what we now know as the Internet.

Also in 1969, International Business Machines (IBM) literally created the software industry overnight when it *unbundled* its products. At the time, IBM had the lion's share of the world market for computers. Software, maintenance, and educational services were included (bundled) with the price of the hardware. When IBM unbundled and sold software separately, the software industry began to flourish.

Courtesy of NASA

1971: INTEGRATED CIRCUITS AND THE FOURTH GENERATION OF COMPUTERS

Although most computer vendors would classify their computers as fourth generation, most people pinpoint 1971 as the generation's beginning. That was the year large-scale integration of circuitry (more circuits per unit of space) was introduced. The base technology, though, is still the integrated circuit. This is not to say that two decades have passed without significant innovations. In truth, the computer industry has experienced a mind-boggling succession of advances in the further miniaturization of circuitry, data communications, and the design of computer hardware and software.

Courtesy of International Business Machines Corporation.
Unauthorized use not permitted.

1969 *Apollo 11* lands on moon

1975: MICROSOFT AND BILL GATES

In 1968, seventh grader Bill Gates and ninth grader Paul Allen were teaching the computer to play monopoly and commanding it to play millions of games to discover gaming strategies. Seven years later, in 1975, they were to set a course that would revolutionize the computer industry. While at Harvard, Gates and Allen developed a BASIC programming language for the first commercially available microcomputer, the MITS Altair. After successful completion of the project, the two formed Microsoft Corporation, now the largest and most influential software company in the world. Microsoft was given enormous boost when its operating system software, MS-DOS, was selected for use by the IBM PC. Gates, now the richest man in America, provides the company's vision on new product ideas and technologies.

Courtesy of Microsoft Corporation

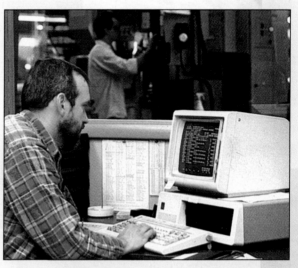

1981: THE IBM PC

In 1981, IBM tossed its hat into the personal computer ring with its announcement of the IBM Personal Computer, or IBM PC. By the end of 1982, 835,000 had been sold. When software vendors began to orient their products to the IBM PC, many companies began offering *IBM PC compatibles* or *clones*. Today, the IBM PC and its clones have become a powerful standard for the personal computer industry.

Courtesy of International Business Machines Corporation.
Unauthorized use not permitted.

1977: THE APPLE II

Not until 1975 and the introduction of the *Altair 8800* personal computer was computing made available to individuals and very small companies. This event has forever changed how society perceives computers. One prominent entrepreneurial venture during the early years of personal computers was the Apple II computer (shown here). Two young computer enthusiasts, Steven Jobs and Steve Wozniak (then 21 and 26 years of age, respectively), collaborated to create and build their Apple II computer on a makeshift production line in Jobs' garage. Seven years later, Apple Computer earned a spot on the Fortune 500, a list of the 500 largest corporations in the United States.

Courtesy of Apple Computer, Inc.

1982: MITCHELL KAPOR DESIGNS LOTUS 1-2-3

Mitchell Kapor is one of the major forces behind the microcomputer boom in the 1980s. In 1982, Kapor founded Lotus Development Company, now one of the largest applications software companies in the world. Kapor and the company introduced an electronic spreadsheet product that gave IBM's recently introduced IBM PC (1981) credibility in the business marketplace. Sales of the IBM PC and the electronic spreadsheet, Lotus 1-2-3, soared.

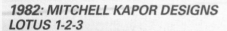

1976 United States 200th birthday

1983 Compact disc (CD) introduced for recorded music

1984: THE MACINTOSH AND GRAPHICAL USER INTERFACES

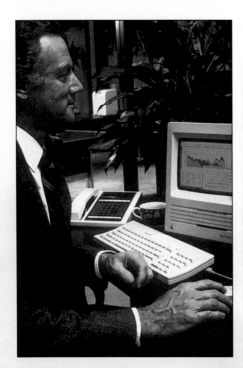

In 1984 Apple Computer introduced the Macintosh desktop computer with a very "friendly" graphical user interface—proof that computers can be easy and fun to use. Graphical user interfaces (GUIs) began to change the complexion of the software industry. They have changed the interaction between human and computer from a short, character-oriented exchange modeled on the teletypewriter to the now familiar WIMP interface—Windows, Icons, Menus, and Pointing devices.

Courtesy of Apple Computer, Inc.

1985–PRESENT: MICROSOFT WINDOWS

Microsoft introduced Windows, a GUI for IBM PC-compatible computers in 1985; however, Windows did not enjoy widespread acceptance until 1990 with the release of Windows 3.0. Windows 3.0 gave a huge boost to the software industry because larger, more complex programs could now be run on IBM PC compatibles. Subsequent releases, including Windows 95, Windows 98, Windows 2000, and Windows XP made personal computers even easier to use, fueling the PC explosion of the 1990s.

1993: THE PENTIUM PROCESSOR AND MULTIMEDIA

The IBM PC-compatible PCs started out using the Intel 8088 microprocessor chip, then a succession of ever more powerful chips, including the Intel 80286, 80386, or 80486 chips. But not until the Intel Pentium (shown here) and its successors, the Pentium Pro and Pentium II, did PCs do much with multimedia, the integration of motion video, animation, graphics, sound, and so on. The emergence of the high-powered Pentium processors and their ability to handle multimedia applications changed the way we view and use PCs.

Photo courtesy of Intel Corporation

1989: THE WORLD WIDE WEB

Former Swiss physicist Tim Berners-Lee invented the World Wide Web, an Internet application that allows us to view multimedia Web pages on the Internet. Berners-Lee and a small team of scientists conceived HTML (the language of the Internet), URLs (Internet addresses), and put up the first server supporting the new World Wide Web format. The World Wide Web, one of several Internet-based applications, came of age as Web traffic grew 341,634% in its third year, 1993. The "Web" was unique and inviting in that it enabled "Web pages" to be linked across the Internet. Today, the World Wide Web is the foundation for most Internet communications and services.

Courtesy of CERN

1993: THE INTERNET BROWSER

The 1995 bombing of the Murrah Federal Building in Oklahoma City stirred the emotions of the people throughout the world. This picture by Liz Dabrowski, staff photographer for *The Oklahoma Daily* (the student voice of the University of Oklahoma in Norman), speaks volumes about what happened and reminds us that we must never forget. In retrospect, we now view 1993 through 1995 as turnaround years for the Internet when millions of people began to tune into it for news of the bombing and other events and for a wealth of other information and services. A number of Internet browsers were introduced during this time, including the Prodigy (a commercial information service) browser shown here and Netscape Navigator. These browsers enabled users to navigate the World Wide Web with ease.

1996: THE HANDHELD COMPUTER

The PalmPilot handheld computer was introduced and signaled to the world that you could place tremendous computing power in the palm of your hand. Now millions of people rely on PalmPilots and other similar handhelds for a variety of personal information management applications, including e-mail.

3Com and the 3Com logo are registered trademarks. PalmIII™ and the PalmIII™ logo are trademarks of Palm Computing, Inc., 3Com Corporation, or its subsidiaries.

1996: U.S. STAMP COMMEMORATES HALF CENTURY OF COMPUTING

The dedication of this U.S. Postal Service stamp was unique in that it was the first to be broadcast live over the Internet so that stamp collectors throughout the world could see and hear the ceremony. The USPS issued the stamp to commemorate the 50th anniversary of the ENIAC (the first full-scale electronic computer) and the 50 years of computer technology that followed. The dedication was held at Aberdeen Proving Ground, Maryland, the home of the ENIAC. In 1999, the U.S. Postal Service granted permission to E-stamp Corporation to issue electronic stamps, stamps sold over the Internet that can be printed along with the name and address on an envelope (shown here). This entrepreneurial effort reminds us that in the new millennium, anything that can be digitized will eventually be distributed over the Internet.

Courtesy of E-Stamp Corporation

1995 Bombing of the Murrah Federal Building in Oklahoma City

1998–2000: THE YEAR 2000 PROBLEM

The year 2000 problem, the millennium bug known as Y2K, may have been one of the biggest challenges ever to confront the businesses of the world. Y2K's historical significance is that it heightened management's awareness of how critical information technology is to the ongoing operation of any organization. Y2K occurred because early programmers wanted to save keystrokes. For most of the twentieth century, information systems had only two digits to represent the year (for example, 99 for 1999). But what would happen when the twentieth century ended and a new one began? At the stroke of midnight on December 31, 1999 (12/31/99), millions of non-Y2K-compliant computer systems would interpret 01/01/00 (January 1, 2000), as being January 1, 1900! If the problem was not resolved, many computers would cease to work, including those at air traffic control centers and those in hospital intensive care units.

The complexity and cost of repairing the year 2000 problem is mind boggling. Millions of programs were affected, and Y2K fixes cost the U.S. economy about $200 billion. During the late 1990s, most new system development was delayed so programmers could devote more time to Y2K.

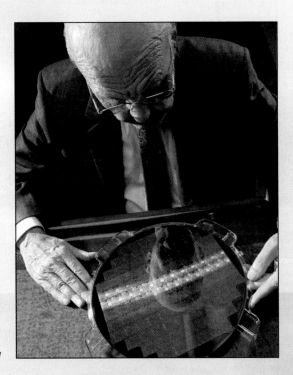

2000: SMALLER, MORE POWERFUL CHIPS

Jack Kilby's first integrated circuit contained a single transistor. Tens of thousands of engineers around the world have built on Mr. Kilby's invention, such that each year our information society is the beneficiary of smaller, more powerful, cheaper chips. In 2000, the industry introduced the 300-millimeter wafer (shown here by Mr. Kilby). This process and the accompanying cost savings opened the door for smaller, more powerful chips to be installed in a greater variety of devices.

Texas Instruments Incorporated

IT ILLUSTRATED SELF-CHECK

1   Lady Ada Lovelace suggested the use of punched cards to Charles Babbage during the 19th century. (T/F)

2   According to a federal court ruling, John Atanasoff is credited with the invention of the automatic electronic digital computer. (T/F)

3   The first significant use of binary automation was Blaise Pascal's Pascaline. (T/F)

4   The first family of computers with upward compatibility was introduced in 1964 by IBM. (T/F)

5   The Internet evolved from ARPANET, a U.S. government-sponsored project. (T/F)

6   The first commercially viable computer was introduced in: (a) 1937, (b) 1951, (c) 1978, or (d) 1984.

7   The punched card tabulating machine used in the 1890 census was invented by: (a) Babbage, (b) Gates, (c) Hollerith, or (d) Kapor.

8   The first operational electronic computer was named the: (a) ENIAC, (b) UNIVAC III, (c) IBM 650, or (d) Monrobot.

9   The first integrated circuit was invented in what decade: (a) 1940s, (b) 1950s, (c) 1960s, or (d) 1970s?

10 Apple Computer was started by two young computer enthusiasts in what decade: (a) 1940s, (b) 1950s, (c) 1960s, or (d) 1970s?

2001 September 11 terrorist attack on the United States

SOFTWARE

CHAPTER 2

LEARNING OBJECTIVES

Once you have read and studied this chapter, you will be able to:

- Describe the purpose and objectives of an operating system, plus common operating system platforms (Section 2-1).

- Grasp the fundamental concepts and terminology associated with the Windows operating environment (Section 2-2).

- Appreciate the function of software suite applications (word processing, presentation, spreadsheet, database, and personal information management) (Section 2-3).

- Appreciate the scope of popular personal computing applications for home and family, education and edutainment, reference, and business and financial management (Section 2-4).

- List graphics applications and explain multimedia terminology and concepts. (Section 2-5).

To be an effective personal computer user, you must know your way around its operating system, such as the popular Microsoft Windows operating systems. Once you have read and studied this chapter, you'll be better prepared to interact with the Windows environment, something that most knowledge workers and PC enthusiasts do for several hours each day.

Also in this chapter is an introduction to applications software that is commonly used in business and the home, including software associated with software suites and a variety of popular personal computing applications. In this chapter, you will learn that almost anything involving the manipulation of text and images can be done more easily and professionally with word processing software. You'll learn that you can prepare professional-looking visual aids that can boost the effectiveness of any presentation. You'll learn how spreadsheet and database software can help you organize, analyze, and present all kinds of information. Perhaps most importantly, you will learn that many personal computing tools exist for work and home that can save you lots of time, make you more productive, and help you present yourself in a more professional manner.

2-1   THE OPERATING SYSTEM

Why this section is important to you.

To interact effectively with your PC's operating system and its applications, you will need a working knowledge of the operating system's function and use. Several operating system options await you. The following discussion will give you insight into the operating system decision process.

Software refers to any program that tells the computer system what to do. Of course, there are many different types of software. Actually, understanding software is a lot like being in a big house—once you know its layout, you're able to move about the house much more easily.

THE HOUSE OF SOFTWARE

Once but a cottage, the house of software is now a spacious eight-room house (in a few years, it will be a mansion). Just as there are rooms in the house built for specific purposes, there are categories of software designed to perform specific functions. Figure 2-1 shows the blueprint for today's house of software, with the rooms arranged by function. The entryway in the house of software consists of *system software*. When you turn on the computer, the first actions you see are directed by system software. It takes control of the PC on startup, and then plays a central role in all interactions with the computer. The software from the other rooms, collectively known as *applications software*, is designed and created to perform specific personal, business, or scientific processing tasks, such as word processing, tax planning, or interactive gaming. We'll visit every room in the house by the time you finish this book, but you enter the house through system software and the operating system.

DIRECTING THE ACTION IN A COMPUTER

Movie audiences can become adoring fans of glamorous actors, but they tend to forget the others involved in the film, even the director who is the person who ties it all together and makes it happen. It's much the same with software. As software users, we tend to shower our praise on helpful *applications software*. However, *system software*, like the film director, stays in the background and ties it all together. The most prominent of these behind-

FIGURE 2-1 THE HOUSE OF SOFTWARE

This blueprint shows the layout of the house of software. Notice that access to the seven application software rooms is through the front room and system software. Each room illustrates a few of the many types of software for that software category.

Business Software
- General business
- Applications by business/interest area
- Desktop publishing
- Project management
- Image processing

Home and Personal Software
- Personal finance
- Creative design
- Home design
- Entertainment/gaming

Productivity Software
- Word processing
- Spreadsheet
- Database
- Presentation graphics
- Personal information management

Multimedia Software
- Photo editing
- Authoring software
- Animation
- Special effects
- Music/MIDI
- Media player
- Video capture and editing

System Software
- Operating systems
- Communications
- Device drivers and utilities
- Performance management

Development Software
- Programming languages
- Computer-assisted software engineering
- Web site development software

Education and Reference Software
- Topical computer-based education
- Encyclopedia
- Map/Travel
- Medical advice

Communications/Internet software
- Internet browser
- E-mail
- Instant messenger
- Chat
- Remote PC-PC connect

the-scenes players is the *operating system,* the software that controls everything that happens in a computer. Its **graphical user interface** (**GUI;** pronounced *"G-U-I"* or *"gooey"*), provides a user-friendly interface to the operating system. *System software* also includes a variety of **utility programs** that are available to help you with the day-to-day chores associated with personal computing (such as disk and file maintenance) and to keep your system running at peak performance. Figure 2-2 illustrates the relationship between the operating system and applications software.

Just as the processor is the nucleus of the computer system, the *operating system* is the nucleus of all software activity (see Figure 2-2). The operating system is actually a family of *system software* programs that monitor and control all I/O and processing activities within a computer system. One of the operating system programs loads other operating system and applications programs to RAM as they are needed. The program, called a **kernel,** is loaded to RAM on system startup and remains in RAM until the system is turned off.

If you purchase a PC off the shelf, you get whatever operating system is installed. When you order a PC, you may have several operating systems from which to choose. One might be business oriented (set up for business networking) and one might be less expensive and more appropriate for home computing.

OPERATING SYSTEM FUNCTIONS

The operating system is what gives a *general-purpose computer,* such as a PC or a company's Internet server computer, its flexibility to tackle a variety of jobs. Most *dedicated computers,* such as those that control devices (dishwashers, car ignition systems, and so

FIGURE 2-2

RELATIONSHIP BETWEEN THE OPERATING SYSTEM AND APPLICATIONS SOFTWARE

The operating system coordinates all software activity within a computer system. Our interaction with the operating system is through the graphical user interface, the GUI.

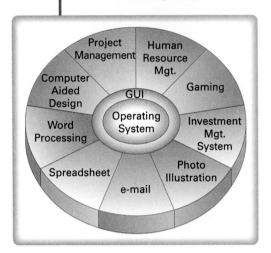

on) and arcade games, are controlled by a single-function program and do not need an operating system.

One of the best ways to understand an operating system is to understand its functions, which are listed and explained in Figure 2-3. All operating systems are designed with the same basic functions in mind. However, server and PC operating systems differ in complexity and orientation. Let's take a look at one of the more important operating system functions.

ALLOCATING SYSTEM RESOURCES

We all should live within our means, and the same goes for computers. A conscientious shopper can stretch the value of a dollar, and a good operating system can get the most from its limited resources, such as processor and disk capacity. Operating systems get the most from their processors through **multitasking**, the concurrent execution of more than one program at a time. Actually, a single computer can execute only one program at a time. However, its internal processing speed is so fast that several programs can be allocated "slices" of computer time in rotation, making it appear that several programs are being executed at once. The operating system addresses the tasks running at a given time in the most efficient manner, giving priority to the more critical tasks.

Multitasking lets you prepare a graphics presentation in PowerPoint while downloading a new MP3 song via the Internet. The **foreground** is that part of RAM containing the active or current program (PowerPoint in this example) and is usually given priority by the operating system. Other lower-priority programs, such as the MP3 download in this example, are run in the **background** part of RAM.

THE USER INTERFACE

To appreciate the impact of graphical user interfaces, it helps if you know what preceded them. Through the 1980s, the most popular microcomputer operating system was **MS-DOS**. The *MS* is short for *Microsoft* and *DOS* is an abbreviation for *disk operating system,* meaning that it is loaded from disk. MS-DOS was strictly *text-based, command-driven* software. That is, we issued commands directly to DOS (the MS-DOS nickname) by entering them on the keyboard, one character at a time. This command copied a word processing document from a hard disk to a floppy disk (see Figure 2-4).

```
copy c:\myfile.txt a:\yourfile.txt
```

Modern operating systems offer a graphical user interface (see Figure 2-4) that lets you "point and click" with a mouse to enter commands. GUI users interact with their computers by using a pointing device, such as a *mouse* on desktop PCs or a *touchpad* on notebook PCs. You can also issue commands on a keyboard. Rather than enter a command directly, you choose from by pointing to and choosing one or more options from menus or by pointing to and choosing a graphics image, called an icon. An **icon** is a picture that represents a processing activity or a file.

PC OPERATING SYSTEMS AND PLATFORMS

In Chapter 1, we learned that the *processor* and an *operating system* define a *platform*. Software created to run on a specific platform will not run on other platforms. The typical computer system, large or small, runs under a single platform. The selection of a platform is important because it sets boundaries for what you can and cannot do with your computer system. For example, the platform defines what type of applications software can be run, the level of network/Internet security, and the level of compatibility with other computers.

FIGURE 2-3   OBJECTIVES OF AN OPERATING SYSTEM

OPERATING SYSTEM OBJECTIVES

1. *To facilitate communication between the computer system and its users.*

   Users issue system-related commands via the graphical user interface (GUI).

2. *To facilitate communication among computer system components.*

   The operating system controls the movement of internal instructions and data between I/O peripheral devices, the processor, programs, and storage.

3. *To facilitate communication between linked computer systems.*

   The operating system enables linked computers to communicate.

4. *To maximize throughput.*

   System resources are employed to maximize throughput.

5. *To optimize the use of computer system resources.*

   The operating system is continually looking at what tasks need to be done and what resources are available to accomplish these tasks; then it makes decisions about what resources to assign to which tasks.

6. *To keep track of all files in disk storage.*

   The operating system enables users to perform such tasks as making backup copies of disks, erasing disk files, making inquiries about files on a particular disk, and preparing new disks for use. The operating system also handles many file- and disk-oriented tasks that are transparent (invisible) to the end user (for example, keeping track of the physical location of disk files).

7. *To provide an envelope of security for the computer system.*

   The operating system can allow or deny user access to the system as a whole or to individual files.

8. *To monitor all systems capabilities and alert the user of system failure or potential problems.*

   The operating system is continually checking system components for proper operation.

FIGURE 2-4   **TEXT-BASED AND GRAPHICS-BASED INTERFACES**

MS-DOS (shown here), the primary PC operating system from 1981 through the mid-1990s, has a text-based, command-driven interface. Windows XP has a graphical user interface (GUI) in which files can be dragged with a mouse between disk icons. Each has its pros and cons.

PC Platforms Overview

IT specialists choose the platforms for server computers, but you—the individual user—are normally responsible for selecting the PC's platform. The following discussion focuses on the most common personal computing environments—those developed for PC-compatible computers. Microsoft Windows, Mac OS X, UNIX, Linux, and LindowsOS are popular operating systems for PCs and workstations.

The PC/Windows Platforms

Most personal computer users choose the *Wintel* platform, which combines one of the Microsoft Windows operating systems (see Figure 2-5) with an Intel-compatible processor. All members of the Windows family have a similar look and feel.

- *Early Versions of Windows.* **Windows 95, Windows 98,** and **Windows Me** (Millennium Edition) operating systems are older version of Windows, but are still widely used in the home and in both small and large business. These older Windows operating systems emerged from **MS-DOS,** a text-based operating system. **Windows NT** was the first Windows operating system to divorce itself from the limitations of MS-DOS, thus beginning a new era for PCs. **Windows 2000** was the successor to Windows NT.

- *Modern PC Operating Systems.* For the foreseeable future, **Windows XP** and its successor will be the foundation of the PC/Windows family of client computer operating systems. Windows XP works with **Windows 2003 Server,** the server-side portion of the operating system (which runs on the server computer) to make client/server computing possible. Windows XP comes in several versions, including versions for the home and the office and for tablet PCs. Popular features of Windows XP include **plug-and-play,** which permits users to plug in a peripheral device even when the PC is running, and **home networking,** the linking of PCs in a home or small office to share information and resources.

- *Windows CE .NET.* The **Windows CE .NET** operating system is designed for handheld, pocket PCs, and other small-footprint devices (see Figure 2-6). Its look and feel are similar to those of the other members of the family. Windows CE .NET users can share information with other Windows-based PCs and they can connect to the Internet.

The Macintosh/Mac OS X Platform

The Apple family of microcomputers (including the Power Mac G4, iMac, eMac desktops and the PowerBook G4 and iBook notebooks) and its operating system, **Mac OS X** (see Figure 2-5), define another major platform. About one in every 10 PCs runs under this platform. The Apple line of microcomputers is based on the Motorola family of microprocessors. One inviting feature of Apple's Mac OS X is that it can be adjusted to fit the user's level of expertise.

UNIX, Linux, and LindowsOS

Created in the 1970s, **UNIX** was one of the first operating systems with the flexibility to be used on almost any computer. UNIX, a multiuser operating system, became very popular in universities and eventually emerged as the operating system of choice for powerful workstations. However, the UNIX

FIGURE 2-5   THE MICROSOFT WINDOWS TIMELINE

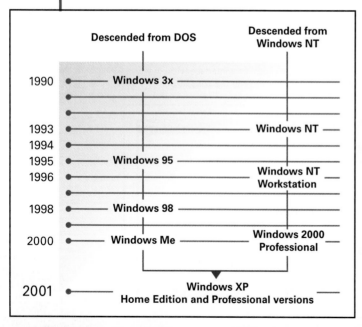

movement to PCs has been slow until recently. Linux (see Figure 2-7), a UNIX spin-off, is gaining momentum as an alternative to Windows. **Linux** is an open source operating system that was developed over the last decade via a worldwide consortium of developers, all working with the same programs. **Open source software** is software for which the actual source programming code (the instructions) is made available to users for review and modification. The significance of the rapid growth of this operating system is that it has the potential to become a competitor to Microsoft Windows client and server programs.

LindowsOS, a commercial Linux-based operating system for PCs, has a Windows-like interface and offers file-level compatibility with many popular Windows-based applications, such as Word and Excel. That is, a Windows-base Word or Excel file can run on a LindowsOS system.

Platforms for Businesses

When you decide on a particular platform, you begin to purchase and create resources for that platform. The investment required in selecting a platform demands a long-term commitment—at least five years. This type of commitment makes choosing a platform at the individual or company level a very important decision.

Companies that standardize on platforms can enjoy the benefits of easily shared resources (from data to printers). Those that do not must do some work to achieve **interoperability,** the ability to run software and exchange information in a **multiplatform environment,** that is, a computing environment of more than one platform.

With interoperability as an objective, Microsoft created and supports what they call the **.NET** (pronounced "dot net") **platform**. The .Net platform encompasses the operating system plus a suite of software tools and services that enable seamless interaction between people, networked computers, applications, and the Internet. One of the principles of dot net is that users will have access to personal/corporate information from any linked device—anytime and anywhere.

UTILITY PROGRAMS

A wide variety of system software *utilities* is available to help you with the day-to-day chores associated with personal computing (disk and file maintenance, system recovery, security, backup, virus protection, and so on) and to keep your system running at peak performance. Figure 2-8 gives you a sampling of common utilities programs you might use to enhance your personal computing environment.

THE WINDOWS CE .NET PLATFORM

This pocket PC runs the Windows CE .NET operating system and has full Internet connectivity. You can check stock quotes from the airport, send an e-mail from a taxi, or read the news from almost anywhere, anytime.

Courtesy of Sun Microsystems, Inc.

PC Platforms
- Legacy PC-Compatible
  - MS-DOS
  - Windows 95/98/Me
  - Windows NT/2000
- Current PC-compatible
  - Windows XP
  - Windows CE .NET (handheld PCs)
- Apple Mac OS X
- UNIX, Linux, and LindowsOS

---

1 The kernel is loaded to RAM on system start-up. (T/F)

2 The concurrent execution of more than one program at a time is called: (a) double duty, (b) multitasking, (c) multilayering, or (d) multiple kerneling.

3 Programs designed to be used by the end user are: (a) system software, (b) systemware, (c) personware, or (d) applications software.

4 Making an input device immediately operational by simply plugging it into a port is referred to as: (a) plug-and-play, (b) cap-and-cork, (c) pop-and-go, or (d) plug-and-go.

5 Which of the following is not in the PC/Windows platform family: (a) Windows 98, (b) Windows TN, (c) Windows XP, or (d) Windows 2000?

6 Software that provides detailed information with regard to available memory and disk space would be considered utility software. (T/F)

7 Utility software would be considered: (a) applications software, (b) system software, (c) utilitarian software, or (d) operating system software.

SELF-CHECK

SECTION

FIGURE 2-7   OPERATING SYSTEMS: WINDOWS XP, LINUX, AND MAC OS X

The interfaces for three popular PC operating systems are shown here. Windows XP represents the Windows family of operating systems. Linux is the open source operating system and Mac OS X is used with Apple computers.

WINDOWS XP

APPLE MAC OS X

LINUX

Screen shot copyright 2001 Red Hat, Inc. All rights reserved. Reprinted with permission from Red Hat, Inc.

APPLE MAC OS X, EMULATING MICROSOFT WINDOWS OPERATING SYSTEMS (XP, 2000, AND 98)

Courtesy of Connectix

FIGURE 2-8 UTILITY SOFTWARE

THE DISK DOCTOR

The *Norton Utilities* Disk Doctor and System Doctor utilities determine the health of your disks and system, checking areas that could cause problems. After diagnosing a problem, the "doctor" corrects it and/or recommends ways to optimize the PC for peak performance.

SYSTEM INFORMATION

The *Norton Utilities* System Information tool gives you detailed information about your PC, its peripherals, and any Internet or network connection.

SYSTEM UNIT TEMPERATURE MONITOR

The Intel Active Monitor utility monitors the temperature of the processor and the system unit and alerts you when temperature is high or fan speeds are low.

VIRUS PROTECTION

Norton AntiVirus, a popular virus vaccine, scans your disk drive(s) for viruses. It alerts you to problems, and then removes the virus.

FIGURE 2-8 continued

INTERNET PRIVACY PROTECTION

Internet Explorer gives users the option to set the level of Internet privacy protection.

SCREEN SAVERS

Originally designed to eliminate burning an image into a screen display, a screen saver program takes over the display screen when there is no key or mouse input for a specified time, say 10 minutes.

2-2 WINDOWS CONCEPTS AND TERMINOLOGY

The Windows operating system series has introduced a number of concepts and terms, all of which apply to the thousands of software packages that have been and are being developed to run on the Windows platforms. The terms, concepts, and features discussed in this section generally apply to Windows 9x/Me/2000/XP; however, the examples are based on Windows XP. The name *Windows* describes basically how the software functions and what you see on the screen—one or more windows. The GUI-based Windows series runs one or more applications in **windows**—rectangular areas displayed on the screen.

Why this section is important to you.

When you learn the Windows GUI, along with related terms and concepts, you also learn the GUI for all Windows-based software packages.

THE DESKTOP

The Windows screen upon which icons, windows, and so on are displayed is known as the **desktop.** The Windows desktop (see Figure 2-9) was introduced in *Getting Started*. People

---

FIGURE 2-9   **THE WINDOWS DESKTOP**

The appearance of this Windows XP desktop depends on the user's application mix and visual wishes at a particular time. To personalize the desktop, right-click anywhere on the desktop, select Properties, and then change the color scheme, the background, the resolution, or other desktop features.

Network Neighborhood
If your PC is on a LAN, the *My Network Places* icon provides ready access to its resources.

Plug-and-Play
All you have to do to add a new device, such as a video camera, is "plug" and "play" it.

Icons and Shortcuts
Program icons, files, and folders (groups of related files) can be displayed directly on the desktop. The My Computer icon provides access to all files and folders. An icon with a tiny arrow is a shortcut or a pointer to a file.

Recycle Bin
Deleted items remain in the *Recycle Bin* until you empty it.

Start Button
A Start button provides access to most of the Windows tools and commonly used applications.

Active Desktop Content
Active desktop content, such as a stock ticker or the local weather (shown here), changes on your screen to reflect updated circumstances.

Internet Explorer
The Window XP Internet Explorer is an integrated file management tool and Web browser.

Taskbar
The *Taskbar* shows active applications.
The *Quick Launch Bar* on the left gives you single-click access to user-selected programs.
The *System Tray* on the right displays the icons of programs that are loaded on system start-up.

DOS Window
Windows XP offers backward compatibility for MS-DOS (shown here) and earlier Windows programs.

usually customize their desktops to reflect their personalities as well as their processing and information needs, so no two desktops are the same.

The Window

Figure 2-9 shows how several **application windows** can be open at the same time, but there is only one **active window** (the one in use) at any given time. An application window contains an **open application** (a running application), such as Paint or Word. Application commands issued via the keyboard or the mouse apply to the active window. The active window's title bar (at the top of each application) is highlighted.

The Workspace

The application **workspace** is the area in a window in which the document, graph, spreadsheet, and so on is created. At the top of each window is the horizontal *title bar* (see Figure 2-10), which includes the *application icon, window title, Minimize button* (![min]), *Maximize/Restore button* (run full screen ![max] or in a window ![restore]), *Close button* (![close]), and the *title area*. In the example in Figure 2-10, two *document windows* are displayed in the application workspace. A **document window** is a rectangular area within the workspace that contains a document. Both documents are photo images and each is shown in a document window.

When document content is more than can be displayed in a window, the window is outfitted with *vertical* and/or *horizontal scroll bars* (see Figure 2-10). Each bar contains a *scroll box* and two *scroll arrows*. Use the mouse or keyboard to move a box up/down or left/right on a scroll bar to display other parts of the application. This movement is known as **scrolling.**

You can have the document windows or application windows automatically presented as **cascading windows** or **tiled windows,** both of which are illustrated in Figure 2-11.

Menus and Toolbars

The menu bar (see Figure 2-10) lists the menus available for that application. Choosing an option from the menu bar results in a **pull-down menu.** The *File, Edit, View,* and *Help*

FIGURE 2-10   **ELEMENTS OF AN APPLICATION WINDOW**

In this example display, the workspace in this *Microsoft PhotoDraw* application has two open document windows, both showing processor chips.

Photo courtesy of Intel Corporation

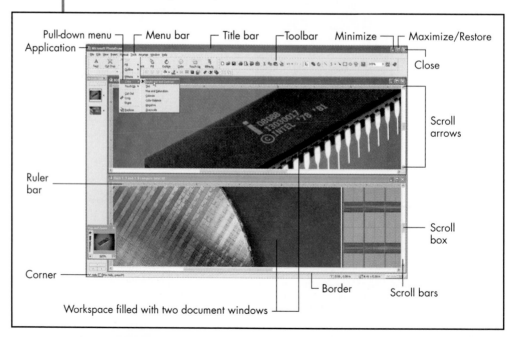

FIGURE 2-11 ARRANGEMENT OF WINDOWS

Here, four open applications are tiled on the Windows XP desktop (clockwise from top left: *Microsoft PhotoDraw, Outlook, Internet Explorer*, and *Microsoft Visio*). The applications, as well as documents within an application's work-space, can be presented as tiled documents (in top left Microsoft PhotoDraw images) or cascading (bottom left Visio documents are overlapped such that all title bars are visible).

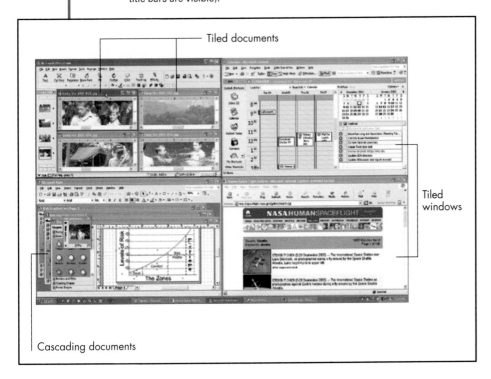

Tiled documents

Tiled windows

Cascading documents

menus are available for most applications. Other menu options depend on the application. Only the undimmed options can be chosen. Corresponding **shortcut keys** (for example, Alt+F4 to *Exit* and Ctrl+C to *Copy*) are presented next to many options in Windows menus.

Toolbars give you ready access to these frequently used menu items. Tool-bars contain multiple buttons with graphics that represent related menu options or commands.

The Dialog Box

You will encounter scores of **dialog boxes** in Windows (such as the Display Properties dialog box) and in user applications. Often, you, the user, must okay or revise entries in the dialog box before you can continue with a particular operation (see Figure 2-12).

SHARING INFORMATION AMONG APPLICATIONS

Windows offers several methods for sharing information among applications, but the easiest way is to use the Windows **Clipboard** and the *Edit* option in the menu bar. Think of the Clipboard as a holding area for information. The information in the Clipboard can be en route to another application, or it can be copied anywhere in the current document. Choosing *Edit* lets you *Cut, Copy*, or *Paste* information in the Clipboard. The *source application* and *destination application* can be the same, or they can be entirely different applications.

The procedure for transferring information via the Clipboard is demonstrated in Figure 2-13. This example illustrates the *Copy* procedure. Choosing the *Cut* option causes the specified information to be removed from the source application and placed on the Windows Clipboard.

FIGURE 2-12

ELEMENTS OF A DIALOG BOX
Many common dialog box elements are shown in the Display Properties dialog box. Not shown are the option button and scroll bar adjustment elements.

WORKING WITH FILES

Personal computing revolves around the file—the word document, the PowerPoint presentation, and so on. The **file** is a permanent, electronically accessible, recording of information. To a computer, a file is a string of 0s and 1s (digitized data) that are stored and retrieved as a single unit. Each file has a user-supplied filename by which it is stored and retrieved.

Types of Files: ASCII to Video

There are many types of files (see Figure 2-14), most of which are defined by the software that created them (for example, a spreadsheet). The following are among the more popular types of files.

- *ASCII file*. An *ASCII file* is a text-only file that can be read or created by any word processing program or text editor.
- *Data file*. A *data file* contains data in any format.
- *Document file*. All word processing and desktop publishing *document files* contain text and, often, embedded images.
- *Spreadsheet file*. A *spreadsheet file* contains rows and columns of data.
- *Web page file*. A *Web page file* is compatible with the World Wide Web and Internet browsers.
- *Source program file*. A *source program file* contains user-written instructions to the computer.
- *Executable program file*. An *executable program file* contains executable machine language code.
- *Graphics file*. A *graphics file* contains digitized images.
- *Audio file*. An *audio file* contains digitized sound.
- *Video file*. A *video file* contains digitized video frames that when played rapidly (for example, 30 frames per second) produce motion video.

FIGURE 2–13   COPY AND PASTE VIA THE CLIPBOARD

This walkthrough demonstrates the procedure for transferring information among multiple Windows applications: Paint (a paint program), Word (a word processing program), and an Internet-based encyclopedia. In the example, the Eiffel Tower image in a Paint document is marked and copied (to the Clipboard), then pasted to a Word document. Supporting text in the online *Encarta Encyclopedia* is marked and copied to the same Word document via the Clipboard.

1. ***Mark the information.*** Drag the select cursor (the Pick tool in Paint) from one corner of the information to be copied to the opposite corner of the area and release the mouse button.

2. ***Copy the marked information to the Clipboard.*** Choose Copy in the Edit menu to place the specified information on the Windows Clipboard.

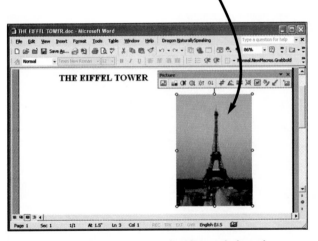

5. ***Mark the information.*** Highlight the information to be copied in the source application (Encarta Encyclopedia).

6. ***Copy the marked information to the Clipboard.***

3. ***Switch to the destination application and place the graphics cursor at the desired insertion point.***

4. ***Paste the marked information.*** Choose the Paste option in the Edit menu to copy the contents of the Clipboard to the cursor position in the destination application.

7. ***Switch to the destination application and place the graphics cursor at the desired insertion point.***

8. ***Paste the marked information.***

FIGURE 2–14 **STORING DIGITIZED RESOURCES**

Anything we digitize and store permanently takes up space on a disk or disc. Shown here are disk/disc storage requirements for a representative clip art image (hot air balloon), a 4.88-second digital recording of an audio greeting (Sound Recorder software), and a computer artist's surreal drawing.

Photo courtesy of Intel Corporation

Disk space: 94 KB

Disk space: 18 KB

Disk space: 7.127 MB

Photo courtesy of Intel Corporation

Files and Parking Lots

Disk storage is much like a parking lot for files. In a parking lot, a variety of vehicles—cars, buses, trucks, motorcycles, and so on—are put in parking places to be picked up later. Similarly, all sorts of files are "parked" in individual spots in disk storage, waiting to be retrieved later. To help you find your vehicle, large parking lots are organized with numbered parking places in lettered zones. The same is true with files and mass storage. Files are stored in numbered "parking places" on disk for retrieval. Fortunately, we do not have to remember the exact location of the file. The operating system does that for us. All we have to know is the name of the file. We assign user names to files, then recall or store them by name. Filenames in the Windows environment can include spaces, but some special characters, such as the slash (/) and colon (:), are not permitted. An optional three-character extension identifies the type of file and associates it with a program.

- *Readme.txt* is an *ASCII* file.
- *Student-Course.mdb* is a file containing a Microsoft Access *database*.
- *Letter.doc* is a Microsoft Word *document* file.
- *Income Statement.xls* is a Microsoft Excel *spreadsheet* file.
- *Adams School Home Page.htm* is a *Web page* file.
- *Module 1-1.vbp* is a Visual Basic *source program* file.
- *Play Game.exe* is an *executable program* file.
- *Family album.gif*, *Vacation Banff.bmp*, *Logo.jpg*, and *Sarah.tif* are *graphic* files.
- *My_song.wav* is an *audio* file.
- *Introduction Sequence.mov* is a *video* file.

Figure 2-15 lists the common types of files and their associated programs. Many applications can work with a variety of file formats. For example, photo illustration programs can load *jpg, gif, tif,* and other graphics file formats. However, most popular applications programs have at least one **native file format** that is associated with that program—Microsoft Word is *doc,* Microsoft Excel is *xls,* and Adobe Acrobat is *pdf.*

What to Do with a File

Everything we do on a computer involves a file and, therefore, disk storage. But what do we do with files?

- We create, name, and save files.
- We copy, move, and delete files.
- We retrieve and update files.
- We display, print, or play files (audio and video files are played).
- We execute and run files (a program is a file).
- We download and upload files over the Internet or a network.

FIGURE 2–15   COMMON FILE EXTENSIONS AND THEIR ASSOCIATED PROGRAMS

Word Processing and Text Documents

.DOC	Microsoft Word and WordPad
.WPD	WordPerfect
.WKS	Microsoft Works
.TXT	Plain ASCII text/unformatted
.PDF	Adobe Acrobat

Spreadsheets

.XLS	Microsoft Excel
.WQ1	Corel Quattro Pro
.WK1	Lotus 1-2-3
.WK3	
.WK4	

Database

.MDB	Microsoft Access

Presentation Graphics

.PPT	Microsoft PowerPoint

Graphics Formats (graphics programs typically open a variety of file types)

.GIF	CompuServe graphics interchange format
.JPG	JPEG compressed graphics format
.BMP	Windows bitmap
.PCT	PICT format
.TIF	Tagged image format (TIFF)
.PCX	PCX format
.WMF	Windows Meta File
.EPS	Encapsulated PostScript
.CGM	Computer Graphics MetaFile

Sound & Video Formats

.WAV	Widows WAV sound
.AIF	Macintosh AIFF sound
.RA	RealAudio sound
.AVI	Windows Video File
.MOV	Macintosh Quicktime video
.MPG	MPEG video format

Compressed Formats

.ZIP	PKzip/WinZIP compression
.HQX	BinHex compression (Macintosh)
.BHX	

System and Miscellaneous Files

.HTM	HTML code (Web pages)
.EXE	Executable file
.COM	
.BAT	MS-DOS batch file
.INI	Windows initialization file
.SYS	System file
.VBP	Visual Basic program file

- We import files (for example, when Word imports an Excel spreadsheet file it converts the spreadsheet file to a table in a Word document).
- We compress files (make them smaller).
- We protect files (by limiting access to authorized persons).

File compression needs a little more explanation. When the air is squeezed out of a sponge, it becomes much smaller. When you release it, the sponge returns to its original shape—nothing changes. File compression works in a similar fashion. File formats for most software packages are inefficient, resulting in wasted disk space when you save files. Using file compression, a repeated pattern, such as the word *and* in text documents, might be replaced by a one-byte descriptor in a compressed file, saving two bytes for each occurrence of *and*. For example, "A band of sand stands grand in this land" might be compressed to "A bδ of sδ stδs grδ in this lδ," where the symbol "δ" replaces "and" in the stored file. One technique used when compressing graphics files replaces those portions of an image that are the same color with a brief descriptor that identifies the color only once and the area to be colored. Depending on the type and content of the file, file compression can create a compressed file that takes 10% to 90% less mass storage (the average is about 50%). The most popular file compression format is the zip format, which is supported by a variety of programs and results in a **zip file.** A zipped file, which usually has a zip extension (such as longfile.zip), is compressed and must be unzipped before it can be used.

FILE MANAGEMENT

FILE MANAGEMENT

The *Windows Explorer* is an integrated Internet browser and file management tool. Windows Explorer, which opens when you choose the *My Computer* icon on the desktop, lets you view files in several formats (see Figure 2-16). With the Explorer, you can do all of your file management tasks such as creating, copying, moving, and deleting folders and files, as well as other folder/file-related tasks. Folders are created for a specific disk drive. The PC used to capture the screen in Figure 2-16 has a hard disk (C:) and four interchangeable disk drives: a floppy drive (A:), a Zip disk drive (D:), a DVD/CD-ROM drive (E:), and a CD-RW drive (F:).

We create folders to hold documents, programs, images, music, and other types of files. File types can be mixed within a folder; that is, the folder can hold any type of file. Some folders, such as the *Windows* and *Program Files* folders, are created by the Windows operating system during system installation; however, the user creates most folders. Typically, people choose to create their folders in a hierarchical manner to provide a logical structure for their files. For example, the file structure on disk drive D: in Figure 2-17, photos are grouped in four subordinate folders: *Boy Scout Camp, Boys School Photos, Family Reunions,* and *Sports*. The *Sports* folder has four subordinate folders to enable sports images to be grouped by sport. The *Soccer* folder has six subordinate folders so soccer photos can be organized by year. The *Personal* folder at the top of the hierarchy has five subordinate folders, one of which is *Music*. The *Music* folder has four subordinate folders: *Classical, Folk, Jazz,* and *R&B*.

You can store a specific file within a particular folder at any level in the hierarchy. For example, Sports photo images in Figure 2-17 are stored at the bottom of the hierarchy (for example, in the 2003 folder). Since files are stored within a hierarchical structure of folders, you must give the operating system the **path** to follow to store or retrieve a particular file. In Figure 2-17, for example, the image *Brady in KC game 1.jpg* has the following path:

```
Family Photo Album\Sports\Soccer\2003\Brady in KC game 1.jpg
```

The audio file for Beethoven's 5th Symphony (not shown in the figure) is stored in this path:

```
Personal\Music\Classical\Beethovens 5th.mp3
```

In the Mac OS X environment, a colon (:) is used in place of the backslash (\). In UNIX/Linux, it is a forward slash (/).

FIGURE 2-16 MY COMPUTER

Double-clicking on the *My Computer* icon on the desktop opens an Explorer window that shows active storage devices. This PC has a hard disk (C:), and four interchangeable disk drives: a floppy (A:), a zip disk (D:), and two CD-ROM/DVD-ROMs (E: and F:). Right-click on a disk icon and choose Properties to view disk usage information.

As mentioned previously, common file management activities include saving, opening, copying, moving, deleting, and renaming files. The commands used to perform these activities are available in the *File* or *Edit* menus and they are available in the shortcut menu (right click on the file to call up the shortcut menu).

- *Save/Save As.* Files are created and saved to a particular folder via the *Save* or *Save As* option in the *File* menu of an applications program.

- *Open.* In the Explorer, navigate through the path to the filename, then double-click on the filename to open the file in the application program associated with its extension (for example, Word for myfile.doc) or to execute a program file (for example, program.exe).

- *Copy.* Highlight what file you want to duplicate and choose the *Copy* command from the *Edit* menu. To complete the copy operation, navigate to where you want to save the copy (the path), then choose the *Paste* option from the *Edit* menu.

- *Cut (Move).* The *Cut* command option in the Explorer lets you move one or more files or folders. The *Cut* command (in the *Edit* menu) works like the *Copy* command, except that a cut operation deletes the highlighted item(s) from its original folder.

FIGURE 2-17   **DISK DRIVES AND MEDIA**

The Windows Explorer is a versatile utility program that lets you manipulate files and folders. Click on a disk or a folder in the Folders pane (left) and see the contents on the right. Click on the "+" to expand and list subordinate folders. Click on the "-" to hide subordinate folders. In this example, the files for the "Family Photo Album\Sports\Soccer\2003" folder are displayed, both in Thumbnails view (foreground window) and Details view (background window).

- *Delete.* Tap the Delete key or choose *Delete* in the *Edit* menu to delete whatever files/folders are highlighted.
- *Rename.* To rename the file or folder, highlight the desired file or folder, then choose *Rename* in the *File* menu.

Copy and cut operations place whatever has been copied or cut on the Clipboard; therefore, you can paste the Clipboard contents as many times as you want. The shortcut keys, for copy, move, and paste, which are marked on most keyboards, are Ctrl+C, Ctrl+X, and Ctrl+V, respectively.

HELP: F1

Every PC user eventually is stumped and needs help, even Bill Gates. Fortunately, help is readily available.

- *Help for Windows.* All you have to do is click *Start,* then *Help and Support* for operating system help. This feature provides online access to comprehensive support information, including FAQs and step-by-step tutorials.
- *Help for any applications program.* Click on *Help* in the main menu at the top of the application window.
- *Context-sensitive help.* Tap the *F1* key to get *context-sensitive help;* that is, help that relates to the window, object, or whatever is active at the time.

1 In Windows, the active window is highlighted in the background. (T/F)

2 The Close button in a Windows application is indicated with a letter Y. (T/F)

3 A file is to a hard disk as a vehicle is to a parking lot. (T/F)

4 When we convert a file from its foreign format to a format that is compatible with the current program, we: (a) import the file, (b) export the file, (c) bypass the file, or (d) link the file.

5 The shortcut key for Copy is: (a) Alt+C, (b) Shift+C, (c) Tab+C, or (d) Ctrl+C.

6 Who/what must okay or revise entries in the dialog box: (a) the operating system, (b) the system administrator, (c) the user, or (d) the PC manufacturer?

7 One way to reduce the size of a file is called file: (a) deflation, (b) compression, (c) downsizing, or (d) decreasing.

2-3 PRODUCTIVITY SOFTWARE: THE SOFTWARE SUITE

Software suites, such as Microsoft Office 2003 (shown in the illustrations), Corel WordPerfect Office, and Lotus SmartSuite, are introduced in Chapter 1. These suites are made up of several complementary applications that can include word processing, presentation, spreadsheet, database, personal information management, and communications (Internet-related) software. Most new PCs are sold with a full or partial software suite installed on the system. This section is designed to give you an overview of the general functionality and capabilities of the first five on this list. You'll probably learn the specifics of how to use software suite applications in a lab or, perhaps, via interactive computer-based training.

> ### Why this section is important to you.
>
> If your personal computing habits are typical, then you will spend a lot of time with these applications: word processing, presentation, spreadsheet, database, and personal information management. This section provides an overview of these important applications.

The software suite programs give you plenty of help with getting started. For most projects, you don't need to start from scratch to create a document, spreadsheet, or presentation. Much of what we want to do has already been done before, whether it's an expense statement spreadsheet, a fax form, or an important market report presentation. Each of the major productivity software packages offers a variety of templates to help you get a head start on your projects. A **template** is simply a document or file that is already formatted or designed for a particular task. You add the content.

WORD PROCESSING: THE MOST POPULAR PRODUCTIVITY APPLICATION

At work, at home, at school, and even during leisure activities, we spend much of our time writing. Whether an e-mail, a party announcement, a report, a diary entry, or a newsletter, all can be made easier and more presentable through the use of word processing software.

Word processing software lets us create, edit (revise), and format documents in preparation for output. Output can be a document that is printed, displayed on a monitor, faxed, e-mailed, or, perhaps, posted to the Internet for worldwide access.

Word processing is the perfect example of how automation can be used to increase productivity and foster creativity. It reduces the effort you must devote to the routine aspects of writing so you can focus your attention on its creative aspects. For example, a *spelling checker* checks your grammar and spelling, an *online thesaurus* helps you find the right word, and a *grammar and style checker* highlights grammatical concerns.

To create an original document, such as a résumé (see Figure 2-18), you simply begin entering text from the keyboard and, as needed, enter formatting commands that enhance the appearance of the document when it is printed or displayed (spacing, italics, and so on). You can insert images, such as the photo in Figure 2-18, then resize and/or reposition them anywhere within the word processing document. Once you are satisfied with the content and appearance of the document, you are ready to print, send, or display it.

FIGURE 2-18

WORD PROCESSING RÉSUMÉ

Mallory Brooks used Microsoft Word 2003 to help her make a good first impression with prospective employers. The result is this professional-looking résumé that emphasizes her strengths.

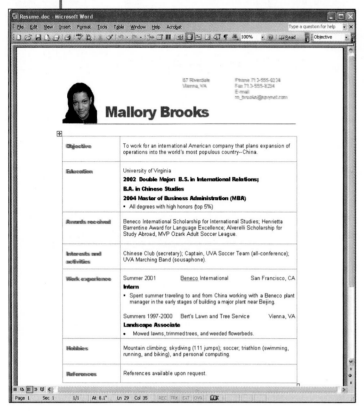

PRESENTATION SOFTWARE: PUTTING ON THE SHOW

Many studies confirm that people who use *presentation software* to create presentations are perceived as being better prepared and more professional than those who do not. Sensible use of this software can help you persuade people to adopt a particular point of view, whether at the lectern or the pulpit. Along with descriptive text, a good slide presentation will include some or all of the following: *photo images, charts* and *graphs,* original *drawings,* a variety of eye-catching *clip art, audio clips,* and even *full-motion video* captured with a digital camera. Typically, presentation software is used in conjunction with an LCD projector that projects images onto a screen for all to see.

Presentation software lets you create highly stylized images for group presentations of any kind; you can create self-running slide shows for PC-based information displays at trade shows, for class lectures (offline or online), and any other situation that requires the presentation of organized, visual information (see Figure 2-19). The software, such as Microsoft PowerPoint, gives you a rich assortment of tools to help you create a variety of charts, graphs, and images for the presentation.

With PowerPoint, you can give the audience a little candy for the eyes and ears using a variety of special effects. For example, the current graph or image can be made to fade out (dissolve to a blank screen) while the text is fading in. An applause sound can be played when a particular image or element is displayed. PowerPoint offers a variety of transitions and sounds, each of which adds an aura of professionalism while helping to hold the audience's attention. Also, text and objects can be animated: they can, for example, be made to fly in from the perimeter of the screen a word or a letter at a time.

Whether you're preparing a report, a speech, a newsletter, or any other form of business, academic, or personal communication, it pays—immediately and over the long term—to take full advantage of presentation software.

SPREADSHEET SOFTWARE: THE MAGIC MATRIX

A spreadsheet is simply a grid for entering rows and columns of data. The typical home or office has scores of applications for organizing tabular information. Instructors' grade books are good uses for spreadsheet software, with student names labeling the rows, quizzes labeling the columns, and scores being the entries. Think of anything that has rows and columns of data and you have identified an application for spreadsheet software: income (profit-and-loss) statements, personnel profiles, demographic data, home inventories, and budget summaries, just to mention a few.

Spreadsheets are organized in a tabular structure with rows and columns. The intersection of a particular row and column designates a **cell.** As you can see in Figure 2-20, the rows are numbered, and the columns are lettered. The user creates a spreadsheet template, which is a model that contains the layout and formulas needed for a particular spreadsheet task (for example, the income summary in Figure 2-20).

Data are entered and stored in a cell. During operations, data are referred to by their **cell address,** which identifies the location of a cell in the spreadsheet by its column and row, with the column designator first. For example, in the BrassCo Income Summary of Figure 2-20, F8 is the address of the total sales cell ($153,000). A given spreadsheet is designed such that the software automatically does the math operations (summing the regional sales to get total sales in the example) and logic operations. Spreadsheet packages let you generate a variety of charts from spreadsheet data (see Figure 2-20).

Spreadsheets can be large, sometimes thousands of rows and hundreds of columns. When document content is more than can be displayed in a window, you can simply scroll vertically or horizontally through the spreadsheet.

DATABASE SOFTWARE: A DYNAMIC DATA TOOL

Hundreds and maybe even thousands of databases contain information about you. The typical knowledge worker interacts with databases all day long. These are good reasons to learn more about databases. Database software lets you enter, organize, and retrieve stored data. With Microsoft Access (see Figure 2-21) and other database software packages you can:

- Create and maintain a database (add, delete, and revise records)
- Extract and list information that meets certain conditions
- Make inquiries (for example, "List all courses taught by Professor Wang")
- Sort records in ascending or descending sequence by key fields (for example, alphabetical by last name)
- Generate formatted reports with subtotals and totals

These are the basic features. They have other features as well, including spreadsheet-type computations, presentation graphics, and programming.

Both database and spreadsheet software packages let you work with data as rows and columns in a spreadsheet and as records in a database, but each has its advantages. Spreadsheet packages are great number crunchers and are very helpful for small database applications. Database software packages may be too cumbersome for any serious number crunching, but they are terrific for creating any kind of personal or business information system. Database concepts and features are discussed in more detail in Chapter 9, E-Commerce, Databases, and Security.

PERSONAL INFORMATION MANAGEMENT SOFTWARE

Personal information management (**PIM**) software is a catch-all phrase that generally refers to messaging and personal information management software that helps you manage your messages, appointments, contacts, and tasks. PIM software, such as Microsoft® Outlook®, may include *calendar* applications for appointment scheduling and reminders; communications applications

FIGURE 2-19 POWERPOINT TRI-PANE VIEW

Microsoft PowerPoint 2003 helps you prepare and present slides for presentations. PowerPoint has a variety of slide templates from which you can choose. The PowerPoint tri-pane view shows the *slide, outline,* and *notes* so you can work with all the elements of the presentation at once.

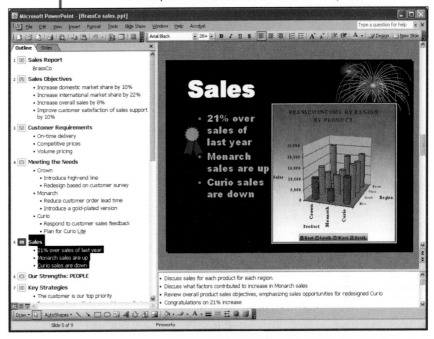

FIGURE 2-20 SPREADSHEET WITH GRAPH OF DATA

Microsoft Excel 2003, shown here, demonstrates how the regional income in the spreadsheet can be graphically illustrated in a three-dimensional bar chart.

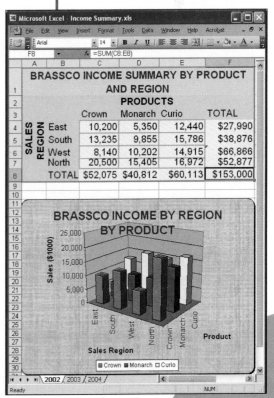

such as *e-mail, phone dialer,* and *fax;* and *databases* for organizing telephone numbers, e-mail addresses, to-do lists, notes, diary entries, and so on. Figure 2-22 gives you an overview of Microsoft Outlook personal information management software.

FIGURE 2-21

EDUCATION DATABASE: COURSE TABLE AND STUDENT TABLE

The Microsoft Access 2003 Education database is comprised of these two tables. The COURSE table contains a record for each course offered by the Computer Information Systems Department. The STUDENT table contains a record for each student who is enrolled in or has taken a course. The COURSE ID field links the two tables.

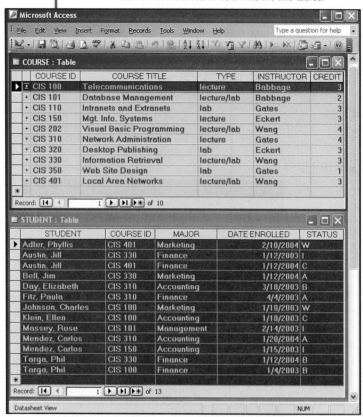

2-4   A CORNUCOPIA OF PC SOFTWARE

You could become a happy PC user and never venture far from software suite applications, e-mail, and browsing the Net. Indeed, there are over a half-million commercial software packages and downloadable shareware, freeware, and public-domain software. **Shareware** is copyrighted software that can be downloaded for free, but its use is based on an honor system where users pay a small fee to the author(s) for using it. **Freeware** is copyrighted software that can be downloaded and used free of charge. **Public-domain software** is not copyrighted and can be used without restriction.

The remainder of this chapter introduces you to a variety of PC software. This section includes an overview of *home and family* software, *education and edutainment* software, *reference* software, and *business and financial* software. Graphics and multimedia software are discussed in more depth in Section 2-5. These, however, are but the tip of the PC software iceberg.

HOME AND FAMILY SOFTWARE

Today, a wide range of software is available for home PCs that can help us with the many activities of day-to-day living, as well as some of the chores of life. Figure 2-23 illustrates but a few of the thousands of software applications that you might find around the home. For example, home *legal advisers* assist you with the creation of a variety of legal documents, from wills to lease agreements. Software is available that is specifically designed for personal advocacy; that is, it helps you make your point to government agencies, political action groups, politicians, and any other organization or individual you wish to influence. There are software packages designed to help college-bound students and their parents find and secure financial aid. And when they graduate, résumé creation software packages can help them put their best foot forward when looking for a job.

Of course, a plethora of software packages has emerged for hobbyists. No matter what your hobby, you are sure to find software that helps you with some aspect of your hobby. For example, tennis software helps you match statistics, create tournament draws, and figure rankings. There are packages for gardeners/landscapers, astronomers, astrologists, bicycling enthusiasts, UFO watchers, golfers, fishing fans, and many more.

EDUCATION AND EDUTAINMENT SOFTWARE

Emerging technologies are prompting fundamental changes in education. The *static, sequential* presentation of books has been the foundation for learning since Gutenberg. Now, however, we are beginning to see *dynamic, linked,* and *interactive technology-based* resources in virtually every discipline. When coupled with online distance learning and personal interaction of the traditional classroom environment, such resources offer a richer learning environment. We need to restate that computer-based education will not replace the classroom or teachers anytime soon, but those who have tried it agree that CBT (computer-based training) will have a dramatic impact on the way we learn.

Computer-based educational resources take many forms and are being embraced by young and old alike. Students can learn anatomy by taking virtual tours of the body. Students can travel through the Milky Way to Cassiopeia and other constellations while an electronic teacher explains the mysteries of the universe. Millions of elementary age students are getting one-on-one instruction on keyboarding skills. Chemistry students are doing lab exercises with bits and bytes rather than dangerous chemicals. Some innovative software packages tease the mind by inviting students to learn the power of logic and creativity.

It did not take long for education software developers to combine *educ*ation and enter*tainment* into a single learning resource. This *edutainment software* gives students an opportunity to play while learning. Figure 2-24 provides examples of education and edutainment software.

REFERENCE SOFTWARE

As soon as the technology gurus figured out that audio CDs could hold 650 MB of digital data, the CD-ROM was born. Almost immediately after the introduction of the CD-ROM, books, dictionaries, encyclopedias, newspapers, corporate manuals, and thousands of other printed materials were being translated to digital media, namely the CD-ROM. Now that CD-RW and DVD+RW (rewritable) are reasonably priced, we at home and in small offices can create our own CD-ROM-based and DVD-based reference material, too.

FIGURE 2-22 **PERSONAL INFORMATION MANAGEMENT SOFTWARE**

Microsoft® Outlook® 2003 provides e-mail, a contact database, a calendar, task list, and other personal information management features. Shown here is the calendar, which gives you a variety of views for your appointments from hour-by-hour to monthly.

PERSONAL COMPUTING
Killer Apps

The killer application, or "killer app," is a PC application that has such a dramatic impact on personal computing that its use can justify the cost of the hardware. The first killer app was the spreadsheet, which legitimized the PC as a business tool. Then came word processing and database software. Eventually, presentation software made the slide and overhead projectors obsolete. E-mail changed the way we communicate and the Web browser gave us ready access to millions of pages of information. Recent killer apps like speech recognition added a new dimension to system interaction. Instant messaging, the most recent killer, allows us to communicate in real time with other people via text, audio, and/or video. Each killer app on your system represents an opportunity to save time and money and to be more productive.

FIGURE 2-23 HOME AND PERSONAL SOFTWARE

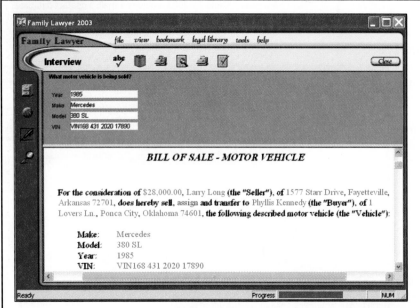

THE FAMILY LAWYER

The Family Lawyer legal software can help you prepare scores of legal documents, including this bill of sale for a motor vehicle, wills, real estate documents, power of attorney, and many more. The software gathers information in much the same way your family lawyer gathers information—through interactive questioning.

BECOME YOUR OWN PRINTER

When you want something special, try doing it yourself with *The Print Shop*. This software helps you create personalized banners (shown here), greeting cards, business cards, letterheads, certificates, calendars, announcements, invitations, and more.

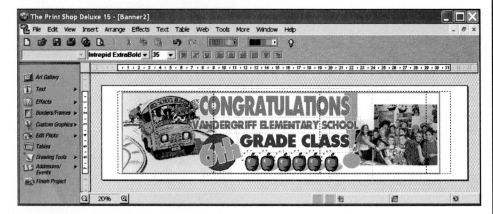

HELP WITH TAXES

Millions of people now prepare their own taxes with tax preparation software, such as *Quicken®* *TurboTax* (shown here). The interactive software guides you, step-by-step, through the process, answering your questions and making suggestions as needed. Upon completion, you are given the option of filing your return the traditional way (via the postal service) or electronically.

FIGURE 2–23 continued

BUILDING A HOUSE?

With *3D Home Architect™* you can create a floor plan for your new home and even see what it might look like when built. You can even "walk through" the inside of the house to see if the design is what you want.

FINANCIAL PLANNING FOR THE FUTURE

Quicken® Retirement Planner guides you step-by-step through the creation personalized plans for retirement, saving for college expenses, buying a vacation home, and much more. The program assists you in deciding how much you should save and where to invest your savings.

Computer-based reference material is much more than simply text on a disk. It is searchable and interactive. Attorneys no longer spend days pouring over scores of cases to prepare for trials. Keyword searches can result in a display of applicable cases within seconds.

Just about any frequently used printed reference material is available on CD-ROM, or it is being considered for CD-ROM publication. We can get detailed geographic information, multilingual dictionaries, state and federal census information, specific entrance requirements for thousands of colleges, Fortune 500 financial information, medical advice and information, and much more. Figure 2-25 gives examples of CD-ROM-based reference materials.

BUSINESS AND FINANCIAL SOFTWARE

There are literally thousands of PC-based business and financial-oriented software packages for the home and small office. In the business community, there are software packages specifically designed for physicians'

PERSONAL COMPUTING
The Worth of the Software Bundle

One of the greatest challenges in choosing between alternative PCs is appraising the worth of the preinstalled software. PC vendors want the quality or variety of their software bundle(s) to either confuse the buyer or be the difference maker, depending on the quality of their offerings. The bundled software frequently is the biggest variable in the PC-purchase decision process. A PC vendor may advertise the worth of their software as $800, but the real value is its "street price," which is probably no more than $50 or $60.

FIGURE 2-24 EDUCATION AND EDUTAINMENT SOFTWARE

PLAYING ROCK GUITAR

Voyetra's Teach Me Rock Guitar™ provides an easy, step-by-step method for learning rock guitar. The Animated Fretboard shows you the fingerings on the guitar neck in real time as you play. You can even jam with the band!

LEARN TO SPEAK SPANISH

Computers and their software have proven to be effective teachers of languages. The Spanish software gives instruction and practice in real-world conversations.

---

clinics, construction contractors, CPAs, churches, motels, law offices, nonprofit organizations, real estate companies, recreation and fitness centers, restaurants, and just about any other organization that has administrative information processing needs. Some business-oriented software for smaller companies can run on a single PC, and other packages are designed for the LAN client/server environment so information can be shared among workers. At home, millions of people now keep family financial records on a PC. Figure 2-26 shows several business/financial software examples.

techtv™
FREEWARE

THE CRYSTAL BALL
Software Updates Overnight

A major headache for businesses and individuals is keeping software up to date. Software and hardware vendors post downloadable updates to the Internet to correct oversights in programming, address security concerns, and add improvements that permit the software to work seamlessly with other new software and devices. The typical PC is filled with software that needs periodic updating. Already, some IT companies alert you when updates are available or they upload and install the updates automatically. This is the beginning of a trend. Within a few of years, users will demand and get software that is updated automatically via the Internet, probably overnight.

FIGURE 2–25   REFERENCE SOFTWARE

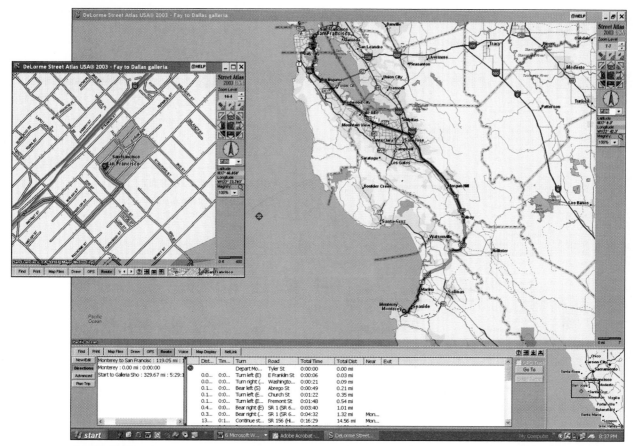

NEVER BE LOST AGAIN

Street Atlas 2003 USA® by DeLorme is a seamless map of the entire country. It offers detail, street address search power, and door-to-door routing. Just identify your start (Los Angeles, CA) and finish (San Francisco, CA) points and the software calculates and then displays the best route (in orange). You can zoom in for street-level maps (downtown San Francisco in the example). The program also interfaces with global positioning systems (GPSs) to pinpoint your location on the map display and to guide you to your destination.

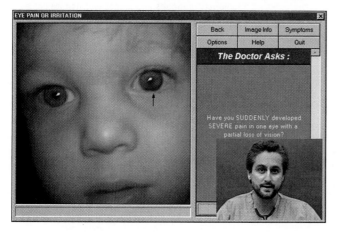

HOME MEDICAL ADVISOR

Home Medical Advisor™ is a practical guide to symptom diagnosis and preventive care. You can even talk to a "video" doctor to get answers to detailed questions (shown here) and then receive possible diagnoses and treatments.

© 2000 TLC Education Properties LLC. All Rights Reserved.

FIGURE 2-26 PERSONAL FINANCE AND BUSINESS SOFTWARE

PROJECT MANAGEMENT

Microsoft's *Project* is a great tool for anyone who oversees a team, plans a budget, juggles schedules, or has deadlines to meet.

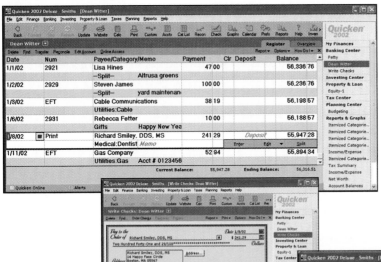

BUSINESS AND HOME FINANCES

Anyone who has attempted to balance a checkbook or consolidate tax information will appreciate *Quicken®*. This financial management system helps you, personally, or it can help a company manage bills, bank accounts, investments, tax records, assets and liabilities, and much more. Quicken offers users a variety of reports and graphs (see itemized categories report).

FIGURE 2-26 continued

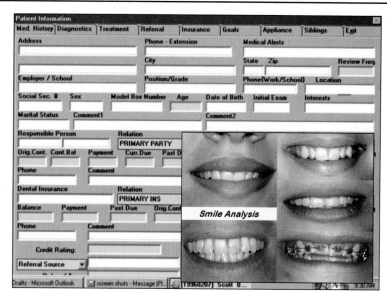

APPLICATION-SPECIFIC SOFTWARE: DENTISTRY

With Dr. Richard Roblee, an expert in aesthetic dentistry and orthodontic techniques and interdisciplinary therapy, information technology is critical to his practice and philosophy of treatment. Dr. Roblee relies on several patient information systems to help him, his staff, and his patients track progress, sometimes for years.

Courtesy of Dr. Richard Roblee, D.D.S., M.S.; IDT Systems, Inc. roblee@idt-network.com

1 Tax preparation software lets you file taxes electronically. (T/F)

2 Mapping software can interface with global positioning systems to pinpoint your location on a map. (T/F)

3 Which of these software applications would not be considered a common application for home use: (a) greeting cards/banners, (b) tax preparation, (c) morphing, or (d) preparing legal documents?

4 It is technologically possible for people at home to put their own reference material on CD-ROM by using what technology: (a) CD-RW and DVD+RW, (b) audio CD, (c) VHS, or (d) PCMCIA.

SECTION

2-5 GRAPHICS SOFTWARE AND MULTIMEDIA

If you wish to add some pizzazz to output and your PC sessions, you will want to familiarize yourself with graphics software and multimedia. That pizzazz could be anything from colorful illustrations for a cyber greeting card to full multimedia class presentations involving sound, animation, and motion video. **Multimedia** is an umbrella term that refers to the capability that allows the integration of computer-based text, still graphics, motion visuals, animation, and sound. This section introduces you to an array of graphics software options and to multimedia concepts.

Why this section is important to you.

More and more, we are living in a multimedia world full of sound, colorful images, and motion. Your multimedia experience is enhanced when you understand the scope of the software used to create, view, and modify multimedia sounds, images, and video.

GRAPHICS SOFTWARE

Graphics software enables the creation, manipulation, and management of computer-based images. Graphics software helps you create line drawings, company logos, maps, clip art, blueprints, flowcharts, or just about any image you can visualize. You can even touch up red eyes in photographs.

Graphic images can be maintained as bit-mapped graphics, vector graphics, or in a metafile format. In **bit-mapped graphics,** the image is composed of patterns of dots called *picture elements,* or **pixels.** The term **raster graphics** is also used to describe *bit-mapped* images. In **vector graphics,** the image is composed of patterns of lines, points, and other geometric shapes (vectors). The **metafile format** is a class of graphics that combines the components of bit-mapped and vector graphics formats. The naked eye cannot distinguish one method of graphics display from another; however, the differences are quite apparent when you try to manipulate images in the various formats.

Paint Software and Bit-Mapped Graphics

Bit-mapped graphics, displayed as dot patterns, are created by graphics paint software (see Figure 2-27), digital cameras, fax machines, and scanners, and when you capture an image on a screen. The term *bit-mapped* is used because the image is projected, or "mapped," onto the screen based on binary bits. Dots, or pixels, on the screen are arranged in rows and columns. The typical PC monitor displays over a million pixels in rows and columns (for example, in 1024 rows and 1280 columns). Each dot or pixel on a monitor is assigned a number that denotes its position on the screen grid (120th row and 323rd column) and its color.

As with all internal numbers in a computer system, the numbers that describe the pixel attributes (position and color) are binary bits (1s and 0s). The number of bits needed to describe a pixel increases with the monitor's resolution and the number of colors that can be presented (from 256 colors in 8-bit color mode to 32-bit true color mode with millions of colors). Images are stored according to a **file format** that specifies how the information is organized in the file. Most of the popular programs that create graphic images have their own file formats. The bit-mapped file format for a specific file is noted by its filename extension (for example, AuntBertha.bmp or CompanyLogo.gif). A few of the many commonly used graphics formats are:

- *JPEG or JPG.* **JPEG,** or **JPG,** is commonly used on Web pages and in digital photography.
- *BMP.* **BMP** is a common format used in the Microsoft Windows environment.
- *GIF.* **GIF,** a patented format, is used in Web pages and for downloadable online images.
- *TIFF and TIF.* **TIFF,** or **TIF,** is the industry standard for high-resolution bit-mapped images used in print publishing.
- *PCX.* **PCX** was introduced for PC Paintbrush (distributed with Windows) but is supported by many graphics packages and by scanners and faxes.
- *PNG.* **PNG** provides a patent-free replacement for GIF.

Paint software, such as the Windows® XP Paint program (see Figure 2-27), gives you a sophisticated electronic canvas for the creation of bit-mapped images. Although you can perform amazing feats with paint software, one important similarity remains between it and the traditional canvas: Whatever you draw on either one

FIGURE 2-27 PAINT: A PAINT PROGRAM

Paint software provides you with a sophisticated electronic canvas for the creation of bit-mapped images. Because the canvas is a bit map, you must erase or draw over any individual part with which you are dissatisfied. This screen shows the steps in creating this PC image: *Step A* (draw image outline); *Step B* (fill in background colors); *Step C* (draw lines as needed); *Step D* (do "free-hand" drawing as needed); *Step E* (draw in PC logo and chart); *Step F* (change colors as needed, add keyboard).

becomes part of the whole drawing. Because the canvas is a *bit map*, you must erase or draw over any individual part with which you are dissatisfied.

Draw Software and Vector Graphics

The vector graphics display, in contrast to the bit-mapped graphics display, permits the user to work with objects, such as a drawing of a computer. Computer-aided design (CAD) software, which is used by engineers and scientists, uses vector graphics to meet the need to manipulate individual objects on the screen. Figure 2-28 illustrates a vector graphics image. Notice how the screen portion of the overall image is actually made up of many objects. Think of a vector graphics screen image as a collage of one or more objects.

Draw software, such as Adobe Illustrator in Figure 2-28, relies on vector graphics instead of the bit-mapped graphics of paint software. As a result, draw software gives you greater flexibility and allows you to alter images more easily. For example, with draw software a specific object can be moved, copied, deleted, rotated, tilted, flipped horizontally or vertically, stretched, and squeezed without affecting the rest of the drawing.

Because vector graphics are defined in geometric shapes, vector graphics images take up less storage space than do bit-mapped images. *CGM* and *EPS* are widely supported vector graphics file formats. A popular metafile format, *WMF,* is used for exchanging graphics between Windows applications.

Photo Illustration Software

Photo illustration software lets you create original images as well as dress up existing digitized images, such as photographs, scanned images, and electronic paintings. Images can be retouched with special effects to dramatically alter the way they appear (see Figure 2-29). Photo illustration software is to an image as word processing software is to text. A word processing package allows you to edit, sort, copy, and generally do whatever can be done to electronic text. Photo illustration software allows you to do just about anything imaginable

Graphic Images
- Bit-mapped (raster) graphics
  - Image as pixels
  - Bit-mapped image
- Vector graphics
  - Image as line patterns and geometric shapes
  - Permits manipulation of objects within image
- Metafiles
  - Combination of bit-mapped and vector

FIGURE 2–28	**ADOBE ILLUSTRATOR: A DRAW PROGRAM**

Adobe® Illustrator®, shown here, is a vector graphics program. The user draws, then integrates objects to create the drawing. This drawing is made up of several vector objects. Some of the many objects that make up the drawing are moved and highlighted to demonstrate what makes up a vector graphics drawing. In the exploded example, each object is highlighted in blue. Adobe Illustrator's interface is similar to Paint's (see Figure 2-37); however, its drawing features are much more sophisticated.

FIGURE 2-29   PHOTO ILLUSTRATION SOFTWARE

Photo illustration software, such as *Microsoft® PhotoDraw®* (shown here), lets you work with digital images, such as those resulting from a digital photograph and scan of an image. With photo illustration software, you can touch up your photographs and apply a wide variety of special effects to all or portions of your images.

CROPPING

You can cut out or crop portions of your image in a variety of shapes (crowns, clover leafs, stars, bells, ovals, and so on).

CONTRAST AND BRIGHTNESS

The contrast and brightness feature can be used to save photographs that may otherwise be too dark (or light) in spots.

SPECIAL EFFECTS

The special effects shown here are but a few of the many that can be applied to give your digital images an artistic touch.

to digitized photos or drawings. The result of a photo illustrator's effort is a composite image with stunning special effects. For example, you can show the changes that take place as one image is modified to become an entirely different image. This process is called **morphing**, a term derived from the word *metamorphosis*.

An interesting application of what photo illustration software can do is the electronic aging of missing children. Artists combine a child's snapshot with a database of measurements showing how human facial dimensions change in a fairly predictable way over time. Such retouched snapshots have helped find hundreds of children since the mid-1980s.

Drag-and-Drop Software

Drag-and-drop software is designed for those who need to create drawings and diagrams but are not graphics specialists and artists. With drag-and-drop software, users drag ready-made shapes from application-specific stencils to the desired position on the drawing area (see Figure 2-30). Each stencil addresses a particular application. For example, the user can select stencils for flowcharting, organizational charts, network diagrams, landscaping, maps, plant layout, bath and kitchen planning, various engineering schematics, marketing, project management, vehicle accident reporting, business graphics, and many more. Even stencils with dinosaurs and castles are available.

In drag-and-drop software, the shapes are intelligent; they can take on different forms, proportions, colors, and other properties, depending on the context in which they are used.

FIGURE 2-30 DRAG-AND-DROP SOFTWARE

Microsoft Visio® lets you create professional-looking drawings. Images are chosen from these templates (on the left), then dragged to the drawing area and dropped.

Animation Software

The next step up from a static display of images is a dynamic display—that is, one that features movement within the display. *Animation*, or movement, is accomplished by the rapid repositioning (moving) of objects on the display screen, giving the illusion of movement. For example, animation techniques give life to video-game characters and it can spice up tutorials and Web sites. **Animation software**, such as Macromedia's Director, is used to create animations.

Most presentation software packages, such as PowerPoint, have several built-in animation features that help you include simple animation in the slides used in a presentation. For example, the *animated bullet build* feature can be applied to a simple text chart to integrate animation into the presentation of the bullet points on the chart.

Video Editing Software

Video editing is the process of manipulating **video** images. Not too long ago, video editing was the exclusive purview of video editing

FIGURE 2-31 VIDEO EDITING

Video editing software, such as Adobe® Premiere®, shown here, lets you manipulate still and video images and audio to create professional-looking video.

specialists working with hardware that cost in excess of $100,000. Now, you can do sophisticated video editing on your home PC (see Figure 2-31). The hardware and software needed over and above a typical PC—a video capture card and video editing software—can be purchased for as little as $100. **Video editing software,** such as Adobe's *Premiere* and Apple's *Final Cut,* lets you pick the video segments you want, sequence the clips, add background music, add scene transitions, place text over video, and employ many other special effects. You can even do fast and slow motion to create exciting "movie" sequences.

THE MULTIMEDIA EXPERIENCE

Dolby sound, colorful digital imagery, tactile feedback, and many other capabilities that tickle our senses have transformed personal computing into a multimedia experience. We see multimedia on the Internet demonstrating "How Things Work," in presentations that open with musical fanfares, in retail kiosks that provide product information, and increasingly in interactive e-books (see Figure 2-32).

Growing with Multimedia

The typical off-the-shelf PC is multimedia ready. The next stage of multimedia growth comes when you decide to pursue sophisticated multimedia applications—perhaps your own multimedia title, an interactive tutorial, or an information kiosk. At this point, you or your company may need to invest in some or all of the following hardware.

- *Digital camera.* To capture high-resolution digital images.
- *Video camera, videocassette recorder/player, audiocassette player, CD-audio player, and television.*
- *CD-RW or DVD+RW.* To "burn" multimedia CD-ROMs or DVDs.
- *Synthesizer.* To reproduce a variety of special effects and sounds and to create source music.
- *Video capture card.* To capture and digitize full-motion color video.
- *Color scanner.* To scan hard copy source material.

Multimedia Resources

Multimedia applications draw content material from a number of sources.

Sound Files

Sound files are of two types: *waveform* and *nonwaveform.* The waveform files, or **wave files,** contain the digital information needed to reconstruct the analog waveform of the sound so it can be played through speakers. The primary Windows waveform files are identified with the WAV extension (for example, SOUNDFIL.WAV).

Another popular sound file format is MP3, which enables CD-quality music to be compressed to about 8% of its original size while retaining CD sound quality. For example, a three-minute song on CD takes 33 MB of disk space, but it can be compressed to 3 MB in MP3 format. The MP3 compression process simply removes sounds outside of the audible range of the human ear, both low and high.

The nonwaveform file contains instructions as to how to create the sound, rather than a digitized version of the actual sound. For example, an instruction might tell the computer the pitch, duration, and sound quality of a particular musical note. The most common nonwaveform file, which is primarily for recording and playing music, is known as the **MIDI file.** MIDI files are identified with the MID extension (for example, MUSICFIL.MID). MIDI stands for Musical Instrument Digital Interface. MIDI provides an interface between PCs and electronic musical instruments, such as the synthesizer (see Figure 2-33).

Image Files

Multimedia is visual, so it uses lots of images. Common sources of images include:

- *You.* You can create your own images using the graphics software and techniques discussed earlier in this chapter.

FIGURE 2–32   **MULTIMEDIA APPLICATIONS**

THE MULTIMEDIA ENCYCLOPEDIA

Far more people are choosing multimedia encyclopedias, such as the Grolier Multimedia Encyclopedia shown here, than traditional print encyclopedias.

Grolier Multimedia Encyclopedia © 2001 by Grolier Interactive Inc.

WINDOWS MEDIA PLAYER

The Windows Media Player software that comes with any Windows operating system lets you play your digital media, including music, videos, DVDs, Internet radio, and audio CDs (shown here).

INFORMATIVE KIOSKS

The manner in which we obtain information is changing rapidly. Virgin Entertainment Group provides kiosks that enable customers to preview hundreds of thousands of CDs, DVDs, and Console Games.

Courtesy of International Business Machines Corporation. Unauthorized use not permitted.

- *Clip art.* Anyone serious about creating multimedia material will have a hefty clip art library of up to 100,000 images.

- *Scanned images.* With a scanner, you can scan and digitize any hard copy image (photographs, drawings, and so on).

FIGURE 2–32 continued

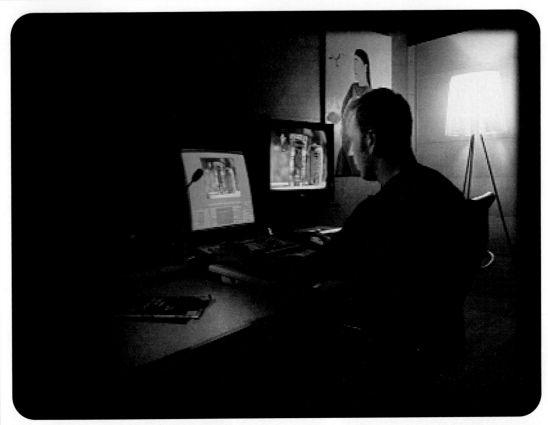

MULTIMEDIA IN THE HOME AND OFFICE

Modern PCs have the computing capacity for a broad range of multimedia applications.
This telecommuter uses his PC to do video editing for a film production studio.

Courtesy of Autodesk, Inc.

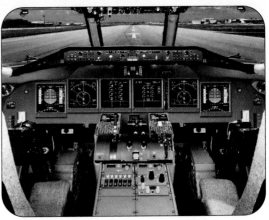

SIMULATION IN EDUCATION

People retain 10% of the information they see; 20% of what they hear; 50% of
what they see and hear; and 80% of what they see, hear, and do. Commercial
airline pilots use flight simulators, such as this one, to learn normal flight
operations and to practice emergency procedures.

Courtesy of Lockheed Martin Corporation

● *Photo images.* Photo image libraries are available commercially as downloadable
files over the Internet or you can create your own with a digital camera.

Motion Video Files

Obtaining relevant motion video for a particular multimedia application can be a challenge. You will need a video camera and a video capture board to produce original motion
video for inclusion in a multimedia application. Depending on your presentation, you may
need actors, props, and a set, as well. For example, you will frequently see video clips of
onscreen narrators in multimedia presentations and tutorials. Videos are produced as you

would any video product (set, actor, and so on), then digitized for storage on a CD-ROM or hard disk.

Motion video files are disk hogs; that is, they take up lots of space, up to a gigabyte per minute of video unless files are compressed. Digital video is functionally like motion picture film, whereby still images are displayed rapidly, from 15 to 60 frames per second, to create the illusion of motion. Video can be compressed up to 20 to 1 by recording and storing that portion of the image that changes from frame to frame. These are the most popular video compression formats in use today (filename extensions are in parentheses).

- *Video for Windows* (avi) from Microsoft Corporation
- *QuickTime* (mov) from Apple Computer Company
- *MPEG* (mpg) is an ISO (International Standards Organization) standard developed by MPEG (Moving Picture Experts Group).

FIGURE 2-33 **DIGITAL AUDIO SEQUENCER AND MIDI**

Digital Orchestrator Pro™ lets you create multitrack recordings from external audio sources, such as the output from a keyboard synthesizer or an audio CD. Digital audio and MIDI tracks exist side by side in perfect sync, making song editing a snap.

Creating a Multimedia Application: Putting the Resources Together

Once you have prepared and/or identified the desired sight and sound resource material, you are ready to put it together. A variety of software packages is available to help you accomplish this task.

- *Presentation software.* As we have seen earlier in this chapter, presentation software such as PowerPoint can help you prepare and create stimulating multimedia presentations.
- *Authoring software.* To create interactive multimedia tutorials and titles, you will need **authoring software,** such as Macromedia Director, which lets you create multimedia applications that integrate sound, motion, text, animation, and images.
- *Multimedia programming.* The creation of sophisticated commercial multimedia titles, such as the multimedia encyclopedia, and Web pages may require the use of several multimedia development tools, including high-end authoring systems and programming languages, such as Visual Basic and C++.

Multimedia possibilities stretch the human imagination to its limits. Already we see that multimedia will change the face of publishing. Many feel that interactive e-books based on multimedia technology have the potential to be more accessible and effective than traditional books, especially as learning tools. Early indications are that passive entertainment, such as TV and movies, may take a back seat to interactive multimedia entertainment that involves the viewer in the action.

1 In bit-mapped graphics, the image is composed of patterns of: (a) vectors, (b) pictures, (c) dots, or (d) objects.

2 MIDI files are: (a) waveform files, (b) nonwaveform files, (c) minidigital files, or (d) minifiles.

3 Which type of graphics software package provides a computer-based version of the painter's canvas: (a) draw, (b) paint, (c) illustrator, or (d) sketch?

4 Which of the following pairs of file formats are used in Web page design: (a) JPG and BMP, (b) TIF and PCX, (c) JPG and GIF, or (d) TIF and PNG?

Chapter Review

CHAPTER SUMMARY

2-1 THE OPERATING SYSTEM

Software falls into two categories, system software and applications software. The operating system, which is system software, and its graphical user interface (GUI) are the nucleus of all software activity. One of the operating system programs, called the kernel, loads other operating system and applications programs to RAM as they are needed.

Early versions of the GUI-based Windows (Windows 95, Windows 98, and Windows Me) emerged from MS-DOS, a text-based operating system. Windows NT and Windows 2000 started a new era. Windows XP and Windows 2003 Server work together to make client/server computing possible. Microsoft's .Net platform encompasses the operating system plus a suite of software tools and services that enable seamless interaction between people, networked computers, applications, and the Internet.

The Apple family of microcomputers and Mac OS X define another major platform.

Linux, a spin-off of the popular UNIX operating system, is a popular operating system for a variety of computers. Linux is open source software. The Linux-based LindowsOS has file-level compatibility with many Windows-based applications.

A wide variety of system software utilities can help with personal computing tasks, such as disk and file maintenance, system recovery, security, backup, and virus protection.

2-2 WINDOWS CONCEPTS AND TERMINOLOGY

The GUI-based Windows series runs one or more applications in windows. The screen upon which icons, windows, and so on are displayed is known as the desktop. The active window displays the application being currently used by the user.

A rectangular application window contains an open application (a running application). Several applications can be open, but there is only one active window at any given time.

Everything that relates to the application noted in the title bar is displayed in the workspace. Several document windows can be displayed in the parent application window's workspace.

The most common method of sharing information among applications is to use the Windows Clipboard and the *Edit* option in the menu bar.

The file is a permanent, electronically accessible, recording of information. The types of files include ASCII, data, document, spreadsheet, web page, source program, executable program, graphics, audio, and video files. Files can be made smaller via file compression.

The Windows Explorer performs file management tasks such as creating folders, copying files, moving files, deleting files, and other folder/file-related tasks. A folder contains a logical grouping of related files and/or subordinated folders.

2-3 PRODUCTIVITY SOFTWARE: THE SOFTWARE SUITE

Software suites can include word processing, presentation, spreadsheet, database, personal information management, and communications (Internet-related) software. Each of the major productivity software packages offers a variety of templates to help you get a head start on your projects.

Word processing lets you create text-based documents into which you can integrate images. Presentation software enables you to create a wide variety of visually appealing and informative presentation graphics.

Spreadsheet software provides an electronic alternative to thousands of traditionally manual tasks that involve rows and columns of data. The intersection of a particular row and column in a spreadsheet designates a cell. During operations, data are referred to by their cell addresses.

Database software lets you enter, organize, and retrieve stored data. Both database and spreadsheet software packages let us work with tabular data and records in a database; however, database software is better for use in personal and business information systems.

Personal information management, or PIM, refers to messaging and personal information management software. PIM software helps you manage your messages, appointments, contacts, and tasks.

2-4 A CORNICOPIA OF PC SOFTWARE

There are over a half-million commercial software packages and downloadable shareware, freeware, and public-domain software.

A wide range of software is available for home PCs that can help us with the many activities of day-to-day living. Popular home applications include greeting cards and banners, tax preparation, and edutainment. Edutainment software combines education and entertainment into a single software package. Most of the reference material distributed on CD-ROM is commercial (for example, encyclopedias) or proprietary; however, with CD-RW and DVD+RW we can create our own CD-ROM or DVD-based reference material. A wide variety of PC-based business and financial-oriented software packages are available for the home and small office.

2-5 GRAPHICS SOFTWARE AND MULTIMEDIA

Multimedia is an umbrella term that refers to the capability that allows the integration of computer-based text, still graphics, motion visuals, animation, and sound.

Graphics software facilitates the creation, manipulation, and management of computer-based images. Graphic images are presented as bit-mapped graphics (file formats include BMP, GIF, TIFF or TIF, PCX, PNG, and JPEG or JPG), vector graphics (CGM and EPS), and metafiles (WMF). In bit-mapped graphics, or raster graphics, the image is composed of patterns of dots (pixels). In vector graphics, the image is composed of patterns of lines, points, and other geometric shapes (vectors).

Paint software, which works with bit-mapped images, provides the user with an electronic canvas. Draw software lets you create a screen image, then isolate and manipulate representations of individual objects within the overall image.

Photo illustration software lets you create original images as well as to dress up existing digitized images, such as photographs and electronic paintings. Drag-and-drop software allows users to drag ready-made shapes from application-specific stencils to the desired position on the drawing area.

Animation software lets you further enhance presentations with animations. Video editing software lets you sequence video clips, add background music, add scene transitions, place text over video, and employ many other special effects.

Multimedia applications draw content material from a number of sources, including sound files, image files, and motion video files. Sound files are of two types: waveform (or wave file) and nonwaveform (or MIDI file).

The most popular video compression formats in use today are Video for Windows (avi), QuickTime (mov), and MPEG (mpg).

There is a variety of software packages available to help you create multimedia applications, including authoring.

KEY TERMS

active window (p. 79)
animation software (p. 103)
application windows (p. 79)
authoring software (p. 107)
background (p. 72)
bit-mapped (raster) graphics (p. 100)
cascading windows (p. 80)
cell (p. 91)
cell address (p. 91)
clipboard (p. 82)
desktop (p. 77)
dialog box (p. 82)
document window (p. 80)
drag-and-drop software (p. 103)
draw software (p. 101)
file (p. 104)
file compression (p. 86)
file format (p. 100)
foreground (p. 72)
freeware (p. 92)
graphical user interface (GUI) (p. 71)

home networking (p. 72)
icon (p. 72)
interoperability (p. 77)
kernel (p. 71)
LindowsOS (p. 75)
Linux (p. 74)
Mac OS X (p. 74)
metafile format (p. 100)
MIDI file (p. 104)
morphing (p. 103)
MS-DOS (p. 72)
multimedia (p. 99)
multiplatform environment (p. 77)
multitasking (p. 72)
native file format (p. 84)
.NET platform (p. 77)
open application (p. 79)
open source software (p. 75)
paint software (p. 100)
path (p. 87)
photo illustration software (p. 101)

pixels (p. 100)
plug-and-play (p. 74)
public-domain software (p. 92)
pull-down menu (p. 80)
scrolling (p. 80)
shareware (p. 92)
shortcut keys (p. 80)
template (p. 90)
tiled windows (p. 80)
toolbars (p. 82)
UNIX (p. 74)
utility programs (p. 71)
vector graphics (p. 100)
video editing software (p. 103)
wave files (p. 104)
windows (p. 77)
Windows 2003 Server (p. 74)
Windows CE .NET (p. 74)
Windows XP (p. 74)
workspace (p. 79)
zip file (p. 86)

MATCHING

_____ 1. Windows CE .NET

_____ 2. Linux

_____ 3. .NET

_____ 4. freeware

_____ 5. JPG

_____ 6. ASCII file

_____ 7. background (windows)

_____ 8. spreadsheet file

_____ 9. zipped file

_____10. folder

a text-only file

b location of inactive windows

c copyrighted software

d operating system for handhelds

e Microsoft platform for interoperability

f spinoff of UNIX

g compressed file

h contains rows and columns of data

i common Web file format

j grouping of related files

TRUE/FALSE

1. MS-DOS is a state-of-the-art operating system. (T/F)

2. All computers, including computers dedicated to a particular application, have operating systems. (T/F)

3. Apple family of PCs is unique in that it does not need an operating system. (T/F)

4. UNIX is a subset of Windows 2003 Server, a more sophisticated operating system. (T/F)

5. The proper use of utility software can help keep a PC running at peak efficiency. (T/F)

6. The universal use of virus vaccine software over the past decade has done away with the threat of computer viruses. (T/F)

7. The cascading windows option fills the workspace in such a way that no document window overlaps another. (T/F)

8. Presentation software allows users to create imaginative slides for use during presentations. (T/F)

9. A Windows folder can contain either files or subordinated folders, but not both. (T/F)

10. The intersection of a particular row and column in a spreadsheet designates a cell. (T/F)

11. Spreadsheet software works only with numbers and does not generate charts. (T/F)

12. Project management software helps you plan and track your projects more effectively. (T/F)

13. Database software gives you greater flexibility in the manipulation of numerical data in rows and columns of data than does spreadsheet software. (T/F)

14. Personal information management is concerned with messages, appointments, contacts, and tasks. (T/F)

MULTIPLE CHOICE

1. A GUI is: (a) text-based, (b) graphics-based, (c) label-based, or (d) paste-based.

2. The operating system for the Apple iMac is: (a) OS Mac, (b) iMac OS, (c) Mac OS X, or (d) The Mac BOSS.

3. Which of these is a spin-off of the popular UNIX multiuser operating system: (a) Bendix, (b) Linux, (c) Linus, or (d) Lucy?

4. Which of the following would not be considered utility software: (a) virus protection, (b) temperature monitoring, (c) disk maintenance, or (d) gaming?

5. Which of these devices is critical to effective interaction with a GUI: (a) printer, (b) CD-ROM, (c) mouse, or (d) scanner?

6. Document windows are displayed in the parent application window's: (a) system window, (b) title bar, (c) scroll area, or (d) workspace.

7. A slide in a slide presentation would not include: (a) photo images, charts, and graphs, (b) clip art and audio clips, (c) content templates, or (d) full-motion video.

8. Which of these is a presentation software special effect: (a) fade out, (b) thumbnail, (c) notes, or (d) export file?

9. Data in a spreadsheet are referred to by their cell: (a) box, (b) number, (c) address, or (d) code.

10. Which of the following is not a characteristic of education software: (a) linked, (b) sequential, (c) interactive, or (d) dynamic?

11. Which type of software gives the student an opportunity to play while learning: (a) education, (b) entertainment, (c) edutainment, or (d) fun-and-learn?

12. In the interactive learning environment, we learn: (a) primarily within workgroups, (b) at our own pace, (c) by the schedule in a syllabus, or (d) only at night.

13. Which of the following is not a characteristic of reference material on CD-ROM: (a) searchable, (b) interactive, (c) multimedia, or (d) limited to public domain content?

14. Another term for bit-mapped graphics is: (a) raster, (b) vector, (c) faster, or (d) geometric?

15. What type of program lets you create multimedia applications that integrate sound, motion, text, animation, and images: (a) authoring, (b) writer, (c) integrator, or (d) direction?

16. What class of graphics combines the components of bit-mapped and vector graphics formats: (a) metafiles, (b) raster files, (c) text files, or (d) MIDI files?

17. Which of these devices would not be listed with multimedia hardware: (a) color scanner, (b) CD+RW, (c) fax machine, or (d) video capture card?

18. The industry standard for high-resolution bit-mapped images used in print publishing is: (a) TIF, (b) JPG, (c) GIF, or (d) WMF.

1. THE QUALITY OF SOFTWARE

The software market is highly competitive even though Microsoft dominates the operating system and productivity software markets. Competition and other market pressures have forced software vendors, including Microsoft, into rushing their products to market, bugs and all. Some industry observers have argued that the quality of software is declining with an increasingly higher percentage of bugs being left intact within commercial software. The end result of this rush to market is that customers lose time and money coping with annoying bugs. Information technology and those who make software decisions are putting pressure on software vendors to raise the quality of their software. Generally, they want a clean product, even if they have to wait for it.

Discussion: What can software vendors do within the context of competition and economic reality to improve software quality?

Discussion: What can those who buy commercial software do to improve software quality?

2. COUNTERFEIT SOFTWARE

In some countries, counterfeit software far outnumbers legitimate proprietary software. Counterfeit software is software that is illegally mass produced from copies of the original manufacturer's software and packaged for retail sales. Counterfeit software may look very much, or exactly, like that distributed by the product's manufacturer. Until recently it was believed that most of this activity was off-shore (outside the United States); however, a counterfeit ring that had produced and sold millions of dollars worth of counterfeit Microsoft was uncovered in California. The sophisticated operation included commercial CD-ROM duplicators, color printing presses, packaging machines, and everything else needed to create the illusion of a legitimate software package worthy of a certificate of authenticity.

Discussion: What would be appropriate punishment for the owner of a company that produced and sold over $50 million worth of counterfeit copyright software? For someone who knowingly sold the counterfeit products to legitimate retail outlets? For someone who worked on the counterfeit company's production line?

Discussion: What can be done to protect intellectual property from counterfeit operations that is not already being done?

Discussion: What, if any, punishment should be given a student who uses CD-RW capability to make a duplicate copy of Microsoft Office, and then gives it to his or her friend. What about the friend who installs and uses the pirated copy of Microsoft Office?

Discussion: Does widespread abuse of copyright laws have any impact on incentives for creating intellectual property, such as software? Explain.

DISCUSSION AND PROBLEM SOLVING

1. Some people contend that the traditional text-based, command-driven operating system interface has some advantages over the modern graphical user interface. Speculate on what these advantages might be.

2. Multitasking allows PC users to run several programs at a time. Describe a PC session in which you would have at least two applications running at the same time.

3. Why is the selection of a platform such an important decision to an organization?

4. How often should you run antivirus software to scan your PC system for viruses?

5. Discuss the consequences of not performing routine disk maintenance with utility software.

6. List and briefly describe four elements of the Windows application window.

7. Describe three situations in which you might use the Clipboard to copy or move information within or between applications.

8. Some organizations may delay their migration from an earlier version of Windows to the most recent version of Windows for several years. What do they lose and what do they gain by delaying this decision?

9. Software vendors list minimum system requirements (processor speed, amount of RAM, etc.) to run their software. Frequently, however, a minimal PC may not permit any real user interaction with the software (too slow, poor graphics, and so on). Why don't vendors publish more realistic system requirements for their software?

10. Identify at least one print document in each of the following environments that would be more effective if distributed as an electronic document: federal government, your college, and any commercial organization.

11. Name five types of charts that can be created with presentation software and illustrate three of them. Describe a situation in which you may need to importing a file into a presentation software file.

12. Identify three applications for spreadsheet software. Then for each application describe the layout specifying at least three column entries and, generally, what would be contained in the rows.

13. If you were asked to create a PC-based inventory management system for a privately owned retail shoe store, would you use spreadsheet software, database software, or both? Why?

14. Describe two types of inquiries to a student database that involve calculations.

15. Under what circumstances is a graphic representation of data more effective than a tabular presentation of the same data?

16. Give examples and descriptions of at least two other fields that might be added to the record for the STUDENT table (Figure 2-21).

17. Describe how you might use personal information management software at home.

18. Describe how you might use personal information management software at work. Which PIM component would be most helpful to you?

19. Why do you suppose there are so many different graphics file formats? Why doesn't the graphics industry standardize a single format for bit-mapped graphics and a single format for vector graphics?

20. What home and family software packages would you like to add to your software portfolio during your first year of PC ownership?

21. Would you feel comfortable creating common legal documents, such as wills and bills of sale, with legal software without input from an attorney? Explain.

22. Some children spend more time playing computer-based games than they do attending school. Would you limit your child's time at playing games? If so, how much time each day would be appropriate?

23. For centuries, the book has been the primary resource for learning. How do you feel about exchanging that tradition for computer-based learning resources that are dynamic, linked, and interactive?

24. What do you think about integrating entertainment with education software for elementary age children? How about doing this with education software for adults?

25. Identify at least three printed reference documents you have used in the past that might be improved if made available as online or CD-ROM-based reference software. Explain why each would be better in electronic format.

26. A diminishing number of attorneys choose to use printed law books. Would you prefer to retain the services of an attorney who prefers books or one who prefers using electronic media? Explain.

27. If you work in a business, briefly describe the personal computing software (other than office suite software) that is most useful to you in your job.

28. Describe the advantages of a multimedia-based encyclopedia over a traditional printed encyclopedia. Describe the advantages of a traditional printed encyclopedia over a multimedia-based encyclopedia.

29. Identify and briefly describe at least three situations where you have witnessed the use of computer animation.

30. Would a music composer work with a wave file or a MIDI file? Explain.

FOCUS ON PERSONAL COMPUTING

1. *Help: Learning about Windows.* Begin a personal computing session. In Windows, click on *Start* then *Help and Support* in any version of Windows, and then choose options that tell you more about the Windows operating system. For example, Windows XP has "Windows Basics" which tells you how to perform core Windows tasks, search for information, protect your computer, and keep Windows up-to-date. Spend a few minutes learning more about Windows and list four things you learned that you did not know before.

2. *Paint Software.* Use paint software, such as Paint or Paintbrush (in legacy versions of Windows), to create an image of your choice. Use at least five different paint software features in the creation of the image. Discuss the capabilities and limitations of Paint.

3. *Discovering Personal Computing Software.* Go to a local PC software store, or, if you have access to the Internet, go online and navigate to a software e-tailer, such as Amazon.com (www.amazon.com). Identify at least one commercial software package in each of these categories: graphics, home and family, education, and reference. Which would you purchase first to begin building your software portfolio? Why? How about second? Why?

ONLINE EXERCISES @ www.prenhall.com/long

1. The Online Study Guide (multiple choice, true/false, matching, and essay questions)

2. Internet Learning Activities
   - Operating Systems
   - The Windows Environment
   - Word Processing

   - Spreadsheet/Database
   - Graphics

3. Serendipitous Internet Activities
   - Humor
   - Hotels and Restaurants
   - Money Management

CHAPTER

LEARNING OBJECTIVES

Once you have read and studied this chapter, you will be able to:

- Comprehend the vast scope of the online world and basic Internet concepts, including how to go online and the makeup of an Internet address (Section 3-1).

- Use Internet browsers and to access a wealth of information on the Internet (Section 3-2).

- Access and use various types of Internet applications, including the World Wide Web, FTP, e-mail, instant messaging, newsgroups, videoconferencing, and electronic publishing (Section 3-3).

- Be sensitive to critical Internet issues that must be confronted by our information society (Section 3-4).

To say that the Internet has had a profound impact on our lives is truly an understatement. How we work, how we learn, and how we play have changed dramatically during the short-lived public Internet era. The virtual classroom, where students can attend classes online, is remaking our college and university system. Each year millions more people telecommute to work from their homes. Many more people make their résumé available to millions by posting it to the Internet, then using searchable job databases to find employment. Many people stay connected to the Internet all day long, taking advantage of its latest resources to get help with daily activities—planning a vacation, getting the best deal on an airline ticket, communicating with friends via e-mail or instant messaging, and so on. More and more, we rely on the Internet to get our news and weather, and even to play games with other cybersurfers.

In this chapter, you'll learn about online information services and the Internet, what you'll need to do to get on, what you'll find when you get there, and how you travel to what seems to be an endless variety of cybersites. For those of you who have not had an opportunity to browse the Internet, this chapter should unlock the door to information and services that can stagger your imagination.

3-1   THE INTERNET

Why this section is important to you.

Once on the Internet, you can talk with friends in Europe, send Grandma a picture, schedule a study group, pay your utility bills, play games with people you've never met, listen to a live radio broadcast of your favorite sporting event, or conduct research for a report. The possibilities are endless.

Imagine being able to explore an entire universe of information databases, forums for discussions on everything from autos to Zimbabwe, online chat, free downloadable files of every conceivable type, countless free and pay-for-use information services, real-time (as it happens) statistics on sporting events, the latest music videos, college courses and degrees, real-time stock quotes, new and classic electronic books (e-books), the biggest mall in the world, and so much more (see Figure 3-1)—all without leaving home or the office. That's the *Internet*.

THE INTERNET: INTERCONNECTED NETWORKS

The **Internet** is a worldwide collection of *inter*connected *net*works. It's actually composed of millions of independent networks at academic institutions, military installations, government agencies, commercial enterprises, Internet support companies, and just about every other type of organization. Just how big is the Internet? The number of people using the Internet is now in the billions. The Net links over a million networks with Internet host server computers in every country in the world. Each host computer, an Internet server computer, is connected to the Internet 24 hours a day. Thousands more link up to this global network each month. In America, over 99% of the schools have Internet access that is made available to students. The Internet has created a global village in which nations around the world are taking steps to increase Internet access. Within the decade, the whole world will be wired.

ARPANET TO THE INTERNET

A lot happened in 1969, including the first landing on the moon and Woodstock. Amidst all of this activity, the birth of what we now know as the Internet went virtually unnoticed. A small group of computer scientists on both coasts of the United States was busy creating

FIGURE 3-1

THE INTERNET'S IMPACT

VIDEOCONFERENCING

Others throughout the world were able to "attend" this presentation at the annual Intel Developer Forum via Internet-based videoconferencing.

Courtesy of Intel Corporation

CHANGING THE WAY WE COMMUNICATE

Ten years ago, virtually all U.S. mail was processed by the U.S. Postal Service (shown here at the San Diego Post Office). Today, several hundred e-mails (see inset) are sent via the Internet for each letter processed by the Postal Service.

Courtesy of Lockheed Martin Corporation

a national network that would enable the scientific community to share ideas over communications links. The government-sponsored project, named ARPANET, worked to use technology to unite a community of geographically dispersed scientists. In 1981, the ARPANET linked 200 sites. By 1990, the idea had caught on. ARPANET was eliminated, leaving behind a legacy of networks that evolved into the Internet. At that time, commercial accounts were permitted access to what had been a network of military and academic organizations. See the *IT Illustrated: The History of Computers* following Chapter 1 for more information on ARPANET.

What we now know as the Internet is one of the federal government's success stories. Although market forces now drive the Internet, along with its policies and technologies, the United States government remains active in promoting cooperation between communications, software, and computer companies.

WHO GOVERNS THE INTERNET?

When the ARPANET was conceived, one objective of its founders was to create a network in which communications could continue even if parts of the network crashed. To do this, it was designed with no central computer or network. This is still true today. The U.S. **Internet backbone,** the major communications lines and nodes to which thousands of host computers are connected, crisscrosses the United States, with no node being the central focus of communications.

As a result, there is no single authoritative organization. The Internet is coordinated, however, by volunteers from many nations serving on various advisory boards, task groups, steering committees, and so on. The volunteer organizations set standards for and help coordinate the global operation of the Internet. Each autonomous network on the

Internet makes its own rules, regulations, and decisions about which resources to make publicly available. Consequently, the people who run these independent networks are reinventing the Internet every day.

Although no one organization runs the Internet, several organizations such as *The Internet Society*, *ICANN* (the Internet Corporation for Assigned Names and Numbers) and the *W3C* (World Wide Web Consortium) help coordinate Internet activities. The Internet Society's mission is "To assure the open development, evolution, and use of the Internet for the benefit of all people throughout the world." ICANN is a global non-profit corporation that has the responsibility of coordinating the assignment and allocation of names and Internet addresses for Web server computers. W3C, founded by Tim Berners-Lee, the inventor of the Web, creates technical specifications to keep pace with the changing technologies used for the Internet's continuously changing infrastructure.

CONNECTING TO THE INTERNET: NARROWBAND AND BROADBAND

A variety of communication channels, wired and wireless, carry digital signals between computers and over the Internet. Each is rated by its *channel capacity* or **bandwidth,** which refers to the amount of digital information that can be pushed through the channel. Bandwidth or channel capacity is the number of bits a line can transmit per second. Domestic channel capacities vary from 56,000 **bits per second** (**bps**), or 56 K bps (thousands of bits, or kilobits, per second), to 9 M bps (millions of bits, or megabits, per second). Commercial channels carry up to 622 M bps.

Channels with high bandwidth are called *broadband*. A channel with a low bandwidth is called *narrowband*. Broadband and narrowband channels are analogous to interstate highways and county roads, respectively. The former carry considerably more traffic, bits or automobiles, than the latter. The generic term for high-speed Internet access is **broadband access.**

Narrowband: Dialup Service

A dialup link is a temporary connection established by using a modem to dial up the number of the Internet service provider's (ISP's) remote computer (over a regular telephone line). Dialup access is available to anyone with **POTS** (plain old telephone services). This analog line permits voice conversations and digital transmissions with the aid of a modem. Traditional modem technology permits data transmission up to 56 K bps (thousands of bits per second).

Broadband: Fast Internet Service

For most of the public Internet era, dialup service was the only option. Now millions are enjoying broadband access, which is 15 to 30 times faster than narrowband access. As anyone who is familiar with click-and-wait narrowband access can attest, Internet access via broadband offers an entirely different experience. A Web page that might take one minute to load at narrowband speeds takes only three seconds on a broadband line.

Broadband opens the door for some amazing applications, including support for full-motion video (movies, music videos, and so on), videoconferencing, high-speed transfer of graphics, and real-time applications involving a group of online participants. Broadband has become popular for telecommuters who work at home but need to be networked to their office's computer system.

Broadband is "always on," so there is no need to dial up and logon. Generally, the broadband access fee is about double that of narrowband. The most common broadband options are, in order of popularity, cable, DSL, satellite, and wireless.

- *Cable*. Cable television systems originally were designed to deliver television signals to subscribers'

PERSONAL COMPUTING
Broadband vs. Narrowband

For about double the monthly subscription cost of dialup Internet access you can have broadband access at 20 to 30 times the speed. The click-and-view Internet (broadband) is a different world than the click-and-wait Internet (at 56 K bps). Broadband changes your perspective on what you can do on the Internet. When you can go more places in less time, you become a cyberexplorer. You don't hesitate to download a 3 MB demo song from a new album. You can enjoy streaming video at broadband resolutions (near TV quality). You tend to take advantage of more online services. Plus, broadband access can be enjoyed by everyone in the family via home networking. If your pocketbook will allow, broadband offers a truly different Net experience.

homes. However, cable companies everywhere are updating their analog cable infrastructure to enable delivery of digital service that offers crystal-clear television signals and high-speed Internet access. Initially, cable Internet access companies are offering 1 M bps (megabits per second) up to 10 M bps service, significantly faster than POTS service and only slightly more expensive. Linking to cable TV for Internet access requires that you be a cable subscriber and have a *cable modem.*

- *DSL*. Another technology, **DSL (Digital Subscriber Line)**, has made it possible to receive data over POTS lines at 1.5 to 9 M bps, the downstream rate. The **downstream rate** is the data communications rate from server computer to client computer. In a few years, the downstream rate will be 52 M bps. The **upstream rate,** the data communications rate from client computer to server computer, is 128 K bps to 1.5 M bps. Like cable, DSL requires a special *DSL modem;* however, it can share an existing telephone line such that voice conversations and digital transmission can occur at the same time.

- *Satellite*. Broadband Internet access via cable or DSL is not universally available, even for people living in some metropolitan areas. However, satellite service is available to anyone in America with a southern exposure to the sky, a digital *satellite dish,* and a *satellite modem*. Digital satellite access offers downstream speeds of 400 K bps to 1.5 M bps and upstream rates of 56 K bps to 1.5 M bps. Satellite has a built-in lag in response time of about a quarter of a second, because of the time it takes the signal to travel to the satellite and back (about 47,000 miles). This latency can cause problems for real-time interaction, such as in online multiplayer gaming. Also, satellite access may not be available when the cloud cover is dense (thunderstorms). The latency problem and its dependence on weather make satellite Internet access a good choice only when cable and DSL Internet service are not available.

- *Wireless*. Wireless communication lets users take their PC and a link to a local area network (LAN) (and therefore the Internet) with them to the classroom, conference room, the boss's office, poolside, or wherever they want to go within the limited range of the wireless link (see Figure 3-2). For example, hundreds of colleges make wireless LANs available to students and professors from wherever they might be on campus. Access points are scattered throughout campus to extend the reach of the wireless LAN. **Access points** are communications hubs that enable users of PCs and other devices with wireless capabilities to link with the campus LAN via short-range radio waves. Each wireless device must be equipped with a **wireless LAN PC card** or equivalent device to transmit and receive radio signals. The most popular standard used for short-range wireless communication is **Wi-Fi** (wireless fidelity), a name given to any IEEE 802.11 communications standard. The **IEEE 802.11b** standard (*Wireless-B*) permits wireless transmission at 11 M bps up to about 300 feet from an access point. The **IEEE 802.11a** standard (*Wireless-A*) permits a transmission rate of 54 M bps, but more access points are needed since the effective range is only 50 feet. The emerging **IEEE 802.11g** (*Wireless-G*), a third alternative which may make IEEE 802.11a obsolete, offers IEEE 802.11a speeds over longer distances.

FIGURE 3–2

WIRELESS LOCAL AREA NETWORK

From anywhere within the hospital, this doctor has a wireless link between his notebook PC and the hospital's local area network.

Courtesy of Raytheon Company

THE LINK TO THE INTERNET

The three most popular ways to connect your PC to the Internet are introduced in Getting Started and discussed in detail in this section. To go online, you will need to connect your PC to the global network we call the Internet.

Connect via an Internet Service Provider

An **ISP** (Internet service provider) is an organization that provides individuals and other organizations with access to, or presence on, the Internet via *dialup* service or *broadband* service (cable, DSL, satellite, or wireless service). ISPs usually are commercial enterprises, but they can be colleges, churches, or any organization with an Internet account and willingness to share or sell access to the Internet. There are thousands of Internet service providers, ranging from local elementary schools making unused line capacity available to students and parents to major international communications companies, such as SBC and Sprint.

Connect via an Information Service Gateway

Another way to gain access to the Internet is to subscribe to a commercial information service, such as America Online or Compuserve. About one-third of the American households with PCs subscribe to America Online (AOL) and other major information services, such as CompuServe or MSN (Microsoft Network). These information services provide an electronic *gateway* to the Net; that is, you are linked to the information services network that, in turn, links you to the Internet.

Commercial information services have an array of powerful server computer systems that offer a variety of online services, from hotel reservations to daily horoscopes. Some information services cater to niche markets, providing specific services to customers with special information needs. For example, LEXIS-NEXIS provides legal information and Dow Jones Business Information Service gives its users fast and easy financial news. Information services have grown with the Internet at a rate of 30% per year since 1990.

To take advantage of information services, you need a communications-equipped PC (that is, one with a modem and communications software) and a few dollars for the monthly service charge. Initially, you get:

- *Communications software.* Some information services, such as AOL, give you communications software packages designed specifically to interface with their information service network. Others rely on Internet browsers to deliver the service.
- *A user ID and password.* To obtain authorization to connect with the online information service, you need to enter your user ID and a password to **logon,** or make the connection with the server computer. The **user ID,** sometimes called a **screen name** for AOL users, identifies the user during personal communications and it identifies the user to the server computer. The **password** is a word or phrase known only to the user. When entered, it permits the user to gain access to the network or to the Internet.

AOL (see Figure 3-3), which is sometimes referred to as an "ISP with training wheels," is often the choice of Internet *newbies,* or novice Internet users. In contrast, an ISP simply offers Internet access—finding and retrieving Internet resources is up to the subscriber.

Direct via Network Connection

A direct connection to the Internet via a local area network generally is preferable to a dialup link because it gives you faster interaction with the Internet. With a direct LAN connection, your PC is linked directly to the Internet via a local area network. A LAN will normally have a broadband link to the Internet, which is shared by the users on the LAN. Depending on the size of the LAN and the extent of Internet usage, the LAN may be connected to a DSL line (up to 9 M bps), a **T-1 line** (1.544 M bps), or a **T-3 line** (44.736 M bps). A dialup connection can take from 15 seconds to about 45 seconds to establish, whereas a direct connection via a LAN is "always on."

TCP/IP and Packet Switching

TCP/IP (**Transmission Control Protocol/Internet Protocol**) is the communications protocol that permits data transmission over the Internet. A **protocol** is a set of rules computers use to talk to each other. The protocol sets the stage for communication; that is, each device uses a common format for messages and a standard method (queries and responses) for communicating with one another. Any operating system (for example, Window or Mac OS X)

FIGURE 3–3   **TOURING AMERICA ONLINE**

SIGN ON TO AMERICA ONLINE

America Online software, shown here, provides the interface for over 30 million AOL users. When you sign on to America Online you enter a screen name, usually an alias, like SkyJockey or PrincessLea, and a password.

PEOPLE CONNECTION

People "enter" AOL chat rooms, the most popular service on AOL, and talk with real people in real time. It's like having a conference call, except the people involved key in their responses.

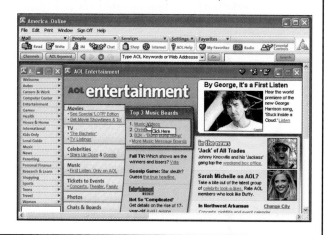

ENTERTAINMENT

The Entertainment channel offers movie reviews, TV guide listings, photos of celebrities, and songs from any style of music, and much more.

---

comes with the software needed to handle TCP/IP communications. Communications over the Net are built around this two-layer protocol—the TCP protocol and the IP protocol. A working knowledge of TCP/IP and associated terminology will come in handy when you work through the process of setting up an Internet connection.

The *Transmission Control Protocol* (the TCP of the TCP/IP) sets the rules for the packaging of information into packets. A **packet** is a piece of the message that contains the Internet address of the destination in addition to the data. Each message, file, and so on to be sent over the Internet is disassembled and placed into packets for routing over the Internet.

The *Internet Protocol* (the IP of the TCP/IP) handles the address, such that each packet is routed to its proper destination. Here is how it works. When you request a file from an Internet server computer, the TCP layer divides the file into one or more packets, associates a number with each packet, and then routes them one-by-one through the IP layer. Each packet has the same destination *IP address*, but the packets are independent of one another as they travel through the Internet and may take different paths to their destination. At the destination, the TCP layer waits until all the packets arrive, reassembles them, and then forwards them to users as a single file. This approach to communications is known as *packet switching*.

Each **point-of-presence** (POP) on the Internet, such as an Internet service provider, has a unique **IP address** that consists of four numbers (0 to 255) separated by periods (for example, 206.28.104.10). A POP is an access point to the Internet. An ISP may have many POPs for use by their subscribers. Typically, when you log on to an ISP, your PC is assigned a temporary IP address, called a **dynamic IP address.** Your computer has this address for as long as you are connected. By assigning IP addresses as they are needed, the number of IP addresses needed to serve customers is minimized since not all customers are online at any given time.

Going Online Without a PC

You don't have to have a PC to connect to the Internet. Access to the Internet is becoming so much a part of our lives that engineers are finding new ways to give us Internet access. The most popular devices are those associated with TV. Some new TVs have built-in modems, Web browsers, and e-mail software. Or, if you don't need a new TV, these capabilities can be purchased in a set-top box and linked to existing TVs. Each TV option comes with a remote keyboard for input.

Entrepreneurs are becoming very imaginative about delivery of Internet service. There's even a plug-in cartridge that turns a Sega video game into a Web browser. The telephone Internet appliance is another path to Internet access. Such devices are used primarily for checking e-mail. Some cellular phones with small embedded displays, called data phones, let you tap into the Internet (see Figure 3-4). Some ISPs offer an **Internet appliance,** an inexpensive communications device with a monitor and keyboard that is primarily for families that do not have a PC. The typical Internet appliance integrates access to the Internet, e-mail, a built-in telephone, and home organization applications.

RETRIEVING AND VIEWING INFORMATION ON THE INTERNET

Once you have established an Internet connection, you're ready to explore the wonders of the Internet—almost. First, you need to open a *client program* that will let you retrieve and view Internet resources. The **client program,** an *Internet browser,* runs on your PC, the *client computer,* and works in conjunction with a companion **server program** that runs on the Internet *server computer.* The client program contacts the server program, and they work together to give you access to the resources on the Internet server. The operation of browsers is discussed in detail in Section 3.2.

The Domain Name

Any person or organization desiring to connect a computer to the Net must register its **domain name** (for example, www.ibm.com, www.yahoo.com, and so on) and computer. The domain name is usually the name of the organization, an abbreviation of the name, or a something similar. The Internet is transitioning to a privatization of the domain name registration process. Now, if you or your company would like to secure a domain name, you would contact any of a number of domain name registration service providers from around the world. Collectively, these organizations keep track of the computers connected to the Net (site names and addresses). They also provide assistance to users concerning policy and the status of their existing registrations. Registered Internet hosts must pay an amount based on Internet usage to support the Internet's backbone.

Domain names are alphabetic and, therefore, easy to remember—whitehouse.gov, notredame.edu, and ford.com. Each of them, however, is assigned a four-number IP address because these IP addresses are the basis for packet switching. An Internet service known as the *Domain Name System* (DNS) interprets user-entered domain names, such as www.howstuffworks.com, into IP addresses, such as 209.116.69.97, so packets can be routed to their destinations. The DNS system supports one of the largest and most volatile databases in the world, yet it does it in such a manner that the typical Internet user is unaware of its existence.

FIGURE 3-4

THE INTERNET ON A PHONE

The Internet is now available via a variety of devices, including the telephone. This woman is using her Nokia cellular phone to access services and text information over the Internet. The data phone even lets you check and send e-mail. Communication is at 14.4 K bps, relatively slow for graphics, but fast for text on its small display (96 by 65 pixels).

Courtesy of Nokia

techtv

DECIPHER WEB ADDRESSES

THE CRYSTAL BALL

The Ubiquitous Internet

The Internet is woven into the fabric of millions of lives. Since we use the Net all the time, it's natural to want to take it with us everywhere we go. And so, the Internet is becoming portable. Some people already have limited access via their cellular phones. Many college students can access the Net from anywhere on campus. Within this decade, evolving wireless technology and a rapidly expanding network of wireless access points will enable us to access a growing number of rich applications from a variety of Internet-enabled devices, including cell phones, portable PCs of all sizes, automobile entertainment/information systems, wristwatches, and many that are yet to be developed.

The Internet Address: URL

The **URL,** or **uniform resource locator** (pronounced "*U-R-L*" or sometimes "*earl*") is the Internet equivalent of a postal service street address. The URL gives those who make information available over the Internet a standard way to designate where Internet elements, such as server sites, documents, files, newsgroups, and so on, can be found. Let's break down one of the following URLs from a proposed companion Internet site for this book (see Figure 3-5).

- *Access method or protocol—**http:**//*www.prenhall.com/long/12e/main.html. That portion of the URL before the first colon (*http* in the example) specifies the access method or protocol. This indicator tells your client software, your Internet browser, how to access that particular file. The *http* tells the software to expect an **http** (HyperText Transport Protocol) file. Http is the primary access method for interacting with the Internet's World Wide Web. Other common access methods, which are discussed later, include *ftp* (File Transfer Protocol) for transferring files, and *news* for newsgroups.

- *Domain name—*http://***www.prenhall.com***/long/12e/main.html. That portion following the double forward slashes (*//*), www.prenhall.com, is the server address, or the domain name. The *domain name*, which identifies an Internet host site, will always have at least two parts, separated by dots (periods). This host/network identifier adheres to rules for the domain hierarchy. At the top of the domain hierarchy (the part on the right) is the *country code* for all countries except the United States. For example, the address for the Canadian Tourism Commission is *info.ic.gc.ca*. Other common country codes are *au* (Australia), *dk* (Denmark), *fr* (France), and *jp* (Japan). The United States is implied when the country code is missing. The **top-level domains** or **TLDs,** such as *com*, denote affiliations. Colleges are in the *edu* TLD. Other TLDs are shown in Figure 3-6. The next level of the domain hierarchy identifies the host network or host provider, which might be the name of a business or college (*prenhall* or *stateuniv*). Large organizations might have networks within a network and need subordinate identifiers. The example Internet address *cis.stateuniv.edu* identifies the *cis* department's local area network at *stateuniv*. The Physics Department LAN at State University might be identified as *physics.stateuniv.edu*. An optional *www* prefaces most World Wide Web domain names.

- *Folder—*http://www.prenhall.com/***long/12e***/main.html. Following the domain name is a folder or path containing the resources for a particular topic. The resource folder, */long* in this example, refers to the proposed Long and Long companion Internet site for all Prentice Hall books by Larry and Nancy Long. Several books are covered within this resource, so subordinate directories are needed to reference a specific book (*long/12e*, implying *Computers*, twelfth edition, folder within the */long* folder).

FIGURE 3-5   **THE URL WEB ADDRESS**

A Web page is accessed by its URL or Uniform Resource Locator.

http://www.prenhall.com/long/12e/main.html			
http:	**www.prenhall.com**	**long/12e**	**main.html**
World Wide Web access method or protocol.	Address, or the domain name, of server at the Internet host site. It will always have at least two parts, separated by dots.	The name of the folder (Long) and, if needed, the subordinate folder (12e) on the server computer's disk that contains the html (Web) document or file to be retrieved.	The name of the document to be retrieved and displayed, in this case an html Web page. This could be a jpg file, pdf file, or some other type of file.

FIGURE 3-6

TOP-LEVEL DOMAINS

The domain name that comes before these top-level domains can contain only letters, numbers, and hyphens (but not consecutive hyphens or hyphens at the beginning or end) and have at least 3 but no more than 63 characters (for example, www.3-to-63-letters-or-numbers.com).

U.S. Top-Level Domain Affiliation ID	Affiliation
aero	Airline groups
biz	Businesses
com	Commercial
coop	Business cooperatives
edu	Education
gov	Government
info	Purveyors of information
mil	Military
name	Personal Web sites
net	Network resources
org	Usually nonprofit organizations
museum	Museums
pro	Professional

- *Filename*—http://www.prenhall.com/long/12e/***main.html***. At the end of most URLs is the specific filename of the file that is retrieved from the server (the server named www.prenhall.com in this example) and sent to your PC over the Internet. The *html* (or *htm*) extension (after the dot) in the filename *main.html* indicates that this is an html file. **HTML (HyperText Markup Language)** is the language used to compose and format most of the content you see when cruising the Net, and is discussed in greater detail in the next section. Some Web files have a *shtml* extension, indicating that the Web site includes extra security to preclude unauthorized access of sensitive information being passed between client and server computers. Of course, the file being retrieved can be an image file, an audio file, a video file, or some other type of file. Entering a URL domain name (www.prenhall.com) without the *http://* access method identifier or without a filename causes the site's home page to be displayed.

HTML: Putting the Page Together

HTML is a **markup language** that tells the client computer how the Web page is to be formatted. An Internet browser such as Internet Explorer, the *client program* on your PC, interprets the HTML instructions and then interacts with the server program in accordance with those instructions to download the necessary elements (text, graphics, and so on) and display the Web page. Figure 3-7 shows an HTML source document and the resulting Web page. HTML documents are text (ASCII) files that can be created with any text editor or word processing package. In HTML, each element in the electronic document is tagged and described (for example, left or right justification or centered). Elements include title, headings, tables, paragraphs, lists, and so on. In this example, the title and a paragraph are tagged.

```
<TITLE ALIGN&equals;CENTER&gt;A Centered Title of
an Electronic Document&lt;/TITLE>

<P>This paragraph is displayed in standard
paragraph format.</P>
```

Tags always come in pairs, with the last one including a forward slash (/). Tags can include attributes, which further describe the presentation of the element. For example, the title in the example is to be centered on the screen (ALIGN=CENTER). The HTML language also permits the identification of inline (inline with the text) graphic images to be inserted in the document. Inline images are retrieved from the server and inserted as per the HTML instructions (position and size).

HTML can be rather cryptic. Fortunately, there are a number of user-friendly development tools that allow you to generate HTML documents using drag-and-drop techniques along with fill-in-the-blank dialog boxes. The tags are inserted automatically for you. For example, you can create a word processing document in Microsoft Word, then save it as an html file, which can be posted to a Web server computer and made available over the Internet.

Over the last decade, billions of Web pages have been created with HTML. Now, however, the World Wide Web Consortium has posted a more feature-rich standard—**XHTML**. HTML and XHTML are both widely accepted and used by Web developers.

PERSONAL COMPUTING
Choosing a Broadband Service

For most of us, the broadband alternatives are DSL, cable, or satellite. Availability may dictate your decision since DSL and cable are not universally available. Satellite service, however, is available from anywhere in United States. People usually choose DSL or cable over satellite because satellite service has a significant upfront cost and satellite service can be intermittent in bad weather. Research and compare installation/equipment costs and monthly fees, but also ask your neighbors if they are getting the advertised speeds from their provider before making a choice.

FIGURE 3-7   **A WEB PAGE AND ITS HTML SOURCE DOCUMENT**

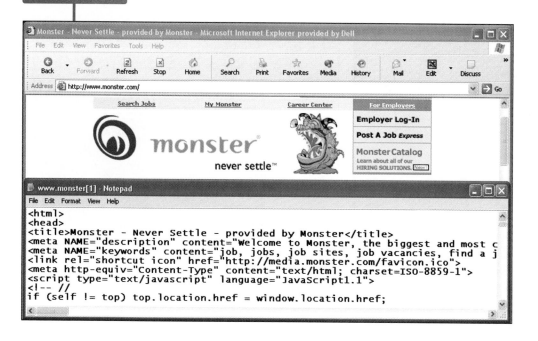

1. A dialup connection to the Internet is considered broadband access. (T/F)

2. These communications channels are listed by capacity (from least to most): dialup, T-1, and T-3. (T/F)

3. In an Internet address, levels in the host/network identifier are separated by a(n): (a) period, (b) comma, (c) @ symbol, or (d) colon.

4. TCP/IP is the communications protocol for: (a) the Net, (b) sending faxes, (c) all internal e-mail, or (d) spherical LANs.

5. The Internet is short for (a) International Network, (b) interconnected networks, (c) internal net e-mail terminal, or (d) inner net.

6. Which of these communications services is distributed over POTS: (a) cable, (b) Wi-Fi, (c) 802.11b, or (d) DSL?

7. In the URL, http://www.abccorp.com/pr/main.htm, the domain is: (a) http, (b) www.abccorp.com, (c) pr/main.htm, or (d) www.

3-2   INTERNET BROWSERS

The Internet browser, or *Web browser,* is a software tool that makes it possible for you to tap the information resources of the Internet. All new PCs come with browser software already installed, usually Internet Explorer and/or Netscape Navigator. Browser software is different from other application software in that you are not creating a document. Browsers have several main functions.

> ### Why this section is important to you.
>
> There's a good chance that you will spend a good deal of time with an Internet browser once you get a taste of the Internet. Understanding browser basics will help you make the most of the Internet's resources.

- *Retrieve and view Internet-based information.* They enable us to retrieve and view information from World Wide Web (Figure 3-8) and FTP server computers on the Internet, on internal (within an organization) intranets, and on any disk/disc medium with HTML-based content (for example, some books, magazines, and company manuals are distributed as electronic versions in HTML format on CD-ROM).

- *Interact with servers.* They allow us to interact with server-based systems; that is, we can submit and receive information (for example, obtaining an airline ticket).

FIGURE 3-8 SURFING THE WORLD WIDE WEB

THE YELLOW PAGES

Use the online "Yellow Pages" to find quickly any business in the United States. This SuperPage site lets you search for individuals, as well.

THE LIBRARY OF CONGRESS

Washington, D. C., has much to see, including the exhibits at the Library of Congress <www.loc.gov>.

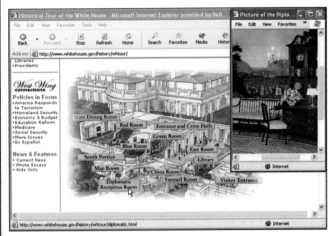

WHITE HOUSE TOUR

When you take your cybertour of the White House <www.whitehouse.gov> be sure to sign the guest book.

ENCYCLOPEDIA BRITANNICA

For decades, the 30-volume *Encyclopedia Britannica* <www.britannica.com> was a fixture in homes all over the world. Now it's online, available to anyone with Internet access.

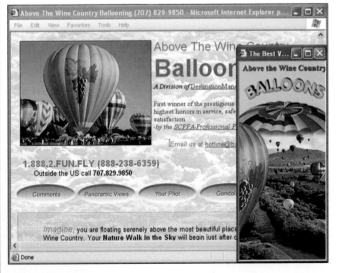

SPECIAL-INTEREST PAGES

No matter what your interests or hobbies, whether whitewater rafting, bungee jumping, or ballooning, there is a wealth of information, including images, about it (or them) on the Internet.

- *Download and upload information.* They let us download and upload digital information (video, images, music, and so on).

The viewing area of a browser can be filled with documents containing any combination of text, images, motion video, and animation. The visual information can be enhanced with real-time audio. These various forms of communication are presented within HTML documents. The browser opens an HTML document and displays the information according to HTML instructions embedded in the document. The HTML document pulls together all the necessary elements, including image files, audio streams, and small programs. The browser accepts the program in the form of **applets** or **ActiveX controls,** and then it interprets and executes them. These applets or ActiveX controls give Web developers added flexibility to create imaginative animation sequences or interactive multimedia displays. Browsers can be used with or without an Internet connection; however, an Internet link is needed to access files other than those on your PC or your local area network.

CONCEPTS AND FEATURES

Compared to the other productivity tools, browsers are easy to use, almost intuitive. It's not unusual for non-IT-competent people, unfamiliar with browsers, to be cruising the Internet within minutes after their first exposure to the software. The first step to using a browser effectively is to understand how the web is organized so you know where you need to go. Next, you must learn to use its navigational tools to get there.

The Web Site

At the top of the Internet's organization are the Internet servers, the computers that provide on-demand distribution of information. Information on the Web, which may be graphics, audio, video, animation, and text, is viewed in **pages.** Think of a Web page as a page in an alternative type of book, one with nonsequential linked documents at a Web site. A Web page can contain text plus any or all of these multimedia elements. A page has no set length and can be a few lines of text, or it can be thousands of lines with many graphic images. Each Web page is actually a file with its own URL. A page is a scrollable file; that is, when it is too large for the viewing area, you can scroll up or down to view other parts of the page.

When you navigate to a particular Web site (perhaps that of your college), the first page you will normally view is the site's **home page.** The home page is the table of contents for the resources at a server site, and will often provide hyperlinks to help you navigate the site. **Hyperlinks,** in a form of *hypertext* (usually a colored, underlined word or phrase), *hot images,* or *hot icons,* permit navigation between pages and between other resources on the Internet. Click on a hyperlink to jump (link) to another place in the same page or to another Web site on the Internet. All hyperlinks are hot; that is, when you click on one with your mouse, the linked page is retrieved for viewing. An image or icon is hot if the cursor pointer turns into a hand image when positioned over it. A home page will have links to many other pages. For example, the home page for this book <http://www.prenhall.com/long> has hundreds of pages and links to other pages (for example, a tutorial on html).

Internet Servers and Addresses

Browsers can accommodate information retrieval for any type of server, but the World Wide Web (WWW), or Web server, with its appealing multimedia capability, has emerged as the most popular server type on the Internet. The FTP server provides a storehouse for information (in downloadable files) and a convenient way to transfer files between computers.

FIGURE 3–9

THE HIERARCHY OF URLS AT A SERVER SITE

This figure shows three levels of URLs at the United States Air Force site: the Air Force Link home page <www.af.mil> (top); the photos page <www.af.mil/photos> (middle); and the Photos-Fighters page <www.af.mil/photos/fighters.shtml> (bottom). Choosing a particular photo (each is a hyperlink) takes you to the next level that displays caption information and a larger image.

The pages at a server site are set up within a hierarchy of URLs. At the top in the following example is the company URL, for example, Prentice Hall. Special-topic directories, such as home pages for various Prentice Hall authors (Kotler, Long, Macionis, and Morris in the following example), are subordinate to the company URL but have their own URLs. These directories have subdirectories, which may also have subdirectories, and so on, each of which has its own unique URL. This subset of some of the URLs at the Prentice Hall server site illustrates one hierarchy of URLs.

HOME PAGE *http://www.prenhall.com* (Prentice Hall home page URL)

- *http://www.prenhall.com/kotler* (home page URL for Kotler books)
- *http://www.prenhall.com/long* (home page URL for all Long books)
  - *http://www.prenhall.com/long/computers11e/index.html* (the opening page for a Long book)
    - ▲ *http://* . . . (other pages associated with the above book)
  - *http://www.prenhall.com/long/computers12e/index.html* (the opening page for another Long book)
    - ▲ *http://* . . . (other pages associated with the above book)
- *http://www.prenhall.com/macionis* (home page URL for Macionis books)
- *http://www.prenhall.com/morris* (home page URL for Morris books)

Here's the good news. For most of your navigation around the Internet, you'll simply click on a named hyperlink to go to a URL. Occasionally, you will need to enter a URL, usually a home page. This hierarchy of URLs is illustrated in Figure 3-9.

Navigating the Internet

Microsoft Internet Explorer and Netscape, the dominant browsers, are shown in Figure 3-10. Internet Explorer is the Internet client of choice for four of every five users in the world. Although both browser have unique features that you will learn with use and experience, both have essentially the same easy-to-use interface. The main buttons in their respective toolbars are shown in Figure 3-10: *Back* (to last page viewed), *Forward* (to next in a string of viewed site), *Stop* (transfer of information), *Refresh* (reload page). Click on the Favorites button (in Internet Explorer) or Bookmarks button (Netscape) to view a list of sites that you placed in your Favorites or Bookmarks folder. Typically, these are the sites that you visit frequently.

The URL/Search bar (see Figure 3-10), sometimes called the location bar, lets you key in the URL of the desired Web site, it displays the URL of the page onscreen, and it permits keyword searches of Internet resources. The status bar displays the status of transmissions to and from Internet servers.

BROWSER PLUGINS

The browser is a very versatile piece of software, but it can't do it all. Plugins help browsers keep pace with the technological innovations on Internet. A **plugin** is a software module that is

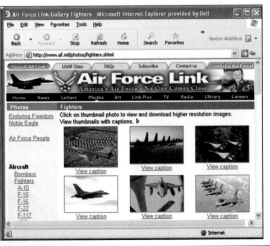

The functionality and appearance of these two browsers is similar and they have the same basic elements.

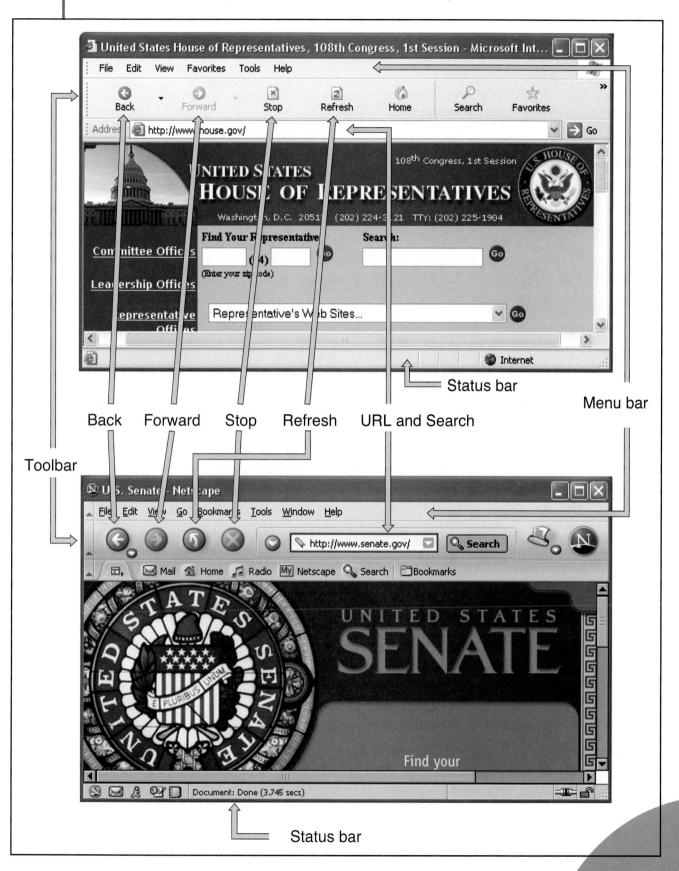

Status bar

Menu bar

Back   Forward   Stop   Refresh   URL and Search

Toolbar

Status bar

FIGURE 3-11

**BROWSER PLUGINS: IPIX®
MOVIES**

The iPIX browser plugin is one of
several Internet browser plugins.
This one lets Net surfers view an
image from every direction by simply moving a pointing hand to the
edge of the image to look up,
down, and all around.

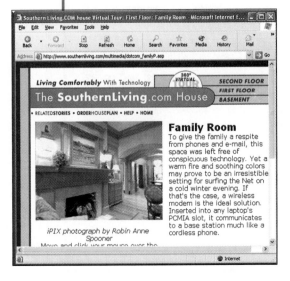

iPIX photograph by Robin Anne
Spooner

integrated into an application, such as a browser, to give the application added capabilities. Here's a list of popular browser plugins.
The download Web sites for these plugins are listed in parentheses.

- *Shockwave Player (www.macromedia.com)*. Displays dynamic
  Web content created with Macromedia Shockwave software
  (for example, interactive multimedia product demos).
- *Flash Player (www.macromedia.com)*. Displays dynamic Web
  content created with Macromedia Flash (for example,
  animations).
- *RealJukebox (www.real.com)*. Provides the tools you need to
  play and record MP3 music.
- *Liquid Player (www.liquidaudio.com)*. Lets you play and
  record MP3 music.
- *Windows Media Player (www.microsoft.com)*. Plays digital
  media, including music, video, CDs, DVDs, and Internet radio.
- *QuickTime (www.apple.com)*. Plays many different kinds of
  files, including video, audio, graphics, and virtual reality (VR)
  movies.
- *iPIX® Movies (www.ipix.com)*. Lets you view an image from
  every direction (up, down, and all around) by simply pointing
  where you wish to view (see Figure 3-11).
- *Acrobat Reader (www.adobe.com)*. Reads and displays PDF-
  format electronic documents.

Audio/video oriented plugins, such as Windows Media Player and QuickTime, play
streaming audio and streaming video. **Streaming audio** and **streaming video** are different
from downloading and saving an audio/video file for replay in that the media is presented
in a continuous "streamed" and played in real time, with nothing being saved to disk.

SECTION

1 The Internet browser is also called a Web browser. (T/F)

2 To eliminate the spread of viruses, the uploading of files is no longer permitted on the
Internet. (T/F)

3 Small programs called within HTML documents are called: (a) apples, (b) applets, (c) applications, or (d) omelets.

4 A URL that begins with http:// begins the address for what type of Internet server: (a) Web,
(b) e-mail, (c) file transfer protocol, or (d) news?

3-3 INTERNET RESOURCES AND APPLICATIONS

**Why this section
is important to you.**

Some say that the Internet has it all, but first you have to find
it. Read this section to learn how to find and use the
information that's important to you.

The Internet offers a broad spectrum of resources, applications, and capabilities (see Figure 3-12). In this section,
we'll discuss how to find what you need, the major Internet
applications, and ways you can use the Internet to communicate with people.

FINDING RESOURCES AND INFORMATION ON THE NET

The Internet has thousands of databases, such as the *Congressional Record*, NIH clinical
information, a list of job openings for the entire United States, and the lyrics to
"Yesterday" by the Beatles. You name it and, if it can be digitized, there is a good chance
that it is on the Net. The information on the Internet is out there, but getting to it can be
challenging—and a lot of fun.

PERSONAL COMMUNICATIONS

E-mail	Send/receive personal and work-related electronic mail
Instant messaging	Real-time text, audio, and/or video communication
Chat	Normally, text-based interaction among groups of people in virtual chat rooms

BROWSING AND SEARCHING FOR INFORMATION

News	Newspapers, television stations, magazines, Internet portals, and other sites offer up-to-the-minute state, local, national, and international news, as well as topic-specific news, such as the stock market analysis and results
Sports	All professional leagues and teams, as well as all colleges, provide continuously-updated sports information and statistics to complement major sports news organizations, such as ESPN
Weather	Up-to-the-minute weather and weather forecasting is available for any city or region
Research for school or job	Billions of pages of information are available on almost any subject
Travel information	A breadth of information is available for tens of thousands of destinations, including cities, specific sites, resorts, and so on, including how to get there
Medical information	The Net has a plethora of medical data, advice, and information

DOWNLOADING AND FILE SHARING

Images and video	These include any kind of still image, from NASA space shots to family baby photos and a variety of brief videos from music videos to family clips
Music	Millions of songs are downloaded and shared, both legally and illegally, each day
Movies	That legal and illegal downloading/sharing of commercial and private movies is growing

STREAMING MEDIA

Video clips	News events, movie trailers, sports highlights, and so on
Audio	Speeches, radio station broadcasts, electronic greeting-card songs, and so on, are streamed over the Net
Movies	On-demand movies may someday threaten the existence of the video store

ONLINE TRANSACTIONS

Online shopping	Shop and buy almost anything on the Internet, from groceries to automobiles
Online auctions	Bid on any of thousands of new and used items on the virtual auction block or place your own items up for auction
Online banking	Most bricks-and-mortar banking transactions can be done online
Making reservations	All types of travel reservations, including airline, train, hotel, auto rental, and so on, can be made online
Stock trading	Stocks can be bought and sold online
Gambling	Place real bets on virtual casino games and win/lose real money

ENTERTAINMENT

Multiplayer gaming	Play bridge or fight galactic battles with other Net-based gamers
Serendipitous browsing	Surf the Net just for fun to see where it leads you
Adult content	Adult entertainment is a major dot.com industry
Hobbyist	All popular hobbies are supported by sites that contain information and related activities

The function of a browser is to take you somewhere in the electronic world. Where you go and how you get there is entirely up to you. There are two basic approaches to using a browser: *browsing* and *searching*. The difference between browsing and searching is best explained through an analogy to a print book. When you leaf through a book, you're browsing. When you select a topic from the index and open the book to the indicated page, you're searching.

Browsing the Net

Browsing is when you use your browser to poke around the Internet with no particular destination in mind. Some people just get on the Internet and travel to wherever their heart leads them. An Internet portal is always a good place to start. A **portal** is a Web site that offers a broad array of information and services, including a menu tree of categories, a tool that lets you search for specific information on the Internet, and a variety of services from up-to-the-minute stock quotes to horoscopes. Infoseek, Excite, and Yahoo! are portals. The categories for Yahoo! are representative.

Arts & Humanities	Entertainment	Recreation & Sports	Social Science
Business & Economy	Government	Reference	Society & Culture
Computers & Internet	Health	Regional	
Education	News & Media	Science	

You would click on one of these main categories, each a hyperlink on the Yahoo! home page, to view subcategories. For example, clicking on Yahoo!'s "Arts & Humanities" displays subcategories: Art History, Artists, Arts Therapy, and so on. You may navigate through several levels of categories before reaching the pages you want. The typical portal will have a variety of service options as well, such as shopping, news and sports, new/used automobile research, job search, classified ads, games, horoscopes, people search, yellow pages, stock quotes, chat rooms, television listings, map search (maps and driving instructions), personals, and more. In addition to the general portals, the net has hundreds of specialized portals that focus on a particular topic, such as news (www.cnn.com), personal computing (www.ZDNet.com), or motorcycles (www.themotorcycleportal.com).

Most of us have at least one general interest area in mind, even when browsing. For example, let's say you want to go shopping for holiday gifts. You can do this by going to the various "shop" categories, moving from virtual store to virtual store. Whether shopping or just surfing the Internet, browsing is always fun because you never know what you will find or where you will end up.

Using Search Engines to Search the Net

techtv™
GET THE MOST
OUT OF GOOGLE

Another more direct way to find what you need on the Internet is searching. For example, if you knew that you wanted to buy your parents sterling silver candlesticks for their twenty-fifth anniversary, then you would want to go directly to a site that sells them—the quicker the better.

Each major portal, such as Excite, provides a resource discovery tool, called a **search engine**, to help you find the information or service you need. Most of them let you find information by keyword(s) searches. You can search the Net by keying in one or more keywords, or perhaps a phrase, that best describes what you want (perhaps, information on "Julia Roberts" or who might offer a "masters degree biomedical engineering"). The rules by which you enter the keywords and phrases vary slightly among the search engines (see Figure 3-13). These hints may reduce your search time.

- *Read the search rules.* Click on "help" and read the instructions first.
- *If you don't get results with one search engine, try another.* Results vary significantly between search engines because their databases are compiled in completely different manners. For example, Yahoo!'s database is organized by category, encouraging topical searches such as "White House AND press room." In contrast, Google's database is created from actual content on the Web, enabling searches for specific phrases, such as "Penn State Nittany Lions." So if you don't find what you need with your first search, don't give up. The right results could be as close as the next search engine.
- *The results of the search are seldom exhaustive.* You may need to go to one of the listed sites, and then follow the hyperlinks to find the information you need.
- *Choose search words carefully.* The keywords and phrases you enter are critical to the success of your search. Try to be as specific as you can. You may wish to try the portal's advanced search options which enable you to narrow your search. For

FIGURE 3-13 AN INTERNET SEARCH ENGINE

At the Yahoo! portal and search engine, users can enter keywords or phrases (such as "bed and breakfast and Berkshires" in the search box) to get a list of applicable pages (see middle window). Clicking on the "Bed and Breakfast in the Berkshires" hyperlink takes the user to the linked Web site (foreground window).

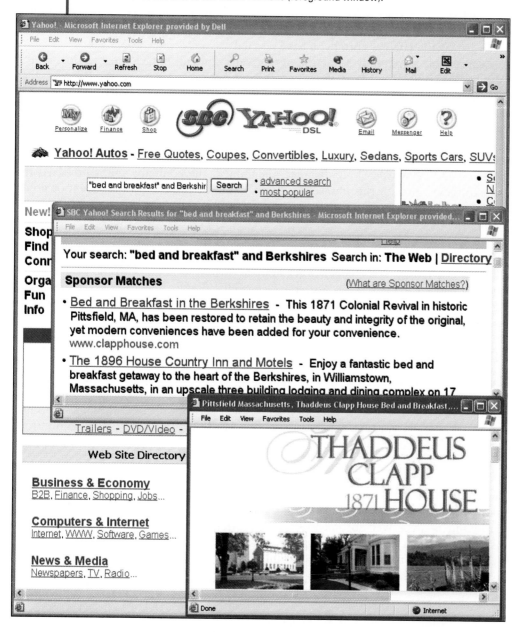

example, Yahoo! lets you limit your search to a particular language or country, or to a particular time frame (for example, past 3 months).

- *Be persistent.* Many of your searches will result in something like "Search item not found." This doesn't mean that the information you need is not on the Internet. It means only that you need to extend your search to other search criteria and/or other search engines.

The Internet has hundreds of search tools, some of which focus on a particular area, such as technology or medicine. These are among the more popular search tools.

Yahoo! (www.yahoo.com)	HotBot (www.hotbot.com)
Infoseek (www.infoseek.com)	Ask Jeeves (www.askjeeves.com)
Google (www.google.com)	MSN Internet Search (search.msn.com)

AltaVista (www.altavista.com)	Netscape Search (search.netscape.com)
Search.com (www.search.com)	Lycos (www.lycos.com)
Excite (www.excite.com)	Metacrawler (www.metacrawler.com)
Northern Light (www.northernlight.com)	Dogpile (www.dogpile.com)

The last two, Metacrawler and Dogpile, search a number of search engines in parallel, then display the result for each search tool. Click on the *Search* button in the browser toolbar to display the Internet portal you have selected as your default search site.

Search tools search only a fraction of the Web's content. In fact, most engines search less than 10% of it. Why? First, search engines tend to index the more popular sites, that is, those sites with the most **hits** and links to them. A hit is either when a Web page is retrieved for viewing or when a page is listed in results of a search. Another reason why searches are so limited is because portals with search engines are business ventures. Keep in mind that the companies sponsoring these widely used portals make money by selling advertising and by selling priority rights to a particular word or phrase. For example, if you enter the keywords "long-distance telephone," the company that purchased the rights to these words or this phrase would be listed in a priority position (first or possibly alone). For these reasons, it pays to tap into several portals to get the most thorough search available.

Asking Someone

When all else fails, ask someone. Don't hesitate to post an inquiry to the people in the cyberworld when you need help. Also, the Net is full of **FAQs (frequently asked questions)** pages and files that you can view or download. There is a good chance that your question has probably been asked and answered before.

INTERNET APPLICATIONS

The terms *Internet* and *World Wide Web* are used interchangeably, as are the Net and the Web, but they are not the same. In fact, the World Wide Web is but one way of accessing information over the Internet. The Internet, a global network of computers and transmission facilities, is the medium for information exchange via the Web, e-mail, and instant messaging, and other Internet applications.

Web Servers

The World Wide Web, affectionately called *the Web*, is an Internet system that permits linking of multimedia documents among servers on the Internet. By establishing a linked relationship between Web documents, related information becomes easily accessible. These linked relationships are completely independent of physical location. These attributes set Web servers apart from other Internet servers.

- *User-friendly*. With Internet browsers, we can point-and-click our way around the Web.
- *Multimedia documents*. A Web page can contain all of these multimedia elements: graphics, audio, video, animation, and text.
- *Hyperlinks*. Multimedia resources on the Web are linked via hyperlinks.
- *Interactive*. The Web system enables interactivity between users and servers. The most common way to interact with the Web is by clicking on hyperlinks to navigate around the Internet. In addition, some pages have input boxes into which you can enter textual information. You can even click on *option buttons* (circle bullets) to select desired options. Finally, browser plugins offer a variety of ways for you to interact with the Web.
- *Frames*. Some Web sites present some or all of their information in frames. The frames feature enables the display of more than one independently controllable section on a single Web page (see Figure 3-14). When you link to a Web page that uses frames, your request results in multiple HTML files being returned from the Web server. The frames capability may be used to display the main site options in one

FIGURE 3-14   A WEB PAGE WITH FRAMES

The home page for Slate, an e-zine (online magazine), uses frames to list the e-zine's departments (the vertical frame on the left) and the options for their affiliate MSN (the vertical frame on the right).

small frame and the primary information page in another larger frame. Sometimes a third frame displays context-sensitive instructions.

FTP Servers

The **File Transfer Protocol** (**FTP**) allows you to download and upload files on the Internet, in much the same way you might manipulate files in folders on your PC. FTP, which pre-dates the Web, has been useful as a file transfer application on the Net for more than two decades. You can download exciting games, colorful art, music from up-and-coming artists, statistics, published and unpublished books, maps, photos, utility and applications programs—basically anything that can be stored digitally. Many FTP sites invite users to contribute (upload) files of their own.

You must be an authorized user (know the password) to access protected FTP sites. Most, however, are anonymous FTP sites that maintain public archives. *Anonymous FTP* sites allow anyone on the Net to transfer files without prior permission. If you are asked to enter a user ID and a password, don't panic. Just enter "anonymous" or "ftp" at the user ID prompt and enter your e-mail address (or just tap the Enter key) at the password prompt. Although most files on an FTP server might be restricted to the server computer and its users, often there is a public or "pub" directory that contains files accessible to all Internet users.

The trick to successful FTPing is knowing where to look. Fortunately, you can search for topical FTP sites on search engines and connect to FTP sites using a browser. Figure 3-15 demonstrates the hierarchical organization of FTP files.

Communicating with People over the Net

The Internet is not just a resource for information and services, it is also an aid to better communication. There are several ways for people to communicate over the Internet,

FIGURE 3-15 FTPING ON THE INTERNET

The browser image illustrates how you might navigate through the directories of an anonymous FTP site. The user proceeded from the /graphics/ directory to the /graphics/train/ directory to the /graphics/train/diesel/ directory to the 1189-1.GIF file (the train engine). The FTP site shown here, however, has been converted to a user-friendlier World Wide Web format (right).

including e-mail, audio mail, newsgroups, mailing lists, chat rooms, instant messaging (IM), Internet telephone, and videophone.

E-mail

You can send and receive e-mail with anyone who has an Internet e-mail address. There are two ways to send/receive e-mail—via *e-mail client software* or via *Web-based e-mail*. E-mail client software, such as Microsoft Outlook, enables e-mail through a program running on your computer. The *Getting Started* at the beginning of the book provides an overview of how e-mail client software works.

Web-based email is handled through interaction with a Web site, such as Yahoo! (see Figure 3-16) or Hotmail. The main advantages of the e-mail client approach are that e-mail can be integrated with other applications such as a calendar and task list, and all of these related applications can be incorporated with other e-mail client users on an organization's local area network. The big advantage of Web-based e-mail is that it is easily accessible from any Internet-connected computer in the world—at a coffee house in Tokyo, a public library, a friend's house, and so on.

Your Internet e-mail address is your online identification. Once you get on the Internet, you will need to let other users and other computers know how to find you. The Internet address has two parts and is separated by an @ symbol. Consider this example Internet address for Kay Spencer at State University in CIS:

kay_spencer@cis.stateuniv.edu

- *Username—kay_spencer@cis.stateuniv.edu.* On the left side of the @ separator is the username (usually all or part of the user's name). Organizations often standardize the format of the username to make addresses easy to remember. One of the most popular formats is simply the first and last name separated by an underscore (kay_spencer).

- *Domain name for the host/network—kay_spencer@**cis.stateuniv.edu.*** The portion to the right of the @ identifies the host or network that services your e-mail, sometimes called the **e-mail server.** This is normally the address for your Internet service

FIGURE 3-16 WEB-BASED E-MAIL

The interaction through Yahoo! Mail is via a Web site. Web-based e-mail is sent and delivered via a Web site versus an e-mail client. An advantage of this type of e-mail is that it provides seamless integration of your e-mail and the World Wide Web. With Web-based e-mail, folders containing your e-mail (inbox, sent, and so on) are maintained at the server site (for example, Yahoo!). This allows you to send and receive e-mail from any PC with an Internet connection and a browser.

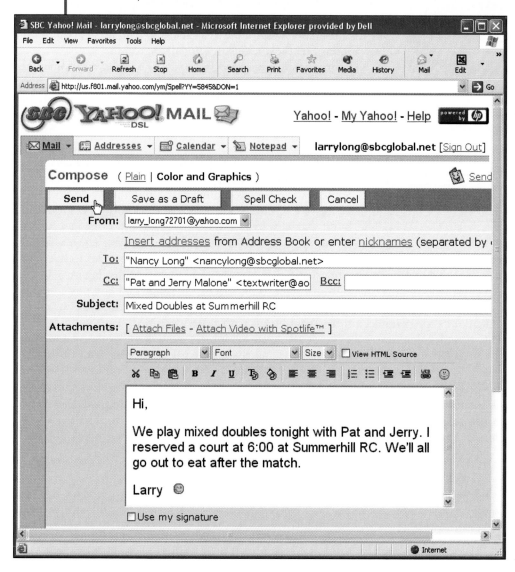

provider (for example, sbcglobal.net), your information service (for example, aol.com), your college (for example, stateuniv.edu), or your company (for example, wal-mart.com).

Most modern e-mail client software and Web-based e-mail let you embed graphics and fancy formatting as you might in a word processing document. Also, you can attach files to an e-mail message. For example, you might wish to send a program or a digitized image along with your message. The **attached file** is routed to the recipient's e-mail server along with the message. It and the message are downloaded to your PC when you retrieve your e-mail. E-mail features and services continue to grow (see Figure 3-17). One of the information services translates e-mail messages posted in French and German into English, and vice versa.

The U.S. Postal Service is losing ground to electronic communications. More and more people send birthday invitations and greeting cards via e-mail, and business communications use less and less "snail mail" everyday. E-mail has resulted in tremendous changes in

FIGURE 3-17

WIRELESS INTER-TAINMENT COMPUTER

With new Cybiko portable wireless inter-tainment system kids can chat with friends, play interactive games, send and receive e-mails, and enjoy hundreds of applications. The manufacturer has teamed with a number of shopping malls so that youth shoppers can receive and send your e-mail wirelessly.

Courtesy of Cybiko, Inc.

the business world because e-mail can be one-to-one, one-to-many, or many-to-many—and it's written, documented information.

Newsgroups

A **newsgroup** is the cyberspace version of a bulletin board. Tens of thousands of newsgroups entertain global discussions on thousands of topics, including your favorite celebrities or professional teams. For example, *alt.fan.letterman* (the newsgroup's name) is one of the David Letterman newsgroups. Real Elvis fans can learn about recent Elvis sightings on the *alt.elvis.sighting* newsgroup.

Newsgroups are organized by topic. The topic, and sometimes subtopics, is embedded in the newsgroup name. Several major topic areas include news, *rec* (recreation), *soc* (society), *sci* (science), and *comp* (computers). For example, *rec.music.folk* is the name of a music-oriented newsgroup in the recreation topic area whose focus is folk music.

To participate in a newsgroup, you'll need *newsreader client software* or similar software that is built into most Internet browser clients. Some newsgroups are maintained within the World Wide Web and newsreader software is not required. Generally, newsgroups are public, but if you wish to keep up with the latest posting in a particular newsgroup, you can subscribe to it (at no charge). The newsreader software lets you read previous postings (messages), add your own messages to the newsgroup, respond to previous postings, and even create new newsgroups (see Figure 3-18).

People who frequent newsgroups refer to the original message and any posted replies to that message as a **thread**. The newsreader sorts and groups threads according to the original title. For example, a thread that begins with a message titled "Pete Sampras' forehand" includes all of the replies titled "RE: Pete Sampras' forehand." If you post a message with an original title or reply to a message and change the title, you start a new thread.

Mailing Lists: Listservs

The Internet **mailing list** is a cross between a newsgroup and e-mail. Mailing lists, which are also called *listservs*, are like newsgroups in that they allow people to discuss issues of common interest. However, like most Internet applications, newsgroups employ **pull tech-**

FIGURE 3-18   NEWSGROUPS ON THE INTERNET

People frequenting the highlighted newsgroup (rec.music.fold) post messages related to aerobic fitness. This person has subscribed to this and eight other newsgroups (see list in folders window). In the example, a newsgroup subscriber was viewing a thread dealing with the subject "George—exceptionally talented, and Way under-credited and under-appreciated..." This user can reply as well and have his reply added to this thread for all subscribers to see.

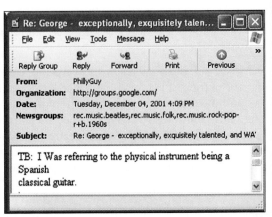

nology, whereby the user requests information via a browser, while mailing lists are **push technology;** that is, information (in this case, mailing list content) is delivered automatically from the automated server site to your e-mail address.

There are mailing lists for most, if not all, of your personal interest areas. To find one of the interest areas, you scan or search available mailing lists from a number of sources. For example, portals, such as Infoseek, summarize and describe thousands of listserv's by description, name, and subject (just search on "mailing list"). When you find one you like, you simply send an e-mail message containing the word *subscribe* plus your name to the mailing list sponsor, and the sponsor puts you on the list. Mailing lists have two addresses, one to send instructions like subscribe (and unsubscribe) to the list (for example, listserv@someplace.com). The other address is where you send e-mail messages to be distributed to others on the list (for example, talk@somplace.com).

Generally, there is no subscription fee. Once on the list, you receive every e-mail message sent out by the sponsor of the mailing list. Some mailing lists are one-way from the list's sponsor. Others accept and redistribute all e-mail received from subscribers. Sending mail to the list is as easy as sending an e-mail message to its mailing list address.

Subscribing to a mailing list can be stimulating and, possibly, overwhelming. Remember, each message posted is broadcast to all on the list. If you subscribe to a couple of active mailing lists, your Internet mailbox could be filled with dozens if not hundreds of messages—each day!

Chat

At any given time, the Internet is filled with virtual chat sessions where people talk about anything from vintage muscle cars to yoga. The **Internet Relay Chat (IRC)** protocol allows users to join and participate in group chat sessions; that is, two or more Internet users carry on a typed, real-time, online conversation. Chatting is a favorite pastime of millions of cybernauts who use their *IRC client software* to establish a link with a chat server; that is, an Internet server that runs the IRC protocol. When you log into a chat session, you can "talk" by keying in messages that are immediately displayed on the screens of other chat participants (see Figure 3-19) people in the chat room.

Chat servers let users join chat sessions called *channels*. A single chat server can have dozens, even thousands, of chat channels open at the same time. The name of the channel will usually reflect the general nature of the discussion. Usually channel names are unchanged, but topics on the channels are continuously changing. For example, in a channel called "Personal Computing," the topic might be "iMac tips" one day and "Windows XP troubleshooting" the next day.

Instant Messaging

Instant messaging, which was introduced in *Getting Started,* is a logical outgrowth of e-mail and chat. IM is a convenient way for you to know when your friends, family, and colleagues are online so you can communicate with them in real time. America Online popularized instant messaging, but now several Internet companies, including Yahoo! and Microsoft, provide instant messaging services.

To participate in instant messaging, you must first sign up with one of the instant messaging services and install its client software. Then you must create a contact list that contains the online identities of the people you wish to track for instant messaging. When you go online and sign in to the IM service, you are notified when your "buddies" (the people on your list) are online and they are notified that you are online. You can then send instant messages, and even images, to those "buddies" currently online. Also, instant messaging software lets you initiate a telephone-type conversation with people on the contact list, if you wish to talk, rather than key in the words. Some instant messaging programs even permit video conversations (see Figure 3-20).

Originally designed to enable casual online interaction, instant messaging is rapidly becoming a viable business tool (see Figure 3-21). People in the business community have the same problem getting hold of their colleagues as the rest of us do communicating with our friends and neighbors. In fact, telephone tag may be the most played game in the corporate world. Instant messaging offers a new level of connectivity not available in e-mail or

FIGURE 3-19   AN AOL CHAT SESSION

One of the most popular destinations on AOL is the thousands of chat rooms. AOL and other Chat programs let you "enter" a chat room and have real-time conversations with other people from all over the world.

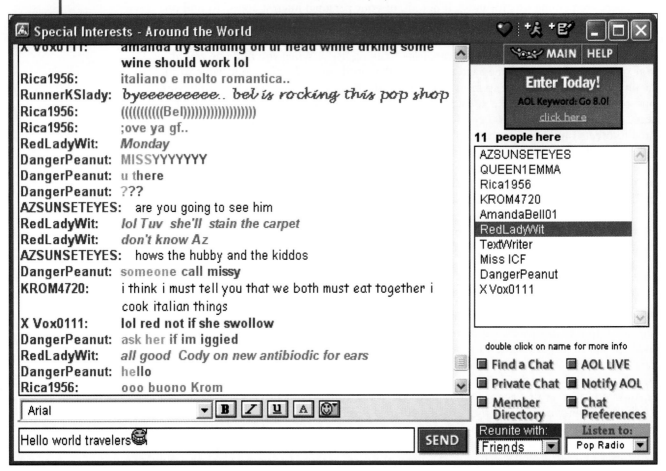

telephone exchanges. What instant messaging offers is a real-time link between people who routinely interact with one another in a business environment. IM immediately informs the others when one of their colleagues is available. Also, the most recent versions of instant messaging software permit sophisticated communication that includes file/application sharing, whiteboarding, and the ability to have audio and video conferencing. **Whiteboarding** enables participants to sketch and illustrate ideas. When one person runs the whiteboard option, it automatically appears on everyone's screen. Everything that is written or drawn on the whiteboard is displayed for all to see.

The Internet Telephone

To make a traditional phone call we simply pick up a telephone, which is linked to a world-wide communications network, and speak into its microphone and listen through its speaker. Guess what? Millions of Internet users with multimedia PCs have these same capabilities: access to a worldwide network (the Internet), a mike, and a speaker. The Internet telephone application is becoming so popular that is being bundled with other popular Internet communications software, such as instant messaging (see Figure 3-20). Internet phone software capability lets you call people at other computers on the Internet with the same capabilities. People routinely use this feature to talk for hours on international calls!

Here is how the Internet telephones work. First, you establish a connection with the Internet, then open your Internet telephone software. The software automatically notifies the host server that you are available for calls. If you and your brother, who lives in Germany, wanted to talk via Internet telephone, you would both have to be online with Internet telephone software running and be registered with the same server.

On the Internet

- Accessing Information and Services
  - World Wide Web (the Web)
  - FTP
  - Webcasting
  - Digital jukebox
- Communicating with People
  - E-mail
  - Newsgroups
  - Mailing list (listserv)
  - IRC (chat)
  - Instant messaging
  - Internet telephone

FIGURE 3–20   INSTANT MESSAGING: VIDEO CONVERSATION

The Windows Messenger instant messaging software permits text, audio, and video conversations (shown here).

FIGURE 3–21

INSTANT MESSAGING AT THE OFFICE

The use of instant messaging is growing at the office. Employees "sign-in" and "sign-out" depending on their availability for electronic interaction.

Cybertalk and Netiquette

Typically, we key in, rather than speak, our words and emotions when we communicate online. People who frequent chat rooms, do instant messaging, send e-mail, and participate in newsgroups have invented keyboard shortcuts and **emoticons** (emotion icons), which are sometimes called *smileys*, to speed up the written interaction and convey emotions. Some of the most frequently used keyboard shortcuts and smileys are illustrated in Figure 3-22.

In cyberspace there is no eye contact or voice inflection, so cybernauts use smileys to express emotions. They must be effective, because many couples who meet on the information highway are eventually married. There are some basic rules of *netiquette*, Internet etiquette.

- Avoid using all capital letters, unless you wish to shout.
- Never send spam, unsolicited e-mail, as this is the ultimate Internet faux pas.
- Be sensitive to the moral compass of your recipients when forwarding Internet content, especially jokes.
- Never send e-mail containing the personal information of others without their permission.
- Use the "returned receipt requested" option sparingly.
- Be patient with newbies and recognize that they are working up the learning curve.
- Some people prefer a casual style of communication, so avoid making comments about keyboarding style, spelling, or grammar.

FIGURE 3–22 **CYBERTALK: KEYBOARD SHORTCUTS AND EMOTICONS**

To learn more emoticons, also called smileys, search for "emoticons" or "smileys" on any Internet search engine.

INTERNET SHORTHAND

AFJ	April fool's joke	**L8R**	Later
<-AFK	Away from keyboard	**LOL**	Laughing out loud
BRB	Be right back	**ROFL**	Rolling on the floor laughing
BTW	By the way...	**SPST**	Same place, same time
CU	See you	**TPTB**	The powers that be
CUL8R	See you later	**TTYL**	Talk to you later
F2F	Face-to-face	**<VBG>**	Very big grin
FAQs	Frequently asked questions	**WAG**	A guess
GR8	Great	**Wizard**	A gifted or experienced user
IMHO	In my humble opinion...	**YKYBHTLW**	You know you've been hacking too long when
IRL	In real life		

EMOTICONS: EMOTION ICONS

(:-*	Kiss	:-~)	User with a cold
:-)	Smiling	:-@	Screaming
:'-(	Crying (sad)	:-&	Tongue tied
:'-)	Crying (happy)	:-Q	Smoker
:-(	Sad	:-D	Laughing
<:(	Dunce	:-/	Skeptical
:-o	Amazed	O :-)	Angel
:-|	Bored	;-)	Wink
:-I	Indifferent	:c)	Pigheaded
8-)	Wearing sunglasses	@->->-	A rose
::-)	Wearing glasses	[[[***]]]	Hugs and kisses
#-)	Partied all night	(:&	Angry
#:-o	Shocked	~ :-(	Steaming mad
%-6	Brain-dead	:-| :-|	Déjà vu
%-(	Confused	:-}	Mischievous smile
>:)	Little devil	^5	High five

EMOTICONS: POP ART

+-(:-)	The Pope
==:-D	Don King
[8-]	Frankenstein
= =):-)=	Abe Lincoln
@@@@@@@:)	Marge Simpson
/:-)	Gumby
7:-)	Ronald Reagan
\	
8-]	FDR
*<(:')	Frosty the Snowman
(8-o	Mr. Bill
~8-)	Alfalfa
@;^D	Elvis
*<:-)	Santa
Q:-)	College graduate
~:o	Baby

- Honor someone's private communication with you and keep it private.
- Think twice before attaching a large file to an e-mail going to someone who has slow dialup service.
- Never forward a virus warning without confirming it with reliable sources because most virus warnings are hoaxes.
- Use antivirus software to maintain a virus free environment, as most viruses are passed via e-mail.

Webcasting

Several companies, including *USA Today*, use push technology to webcast, or broadcast news and other information in real time that can be customized to your information needs. For example, you can request news on a particular topic (personal computing, politics) or from a particular country, weather for a particular region, stock quotes for selected companies, business

THE CRYSTAL BALL

Audio Mail: An Alternative to Text E-mail

Audio mail is just evolving, but it's inevitable that this system of worldwide audio messaging will continue to grow and mature. With audio mail, you speak your message instead of keying it. Users send sound files (rather than text-based e-mail) over the Internet, thus producing a form of worldwide audio messaging. Proponents of audio mail tout it as a faster and more effective way to communicate over the Internet. It eliminates the need to key in, edit, and spell-check text before sending a message, a time-consuming task for many of us. Also, audio mail conveys humor and other emotions that may be lost in e-mail messages.

FIGURE 3–23 **PUSH TECHNOLOGY**

The *USA Today* NewsTracker gathers news, weather, sports, and financial information according to preset user specifications and then delivers it in real-time via the Internet via push technology. The NewsTracker banner (top) can remain active at the top of the screen and other applications and the NewsTracker screen saver (bottom) presents hyperlinks to current news on user-selected topics.

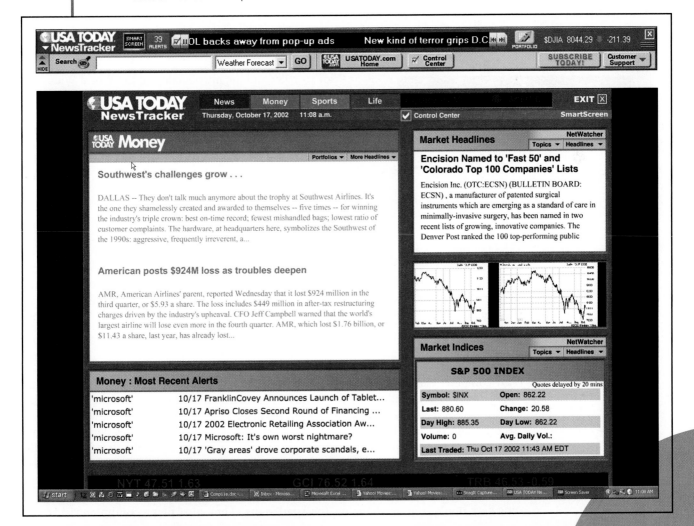

news for selected industries, sports news relating to a particular sport (even to your teams), and so on. The company periodically scans available Net sources then automatically delivers information to you via push technology for viewing (see Figure 3-23).

The Jukebox

Now that virtually all music is digital, the Internet may be emerging as the primary delivery system for music in the near future. **Jukebox** software (see Figure 3-24) records, stores, and plays music on the PC. The software can also download stored music to portable players. The Internet is truly alive with music, with lots of MP3 music files, and thousands of radio stations and other sites offering online music. The digital jukebox can help you gather MP3 and other audio files from Internet music resources. Use it to play stored music or real-time music from the Internet or from CDs based on user-defined playlists. Jukebox software also has a capability to play popular videos along with the music.

SECTION

1 The IRC protocol enables users to join and participate in group chat sessions. (T/F)
2 All Internet search engines have the same rules for formulating the inquiry. (T/F)
3 Which of these would not be considered an Internet portal: (a) Yahoo!, (b) Google, (c) Webcast, or (d) Excite?
4 What FTP feature allows anyone on the Net to use FTP sites without prior permission: (a) unsigned FTP, (b) secret FTP, (c) unnamed FTP, or (d) anonymous FTP?
5 Which of these applications is associated with text chat: (a) Internet telephone, (b) IRC, (c) e-mail, or (d) newsgroups?
6 The two ways e-mail is delivered are: (a) client software and FTP, (b) Web-based and FTP, (c) Web-based and client software, or (d) client and consumer.

3-4 INTERNET ISSUES

Why this section is important to you.

People on the Internet reflect real life—most are good and a few are bad. Crackers, hate mongers, stalkers, and other unpleasant elements have Net access just like you. Awareness of all sides of the Internet makes you a better informed netizen and reduces the chances of you being a target for abuse on the Internet.

Prior to 1989 and the introduction of the World Wide Web and its user-friendly interface (see Figure 3-25), the Internet was used mostly by technical people who were willing to learn its cryptic text interface. The Web opened the Internet to the masses and to inevitable abuse. The Internet remains a digital Wild West, largely without law and order. Nevertheless, the lure of this new frontier has an endless stream of wagon trains "heading west."

THE SHADY SIDE OF THE INTERNET

The Internet is public land; therefore, this accessibility is one of the inherent problems on the Internet. Bigots and cranks who push everything from neo-Nazi propaganda to pornographic images dominate some Internet newsgroups. Electronic lechers sometimes hound women on the Internet, and the language spoken in the heat of a passionate electronic debate can range from rude to libelous. With unlimited accessibility come mischievous hackers, hate mongers, and pornography.

Hackers and Crackers

Any computer enthusiast who enjoys the lawful excesses of personal computing (programming, building PCs, and so on) would qualify as a **hacker.** Hackers created the term **cracker** to distinguish themselves from overzealous hackers, who "crack" through network/Internet security and tap into everything from local credit agencies to top-secret defense systems. Crackers are continually doing what they can to disrupt the flow of information on the Internet. Often these electronic assaults are on Internet servers and the other communications devices that route data from node to node on the Net. These actions are like changing the road signs along the interstate highway system. Unfortunately, overzealous hackers and crackers don't stop at changing the road signs. They also plant computer viruses on

FIGURE 3-24 **DIGITAL JUKEBOXES**

Millions of songs flow throughout the Internet everyday. Digital Jukeboxes, such as RealJukebox shown here in full and "skin" (not within a window) views, enable downloading, cataloging, playing, and visualization of songs, along with artist information and Internet links to related sites.

THE FIRST WEB SERVER COMPUTER

The World Wide Web originated here in 1989 at the CERN computer center. CERN is the European Organization for Nuclear Research. Did Web inventor Tim Berners-Lee envision the many serious issues that would result from millions of interconnected Web servers?

Courtesy of CERN

the Internet disguised as enticing downloadable files or distributed as e-mail. Once downloaded or opened as an e-mail attachment, the virus infects the PC and creates havoc, often destroying files and sometimes even entire hard disks. Crackers have stolen valuable software, traded corporate and country secrets, hijacked telephone credit card numbers, distributed copyrighted photos and songs, and run online securities scams.

Hate Mongers

The Internet is filled with hate mongers—those who spew venom designed to foster hate, discrimination, prejudice, and/or intolerance. Before the Internet, these extremists would typically reach a few dozen or, maybe, a few thousand people by marching on courthouses, distributing leaflets, renting space on roadside signs, speaking on street corners, or doing whatever they could to get media attention. In this new Internet era, they can create hate sites espousing their messages to millions throughout the world.

Hate and lies can be spread over cyberspace with anonymity. However, according to our courts and the sentiments of most people, anonymous speech is part of the price we pay for a democracy. Unfortunately, the privilege of anonymity on the Net is abused routinely.

Hate is easy to find on the Internet. To put Internet hate into perspective, these are just a few of the themes you might find on the Internet: antiwhite, antiblack, anti-Semitic, Anti-Judeo-Christian, anti-Muslim, antigay, antiwomen, antimen, anti-AOL, anti-Spice Girls, anti-Beatles, anti-Star Trek, anti-Survivor (the TV show), anti-Olympics, anti-Ford, and anti-Chevy. There are even "I hate you" sites. Hate also is promoted through newsgroups, mailing lists, and aggressive spam campaigns.

By definition, these hate sites represent extremist views. Some, however, get very personal, often attacking public figures in politics, sports, and the film industry, often to the point of libel. Some hate sites are parodies that are meant to be "funny," but at the expense of those people, ideas, institutions, etc., being attacked. Typically, the small groups of people who help sling the mud see the humor; but most people are repulsed.

What can or should be done to thwart the efforts of hate mongers? Some say nothing. After all, the Internet is free and generally unrestricted regarding content. Others cannot understand why these users would be allowed to maintain a presence on the Internet. Under pressure, several major Internet portals have decided not to include such sites in their indices (the sites they categorize for their menus and search engines). But this action doesn't make them go away; it just makes them harder to find. Also, the United States government is beginning to crack down on hate mongers who threaten physical harm or damage. Several people have been imprisoned for the words and/or images they included on their hate sites.

Pornography

It's possible to get hundreds of thousands, if not millions, of hits when you enter sex-related keywords into a major Internet portal's search engine. Sexually explicit material comprises 1.5% of all Internet content—that's a lot when you consider that the Internet has billions of pages.

Any conceivable type of sexually explicit content that can be digitized is on the Internet. Much of this is available to whoever wishes to explore the sites, but mostly, sexually explicit sites require users to subscribe to their fee-based services. The services might include adult language, links to nudity, still images, live video, and interactive sessions where users have a video and voice/text link with the site. Sadly, the online sale of pornography is one of e-commerce's biggest businesses.

The controversy about whether sexually explicit material on the Internet should be banned or controlled has been debated by local library boards and in the highest courts of the land. The debate will rage on because controlling Net content is difficult, if not impossible, in the current environment. Therefore, parents with children who go online and facilities that make the Internet available to the public, such as libraries, can opt to use **filtering programs** that deny access to certain types of "undesirable" content (sexually explicit material, sites that foster terrorism, gambling, and so on). Because Internet pornography has become an international issue, these sites are at least making an effort to discourage viewing by minors (young people). They do this by asking visitors to confirm that they are adults and that they understand exactly what is contained at the Web site. As you might imagine, many ignore the warnings and just click through to the content pages.

GAMBLING

Internet gambling, also called online gambling, is simply placing bets on sports contests or the playing of casino-type games (roulette, slot machines, lotteries, bingo, Keno, video poker, and so on) over the Internet (see Figure 3-26). The betting, playing, and passing of money is done online, so all gambling sites require that you deposit money before gambling with them. Winnings are deposited to your account and losses are deducted. Even though gambling is illegal in most areas of the United States, Internet technology has rendered state and country boundaries to be nothing more than lines on a map. Several hundred sites offer Internet gambling, and all of these casinos are located offshore in countries that promote gambling as a way to improve their economies.

SPAM

Another downside of the Internet is spam, the cyberworld's version of junk mail (see Figure 3-26). **Spam** is unsolicited junk e-mail, usually advertising for worthless, deceptive, and/or fraudulent commercial products or services. Some spam messages provide information on legitimate services, but most spams are scams (for example, earn $50,000 with only a $20 investment, obtain a university diploma without studying, or become a legally ordained minister). The term *spam* was derived from an old Monty Python comedy routine where Vikings howled "spam spam spam spam" to drown out other conversations. Similarly, spam tends to overwhelm people's e-mail inboxes, making important messages difficult to find.

Spammers, or those who send spam, get your e-mail address in a variety of ways. For example, many Web sites sell their "hit lists" (e-mails of those who visit a site) to spammers. Of course, spammers sell their "response list" (e-mails of those who respond to their spam messages) to other spammers. Unfortunately, it's often as difficult to get off a spammer's list as it is to figure out how you got on it. To date, there is no central clearinghouse to which you can write to get your name taken off a direct e-mail advertiser's mailing list. However, a number of spammers advertise such a service as a way of adding names to their spam database. Some of the more ethical online advertisers give users a legitimate option to be removed from their mailing lists. At the other end of the spectrum are those spammers who ask you to call them to be removed. What they don't tell you is that you are being charged $2 per minute for the call.

Not only is spam filling our e-mail boxes, it's also problematic. Millions of spam messages are sent each day to AOL users, who spend up to 10 cumulative person-years simply deleting these unwanted messages. In addition, Internet users are increasingly concerned that spam is taking up valuable bandwith in the Net, stressing its capacity for information.

Though most of us would prefer not to be spammed, it's as difficult to rid the public Internet of spam as it is to rid our mail boxes of junk mail. Commercial information services, such as AOL and ISPs use sophisticated filters, which are continually updated, to

FIGURE 3-26 NET CONCERNS AND ISSUES

ONLINE GAMBLING

Gambling is one of the more established e-commerce applications and is readily available for those who wish to gamble. An online gambling casino gives you up to $50 in chips to get you started.

ATMS EVERYWHERE

Many cyberworld issues are not apparent, such as the existence and/or location of ATMs. While most of us see ATMs as a convenience, others see them as unsafe and a threat to their money or as a future crime site.

Courtesy of Diebold, Incorporated

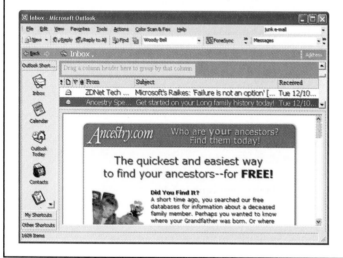

TYPICAL SPAM

Anybody with an e-mail address gets it—spam, or unsolicited e-mail.

minimize the amount of spam that reaches their customers. Most e-mail client software, such as Microsoft Outlook, has filters capable of deleting much of the pornography-related spam. The client filter also routes spam to a junk e-mail folder for review if user-specified keywords or phrases are in the subject and/or message ("100%," "guaranteed," "best mortgage," "refinance," "FREE," "!!!," and so on).

Regrettably, spammers are very imaginative and do what they can to stay one step ahead of efforts to stop them. For example, often spammers use the "hit and run" approach where they open an account with an ISP, send thousands of unsolicited e-mail messages, then leave town and do it again somewhere else. Spammers don't stay put long enough to be *flamed,* or barraged with scathing e-mails from irate Internet users, although recipients sometimes try. Others who might be outraged at happenings on the Internet are fighting back through the legal system. They're placing pressure on legislatures, often through e-mail campaigns, to make laws more in line with societal norms. Others are simply choosing not to frequent or shop at sites they believe offer inappropriate content in hopes that boycotting will cause the site to fold.

As we change, the Internet changes. The Internet is a worldwide work-in-progress. It is our duty to promote positive change, but we must at all times recognize that it will continue to shape us as individuals and as a society. In time, this information medium, like its predecessors, newspapers, radio, and television, will be taken for granted like the air we breathe. It's incumbent upon us to ensure that we continue to breathe clean air, both in the real world and in cyberspace.

1 The Internet is now secure and no longer vulnerable to malicious hackers. (T/F)

2 Internet law and order is refined and explicit. (T/F)

3 Conducting business online is called: (a) electronic business, (b) cyber commerce, (c) e-commerce, or (d) cyber business.

4 Unsolicited junk e-mail is called: (a) spam, (b) pam, (c) weanies, or (d) flames.

Chapter Review

CHAPTER SUMMARY

3-1 THE INTERNET

The Internet (a worldwide collection of *inter*connected *networks*) is composed of thousands of independent networks in virtually every type of organization. The Department of Defense's ARPANET project was the genesis of the Internet. Volunteers from many nations serving on various advisory boards, task groups, steering committees, and so on, coordinate the Internet.

You can connect to the Internet via high-speed broadband or narrowband. Communication channels are rated by their bandwidth. Channel capacities range from 56,000 bits per second (bps) for dialup service to broadband access at 622 M bps for commercial service. Narrowband dialup access is available to anyone with POTS—plain old telephone services. Common broadband options, which are up to 30 times faster than narrowband access, include cable, DSL, satellite, and wireless. A cable modem is required for cable access. DSL shares an existing telephone line and can provide access speed up to 9 M bps (the downstream rate) with an upstream rate (sending) of up to 1.5 M bps. Wireless communication lets users take their PC anywhere within the range of a wireless signal and a link to a LAN via an access point, a wireless communications hub.

The most popular Wi-Fi standard used for short-range wireless communication is the IEEE 802.11b communications standard. The IEEE 802.11a and the emerging IEEE 802.11g standards permit a higher transmission rate. Wireless devices must be equipped with a wireless local area network (LAN) PC card.

The three most popular ways to connect your PC to the Internet are subscribing to the services of an ISP (Internet service provider), subscribing to a commercial information service, such as America Online, and using a direct connection to the Internet via a local area network. When you logon, you will need to enter a user ID (or a screen name) and a password.

The Transmission Control Protocol/Internet Protocol (TCP/IP) is the communications protocol that permits data transmission over the Internet. The *Transmission Control Protocol* sets the rules for the packaging of information into packets. The *Internet Protocol* handles the address, such that each packet is routed to its proper destination. Each point-of-presence (POP), an access point on the Internet, has a unique IP address that consists of four numbers (0 to 255). When you log on to an ISP, your PC is assigned a dynamic IP address.

A client program runs on your PC and works in conjunction with a companion server program that runs on the Internet host computer. The client program contacts the server program, and they work together to give you access to the resources on the Internet server. An *Internet browser* is one kind of client. The dominant browsers are Microsoft Internet Explorer and Netscape.

The URL (uniform resource locator), which is the Internet equivalent of an address, progresses from general to specific. That portion of the URL before the first colon (usually *http*) specifies the access method. The *http* tells the software to expect an http (HyperText Transport Protocol) file. That portion following the double forward slashes (//) is the server address, or the domain name. It has at least two parts, separated by dots (periods). The top-level domains or TLDs, such as *com* and *org,* denote affiliations. What follows the domain name is a folder or path containing the resources for a particular topic. At the end of the URL is the specific filename of the file that is retrieved from the server.

HTML (HyperText Markup Language) is a markup language used to compose and format most files on the Net. A more feature-rich XHTML is to become the new standard.

3-2 INTERNET BROWSERS

Internet browser, or Web browser, software lets us tap the information resources of the electronic world. It enables us to retrieve and view Internet-based information, interact with server-based systems, view electronic documents, pass digital information between computers, send and receive e-mail, and join newsgroups. The browser opens an HTML/XHTML document and displays the information according to HTML/XHTML instructions embedded in the document.

At the top of the Internet organization scheme are the Internet servers. Each World Wide Web server has one or more home pages, the first page you will normally view when traveling to a particular site. Web resources, which may be graphics, audio, video, animation, and text, are viewed in pages.

Each Web page is actually a file with its own URL. We navigate to an address on the Internet just as we drive to a street address. Hyperlinks permit navigation between pages and between other resources on the Internet. The pages at a server site are set up within a hierarchy of URLs.

There are a number of complementary applications, called plugins, which can enhance the functionality of browsers. Examples include *Shockwave Player, QuickTime,* and *RealPlayer,* which let you listen to streaming audio and view streaming video.

3-3 INTERNET RESOURCES AND APPLICATIONS

There are two basic approaches to using a browser: *browsing* and *searching.* You can browse through menu trees of *categories* or you can search using a variety of resource discovery tools, including search engines. Portals are Web sites that offer a broad array of information and services, including a menu tree of categories and a capability that helps us find online resources.

The World Wide Web is an Internet application that permits linking of multimedia documents among Web servers on the Internet. By establishing a linked relationship between Web documents, related information becomes easily accessible. Web resources are designed to be accessed with easy-to-use browsers.

The File Transfer Protocol (FTP) allows you to download and upload files on the Internet. Most are anonymous FTP sites.

The Internet is an aid to better communication. You can send e-mail to and receive it from anyone with an Internet e-mail address. The two ways to send/receive e-mail are via e-mail client software or via Web-based e-mail, which is handled through interaction with a Web site.

The Internet e-mail address has two parts, the username and the domain name, and is separated by an @ symbol. The domain name identifies the e-mail server. An attached file can be sent with an e-mail message.

A newsgroup is the cyberspace version of a bulletin board. People who frequent newsgroups refer to the original message and any posted replies to that message as a thread. The Internet mailing list (listserv) is a cross between a newsgroup and e-mail.

The Internet Relay Chat (IRC) protocol allows users to participate in group chat sessions. A chat session is when two or more Internet users carry on a typed, real-time, online conversation.

Instant messaging is a convenient way for you to know when your friends are online so you can communicate with them in real time. Some versions of instant messaging software permit file/application sharing, whiteboarding, and the ability to have audio and video conferencing. The Internet phone capability lets you call people at other computers on the Internet.

People who communicate online have invented keyboard shortcuts and emoticons to speed up the written interaction and convey emotions. Rules of netiquette, Internet etiquette, demand sensitivity and concern for others in cyberspace.

Webcasting (Internet broadcasting) has emerged as a popular Internet application. With pull technology, the user requests information via a browser. With push technology, information is sent automatically to a user.

Digital jukebox software records, stores, and plays music on the PC. It can help you gather MP3 and other audio files from Internet music resources.

3-4 INTERNET ISSUES

The Internet is a digital Wild West. Mischievous hackers and crackers are continually doing what they can to disrupt the flow of information on the Net. In addition, the Internet is filled with hate mongers, whose objective is to foster hate, discrimination, prejudice, bigotry, and/or intolerance.

The controversy about whether sexually explicit material on the Internet should be banned or controlled is debated, but the use of filtering programs can deny access to certain types of "undesirable" content. Internet gambling is one of those issues whose growth is much faster than the legal system can accommodate.

Spammers send spam, the electronic equivalent of junk mail and, at present, there is no foolproof way for netizens to keep spam out of the received e-mail list. People who send discourteous communications over the Net are frequently flamed.

KEY TERMS

Access points (p. 117)
ActiveX control (p. 125)
applets (p. 125)
attached file (p. 135)
bandwidth (p. 116)
bits per second (bps) (p. 116)
broadband access (p. 116)
client program (p. 120)
cracker (p. 142)
domain name (p. 120)
downstream rate (p. 117)
DSL (Digital Subscriber Line) (p. 117)
dynamic IP address (p. 120)
e-mail server (p. 134)
emoticons (p. 140)
FAQs (frequently asked questions
    (p. 132)
File Transfer Protocol (FTP) (p. 133)
filtering program (p. 145)
hacker (p. 142)
hits (p. 132)
home page (p. 125)
HTML (HyperText Markup
    Language) (p. 122)

http (HyperText Transport Protocol
    (p. 121)
hyperlink (p. 125)
IEEE 802.11a (p. 117)
IEEE 802.11b (p. 117)
IEEE 802.11g (p. 117)
Internet (p. 114)
Internet appliance (p. 120)
Internet backbone (p. 115)
Internet Relay Chat (IRC) (p. 137)
IP address (p. 119)
ISP (p. 118)
jukebox (p. 142)
logon (p. 118)
mailing list (p. 136)
markup language (p. 122)
newsgroup (p. 136)
packet (p. 119)
pages (p. 125)
password (p. 118)
plugin (p. 126)
point-of-presence (POP) (p. 119)
portal (p. 130)
POTS (p. 116)

protocol (p. 118)
pull technology (p. 136)
push technology (p. 137)
screen name (user ID) (p. 118)
search engine (p. 130)
server program (p. 120)
spam (p. 145)
streaming audio (p. 128)
streaming video (p. 128)
T-1 line (p. 118)
T-3 line (p. 118)
TCP/IP (p. 118)
thread (p. 136)
top-level domain (TLD) (p. 121)
upstream rate (p. 117)
URL, or uniform resource locator
    (p. 121)
whiteboarding (p. 138)
Wi-Fi (p. 117)
wireless LAN PC card (p. 117)
XHTML (p. 122)

MATCHING

_____ 1. broadband access

_____ 2. search engine

_____ 3. TCP/IP

_____ 4. ARPANET

_____ 5. instant messaging

_____ 6. plugin

_____ 7. bandwidth

_____ 8. HTML

_____ 9. Wi-Fi

_____10. Satellite

a IEEE 802.11b

b high-speed Internet

c linking people in real-time

d rules for Internet packets

e early Internet

f enhances browser functionality

g source for remote Internet access

h channel capacity

i markup language

j Net resource discovery tool

CHAPTER SELF-CHECK

TRUE/FALSE

1. One way to go online is to subscribe to a commercial information service. (T/F)

2. ARPANET was the first commercially available communications software package. (T/F)

3. A newbie is anyone with a fear of cyberspace. (T/F)

4. Every home user is assigned a permanent IP address on the Internet. (T/F)

5. Narrowband has slightly more capacity than broadband. (T/F)

6. On the Internet, only hypertext hyperlinks are hot. (T/F)

7. Internet portals are designed to permit searches by category or by keyword, but never both. (T/F)

8. Yahoo! is a site on the Internet that can be used to browse the Net by content category. (T/F)

9. Subscribing to a popular mailing list would result in more Internet e-mail than posting a message to a newsgroup. (T/F)

10. A file attached to an e-mail is routed to the recipient's e-mail server computer along with the message. (T/F)

11. All hackers are crackers, too. (T/F)

12. Hate can be spread over the Internet with anonymity. (T/F)

MULTIPLE CHOICE

1. Which of the following is not a link to the Internet: (a) interstate bonds, (b) DSL, (c) cable, or (d) wireless satellite?

2. Which of the following is not included with a subscription to an information service: (a) communications software, (b) a user ID, (c) speech-recognition software, or (d) a password?

3. Which of the following is not an online commercial information service: (a) Dow Jones Business Information Service, (b) the Web, (c) AOL, or (d) CompuServe?

4. Which of these is not a U.S. top-level domain affiliation ID: (a) moc, (b) edu, (c) gov, or (d) org?

5. What type of company provides people with access to the Internet: (a) PSI, (b) ISP, (c) SPI, or (d) IPS?

6. In the e-mail address, _mickey_mouse@disney.com_, the user ID is: (a) _mickey_mouse_, (b) _mouse_, (c) _disney.com_, or (d) @.

7. A 56,000 bits-per-second channel is the same as a: (a) 56 K bps pipe, (b) 56 K bps line, (c) dual 28000X2 K bps line, or (d) single-channel DSL.

8. A communication channel is rated by its: (a) channel aptitude, (b) bandwidth, (c) flow, or (d) datastream.

9. Which broadband service has a built-in lag in response time: (a) DSL, (b) satellite, (c) cable, or (d) Wi-Fi?

10. Which of these would not be associated with a wireless local area network: (a) access points, (b) Wi-Fi, (c) IEEE 802.11b, or (d) DSL?

11. Which of the following labels might be included with an Internet address: (a) <bps>, (b) ULS, (c) http://, or (d) fpt://?

12. The opening page for a particular Web site normally is the: (a) opener page, (b) home page, (c) flip-flop page, or (d) master page.

13. Which of the following buttons is not one of the main buttons on a browser toolbar: (a) Back, (b) Forward, (c) Refresh, or (d) House?

14. Web pages can be tied together by: (a) cybertext links, (b) hydratext links, (c) hydrolinks, or (d) hyperlinks.

15. Which server on the Internet offers hypertext links: (a) QOQ, (b) Web, (c) Gopher, or (d) FTP?

16. All but which one of these would be a common way to search for information on the Internet: (a) browse, (b) search, (c) push/pull, or (d) ask someone on the Net?

17. What Web features enable the display of more than one independently controllable sections on a screen: (a) borders, (b) windows, (c) frames, or (d) structures?

18. Generally, today's Internet applications are based on what technology: (a) push, (b) pull, (c) place, or (d) draw?

19. Internet-based capabilities that help you find information on the Internet are: (a) seek portals, (b) find files, (c) search motors, or (d) search engines.

20. On a newsgroup, the original message and any posted replies to that message are a: (a) needle, (b) thread, (c) pinpoint, or (d) tapestry?

21. Sexually explicit material comprises what percent of Internet content: (a) .003%, (b) 1.5%, (c) 15%, or (d) 31%?

22. Some organizations use what type of software to deny access to "undesirable" Internet content: (a) sifting, (b) filtering, (c) screening, or (d) straining.

IT ETHICS AND ISSUES

1. E-MAIL ETIQUETTE

E-mail is now as much a part of the business world as the paycheck. How we present ourselves in our e-mails can play a role in how effective we are in business and in what people think of us. You can leave a good or bad impression with your correspondents depending on your understanding of netiquette; that is, *what* you say in your message and *how* you say it.

During face-to-face conversations we use vocal inflections or body movements that clarify words or phrases. In contrast, e-mail is just words, which leave the door open for misinterpretation. Anyone composing e-mail should be aware that it could easily be forwarded, printed, and even broadcast to others, which could be very embarrassing to you and to others. This is why every e-mailer should be careful what he or she writes and follow the basic tenets of e-mail etiquette. For example, you should inform senders when you forward their e-mail. A good e-mail message includes a subject, has a logical flow, and concludes with a signature (name, association, and contact information).

Discussion: What would be considered good netiquette?

Discussion: Describe e-mails that you have received (or seen) that you feel are in poor taste and out of step with good e-mail etiquette. What could the sender have done to modify the e-mail while retaining the essential message?

2. THE UNWANTED CHAT ROOM GUEST

America Online, Yahoo!, and other information services/portals sponsor hundreds of topical chat rooms where participants chat (via text input) with one another about a specific topic. Topics range from auto repair to Little League baseball to "over 60" to Harley-Davidson motorcycles. However, it's not unusual for at least one of the participants to be an unwanted guest. Unwanted guests make rude or obnoxious comments that have nothing to do with the focus of the chat room. Sometimes these comments become inappropriately profane and personal, causing well-meaning participants to leave the chat room.

Discussion: Should those who enter a public chat room have the right to talk about whatever they wish, disregarding the stated topic of the chat rooms?

Discussion: What, if anything, should be done to stop these unwanted guests from wasting the time of the other participants and violating the purpose of the chat room?

3. ADS IN PERSONAL E-MAIL

Marketers continue to search for better ways to reach customers via Internet advertising. One company has introduced a technology that marketers can use to advertise their products and services within your personal e-mail messages. It works like this: your e-mails are intercepted at the mail server and then wrapped with advertising content. In theory, the advertising will be tailored to the individual receiving the e-mail based on his/her demographic profile. Marketers are hoping that e-mail recipients will continue to open personal mail and, whether they like it or not, read the advertisements, as well.

Discussion: Internet companies have found it necessary to integrate advertising within their services. Is this approach to Net advertising justified given the current economic climate of Internet commerce?

Discussion: Is this approach more or less palatable than spam to the e-mail community? Why?

DISCUSSION AND PROBLEM SOLVING

1. Describe at least three things you do now without the aid of online communications that may be done in the online environment in the near future.

2. The federal government is calling for "universal service" such that everyone has access to the "information superhighway." Is this an achievable goal? Explain.

3. Discuss how you would justify spending $15 to $25 a month to subscribe to an ISP for dialup Internet access. How would you justify spending $40 to $60 a month for broadband Internet access?

4. Speculate on how Internet appliances might change your life during the next decade.

5. Briefly describe one of alternative methods of connecting your PC to the Internet.

6. What is the organizational affiliation of these Internet addresses: smith_jo@mkt.bigco.com; politics@washington.senate.gov; and hugh_roman@anthropology.stuniv.edu? Why do we need this "affiliation" distinction?

7. Expand and discuss the meaning of the following acronyms: TCP/IP, ISP, http, and URL.

8. The Microsoft Internet Explorer browser is now the most used browser in the world. A few years ago, the Netscape browser was the dominant browser. Some will argue that Netscape still makes the best browser. Speculate on what might have caused the turnaround.

9. The Internet has over 2 billion pages of information, some of which are placed online and not updated for years. Should there be an effort to purge inactive information on the Internet? Explain.

10. Why are there so many plugins for Internet browsers and why are they not built into the original browser software?

11. What is your favorite portal on the Internet and why?

12. In what ways is the World Wide Web different from other servers on the Internet?

13. Describe circumstances for which you would prefer browsing the Net to using a search engine.

14. Discuss the pros and cons of FTPing on the Internet.

15. Videophones are available on the Internet now. Is this innovation in personal communications something you are looking forward to or dreading? Explain.

16. Would you prefer to receive traditional e-mail or audio mail? Explain.

17. Discuss the advantages and disadvantages of e-mail and instant messaging in a domestic setting and in a business setting.

18. What type of information would you like to be sent to you automatically via Internet push technology?

19. Describe five things you would like to do on the Internet.

20. What is your favorite Internet application and why?

21. The Internet is a digital Wild West. Should presence on the Internet be more tightly controlled to help bring law and order to the Internet?

22. Gambling could be one of the most profitable computer applications ever. Americans spent 70 times as much on gambling last year as they spent on movies. Internet gambling is currently hosted offshore. Argue for or against legalizing Internet gambling within the United States.

23. The Internet is public and much of the readily accessible content on the Internet is considered inappropriate for viewing by young people. Should legislation be enacted to control Internet content?

24. Dissatisfied customers routinely create Web sites devoted to criticizing a company's product or services. The company's name usually is embedded in the domain name in a derogatory manner. Companies being attacked are seeking legislative relief. Should the government get involved?

FOCUS ON PERSONAL COMPUTING

1. *Surfing the Net: Small Waves and Big Waves*. If you have not already done so, spend a few minutes doing some serendipitous surfing on the Internet via a dialup, narrowband Internet link. Do the same on a system with a broadband connection. Briefly describe how your perspective, what you did, and where you went changed when you began the broadband session.

2. *Searching the Net*. On an Internet-enabled PC, do at least two of the following tasks. Search for and play the signal from an Internet radio station based in a country other than your own. Find, download, and play a hit song. Find a long-lost friend (where they live or work). Plan your dream vacation (flight schedules and lodging). Describe your activities.

3. *Communicating on the Net*. Send an e-mail. Find and visit a newsgroup of interest to you. Set up instant messaging with several of your friends. Be a participant in an Internet chat room. If possible, hold a voice conversation over the Internet. Which of these means of Internet communications is of the greatest interest to you? Explain.

ONLINE EXERCISES @ www.prenhall.com/long

1. The Online Study Guide (multiple choice, true/false, matching, and essay questions)
2. Internet Learning Activities
   - The Internet
   - Going Online
3. Serendipitous Internet Activities
   - Magazines

INSIDE THE COMPUTER

CHAPTER 4

LEARNING OBJECTIVES

Once you have read and studied this chapter, you will be able to:

- Show how data are stored and represented in a computer system (Section 4-1).

- Describe the function of and relationships between the internal components of a personal computer, including the motherboard, processor, random-access memory (RAM) and other memories, ports, buses, expansion boards, and PC cards (Section 4-2).

- Distinguish processors by their word size, speed, and memory capacity (Section 4-3).

- Identify new approaches to traditional processor design (Section 4-4).

A PC card here, a DVD+RW drive there, a few GHz, and all of a sudden you are talking significant dollars. A state-of-the-art PC configured with a full complement of peripheral devices will run you between $1,500 and $2,000. Hang on a few extras, add a quality sound system, and you are over $2,500. And that's just the hardware! With Mom, Dad, and the kids all wanting their own PC, it's not unusual for expenditures on hardware and software to top that of the family car. With a significant portion of your budget at stake, you want to make informed decisions when purchasing PCs.

When you purchase a car, you know it will perform its basic function—to carry people over roadways from point to point. Not so with PCs. PCs have thousands of functions, and when you purchase one, you want to be sure that it will do what you want it to do. Most of us can easily grasp the variables involved in buying a house or a car. The average car buyer can assess functionality and style relative to his or her budget constraints and visual tastes, then make a reasonably informed decision. However, to get what you want and need in a PC, and to get the most for your money, you need to have an overall understanding of the essential elements of a computer.

One PC looks about like another, with perhaps a little variation in color, style, and size. Look inside, however, and they can be vastly different. Similar-looking PC boxes can be mansions or efficiency apartments on the inside. One might have a 3.3-GHz processor and another much slower 2.0-GHz processor. Differences in processor speed, RAM capacity, type of RAM, what's embedded on the motherboard, and so on, dictate overall system performance and ability to enhance the system. If you understand these essential elements, you'll be able to make informed decisions when purchasing PCs—and that may be as often as once or twice a year for work and family. Those people who depend on advice from the PC salesperson may end up spending far more than necessary and still not get what they need to do the job.

4-1 DIGITAL: THE LANGUAGE OF COMPUTERS

Why this section is important to you.

Much of what we see, hear, and do is going digital: music, cell phones, photographs, books, movies, catalogues, and much more. This section will help prepare you for immersion into a world filled with computers—all of which are digital with one another.

A computer is a virtual university providing interactive instruction and testing. It's a painter's canvas. It's an entertainment center with hundreds of interactive games. It's a video telephone. It's a CD player. It's a home or office library. It's a television. It's the biggest marketplace in the world. It's the family photo album. It's a print shop. It's a wind tunnel that can test experimental airplane designs. It's a recorder. It can perform thousands of specialty functions that require specialized skills, such as preparing taxes, drafting legal documents, counseling suicidal patients, and much more.

In all of these applications, the computer deals with everything as electronic signals. The two kinds of electronic signals are **analog** and **digital.** Analog signals are *continuous*

FIGURE 4–1

GOING DIGITAL WITH COMPACT DISCS

The recording industry has gone digital. To create a master CD, analog signals are converted to digital signals that can be manipulated by a computer and written to a master CD. The master is duplicated and the copies are sold through retail channels.

waveforms in which variations in frequency and amplitude can be used to represent information from sound and numerical data. Traditionally, the sound of our voice has been carried by analog signals when we talk on the telephone. That, however, is changing because just about everything in the world of electronics and communication is *going digital* to enable compatibility with computers. Digital signals describe everything in two states: The circuit is either *on* or *off*. Generally, the *on* state is expressed or represented by the number 1 and the *off* state by the number 0.

So how do you go digital? You simply need to **digitize** your material. To digitize means to convert data, analog signals, and images into the discrete format that can be interpreted by computers—1s and 0s. For example, Figure 4-1 shows how music can be digitized. Once digitized, you can use a computer to work with (revise and copy, among other things) the music recording, data, image, shape, and so on. Old recordings of artists from Enrico Caruso to the Beatles have been digitized and then digitally reconstructed on computers to eliminate unwanted distortion and static. Some of these reconstructed CDs are actually better than the originals!

BINARY DIGITS: 1 AND 0

The electronic nature of the computer makes it possible to combine the two digital states—*on* and *off*—to represent letters, numbers, colors, sounds, images, shapes, and even odors. An "on" or "off" electronic state is represented by a *bit*, short for binary digit. In the **binary** numbering system (base 2), the *on-bit* is a 1 and the *off-bit* is a 0. Physically, these states are achieved in a variety of ways.

- In RAM (temporary storage), the two electronic states often are represented by the presence or absence of an electrical charge in an integrated circuit—a computer chip (see Figure 4-2).

- In disk storage (permanent storage), the two states are made possible by the magnetic arrangement of the surface coating on magnetic disks (see Figure 4-3).

- In CDs and CD-ROMs, digital data are stored permanently as microscopic pits.

- In fiber optic cable, binary data flow through as pulses of light, and in electrical transmission media, the binary numbers are electrical signals.

FIGURE 4–2

MICROMINIATURIZATION OF THE CHIP'S BIT

During the first generation of computers a bit was represented by a vacuum tube. This silicon wafer contains a number of thumbnail-sized Pentium 4 processor chips, each with the capability to process and store billions of bits.

Photo courtesy of Intel Corporation

Courtesy of International Business Machines Corporation. Unauthorized use not permitted.

Bits may be fine for computers, but human beings are more comfortable with letters and decimal numbers (the base-10 numerals 0 through 9). We like to see colors and hear sounds, not binary representations of colors and sounds. Therefore, the letters, decimal numbers, colors, and sounds we input into a computer system while doing word processing, graphics, and other applications must be translated into 1s and 0s for processing and storage. The computer translates the bits back into letters, decimal numbers, colors, and sounds for output on monitors, printers, speakers, and so on.

CHARACTER ENCODING SYSTEMS: BITS AND BYTES

Computers don't speak to one another in English, Spanish, or French. They have their own languages, which are better suited to electronic communication. In these languages, bits are combined according to a *character encoding system* to represent letters, numbers, and special characters (such as *, $, +, and &), collectively referred to as *alphanumeric* characters.

ASCII and ANSI

ASCII (American Standard Code for Information Interchange—pronounced "*AS-key*") was the most popular character encoding system for PCs and data communication through the 1990s. In ASCII, alphanumeric characters are *encoded* into a bit configuration on input so that the computer can interpret them. This coding equates a unique series of 1s and 0s with a specific character. Figure 4-4 shows the ASCII bit string of commonly used characters. Just as the words *mother* and *father* are arbitrary English-language character strings that refer to our parents, 01000010 is an arbitrary ASCII code that refers to the letter *B*. When you tap the letter *B* on a keyboard, the *B* is sent to the processor as a coded string of binary digits (01000010 in ASCII) as shown in Figure 4-5. The characters are *decoded* for output to a printer or monitor so we can interpret them. The 8-bit combination of bits used to represent a character is called a **byte** (pronounced "*bite*").

The 7-bit ASCII code can represent up to 128 characters (2^7). The PC byte is 8 bits so ASCII usually is presented as 8 bits with a leading zero as shown in Figure 4-4. There are 256 (2^8) possible bit configurations in an 8-bit byte. Hardware and software vendors accept the 128 standard ASCII codes and use the extra 128 bit configurations to represent control characters (such as ringing a bell) or noncharacter images to complement their hardware or software product. Earlier versions of Microsoft Windows use the 8-bit **ANSI** encoding system (developed by the American National Standards Institute) to enable the sharing of text between Windows applications. The first 128 ANSI codes are the same as the ASCII codes, but the next 128 are defined to meet the specific needs of Windows applications.

CHARACTER	ASCII ANSI CODES	UNICODE CODES	NUMERICAL EQUIVALENTS FOR BINARY CODES	
	Binary	Binary	Decimal	Hex
Space	00100000	0000000000100000	32	20
!	00100001	0000000000100001	33	21
"	00100010	0000000000100010	34	22
#	00100011	0000000000100011	35	23
$	00100100	0000000000100100	36	24
%	00100101	0000000000100101	37	25
&	00100110	0000000000100110	38	26
'	00100111	0000000000100111	39	27
(	00101000	0000000000101000	40	28
)	00101001	0000000000101001	41	29
*	00101010	0000000000101010	42	2A
+	00101011	0000000000101011	43	2B
,	00101100	0000000000101100	44	2C
-	00101101	0000000000101101	45	2D
.	00101110	0000000000101110	46	2E
/	00101111	0000000000101111	47	2F
0	00110000	0000000000110000	48	30
1	00110001	0000000000110001	49	31
2	00110010	0000000000110010	50	32
3	00110011	0000000000110011	51	33
4	00110100	0000000000110100	52	34
5	00110101	0000000000110101	53	35
6	00110110	0000000000110110	54	36
7	00110111	0000000000110111	55	37
8	00111000	0000000000111000	56	38
9	00111001	0000000000111001	57	39
A	01000001	0000000001000001	65	41
B	01000010	0000000001000010	66	42
C	01000011	0000000001000011	67	43
D	01000100	0000000001000100	68	44
E	01000101	0000000001000101	69	45
F	01000110	0000000001000110	70	46
G	01000111	0000000001000111	71	47
H	01001000	0000000001001000	72	48
I	01001001	0000000001001001	73	49
J	01001010	0000000001001010	74	4A
K	01001011	0000000001001011	75	4B
L	01001100	0000000001001100	76	4C
M	01001101	0000000001001101	77	4D
N	01001110	0000000001001110	78	4E
O	01001111	0000000001001111	79	4F
P	01010000	0000000001010000	80	50
Q	01010001	0000000001010001	81	51
R	01010010	0000000001010010	82	52
S	01010011	0000000001010011	83	53
T	01010100	0000000001010100	84	54
U	01010101	0000000001010101	85	55
V	01010110	0000000001010110	86	56
W	01010111	0000000001010111	87	57
X	01011000	0000000001011000	88	58
Y	01011001	0000000001011001	89	59
Z	01011010	0000000001011010	90	5A

FIGURE 4–4

ASCII/ANSI AND UNICODE CODES

This figure shows the binary (base 2) ASCII/ANSI and Unicode codes, along with their decimal (base 10) and hexadecimal (hex, base 16) equivalents, for uppercase letters, numbers, and several special characters. The first 128 characters (00000000-01111111), some of which are shown here, are the same for ASCII and ANSI. The codes for uppercase and lowercase letters are similar. Replace the third binary digit with a 1 to get the lowercase equivalent of a capital letter (B is 01000010 and b is 01100010). Except for the eight leading zeros, the Unicode codes are the same for the first 128 characters, too.

FIGURE 4-5 ENCODING

When you tap the B key on the keyboard, a binary representation of the letter *B* is sent to the processor. The processor sends the encoded *B* to the monitor, which interprets and displays a **B**.

Although the English language has considerably fewer than 128 printable characters, the extra bit configurations are needed to represent additional special characters, such as - [hyphen]; @ [at]; | [a vertical bar]; and ~ [tilde]). These extra bit configurations also are used to signal a variety of activities to the computer, such as ringing a bell or telling the computer to accept a piece of datum.

Unicode

ASCII, with 128 character codes, is sufficient for the English language; but we're now a global economy, and ASCII falls far short of the Japanese language requirements (see Figure 4-6). Because of the need to represent more characters, **Unicode,** a 16-bit encoding system, has emerged as the worldwide character-encoding standard. Windows XP uses Unicode exclusively for character manipulation. Universal acceptance of the Unicode standard is making international communication in all areas easier, from monetary transfers between banks to e-mail.

Unicode enables computers and applications to talk to one another more easily and handles most languages of the world (including Hebrew, Japanese, and Greek). Its 16-bit code allows for 65,536 characters (2^{16}). The first 128 Unicode characters are numerically the same as those of the ASCII/ANSI code. For example, the Unicode for the letter *B* is 0000000001000010, the numerical equivalent of the ASCII/ANSI code for *B* (01000010).

The Principles of Numbering Systems

The binary, or base 2, numbering system is based on the same principles as the decimal, or base 10, numbering system, with which we are already familiar. The only difference between the

FIGURE 4-6 THE NEED FOR 16-BIT ENCODING

An 8-bit encoding system, with its 256 unique bit configurations, is more than adequate to represent all of the alphanumeric characters used in the English language. The Japanese, however, need a 16-bit encoding system, like Unicode, to represent thousands of characters.

two numbering systems is that binary uses only two digits, 0 and 1, and the decimal numbering system uses 10 digits, 0 through 9. The equivalents for binary, decimal, and hexadecimal numbers are shown in Figure 4-7.

The value of a given digit is determined by its relative position in a sequence of digits. If you were asked to write the number 124 in decimal, the interpretation is almost automatic because of your familiarity with the decimal numbering system. Binary is no more difficult, but you only have two digits instead of 10. If you were asked to represent the 124 (decimal) in binary, you would go through the same thought process, but using only 1 and 0. This process is illustrated in Figure 4-8.

Hexadecimal: A Shorthand for Expressing Binary Numbers

Perhaps the biggest drawback to using the binary numbering system for computer operations is that human beings occasionally must deal with long and confusing strings of 1s and 0s. To reduce the confusion, the **hexadecimal**, or base 16, numbering system is used as shorthand to display the binary contents of RAM and disk storage.

Notice that the bases of the binary and hexadecimal numbering systems are multiples of 2, 2 and 2^4, respectively. Because of this, there is a convenient relationship between these numbering systems. The table in Figure 4-7 illustrates that a single hexadecimal digit represents four binary digits ($0111_2 = 7_{16}$, $1101_2 = D_{16}$, 1010_2, $= A_{16}$ where subscripts are used to indicate the base of the numbering system). Notice that in hexadecimal, or "hex," *letters* (A, B, C, D, E, and F) are used to represent the six higher-order digits. Two hexadecimal digits can be used to represent an eight-bit byte. The binary and hex ASCII representations of the letter Z are 01011010_2 and $5A_{16}$, respectively.

| FIGURE 4-7 | NUMBERING SYSTEM EQUIVALENCE TABLE |

Binary (Base 2)	Decimal (Base 10)	Hexadecimal (Base 16)
00	0	0
01	1	1
10	2	2
11	3	3
100	4	4
101	5	5
110	6	6
111	7	7
1000	8	8
1001	9	9
1010	10	A
1011	11	B
1100	12	C
1101	13	D
1110	14	E
1111	15	F
10000	16	10

| FIGURE 4-8 | REPRESENTING A BINARY NUMBER |

This figure illustrates the thought process that you might go through to represent the decimal number 124 in binary. For ease of understanding, the arithmetic is done in decimal.

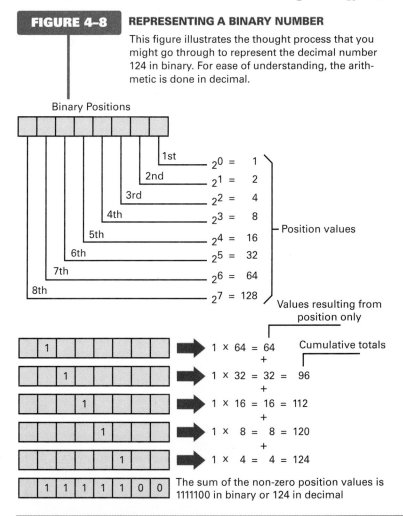

Binary Positions

Position	Value
1st	$2^0 = 1$
2nd	$2^1 = 2$
3rd	$2^2 = 4$
4th	$2^3 = 8$
5th	$2^4 = 16$
6th	$2^5 = 32$
7th	$2^6 = 64$
8th	$2^7 = 128$

Position values

Values resulting from position only

Cumulative totals

1 × 64 = 64
+
1 × 32 = 32 = 96
+
1 × 16 = 16 = 112
+
1 × 8 = 8 = 120
+
1 × 4 = 4 = 124

The sum of the non-zero position values is 1111100 in binary or 124 in decimal

SECTION

1 Data are stored permanently on magnetic disk. (T/F)
2 Binary data flow through fiber optic cable as pulses of light. (T/F)
3 What are the two kinds of electronic signals: (a) analog and digital, (b) binary and octal, (c) alpha and numeric, or (d) bit and byte?
4 The combination of bits used to represent a character is called a: (a) bits on/off, (b) binary config, (c) 0-1 string, or (d) byte.
5 The 16-bit encoding system is called: (a) Unicorn, (b) Unicode, (c) Hexacode, or (d) 10 plus 6 code.

4-2   THE PC SYSTEM UNIT

Why this section is important to you.

If you want to take advantage of ever-advancing PC technology, get the most for your PC dollar, and allow your PC to grow with your capabilities, you will need to know what's inside your PC.

The processor, RAM, and a variety of other electronic components are housed in the *system unit,* usually a metal and plastic upright box (the tower), or inside the notebook's shell. As components get smaller, the system unit is being redefined with the integration of more components, and sometimes the monitor, into a single physical unit. In this section, we'll look inside the box at the major components of a computer system. Figure 4-9 gives you a peek inside the system unit of a PC.

Someday we won't have to worry about what's inside a PC. That day, however, will not be any time soon. So, let's start with the component that ties it all together, the *motherboard.*

Prentice Hall
train &
assess **it**
generation

INSIDE THE BOX

THE MOTHERBOARD: THE CENTRAL NERVOUS SYSTEM

The *motherboard,* a single circuit board, provides the path through which the processor communicates with memory components and peripheral devices. Think of the processor as the PC's brain and the motherboard as the PC's central nervous system. Continuing the analogy, think of the motherboard's chipset as the heart of the system. The **chipset** is a

FIGURE 4–9   **SYSTEM UNIT AND MOTHERBOARD**

The system unit is this box and its contents—the computer system's electronic circuitry, including the motherboard with the processor and various expansion boards (added capabilities discussed later in this chapter), and various storage devices.

- power supply
- cooling fans
- motherboard
- expansion cards
- hard drive
- DVD drive
- DVD+RW±/CD+RW drive
- empty bay
- power-on switch
- disk activity light
- reset button
- empty bays for floppy drives

group of integrated circuits (chips) that control the flow of information between all system components connected to the board, including the hard disk. The chipset is important because it determines what features are supported on the system (including types of processors and memory). In a personal computer, the following are attached to the motherboard (see Figure 4-10):

- Processor (main processor)
- Support electronic circuitry, such as the chipset
- Memory chips (for example, RAM)
- Expansion boards (optional circuit boards, such as a fax/modem)

FIGURE 4-10   **MOTHERBOARD**

Shown here is a motherboard ready to be installed to a PC (top) and the same motherboard installed in a system unit (bottom) and configured with a 2.8-GHz (gigahertz) Intel Pentium 4 processor (under the cooling fan) and 1 GB of RAM in two DIMMs.

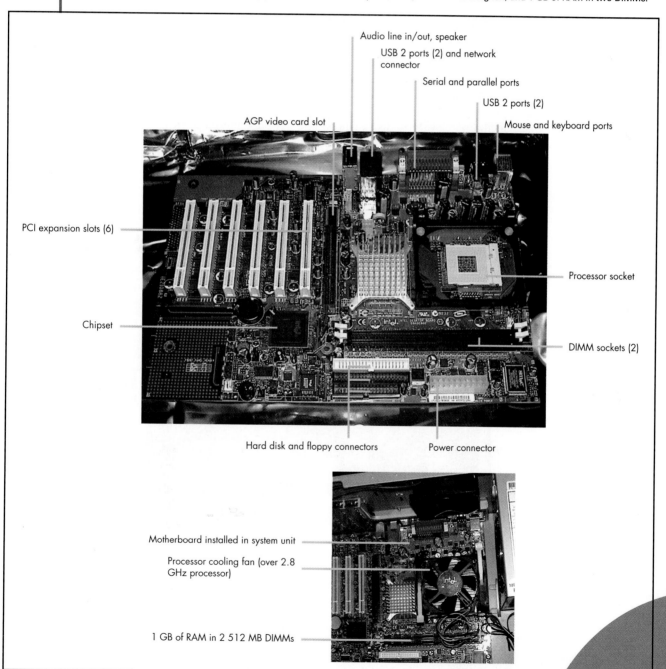

The various chips have standard-sized pin connectors that allow them to be attached to the motherboard and, therefore, to a common **system bus** that permits data flow between the system's various components.

Just as big cities have mass transit systems that move large numbers of people, the computer has a similar system that moves billions of bits a second. All electrical signals travel on a common system bus. The term *bus* was derived from its wheeled cousin because passengers on both buses (people and bits) can get off at any stop. In a computer, the bus stops are the processor, RAM and other types of internal memory, and all of the small computers, called **device controllers,** that control the operation of the peripheral devices.

Relatively little electronic functionality was integrated into motherboards during the first two decades of personal computers. The trend today, however, is to embed more functionality into the motherboard circuitry. For example, prior to 1995, the audio and video interfaces were add-on capabilities. Today, these capabilities are built into many motherboards. Of course, motherboards still have add-in sockets and slots for the more volatile technologies, such as RAM and the processor.

THE PROCESSOR: COMPUTER ON A CHIP

The processor, which is smaller than a postage stamp and found in wristwatches, sewing machines, and CD players, is literally a "computer on a chip." We use the term *chip* to refer to any self-contained integrated circuit. The size of chips varies from fingernail size to postage-stamp size (about 1-inch square). Processors and small processors, called microprocessors, have been integrated into thousands of mechanical and electronic devices—including elevators, dishwashers, and ski-boot bindings. In a few years, virtually everything mechanical or electronic will incorporate processor technology into its design (see Figure 4-11).

FIGURE 4–11

MICROPROCESSORS EVERYWHERE

Microprocessors are present in almost every aspect of our lives. The electrical and mechanical appliances plus a variety of personal computers are networked throughout this Portland, Oregon home.
Microprocessors and structured wiring allows audio, video, computer and Internet signals to be routed anywhere in the home. Several wireless Tablet PCs allow home owners to surf the Web and control the connected products around their home from anywhere in the house.

Photo courtesy of Intel Corporation

Ultimately, the type of processor and the amount of RAM placed on the motherboard define the PC's speed and capacity. The central component of the motherboard, the processor, is generally not made by the manufacturers of PCs. They are made by companies that specialize in the development and manufacture of processors. A number of companies make PC processors, including Intel, Motorola, Advanced Micro Devices (AMD), and IBM.

The motherboard for the original (1981) and most of the *IBM PC-compatible* computers manufactured through 1984 used the Intel 8088 microprocessor chip. Since then, Intel has introduced a succession of increasingly more advanced processors to power the IBM PC-compatible PCs, called *PC compatibles* or, simply, *PCs*. The Intel "286" (Intel 80286), "386," and "486" processors took us into the 1990s followed by the Intel *Pentium®*, *Pentium® Pro*, *Pentium® II*, and *Pentium® III* series. Most new system units have an Intel *Pentium 4®* (see Figure 4-12), *Celeron®*, *Xeon™*, or Itanium™ processor inside. The more

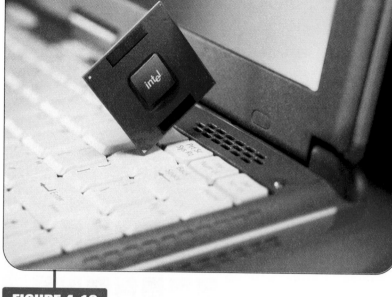

FIGURE 4–12

MOBILE INTEL PENTIUM 4 PROCESSOR

About the size of four keys on a keyboard, this 1.8-GHz Mobile Pentium 4 processor provides the processing capability for this notebook PC.

Photo courtesy of Intel Corporation

expensive Pentium 4, Xeon, or Itanium-based PCs offer the greatest performance, whereas the less expensive Celeron-based PCs offer good value with reduced performance.

Gordon Moore, cofounder of Intel Corporation, made a prediction in 1965 that has proven to be remarkably accurate. Moore's Law states that *the density of transistors on a chip doubles every 18 months.* The density of transistors refers to the number of bits and logic circuits that can be included per unit space on a chip. Often Moore's Law is stated in terms of *processing power,* which is directly related to the density of a chip's transistors. Dr. Andy Grove, the other cofounder of Intel, has said that Moore's Law has become a self-fulfilling prophecy at Intel because no engineer wants to design a chip that would fall below this implied standard. Eventually chip designers will begin to bump up against the laws of physics and the pace of chip evolution may slow, but that may be a few years away. Gordon Moore recently reaffirmed that his law should hold through 2013.

Inside the Processor

The processor runs the show and is the nucleus of any computer system. Regardless of the complexity of a processor, sometimes called the **central processing unit** or CPU, it has only two fundamental sections: the *control unit* and the *arithmetic and logic unit.* These units work together with RAM and other internal memories to make the processor, and the computer system, go. Figure 4-13 illustrates the interaction between computer system components.

The Control Unit

The **control unit** is the command center of the processor. It has three primary functions:

- To read and interpret program instructions
- To direct the operation of internal processor components
- To control the flow of programs and data in and out of RAM

During program execution, the first in a sequence of program instructions is moved from RAM to the control unit, where it is decoded and interpreted by the **decoder.** The control unit then directs other processor components to carry out the operations necessary to execute the instruction.

FIGURE 4–13   INTERACTION BETWEEN COMPUTER SYSTEM COMPONENTS

During processing, instructions and data are passed between the various types of internal memories, the processor's control unit and arithmetic and logic unit, and the peripheral devices over the system bus. A system clock paces the speed of operation within the processor and ensures that everything takes place in timed intervals.

The processor contains high-speed working storage areas called **registers** that can store no more than a few bytes (see Figure 4-13). Because registers reside on the processor chip, they handle instructions and data at very high speeds. One register, called the *instruction register*, contains the instruction being executed. Other general-purpose registers store data needed for immediate processing. Registers also store status information. For example, the *program register* contains the location in RAM of the next instruction to be executed. Registers facilitate the processing and movement of data and instructions between RAM, the control unit, and the arithmetic and logic unit.

The Arithmetic and Logic Unit

The **arithmetic and logic unit** (see Figure 4-13) performs all *computations* and all *logic operations* (comparisons). The results are placed in a register called the **accumulator.**

Computers can add (+), subtract (−), multiply (*), divide (/), and do exponentiation (^). In the payroll system, an instruction in a computer program tells the computer to calculate the gross pay for each employee in a computation operation. The actual program instruction that performs this calculation might look like this:

```
PAY = HOURS_WORKED * PAY_RATE
```

To execute the instruction, the control unit would interpret the instruction and recall values for HOURS_WORKED and PAY_RATE into memory from the personnel master file on the hard disk. The control unit would then instruct the arithmetic and logic unit to calculate PAY (for example, Pay = 40 hours worked * $15/hour = $600).

The arithmetic and logic unit's logic capability enables comparisons between numbers and between words. For example, the processor must use its *logic capability* to decide if an employee is due overtime pay. To do this, hours worked are compared to 40 in a program instruction that might look like this:

```
IF HOURS_WORKED > 40 THEN PAY_OVERTIME
```

Based on the result of the comparison, the program "branches" to one of several alternative sets of program instructions.

RAM: Digital Warehouse

RAM is essentially a high-speed holding area for data and programs. All programs and data must be transferred to RAM from an input device (such as a keyboard) or from disk before programs can be executed and data can be processed. In fact, *nothing really happens in a computer system until the program instructions and data are moved from RAM to the processor*. Programs and data are loaded to RAM from disk storage because the time required to access a program instruction or piece of datum from RAM is significantly less than from disk storage.

RAM enables data to be both read and written to *solid-state* memory. It is **volatile memory** because when the electrical current is turned off or interrupted, the data are lost. In contrast to permanent storage on disk, RAM provides the processor with only *temporary* storage for programs and data. Once a program is no longer in use, the storage space it occupied is assigned to another program awaiting execution.

The processor, according to program instructions, manipulates the data in RAM. A program instruction or a piece of datum is stored in a specific RAM location called an **address.** RAM is analogous to the rows of boxes you see in post offices. Just as each Post Office box has a number, each byte in RAM has an address. Addresses permit program instructions and data to be located, accessed, and processed. The content of each address changes frequently as different programs are executed and new data are processed.

The transfer of data to and from RAM is very fast because solid-state electronic circuitry has no moving parts. Electrically charged points in the RAM chips represent the bits (1s and 0s) that comprise the data and other information stored in RAM. RAM is attached to the motherboard and therefore to the system bus. Over the past two decades, researchers have given us a succession of RAM technologies, each designed to keep pace with ever-faster processors. Most new PCs are being equipped with **DDR SDRAM,** a newer "double data rate" SDRAM (synchronous dynamic RAM).

A state-of-the-art memory chip, smaller than a postage stamp, can store about 128,000,000 bits, or more than 12,000,000 characters of data! Physically, memory chips are installed on *single in-line memory modules,* or *SIMMs,* and on the newer *dual in-line memory modules,* or *DIMMs.* SIMMs are less expensive but have only a 32-bit data path to the processor, whereas DIMMs have a 64-bit data path. The modules are about an inch high and four to six inches long.

Cache and Other High-Speed Memories

Computer designers use very high-speed memory to increase computer system **throughput,** the rate at which work can be performed by a computer system. Data and programs are being continually moved in and out of RAM at electronic speeds—but that's not fast enough. To achieve even faster transfer of instructions and data to the processor, and, therefore, greater throughput, computers are designed with cache memory (see Figure 4-13).

Like RAM, **cache memory** is a high-speed holding area for program instructions and data. However, cache memory uses internal storage technologies that are much faster (and much more expensive) than conventional RAM. With only a fraction of the capacity of RAM, cache memory holds only those instructions and data that are *likely* to be needed next by the processor. Cache memory is effective because, in a typical session, the same data or instructions are accessed over and over. The processor first checks cache memory

---

THE CRYSTAL BALL:
Will Solid-State Memory Replace Rotating Memory?

Many mainframe computers of the 1960s had only 512 KB of RAM. That amount of RAM was housed in refrigerator-size cabinets and could cost up to a million dollars. Today, digital cameras have thumbnail-size memory cards with 1,000 times that amount of RAM (512 MB of RAM) at a millionth the cost per byte. At an internal seminar in 1968, an IBM researcher told IBM employees that all memory (RAM) in all the computers in the world at that time would fit into a brandy snifter by the turn of the century. Well, he was right. Indications are that we are in a transition from the relatively slow rotating disk storage to high-speed solid-state memory.

for needed data and instructions, thereby reducing the number of accesses to the slower RAM. When you purchase a PC, you will see references to level 1 (L1) and level 2 (L2) cache. *Level 1 cache* is built into the processor, whereas *level 2 cache* is on another chip, sitting between the processor and RAM (see Figure 4-13). L2 cache is ultra-fast memory that buffers the transfer of information between the processor and RAM, thereby accelerating internal data movement.

The user cannot alter another special type of internal memory, called *read-only memory* (**ROM**) (see Figure 4-13). The contents of **ROM** (rhymes with *"mom"*) are "hardwired" (designed into the logic of the memory chip) by the manufacturer and can be "read only." When you turn on a microcomputer system, a program in ROM automatically readies the computer system for use and produces the initial display-screen prompt. A variation of ROM is **PROM** (programmable ROM). PROM is ROM into which you, the user, can load read-only programs and data.

Flash memory (see Figure 4-14) is a type of PROM that can be altered easily by the user. Flash memory can be found on all new PCs, I/O devices, and storage devices. It is **nonvolatile memory** that retains its contents after an electrical interruption. The logic capabilities of these devices can be upgraded by simply downloading new software from the Internet or a vendor-supplied disk to flash memory. Upgrades to early PCs and peripheral devices required the user to replace the old circuit board or chip with a new one. The emergence of flash memory has eliminated this time-consuming and costly method of upgrade.

The PC's **BIOS** (Basic Input Output System) is stored in flash memory. The built-in BIOS software contains the instructions needed to boot (start up) the PC and load the operating system to RAM. It also contains specific instructions on the operation of the keyboard, monitor, disk drives, and other devices. A PC's BIOS software should be periodically upgraded to the most recent version so that the PC can recognize new innovations in I/O and disk/disc storage.

The Instruction Set and the Instruction Cycle

We communicate with computers by telling them what to do in their native tongue—the machine language. You may have heard of computer programming languages such as BASIC (in Figure 4-15) and C++. Dozens of these languages are in common usage, but all need to be translated into the only language that a computer understands—its own **machine language**. Typically, each instruction in a human-oriented language, like BASIC, is

FIGURE 4–14

THE FLASH MEMORY CARD

Nonvolatile flash memory cards are being used in many consumer products, such as digital cameras (shown here) and MP3 players.

Photo courtesy of Intel Corporation

Internal Storage
- Volatile memory
  - DDR SDRAM
  - Cache (level 1 and level 2)
  - Registers
- Nonvolatile memory
  - ROM and PROM
  - Flash memory

FIGURE 4–15 THE INSTRUCTION CYCLE

Fetch instruction
The next machine language instruction to be executed is retrieved, or "fetched," from RAM and loaded to the instruction register in the control unit.

Instruction time

Execution time

Place result in memory
The results are placed in the appropriate memory position or the accumulator.

Decode instruction
The instruction is decoded and interpreted.

Execute instruction
Using whatever processor resources are needed (primarily the arithmetic and logic unit), the instruction is executed.

translated automatically by the computer into several machine language instructions. As you might expect, machine language instructions are represented inside the computer as strings of binary digits.

Most processors have a **CISC** (*complex instruction set computer*) design; that is, the computer's machine language has a wide variety of instructions (add, multiply, compare, move data, and so on). However, computer designers have rediscovered the beauty of simplicity and they design some processors around much smaller instruction sets. These **RISC** (*reduced instruction set computer*) computers can have significantly increased throughput for certain applications, especially those that involve graphics (for example, computer-aided design). Many workstations have RISC processors.

Instructions, whether from a CISC or a RISC processor, are executed within the framework of an **instruction cycle**. The timed interval that comprises the instruction cycle is the total of the *instruction time*, or *I-time*, and the *execution time*, or *E-time*. The speed of a processor is sometimes measured by how long it takes to complete an instruction cycle. The actions that take place during the instruction cycle are shown in Figure 4-15.

Most modern processors are capable of **pipelining**; that is, they can begin executing another instruction before the current instruction is completed. In fact, several instructions can be pipelined simultaneously, each at a different part of the instruction cycle. Pipelining improves system throughput significantly.

What Happens Inside: Unraveling the Mystery

BASIC is a popular programming language. The simple BASIC program in Figure 4-16 computes and displays the sum of any two numbers (22 and 44 in the example). The instructions in this example program are intuitive; that is, you don't really need to know BASIC to understand what is happening. Figure 4-16 gives you insight into how a processor works by showing the interaction between RAM, the control unit, and the arithmetic and logic unit during the execution of this program. Figure 4-16 uses only 10 RAM locations and only for data. In practice, both programs and data would be stored in RAM, which usually has a minimum of 128 million storage locations.

The statement-by-statement walkthrough in Figure 4-16 illustrates generally what happens as each BASIC instruction is executed to perform a simple arithmetic task. More complex tasks might involve logic operations (greater than, less than, equal to, and so on). In logic operations, values in RAM and the accumulator compared, then the result of the comparison determines which sequence of instructions is executed next.

PUTTING IT ALL TOGETHER WITH BUSES AND PORTS

The motherboard, with its processor and memory, is ready for work. Alone, though, a motherboard is like a college with no students. The motherboard and its system bus must be linked to input, output, storage, and communication devices to receive data and return the results of processing.

In tech-talk, a bus is the channel that enables information flow between one or more parts of the computer or its devices. A typical PC has the system bus that facilitates the movement of data around the motherboard and supports a variety of bus standards that link internal and external devices to the PCs common system bus. To link a device to a bus, you plug its connector into a socket in much the same way you plug a telephone into a phone jack. The socket, called a *port*, provides a direct link to the PC's system bus on the motherboard via a particular type of bus. A variety of ports shown in Figure 4-17 enable system links with a joystick, a local area network, a digital video camera, the monitor, and other devices.

A Fleet of Buses

A modern PC will have most, if not all, of these popular types of buses.

PERSONAL COMPUTING
Planning for USB

USB 2.0 offers transmission speeds 40 times faster than the original USB standard. The new USB standard, which is available with new PCs, is backwards compatible, so you can continue to use early USB devices. When purchasing peripheral devices, look for the high-speed USB logo to ensure that they meet the emerging de facto standard, USB 2.0. Also, be aware that each USB port is considered an independent path which can transmit information no faster than the lowest performing element on the USB connection (USB devices can linked in a tree of hubs). Avoid mixing and matching USB standards and either select a PC with plenty of USB 2.0 ports (six is usually sufficient) or choose a USB 2.0 hub.

FIGURE 4-16

WHAT HAPPENS INSIDE THE PROCESSOR

Illustrated here is the essence of what happens inside a computer when the five-instruction BASIC program shown here is executed. The RAM in this example has 10 numbered storage locations. The accumulator is part of the arithmetic and logic unit.

10   INPUT "INPUT NO."; X
20   INPUT "INPUT NO."; Y
30   LET SUM = X + Y
40   PRINT "THE SUM IS"; SUM
50   END

Statement 10
INPUT "INPUT NO."; X
Accept a number and store it in RAM location *six*.

The control unit assigns the value to RAM location *six*. Future program references to X recall the content of the storage location whose address is *six*.

Statement 20
INPUT "INPUT NO."; Y
Accept a number and store it in RAM location *seven*.

The control unit assigns the value to RAM location *seven*.

Statement 30
LET SUM = X + Y

STEP 1
Move a number to the accumulator, a part of the arithmetic and logic unit.

STEP 2
Add the other number to the value in the accumulator.

STEP 3
Move the sum to RAM location *eight*.

Statement 40
PRINT "THE SUM IS"; SUM
Display sum.

Statement 50
END
Terminate execution.

power supply on/off button
power cord
keyboard and mouse PS/2 ports
parallel port
serial ports (2)
on-board audio and game port
USB ports (2) and Ethernet port
video card: support for dual monitors and S-video
sound card: 1394/FireWire port, audio out/in, digital out
on-board audio surround card (on motherboard)
Ethernet network interface card: ethernet port
game/MIDI port
SCSI card: SCSI port
USB ports (4)

PS/2 keyboard connector
9-pin RS-232C connector (serial)
25-pin RS-232C connector (parallel)
SCSI connector
Ethernet connector
microphones/headset audio in/out
speaker audio out
video/monitor connector
S-video connector
1394/FireWire connector
USB connector

PCI Local Bus

The **PCI local bus** (Peripheral Component Interconnect) enables circuit boards with extra features to be linked directly to the common system bus. Modern motherboards normally include several PCI local bus **expansion slots** into which **expansion boards** can be inserted, thus connecting them to the system bus. These special-function expansion boards, also called **expansion cards,** are add-on circuit boards contain the electronic circuitry for many supplemental capabilities, such as extra ports, a modem, or video capture capability. Expansion boards are made to fit a particular type of bus.

AGP Bus

The **AGP bus** (Accelerated Graphics Port) is a special-function bus designed to accommodate the throughput demands of high-resolution 3-D graphics. This special bus provides a direct link between the graphics adapter, which feeds video data to the monitor, and RAM.

Universal Serial Bus

The **USB** (Universal Serial Bus) is the primary standard for connecting peripheral devices to a PC. Multiple USB devices can be connected to a single *USB port* with the use of a **USB hub,** a device that connects to a USB port and offers three, four, or five additional USB ports. Hubs can be connected in a "tree" to provide more USB ports than any single user will ever need (see Figure 4-18). Most modern

FIGURE 4–18

PERIPHERALS WORLD RECORD

Television personality Bill Nye, "The Science Guy," helped connect 111 peripheral devices to a single PC via a USB port, setting a new world record. Peripherals ranged from mice, joysticks, and keyboards to digital speakers and video conferencing systems.

Photo courtesy of Intel Corporation

Buses
- PCI local bus
- AGP bus
- USB (Universal Serial Bus) and USB 2.0
- 1394 bus (FireWire)
- SCSI bus

PC peripheral devices provide from 4 to 8 USB ports, enough to meet the need of the typical user.

The USB **hot plug** feature allows peripheral devices to be connected to or removed from the USB port while the PC is running. This is especially helpful to gamers who like to switch types of controllers when they begin a new game. Newer hardware is based on **USB 2.0,** a standard that permits data transfer at 480 M bps, about 40 times faster than the original USB standard.

1394 or FireWire Bus

The **1394 bus** supports data transfer rates of 400M bps for the original standard and 800M bps for the current standard. In the Apple world, this type of bus is called **FireWire.** 1394, or FireWire, is support by some peripheral devices and by many audio/video (A/V) appliances, such as digital camcorders. Up to 63 external devices can be daisy-chained to a *1394 port*. Like USB, 1394 supports hot plugging.

SCSI Bus

The **SCSI bus** (Small Computer System Interface), or "scuzzy" bus, was an early alternative to using expansion slots to expand PC functionality. Up to 15 SCSI peripheral devices can be daisy-chained to a SCSI interface expansion card via the *SCSI port*. That is, the devices are connected along a single cable, both internal and external, with multiple SCSI connectors. The typical off-the-shelf PC compatible will not come with a SCSI bus, the add-on circuitry needed for a SCSI port.

FIGURE 4–19 **SERIAL AND PARALLEL DATA TRANSMISSION**

In serial transmission, outgoing and incoming bits flow one-at-a-time through a single line. In parallel transmission, bytes flow together over eight separate lines.

To processor

010100110101010101010010010010010100000101001100

From processor

001100101000001010010010010010101010101011001010

Serial transmission

To processor

00000000 00000000 00000000
11111111 111111111 11111111
00000000 00000000 00000000
10100000 10100000 10100000
00001101 00001101 00001101
00001111 00001111 00001111
00100000 00100000 00100000
01010010 01010010 01010010

Parallel transmission

Legacy and Other PC Ports

For several decades motherboards have been designed with at least one serial port, one parallel port, a keyboard port, and a mouse port each. Their continued support is primarily to enable backward compatibility with older devices that use these ports. These ports will be phased out in favor of the more versatile and higher-speed USB and 1394 ports.

The **serial port** allows the serial transmission of data, one bit at a time (see Figure 4-19). Imagine a line of fans going single-file through a turnstile at a high school football game. An external modem might be connected to a serial port. The standard for PC serial ports is the 9-pin or 25-pin (male or female) *RS-232C connector*. One of the 9 or 25 lines carries the serial signal to the peripheral device, and another line carries the signal from the device. The other lines carry control signals.

The **parallel port** allows the parallel transmission of data; that is, several bits are transmitted simultaneously. Figure 4-19 illustrates how 8-bit bytes travel in parallel over 8 separate lines. Imagine 8 lines of fans going through 8 adjacent turnstiles at an NFL football game. Extra lines carry control signals. Parallel ports use the same 25-pin RS-232C connector. Printers used parallel ports until USB became widely used. Dedicated keyboard and mouse ports use a round 6-pin connector.

The **IrDA port,** or **infrared port,** transmits data via infrared light waves. Many PCs and devices, such as printers, come with IrDA ports. As long as the devices are within a few feet, data can be transferred without the use of cables.

PC GROWTH: ADDING CAPABILITIES

Today's PCs are designed such that they can grow with your personal computing needs. Initially you purchase what you need and/or can afford, then purchase and install optional capabilities or upgrade existing capabilities as required.

Expansion Boards

The *expansion slots* associated with expansion buses (PCI, SCSI, AGP, etc.) let you add features to your PC by adding *expansion boards*. The number of available expansion slots varies from computer to computer. Keep in mind that an expansion board and/or peripheral device is designed for use with a particular type of expansion bus (PCI, SCSI, and so on). There are literally hundreds of expansion boards from which to choose. These are among the more popular add-on capabilities.

- *Graphics adapter.* This adapter permits interfacing with one or more video monitor and normally is an *AGP board* that is placed in the AGP bus slot.

- *Sound.* The sound card makes two basic functions possible. First, it enables sounds to be captured and stored on disk. Second, it enables sounds, including music and spoken words, to be played through external speakers. The typical sound card will have receptacles for a microphone, a headset, an audio output and most will have a port for a game controller and a MIDI (Music Instrument Digital Interface) port. Basic sound card functionality is built into some motherboards; however, if you wish to have top-quality audio, you might want to upgrade to a feature-rich sound card.

- *Data/voice/fax modem.* A *modem* permits communication with remote computers via a telephone-line link. The **data/voice/fax modem** performs the same function as a regular modem, plus it has added capability. It lets you to receive and make telephone calls, and it enables your PC to emulate a *fax* machine.

- *Network interface card.* The **network interface card** (**NIC**) enables and controls the exchange of data between the PCs in a local area network or a home network. Each PC in a local area or home network must be equipped with an NIC.

- *SCSI interface card.* Devices using the SCSI bus plug into a SCSI port on the mother-board or into one on the SCSI interface card.

- *Video capture card.* This card enables full-motion color video with audio to be captured and played on a monitor or stored on disk. To capture video and convert it to digital format, simply plug the standard cable from the video camera or VCR into the video capture card and play the video. Once on disk storage, video information can be edited; that is, the content can be rearranged and integrated with text, graphics, special effects, and other forms of presentation, as desired. Some all-in-one AGP graphics cards include video capture card functionality, eliminating the need for a separate graphics card.

PC Cards: PCMCIA Technology

The **PCMCIA card,** sometimes called a **PC card,** is a credit card-sized removable expansion module that is plugged into an external PCMCIA expansion slot on a PC, usually a notebook (see Figure 4-20). The PC card functions like an expansion board in that it offers a wide variety of capabilities. PC cards can be expanded RAM, programmable non-volatile flash memory, network interface cards (wireless and wired), data/voice/fax modems, hard-disk cards, and much more. For example, one PC card comes in the form of a mobile **GPS** (global positioning

FIGURE 4-20

PC CARDS FOR NOTEBOOKS

Notebook PCs are designed with PCMCIA expansion slots for PC cards. This PC Card, which is shown with its PCI card counterpart, serves as a wireless network interface card (NIC) or a wireless voice/data/fax modem.

Courtesy of Symbol Technologies, Inc.

system). The mobile GPS card can be used to pinpoint the latitude and longitude of the user within a few feet, anywhere on or near earth. Business travelers use GPS cards in conjunction with computer-based road maps to help them get around in unfamiliar cities.

Notebook computers are equipped with at least one PCMCIA-compliant interface. PDAs (personal digital assistants) and notebook PCs do not have enough space for as many expansion slots as do their desktop cousins. Interchangeable PC cards let laptop users insert capabilities as they are needed. For example, a user can insert a data/voice/fax modem PC card to send e-mail, then do a *hot swap* (PC remains running) with a hard disk card to access corporate maintenance manuals.

BUILD YOUR OWN PC

The biggest name in PCs isn't Apple, Dell, IBM, Gateway, or Hewlett-Packard—it's the "white box." Small companies that custom build no-name, white box PCs and individuals, like you, who make their own PCs account for most of the PCs in use today. Major computer manufacturers, white box companies, and individuals don't actually build PCs from scratch, they assemble the components made by a variety of specialty manufacturers. Scores of high tech companies manufacture the parts and components that make up a personal computer. Processors are made by chip manufacturers. Several companies specialize in motherboards. Some companies build only sound cards and others build only modems. Some parts have little to do with electronic circuitry, such as the case for the system unit that is mostly plastic and metal.

Each year tens of thousands of individuals order PC components, just as manufacturers do, and assemble their own desktop PCs. The primary reasons they do it themselves are:

- *To save money*. If you shop around for good deals, you can save from $200 to $800 by assembling your own high-end PC. It's hard to build a low-end PC for less than you would pay on the open market.

- *To get exactly what you want in a desktop PC*. Manufacturers give you limited options for memory, audio, graphics, cases, and so on. When you build your own, all options are available to you.

Once you have the components, the assembly takes from one to three hours, depending on your level of expertise and experience (see Figure 4-21).

The downside of building your own computer is that there is no system warranty and no help desk. Although the individual components have warranties, there is no warranty on the overall system. Also, the technical support provided by most major PC manufacturers, is only available to their customers. Generally, people who opt to build their own PCs have a sound foundation of hardware knowledge and are comfortable without a system warranty and manufacturer-supplied technical assistance.

1 The arithmetic and logic unit controls the flow of programs and data in and out of main memory. (T/F)

2 The RS-232C connector provides the interface to a USB port. (T/F)

3 The rate at which work can be performed by a computer system is called: (a) system spray, (b) throughput, (c) push through, or (d) volume load.

4 The timed interval that comprises the instruction cycle is the total of the instruction time and: (a) execution time, (b) I-time, (c) X-time, or (d) delivery time.

5 PC components are linked via a common system: (a) train, (b) bus, (c) car, or (d) plane.

4-3 DESCRIBING THE PROCESSOR AND ITS PERFORMANCE

We distinguish one computer from the other in much the same way we would distinguish one person from the other. When describing someone, we generally note gender, height, weight, and age. When describing computers or processors, we talk about *word size, core* speed, *bus speed*, and *memory capacity* because these elements make the biggest contribution to system performance. For example, a computer might be described as a 64-bit, 3.4-GHz, 2-GB PC with an 800 MHz bus. This section will help you understand what all of this means.

WORD SIZE: BUS WIDTH

Just as the brain sends and receives signals through the central nervous system, the processor sends and receives electrical signals through its system bus a word at a time. A **word**, or *bus width*, describes the number of bits that are handled as a unit within a particular computer system's bus or during internal processing (see Figure 4-13). Many popular computers have 64-bit internal processing but only a 32-bit path through the system bus. This disparity in bus width doesn't affect performance because most of the data movement is within the processor. The word size for internal processing for most modern PCs is 64 bits (eight 8-bit bytes). Workstations, server computers, and supercomputers have 64-bit word sizes and up.

CORE SPEED: GHZ, MIPS, AND FLOPS

A tractor can go 22 miles per hour (mph), a minivan can go 90 mph, and a slingshot drag racer can go 300 mph. These speeds, however, provide little insight into the relative capabilities of these vehicles. What good is a 300-mph tractor or a 22-mph minivan? Similarly, you have to place the speed of computers within the context of their design and application. Generally, PCs are measured in *GHz*, workstations and some server computers are measured in *MIPS*, and supercomputers are measured in *FLOPS*.

- *Gigahertz: GHz.* The PC's heart is its *crystal oscillator* and its heartbeat is the *clock cycle.* The crystal oscillator paces the execution of instructions within the processor. A PC's processor speed, or *core speed*, is rated by its frequency of oscillation, or the number of clock cycles per second. The Intel processor timeline in Figure 4-22 gives you some perspective on the evolution of core speed for Intel processors. Legacy PCs are rated in **megahertz**, or **MHz** (millions of clock cycles per second), but modern PCs are measured in **gigahertz**, or **GHz** (billions of clock cycles per second), with high-end PCs running in excess of 3 GHz. The elapsed time for one clock cycle is 1 divided by the frequency. For example, the time it takes to complete one cycle on a 4-GHz processor is 1/4,000,000,000, or 0.00000000025 seconds, or .25 nanoseconds (.25 billionths of a second). Pipelining (processing the next instruction before the current instruction is completed) enables PCs to process several instructions during a single clock cycle. The shorter the clock cycle, the faster the processor.

- *MIPS.* Processing speed may also be measured in **MIPS,** or millions of instructions per second. Although frequently associated with workstations and some server computers, MIPS is also applied to PCs. Computers can operate up to several thousand MIPS. A modern high-end PC is capable of running at around 2000 MIPS. The MIPS measurement is not as accurate as MHz and FLOPS.

- *FLOPS.* Supercomputer speed is measured in **FLOPS**—floating point operations per second (see Figure 4-22). Supercomputer applications, which are often scientific, frequently involve floating point operations. Floating point operations accommodate very small or very large numbers. State-of-the-art supercomputers operate at speeds in excess of a trillion FLOPS.

BUS SPEED: THE PC BOTTLENECK

Modern processors are thousands of times faster than they were 25 years ago. The technology of the system bus, which handles the movement of data between the various

MEMORY BITS

Processor Description
- Word size: Bits handled as a unit
  - 32 bits
  - 64 bits
- Core Speed
  - PCs: MHz and GHz (clock cycles)
  - PCs, workstations, and server computers: MIPS
  - Supercomputers: FLOPS
- Bus Speed
  - MHz and GHz (clock cycles)
- Memory Capacity
  - Kilobyte (KB), kilobit (Kb)
  - Megabyte (MB), megabit (Mb)
  - Gigabyte (GB)
  - Terabyte (TB)

PERSONAL COMPUTING
RAM, Cache, and System Performance

When you purchase a computer, one of your primary considerations is to optimize system performance. The most cost-effective way to do this is to get plenty of RAM, at least 512 MB. New, off-the-shelf PCs often are configured with minimal RAM, perhaps 256 MB. Adding $100 worth of RAM to a basic system has the potential to increase overall system performance up to 50%. Any new PCs should have DIMM sockets for at least 1 GB of RAM. The amount of cache memory can have a dramatic impact on system performance, as well. Make sure that the system you are considering offers state-of-the-art cache.

FIGURE 4–21

BUILDING YOUR OWN PC

Many people of all ages and backgrounds build their own desktop PCs. A junior high school student ordered these components and built his own high-end custom PC. The only tool needed to assemble the components and load the operating system is a screwdriver.

THE TOWER CASE

The tower case has a 400-watt power supply and six cooling fans, two in front, two in the back, and two for the power supply.

THE MOTHERBOARD

This motherboard has six PCI slots (white) for expansion cards, an AGP slot (purple) for the video card, and three DIMM slots (blue), for 512 or 1024 MB DIMMs. The motherboard has a chipset with a cooling fan (gold) and a processor socket (white square) for the 478-pin Intel Pentium 4 processor.

THE SYSTEM UNIT COMPONENTS

Shown here are all of the components that comprise the electronics and storage in the system unit plus a flat-panel monitor, the tower case, and the operating system. The system unit component include a gigabyte motherboard, a 3.06-GHz Intel Pentium 4 processor, a processor heat sink/cooling fan, a 200 GB hard disk, a DVD drive, a combination DVD±RW/CD+RW drive, a PCI 7-channel sound card, an AGP video card, and 1 GB of DDR SDRAM.

FORMATTING THE HARD DISK AND INSTALLING THE OPERATING SYSTEM

After attaching the monitor, keyboard, and mouse, the system is ready for the operating system. The final step in building a PC is to insert the operating system disc and turn on the newly-assembled PC. The software needed to format the disk (prepare the disk to store data and programs) is loaded to RAM. After formatting is complete, the operating system begins the interactive installation process.

THE BUILDER AND HIS PC

After loading Microsoft Office and a full complement of software, this teenager/PC builder chose to configure his system with a keyboard and a wireless mouse, a Webcam, several game controllers, seven speakers (one for each channel), a microphone/ headset, and a scanner. The system is connected to an external router that links other PCs in a home network.

components on the motherboard, has not kept pace with processor speed. This lag in speed has made the system bus the primary bottleneck to processing efficiency within the PC. Like processors, bus speed is measured in cycles per second, but most processors operate at GHz speeds and buses operate at MHz speeds, usually around 400 to 800 MHz for modern PC processors (see Figure 4-22).

MEMORY CAPACITY: MB, GB, AND TB

The capacities of RAM, cache, and other memories are stated in terms of the number of bytes they can store. Memory capacity for most computers is stated in terms of **megabytes** (**MB**) and **gigabytes** (**GB**). One megabyte equals 1,048,576 (2^{20}) bytes, about a million

INSTALLING THE MOTHERBOARD

The motherboard is fastened to the case with six screws.

INSTALLING MEMORY

For this assembly, the processor and its cooling fan (top right) and two 512 MB DIMMs (being installed) were installed before placing the motherboard in the case.

CONNECTING THE DISKS/DISCS AND POWER

The hard disk (middle bottom) is inserted into one of the hard disk shelves. The DVD drive and the DVD±RW/CD+RW drive (the DVD/CD burner) are inserted into open bays used for interchangeable disk/disc drives. After all storage units are installed, the ribbon cables are connected between the disks/discs and their controllers on the motherboard. The power-on switch and disk activity light are connected to the motherboard (lower left). The last step in the assembly processes is to attach the power cords from the power supply to all electrical components, including the nine cooling fans.

INSTALLING THE EXPANSION CARDS

An AGP video card with the cooling fan for its onboard processor and 128 MBs of DDR SDRAM (shown separately) and a PCI sound card are installed in the appropriate expansion slots. Several external ports, including the front and rear USB 2.0 ports (top left and bottom left), are installed and connected to the system bus.

bytes. One gigabyte (2^{30} bytes) is about one billion bytes. Memory capacities of modern PCs range from 128 MB to 3 GB. High-speed cache memory capacities usually are measured in **kilobytes** (**KB**) and megabytes, the most common cache capacities being 512 KB and 1 MB. One kilobyte is 1024 (2^{10}) bytes of storage.

Some high-end server computers and supercomputers have more than 1000 GB of RAM. It's only a matter of time before we state RAM in terms of **terabytes** (**TB**), about one trillion bytes. GB and TB are frequently used in reference to high-capacity disk storage. Occasionally you will see memory capacities of individual chips stated in terms of **kilobits** (**Kb**) and **megabits** (**Mb**). Figure 4-24 should give you a feel for KBs, MBs, GBs, and TBs.

techtv™
**SUPERCOMPUTERS—
SIZE MATTERS**

FIGURE 4-22

THE INTEL® FAMILY OF PROCESSORS

The Intel family of processors has been installed in 9 of every 10 PCs in use today.

Intel Processor Timeline

PROCESSOR	CLOCK SPEED (range)	RELEASE DATES (first, most recent)	NUMBER OF TRANSITORS (millions)	BUS SPEED (range)
Xeon	1.4 GHz / 3.06 GHz	Sep. 2001 / March 2003	42–108	400–533 MHz
Pentium 4	1.4 GHz / 3.06 GHz	Nov. 2000 / April 2003	42–55	400–800 MHz
Mobile Pentium 4	1.4 GHz / 2.55 GHz	March 2002 / April 2003	55	400 MHz
Pentium III	450 MHz / 1 GHz	Feb. 1999 / March 2000	9.5–28	100–133 MHz
Mobile Pentium III	400 MHz / 1.33 GHz	Oct. 1999 / Sep. 2002	28–44	100–133 MHz
Celeron	266 MHz / 2.4 GHz	April 1998 / March 2003	7.5–19	66–400 MHz
Mobile Celeron	266 MHz / 2.2 GHz	Jan. 1999 / April 2003	7.5–19	100–400 MHz
Pentium II	233 MHz / 450 MHz	May 1997 / August 1998	7.5	100–400 MHz
Mobile Pentium II	233 MHz / 400 MHz	April 1998 / June 1999	7.5	100–400 MHz
Pentium Pro	150 MHz / 200 MHz	Nov. 1995 / August 1997	5.5	N/A
Pentium	60 MHz / 233 MHz	March 1993 / June 1997	3.1–4.5	N/A
Mobile Pentium	200 MHz / 300 MHz	Sep. 1997 / Jan. 1999	4.5	N/A
Intel 486	20 MHz / 100 MHz	April 1989 / Nov. 1992	.275–1.6	N/A
Intel 386	16 MHz / 33 MHz	Oct. 1985 / Sep. 1991	.275–1.6	N/A
Intel 286	6 MHz / 12 MHz	Feb. 1982	.134	N/A
Intel 8088	5 MHz / 8 MHz	June 1979	.029	N/A
Intel 8080	2 MHz	April 1974	.0045	N/A
Intel 4004	108 KHz	Nov. 1971	.0023	N/A

FIGURE 4-23

WORLD SPEED RECORD FOR COMPUTERS

This engineer at Sandia National Labs is inspecting a connection in one of the 86 cabinets that house the 9,200 processors. The collective power of thousands of processors enables this supercomputer to perform at more than one trillion operations-per-second (1 trillion FLOPS or TERAFLOPS). This record-setting supercomputer is used to ensure the safety, reliability, and effectiveness of the U.S. nuclear stockpile through computer simulation instead of nuclear testing.

Photo courtesy of Intel Corporation

FIGURE 4-24 **HOW MUCH IS A KB, AN MB, A GB, AND A TB?**

Compare the number of characters in the Gettysburg Address to 1 KB (Kilobyte)

Compare the number of characters in this book to 1 MB (Megabyte)

Compare the number of people in China to 1 GB (Gigabyte)

Compare the number of gallons of water consumed each day in North America to 1 TB (Terabyte)

DIFFERENCES IN PROCESSOR PERSONALITY

Word size, core and bus speeds, and *memory capacity* are the primary descriptors of processors and processor performance. However, computers, like people, have their own "personalities." That is, two similarly described computers might possess attributes that give one more capability than the other. For example, one 64-bit, 3.4-GHz, 2-GB PC with an 800 MHz bus might have 2 MB of cache memory and another with the same specs might have only 512 KB of cache. Remember this: When you buy a PC, the basic descriptors tell most but not the entire story. See the *IT Illustrated: Personal Computing Buyer's Guide* following Chapter 7 for information for how to get the most for your PC dollar.

1 *MIPS* is an acronym for "millions of instructions per second." (T/F)

2 A common bus width for modern PCs is 16 bits. (T/F)

3 Which has the most bytes: (a) a kilobyte, (b) a gigabyte, (c) a megabyte, or (d) a big byte?

4 The time it takes to complete one cycle on a 2-GHz processor is: (a) 1/2,000,000,000 second, (b) .000000005 second, (c) .5 microseconds, or (d) .5 thousandths of a second?

5 Word size is the same as: (a) bus speed, (b) bus width, (c) bus stop, or (d) bus capacity.

SELF-CHECK

SECTION

4-4 PROCESSOR DESIGN

Researchers in IT are continually working to create new technologies and processes that will make processors faster and better utilize resources, thereby improving system throughput. The design process extends to creating processors for use in different environments (see Figure 4-25).

PARALLEL PROCESSING: COMPUTERS WORKING TOGETHER

In a single processor environment, the processor addresses the programming problem sequentially, from beginning to end. Today, designers are building computers that break a programming problem into pieces. Work on each of these pieces is then executed simultaneously in separate processors, all of which are part of the same computer system. The concept of using multiple processors in the same computer system is known as **parallel processing.** In parallel processing, one main processor examines the programming problem and determines what portions, if any, of the problem can be solved in pieces (see Figure 4-26). Those pieces that can be addressed separately are routed to other processors and solved. The individual pieces are then reassembled in the main processor for further computation, output, or storage. The net result of parallel processing is better throughput.

Computer designers are creating some server computers and supercomputers with thousands of integrated processors. Parallel processing on such a large scale is referred to as **massively parallel processing (MPP).** These superfast supercomputers have sufficient computing capacity to attack applications that are beyond the capabilities of traditionally designed computers. For example, researchers can use these supercomputers to simulate trends in global warming over several decades.

GRID COMPUTING: SHARING COMPUTING POWER

During the past few years, the potential of **grid computing** has been compared to that of the Internet—virtually limitless. Grid computing takes advantage of the unused processing capabilities of hundreds, even thousands of personal computers, to address a single programming problem. The typical PC user has a computer that is more powerful than the behemoth mainframe computers of the 1960s and 1970s, but these users use less than 1% of their PC's processing capabilities. Now that the world is networked via the Internet and an increasing number of users are linked to the Net via broadband, it is possible to share vast amounts of unused processing resources via grid computing.

In terms of evolution, grid computing is about where the Internet was in the 1970s. It has devoted fans that expect it to define a new era in information tech-

FIGURE 4–25

PC PROCESSOR DESIGN CONSIDERATIONS

Design considerations for processors used in desktop PCs, such as the Pentium 4 (the microscopic view), and notebook PCs are different. For example, the mobile Intel Celeron processor has a feature that drops the processor power consumption when the laptop is idle or inactive to preserve battery life. Laptop processors must also be designed to dissipate heat within smaller enclosures.

Photos courtesy of Intel Corporation

FIGURE 4–26

PARALLEL PROCESSING

In parallel processing, auxiliary processors solve pieces of a problem to enhance system throughput.

Problem

Result

Problem is solved in pieces.

nology; but grid computing may be several years away from widespread acceptance and use. Here is how it works. People who are willing to share unused computing capacity via a network to solve a large processor-oriented problem, perhaps the analysis of extraterrestrial data, download and install a program. The program enables an interface with the server computer that coordinates the grid computing effort. PCs in the grid system work on a piece of the problem, but only when the PC is not in use. In this way, grid systems can combine unused resources with processing potential greater than some supercomputers. Supercomputers can cost millions of dollars, but grid systems composed entirely of volunteer participants who willingly share their computing resources are routinely performing supercomputer-level processing for virtually nothing.

IBM, Oracle, and other major technology companies are beginning to employ grid computing. The word is out; grid computing works. It offers a way for companies to expand significantly their computing capacity while saving considerable amounts of money. If grid computing continues to grow at the current pace of acceptance and use, it has the potential to change the face of computing.

THE CRYSTAL BALL
Grid Computing Coming of Age

Grid computing is on the brink of widespread acceptance and use. In grid computing, networking enables the capabilities of hundreds, even thousands of personal computers, to be applied to a single programming problem. During its downtime (no user processing), each computer in the grid addresses a piece of a massive problem, such as the simulation of the earth's climate over the next decade. All of the pieces are coming together to launch grid computing into the mainstream of information technology: millions of powerful PCs linked via broadband with 99% of their capacity unused; economic pressures to use existing resources more effectively; a large backlog of huge, socially significant processor-bound problems; and a groundswell of people willing to support these projects.

---

1 In a single processor environment, the processor addresses the programming problem sequentially. (T/F)

2 Parallel processing on a large scale is referred to as massively trapezoidal processing. (T/F)

SELF-CHECK

SECTION

Chapter Review

4-1 DIGITAL: THE LANGUAGE OF COMPUTERS

To make the most effective use of computers and automation, the electronics world is moving from analog to digital electronic signals. Computers are digital and, therefore, work better with digital data.

The two digital states of the computer—on and off—are represented by a bit, short for binary digit. These electronic states are compatible with the binary numbering system. Letters and decimal numbers are translated into bits for storage and processing on computer systems.

Alphanumeric (alpha and numeric) characters are represented in computer storage by unique bit configurations. Characters are translated into these bit configurations, also called bytes, according to a particular coding scheme, called a character encoding system.

The ASCII encoding system was the most popular encoding system for PCs and data communication through the 1990s. Earlier versions of Microsoft Windows use the 8-bit ANSI encoding system. The first 128 of the 256 ANSI codes are the same as the ASCII codes. Because of the need to represent more characters, Unicode, a 16-bit encoding system, has emerged as the worldwide character-encoding standard.

The binary numbering system is based on the same principles as the decimal numbering system, with the only difference being that binary uses only two digits, 0 and 1, and the decimal numbering system uses 10 digits. The hexadecimal, or base 16, numbering system is used as shorthand to display the binary contents of RAM and disk storage.

4-2 THE PC SYSTEM UNIT

The processor, RAM, and other electronic components are housed in the system unit. The processor is literally a computer on a chip. This processor, the electronic circuitry for handling input/output signals from the peripheral devices, and the memory chips are mounted on a single circuit board called a motherboard. The motherboard's chipset controls the flow of information between system components.

The system bus is the common pathway through which the processor sends/receives data and commands to/from RAM and disk storage and all I/O peripheral devices. The bus provides data transportation to all processor components, memory, and device controllers.

The processor is the nucleus of any computer system. A processor, which also is called the central processing unit or CPU, has two fundamental sections, the control unit and the arithmetic and logic unit, which work together with RAM to execute programs.

RAM, or random-access memory, provides the processor with temporary storage for programs and data. In RAM, each datum is stored at a specific address. RAM is volatile memory (contrast with nonvolatile memory); that is, the data are lost when the electrical current is turned off or interrupted. All input/output, including programs, must enter and exit RAM. Other variations of internal storage are ROM, programmable read-only memory (PROM), and flash memory, a nonvolatile memory. The BIOS software is stored in flash memory.

Some computers employ cache memory (level 1 and level 2) to increase throughput (the rate at which work can be performed by a computer system). Like RAM, cache is a high-speed holding area for program instructions and data. However, cache memory holds only those instructions and data likely to be needed next by the processor.

Every machine language has a predefined format for each type of instruction. Most processors have a CISC (complex instruction set computer) design; that is, the computer's machine language has a wide variety of instructions, but some have a RISC (reduced instruction set computer) design.

During one instruction cycle, an instruction is "fetched" from RAM, decoded in the control unit, and executed, and the results are placed in memory. The instruction cycle time is the total of the instruction time (I-time) and the execution time (E-time). Most modern processors are capable of pipelining to speed up processing.

A modern PC will have most, if not all, of these popular types of buses: PCI local bus, AGP bus, Universal Serial Bus (USB and USB 2.0), and 1394 bus (FireWire). The motherboard includes several empty expansion slots so you can plug in optional capabilities in the form of expansion boards or expansion cards. USB peripheral devices can be hot plugged to the PC.

In a PC, external peripheral devices come with a cable and a multipin connector. A port provides a direct link to the PC's system bus. External peripheral devices can be linked to the processor via cables through a USB port, 1394 port, SCSI port, keyboard port, mouse port, serial port, parallel port, or IrDA (infrared) port.

Popular expansion boards include graphics adapters such as the AGP board, sound card, data/voice/fax modem (enables emulation of a fax machine), network interface card (NIC), and video capture card.

The PCMCIA card, sometimes called a PC card, provides a variety of interchangeable add-on capabilities for notebook PCs in the form of credit-card-sized modules.

4-3 DESCRIBING THE PROCESSOR AND ITS PERFORMANCE

A processor is described in terms of its word size (bus width), core speed, bus speed, and memory capacity.

A word, or *bus width*, is the number of bits handled as a unit within a particular computer's system bus or during internal processing.

Personal computer speed, called the core speed, is measured in megahertz (MHz) and gigahertz (GHz). High-end PC, workstation, and server computer speed is measured in MIPS. Supercomputer speed is measured in FLOPS.

Bus speed, which is less than core speed, is measured in cycles per second. Bus speed can be a bottleneck in processing performance.

Memory capacity is measured in kilobytes (KB), megabytes (MB), gigabytes (GB), and terabytes (TB). Chip capacity is stated sometimes in kilobits (Kb) and megabits (Mb).

4-4 PROCESSOR DESIGN

In parallel processing, one main processor examines the programming problem and determines what portions, if any, of the problem can be solved in pieces. Those pieces that can be addressed separately are routed to other processors, solved, then recombined in the main processor to produce the result. Parallel processing on a large scale is referred to as massively parallel processing (MPP).

The basic premise of grid computing is to use available computing resources more effectively. Grid computing addresses a single programming problem by tapping the unused processing capabilities of many PCs via a network.

KEY TERMS

1394 bus (FireWire) (p. 170)
accumulator (p. 164)
address (p. 165)
AGP bus (p. 169)
analog (p. 154)
ANSI (p. 156)
arithmetic and logic unit (p. 164)
binary (p. 155)
BIOS (p. 166)
byte (p. 156)
cache memory (p. 165)
central processing unit (CPU)
   (p. 163)
chipset (p. 160)
CISC (p. 167)
control unit (p. 163)
data/voice/fax modem (p. 171)
DDR SDRAM (p. 165)
decoder (p. 163)
device controllers (p. 162)
digital (p. 154)
digitize (p. 155)
expansion board (p. 169)

expansion card (p. 169)
expansion slot (p. 169)
flash memory (p. 166)
FLOPS (p. 173)
gigabytes (GB) (p. 174)
gigahertz (GHz) (p. 173)
GPS (global positioning system)
   (p. 171)
grid computing (p. 178)
hexadecimal (p. 159)
hot plug (p. 170)
instruction cycle (p. 167)
IrDA (infrared) port (p. 170)
kilobits (Kb) (p. 175)
kilobytes (KB) (p. 175)
machine language (p. 166)
massively parallel processing (MPP)
   (p. 178)
megabits (Mb) (p. 175)
megabytes (MB) (p. 174)
megahertz (MHz) (p. 173)
MIPS (p. 173)
network interface card (NIC) (p. 171)

nonvolatile memory (p. 166)
parallel port (p. 170)
parallel processing (p. 178)
PC (PCMCIA) card (p. 171)
PCI local bus (p. 169)
pipelining (p. 167)
PROM (p. 166)
register (p. 164)
RISC (p. 167)
ROM (p. 166)
SCSI bus (p. 170)
serial port (p. 170)
system bus (p. 162)
terabytes (TB) (p. 175)
throughput (p. 165)
Unicode (p. 158)
USB (Universal Serial Bus) (p. 169)
USB 2.0 (p. 170)
USB hub (p. 169)
volatile memory (p. 165)
word (bus width) (p. 173)

MATCHING

_____ 1. 1394 bus

_____ 2. pipelining

_____ 3. chipset

_____ 4. Moore's Law

_____ 5. grid computing

_____ 6. ASCII

_____ 7. machine language

_____ 8. throughput

_____ 9. hexadecimal

_____ 10. AGP

a doubling of transistors each 1.5 years

b graphics adapter

c encoding

d rate of work by a CPU

e language of computers

f base 16

g motherboard flow control

h networking of unused computing capacity

i FireWire

j overlapping instruction execution

TRUE/FALSE

1. Bit is the singular of byte. (T/F)

2. The hexadecimal numbering system has 26 unique numbers. (T/F)

3. Stereo music cannot be digitized. (T/F)

4. The control unit is that part of the processor that reads and interprets program instructions. (T/F)

5. PC cards can be hot swapped while the PC is running. (T/F)

6. The FireWire 800M bps bus transfers data at a slower rate than the USB 2.0 bus. (T/F)

7. The word size of all PCs is 32 bits. (T/F)

8. Bus speed is always the same as core speed. (T/F)

9. A gigabyte of RAM has more storage capacity than a megabit of RAM. (T/F)

10. In parallel processing, two main processors examine the programming problem and determine what portions, if any, of the problem can be solved in pieces. (T/F)

11. In grid computing, all PCs on the grid must commit their resources until processing is complete. (T/F)

12. Grid computing is well ahead of the Internet in technological evolution. (T/F)

MULTIPLE CHOICE

1. The base of the binary number system is: (a) 2, (b) 8, (c) 16, or (d) 32.

2. How many ANSI bytes can be stored in a 32-bit word: (a) 2, (b) 4, (c) 6, or (d) 8?

3. What is the ASCII code for Q if the code for P is 01010000: (a) 01010011, (b) 01010010, (c) 01010001, or (d) 01011111?

4. A hexadecimal A3 is what in binary: (a) 10100011, (b) 01010011, (c) 00111010, or (d) 11110011?

5. Which of the following memory groups are in order based on speed (slowest to fastest): (a) registers, cache, RAM, (b) cache, RAM, registers, (c) cache, registers, RAM, or (d) RAM, cache, registers?

6. BIOS software is stored permanently: (a) in flash memory, (b) in DDR SDRAM, (c) on hard disk, or (d) on DVD-ROM.

7. Which one of the following would not be attached to a motherboard: (a) RAM, (b) processor, (c) FLOP, or (d) video card?

8. Which port enables the parallel transmission of data within a computer system: (a) serial, (b) parallel, (c) Centronics, or (d) speaker?

9. Which bus enables the daisy-chaining of peripheral devices: (a) SCSI, (b) infrared, (c) PCI local bus, or (d) Greyhound?

10. Which of these would not be a major factor in processor performance: (a) core speed, (b) bus width, (c) size of RAM, or (d) bus strength?

11. A high-capacity hard disk would be measured in: (a) GB or TB, (b) KB or TB, (c) kilobits or megabits, or (d) MB or GB.

12. Supercomputer speed is measured in: (a) LOPS, (b) MOPS, (c) FLOPS, or (d) POPS.

13. The concept of using multiple processors in the same computer system is known as: (a) massive processing, (b) acute processing, (c) parallel processing, or (d) perpendicular processing.

14. Grid computing takes advantage of what capabilities in remote PCs: (a) printing, (b) Net search, (c) unused processing, or (d) lattice uploading?

1. IS WHAT WE SEE AND HEAR REAL OR NOT?

There was a time when photographs could be used as evidence in a court of law. Now that we live in digitized world of powerful computers and photo illustration software, that is not the case. Most image professionals now deal with digital images that can be electronically modified to achieve the desired result. Magazines routinely alter fashion covers to hide the "flaws" of supermodels. For example, a graphics artist might take a little off the thigh or add a little shadow to highlight the cheekbone. Advertisers "fix" deficiencies in product presentations and, generally, enhance the image whenever possible. It is impossible to distinguish the reality from "special effects" in TV commercials and at the movies. All commercial music is digitally recorded and, if needed, digitally enhanced to remove mistakes or to get the right sound.

Discussion: Has the combination of "going digital" and information technology taken away our ability to perceive what is artificial and what is natural? Explain.

Discussion: Is it ethical to present a digitally enhanced still image, video, or song without warning those who might otherwise assume that what they see and hear is real?

2. THE DIGITAL DIVIDE: IS IT RACIAL OR ECONOMIC?

Much has been made in the news about an ever-growing digital divide that heretofore has been described primarily along racial lines. The divide refers to the disparity between groups of people who have computers and access to the Internet and those who do not. Politicians have presented the digital divide as a disparity between races, generally white and African American. A comprehensive study, however, reveals that the digital divide is not so much an issue of race, but of economics. A very high percentage of those with the money to buy PCs and be online make the cyber investment. Those without funds do not have that option.

Discussion: What can be done about the digital divide?

Discussion: Universal access to the Internet is a stated goal of many U.S. politicians. Discuss approaches to achieving this universal access given that only 70% of the population can afford PCs or Internet appliances in their homes.

3.   RECYCLING OLD COMPUTERS

They say a dog year is equal to 7 human years. A continuous string of processor innovations has made one computer year about the same as 20 human years, so computers get "old" very quickly. Old cars of ages 20 or older still get

people from point A to point B and some become desirable antiques. But what do you do with an old computer whose processor and most components are worth virtually nothing? About 80% of those computers, about 300 million worldwide, are sent to landfills and only 20% are recycled. Electronic components in computers are generally not biodegradable and they can contain many toxic substances.

Discussion: Should the government regulate the disposal of obsolete computers? Justify your response.

Discussion: What did you do with your obsolete computer? What will you do with your current PC once it becomes obsolete?

Discussion: Should corporations police themselves and adopt a PC product stewardship policy? If not, why? If so, write a proposed policy.

DISCUSSION AND PROBLEM SOLVING

1. Generally, computers are digital and human beings are analog, so what we say, hear, and see must be converted, or digitized, for processing on a computer. Speculate on how a family photograph might be digitized for storage and processing on a computer system.

2. Create a 5-bit encoding system to be used for storing uppercase alpha characters, punctuation symbols, and the apostrophe. Discuss the advantages and disadvantages of your encoding system in relation to the ASCII encoding system.

3. How many characters can be represented with a 12-bit encoding system?

4. Write your first name as an ASCII bit configuration.

5. List at least 10 products that are smaller than a toaster oven and use microprocessors. Select one and describe the function of its microprocessor.

6. Describe the advantages of a USB port over a parallel port. Also, describe the advantages of a parallel port over a serial port.

7. Distinguish between RAM and flash memory. Be specific.

8. Which two functions does the arithmetic and logic unit perform? Give a real-life example for each function.

9. Explain the relationship between a processor, a motherboard, and a PC.

10. Generally describe the interaction between the processor's control unit, registers, and RAM.

11. Give one example of where each of the memory technologies in question 10 might be used in a personal computer system.

12. Illustrate the interaction between the user RAM and the accumulator in the arithmetic and logic unit for

the following basic program. Use the model shown in Figure 4-16.

```
INPUT "Enter ages for 3 children"; A,
B, C

LET AVGAGE=(A+B+C)/3

PRINT "The average age is"; AVGAGE

END
```

13. List three expansion boards you would like to have on your own PC. How would you use these added capabilities?

14. Describe a hot swap as it relates to a PCMCIA-compliant interface.

15. Why do you suppose PC motherboards are designed to accommodate several types of buses?

16. Would you consider building your own computer? Why or why not?

17. Assume a move data instruction requires five clock cycles. Compute the time it takes, in nanoseconds, to execute a move data instruction on a 3-GHz processor.

18. Convert 5 MB to KB, Mb, and Kb. Assume a byte contains eight bits.

19. Describe the computer you use at home, at work, or in the PC laboratory.

20. Speculate on an application that might be appropriate for parallel processing.

21. Under what circumstances would you be willing to participate in a grid system and share your computing resources?

1. *Looking Inside a PC.* Explore the inside of a PC (yours or a lab computer made available to students for this exercise). Remove the cover on a tower PC to expose the motherboard. Usually, this is no more difficult than loosening a couple of thumbscrews and removing a side panel. Do not touch any electronic components since they are sensitive to static electricity. Identify as many of the motherboard components shown in Figure 4-10 as you can. Look inside and on the back of the computer to identify the number of PCI expansion slots and DIMM sockets on the motherboard. Also, count the number of USB ports.

2. *Speed and Memory Assessment.* Use available system monitoring software and/or system documentation to determine the following information for a particular PC (yours or a lab PC): processor speed, amount and type of RAM, and amount of L1 and L2 cache.

1. The Online Study Guide (multiple choice, true/false, matching, and essay questions)
2. Internet Learning Activities
   - Encoding
   - Processors, Chips, and RAM
3. Serendipitous Internet Activities
   - Popular Culture
   - Online Shopping

The Computer on a Chip

The invention of the light bulb in 1879 symbolized the beginning of electronics. Electronics then evolved into the use of vacuum tubes, then transistors, and now integrated circuits. Today's microminiaturization of electronic circuitry is continuing to have a profound effect on the way we live and work. The increased speed and capability of computers influence all the many services we may take for granted. Where would telecommunications, speech recognition, advanced software applications, and the Internet be without this technology?

Current chip technology permits the placement of hundreds of thousands of transistors and electronic switches on a single chip. Chips already fit into wristwatches and credit cards, but electrical and computer engineers are working to make them even smaller. In electronics, smaller is better. For example, the ENIAC, the first full-scale digital electronic computer, weighed 50 tons and occupied an entire room. Today, a computer far more powerful than the ENIAC can be fabricated within a single piece of silicon the size of a child's fingernail.

Chip designers think in terms of nanoseconds (one billionth of a second) and microns (one millionth of a meter). They want to pack as many circuit elements as they can into the structure of a chip. This is called *scaling,* or making the transistor, and the technology that connects it, smaller. High-density packing reduces the time required for an electrical signal to travel from one circuit element to the next—resulting in faster computers. Circuit lines on early 1980s PC processors were 10 microns wide. Today's circuit lines are .09 microns or 90 nanometers (one billionth of a meter). The reduced size of the circuit lines enables chips to hold over 100 million transistors and provide thousands of times the power of earlier processors.

As transistors become smaller, the chip becomes faster, conducts more electricity, and uses less power. Also, it costs less to produce as more transistors are packed on a chip. The computer revolution will continue to grow rapidly into the twenty-first century as long as researchers find ways to make transistors faster and smaller, make wiring that is less resistive to electrical current, and increase chip density. Each year, researchers have developed radically new techniques for manufacturing chips. For example, IBM recently began developing a logic chip and processor using silicon-on-insulator (SOI) technology, an innovative approach to the chip-making process. The process presented here provides a general overview that is representative of the various techniques used by chip manufacturers (see Figure 4-27).

Chips are designed and manufactured to perform a particular function. Microprocessors, memory, and logic chips are three of the most common kinds of chips. A microprocessor is the "brain" of a personal computer. A memory chip might be for temporary random-access storage (RAM). Logic chips are used in beverage vending machines, televisions, refrigerators, cell phones, and thousands more devices.

The development of integrated circuits starts with a project review team made up of representatives from design, manufacturing, and marketing. This group works together to design a product the customer needs. Next, they go through prototype wafer manufacturing to resolve potential manufacturing problems. Once a working prototype is produced, chips are manufactured in quantity and sent to computer, peripheral, telecommunications, and other customers.

The manufacturing of integrated circuits involves a multistep process using various photochemical etching and metallurgical techniques. This complex and interesting process is illustrated here with photos, from silicon to the finished product. The process is presented in five steps: design, fabrication, packaging, testing, and installation.

1. USING CAD FOR CHIP DESIGN

Chip designers use computer-aided design (CAD) systems to create the logic for individual circuits. Although a chip can contain up to 30 layers, typically there are 10 to 20 patterned layers of varying material, with each layer performing a different purpose. In this multilayer circuit design, each layer is color-coded so the designer can distinguish one layer from another. Some of the layers lie within the silicon wafer and others are stacked on top.

Courtesy of Micron Technology, Inc.

2. CREATING A MASK

The product designer's computerized drawing of each circuit layer is transformed into a *mask,* or *reticle,* a glass or quartz plate with an opaque material (such as chrome) formed to create the pattern. The process used to transfer a pattern or image from the masks to a wafer is called *photolithography.* The number of layers depends on the complexity of the chip's logic. The Intel Pentium processor, for example, contains 20 layers. When all these unique layers are combined, they create the millions of transistors and circuits that make up the architecture of the processor. Needless to say, the manufacturing process forming this sequence of layers is a very precise one!

Courtesy of Micron Technology, Inc.

3. CREATING SILICON INGOTS

Molten silicon is spun into cylindrical ingots, usually from six to eight inches in diameter. Because silicon, the second most abundant substance, is used in the fabrication of integrated circuits, chips are sometimes referred to as "intelligent grains of sand."

M/A-COM, Inc.

4. CUTTING THE SILICON WAFERS

The ingot is shaped and prepared prior to being cut into silicon wafers. Once the wafers are cut to about the thickness of a credit card, they are polished to a perfect finish.

M/A-COM, Inc.

5. WEARING BUNNY SUITS

To help keep a clean environment, workers wear semi-custom-fitted Gortex® suits. They follow a rigorous 100-step procedure when putting the suits on.

Courtesy of Intel Corporation

6. KEEPING A CLEAN HOUSE

Clean air continuously flows from every pore of the ceiling and through the holes in the floor into a filtering system at the manufacturing plant. A normal room contains some 15 million dust particles per cubic foot. A clean, modern hospital has about 10,000 dust particles per cubic foot. A class-1 clean room (the lower the rating, the cleaner the facility) contains less than one dust particle per cubic foot. All of the air in a "clean room" is replaced seven times every minute.

Portions of the microchip manufacturing process are performed in yellow light because the wafers are coated with a light-sensitive material called "photoresist" before the next chip pattern is imprinted onto the surface of the silicon wafer.

Courtesy of AMD

8. ETCHING THE WAFERS

A photoresist is deposited onto the wafer surface creating a film-like substance to accept the patterned image. The mask is placed over the wafer and both are exposed to ultraviolet light. In this way the circuit pattern is transferred onto the wafer. The photoresist is developed, washing away the unwanted resist and leaving the exact image of the transferred pattern. Plasma (superhot gases) technology is used to etch the circuit pattern permanently into the wafer. This is one of several techniques used in the etching process. The wafer is returned to the furnace and given another coating on which to etch another circuit layer. The procedure is repeated for each circuit layer until the wafer is complete.

Some of the layers include aluminum or copper interconnects, which leave a fine network of thin metal connections or wires for these semiconductor chips. The wires are used to link the transistors. Aluminum has long been the standard for semiconductor wiring, but recent innovations with the use of copper wiring, a better conductor of electricity, will help create the next generation of semiconductors.

Courtesy of Micron Technology, Inc.

7. COATING THE WAFERS

Silicon wafers that eventually will contain several hundred chips are placed in an oxygen furnace at 1200 degrees Celsius. In the furnace, the wafer is coated with other minerals to create the physical properties needed to produce transistors and other electronic components on the surface of the wafer.

Photo courtesy of National Semiconductor Corporation

9. TRACKING THE WAFERS

Fabrication production control tracks wafers through the fabricating process and measures layers at certain manufacturing stages to determine layer depth and chemical structure. These measurements assess process accuracy and facilitate real-time modifications.

Courtesy of Micron Technology, Inc.

10. DRILLING THE WAFERS

It takes only a second for this instrument to drill 1440 tiny holes in a wafer. The holes enable the interconnection of the layers of circuits. Each layer must be perfectly aligned (within a millionth of a meter) with the others.

Courtesy of International Business Machines Corporation

13. DICING THE WAFERS

A diamond-edged saw, with a thickness of a human hair, separates the wafer into individual processors, known as die, in a process called dicing. Water spray keeps the surface temperature low. After cutting, high-pressure water rinses the wafer clean. In some situations, special lasers are used to cut the wafers.

Courtesy of Micron Technology, Inc.

P A C K A G I N G

11. REMOVING THE ETCHED WAFERS

The result of the coating/etching process is a silicon wafer that contains from 100 to 400 integrated circuits, each of which includes millions of transistors.

Courtesy of International Business Machines Corporation

14. ATTACHING THE DIE

Individual die are attached to silver epoxy on the center area of a lead frame. Each die is removed from the tape with needles plunging up from underneath to push the die while a vacuum tip lifts the die from the tape. Lead frames are then heated in an oven to cure the epoxy. The wafer map created in probe tells the die-attach equipment which die to place on the lead frame.

Courtesy of Micron Technology, Inc.

12. MOUNTING THE WAFER

Each wafer is vacuum mounted onto a metal-framed sticky film tape. The wafer and metal frame are placed near the tape, then all three pieces are loaded into a vacuum chamber. A vacuum forces the tape smoothly onto the back of the wafer and metal frame.

Courtesy of Micron Technology, Inc.

15. PACKAGING THE CHIPS

The chips are packaged in protective ceramic or metal carriers. The carriers have standard-sized electrical pin connectors that allow the chip to be plugged conveniently into circuit boards. Because the pins tend to corrode, the pin connectors are the most vulnerable part of a computer system. To avoid corrosion and a bad connection, the pins on some carriers are made of gold.

Courtesy of International Business Machines Corporation

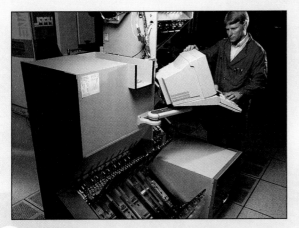

16. TESTING THE CHIPS

Each chip is tested to assess functionality and to see how fast it can store or retrieve information. Chip speed (or access time) is measured in nanoseconds (a billionth, 1/1,000,000,000th of a second). The precision demands are so great that as many as half the chips are found to be defective. A drop of ink is deposited on defective chips.

Courtesy of Micron Technology, Inc.

18. SCANNING

All chips are scanned, using optics or lasers, to discover any bent, missing, or incorrectly formed leads.

Courtesy of Micron Technology, Inc.

17. BURNING IN

This burn-in oven runs performance tests on every chip, simulating actual usage conditions. Each chip is tested by feeding information to the chip and querying for the information to ensure the chip is receiving, storing, and sending the correct data.

Courtesy of Micron Technology, Inc.

19. CREATING CIRCUIT BOARDS

Pick and place equipment precisely positions various chips on the solder and contacts. Completed boards are then heated in reflow ovens, allowing the lead coating and solder to melt together to affix the chip to the printed circuit board.

Courtesy of Micron Technology, Inc.

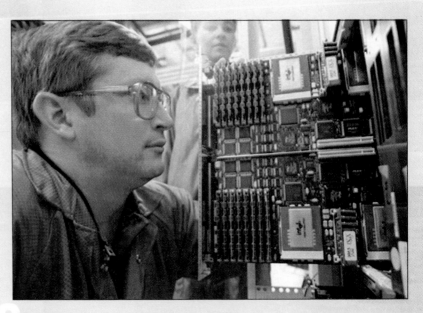

20. INSTALLING THE FINISHED CHIPS

The completed circuit boards are installed in computers and thousands of other computer-controlled devices.

Photo courtesy of Intel Corporation

IT ILLUSTRATED SELF-CHECK

1   The width of circuit lines on today's integrated chip technology is measured in nanometers. (T/F)

2   Modern chip technology calls for at least 1,000 layers of logic for each chip. (T/F)

3   Wafers are cut into individual chips with a diamond-edged saw. (T/F)

4   Which of the following is not a common type of chip: (a) memory, (b) microprocessor, (c) pulsar, or (d) logic?

5   Which substance is the basis of the ingots from which the wafers are made: (a) silicone, (b) uranium, (c) gold, or (d) silver?

6   Integrated circuits are fabricated in: (a) sparkling rooms, (b) semi-clean rooms, (c) semi-soiled rooms, or (d) clean rooms.

INPUT/OUTPUT DEVICES

CHAPTER 5

LEARNING OBJECTIVES

Once you have read and studied this chapter, you will be able to:

- Understand the various types of magnetic disk storage devices and media, including their organization, principles of operation, maintenance, and performance considerations (Section 5-1).

- Understand the operational capabilities and applications for the various types of optical laser disc storage (Section 5-2).

- Describe the operation and application of common input devices (Section 5-3).

- Describe the operation and application of common output devices (Section 5-4).

Not too long ago, we stored things in file drawers, family photo albums, notebooks, recipe boxes, keepsake boxes, calendars, bookshelves, Rolodex name and address files, and many other places. Most of us still store things in these same places, but to a far lesser extent. The family photo album may be scanned and stored on a rewritable CD-ROM. Personal information software is rapidly replacing the Rolodex file. Encyclopedias are pressed into a CD-ROM rather than printed as a 20-volume set. Music is now available from many electronic sources. Much of what used to be physical and tangible is now stored permanently in electronic form on various storage media.

This chapter should help you sort out the storage options and give you some insight as to what (and how much) to buy. Plus, it will help you to know when and how to use various storage alternatives.

When PCs arrived as a viable consumer product in the late 1970s, choices for input/output were limited. Input was mostly via the standard QWERTY keyboard. Output was a small low-resolution monitor, a really slow printer, and a tiny little speaker that made annoying sounds when you tapped the wrong key. Now we have ergonomic keyboards and even speech-recognition software that lets you talk to your PC. Monitors come in many different shapes, sizes, and qualities. All-in-one devices offer fast photo-quality color printing, along with copying, scanning, and faxing capabilities. There is a broad array of input/output devices you can connect to a PC for what seems to be an infinite number of applications.

When it comes to buying PC related hardware, you are generally on your own. Realistically, you cannot depend on salespeople or friends to make these important decisions for you. It takes personal knowledge and research. This chapter should help you get exactly what you want and need in input and output devices, and ultimately, the biggest bang for your PC buck.

5-1 MAGNETIC DISK STORAGE

Did you ever stop to think about what happens behind the scenes when you…

- Request a telephone number through directory assistance?
- Draw money from your checking account at an ATM?
- Check out at a supermarket?
- Download a file from the Internet?

Needed information—such as telephone numbers, account balances, item prices, or stock summary files on the Internet—is retrieved from rapidly rotating disk-storage media and loaded to random-access memory (RAM) for processing. Untold terabytes (trillions of bytes) of information, representing millions of applications, are stored *permanently* for periodic retrieval in magnetic (such as hard disk) and optical (such as DVD+RW) storage media. There they can be retrieved in milliseconds. For example, as soon as the directory assistance operator keys in the desired name, the full name and number are retrieved from disk storage and displayed. Moments later, a digitized version of voice recordings of numbers is accessed from disk storage and played in response to the caller's request: "The number is five, zero, one, five, five, five, two, two, four, nine."

STORAGE TECHNOLOGIES

Within a computer system, programs and information in all forms (text, image, audio, and video) are stored in both *RAM* and permanent **mass storage**, such as *magnetic disk and rewritable optical laser disc* (see Figure 5-1). Programs and information are retrieved from mass storage and stored *temporarily* in high-speed RAM for processing.

Over the years, manufacturers have developed a variety of permanent mass storage devices and media. Today the various types of **magnetic disk drives** and their respective storage media are the state of the art for permanent storage. **Optical laser disc,** such as CD-ROM and DVD±RW, continues to emerge as a means of mass storage. Note that *disk* is spelled with a "k" for magnetic disk media and with a "c" for optical disc media. **Magnetic tape drives** complement disk/disc storage by providing inexpensive *backup* capability and *archival* storage, primarily for the business environment. The tape "data cartridge" is similar in appearance to the audio cassette tape. The focus of this section is magnetic disk storage. Optical laser discs are covered in the next section. Magnetic tape, which seldom is used in personal computing, is including in the backup discussion in Chapter 8.

Random and Sequential Access

Magnetic disks have *random-* or *direct-access* capabilities. You are quite familiar with these access concepts, but you may not realize it. Suppose you have Paul Simon's classic album, *The Rhythm of the Saints,* on both CD and cassette tape. To play the third song on the cassette, "The Coast," you would have to wind the tape forward and search for it sequentially. To play "The Coast" on the CD, all you would have to do is select track number 3. This simple analogy demonstrates the two fundamental methods of storing and accessing data— *random* and *sequential*.

Types of Magnetic Disks: Interchangeable and Fixed

Magnetic disks are very fast, able to seek and retrieve information quicker than a blink of an eye (in milliseconds). This direct-access flexibility and speed have made magnetic disk storage the overwhelming choice of computer users, for all types of computers and all

FIGURE 5–1 **RAM AND MASS STORAGE**

Programs and data are stored permanently in mass storage and temporarily in RAM.

FIGURE 5-2

INFORMATION ON MAGNETIC DISK

Today, most readily accessible information is stored on hard disk. The information provided by these interactive ATMs and kiosks is stored on disk and all transactions are recorded on disk.

Courtesy of Diebold, Incorporated

types of applications (see Figure 5-2). A variety of magnetic disk drives, the *hardware device,* and magnetic disks, the *medium* (the actual surface on which the information is stored), are manufactured for different business requirements and are discussed in the following sections.

Generally, magnetic disks are classified as *interchangeable* or *fixed.*

- *Interchangeable disks.* The classic "floppy" diskette is an example of an **interchangeable disk.** These types of disks can be stored offline and loaded to the magnetic disk drives as they are needed. A disk or device is **offline** if it is not accessible to and under the control of a computer system.

- *Fixed disks.* **Fixed disks,** also called **hard disks,** usually are permanently installed. Typically, the hard disk is a fixed part of a computer system and is **online** at all times; that is, the disk and its information are under the control of the computer system. All hard disks are rigid and usually made of aluminum with a surface coating of easily magnetized elements, such as iron, cobalt, chromium, and nickel.

Figure 5-3 shows some of the different types of interchangeable disks and fixed disks. The type you (or a company) should use depends on the volume of data you have and the frequency with which those data are accessed.

Interchangeable Disks

Three types of interchangeable disk drives are commonly used on PCs—the traditional *floppy disk* and the newer high-capacity *SuperDisk* and *Zip disk.* These disk drives accept interchangeable disks.

The traditional 3.5-inch **floppy disk** is a thin, Mylar disk that is permanently enclosed in a rigid plastic jacket. The widely used standard for traditional "floppies," also called *diskettes,* permits only 1.44 MB of storage, not much in the modern era in which 4-MB images and 30-MB programs are commonplace. A newer version, called a **SuperDisk,** can store 120 MB of information. The diskette and the SuperDisk are the same size but have different disk densities. **Disk density** refers to the number of bits that can be stored per unit of area on the disk-face surface. In contrast to a hard disk, the diskette and the SuperDisk are set in motion only when a command is issued to read from or write to the disk. The 120-MB SuperDisk combines floppy and hard disk technology to read from and write to specially formatted floppy-size disks. The SuperDisk drive reads from and writes to the traditional diskette, as well.

The original **Zip**® **drive** reads and writes to 100-MB **Zip**® **disks.** The most recent innovation, a 750-MB Zip drive, handles all versions of Zip disks (100, 250, and 750 MB). The SuperDisk and 750-MB Zip disk have storage capacities of 70 and 521 floppy diskettes, respectively.

Soon, the 3.5-inch floppy may become a historical artifact. Many major PC manufacturers no longer include the traditional floppy disk drive with their computers. Instead, they rely on DVD±RW/CD-RW drives, local area networks, and the Internet as vehicles for the transfer of information and programs.

A blank interchangeable disk has a very modest value. But once you save your files on it, its value, at least to you, increases greatly. Such a valuable piece of property should be handled with great care. Here are a few commonsense guidelines for handling interchangeable disks.

- Avoid temperature extremes.
- Store disks in a protected location, preferably in a storage tray away from direct sunlight and magnetic fields (for example, magnetic paperclip holders).

FIGURE 5-3   DISK DRIVES AND MEDIA

SUPERDISK

This illustration compares the capacity of a 120-MB SuperDisk (right) to the traditional floppy disk. The SuperDisk drive is compatible with the traditional 1.44-MB diskette.

Courtesy of Imation Corporation

ZIP DISK

An alternative high-capacity interchangeable disk is the 100-, 250-, or 750-MB Zip disk (shown here) with an external Zip drive.

Courtesy of Iomega Corporation

HARD DRIVE

This 150-GB hard drive is exposed to show its inner workings (2 platters with 4 read/write heads).

Courtesy of Seagate Technology

MICRODRIVE

IBM unveiled the world's smallest and lightest hard-disk drive with a disk platter that will fit into an egg. The IBM Microdrive, which weighs less than an AA battery and holds 340 MB, is designed for use in PDAs and palmtop PCs.

Courtesy of International Business Machines Corporation. Unauthorized use not permitted.

PORTABLE HARD DISK

The external portable hard disk lets you take your files with you and access them on any PC with a USB port.

Courtesy of Iomega Corporation

- Remove disks from disk drives before you turn off the computer, but only when the "drive active" light is off.
- Use an interchangeable drive cleaning kit periodically.
- Avoid force when inserting or removing a disk, as there should be little or no resistance.
- Don't touch the disk surface.

The Hard Disk

Hard disk manufacturers are working continuously to achieve two objectives: (1) to put more information in less disk space and (2) to enable a more rapid transfer of that information to/from RAM. Consequently, hard-disk storage technology is forever changing. There are two types of hard disks in common use—those that are permanently installed and those that are portable.

Generally, the 1- to 5.25-inch (diameter of disk) hard disks have storage capacities from about 40 GB (gigabytes) to over 300 GB. A 300-GB hard disk stores about the same amount of data as 63 DVDs or 462 CD-ROMs.

A hard disk contains up to 12 disk platters stacked on a single rotating spindle. PC-based hard disks will normally have from one to four platters. Data are stored on all *recording surfaces*. For a disk with four platters, there are eight recording surfaces on which data can be stored (see Figure 5-4). The disks spin continuously at a high speed (from 7,200 to 15,000 revolutions per minute) within a sealed enclosure. The enclosure keeps the disk-face surfaces free from contaminants (see Figure 5-5), such as dust and cigarette smoke. This contaminant-free environment allows hard disks to have greater density of data storage than the interchangeable diskettes.

The rotation of a magnetic disk passes all data under or over a **read/write head,** thereby making all data available for access on each revolution of the disk (see Figure 5-4). A fixed disk will have at least one read/write head for each recording surface. The heads are mounted on **access arms** that move together and literally float on a cushion of air over (or under) the spinning recording surfaces.

The **portable hard disk** is an external device that is connected easily to any personal computer via a USB port or FireWire port. Portable hard disks are popular in the business world where knowledge workers can take their user files with them to their home office or to a PowerPoint presentation in San Francisco. Portable hard disk capacities are similar to those of fixed hard disks and they weigh from .5 to 2 pounds.

One of the most frequently asked questions is "How much hard drive capacity do I need?" The answer you hear most is "As much as you can afford." Disk space is like closet space—you never seem to have enough. If it's there, you tend to fill it with some-

---

FIGURE 5–4   **FIXED HARD DISK WITH FOUR PLATTERS AND EIGHT RECORDING SURFACES**

A cylinder refers to similarly numbered concentric tracks on the disk-face surfaces. In the illustration, the read/write heads are positioned over Cylinder 0012. At this position, the data on any one of the eight tracks numbered 0012 are accessible to the computer on each revolution of the disk. The read/write heads must be moved to access data on other tracks/cylinders. Next to the illustration is a highly magnified area of a magnetic disk-face surface shows elongated information bits recorded serially along 8 of the disk's 1774 concentric tracks.

Courtesy of International Business Machines Corporation. Unauthorized use not permitted.

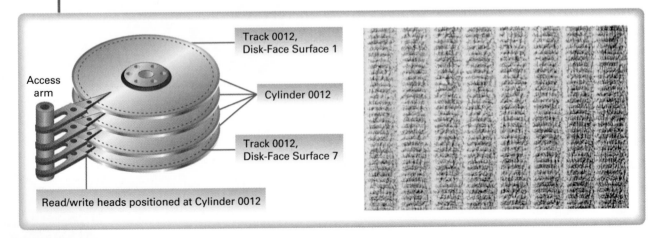

Track 0012, Disk-Face Surface 1

Access arm

Cylinder 0012

Track 0012, Disk-Face Surface 7

Read/write heads positioned at Cylinder 0012

FIGURE 5-5

DISK READ/WRITE HEAD FLYING DISTANCE
When the disk is spinning at 10,000 rpm, the surface of the disk travels across the read/write head at approximately 130 mph.

thing. If you don't, the software vendors will. The original MS-DOS operating system was 160 KB, Windows 3.1 was 10 MB, and Windows XP is over 100 MB—over 600 times the size of MS-DOS.

DISK ORGANIZATION

Typically, the PC owner maintains his or her own hard disk—that, probably, would be you. To keep your disk running at peak performance and to understand warnings and error messages that pertain to your hard disk, you will need to understand the fundamentals of disk organization.

The way in which data and programs are stored and accessed is similar for all disks. Conceptually, a floppy disk looks like a hard disk with a single platter. Both media have a thin film coating of one of the easily magnetized elements (cobalt, for example). The thin film coating on the disk can be magnetized electronically by the read/write head to represent the absence or presence of a bit (0 or 1).

Tracks, Sectors, and Clusters

Data are stored in concentric **tracks** by magnetizing the surface to represent bit configurations (see Figure 5-6). Bits are recorded using *serial representation;* that is, bits are aligned in a row in the track. The number of tracks varies greatly between disks, from as few as 80 on a diskette to thousands on high-capacity hard disks. The spacing of tracks is measured in **tracks per inch,** or **TPI.** The 3.5-inch floppies are rated at 135 TPI. The TPI for hard disks can be in the thousands. The *track density,* which is measured in TPI, tells only part of the story. The *recording density* tells the rest. Recording density, which is measured in *megabits per inch,* refers to the number of bits (1s and 0s) that can be stored per linear inch of track. High-density hard disks have densities in excess of 3 megabits per inch.

PC disks use **sector organization** to store and retrieve data. In sector organization, the recording surface is divided into pie-shaped **sectors** (see Figure 5-6). The number of sectors depends on the density of the disk. A hard disk may have hundreds of sectors. Typically, the storage capacity of each sector on a particular track is 512 bytes, regardless of the number of sectors per track. Adjacent sectors are combined to form **clusters,** the capacity of which is a multiple of 512. Typically, clusters range in size from 4,096 bytes up to 32,768 bytes (that's 8 up to 64 sectors). The cluster is the smallest unit of disk space that can be allocated to a file, so every file saved to disk takes up one or more clusters.

Each disk cluster is numbered, and the number of the first cluster in a file comprises the **disk address** on a particular file. The disk address represents the physical location of a particular file or set of data on a disk. To read from or write to a disk, an access arm containing the

FIGURE 5-6

CUTAWAY OF A DISKETTE

The access arm on this 3.5-inch disk drive is positioned at a particular track (Track 2 in the example). Data are read or written serially in tracks within a given sector. Below, the flexible 3.5-inch recording disk spins between two soft liners when accessed. The recording surface is sandwiched in a rigid plastic jacket for protection. When inserted, the metal shutter slides to reveal the recording window.

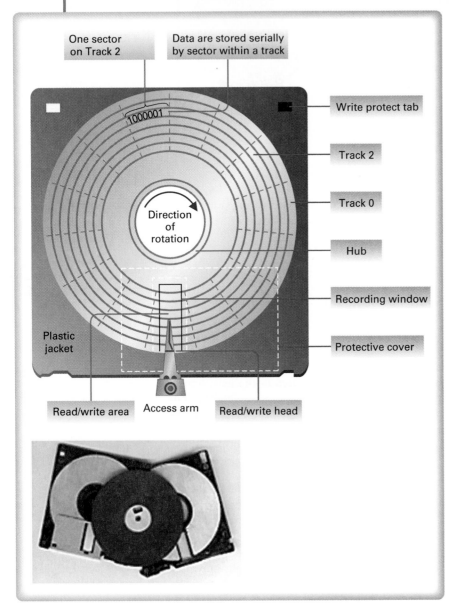

One sector on Track 2

Data are stored serially by sector within a track

1000001

Direction of rotation

Write protect tab

Track 2

Track 0

Hub

Recording window

Protective cover

Plastic jacket

Read/write area   Access arm   Read/write head

read/write head is moved, under program control, to the appropriate *track* or *cylinder* (see Figures 5-4 and 5-6). A particular **cylinder** refers to the same-numbered tracks on each recording surface (for example, Track 0012 on each recording surface; see Figure 5-4). When reading from or writing to a hard disk, all access arms are moved to the appropriate *cylinder*. For example, each recording surface has a track numbered 0012, so the disk has a cylinder numbered 0012. If the data to be accessed are on Recording Surface 01, Track 0012, then the access arms and the read/write heads for all eight recording surfaces are moved to Cylinder 0012. When the cluster containing the desired data passes under or over the read/write head, the data are read or written. Fortunately, software automatically monitors the location, or address, of our files and programs. We need only enter the name of the file to retrieve it for processing.

One of the major limitations of traditional sector organization is that recording space is wasted on the outer tracks. To overcome this limitation, some high-performance disk manufacturers employ a technique called **zoned recording**. In zoned recording, tracks are grouped into zones and all tracks in a particular zone have the same number of sectors (see Figure 5-7). A zone contains a greater number of sectors per track as you move from the innermost zone to the outermost zone. This approach to disk organization enables a more efficient use of available disk space.

The File Allocation Table

Each disk used in the Windows environment has a **Virtual File Allocation Table** (**VFAT**) in which information about the clusters is stored (it was a FAT in early operating systems). The table includes an entry for each cluster that describes where on the disk it can be found and how it is used (for example, whether the file is open or not). Here's what happens when you or a program on your PC makes a request for a particular file.

1. The operating system searches the VFAT to find the physical address of the first cluster of the file.

2. The read/write heads are moved over the track/cylinder containing the first cluster.

3. The rapidly rotating disk passes the cluster under/over the read/write head, and the information in the first cluster is read and transmitted to RAM for processing.

4. The operating system checks an entry within the initial cluster that indicates whether the file consists of further clusters, and if so, where on the disk they are located.

5. The operating system directs that clusters continue to be read and their information transmitted to RAM until the last cluster in the chain is read (no further chaining is indicated).

The trade-off between system performance and efficient use of disk space is a major consideration during the disk design process. A 100-KB file being stored on a disk with 32,768 byte clusters would require four clusters (three clusters will store only 98,304 bytes). Most of the space in the fourth cluster is wasted disk space. Large clusters may improve overall system performance, but, because of their size, they tend to make more space inaccessible.

Eventually your PC will give you a "lost clusters found" message, indicating that the hard disk has orphan clusters that don't belong to a file. Typically, lost clusters are the result of an unexpected interruption of file activity, perhaps a system crash or loss of power. Periodically Windows users should run the **ScanDisk** utility program, a program that periodically "scans" the disk for lost clusters and, if any are found, lets the user return them to the available pool of usable clusters.

Defragmenting the Disk to Enhance Performance

Ideally, all files would be stored on disk in contiguous clusters, but such is not the case with computing. Over time, files are added, deleted, and modified such that, eventually, files must be stored in noncontiguous clusters. When clusters that make up a particular file are scattered, the read/write heads must move many times across the surface of a disk to access a single file. This excess mechanical movement slows down the PC because it takes longer to load a file to RAM for processing.

In fact, the mechanical movement of the disk read/write heads is the most vulnerable part of a PC system—the greater the fragmentation of files, the slower the PC. Fortunately, we can periodically reorganize the disk such that files are stored in contiguous clusters. This process, appropriately called **defragmentation,** is done with a handy utility program (see Figure 5-8) called a **disk defragmenter.** The program consolidates files into contiguous clusters; that is, the clusters for each file are chained together on the same or adjacent tracks (see Figure 5-9), thereby minimizing the movement of the read/write head. After running the program, each file stored on a disk is a single cluster or a chain of clusters.

How often you run a "defrag" program depends on how much you use your PC. The fragmentation problem and the defragmentation solution are illustrated in Figure 5-9. In the example, five files are loaded to a disk, each in contiguous clusters. A file is modified, another is deleted, and another is added, resulting in fragmentation of several files and a need for defragmentation. The defragmentation process rewrites fragmented files into contiguous clusters (see Figure 5-9).

Formatting: Preparing a Disk for Use

A new disk is coated with a surface that can be magnetized easily to represent data. However, before the disk can be used, it must be **formatted.** The formatting procedure causes the disk to be initialized with a recording format for your operating system. Specifically, it

- Creates sectors and tracks into which data are stored.
- Sets up an area for the virtual file allocation table.

FIGURE 5-7

ZONED RECORDING ON A HARD DISK

Zoned recording groups tracks into concentric zones (three of them in the illustration) such that the number of sectors in each track increases as the zones spread to the outer edge of the disk (9, 12, 16), thus enabling a more efficient use of storage space on the disk space surface.

Characteristics of a Magnetic Disk

- Media
  - Fixed (hard) and interchangeable disks
- Type access
  - Direct (random) or sequential
- Data representation
  - Serial
- Storage scheme
  - Clusters on tracks

FIGURE 5-8   **DEFRAG SUMMARY**

The Speed Disk utility program within Symantec's Norton SystemWorks optimizes the disk by performing the defragmentation process. During the process, the utility program gives a visual overview of the status of each cluster, with colors indicating cluster status (used, bad, frequent access, applications, and so on).

If you purchased a PC today, the hard disk probably would be formatted and ready for use. However, if you added a hard disk or upgraded your existing hard disk, the new disk would need to be formatted.

DISK SPEED

Data access from RAM is performed at electronic speeds—approximately the speed of light. But the access of data from disk storage depends on the movement of mechanical apparatus (read/write heads and spinning disks) and can take from 4 to 8 milliseconds—still very slow when compared with the microsecond-to-nanosecond internal processing speeds of computers. The disk engineer's quest in life is to improve disk performance by reducing *access time* and increasing the *data transfer rate*.

Access time is the interval between the instant a computer makes a request for the transfer of data from a disk-storage device to RAM and the instant this operation is completed. The read/write heads on the access arm in the illustration of Figure 5-4 move together. Some hard disks have multiple access arms, some with two read/write heads per disk-face surface. Having multiple access arms and read/write heads results in less mechanical movement and faster access times.

The **data transfer rate** is the rate at which data are read from mass storage to RAM or written from RAM to mass storage. Even though the data transfer rate from magnetic disk to RAM may be 400 million bytes per second, the rate of transfer from one part of RAM to another is much faster. **Disk caching** (pronounced *"cashing"*) is a technique that improves system speed by taking advantage of the greater transfer rate of data within RAM. With disk caching, programs and data that are *likely* to be called into use are moved from a disk into a separate disk caching area of RAM. For example, if you close the Internet Explorer browser, the browser program might remain in unused RAM ready for immediate reload in case you decide to open it again. When an application program calls for the data or programs in the disk cache area, the data are transferred directly from RAM rather than from the slower disk. Updated data or programs in the disk cache area eventually must be transferred to a disk for permanent storage. All modern PCs take full advantage of disk caching to improve overall system performance.

FIGURE 5-9

DISK DEFRAGMENTATION

(a) Initially, five files are stored ideally in contiguous clusters. (b)The user adds a few objects to a graphics file (blue), increasing its size and the number of clusters needed to store it. Note that file clusters are no longer contiguous. Then, a file (green) is deleted. (c) A new file (orange) is stored in noncontiguous clusters. (d)The disk is defragmented, resaving all files in contiguous clusters.

A. All files stored in contiguous clusters.

B. ■ File is modified and increased in size, then ■ file is deleted.

C. ■ File is added.

D. Result of defragmentation.

VIRTUAL MEMORY: DISK IMITATING RAM

RAM is a critical factor in determining a computer system's performance because all data and programs must be resident in RAM to be processed. Once RAM is full, no more programs can be executed until a portion of RAM is made available. **Virtual memory** effectively expands the capacity of RAM through the use of software and hard disk storage. The amount of virtual memory (hard disk capacity) you set aside as virtual memory is a user option in the Windows environment. In most personal computing situations, increasing the amount of disk space allocated for virtual memory can improve overall system performance, especially when running multiple applications.

The principle behind virtual memory is quite simple. Remember, a program is executed sequentially—one instruction after another. The operating system breaks programs into *pages* so only those pages of the program being executed are resident in RAM. The rest of the program is on disk storage. The pages are transferred into RAM from disk storage as they are needed to continue execution of the program.

1 Data are retrieved from temporary disk storage and stored permanently in RAM. (T/F)

2 The capacity of a floppy disk is about that of a portable hard disk. (T/F)

3 Which has the greatest storage capacity: (a) the traditional floppy, (b) the latest Zip disk, (c) the SuperDisk, (d) or the 3.5-inch diskette?

4 The defragmentation process rewrites fragmented files into: (a) contiguous clusters, (b) continuous clusters, (c) circular clusters, or (d) Cretan clusters.

5 The rate at which data are read from disk to RAM is the: (a)TPI, (b) caching rate, (c) data transfer rate, or (d) streaming velocity.

SELF-CHECK

SECTION

Why this section is important to you.

CD, CD-ROM, CD-R, CD-RW, DVD-audio, DVD-video, DVD-ROM, DVD-R, DVD-RAM, DVD+RW, DVD-RW, and DVD±RW. Life will be less confusing when you are able to sort out these optical laser disc options.

Optical laser disc technology (see Figure 5-10) complements hard disk storage in that it provides a compact, interchangeable, high-capacity alternative for the permanent storage of programs and data. The tremendous amount of low-cost direct-access storage made possible by optical laser discs has opened the door to many new applications. The most visible application for optical discs is the DVD movie that you can buy or rent and play on your DVD player or your PC. Another very visible application is that they have emerged as the media-of-choice for the distribution of software. Many of the thousands of commercially produced CD-ROM/DVD discs contain reference material, such as encyclopedias and dictionaries. The books that traditionally lined the walls of attorneys have given way to disk-based law libraries that can be easily updated as laws change in cases are added. Businesses periodically back up their data to DVD±RW discs. Companies produce their own CD-ROM-based procedures manuals and individuals burn their own audio and video discs.

Optical laser disc technology continues to evolve and may never slow down long enough for a standard to emerge. The read-only audio CD, the data CD-ROM, and the DVD movie were our only options 10 years ago. Now, we have many more optical laser disc options, including rewritable discs (see Figure 5-10).

FIGURE 5-10   **OPTICAL LASER DISC TECHNOLOGIES**

APPLICATION	CD Formats (650 MB)	DVD Formats (4.7 GB or 9.4 GB for double sided)
Audio/video consumer products	CD audio	DVD audio DVD video (movies)
Commercially distributed content (*software, reference material, and so on*)	CD-ROM	DVD-ROM
CD or DVD burner (*write once, read many times*)	CD-R	DVD-R DVD+R
CD and/or DVD burner plus CD and/or DVD rewritable applications (*write many times, read many times*)	CD-RW	DVD-RW DVD+RW (plus CD-RW capability)

CD-ROM AND DVD-ROM

CD-ROM and DVD-ROM technologies have had a dramatic impact on personal computing and IT during the past decade because these technologies continue to provide ever-increasing storage capacity at ever-decreasing cost.

CD-ROM History

Introduced in 1980 for stereo buffs, the *CD*, or *compact disc*, is an optical laser disc designed to enhance the reproduction of recorded music. To make a CD recording, the analog sounds of music are digitized and stored on a plastic 4.72-inch optical laser disc about 1 millimeter thick. Seventy-four minutes of music can be recorded on each disc in digital format in 2 billion bits. With its tremendous storage capacity per square inch, computer industry entrepreneurs immediately recognized the potential of optical laser disc technology. In effect, anything that can be digitized can be stored on optical laser disc: data, text, voice, still pictures, music, graphics, and motion video.

CD-ROM and DVD-ROM Technology

CD-ROM, a spin off of audio CD technology, stands for *compact disc–read-only memory.* The name implies its application. Once inserted into the *CD-ROM drive,* the text, video images, and so on can be read into RAM for processing or display. However, the data on the disc are fixed—*they cannot be altered.* This is in contrast, of course, to the read/write capability of magnetic disks.

The capacity of a single CD-ROM is up to 650 MB. To put the density of CD-ROM into perspective, the words in every book ever written could be stored on a hypothetical CD-ROM that is 8 feet in diameter.

Magnetic disks store data in concentric tracks, each of which is divided into sectors (see Figure 5-6). In contrast, CD-ROMs store data in a single track that spirals from the center to the outside edge (see Figure 5-11). The ultra thin track spirals around the disc thousands of times.

With optical laser disc, two lasers replace the mechanical read/write head used in magnetic storage. One laser beam writes to the recording surface by scoring microscopic *pits* in the disc, and another laser reads the data from the light-sensitive recording surface. A bit is represented by the presence of a pit or a *land,* the flat area separating the pits (see

FIGURE 5-11 **OPTICAL LASER DISC ORGANIZATION**

A laser beam detector interprets pits and lands, which represent bits (1s and 0s), located within the sectors in the spiraling track on the CD-ROM reflective surface. Next to the illustration is a microscopic view of the pits and lands on the surface of a CD-ROM.

Figure 5-11). Together they record binary (1s and 0s) information that can be interpreted by the computer as text, audio, images, and so on.

Popular CD-ROM drives are classified simply as 32X, 40X, or 75X. These spin at 32, 40, and 75 times the speed of the original CD standard. The faster the spin rate, the faster data are transferred to RAM for processing. The slower speeds may cause program/image load delays and the video can be choppy. The original 1X CD-ROM data transfer rate was 150 KB per second, so the 75X CD-ROM data transfer rate is 75 times that, or 11.25 MB per second. The speed at which a given CD-ROM spins depends on the physical location of the data being read. The data pass over the movable laser detector at the same rate, no matter where the data are read. Therefore, the CD-ROM must spin more quickly when accessing data near the center (about 450 rpm) and more slowly for data near the edge (about 250 rpm). Listen carefully and you can hear the spin motor adjusting the spin rate of the CD-ROM during read operations.

The laser detector is analogous to the magnetic disk's read/write head. The relatively slow spin rates make the CD-ROM access time much slower than that of its magnetic cousins. A CD-ROM drive may take 10 to 50 times longer to ready itself to read the information. Once ready to read, the transfer rate also is much slower.

Just as CD-ROMs have become mainstream equipment, DVD-ROMs with much greater capacities are poised to replace them. **DVD** stands for *digital video disc*. The DVD-ROM has the same physical dimensions as the CD and the CD-ROM, but it can store from 7 to 14 times as much information. The pits and lands are more densely packed on *DVD-ROM,* enabling 4.7 GB of storage. A *double-sided* DVD-ROM has a 9.4 GB capacity. Because data are packed more densely on a DVD-ROM, the data transfer rate is nine times that of a CD-ROM spinning at the same rate. For example, an 8X DVD-ROM drive transfers data at about the same rate as a 75X CD-ROM.

DVD-ROM drives are *backward compatible;* that is, they can play all of your CD-ROMs and CDs. They can read or play other DVD formats, too, including *DVD-video* and *DVD-audio,* which are expected to make videotapes and traditional CDs obsolete in a few years. This home entertainment version of DVD-ROM usually is shortened to simply DVD.

Creating CD-ROMs and DVD-ROMs for Mass Distribution

Most CD-ROMs and DVD-ROMs are created by commercial enterprises and sold to the public for multimedia applications and reference. Application developers gather and create source material, then write the programs needed to integrate the material into a meaningful application. The resulting files are then sent to a mastering facility. The master copy is duplicated, or "pressed," at the factory, and the copies are distributed with their prerecorded contents (for example, the complete works of Shakespeare or the movie, *Gone with the Wind*). Depending on the run quantity, the cost of producing and packaging a CD-ROM or DVD-ROM for sale can be less than a dollar apiece. These media provide a very inexpensive way to distribute applications and information.

REWRITABLE OPTICAL LASER DISC OPTIONS

Optical laser technologies are now in transition from write-only technologies, such as CD-ROM and DVD-ROM, to read and write technologies. This means that we, the end users, can make our own CD-ROMs and DVD-ROMs.

CD-R and CD-RW

Most of the world's PCs have CD-ROM or DVD-ROM drives. This rapid and universal acceptance of CD-ROM gave rise to another technology—**CD-R** (compact disc-recordable). Ten years ago, the capability to record on CD-ROM media cost over

$100,000. CD-R drives, at less than $100, brought that capability to any PC owner. While people were celebrating the arrival of CD-R, another more flexible CD technology was introduced—**CD-RW** (CD-ReWritable). This technology goes one step further, allowing users to rewrite to the CD-sized media, just as is done on magnetic disk media. With the cost of CD-R and CD-RW technologies converging, CD-R drives have disappeared from the optical drive landscape. CD-RW discs can be inserted and read on modern CD-ROM drives, but they will not work with the older models.

DVD+RW and DVD-RW

Like CD-ROM technology, recordable and read/write capabilities are emerging for DVD technology as well. **DVD+R** and **DVD-R** are like CD-R but with the recording density of DVD-ROM. **DVD+RW** and **DVD-RW** are like CD-RW, giving us rewritable capabilities for high-capacity DVD technology. DVD-RW (DVD-R) and DVD+RW (DVD+R) are competing technologies, with the most recent technology, DVD+RW (DVD+R), appearing to emerge as the technology of choice for most PC vendors. DVD rewritable alternatives are more costly than CD-RW, but as the price drops, DVD rewritable drives might become a standard storage device on new PCs.

State-of-the-art DVD rewritable drives can read all DVD and CD-ROM formats. The DVD±RW drive can read and write to either DVD format. All rewritable DVD drives have CD-RW capability, as well. You can rewrite to rewritable discs thousands of times.

OPTICAL DISCS IN YOUR PC

The typical PC will have one or two optical drives. At a minimum, users want a PC with a DVD-ROM drive so they have full optical read capability and can enjoy all CD-ROM and DVD applications, including playing DVD movies. One of the most popular optical storage options is the *DVD-ROM/CD-RW combination drive* which gives users the flexibility to read CD-ROM and DVD-ROM format discs (including audio CDs and DVD movies) and to burn their own audio and video CDs, to burn discs for data transfer, and to provide read/write backup of user files. Some people choose to configure their PCs with both a DVD-ROM drive and a DVD-ROM/CD-RW combination drive to enable easy duplication of optical media.

Those users with a few extra dollars to spend and expanded application needs are choosing a *DVD±RW/CD-RW combination drive*. You can use it to store original videos on DVD disc or archive up to 4.7 GB of data to a DVD+RW or a DVD+RW disc. People who spend the money on this high-end rewritable disk combo drive will usually add a DVD-ROM drive as well, to facilitate duplication tasks.

Optical storage technology has experienced many changes in the past decade. It's inevitable that we will continue to see new optical storage technologies that offer greater capacities and faster access times (see Figure 5-12).

WHAT'S THE BEST MIX OF STORAGE OPTIONS?

The choice of which technologies to choose for a system or an application is often a trade-off between storage capacity, cost (dollars per megabyte), and speed (access time). You can never really compare apples to apples when comparing storage media because one might have an advantage in access time, portability, random access, nonvolatility, and so on. Solid-state storage (RAM) is the fastest and most expensive (about $0.10 per MB), but it's volatile. Hard disk offers fast, permanent storage for a hundredth the cost of RAM. You can get 1 MB of interchangeable DVD±RW storage for slightly more than the cost of hard disk storage, but it is relatively slow. A well-designed system will have a mix of storage options. Each time you purchase a PC, you should spend a little extra time assessing your application and backup needs so you can configure your system with an optimum mix of storage options.

FIGURE 5-12

AN EVOLVING OPTICAL LASER DISC TECHNOLOGY: FMD-ROM

A single FMD-ROM disc, an emerging new optical storage technology, can store an amount of printed documentation that, if stacked, would stretch almost two miles into the sky.

Courtesy of Constellation 3D

FIGURE 5-13 SOLID STATE STORAGE

THE MINI USB DRIVE

About the size of a car key, the solid-state, flash memory Iomega® Mini USB drive is a portable solution for transporting and sharing 128 MB of data.

Courtesy of Iomega Corporation

SOLID-STATE STORAGE APPLICATIONS

This RCA eBook uses solid state flash memory, rather than disk, to hold more than 5,000 pages of material. Popular magazines, novels, and periodicals are readily available for downloading and viewing on the eBook.

Photo courtesy of RCA Corporation

Rotating storage media may go the way of the steam engine when low-cost nonvolatile, solid-state memory, such as *flash memory,* can store as much in less space. Already, flash memory chips, such as the Mini USB drive, are being developed that will have many times more storage capacity than the largest flash chips currently available (see Figure 5-13). Plug the thumb-size Mini USB drive it into any computer's USB port and it is immediately recognized as an active storage drive, enabling applications to be launched and run directly from the drive. Flash memory is also already the basis for e-book (electronic book) readers that hold many books, magazines, and so on (see Figure 5-13). Perhaps someday the only moving part on PCs will be the cooling fan.

What does being able to store more information in less space mean to you? It means videophones that can be worn like wristwatches. It means that you can carry a floppy-sized reader and all your college "textbooks" in your front pocket. Each new leap in storage technology seems to change much of what we do and how we do it.

SELF-CHECK

SECTION

1. CD-ROM is read-only. (T/F)
2. A double-sided DVD-ROM has a capacity of 22 GB. (T/F)
3. DVD+RW technology is: (a) rewritable, (b) read-only, (c) write-only, or (d) nonwritable.
4. Which of these is poised to replace the CD-ROM: (a) VVV, (b) jukebox, (c) CD-R, or (d) DVD-ROM?
5. Which disc drive offers the PC user the greatest flexibility: (a) DVD±RW/CD-RW, (b) DVD-ROM, (c) DVD-ROM/CD-RW, or (d) CD-R?

5-3 INPUT DEVICES

Why this section is important to you.

Computers work in binary, bits and bytes; but we don't, so we need input devices to communicate our data and wishes to computers. The more you know about the variety of available input devices, the easier it is for you to enter information to your PC.

Even people who have never sat in front of a PC communicate with computers. Perhaps you have had one of these experiences.

- Have you ever been hungry and short of cash? No problem. Just stop at an automatic teller machine (ATM) and ask for some "lunch money." The ATM's keyboard and monitor enable you to hold an interactive conversation with the bank's computer. The ATM's printer provides you with a hard copy of your transactions when you leave. Some ATMs talk to you as well.

- Have you ever called a mail-order merchandiser and been greeted by a message like this: "Thank you for calling BrassCo Enterprises Customer Service. If you wish to place an order, press one. If you wish to inquire about the status of an order, press

FIGURE 5-14 **INPUT/OUPUT ON AUTOMATIC TELLER MACHINES**

The widely used automatic teller machine (ATM) supports a variety of input/output methods.

two." The message is produced by a computer-based voice-response system, which responds to the buttons you press on your telephone keypad.

We routinely communicate directly or indirectly with these computers through input/output devices. *Input devices* translate our data and communications into a form that the computer can understand. The computer then processes these data, and an *output device* translates them back into a form we can understand. In our two examples, the ATM's keypad, touch screen monitor, and the telephone keypad serve as input devices, and the ATM's monitor, printer, and the voice-response system serve as output devices (see Figure 5-14).

Input/output devices are quietly playing an increasingly significant role in our lives. The number and variety of I/O devices are expanding even as you read this, and some of these devices are fairly exotic (see Figure 5-15). For example, there is an electronic nose that can measure and digitally record smells. It's used to analyze aroma in the food, drink, and perfume industries. Commuters enjoy another benefit of I/O as they drive through toll plazas at highway speeds. For each passing car, toll road computers grab the customer number from a credit card-sized transmitter mounted on the car windshield, then process the transaction and flash a "Thank You" message.

This part of the chapter is about I/O devices. This first section is on input devices, and we will begin with the *keyboard* and the *mouse,* the most popular input devices.

THE KEYBOARD

Every notebook and desktop PC comes with a keyboard. There are two basic types of keyboards: alphanumeric keyboards and special-function keyboards.

FIGURE 5-15

INNOVATIONS IN INPUT/OUTPUT

This PC is evolutionary in its approach to user interaction in that it provides a variety of I/O options and is converted easily from a notebook PC to a tablet PC—just twist the screen and close.

Photo courtesy of Intel Corporation

Traditional Alphanumeric Keyboards

The traditional *QWERTY* (the first six letters on the third row) keyboard has 101 keys, 12 function keys, a numeric keypad, a variety of special-function keys, and dedicated cursor-control keys (see Figure 5-16). Some of the innovations in keyboard technology are illustrated in Figure 5-17. The keyboard is either attached to the computer by a cable or linked via a wireless connection (either infrared or radio wave as shown in Figure 5-18).

Special-Function Keyboards

Some keyboards are designed for specific applications. For example, the cash-register-like terminals at most fast-food restaurants have special-purpose keyboards. Rather than key in the name and price of an order of French fries, attendants need only press the key marked "French fries" to record the sale. Such keyboards help shop supervisors, airline ticket agents, retail salesclerks, and many others interact more quickly with their computer systems.

FIGURE 5-16 A REPRESENTATIVE PC KEYBOARD

FIGURE 5-17 KEYBOARD INNOVATIONS

ALTERNATIVE KEYBOARD

The DataHand System is designed ergonomically as two independent units molded to fit the shape of the human hand such that fingers move no more than .1 inch, 88% less travel than on a standard keyboard.

Courtesy of DataHand

FOLDUP KEYBOARD FOR HANDHELDS

This ultra slim keyboard is designed for use with handheld PCs. It folds into a 5 oz. package that can easily slip into a shirt pocket.

Courtesy of Logitech

KEYBOARD INPUT AND BRAILLE OUTPUT

Special input/output devices, called assistive technology, are available for disabled people. This traditional keyboard is used in conjunction with an electronic Braille display enabling this blind man real-time two-way interaction with his PC.

Courtesy of Sun Microsystems, Inc.

THE MOUSE AND OTHER POINT-AND-DRAW DEVICES

A point-and-draw device, such as a mouse, complements the keyboard in a *graphical user interface* (**GUI**), allowing users to *point* to and select (click) a particular user option quickly and efficiently. Also, such devices can be used to *draw*.

When the mouse, which can be wireless or tethered via a cable (its tail), is moved across a desktop, the *mouse pointer* on the display moves accordingly. The mouse pointer is displayed as an arrow, a crosshair, or a variety of other symbols, depending on the current application and its position on the screen. Figure 5-19 illustrates several of the many mouse pointer schemes available to users. The text cursor and mouse pointer may be dis-

FIGURE 5-18

WIRELESS PC

This PC is wireless—the mouse, keyboard, and monitor are no longer tethered to the system unit by wires.

Photo courtesy of Intel Corporation

FIGURE 5-19 **MOUSE POINTER SCHEMES**

This figure shows three of many predefined mouse pointer schemes available to Windows users. Each mouse pointer shape provides a visual clue showing what Windows is doing or what you can do in various situations.

played on the screen at the same time in some programs, such as word processing.

Mice and other point-and-draw devices have one or two buttons. Mice used with Wintel PCs typically will have a left and right button plus a wheel between the buttons to facilitate scrolling. Mouse operations are introduced in Chapter 2.

For the moment, the mouse remains the most popular point-and-draw device. However, a variety of devices is available and each has its advantages and disadvantages. Here are a few of the more popular ones, all of which are illustrated in Figure 5-20.

- *Trackpad.* The **trackpad** has no moving parts and is common on notebook PCs. Simply move your finger about a small touch-sensitive pad to move the mouse pointer.
- *Trackpoint.* A **trackpoint** usually is positioned in or near a notebook's keyboard. Trackpoints function like miniature joysticks but are operated with the tip of the finger.
- *Trackball.* The **trackball** is a ball inset in a notebook PC or as a separate unit. The ball is rolled with the fingers to move the mouse pointer.
- *Joystick.* The **joystick** is a vertical stick that moves the mouse pointer in the direction the stick is pushed.
- *Digitizer tablet and pen.* The **digitizer tablet and pen** is a pen and a pressure-sensitive tablet whose *X-Y* coordinates correspond with those on the computer's display screen. Some digitizing tablets also use a crosshair device instead of a pen. Digitizer tablets are used to enable drawing or sketching of images, such as X-rays, and for many other drawing and engineering applications.

SCANNERS

Scanners read and interpret information on printed matter and convert it to a format that can be stored and/or interpreted by a computer (see Figure 5-21). Some scanners automate the data entry process, such as those at the grocery store checkout counter, and some scan and digitize images, such as photographs.

Scanners for Source Data Automation

In **source data automation,** data are entered directly to a computer system at the source without the need for key entry transcription. For example, scanners read preprinted bar codes on consumer products, eliminating the need for most key entry at checkout counters in retail stores.

Two types of scanners—*contact* and *laser*—read information on labels and various types of documents. Both bounce a beam of light off an image, and then measure the reflected light to interpret the image. Contact scanners must make contact as they are brushed over the printed matter to be read. Laser-based scanners are more versatile and can read data passed near the scanning area. Scanners of both technologies can recognize printed characters and various types of codes. Generally, scanners used for source data automation are in three basic categories.

FIGURE 5-20   POINT-AND-DRAW DEVICES

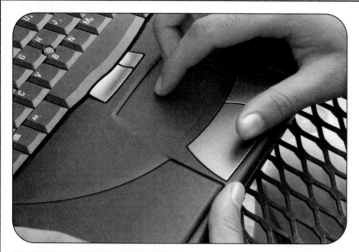

TRACKPAD AND TRACKPOINT

This notebook PC has both a trackpad and a trackpoint (between the B, G, and H keys) to enable mouse pointer movement with the tip of the finger.

Long and Associates.

THE IN-AIR MOUSE

This wireless mouse uses gyroscopic, motion-sensing technology that lets you use it in the traditional manner or away from the desktop. The mouse's gyroscope lets you use in-air gestures to control the movement of the mouse pointer.

TRACKBALL

This cordless, optical track-ball is a mouse alternative that reduces wrist and elbow fatigue.

Courtesy of Kensington Technology Group

PEN WITH TOUCH-SENSITIVE DISPLAY

These students are using a pen with a tablet PC's touch-sensitive display to interact remotely via a wireless link to the school's server computer and the Internet.

Courtesy of Xybernaut

CROSSHAIR AND DIGITIZER

This ALTEK digitizer uses a crosshair for medical imaging. The backlighting system enables the digitizing of x-rays for such applications as radiation treatment planning.

Courtesy of ALTEK Corporation

FIGURE 5-20 continued

JOYSTICK AND GAME PAD

This Microsoft Sidewinder Force Feedback Pro (joystick) and the Gravis Stinger (game pad) are designed specifically for PC action games and flight simulation programs. The Sidewinder is both an input and output device in that it provides tactile feedback (vibration and pressure).

Courtesy of Advanced Gravis Computer Technology Ltd.

DIGITIZER TABLET AND PEN

Infrared technology enables handwritten notes and drawings to be transferred to Palm organizers, such as the Palm VII shown here. As users write on the notepad with the SmartPen™, their notes and drawings are instantly transferred to the Palm.

Courtesy of Seiko Instruments USA Inc.

- *Handheld label scanners.* These devices read data on price tags, shipping labels, inventory part numbers, book ISBNs, and the like. **Handheld label scanners,** sometimes called **wand scanners,** use either contact or laser technology. You have seen both types used in libraries and various retail stores.

- *Stationary label scanners.* These devices, which rely exclusively on laser technology, are used in the same types of applications as wand scanners. **Stationary scanners** are common in grocery stores and discount stores.

- *Document scanners.* **Document scanners** are capable of scanning documents of varying sizes. Document scanners read envelopes at the U.S. Postal Service, and they also read turnaround documents for utility companies. A **turnaround document** is computer-produced output that we can read and, ultimately, is returned as computer-readable input to a computer system. For example, the stub you return with your utility bill is a turnaround document.

Bar Code and OCR Technology

Bar codes represent alphanumeric data by varying the size of adjacent vertical lines. One of the most visible bar-coding systems is the Universal Product Code (**UPC**). The UPC, originally used for grocery items, is now being printed on other consumer goods. See other applications in Figure 5-21.

OCR (**optical character recognition**) technology permits the reading of coded and text information into a computer system, including reading your handwriting. The United States Postal Service relies on both OCR and bar code scanning to sort most mail. At the Postal Service, light-sensitive scanners read and interpret the ZIP code and POSTNET bar code on billions of envelopes each day. The ZIP information then is sent to computer-based sorting machines that route the envelopes to appropriate bins for distribution.

The advantage of bar codes over OCR is that the position or orientation of the code being read is not as critical to the scanner. In a grocery store, for example, the UPC can be recorded even when a bottle of ketchup is rolled over the laser scanner. Most retail

FIGURE 5-21 | SCANNERS AND SCANNER APPLICATIONS

BAR CODES IN MANUFACTURING

Here at the Dell Computer Corporation manufacturing facility in Austin, Texas, bar codes on boxed parts are scanned as they are moved throughout the warehouse to ensure efficient inventory management, a goal of every manufacturing company.

Courtesy of Dell Computer Corp.

THE INTACTA.CODE™

The bar-code has taken on a new meaning with the recent invention of the INTACTA.CODE™. This print bar code is capable of storing photo images, MP3 music files, gaming software demos, or anything else that can be digitized. When newspaper or magazine readers scan the printed INTACTA.CODE™ into their computers, special software, working with standard scanners, decodes the dot pattern to the original electronic file.

Courtesy of Intacta Technologies

PERSONAL SCANNERS

This tiny scanner, which is small enough to hang on a keychain, allows consumers to scan products and services anywhere, anytime. Transactions such as purchases, inquiries, and payments can be made while commuting on a train or anywhere else. To retrieve the data contained in the scanner, the unit synchs up (synchronizes) with a PC, and uploads the data stored in its memory.

Courtesy of Symbol Technology, Inc.

stores and distribution warehouses, and all overnight couriers, use scanners for source data automation. Salespeople, inventory management personnel, and couriers would much prefer to wave their "magic" wands than enter data one character at a time.

Magnetic-Ink Character Recognition: Banking Exclusive

Magnetic-ink character recognition (MICR) is similar to optical character recognition and is used exclusively by the banking industry. MICR readers are used to read and sort checks and

FIGURE 5-21 continued

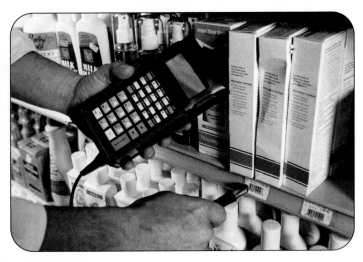

SCANNERS IN THE SUPERMARKET: STATIONARY AND HANDHELD

Supermarket checkout systems are now an established cost-saving technology. The automated systems use stationary laser scanners to read the bar codes that identify each item (left). Price and product descriptions are retrieved from a database and recorded on the sales slip. Stockers use handheld scanners to order products and update the database (right).

Courtesy of International Business Machines Corporation

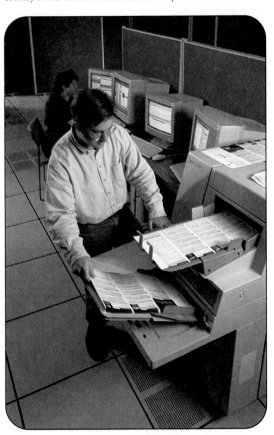

EXPEDITING THE 2000 U.S. CENSUS

One of the reasons the 2000 U.S. census went smoothly is that millions of completed mark-sense census forms were read by document scanners, thus enabling the data to be entered directly to the system for processing.

Courtesy of Lockheed Martin Corporation

WIRELESS SCANNERS

UPS maintains a worldwide wireless network, including wireless scanners (shown here), to facilitate the movement of 13 million packages each day.

Courtesy of UPS

deposits. You probably have noticed the *bank number,* the *account number,* and the *check number* encoded on all your checks and personalized deposit slips. The *date* of the transaction is automatically recorded for all checks processed that day; therefore, only the *amount* must be entered. The **MICR reader-sorter,** a MICR scanner especially designed to interpret MICR characters, reads the data on the checks and sorts the checks for distribution to other banks and customers or for further processing.

Optical Mark Recognition

You are probably familiar with one of the oldest scanner technologies, *optical mark recognition* (**OMR**). One of the most popular applications for these scanners is grading tests. All of us at one time or another has marked answers on a preprinted multiple-choice test answer form. The marked forms are scanned and corrected, comparing the position of the "sense marks" with those on a master to grade the test. The results of surveys and questionnaires often are tabulated with OMR technology.

Image Scanners

Image scanners can read written text and hard copy images, then translate the information into an electronic format that can be interpreted by and stored on computers. The image to be scanned can be a photograph, a drawing, an insurance form, a medical record—anything that can be digitized. Once an image has been digitized and entered into the computer system, it can be retrieved, displayed, modified, merged with text, stored, sent via data communications to one or several remote computers, and even faxed. Manipulating and managing scanned images is known as **image processing**.

Organizations everywhere are replacing space-consuming metal filing cabinets and millions of hard copy documents, from tax returns to warrantee cards, with their electronic equivalents. Image processing's space-saving incentive, along with its ease of document retrieval, are making the image scanner a must-have peripheral in the office. The same is true of the home as people begin converting their family photo albums and other archives to electronic format.

The Page and Hand Image Scanners

Image scanners are of two types: *page* and *hand.* Virtually all modern scanners can scan in both black and white images and color images.

- *Page image scanners.* **Page image scanners** work like copy machines. The scanned result is a high-resolution digitized image. Inexpensive sheet-fed page scanners weighing less than two pounds accept the document to be scanned in a slot.

- *Hand image scanners.* The **hand image scanner** is rolled manually over the image to be scanned. About five inches in width, hand image scanners are appropriate for capturing small images or portions of large images.

In addition to scanning photos and other graphic images, image scanners can also use OCR technology to scan and interpret the alphanumeric characters on regular printed pages. For applications that demand this type of print-to-word processing document translation, page scanners can minimize or eliminate the need for key entry. Today's image scanners and the accompanying OCR software are very sophisticated. Together they can read and interpret the characters from most printed material, such as a printed letter or a page from this book. They do a respectable, but less than perfect, job with handwritten material.

Image Processing: Eliminating the Paper Pile

In some organizations, paper files take up most of the floor space. Finding paper documents is always time consuming and, sometimes, you never find what you want. Image processing applications scan and index thousands, even millions, of documents (see Figure 5-22). Once scanned documents are on the computer system, they can be easily retrieved and manipulated. For example, banks use image processing to archive canceled checks and documents associated with mortgage loan servicing. Insurance companies use image processing in claims processing applications.

FIGURE 5-22 IMAGE PROCESSING

PAGE SCANNER

Inexpensive image scanners have given rise to a variety of image processing applications. Here, a graphic artist scans an image into the system on a page scanner.

Photo courtesy of Hewlett-Packard Company

HAND SCANNER

A manager uses a hand scanner to convert text in a magazine into electronic text that can be inserted into a word processing document.

Courtesy of Caere Corporation

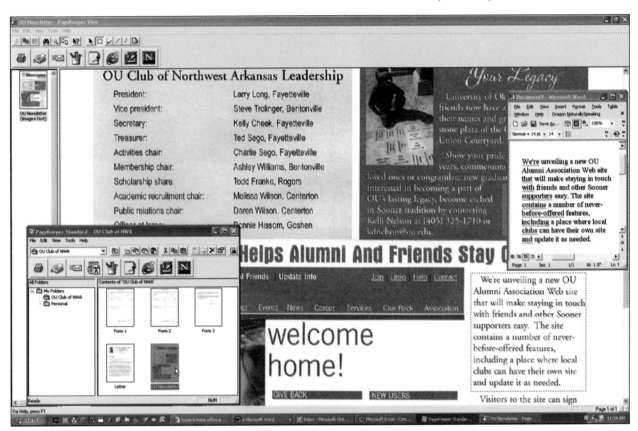

IMAGE PROCESSING SOFTWARE

PageKeeper image processor software helps you organize documents in your computer. The software lets you scan documents, such as this newsletter, into a folder system (bottom left). Once in the system, documents are retrieved and viewed easily (background). You also can make annotations on documents and copy contents to other documents (see the Word document on the right).

A decade's worth of hospital medical records can be scanned and stored on magnetic disks in an area the size of a file cabinet drawer. The images are organized so they can be retrieved in seconds rather than minutes or hours. Medical personnel who need a hard copy can simply print one out in a matter of seconds.

The real beauty of image processing is that the digitized material can be easily manipulated. For example, any image can be faxed easily to another location (without being printed). A fax is sent and received as an image. The content on the fax or any electronic image can be manipulated in many ways. OCR software can be used to translate any text on the stored bit-mapped image to an electronic format (see Figure 5-22). For example, a doctor might wish to pull selected printed text from various patient images into a word processing document to compile a summary of a patient's condition. The doctor can even select specific graphic images (X-rays, photos, or drawings) from the patient's record for inclusion in the summary report.

FIGURE 5-23

INTELLIGENT PLASTIC

Smart cards and magnetic stripe cards have a variety of applications, including banking, medical records, security, and more. In the photo, a girl uses her card to gain access to the library's automated resources.

Courtesy of Sun Microsystems, Inc.

MAGNETIC STRIPES AND SMART CARDS

Most of us carry this method of input with us—magnetic stripes. The magnetic stripes on the back of charge cards and badges offer another means of data entry. The magnetic stripes are encoded with data appropriate for specific applications. For example, your account number and personal identification number are encoded on a card for automatic teller machines.

Magnetic stripes contain much more data per unit of space than do printed characters or bar codes. Plus, because they cannot be read visually, they are perfect for storing confidential data, such as a personal identification number. Employee cards, security badges, and library cards (see Figure 5-23) often contain authorization data for access to physically secured areas, such as a computer center, or to protected resources, such as e-books in a library. To gain access, an employee or patron inserts a card or badge into a **badge reader,** a device that reads and checks the authorization code before permitting the individual to enter a secured area. When badge readers are linked to a central computer, that computer can maintain a chronological log of people entering or leaving secured areas.

What looks like any garden-variety credit card, but with a twist? The **smart card** has an embedded microprocessor with up to 64 KB of nonvolatile memory (see Figure 5-24). Because the smart card can hold more information, has processing capability, and is almost impossible to duplicate, smart cards may soon replace cards with magnetic stripes. Already, smart cards are gaining widespread acceptance in Europe and in the United States, especially smart cards with *stored value*. The dual-function stored-value smart card serves as a credit card and as a replacement for cash. Customers with these cards can go to automatic teller machines to transfer electronic cash from their checking or savings accounts to the card's memory. They are used like cash at the growing number of stores that accept stored-value cards. Each time the card is used, the purchase amount is deducted from the card's stored value. To reload the card with more electronic cash, the card's owner must return to an automatic teller machine. The stored-value smart card is another big step toward the inevitable elimination of cash.

SPEECH RECOGNITION

Generally, input technology has lagged behind that of output, processing, and storage, but one input area is starting to take wings: speech recognition. In fact, the power of PCs has finally caught up with speech-recognition technology. With the modern speech-recognition software and a quality microphone, the typical off-the-shelf PC is able to accept spoken words in continuous speech (as you would normally talk) at speeds of up to 125 words a minute. Speech recognition has made hands-free interaction possible for surgeons during operations and for quality control personnel who use their hands to describe defects as they are detected. Many executives now dictate, rather than keyboard, their e-mail messages. Also, speech recognition is a tremendous enabling technology for the physically challenged. The two types of speech recognition technology are speaker-dependent and speaker-independent.

techtv
TALK TO YOUR PC

Speaker-Dependent Speech Recognition

Speaker-dependent speech-recognition systems, which usually are associated with PCs, interpret spoken words from one person at a time. A PC-based speech-recognition system consists of software, a generic vocabulary database, and a high-quality microphone with noise-canceling capabilities. Speech recognition capability is now built into modern versions of the Microsoft Office suite. Several software companies offer more sophisticated and/or application-specific speech recognition software (law, medicine, engineering, and so on). The size of the vocabulary database ranges from 30,000 words for general dictation to more than 300,000 words for legal, medical, or technical dictation.

Already, thousands of attorneys, doctors, journalists, and others who routinely rely on dictation and writing are enjoying the benefits of speech recognition. The basic steps in speech recognition are illustrated in Figure 5-25. The system will accept most of your spoken words (see Figure 5-26). However, you can *train* the system to accept virtually all of your words. It helps to train the system to recognize your unique speech patterns. We all sound different, even to a computer. To train the system, simply read to it for about an hour—the longer the better. Even if a word is said twice in succession, it will probably have a different inflection or nasal quality. The system learns your speech patterns and updates the vocabulary database accordingly. The typical speech-recognition system never stops learning, for it is always fine-tuning the vocabulary so it can recognize words with greater speed and accuracy. Each user on a given PC would need to train the system to customize his or her own vocabulary database. To further customize your personal vocabulary database, we can add words that are unique to our working environment, such as acronyms or product names (for example, QRCV or Xbox).

It is only a matter of time before we all will be communicating with our PCs in spoken English rather than through time-consuming keystrokes. Soon, one of the speech recognition options available to us, as users, would be to give our PCs a personality. What kind of personality would you give your computer: somber, serious, happy-go-lucky, polite, rude, frivolous, Valley girl, punk? The possibilities are endless.

Speaker-Independent Speech Recognition

Speaker-independent speech-recognition systems accept words spoken by anyone. Such systems typically are server-based and are restricted to accepting only a limited number of words and tasks. Today, speech-enabled applications are being implemented in all types of industries. For example, thousands of salespeople in the field can enter an order simply by calling in to the company's computer and stating the customer number, item number, and quantity. Several airline companies offer a speech-enabled airline reservation system. Telephone companies have introduced speech-enabled directory service.

FIGURE 5-24

SMART CARD PRODUCTION

Each smart card has embedded nonvolatile memory and a processor (shown here) that can be loaded with information and programmed for a wide variety of applications.

Courtesy of Sun Microsystems, Inc.

DIGITAL CAMERAS: DIGICAMS

We all know that a picture is worth 1000 words, whether at home or the office. We now have the tools to capture still and video imagery, easily and economically. Personal computing and the Net have made it easy to share these images and video with our neighbors or with friends around the world.

Digital Cameras: Digicams

Photo images are an effective way to communicate. The **digital camera** (or **digicam**), which records images digitally rather than on traditional film, has become a popular consumer item. When you take a picture with a modern digicam, a digitized image goes straight to onboard flash memory in the form of a *memory stick*. Once in the interchangeable memory cards, or "stick," it can be uploaded to a PC and manipulated (viewed, printed, modified, and so on) as you would other graphic images (see Figure 5-27).

There are many applications for digital cameras. For example, customers from all over the world make special requests to a designer jewelry store. Store personnel take photos of available merchandise from various angles, and then they e-mail the photos to the customer. An automobile repair center takes photos of all major repair jobs to show customers exactly what the problem was and for training purposes. To help them to adjust braces better, orthodontists use digital cameras to track the migration of patients' teeth. Online retailers use digital cameras when preparing product Web pages, thereby skipping the film developing and scanning process altogether. One of the most popular applications is expanding the family photo album.

PERSONAL COMPUTING
Using Digital Cameras for File Transfer

Modern digital cameras have memory sticks (flash memory) that can store hundreds of images. When a digital camera is connected to a PC via a USB port, its memory stick is treated as another disk, enabling you to upload and download information, as needed. This capability makes digital cameras a convenient alternative for transferring files between PCs.

MEMORY BITS

Input Devices
- Keyboard
- Point-and-draw devices
- Scanners
- Image scanners (*page* and *hand*)
- Badge reader (for magnetic stripes and smart cards)
- Speech-recognition systems
- Digital cameras
- Digital video cameras
- Digital camcorders
- Handheld and wearable data entry devices

FIGURE 5-25	SPEECH RECOGNITION

The sound waves created by the spoken word *Move* are digitized by the computer. The digitized template is matched against templates of other words in the electronic dictionary. When the computer finds a match, it displays a written version of the word.

FIGURE 5-26 **TALKING TO COMPUTERS**

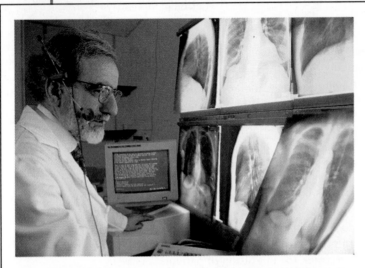

SPEECH RECOGNITION IN A MEDICAL CLINIC

This radiologist (right) is dictating his findings directly to the computer. He can also issue commands, such as "move left," "paste that," or "give me help."

Courtesy of Dragon Systems, Inc.

SPEECH RECOGNITION SOFTWARE

Dragon Systems® Dragon NaturallySpeaking™ allows users to input text and control applications by speaking naturally instead of key entry. The speech-recognition program displays a word or phrase that contains its best guesses when a spoken word or phrase has several interpretations. In this example, the only phrase not interpreted correctly was "a quality," which was interpreted as "equality."

With the cost of high-resolution digital cameras, about that of a quality 35-mm camera, a lot more people are going digital for photography. Once you own a digital camera, the cost of photography plummets because the costly, time-consuming developing processing is eliminated. With digital cameras, you can take all the photos you want and just keep the really good ones.

Desktop Digital Video Cameras

The **desktop digital video camera** lets you capture motion video in the area of the PC. Two popular uses for these cameras are as Webcams and to capture video for real-time Internet-based videophone conversations. **Webcams** are digital video cameras that are continuously linked to the Internet, providing still and video imagery from thousands of sites, usually 24 hours a day. Webcams are located in zoos, classrooms, offices, living rooms, forests, on top of tall buildings, and just about any other place you can imagine beaming stills or video of whatever is happening into cyberspace. If you have a PC, videophone software, an Internet connection, and a digital video camera, you are set to have videophone conversations, whereby you both see and hear the other party.

Digital video cameras have many applications. They are used to create video content for Web pages. People use them to capture still images. More and more companies are opting to save the airfare and have videoconferences instead. Already the relative inexpensive digital video camera (around $70) is standard on some PCs. The emergence of low-cost rewritable optical disc storage means that you can use digital video cameras for the family video, too. Digital video imagery can eat up the megabytes on a hard disk, so people often move captured video to optical laser discs. A CD-R will hold about 15 minutes of video.

Digital Camcorders

Handheld **digital camcorders** offer another way to capture video (see Figure 5-28). Video is stored on digital tape, but it can be

FIGURE 5-28

DIGITAL MOVIEMAKER

This digital camcorder can capture favorite scenes that can be shared with your friends and relatives. The digital video can be viewed via TV or PC.

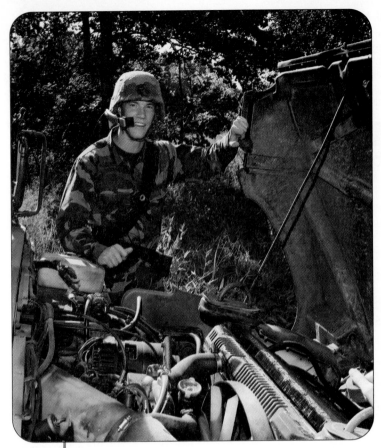

WEARABLE INFORMATION RETRIEVAL AND DATA ENTRY HARDWARE

This wearable PC is worn around the head and on the waist. This U.S. Army mechanic enters data and retrieves information in a hands-free environment, eliminating the need to carry maintenance manuals during field maneuvers.

Courtesy of Xybernaut

uploaded to a PC for digital video editing. Digital video is edited easily, that is, parts can be deleted, moved, or copied to meet application needs. Digital camcorders offer greater portability and the quality of the video is higher than that of desktop cameras, but so is the price ($500 to $1,000).

Another way to capture video is to use a standard analog camcorder or VCR in conjunction with a *video capture card*, an expansion card that enables full-motion color video with audio to be captured and stored on disk. Simply plug the cable from the camera or VCR into the expansion card and hit the record or play button. The analog signal is sent to the video capture card where it is digitized for viewing, editing, and storage.

HANDHELD AND WEARABLE DATA ENTRY DEVICES

Handheld and wearable computers, introduced in Chapter 1, frequently are used as data entry devices (see Figure 5-29). Some data entry tasks still require the use of some keystrokes and are performed best on handheld data entry devices. The typical *handheld data entry device*, which is actually a small computer, has the following:

- A limited external keyboard or a soft keyboard (displayed on a touch-sensitive screen)
- A small display that may be touch sensitive
- Some kind of storage capability for the data, usually solid-state nonvolatile flash memory
- A scanning device, capable of optical character recognition

After the data have been entered, the portable data entry device is linked with a central computer, and data are *uploaded* for processing. Although most handheld data entry devices have these or similar characteristics, new innovations keep this type of handheld input device in a continual state of evolution (see Figure 5-30).

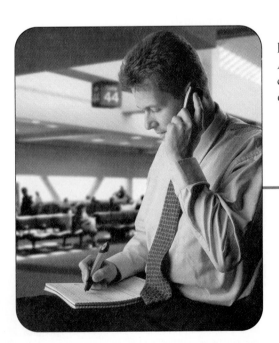

A NEW ERA FOR BALL POINT PENS

With the Logitech io pen, write down whatever you want—up to 40 pages at a time. When you place your pen into its cradle, your drawings, handwritten notes, or whatever you enter on the paper is digitized and transferred to your PC. The images can be integrated with such applications as Microsoft Outlook.

Courtesy of Logitech

Stock clerks in department stores routinely use handheld devices to collect and enter reorder data. As clerks visually check the inventory level, they identify the items that need to be restocked. They first scan the price tag (which identifies the item), and then enter the number to be ordered on the keyboard.

5-4 OUTPUT DEVICES

Output devices translate bits and bytes into a form we can understand. There are many output devices, including monitors, printers, plotters, multimedia projectors, and voice-response systems, all presented in this section.

> ### Why this section is important to you.
>
> There are hundreds of output devices that provide hard copy output, video, and audio, all with different features and price tags. It's up to you to determine how big, clear, fast, or loud you want these devices to be. Familiarizing yourself with the options should help you get exactly those devices that meet your personal computing output needs.

MONITORS

Monitors are amazing in that their gray surfaces can spring to life as an artist's drawing, an engineer's design, an author's novel, and even a virtual world. Monitors come in all shapes and sizes to meet a variety of application needs (see Figure 5-31). The primary descriptors for modern monitors are the following:

- Technology
- Graphics adapter (the electronic link between the processor and the monitor)
- Size (viewable area)
- Resolution (detail of the display)

Technology: CRT and Flat-Panel

The basic technology employed in the bulky, boxy **CRT monitors** that you see used with most desktop personal computers has been around since the 1940s. These monitors offer excellent resolution at a very competitive price. However, their footprint, the amount of space they take up on a desk, remains a user concern. The alternative, the **flat-panel monitor**, which is found on all notebook PCs and with many modern desktop PCs, has a much smaller footprint. Some of the space-saving flat-panel monitors are less than 1/4-inch thick. The flat-panel monitor is becoming an increasingly viable option for the PC user as the price continues to drop toward that of the CRT. You must still pay a premium to save desk space and energy, as much as two to three times the cost per unit of viewing area. It is inevitable that the space-saving, energy-saving flat-panel displays will eventually displace the traditional CRT-type monitors for desktop PCs.

FIGURE 5–31 MONITORS

46-INCH TFT LCD PANEL DISPLAY

This 46-inch TFT LCD panel offers 1280 by 720 resolution and a 170 viewing angle in all directions.

Courtesy of Samsung Electronics Co., Ltd.

DURABLE MONITORS

In video arcades, the action takes place on large, durable monitors.

Photo courtesy of Intel Corporation

FLAT-PANEL MONITORS

Flat-panel LCD monitors may be the wave of the future for desktop PCs.

Photo courtesy of Intel Corporation

MULTIPLE-MONITOR ENVIRONMENTS

Monitors are an integral component of virtually all computer-based applications, including video editing. This one-person studio employs a variety of high-resolution CRT and flat-panel monitors.

Photo courtesy of Hewlett-Packard Company

TOUCH SCREEN MONITORS

A growing number of ATMs (shown here) and public information kiosks use touch screen monitors with input/output capabilities.

Courtesy of Diebold, Incorporated

WEARABLE MONITORS

This tiny wearable monitor is worn on a wireless headset and linked to a wearable PC, and lets this pipe fitter view a schematic of the lattice work of pipes at an oil refinery.

Courtesy of Xybernaut

Flat-panel monitors use a variety of technologies, the most common being *LCD* (liquid crystal display). LCD monitors are *active matrix* or *passive matrix*. Active matrix, which has the more brilliant display, also is known as TFT (thin film transistor) LCD monitors. Millions of transistors are needed for TFT LCD monitors. Color monitors need three transistors for each pixel: one each for red, green, and blue. Active matrix LCD displays are more expensive than passive matrix displays; therefore, these displays are usually associated with the better desktop monitors and notebook PCs.

Graphics Adapters

The **graphics adapter** is the device controller for the monitor. Some are built into the motherboard. On desktop PCs, graphics adapters usually are inserted into an *AGP bus* expansion slot on the motherboard. The monitor cable is plugged into the graphics adapter board to link the monitor with the processor. All display signals en route to the monitor pass through the graphics adapter, where the digital signals are converted to signals compatible with the monitor's display capabilities.

Most existing graphics adapters have their own RAM, called **video RAM** or **VRAM**, whereby they prepare monitor-bound images for display. The size of the video RAM is important in that it determines the number of possible colors and resolution of the display, as well as the speed at which signals can be sent to the monitor. Gamers, those who do video editing, and others who place extreme demands on graphics adapters will want to upgrade the standard graphics adapter to one with enough VRAM to handle heavy video demands.

The better graphics adapters enable *dual monitor* support; that is, two monitors can be connected to a single PC. Dual monitor support effectively expands the viewing area by an additional display. The mouse pointer and application windows can be moved seamlessly between the two displays. An application window, perhaps a wide spreadsheet, can be expanded into an adjacent screen. The use of dual monitors is popular with gamers, graphics designers, video editors, accountants, engineers, and others who routinely require extra viewing area or switch between a variety of open applications.

Monitor Size

Display screens vary in size, the viewing area, from 5 to 60 inches (measured diagonally). The monitor size for newly purchased desktop PCs has inched up from 14 inches to 17 inches and is now moving toward 19 inches. If your applications demand a large viewing area or you routinely switch between a variety of open programs, you might want to consider a 20-plus inch monitor or a dual monitor set up. The larger displays, 30 inches and up, usually are designed for viewing by two or more people.

Monitor Resolution

Monitors vary in their quality of output, or *resolution*. Resolution depends on:

- The number of pixels that can be displayed
- The number of bits used to represent each pixel
- The dot pitch of the monitor

A *pixel*, short for *picture element* (see Figure 5-32), is an addressable point on the screen, a point to which light can be directed under program control. Every computer-generated image is composed of a grid of pixels in which the pixels are so close they appear to be connected. The typical monitor is set to operate with a *screen area* of 786,432 addressable points in 1024 columns by 768 rows; however, most can have screen area up to 2000 by 1600. This setting has over three million addressable points. The higher the number of pixels, the more information you can display on your screen. Use a magnifying glass to examine the pixels and observe the pixel grid on your computer's monitor.

Each pixel can be assigned a color or, for monochrome monitors, a shade of gray. **Gray scales** refer to the number of shades of a color that can be shown on a monochrome monitor's screen. Most color monitors mix red, green, and blue to achieve a spectrum of colors,

Output Devices

- Monitors
  - CRT
  - Flat-panel
  - Touch screen (input and output)
  - Wearable display
- Printers
  - Laser (page) printers
  - Ink-jet printers
  - Large-format ink-jet printers (plotters)
  - All-in-one multi-function devices (print, fax, scan, and copy)
- LCD projectors (screen image projection for groups)
- Sound systems (speakers and sound card)
- Voice-response systems
  - Recorded voice
  - Speech synthesis

FIGURE 5-32

PIXELS

This photo of children enjoying a snow day off from school illustrates how computers use picture elements, or pixels, arranged in rows and columns to portray digital images. In the inset image, the pixels are so close together they portray continuous color.

and are called **RGB monitors.** One of the user options is the number of bits used to display each pixel, sometimes referred to as **color depth.** Differences in color depth are illustrated in Figure 5-33. In 8-bit color mode, 256 colors are possible ($2^8 = 256$). The 16-bit mode *high-color* mode yields 65,536 colors. *True color* options, either 24-bit or 32-bit mode, provide photo-quality viewing with over 16 million colors. There is a trade-off between the color depth being used and system performance. Greater depth of color demands more of the processor, leaving less capacity for other processing tasks.

Its **dot pitch,** or the distance between the centers of adjacent pixels, also affects a monitor's resolution—the lower the dot pitch number, the greater the number of pixels in the display. Any dot pitch equal to or less than .28 mm (millimeters) provides a sharp image. A dot pitch of .25 is even better, enabling 10,000 pixels per square inch.

Touch Screen Monitors

A special input/output version of the monitor is the touch screen monitor. **Touch screen monitors** have pressure-sensitive overlays that can detect pressure and the exact location of that pressure. Users simply touch the desired icon or menu item with their finger. Interactive touch screen systems are installed in shopping centers, zoos, airports, grocery stores, post offices, and many other public locations.

LCD PROJECTORS

Screen images can be displayed on a monitor or they can be projected onto a large screen to be viewed by a group of people or an audience with the aid of a **LCD projector** (see Figure 5-34). The need for overhead transparencies and 35-mm slides is beginning to fade as presenters discover the ease with which they can create dynamic multimedia presentations, then present them with LCD projectors. LCD projectors use their own built-in lens and light source to project the image on the screen.

LCD projectors are expensive, costing as much as a quality PC. Because of their high cost, they are considered business-oriented hardware. The price, however, continues to drop, and we can expect LCD projectors to eventually become a consumer item. It won't belong before we at home can splash games, DVD movies, and whatever else is on our monitor across the living room wall.

PRINTERS

There is a printer to meet the hard copy output requirements of any individual or company, and almost any combination of features can be obtained (see Figure 5-35)—size (some weigh less than a pound), speed, quality of output, color requirements, and even noise level. Printers sell for as little as a pair of shoes or as much as a house. Think about these considerations as you read about various printer options. Keep in mind that additional features, such as two-sided printing, and each increment in speed and quality of output add to the cost of the printer. The most popular technologies for PC-based printers are *laser* and *ink-jet*.

Laser Printers

Nonimpact **laser printers** use laser, LED (*light-emitting diode*), LCS (*liquid crystal shutter*), and other laser-like technologies to achieve high-speed hard copy output by printing *a page at a time*. The operation of laser printers, sometimes called *page printers*, is illustrated in Figure 5-36. Most of the laser printers in use print shades of gray; however, color laser printers are becoming increasingly popular as their price continues to drop. Economically priced laser printers have become the standard for office printing on a local area network. These printers can run through up to six feet of paper during a business day.

The resolution (quality of output) of the low-end desktop page printer is 600 *dpi* (dots per inch). High-end desktop page printers are capable of at least 1200 dpi. The dpi qualifier refers to the number of dots that can be printed per linear inch, horizontally or vertically. That is, a 600-dpi printer is capable of printing 360,000 (600 times 600) dots per square inch.

Ink-Jet Printers

To the naked eye, there is little difference between the print quality of nonimpact **ink-jet printers** and laser printers, but they print in very different ways. The ink-jet printer has a print head that moves back and forth across the paper to write text and create the image (see Figure 5-37). Several independently controlled injection chambers squirt ink droplets on the paper.

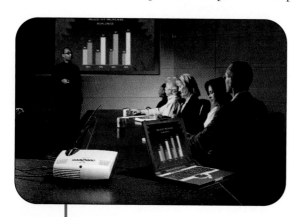

FIGURE 5–34

LCD PROJECTORS

LCD projectors are used in conjunction with presentation software, such as Microsoft PowerPoint, and notebook PCs.

Photo courtesy of Hewlett-Packard Company

FIGURE 5-33 COLOR DEPTH

The same Niagara Falls image is shown at three levels of color depth: 8 bit with 256 (2^8) possible colors, 16-bit *high color* with 65,536 (2^{16}) possible colors, and 32-bit *true color* with over 4 billion (2^{32}) possible colors.

FIGURE 5-35 PRINTERS

INK-JET PRINTER

During a break in the competition, Miss America Pageant contestants Casey Preslar, Miss Oklahoma; Morgan O'Murray, Miss Colorado; and Stephanie Moore, Miss Iowa, look over photographs printed on this high-resolution ink-jet printer.

Courtesy of Epson America, Inc. Photo by Bruce Boyajian

LASER PRINTER

Laser printers, such as this, often are on a local area network and service the printing needs of all people on the LAN.

Photos courtesy of Hewlett-Packard Company

LARGE-FORMAT PRINTERS

Typical applications for this large-format ink-jet printer include point-of-sale displays, billboards, banners, backlit signs, backdrops for photography or video, and trade show graphics.

Courtesy of Xerox Corporation

IT'S A FAX, A PRINTER, A COPIER, AND A SCANNER

This compact and lightweight all-in-one multifunction device lets road warriors take the office with them.

Photo courtesy of RCA

SPECIAL-FUNCTION PRINTERS

There is a printer for every job. This printer prints wristbands for hospital patients. The wristbands include bar-coded patient information that can be read with wand scanners.

Courtesy of Diebold, Incorporated

ENTERPRISE PRINTERS

Enterprise printers are designed for high-volume printing (telephone bills, financial statements, insurance coverage summaries, and so on). This IBM printer can print over 400 miles of cut sheet paper per month at 600 dpi resolution.

Courtesy of International Business Machines Corporation. Unauthorized use not permitted.

FIGURE 5-36   **LASER PRINTER OPERATION**

(A) Prior to printing, a laser printer applies an electrostatic charge to a drum. Then the laser beam paths to the drum are altered by a spinning multisided mirror. The reflected beams selectively remove the electrostatic charge from the drum.

(B) Toner is deposited on those portions of the drum that were affected by the laser beams. The drum is rotated and the toner is fused to the paper to create the image.

A

Prior to printing, a laser printer applies an electrostatic charge to a drum. Then laser beam paths to the drum are altered by a spinning multisided mirror. The reflected beams selectively remove the electrostatic charge from the drum.

B

Toner is deposited on those portions of the drum that were affected by the laser beams. The drum is rotated and the toner is fused to the paper to create the image.

The droplets, which dry instantly as dots, form the letters and images. Resolutions for the typical ink-jet printer are about that of laser printers, 1200 dpi for regular black and white printing and up to 4800 dpi for color printing on premium photo paper.

Large-Format Ink-Jet Printers

Laser and ink-jet are capable of producing page-size graphic output, but are limited in their ability to generate large-scale, high-quality, perfectly proportioned graphic output, such as a blueprints and commercial posters. **Large-format ink-jet printers,** also called **plotters,** use ink-jet technology to print on roll-feed paper up to 4 feet wide and 50 feet in length (see Figure 5-35).

The All-in-One Device: Print, Fax, Scan, and Copy

Traditionally, businesses and individuals with home offices have purchased separate machines to handle printing, facsimile (fax), scanning, and copying (duplicating). The considerable overlap in the technologies used in these machines has enabled manufacturers to create **all-in-one multifunction devices** that perform all of these functions (see Figure 5-35), which include both input and output. These multifunction devices are popular in the small office/home office environments and in other settings where the volume for any of their functions is relatively low. The laser all-in-one peripheral is faster and more expensive than the ink-jet all-in-one.

You can easily pay in excess of $1,000 for a printer, a scanner, a copier, and a fax machine. Many people with low volume needs are choosing the all-in-one device for 20 to 40% of the cost of separate peripherals. It's an easy choice when you consider that there is relatively little loss of functionality when compared to separate devices. The popularity of the all-in-one device has exploded since the print/scan/copy quality and the speeds of the all-in-one are

PERSONAL COMPUTING
What Input/Output Peripheral Devices Do You Need?

The I/O peripherals you select depend on your *specific needs, usage volumes,* and the *amount of money you are willing to spend.* Each increment in expenditure gets you a device that is faster, bigger, more durable, and/or provides higher quality I/O. A good mix of peripheral devices would include these devices: an all-in-one multifunction device (print, scan, fax, and copy), a *quality* keyboard and mouse (good ones last longer), a 17-inch monitor (preferably a 19-inch), surround-sound speakers, a *quality* headset with a mike (for speech recognition), and a digital Web camera (for videophone).

THE CRYSTAL BALL
The Paperless Society

Forecasters have been predicting a movement to a paperless society for 30 years. It hasn't happened. However, the forces of the economy have given this latent trend new life. The cost of producing and handling paper, whether it is a utility bill, a college textbook, or a company manual, is becoming prohibitive. Adding fuel to the trend, an increasingly IT-competent population is demanding quick and easy access to information in electronic documents. Businesses and government agencies are providing incentives for customers to opt for electronic alternatives to paper. Finally, the paperless society is on the horizon.

FIGURE 5-37 INK-JET PRINTER OPERATION

(A) Ink-jet printers use interchangeable cartridges with up to 100 nozzles for each of the four colors. Frequently, black has its own cartridge (left cartridge), whereas the other colors share a separate cartridge (right cartridge). Tiny droplets of ink, about one millionth the volume of a drop of water, in blue, red, yellow, or black, are positioned with great precision on the paper to form characters and images. The droplets, which are mixed to form a wide range of possible colors, are squirted from a nozzle less than the width of a human hair.

(B) Movement of the print heads and paper are coordinated under program control to squirt the dots to form the text and images. Several methods are used to squirt the droplets onto the paper. One method involves superheating ink in a tiny chamber such that it boils and the pressure forces droplets out the nozzle. The chamber cools, ink flows into the chamber, and a process is repeated every few millionths of a second. The dots of color are overlapped to increase the density and, therefore, the quality of the image.

A
Ink-jet printers use interchangeable cartridges with up to 100 nozzles for each of the four colors. Frequently, black has its own cartridge (left cartridge), whereas the other colors share a separate cartridge (right cartridge). Tiny droplets of ink, about one millionth the volume of a drop of water, in either blue, red, yellow, or black, are positioned with great precision on the paper to form characters and images. The droplets, which are mixed to form a wide range of possible colors, are squirted from a nozzle less than the width of a human hair.

B
Movement of the print heads and paper are coordinated under program control to squirt the dots to form the text and images. Several methods are used to squirt the droplets onto the paper. One method involves superheating ink in a tiny chamber such that it boils and the pressure forces droplets out the nozzle. The chamber cools, ink flows into the chamber, and a process is repeated every few millionths of a second. The dots of color are overlapped to increase the density and, therefore, the quality of the image.

now comparable to that of the separate devices. The pros and cons of laser, ink-jet, and all-in-one multifunction devices are summarized in Figure 5-38.

SOUND SYSTEMS

For the first decade of personal computing, small, tinny-sounding speakers came with PCs, primarily to "beep" users when an operation was completed or interaction was needed. Today we watch DVD movies, listen to CDs and MP3 music, play games, and do multimedia presentations on our PCs.

The two parts of a PC's sound systems are the *sound card* and the *speaker system*. As with any sound system, these components can be purchased at various levels of quality. Speaker and sound card capabilities must be compatible; that is, a high-end speaker system requires a high-end sound card. Sound systems vary from a couple of small speakers embedded in notebook PCs to sophisticated sound systems that provide 6.1 surround sound with seven channels of audio. The 6.1 sound systems, which have seven speakers (3 front, 3 rear, and a subwoofer), can provide thunderous Dolby Digital Surround audio and a true cinematic experience.

VOICE-RESPONSE SYSTEMS

Anyone who has used a telephone has heard "If you wish to speak to customer service, press 1. If you wish to speak to…" You may have driven a car that advised you to "fasten your seat belt." These are examples of talking computers that use output from a

FIGURE 5-38 **PRINTER SUMMARY**

	Pros	Cons	Outlook
Page/laser printers	• High-resolution output • Fast (up to 32 ppm) • Quiet • Low cost per page	• High purchase price • Cut sheet only	• High-speed, high-quality page printers will remain the mainstay of office printing for the foreseeable future.
Ink-jet printers	• High-resolution output • Quiet • Small footprint • Energy-efficient	• Higher cost per page than laser • Slower than laser (up to 20 ppm) • Cut sheet only • High cost of print cartridges	• Ink-jet printers will remain the choice for any environment, home or office, with low-volume printing needs.
All-in-one (multifunction) printers	• Can function as a printer, a scanner, a copier, and a fax machine • Get four functions for the price of 1 or 2 • Functional specifications close to separate devices (output quality, speed, and so on)	• Can handle only one function at a time • Larger footprint than a comparable printer	• The all-in-one printer has emerged as the choice in the home or home office with copier, scanner, and fax needs, too.

voice-response system. A **voice-response system** is a device that enables output in the form of user-recorded words, phrases, music, alarms, and so on. There are two types of voice-response systems: One uses a *reproduction* of a human voice and other sounds, and the other uses speech synthesis.

In the first type of voice-response system, the actual analog recordings of sounds are converted into digital data, then permanently stored on disk or in a memory chip. When output occurs, a particular sound is routed to a speaker. Sound chips are mass-produced for specific applications, such as output for automatic teller machines, microwave ovens, smoke detectors, elevators, alarm clocks, automobile warning systems, video games, and vending machines, to mention only a few. When sounds are stored on disk, the user has the flexibility to update them to meet changing application needs.

Speech synthesis systems convert raw data into electronically produced speech. All you need to produce speech on a PC are a sound expansion card, speakers (or headset), and appropriate software. *Text-to-speech software* often is packaged with speech recognition software and produces speech by combining phonemes (from 50 to 60 basic sound units) to create and output words.

Despite limitations such as limited vocal inflections and phrasing, the number of speech synthesizer applications is growing. For example, a visually impaired person can use the speech synthesizer to translate printed words into spoken words. Some people use their notebook PCs to "read" their e-books to them. Translation systems offer one of the most interesting applications for speech synthesizers and speech-recognition devices. Researchers are making progress toward enabling conversations among people who are speaking different languages.

1   Ink-jet printers are nonimpact printers. (T/F)
2   The passive matrix LCD monitor provides a more brilliant display than those with active matrix technology. (T/F)
3   What type of printer would most likely be found in a busy office: (a) laser printer, (b) ink-jet printer, (c) multifunction duplicator system, or (d) glove box printer?
4   What technology converts raw data into electronically produced speech: (a) voice response, (b) reproduction analysis, (c) speech synthesis, or (d) sound duping?
5   All other things being equal on a monitor, which dot pitch would yield the best resolution: (a) .24 dot pitch, (b) .26 dot pitch, (c) .28 dot pitch, or (d) .31 dot pitch?

SELF-CHECK
SECTION

5-1 MAGNETIC DISK STORAGE

Data and programs are stored permanently in mass storage. Magnetic disk drives are popular devices for mass storage. Magnetic tape drives are used mostly for backup capability and archival storage. Optical laser disc technology continues to emerge as a mass storage medium.

Data are retrieved and manipulated either sequentially or randomly. There are two types of magnetic disks: interchangeable disks and fixed disks. Magnetic disk drives enable random- and sequential-processing capabilities.

Popular types of interchangeable disks include the 3.5-inch floppy disk, the 120-MB SuperDisk, and the 100-, 250-, or 750-MB Zip disk. The floppy disk and the SuperDisk are the same size but have different disk densities.

There are two types of hard disks—those that are permanently installed and those that are portable. Hard disks contain at least one platter and usually several disk platters stacked on a single rotating spindle. The rotation of a magnetic disk passes all data under or over read/write heads, which are mounted on access arms. The portable hard disk is an external device that is connected easily to any personal computer via a USB port or FireWire port.

The way in which data and programs are stored and accessed is similar for both hard and interchangeable disks. Data are stored via serial representation in concentric tracks on each recording surface. The spacing of tracks is measured in tracks per inch (TPI). In sector organization, the recording surface is divided into pie-shaped sectors, and each sector is assigned a number. Adjacent sectors are combined to form clusters.

Each disk cluster is numbered, and the number of the first cluster in a file comprises the disk address on a particular file. The disk address designates a file's physical location on a disk. A particular cylinder refers to every track with the same number on all recording surfaces.

Some high-performance disk manufacturers employ zoned recording where zones contain a greater number of sectors per track as you move from the innermost zone to the outermost zone.

Each disk used in the Windows environment has a Virtual File Allocation Table (VFAT) in which information about the clusters is stored. Clusters are *chained* together to store file information larger than the capacity of a single cluster. The ScanDisk utility lets you return lost clusters to the available pool of usable clusters.

The defragmentation process rewrites fragmented files into contiguous clusters. A Windows utility program called Disk Defragmenter consolidates files into contiguous clusters.

Before a disk can be used, it must be formatted. Formatting creates *sectors* and *tracks* into which data are stored and establishes an area for the VFAT.

The access time for a magnetic disk is the interval between the instant a computer makes a request for transfer of data from a disk-storage device to RAM and the instant this operation is completed. The data transfer rate is the rate at which data are read from (written to) mass storage to (from) RAM. Disk caching improves system speed.

Virtual memory effectively expands the capacity of RAM through the use of software and hard disk storage.

5-2 OPTICAL LASER DISCS

Optical laser disc storage is capable of storing vast amounts of data. The main categories of optical laser discs are CD, CD-ROM, CD-R, CD-RW, DVD-audio, DVD-video, DVD-ROM, DVD-R, DVD-RAM, DVD+RW, DVD-RW, and DVD±RW.

A CD-ROM is inserted into the CD-ROM drive for processing. Most of the commercially produced read-only CD-ROM discs contain reference material or multimedia applications.

A blank compact disc-recordable (CD-R) disc looks like a CD-ROM and once information is recorded on it, it works like a CD-ROM. CD-RW (CD-ReWritable) allows users to rewrite to the same CD media and "burn" discs, such as audio CDs.

The DVD (digital video disc) looks like the CD and the CD-ROM, but it can store up to about 17 GB. DVD drives can play CD-ROMs and CDs. DVD+R and DVD-R are like CD-R but with the recording density of DVD-ROM. DVD+RW and DVD-RW are like CD-RW, giving us rewritable capabilities for high-capacity DVD technology.

The typical PC will have at least a DVD-ROM drive and possibly another read/write disc drive. Most people who want to burn discs and use optical media for backup and transfer purposes are installing a versatile rewritable combination drive, such as the DVD±RW/CD-RW drive.

The choice of which technologies to choose for a system or an application is often a trade-off between storage capacity, cost (dollars per megabyte), and speed (access time).

5-3 INPUT DEVICES

A variety of input/output (I/O) peripheral devices provides the interface between the computer and us. There are two basic types of keyboards: traditional alphanumeric QWERTY-style keyboards and special-function keyboards, which are designed for specific applications. The mouse and its cousins enable interaction with the operating system's graphical user interface (GUI) and they help us to draw. These devices include the trackball, trackpad, joystick, trackpoint, and digitizer tablet and pen.

The trend in data entry has been toward source-data automation. A variety of scanners reads and interprets information on printed matter and converts it to a format that can be interpreted directly by a computer. Two types of scanners—*contact* and *laser*—read information on labels and various types of documents. Generally, scanners used for source data automation are in three basic categories—

handheld label scanners (called wand scanners), stationary label scanners, and document scanners (which are often used with turnaround documents).

OCR (optical character recognition) is the ability to read printed information into a computer system. Bar codes represent alphanumeric data by varying the size of adjacent vertical lines.

Bar codes, such as UPC, represent alphanumeric data by varying the size of adjacent vertical lines. OCR (optical character recognition) technology permits the reading of coded and text information into a computer system, including reading your handwriting. Two types of OCR or bar code scanners—*contact* and *laser*—read information on labels and various types of documents.

MICR scanning technology is used exclusively by the banking industry. The most popular application for optical mark recognition (OMR) is for grading sense-mark tests.

An image scanner uses laser technology to scan and digitize an image. Image scanners provide input for image processing. Image scanners are of two types: *page* and *hand*.

Magnetic stripes, smart cards, and badges provide input to badge readers.

Speech-recognition systems can be used to enter spoken words by comparing digitized representations of words to similarly formed templates in the computer system's electronic dictionary. Usually, PC-based speech-recognition systems are speaker dependent. Server-based systems that accept words spoken by anyone are speaker dependent.

Digital cameras (digicams) are used to take photos that are represented digitally (already digitized). The desktop digital video camera lets you capture motion video in the area of the PC. The Webcam is a popular application for these cameras. Handheld digital camcorders offer another way to capture video. Use a video capture card to capture video from a standard analog video camera or VCR.

Handheld and wearable data entry devices have a limited external keyboard or a soft keyboard, a small display that may be touch-sensitive, nonvolatile RAM, and often a scanning device.

5-4 OUTPUT DEVICES

Output devices translate bits and bytes into a form we can understand. Common output only devices include monitors, printers, plotters, LCD projectors, sound systems, and voice-response systems.

Monitors are defined in terms of their technology (CRT monitor or flat-panel monitor), graphics adapter (which has video RAM or VRAM), size (viewing area), and resolution (number of pixels, number of bits used to represent each pixel, and dot pitch).

Gray scales are used to refer to the number of shades of a color that can be shown on a monochrome monitor's screen. RGB monitors mix red, green, and blue to achieve a spectrum of colors. One user option is the number of bits used to display each pixel, sometimes referred to as color depth.

Flat-panel monitors are used with notebook PCs and some desktop PCs, many of which use LCD technology. Wearable displays give us freedom of movement. Touch screen monitors permit input as well as output.

The most popular technologies for PC-based printers are laser and ink-jet. Laser printers (page printers) use several technologies to achieve high-speed hard copy output by printing a page at a time. Ink-jet printers have print heads that move back and forth across the paper, squirting ink droplets to write text and create images.

Large-format ink-jet printers, also called plotters, use ink-jet technology to print on roll-feed paper up to four feet wide.

Multifunction all-in-one peripheral devices are available that handle several paper-related tasks: computer-based printing, facsimile (fax), scanning, and copying.

PC sound systems include the speakers, up to seven on seven channels, and the sound card.

Voice-response systems provide recorded or synthesized audio output (via speech synthesis). Text-to-speech software enables you to produce speech on a PC.

KEY TERMS

MATCHING

_____ **1.** fixed disk

_____ **2.** LCD projector

_____ **3.** zoned recording

_____ **4.** disk clusters

_____ **5.** mouse pointer

_____ **6.** DVD+RW

_____ **7.** cylinder

_____ **8.** joystick

_____ **9.** smart card

_____ **10.** all-in-one peripheral device

a chained together

b hard disk

c gaming control

d uses disk space efficiently

e fax, copy, print, and scan

f provides screen image display for groups

g has multiple tracks

h moved with a point-and-draw device

i rewritable optical disc

j embedded processor

CHAPTER SELF-CHECK

TRUE/FALSE

1. Magnetic disks have sequential-access capabilities only. (T/F)

2. The terms hard disk and fixed disk are used interchangeably. (T/F)

3. Both the floppy disk and the SuperDisk disk are the same size but have different disk densities. (T/F)

4. Information on interchangeable disks cannot be stored offline. (T/F)

5. The capacity of clusters is based on a multiple of 521 bytes. (T/F)

6. In a disk drive, the read/write heads are mounted on an access arm. (T/F)

7. Before a disk can be used, it must be formatted. (T/F)

8. The innermost zone has fewer sectors than the outermost zone in zoned recording. (T/F)

9. CD-ROM is a spinoff of audio CD technology. (T/F)

10. Optical laser discs store data in spiraling tracks. (T/F)

11. DVD+RW technology is faster—for read and write—than hard disk storage. (T/F)

12. The primary function of I/O peripherals is to facilitate computer-to-computer data transmission. (T/F)

13. Use the keyboard's numeric keypad for rapid numeric data entry. (T/F)

14. Only those keyboards configured for notebook PCs have function keys. (T/F)

15. Speech-recognition systems can be trained to accept words not in the system's original dictionary. (T/F)

16. Desktop ink-jet printers generate graphs with greater precision than plotters. (T/F)

17. The graphics adapter is the device controller for a high-resolution speech synthesizer. (T/F)

MULTIPLE CHOICE

1. Which of these statements is *not* true: (a) the rotation of a disk passes all data under or over a read/write head; (b) the heads are mounted on access arms; (c) the standard size for PC hard disks (diameter) is 8 inches; (d) a hard disk contains several disk platters stacked on a single rotating spindle?

2. The standard size for common diskettes is: (a) 3.25 inches, (b) 3.5 inches, (c) 3.75 inches, or (d) 5.25 inches.

3. The VFAT is searched by the operating system to find the physical address of the (a) first cluster of the file, (b) read/write head, (c) microprocessor, (d) midsector of the file.

4. What denotes the physical location of a particular file or set of data on a magnetic disk: (a) cylinder, (b) data compression index, (c) CD-R, or (d) disk address?

5. TPI refers to: (a) sector density, (b) cylinder overload, (c) track density, or (d) bps thickness.

6. The disk caching area is: (a) on a floppy disk, (b) in RAM, (c) on a hard disk, or (d) on the monitor's expansion board.

7. In zoned recording, tracks are grouped into: (a) sectors, (b) regions, (c) zones, or (d) partitions.

8. Using disk capacity to expand RAM capacity is called: (a) virtual memory, (b) RAM-expand, (c) actual disk, or (d) mystic RAM.

9. The CD-ROM drive specifications 32X, 40X, or 75X refer to its: (a) speed, (b) diameter, (c) number of platters, or (d) sector groupings.

10. The data transfer rate for an 8X DVD-ROM is about how many MB per second: (a) 3, (b) 6, (c) 11, or (d) 124?

11. Which optical laser disc has the greatest storage capacity: (a) double-sided DVD-ROM, (b) DVD+RW, (c) 75X CD-ROM, or (d) CD-RW?

12. Which of the following is not a point-and-draw device: (a) joystick, (b) document scanner, (c) trackpad, or (c) trackpoint?

13. Banks use which technology to scan checks: (a) OCR, (b) UPC, (c) MICR, or (d) e-commerce?

14. The enhanced version of cards with a magnetic stripe is a(n): (a) badge card, (b) intelligent badge, (c) smart card, or (d) debit card.

15. Which of these is not a type of scanner: (a) document scanner, (b) stationary label scanner, (c) wand scanner, or (d) magnetic scanner?

16. Manipulating and managing scanned images would be considered: (a) image processing, (b) parallel processing, (c) scanner management, or (d) image administration.

17. Which of the following is not true of digital cameras: (a) uses the same film as 35-mm cameras, (b) digitized images are uploaded from the camera, (c) uses flash memory to store images, or (d) can be purchased for as little as $200?

18. Which of these is not one of the capabilities of all-in-one multifunction devices: (a) duplicating, (b) faxing, (c) scanning, or (d) vision input?

19. Which of these does not play a part in determining a monitor's resolution: (a) number of colors mixed within a pixel, (b) number of pixels, (c) number of bits that represent a pixel, or (d) dot pitch?

20. Which of these would not be a pixel density option for monitors: (a) 1024 by 768, (b) 640 by 480, (c) 84 by 123, or (d) 1600 by 1200?

21. Flat-panel monitors always are used in conjunction with which computer systems: (a) server computers, (b) tower PCs, (c) notebook PCs, or (d) desktop PCs?

22. Which of these I/O devices produces hard copy output: (a) monitor, (b) printer, (c) LCD projector, or (d) voice-response system?

23. In text-to-speech technology, speech is produced by combining: (a) firmware, (b) synonyms, (c) phonemes, or (d) digitized templates.

24. Gamers looking to purchase a new PC would pay special attention to the amount of what: (a) gray scales, (b) VRAM, (c) image RAM, or (d) ppm of output?

IT ETHICS AND ISSUES

1. ASSISTIVE TECHNOLOGY IN THE IT WORKPLACE

The Americans with Disabilities Act of 1990 prohibits discrimination that might limit employment or access to public buildings and facilities. Under the law, employers cannot discriminate against any employee who can perform a job's "essential" responsibilities with "reasonable accommodations." Increasingly, these "accommodations" take the form of a personal computer with special input/output peripherals and software, called *assistive technology*. Almost 20,000 assistive technology-based products are available for the disabled. Assistive technology in its many forms has enabled people with disabilities greater freedom to work and live independently.

Discussion: Employers can easily spend from $20,000 to $50,000 on assistive technology for a single disabled employee. What is the payback to the employer? To the disabled employee?

Discussion: Surveys show that employers who provide "assistive technologies" to their employees gain highly motivated and productive workers. Discuss strategies for encouraging managers to invest in assistive technology and hire disabled workers.

2. FILE SHARING

Today's high-capacity hard disk and optical disc storage options enable PC users to storage thousands of huge files, including music and movies. The music industry, which has relied almost exclusively on CD and cassette tape media to market and distribute its products in recent years, is now confronted with millions of music-hungry people who routinely share MP3 files (via the Internet by burning CDs). In the same vein, netizens have begun to share movies, as well (over a half-million a day).

Discussion: In the eyes of the music industry, if you receive an MP3 file containing copyrighted music, then you are receiving stolen goods. Do listeners share this view? Why or why not?

Discussion: Sometimes people attend concerts and tape parts of the concerts, make MP3 files of the music, then send these MP3 files to friends. Is this practice unethical or illegal, or both? Explain.

Discussion: People routinely use digital cameras and illegally tape first-run movies at theaters. They then post the movie file to the Internet. Would you download and view an illegal movie video? Why or why not?

Discussion: Violating copyright laws is punishable by up to five years in prison and a $250,000 fine. Describe what someone would have to do to get the maximum sentence for copyright violations.

Discussion: The upside to MP3 file sharing is that an aspiring artist can place his or her music on the Internet and make it available at little or no charge. Would it be ethical

for an artist to change his or her mind and ask users to pay a fee for music that was offered previously for free?

3. THE SPYCAM

Wireless technology for peripheral devices and the proliferation of small, inexpensive, wireless video cameras has created many new applications for personal computing—some good and many bad. The video cameras can be placed within 100 feet of the host unit and can return clear streaming video images. Moreover, the camera is tiny and is hidden easily from view. You can imagine where pranksters and the lower elements of our society might have placed these cameras. Restrooms, college communal showers, conference rooms, the doctor's office, every room in the house, and so on, are now vulnerable to the spycam.

Discussion: Should those who purchase wireless video cameras be warned of the legal consequences of using this technology to "spy" on people, perhaps by a label similar to those on cigarette packaging? Explain why or why not.

Discussion: What would you do if you had a wireless video camera that could be placed discretely anywhere within 100 feet of your PC?

DISCUSSION AND PROBLEM SOLVING

1. Traditionally, personal computers have had a floppy disk drive. However, some personal computers no longer come with a floppy drive. Is the floppy drive needed anymore? Explain.

2. A program issues a "read" command for data to be retrieved from hard disk. Describe the resulting mechanical movement and the movement of data.

3. What happens during formatting? Why must hard disks and diskettes be formatted?

4. The SuperDisk and Zip disk serve similar purposes on a computer system. The SuperDisk drive is compatible with the traditional floppy diskette, but the Zip disk reads and writes data more rapidly and has a higher capacity. Costs are comparable. Which one would you choose and why?

5. What would determine the frequency with which you would need to defragment your hard drive? Explain.

6. Describe the danger of having too little hard disk capacity allocated to virtual memory. Of having too much.

7. List six content areas that are distributed commercially on CD-ROM (for example, electronic encyclopedias).

8. Describe the potential impact of optical laser disc technology on public and university libraries. On home libraries.

9. Describe at least two applications where CD-RW or DVD+RW would be preferred over a hard disk for storage.

10. The DVD+RW drive also has the capabilities of the CD-RW drive, the "CD burner." Currently the DVD+RW drive is more expensive than the CD-RW drive, but prices are converging. Speculate on when or if DVD+RW will replace CD-RW.

11. With the capability to store digital music, the audio CD has revolutionized the way we play and listen to recorded music. Now music can be downloaded over the Internet and played on PCs, solid-state MP3 players, and other electronic devices. Does this signal the beginning of the end of the audio CD? Explain.

12. The only internal mechanical movement in a typical notebook PC is associated with the disk and optical drives. Someday soon, both may be replaced with solid-state nonvolatile memory. Speculate on how this might change the appearance of notebook PCs and on how we use and what we do with them.

13. Describe two instances during the past 24 hours in which you had indirect communication with a computer; that is, something you did resulted in computer activity.

14. Describe an automated telephone system with which you are familiar that asks you to select options from a series of menus. Discuss the advantages and disadvantages of this system.

15. Name four types of point-and-draw devices. Which one do you think you would prefer? Explain your reasoning.

16. The QWERTY keyboard, which has been the standard on typewriters and keyboards for decades, actually was designed to keep people from typing especially rapidly. Speculate on why built-in inefficiency was a design objective.

17. Today's continuous speech-recognition systems are able to interpret spoken words more accurately when the user talks in phrases. Why would this approach be more accurate than discrete speech where the user speaks one word at a time with a slight separation between words?

18. In the next generation of credit cards, the familiar magnetic stripe probably will be replaced by embedded microprocessors in smart cards. Suggest applications for this capability.

19. Some department stores use handheld label scanners, and others use stationary label scanners to interpret the bar codes printed on the price tags of merchandise. What advantages does one scanner have over the other?

20. Today, literally billions of pages of documentation are maintained in government and corporate file cabinets. Next year, the contents of millions of file cabinets will be digitized via image processing. Briefly describe at least one situation with which you are familiar that is a candidate for image processing. Explain how image processing can improve efficiency at this organization.

21. Describe how your photographic habits might change (or have changed) if you owned a digital camera.

22. Four PCs at a police precinct are networked and currently share a 5 ppm ink-jet printer. The captain has allocated money in the budget to purchase one laser printer (20 ppm) or two more 5 ppm ink-jet printers. Which option would you suggest the precinct choose and why?

23. Describe the input/output characteristics of a workstation/PC that would be desirable for engineers doing computer-aided design (CAD).

24. By purchasing 17-inch low-quality monitors rather than 19-inch high-quality monitors, a large company can save up to $300 per employee on the cost of new PCs. In the long run, however, health and overall efficiency implications of this decision may result in costs that exceed any savings. Explain.

25. In five years, forecasters are predicting flat-panel monitors less than .25-inch thick may be placed everywhere around the home and office. Speculate on how these ultra thin monitors might be used in the home. In the office.

26. Would an all-in-one multifunction device be appropriate in your home or would you prefer purchasing separate devices for the various document-handling functions (duplicating, faxing, printing, and scanning)? Explain your reasoning.

27. Describe the benefits of using a notebook PC in conjunction with an LCD projector during a formal business presentation as opposed to the traditional alternative (transparency acetates and an overhead projector).

28. Some people are calling PC-based speech-recognition software a "killer app." Why?

FOCUS ON PERSONAL COMPUTING

1. *Organizing Your Folders and Files*. The typical user's folder/file structure needs some cleanup. Set up a hierarchical file structure (on paper or on your PC) that includes specific folder categories within general areas of usage. For example, one major folder might be "State University" with subfolders for each semester. Each semester subfolder would have subfolders for your classes and perhaps a miscellaneous folder with subfolders for your extracurricular activities. Rename folders/files as needed.

2. *Hard Disk Maintenance*. If you are an active user and have not defragmented your hard disk, use a disk defragmenter utility and "defrag" your hard disk. Defragmenting the hard disk can substantially improve system performance.

3. *Customizing Preferences for I/O Devices*. Too often, we do not take time to assess and, if needed, adjust I/O features to meet our needs more effectively. Open your Control Panel and open the settings for any I/O device. Familiarize yourself with the device's features and settings and customize them as you see fit. For example, you might prefer the "nature" scheme for the mouse pointer or you might opt for a higher resolution on your display. Examine and customize all input/output devices on your system, including sound and audio devices.

4. *Exploring Available Assistive Technologies*. Modern operating systems provide a minimum level of functionality for people with disabilities. For example, one utility provides visual warnings for system-produced sounds. Another enables the keyboard to perform mouse functions. Search for "accessibility" in the Windows Help and Support Center and learn more about these capabilities. Open and experiment with the Magnifier utility and/or use your system's text-to-speech capabilities. These may not be available with all operating systems or they may need to be installed.

1. The Online Study Guide (multiple choice, true/false, matching, and essay questions)
2. Internet Learning Activities
   - Magnetic Disk
   - Optical Storage
   - Input
   - Output
   - Printers
3. Serendipitous Internet Activities
   - Travel

NETWORKS AND NETWORKING

6

CHAPTER

LEARNING OBJECTIVES

Once you have read and studied this chapter, you will be able to:

- Apply the concept of connectivity to your life (Section 6-1).

- Discuss the function and operation of data communications hardware (Section 6-2).

- Identify alternatives and sources of data transmission services that enable the networking of our world (Section 6-3).

- Understand the various kinds of network topologies and essential local area network concepts and terminology (Section 6-4).

- Recognize the scope and potential of home networking and to grasp related concepts (Section 6-5).

Each day our world is becoming increasingly connected—electronically. If you are not already online, you, too, will eventually be connected. When you are, you can save yourself both time and money by knowing the basics of data communications and networking.

During the first 25 years of the communications era, data communications was an experts-only domain. Now, millions of PC users purchase, install, and maintain their own communications hardware and channels. Usually the hardware is no more involved than a modem and a telephone line. However, this is beginning to change as homes and small offices begin to network multiple PCs and upgrade to broadband (high-speed) Internet connections.

This chapter introduces you to data communications and networking concepts that will prove helpful at home and make you a more informed employee at work. You'll learn about communications-related hardware and be introduced to various delivery alternatives, including transmission options over traditional voice-grade telephone lines, cable TV lines, and wireless alternatives.

6-1 OUR WIRED WORLD

Why this section is important to you.

People who understand information technology trends, such as global connectivity, are better prepared to cope with our increasingly wired society.

As knowledge workers, we need ready access to information. In the present competitive environment, we cannot rely solely on verbal communication to get that information. For example, corporate presidents cannot wait until the Monday morning staff meeting to find out whether production is meeting demand. We rely on *computer networks* to retrieve and share information quickly. Of course, we will continue to interact in a variety of ways with our coworkers, but computer networks simply enhance the efficiency and effectiveness of that interaction.

It's official: We now live in a weird, wild, wired world where computer networks are networked to one another and we are never far from a computer network (see Figure 6-1). This ever-expanding worldwide network of computers, when combined with digital convergence, is enabling our society to take one giant leap into the future. This chapter is devoted to concepts relating to computer networks and communications technology. Once you have a grasp of this technology, you will find it easier to understand the many and varied applications of networks.

CONNECTIVITY

To realize the potential of a universe of digital information, the business and computer communities are continually seeking ways to interface, or connect, a diverse set of hardware, software, and databases. This increased level of connectivity brings people from as close as the next room and as far as the other side of the world closer together. **Connectivity** pertains to the degree to which hardware devices, software, and databases can be functionally linked to one another. Connectivity also means that:

THE CRYSTAL BALL
24/7 Connectivity

Some will embrace it and others will refuse it, but around-the-clock connectivity is on the horizon. Advances in wireless technology and the trend to digital conversion have set the stage for a world in which we are linked 24/7 to each other, myriad devices, thousands of services, and an Internet's worth of information. Within this decade, most of us will carry an amazing multifunction device that will fit easily in a pocket. The yet-unnamed device will serve as an Internet-ready computer, a telephone, a complete entertainment center (on-demand TV and music), an electronic billfold, and a remote-control for dozens of devices (home/office air-conditioning, lawn sprinklers, swimming pool heaters, lighting, and so on).

FIGURE 6-1 **YESTERDAY AND TODAY**
When you contrast businesses of today with those of yesterday, one thing sticks out—communications and networking. Today, service station customers can pay at the pump via credit card or via a wireless "billfold."
Photo courtesy of Phillips Petroleum Company

- A marketing manager can use a PC to access information in the finance department's database.
- A network of PCs can route output to a shared page printer.
- A manufacturer's server computer can communicate with a supplier's server computer.
- You can send your holiday newsletter via e-mail.
- The appliances, including PCs, in your home can be networked.

Connectivity is implemented in degrees. We can expect to become increasingly connected to computers and information both at work and at home during the coming years. Thirty years ago, there were tens of thousands of computers. Today, there are hundreds of *millions* of them! Plus, we have the Internet! Our challenge is to connect them.

THE ERA OF COOPERATIVE PROCESSING

We are living in an era of *cooperative processing*. Companies have recognized that they must cooperate internally to take full advantage of company resources, and that they must cooperate externally with one another to compete effectively in a world market. To promote internal cooperation, businesses are setting up intracompany networking (see Figure 6-2). **Intracompany networking** allows people in, say, the sales department to know the latest information from the production department. Companies cooperate externally with customers and other companies via **intercompany networking** (see Figure 6-2).

Increasingly, business between companies is being moved to the Internet, often via an intranet. An **intranet** is essentially a closed or private version of the Internet that is based on TCP/IP protocols (see Figure 6-3). Employees use the same browser that they use for the Internet, so an intranet looks and feels like the Internet. In fact, employees can browse seamlessly between their intranet and the Internet. However, it is accessible only by those people within the company. For most organizations, building an intranet is relatively easy because

FIGURE 6–2 **INTRACOMPANY AND INTERCOMPANY NETWORKING**

FIGURE 6–3

THE INTERNET, INTRANETS, EXTRANETS, AND VPNS

This figure illustrates how VPNs use tunneling technology and the Internet. The graphical communications overview also shows the relationships between TCP/IP-based intranets and extranets, both with and without Internet access.

the typical organization provides Internet service and, therefore, has everything in place for the intranet—servers, support for TCP/IP, browser software, local area networks (LANs), and so on. A wealth of company information is made available on intranets, including daily announcements, the sales/marketing database, the menu for the company cafeteria, human resources information (benefits, job openings, and so on), corporate policies, and so on.

An **extranet** is simply an extension of an intranet such that it is partially accessible to authorized outsiders, such as customers and suppliers (see Figure 6-3). In practice, an extranet is two or more overlapping intranets. Invoices, orders, and many other intercompany transactions can be transmitted via an extranet. For example, at major retail chains, such as Wal-Mart, over 90% of all orders are processed directly—business to business—often via an extranet.

For decades, companies have leased communications lines from telecommunications companies to create their own private networks that link offices in remote locations, suppliers, and, sometimes, customers. This type of private network, however, is an expensive proposition, primarily because of the cost of leasing lines. An alternative is the **virtual private network,** or **VPN,** which has evolved as a less expensive alternative to the private network. The cost savings for VPNs is realized because its channels for communications are over a public infrastructure—the Internet (see Figure 6-3). The VPN employs encryption and other security measures to ensure that communications are not intercepted and that only authorized users are allowed access to the network. VPN uses tunneling technology. In **tunneling,** one network uses the channels of another network to send its data. In the case of VPNs, transmissions are "tunneled" through the Internet. VPNs have been a boon to companies whose policies encourage telecommuting and want knowledge workers on the go to stay connected.

The phenomenal growth of the use of PCs in the home is causing companies to expand their information system capabilities to allow linkages with home and portable PCs, primarily via the Internet. This form of cooperative processing increases system efficiency while lowering costs. For example, in many banks, services have been extended to home PC owners in the form of online banking. Subscribers to an online banking service use their personal computers as terminals linked to the bank's server computer system, either directly or via the Internet, to pay bills, transfer funds, and ask about account status.

1 The degree to which hardware devices, software, and databases can be functionally linked to one another is called connectivity. (T/F)

2 With intracompany networking, companies cooperate externally with customers and other companies. (T/F)

3 VPN uses what type of technology for its channels: (a) conduit, (b) tunneling, (c) canals, or (d) subway?

4 An intranet is a closed and private version of: (a) an extranet, (b) the Internet, (c) connectivity, or (d) a VPN.

SELF-CHECK

SECTION

6-2 DATA COMMUNICATIONS HARDWARE

Data communications, or **telecommunications,** is the electronic collection and distribution of information between two points. Information can appear in a variety of formats—numeric data, text, voice, still pictures, graphics, and video. As we have already seen, raw information must be digitized before we can input it into a computer. For example, numerical data and text might be translated into their corresponding ASCII codes. Once the digitized information has been entered into a computer, that computer can then transfer the information to other computers connected over a network. Ultimately, all forms of digitized information are transmitted over the transmission media (for example, fiber optic cable) as a series of binary bits (1s and 0s).

Data communications hardware is used to transmit digital information between terminals and computers or between computers and other computers. With the trend toward digital convergence, the number and variety of network hardware components continue to evolve, with new devices being introduced almost monthly. Because of this, networks are a lot like snowflakes—no two are alike. We will examine some of the visible devices, starting with the foundation components of any network, the *client* and *server computers.* We will also discuss common support devices, such as the various types of *modems, routers, gateways,* and *network interface cards.* These special-function devices route, convert, and format/reformat bits and bytes traveling along communications links.

CLIENT AND SERVER COMPUTERS

The essential elements in any network are the computers. One or more central computers, called *server computers,* manage the resources on a network and perform a variety of functions for the other computers on the network, called *client computers.* The client computers, which usually are PCs or workstations, are linked to the server computer, which can be anything from a PC to a supercomputer, to form the network. In **client/server computing,** a server computer supports many client computers (see Figure 6-4) A server computer performs a variety of functions for its client computers, such as maintenance of the enterprise

THE CRYSTAL BALL

Fax on the Brink of Extinction

Facsimile or fax was invented in 1842, by the Scotsman Alexander Bain; however, the first wire photo was sent from Cleveland to New York in 1924. By the mid-1950s, the fax had become a mainstream business tool and its use has increased steadily until now. Everything the fax does can be done more quickly, more efficiently, and at less cost within the context of online systems, image processing, networking, and the Internet. As people familiarize themselves with the alternatives, look for fax machines to take their place alongside the typewriter and other obsolete offline business equipment.

FIGURE 6-4

HARDWARE COMPONENTS IN DATA COMMUNICATIONS

Shown here are some of the devices that handle the movement of data in a computer network. Also in the figure, electrical digital signals are modulated (via a modem) into analog signals for transmission over telephone lines and then demodulated for processing at the destination.

database. The client computer, which typically is a PC or a workstation, requests printing, remote communication, or another type of service from one or more server computers.

Client/server environments with heavy traffic, such as America Online or a medium to large company, might use a **proxy server computer.** This computer sits between the client PC and a normal server, handling many client requests and routing only those requests that it cannot handle to the real server. The proxy server improves overall performance by reducing the number of tasks handled by the real server. Proxy servers also are used as filters to limit outside access to the server and to limit employee access to specific Web sites.

THE STANDARD TELEPHONE-LINK MODEM

Even if your PC is not connected to a corporate local area network with a digital line to cyberspace, you can establish a communications link between it and any remote computer system in the world, assuming you have the authorization to do so. However, you must first have ready access to a *telephone line,* and your PC must be equipped with a *modem.*

Telephone lines were designed to carry *analog signals* for voice communication, not the binary *digital signals* (1s and 0s) needed for computer-based data communication. The modem (modulator-demodulator) converts (modulates) *digital* signals into *analog* signals so data can be transmitted over telephone lines (see Figure 6-4). Upon reaching their destination, these analog tone signals are demodulated into computer-compatible digital signals for processing. A modem is always required for two computers to communicate over a telephone line. It is not needed when the PC is wired directly to a computer network (for example, cabling between embedded network interface cards) or another PC (for example, via USB cables).

Modems for PCs and terminals are *internal* and *external*. Most PCs have internal modems; that is, the modem is on an optional add-on circuit board that is simply plugged into an empty expansion slot in the PC's motherboard. On notebooks, modems are on interchangeable PC cards or built into the motherboard. The external modem is located outside the PC's system unit, as illustrated in Figure 6-4, and is connected to a USB port. To make the connection with a telephone line and either type of modem, you simply plug the telephone line into the modem just as you would when connecting the line to a telephone.

The typical modem is a *voice/data/fax modem*. Besides the data communications capabilities, it allows you to make telephone calls through your PC and modem hookup (using a microphone, speakers, and/or a headset). The fax feature enables a PC to simulate a *fax machine*. Instead of sending a document to a printer, you simply send it to the fax modem along with a destination fax number.

OTHER MODEMS

Traditional modems are largely unused by those people with broadband Internet access. Instead, they use a cable modem, a DSL modem, or a satellite modem. Typically, these broadband modems are external and connect to the PC via a USB port; however, they may be installed in an expansion slot or linked via a network interface card, too.

The *cable modem* enables Internet access over cable TV lines. It is similar to the telephone modem, but instead of modulating the PC's digital signals to analog tone signals, it modulates the digital signals to radio-frequency (RF) carrier signals. The RF carrier signals are demodulated by another cable modem to digital information upon arrival at their destination.

The *DSL modem* isn't actually a modem. It is a DSL transceiver, but tradition calls for the "modem" designation. Regardless of what it is called, it provides the connection between the user's computer or network and the DSL line. All DSL signals are routed to a telephone company's *DSLAM* (Digital Subscriber Line Access Multiplexor). The DSLAM combines outbound DSL signals into a very-high speed Internet connection, usually a fiber-optic cable. It also separates the inbound signals for routing to DSL customers.

A *satellite modem* is a device that enables uplink and downlink from a satellite. A satellite modem is actually two modems, one for the uplink signal conversion and one for the downlink signal conversion.

NETWORK INTERFACE CARDS

A *network interface card* (NIC), which we introduced in Chapter 4, "Inside the Computer," is an add-on board or PC card (for notebooks) that enables and controls the exchange of data between PCs in a LAN. NICs also are called *network cards* and *network adapters*. Each PC in the LANs in Figure 6-4 must be equipped with a NIC. The cables or wireless transceivers that link the PCs are connected physically to the NICs. Whether as an add-on board or a PC card, a NIC is connected directly to the PC's internal bus. With the Ethernet standard for LAN architecture a de facto standard, the Ethernet NIC is simply the **Ethernet Card.** The Ethernet standard is discussed in Section 6-4. Usually, NICs are designed to support a particular type of network (for example, Ethernet) and communications channel (for example, coaxial cable or twisted-pair telephone wire). Some, however, support several network and/or media options.

GATEWAYS AND ROUTERS

Computer networks are everywhere—in banks, in law offices, in the classroom, and in the home. In keeping with the trend toward greater connectivity, computer networks are themselves being networked and interconnected to give users access to a greater variety of applications and to more information. For example, the typical medium-to-large company links several PC-based networks to the company's enterprise-wide network. This enables end users on all networks to share information and resources.

Cyberspace is a network of millions of computer networks. Linking the networks poses a technical challenge in that networks use a variety of communications protocols and operating systems. The primary hardware/software technologies used to link these networks and facilitate the routing of information among networks are the *router* and the *gateway*. The **router** enables communications links between networks by performing the necessary protocol conversions to route messages to their proper destinations (see Figure 6-4). A **gateway** permits networks using different communications protocols to "talk" to one another. In practice, these functions often are housed in a single unit called a **gateway router.**

The terminal/PC or computer sending a **message** is the *source*. The terminal/PC or computer receiving the message is the *destination*. The router establishes the link between the source and destination in a process called **handshaking.** If you think of messages as mail to be delivered to various points in a computer network, the router is the post office. Each computer system and terminal/PC in a computer network is assigned a **network address.** The router uses these addresses to route messages to their destinations. The content of a message could be a prompt to the user, a user inquiry, a program instruction, an "electronic memo," or any type of information that can be transmitted electronically—even the image of a handwritten report.

Organizations that are set up to interconnect computer networks do so over a *backbone*. The **backbone** is a collective term that refers to a system of routers, gateways, and other communications hardware and the associated transmission media (cables, wires, and wireless links) that link the computers in an organization.

Routers and gateways, once limited to the business environment, are becoming popular in the home, too. Broadband ISPs often sell routers (or gateway routers) to their customers to enable sharing of the Internet signal on a home network. If you wish to share an Internet signal among several PCs in your home network, ask your ISP if you will need a router or if you can share the Internet through your PC's peer-to-peer networking capability.

HUBS AND SWITCHES

A **hub** is a multiport device that expands the number of nodes that can be linked to a network (usually from 4 to 24 devices). A LAN cable is connected to a hub, then multiple PCs or network devices can be linked to the hub. A hub is a *half-duplex* device, that is, it transmits data in either direction, but not at the same time. A hub transmits whatever information it receives to all PCs on the LAN, but only the destination hub accepts the transmission. Hubs can be linked in a tree structure to expand the network.

A **switch** is like a hub in that it is a multiport device for a LAN. Switches are *full-duplex,* enabling transmission in both directions at the same time to improve overall network performance. Also, a switch transmits information only to its intended destination. Some multifunction routers include the hub/switch function.

TERMINALS

A variety of terminals enables both *input to* and *output from* a remote computer system. Interactions via a terminal form the foundation for a wide variety of applications, from airline reservations to point-of-sale systems in retail outlets.

VDTs and Thin Clients: Dumb and Smart Terminals

Terminals come in all shapes and sizes and have a variety of input/output capabilities (see Figure 6-5). The most popular general-purpose terminal is the traditional **video display terminal** (VDT) that you see in hospitals and airports. The primary input mechanism on the *VDT*, or simply the *terminal*, is a *keyboard*. Output is displayed on a *monitor*. Most of these terminals are dumb; that is, they have little or no intelligence (processing capability).

A **thin client** is a smart terminal (see Figure 6-5); that is, it has some processing capabilities and RAM. These smart terminals are configured with some type of point-and-draw device, such as a mouse, to permit efficient interaction with the GUI. It is "thin" because it is has fewer features than a PC and is a client of (dependent on) server computers for certain resources, such as storage and some processing. Also, they do not have permanently installed disks. Because thin clients perform many basic processing tasks locally, the server computer can devote more processing capability to priority tasks.

Some companies prefer that their network clients be full-feature personal computers, but others prefer thin clients. Exchanging PCs for thin clients eliminates the expensive and time-consuming task of installing and maintaining PC-based software, but all "clients" are dependent on the server computer. If the server crashes and goes down, all thin clients depending on it go down, too. In contrast, the more costly PC clients can continue to operate as stand-alone units.

FIGURE 6–5   **THE EVOLUTION OF TERMINALS**

WEARABLE DISPLAY TERMINAL

The terminal is being redefined with recent technological innovations. This wearable display is integrated into eyeglasses. The system enables the display of an image that doesn't block the surgeon's view but will, instead, superimpose a color image on top of it.

Photo courtesy of Microvision Incorporated

AIRLINE CHECK-IN KIOSK

Many airlines are making a terminal available to their customers in the form of a self-service check-in kiosk, such as this one with a touch screen monitor.

Courtesy of International Business Machines Corporation. Unauthorized use not permitted.

THIN CLIENTS

Thin clients, such as this one, have replaced terminals and PCs in some networks.

Courtesy of Sun Microsystems, Inc.

techtv
TRANSFER DVDS
IN SECONDS

Telephone Terminals and Telephony

Because of its widespread availability, the telephone is often used as a terminal. You can enter alphanumeric data on the touch-tone keypad of a telephone or by speaking into the receiver (voice input via speech recognition). You would then receive computer-generated voice output from a voice-response system. Salespeople use telephones as terminals for entering orders and inquiries about the availability of certain products into their company's server computer. Brokerage firms allow their clients to tap into the firm's computers via telephone.

The telephone by itself has little built-in intelligence; however, when linked to a computer, potential applications abound. **Telephony** is the integration of computers and telephones, two essential instruments of business. In telephony, the computer, often a PC, acts in concert with the telephone. For example, a PC can analyze incoming telephone calls and take appropriate action (take a message, route the call to the appropriate extension, and so on).

Special-Function Terminals: ATMs and POSs

Special-function terminals are designed for a specific application, such as convenience banking. You probably are familiar with the *automatic teller machine* (ATM) and its input/output capabilities.

The ATM idea has caught on for other applications. A consortium of companies is installing thousands of ATM-like terminals that will let you order and receive a wide variety of documents on the spot. For example, you can now obtain an airline ticket, your college transcript, and an IRS form electronically, and many more applications are on the way.

Another widely used special-function terminal is the *point-of-sale* (POS) terminal. Clerks and salespeople in retail stores, restaurants, and other establishments that sell goods and services use POS terminals. POS terminals have a keypad for input, at least one small monitor, and a printer to print the receipt. Some have other input/output devices, such as a badge reader for credit cards, a wand or stationary scanner to read price and inventory data, and/or a printer to preprint checks for customers.

SELF-CHECK
SECTION

1 The electronic collection and distribution of information between two points is referred to as telecommunications. (T/F)

2 What type of computer sits between the client PC and a normal server: (a) proxy server, (b) roxy server, (c) loxie server, or (d) foxy server?

3 The communications device that permits networks using different communications protocols to "talk" to one another is: (a) a server, (b) a client, (c) a DSL line, or (d) a gateway.

4 Each computer system and PC in a computer network is assigned: (a) a network address, (b) a mailbox, (c) a P.O. address, or (d) an alphabetic identifier.

5 The integration of computers and telephones is known as: (a) telecommunications, (b) telephony, (c) autophony, or (d) IT phoning.

6-3 THE DATA COMMUNICATIONS CHANNEL

Why this section is important to you.

You have plenty of options for connecting to networks and the Internet. People who know these communications options tend to make better-informed decisions, decisions that fit their pocketbook and computing habits.

A **communications channel** is the medium through which digital information must pass to get from one location in a computer network to the next. People often use slang terms for communications channel, such as *line, link,* or *pipe.* Communications channels link client computers, servers, and other devices in a network. They provide links between networks, whether between rooms at home or between remote offices. And they enable you, other individuals, and companies to access the Internet, which, itself, is made up of a variety of communications links.

TRANSMISSION MEDIA

Some communication channels involve a physical link (wire or cable) and others are wireless. Channels are rated by their capacity to transmit information, which is cited in terms of *bits per second* (bps).

Twisted-Pair Wire: Telephone Line and Cat5

Regular telephone wire is **twisted-pair wire.** Each twisted-pair wire is actually two insulated copper wires twisted around each other. At least one twisted-pair line provides POTS (plain old telephone services) to just about every home and business in the United States (see Figure 6-6). Telephone companies offer two different levels of twisted-pair service.

- *POTS.* When you call the telephone company and request a telephone line, it installs POTS. This analog line permits voice conversations and digital transmissions with the aid of a modem. Traditional modem technology permits data transmission up to 56 K bps.
- *DSL. Digital Subscriber Line* (DSL) is delivered over a POTS line. Data can stream along the same line while you talk. DSL, one of the broadband options, is introduced in Getting Started and discussed further in Chapter 3.

Twisted-pair wire is a common conduit for data transmission in home and office networks. Computers in home networks often are linked via common telephone wires terminating with *RJ-11 connectors* (see Figure 6-6). Most business LANs use Cat5 cabling with *RJ-45 connectors* (see Figure 6-6). **Cat5 cabling,** which uses four twisted pairs of wire, is capable of transmission speeds up to 100 M bps. **Cat5e cabling** (Cat5 Enhanced) enables speeds up to 1 G bps.

Coaxial Cable

Most people know coaxial cable as the cable in "cable television." **Coaxial cable,** or "coax," contains electrical wire (usually copper wire) and is constructed to permit high-speed data transmission with a minimum of signal distortion. It is laid along the ocean floor for intercontinental voice and data transmission; it's used to connect terminals and computers in a "local" area (from a few feet to a few miles); and it delivers TV signals to close to 100 million homes in America alone. Coaxial cable is said to be a "wide pipe." That is, it is a high-capacity channel that can carry digital data at up to 10 M bps, as well as more than 100 analog TV signals. Internet access via cable TV coax cable is at least 30 times faster than POTS. Cable modem broadband access, introduced in Getting Started and Chapter 3, is comparable to DSL.

Fiber Optic Cable: Light Pulse

Twisted-pair wire and coaxial cable carry data as electrical signals. **Fiber optic cable** carries data as laser-generated pulses of light (see Figure 6-7). Made up of bundles of very thin, transparent, almost hair-like fibers, fiber optic cables transmit data more inexpensively and much more quickly than do copper wire transmission media. The Internet backbone, the primary channels for Internet transmissions, is mostly fiber optic cable. In the time it takes to transmit a single page of *Webster's Unabridged Dictionary* over twisted-pair copper wire (about 3 seconds) over a regular modem, the entire dictionary could be transmitted over a single optic fiber! Businesses that demand very high-speed business-to-business communications have fiber optic cable linked directly to their server computers.

Each time a communications company lays a new fiber optic cable, the world is made a little smaller. In 1956, the first transatlantic cable carried 50 voice circuits. Then, talking to someone in Europe was a rare and expensive experience. Today, a single fiber can carry over 32,000 voice and data transmissions, the equivalent of 2.5 billion bits per second. Nowadays, people call colleagues in other countries or link up with international computers as readily as they call home.

A. Coaxial cable with BNC connector

B. Cat5 cabling with RJ-45 connector

C. Twisted-pair wire (4 pairs)

D. Phone line wire with RJ-11 connector

FIGURE 6–6

COMMON PHYSICAL CHANNELS FOR LOCAL AREA NETWORKS

Common physical channels for LANs include: A. coaxial cable (shown with a BNC twist-on connector), B. Cat5 cabling with RJ-45 connector (Registered Jack-45, an 8-wire cable used with Ethernet cards), C. twisted-pair wire in a 4-pair cable, and D. Phone line wire with RJ-11 connector (the common telephone jack).

FIGURE 6-7

FIBER OPTIC CABLE

Wherever possible, telephone poles and twisted-pair wire are being replaced by the more versatile fiber optic cable. More than 90% of long-distance telephone and Internet traffic in the United States is carried over 15 million miles of fiber optic cable, the hair-thin strands of glass that make up fiber optic cable.

Courtesy of International Business Machines Corporation. Unauthorized use not permitted.
Courtesy of Corning, Inc.

Another of the many advantages of fiber optic cable is its contribution to data security. It is much more difficult for a computer criminal to intercept a signal sent over fiber optic cable (via a beam of light) than it is over copper wire (an electrical signal).

Fiber optic technology is taking giant leaps. Already scientists are able to transmit data over a special fiber optic cable at 3.28 terabits per second (trillion bps), but only over a distance of a city block. At that rate, the new high-tech fiber can transmit the equivalent of three days' worth of Internet traffic (worldwide) in a single second! This technology is still in the laboratory, but this new technology may give us a very big "pipe" through which to receive information in the near future.

Although most fiber optic cable is laid and maintained by commercial enterprises that sell communications capabilities (MCI, Sprint, AT&T, and so on), many businesses lay their own fiber optic cable to provide high-speed links between their LANs and enterprise computers.

Wireless Communication

High-speed communications channels do not have to be wires or fibers. Data also can be transmitted via microwave signals or radio-frequency signals in much the same way that signals travel from a remote control to a TV or VCR or between a cellular telephone tower and a cell phone. A **microwave signal** is a high-frequency electromagnetic wave used in wireless communications. **Radio-frequency (RF) signals** enable data communication between radio transmitters and receivers. Transmission of these signals is line-of-sight; that is, the signal travels in a straight line from source to destination.

Microwave signals are transmitted between transceivers. Because microwave signals do not bend around the curvature of the earth, signals may need to be relayed several times by microwave repeater stations before reaching their destination. Repeater stations are placed on the tops of mountains, tall buildings, and towers, usually about 30 miles apart.

Communications Satellites: Sky High Repeater Stations

Communications satellites eliminate the line-of-sight limitation because microwave signals are bounced off the satellites, avoiding buildings, mountains, and other signal obstructions. One of the advantages of communications satellites is that data can be transmitted from one location to any number of other locations anywhere on (or near) our planet. Satellites routinely are launched into orbit for the sole purpose of relaying data communications signals to and from earth stations (see Figure 6-8). A **communications satellite,** which is essentially a repeater station for microwave signals, is launched and set in a geosynchronous orbit. A **geosynchronous orbit** at 22,300 miles above the earth permits the communications satellite to maintain a fixed position relative to the earth's surface. Each satellite can receive and retransmit signals to slightly less than half of the earth's surface; therefore, three satellites are required to cover the earth effectively (see Figure 6-9). Internet access via satellite is available to companies and to individuals at speeds up to 48 M bps. Broadband digital satellite Internet access, which is introduced in Getting Started and Chapter 1, is comparable to cable modem and DSL access speeds.

FIGURE 6–8 **WIRELESS COMMUNICATION**

INTERNET ACCESS VIA DIGITAL SATELLITE
This digital satellite dish enables two-way high-speed access to the Internet.

Long and Associates

SATELLITE COMMUNICATIONS
Common carriers rely heavily on communications satellites and a network of earth stations to help them offer high-speed data communications to customers.

Courtesy of Lockheed Martin Corporation
Courtesy of Orbital Sciences Corporation

FIGURE 6-9   SATELLITE DATA TRANSMISSION

Three satellites in geosynchronous orbit (staying over the same point on earth) provide worldwide data transmission service.

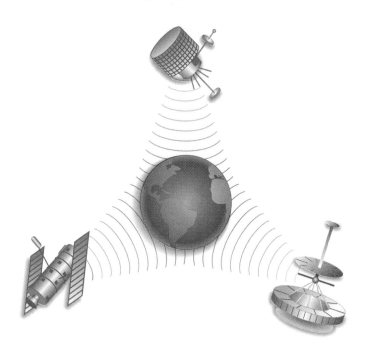

Down to Earth Wireless: Wi-Fi and Bluetooth

Wireless technology is redefining the way we experience connectivity (see Figure 6-10). The most popular communications standards used for enabling devices and PCs to talk to one another are *Wi-Fi* and *Bluetooth*. Wi-Fi is introduced in Chapter 3 as a wireless alternative for Internet access. Wi-Fi (*wireless fidelity*) is a generic reference to any IEEE 802.11 network. These include *Wireless-B* (based on the *IEEE 802.11b* standard), *Wireless-A* (based on the *IEEE 802.11a* standard), and *Wireless-G* (based on the *IEEE 802.11g* standard).

Wireless-B, Wireless-A, and Wireless-G offer a way to meet one of the greatest challenges and biggest expenses in a computer network—installing the physical links between its components. These wireless communications standards are a wireless replacement for physical cabling (Cat5, coaxial cable, and so on) in a LAN. To gain access to a wireless LAN, you need a PC with a wireless LAN PC card and network rights (be an authorized user).

The wireless LAN PC card is a transceiver with a limited range (about 50 to 300 feet). It links computers via omnidirectional (traveling in all directions at once) radio waves to communications hubs, called *access points*. Access points are hardwired to a central server computer and are positioned throughout a building, a neighborhood, or a college campus to extend the reach of the wireless LAN. Transceivers at access points work together with wireless LAN PC cards to provide users with tremendous mobility within the operational area of the LAN.

Microsoft's Redmond campus is entirely wireless. The company's 7000 employees at the site have wireless enabled notebook PCs. Wireless technology enables these laptops to maintain a wireless link to any of 3000 *access points*. The access points, which are linked physically to company servers, are strategically located such that a wireless PC on the campus is never out of Wi-Fi range. Microsoft attributes a 30-minute gain in productivity per employee per day to its wireless network. "Connected" mobility is a tremendous advantage for the modern knowledge workers and people who rely on their PCs. These advantages have prompted many business and college campuses to install or convert to wireless networks.

Wi-Fi is the most popular "longwire" replacement technology in LANs. Wireless-B offers reasonable transmission speed (11 M bps) and excellent range from an access point (up to about 300 feet). Wireless-A offers 54 M bps, but has an effective range of only 50 feet. The emerging Wireless-G standard may render both earlier standards obsolete by providing Wireless-A speed and Wireless-B range.

Bluetooth is a considerably slower (1 M bps) "shortwire" replacement technology with a range of 30 feet. Bluetooth was named after tenth century King Harald Blåtland (translated Bluetooth) of Denmark, a good king who united the warring factions in Denmark and Norway. The modern day Bluetooth "unites" a variety of personal devices via wireless links. These include portable PCs, cellular telephones and headsets, handheld PCs, personal digital assistants (PDAs), printers, digital cameras, MP3 players, and so on. As Bluetooth matures and gains acceptance, we can expect to see more Bluetooth enabled devices around the home and office. The official Bluetooth industry organization has almost 2000 member

FIGURE 6-10

COMBINING BLUETOOTH AND WI-FI TECHNOLOGIES

United Parcel Service (UPS) has implemented a wireless network which combines Bluetooth and Wi-Fi wireless technologies. Over 50,000 package handlers use the short-range Bluetooth enabled barcode readers (worn on a finger) to scan package labels. That information is sent to a Wi-Fi radio on the handler's belt, which in turn, is sent via a Wi-Fi link to a central computer for processing.

companies, all of whom would like to eliminate dependence on wires. For example, these companies currently are developing hundreds of Bluetooth enabled devices such as heating/air conditioning units, lighting, lawn sprinklers, televisions, pacemakers, automobile entertainment centers, elevators, washer/dryers, garage door openers, and many more. The Bluetooth chip is relatively inexpensive (about $5), so it is an economically feasible add-on to almost any electronic device. Forecasters are predicting that two billion Bluetooth enabled devices will be in service in 2006.

Bluetooth has the potential to have a dramatic impact in the not-too-distant future. Imagine being able to sit at the kitchen table and, from your PDA, open the garage door, start your car, and turn on the seat heater. Your refrigerator's inventory system can post grocery needs to your to-do list. Your contact list and calendar on your cell phone, handheld PC, and notebook PC are synchronized automatically when in close proximity to each other. Before this can happen, however, the Bluetooth organization will need to resolve security concerns. Currently, any device within its range can easily intercept sensitive files on another Bluetooth device.

Wireless will continue to evolve to offer faster data rates over longer distances. Already, many major technology companies are promoting the development of the 802.16 standard. This standard will permit 70 M bps over a 30-mile range. The only hardware needed to access the service would be an inexpensive wireless network adapter.

WAP: Wireless Application Protocol

The technology often associated with wireless capabilities is **WAP**, the Wireless Application Protocol. WAP, however, is not a communications protocol, but an application protocol. WAP is the de facto standard for wireless Internet access via handheld devices, such as cellular telephones. It enables the creation of Web applications for mobile devices. These applications are viewed on a micro browser, which is designed for use with smaller displays.

The Future of Wireless

Very high speed wireless Internet service may be headed to our doorstep. Line-of-sight microwave wireless technologies **MMDS** (Multichannel Multipoint Distribution Service) and **LMDS** (Local Multipoint Distribution Service) provide for network access at fiber optic-level speeds. Industry forecasters are predicting that MMDS will provide Internet services at 1 G bps (gigabits per second) for 70% of the residential and small office market within 5 years. That is about 1000 times faster than current domestic broadband options. ISPs are very interested in MMDS because it can offer high-speed Internet service within a 35-mile radius with minimal investment in equipment. LMDS is a wireless solution to bringing very high bandwidth to homes and offices on the last mile of connectivity.

COMMON CARRIERS

It is impractical for individuals and companies to string their own fiber optic cable between distant locations, such as Hong Kong and New York City. It is also impractical for them to set their own satellites in orbit, although some companies have. Therefore, most people and companies turn to communications **common carriers**, such as AT&T, MCI, and Sprint, to provide communications channels for data transmission. Organizations pay communications common carriers for *private* or *switched* data communications service.

A **private line** (or **leased line**) provides a dedicated data communications channel between any two points in a computer network. The charge for a private line is based on channel capacity (bps) and distance. Some companies have private lines that link remote offices, primarily with fiber optic cable.

A **switched line** (or **dialup line**) is available strictly on a time-and-distance charge, similar to a long-distance telephone call. You (or your computer) make a connection by "dialing up" a computer, then a modem sends and receives data. Switched lines offer greater flexibility than do private lines because they allow you to link up with any communications-ready computer. A regular POTS telephone line is a switched line.

MEMORY BITS

Transmission Media
- Twisted-pair wire
  - Telephone lines
  - Cat5 and Cat5e cabling
- Coaxial cable
- Fiber optic cable
- Wireless
  - Microwave
    - MMDS
    - LMDS
  - Wi-Fi (longwire radio-frequency, RF, signals)
    - Wireless-B (802.11b)
    - Wireless-A (802.11a)
    - Wireless-G (802.11g)
  - Bluetooth (shortwire radio-frequency, RF, signals)

The number and variety of common carriers is expanding. For decades, it was just the telephone companies. Now cable TV and satellite companies provide common carrier services. Data rates offered by common carriers range from voice-grade POTS (up to about 56 K bps with a modem) to the widest of all pipes, the massive 622 M bps channel.

The emergence of Internet-connected intranets, extranets, and VPNs has changed the way companies link with remote locations and other companies. Although the leased line is still the corporate choice when very high-speed communication is required, most companies opt for cost-saving Internet-based alternatives for all other communication needs.

COMMUNICATIONS PROTOCOLS

Computers must adhere to strict rules when transmitting information between computers. **Communications protocols** are rules established to govern the way data are transmitted in a computer network. A protocol describes how these data are transmitted. Communications protocols are defined in *layers*, the first of which is the physical layer. The physical layer defines the manner in which nodes in a network are connected to one another. Subsequent layers, the number of which varies between protocols, describe how messages are packaged for transmission, how messages are routed through the network, security procedures, and the manner in which messages are displayed. A number of different protocols are in common use. The protocol you hear about most often is TCP/IP (Transmission Control Protocol/Internet Protocol), which actually is a collective reference to the protocols that link computers on the Internet (TCP and IP). These protocols are discussed in Chapter 3, "Going Online."

Protocols fall into two general classifications: *asynchronous* and *synchronous* (see Figure 6-11). In **asynchronous transmission,** data are transmitted at irregular intervals on an as-needed basis, usually a single character at a time. Most communication between computers and devices is asynchronous, occurring as needed at irregular intervals. Internet interaction is asynchronous. Asynchronous transmission, sometimes called *start/stop transmission,* is best suited for low-speed data communications, such as that between the Internet and a PC with a standard 56 K bps modem. *Start/stop bits* are appended to the beginning and end of each message. The start/stop bits signal the receiving terminal/computer at the beginning and end of the message. In PC data communications, the message is a single byte or character.

Start/stop bits are not required in synchronous transmission. In **synchronous transmission,** the source and destination operate in timed synchronization to enable high-

FIGURE 6-11 **ASYNCHRONOUS AND SYNCHRONOUS TRANSMISSION OF DATA**

Asynchronous data transmission takes place at irregular intervals. Synchronous data transmission requires timed synchronization between sending and receiving devices.

FIGURE 6-12 DATA TRANSMISSION PATH

It's more the rule than the exception that data are carried over several transmission media between source and destination.

Microwave

Fiber optic cable

Cat-5

Wi-Fi

PC and computer in the same
building in downtown Seattle

Notebook PC and computer in the same
building in downtown Orlando

speed data transfer. The message is typically a block of characters. Data transmission between computers and hardware that facilitates high-speed data communications is normally synchronous.

DATA TRANSMISSION IN PRACTICE

A communications channel from a PC in Seattle, Washington, to a notebook PC in Orlando, Florida (see Figure 6-12), usually would consist of several different transmission media and, perhaps, multiple protocols. The connection between the Seattle PC and its server is Cat5. The Seattle company might use a common carrier company such as AT&T to transmit the data via a leased line. AT&T would then send the data through a combination of transmission facilities that might include twisted-pair wire, microwave signals, radio-frequency signals, and fiber optic cable. The final link from the Orlando server to the notebook PC is via Wi-Fi.

1 The wireless transceiver will never replace the physical link between the source and the destination in a network. (T/F)

2 Synchronous transmission is best suited for data communications involving low-speed I/O devices. (T/F)

3 Which of these is not a wireless communications standard: (a) IEEE 802.11g, (b) Greentooth, (c) IEEE 802.11g, or (d) IEEE 802.11a?

4 Communications satellites in geosynchronous orbit are how many miles above the earth: (a) 200, (b) 2,200, (c) 22,300, or (d) 100,000?

SELF-CHECK

SECTION

6-4   NETWORKS

Networks are about sharing and communication. Networks facilitate the sharing of hardware (from printers to backup disk storage to server computers), software, data, and Internet access. They also make it easier for us to share ideas and communicate all kinds of information, from meeting schedules to product design data. The telephone system is the world's largest computer network, so you have been sharing and communicating on a network for most of your life. A telephone is an endpoint, or a **node**, connected to a network of computers that routes your voice signals to any one of a billion telephones (other nodes) in the world.

In a computer network, the node can be a terminal, a computer, or any destination/source device (for example, a printer, an automatic teller machine, or even a telephone). Computer networks can have three nodes or 10,000 nodes, depending upon the specific requirements of an organization. Each network is one of a kind (see Figure 6-13). We

FIGURE 6–13 **NETWORKS IN PRACTICE**

VISUAL AREA NETWORKING

Using a wireless tablet PC, Dr. Eng Lim Goh of SGI demonstrates Visual Area Networking. Visual Area Networking allows users to interact with visualization supercomputers anywhere they are, with any client device.

Courtesy of SGI. Tablet image courtesy of SONICblue, Inc. Screen images courtesy of Landmark Graphics Corporation.

NETWORK CONTROL CENTER

This Global Network Control Center controls the entire ORB-COMM satellite constellation. The satellites envelop the earth in low-altitude orbits, which allows messages to be sent and received by small, low-power access devices.

Courtesy of Orbital Sciences Corporation

HOSPITALS LINK UP

The workstations and PCs at this hospital are on a network. A computerized patient records system allows physicians to access up-to-date patient chart information from workstations throughout the hospital.

Courtesy of Harris Corporation

have already seen the hardware and transmission media used to link nodes in a network. In this section, we introduce network topologies and the various types of networks. LANs, the most popular type of network, are discussed in more detail.

NETWORK TOPOLOGIES

A **network topology** is a description of the possible physical connections within a network. The topology is the configuration of the hardware and shows which pairs of nodes can communicate. The basic computer network topologies—star, ring, and bus—are illustrated in Figure 6-14. However, a pure form of any of these three basic topologies is rare in practice. Most computer networks are *hybrids*—combinations of these topologies.

Star Topology

The **star topology** involves a centralized host computer connected to several other computer systems, which are usually smaller than the host. The smaller computer systems communicate with one another through the host and usually share the host computer's database. The host could be anything from a PC to a supercomputer. Any computer can communicate with any other computer in the network. Banks often have a large home-office computer system with a star network of smaller server computer systems in the branch banks.

Ring Topology

The **ring topology** involves computer systems of approximately the same size, with no one computer system as the focal point of the network. When one system routes a message to another system, it is passed around the ring until it reaches its destination address.

FIGURE 6-14	NETWORK TOPOLOGIES

Network topologies include (A) star, (B) ring, and (C) bus.

The **bus topology** permits the connection of terminals, peripheral devices, and PCs along a common cable called a **network bus.** The term *bus* is used because people on a bus can get off at any stop along the route. In a bus topology, a signal is broadcast to all nodes, but only the destination node responds to the signal. It is easy to add devices or delete them from the network, as devices are simply daisy-chained along the network bus. Bus topologies are most appropriate when the linked devices are physically close to one another.

TYPES OF NETWORKS

Networks tend to be classified by the proximity of their nodes.

- The **personal area network (PAN)** is a new concept made possible by the introduction of Bluetooth technology, the short-range, low-cost, low-speed wireless technology. The PAN spans an individual's personal world of electronics, including the cell phone, notebook PC, PDA, MP3 player, printer, and so on. The PAN would let you synchronize your appointments on your notebook PC with your PDA, download songs from your notebook to your MP3 player, and pass your medical history from PDA to a computer at an emergency room via a wireless link.
- The **local area network (LAN),** or **local net,** connects nodes in close proximity, such as in a suite of offices or a building.
- The **MAN,** or **metropolitan area network,** is a network designed for a city. MANs are more encompassing than LANs, but smaller than wide area networks (WANs).
- A **WAN,** or **wide area network,** connects nodes, usually LANs, in widely dispersed geographic areas, such as cities, states, and even countries. Wal-Mart, the largest retailer in the world, links the LANs in over 2000 stores and warehouses. The WAN often depends on the transmission services of a common carrier to transmit signals between nodes in the network. The emergence of virtual private networks and the potential for cost savings have resulted in many WANs being setup as VPNs over the world's grandest WAN, the Internet.

When we refer to PANs, LANs, MANs, and WANs, we refer to all hardware, software, and communications channels associated with them.

LAN OVERVIEW

Local nets, or LANs, are found in just about any office building. The local net, including all data communications channels, is owned by the organization using it. Because of the proximity of nodes in local nets, a company can install its own communications channels (such as Cat5, coaxial cable, fiber optic cable, wireless transceivers, and so on). Therefore, LANs do not need common carriers.

Strictly speaking, any type of computer can be part of a LAN, but in practice, PCs, thin clients, and workstations provide the foundation for local area networks. PCs in a typical LAN are linked to each other and share resources such as printers, disk storage, and Internet access. The basic hardware components in a PC-based LAN are the network interface cards, or NICs, in the PCs; the transmission media that connect the nodes in the network; and the servers. LANs may also have routers, modems, and other network hardware. The distance separating devices in the local net may vary from a few feet to a few thousand feet. As few as two and as many as several hundred PCs can be linked on a single local area network.

Most corporate PCs are linked to a LAN to aid in communication among knowledge workers. LANs make good business sense because these and other valuable resources can be shared.

- *Applications software.* The cost of a LAN-based applications software (for example, Microsoft Word) is far less than the cost of installing the software on each PC in the LAN.

- *Links to other LAN servers.* Other LANs become an accessible resource. It is easier to link one or more LANs to a single LAN than to many individual PCs.
- *Communications capabilities.* Many users can share a dedicated communications line or broadband Internet access.
- *I/O devices.* With a little planning, a single page printer, plotter, or scanner can support many users on a LAN with little loss of office efficiency.
- *Storage devices.* Databases on a LAN can be shared.
- *Add-on boards.* Add-on boards, such as video capture boards, can be shared by many PCs.

Like computers, automobiles, and just about everything else, local nets can be built at various levels of sophistication. At the most basic level, they permit the interconnection of PCs in a department so that users can send messages to one another and share files and printers. The more sophisticated local nets permit the interconnection of server computers, PCs, and the spectrum of peripheral devices throughout a large but geographically constrained area, such as a cluster of buildings.

LAN Access Methods

Only one node on a LAN can send information at any given time. The other nodes must wait their turn. The transfer of data and programs between nodes is controlled by the access method embedded in the network interface card's ROM. A **network access method** is the set of rules by which networks determine usage priorities for a shared medium. Think of a network access method as the network's *logical topology.*

We have traffic lights on busy streets to keep cars from crashing into each other. It's the same with networks. The access methods keep messages from colliding along the transmission medium. The most popular access methods are *Ethernet* and *token.*

Ethernet

Ethernet, the most widely used network access method, uses the **CSMA/CD protocol** (*Carrier Sense Multiple Access/Collision Detection*). In an Ethernet network, the nodes on the LAN must compete for the right to send a message. A node with a message sends a message and its signal is broadcast over the entirety of the network (all links), passing all nodes. Only the addressee node recognizes and accepts the message; the other nodes ignore it. Ethernet transmits messages at 10 M bps, 100 M bps (sometimes called Fast Ethernet), or 1 G bps.

Occasionally, two messages collide en route to their destination, at which time the network returns a "line busy" signal to the senders. When this happens, the node waits a random amount of time and tries again, and again, until the line is free. This all happens much faster than the blink of an eye and is transparent to the user. Ethernet LANs operate like a conversation between polite people. When two people begin talking at the same time, one must wait until the other is finished.

Token Access Method

When a LAN with a *ring* topology uses the **token access method,** an electronic *token* travels around a ring of nodes in the form of a header. The header contains control signals, including one specifying whether the token is "free" or carrying a message. A sender node captures a free token as it travels from node to node, changes it to "busy," and adds the message. The resulting *message frame* travels around the ring to the addressee's NIC, which copies the message and returns the message frame to the sender. The sender's NIC removes the message frame from the ring and circulates a new free token. Figure 6-15 demonstrates the token-passing process for this type of LAN. When a LAN with a *bus* topology uses the token access method, the token is broadcast to the nodes along the network bus. Think of the token as a benevolent dictator who, when captured, bestows the privilege of sending a transmission.

FIGURE 6-15 THE TOKEN ACCESS METHOD IN A LAN WITH A RING TOPOLOGY

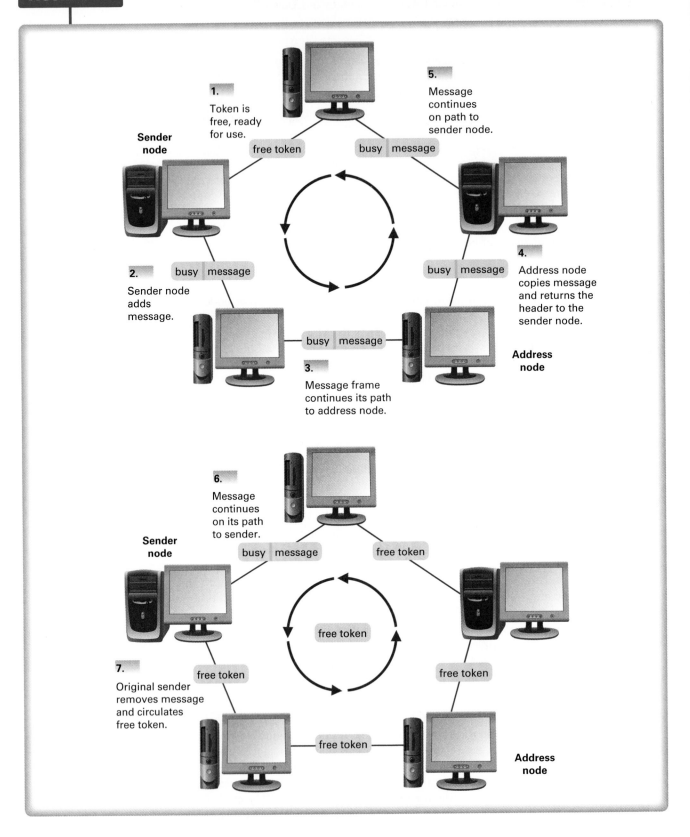

The token ring access method defines data rates of 4 and 16 M bps, considerably slower than Ethernet. Although token ring is still used, the faster Ethernet has emerged as the de facto standard network access method.

LAN Transmission Media and Servers

Several kinds of physical transmission media can be connected to the network interface cards, including twisted-pair wire (Ethernet Cat5 and telephone line), coaxial cable, and fiber optic cable. Cables are not needed in wireless LANs. Figure 6-16 illustrates how nodes in a LAN are connected in a bus topology with a wiring hub at the end that allows several more nodes to be connected to the bus.

In a LAN, a *server* is a computer that can be shared by users on the LAN. The three most popular servers are the file server, the print server, and the communications server.

- *File server.* The **file server** normally is a dedicated computer, sometimes a high-performance PC or a workstation, with one or more high-capacity hard disks for storing the data and programs shared by the network users. For example, the master customer file, word processing software, spreadsheet software, and so on would be stored on the server disk.

FIGURE 6-16 **LAN LINKS**

Nodes in this LAN are linked via a bus topology. One of the nodes is linked to a wiring hub that enables several PCs to be connected to the network bus. The LAN is linked to other LANs with fiber optic cable.

- *Print server.* The **print server** typically is housed in the same dedicated PC as the file server. The print server handles user print jobs and controls at least one printer. If needed, the server *spools* print jobs; that is, it saves print jobs to disk until the requested printer is available, then routes the print file to the printer.

- *Communications server.* The **communications server** provides communication links external to the LAN—that is, links to other networks. To accomplish this service, the communications server controls one or more modems, or perhaps access to a DSL line.

These server functions may reside in a single PC or be distributed among the PCs that make up the LAN. When the server functions are consolidated, the server PC usually is *dedicated* to servicing the LAN. Some PCs are designed specifically to be dedicated **LAN servers,** high-end PCs whose resources are shared by users on the LAN. Using a PC continues to be an option with small- to medium-sized LANs, but not in large LANs with 100 or more users. Now, PC vendors manufacture powerful computers designed, often with multiple processors, specifically as LAN servers. LAN servers are configured with enough RAM, storage capacity, and backup capability to handle the resource needs of hundreds of PCs.

LAN SOFTWARE

In this section, we explore LAN-based software, including LAN operating systems alternatives and a variety of applications software.

Network Operating Systems

Network operating systems (**NOS**), the nucleus of a local net, come in two formats: *peer-to-peer,* sometimes called *P2P,* and *dedicated server.* In both cases, the LAN operating system is actually several pieces of software. Each processing component in the LAN has a piece of the LAN operating system resident in its RAM. The pieces interact with one another to enable the nodes to share resources and communication. Novell's *NetWare,* Microsoft's *Windows Server 2003,* and *UNIX* are popular network operating systems. Each offers a family of network operating system, or "server," software to meet a variety of networking and Internet-based processing needs.

The individual user in a LAN might appear to be interacting with an operating system, such as Windows XP. However, the RAM-resident LAN software *redirects* certain requests to the appropriate LAN component. For example, a print request would be redirected to the print server.

Peer-to-Peer LANs

In a **peer-to-peer LAN,** all PCs are peers, or equals. Any PC can be a client to another peer PC or any PC can share its resources with its peers. Peer-to-peer LANs are less sophisticated than those that have one or more dedicated servers in support of client/server networking. Because they are relatively easy to install and maintain, peer-to-peer LANs are popular when small numbers of PCs are involved (for example, from 2 to 20). PCs running the Windows operating system can be linked together in a peer-to-peer LAN. Most home networks are Windows-based peer-to-peer networks.

Client/Server LANs

In LANs with dedicated servers, the controlling software resides in the file server's RAM. LANs with dedicated servers can link hundreds of clients (PCs and thin clients) in a LAN while providing a level of system security that is not possible in a peer-to-peer LAN. Control is distributed among the clients in the LAN.

Applications Software for LANs

LAN-based PCs can run all applications that stand-alone PCs can run, plus those that involve electronic interaction with groups of people.

Client/Server LAN Applications Software

In client/server computing, both client and server computers perform processing to maximize system efficiency. For example, the client computer system might run a database application *locally* (on the client computer) but access data on a *remote* (not local) server computer system. In client/server computing, applications software has two parts—*the front end* and *the back end*.

- Client computers run **front-end applications software,** which performs processing associated with the user interface and applications processing that can be done locally. For example, the front-end software might enable inquiry and data entry to an enterprise customer database.

- The server computer's **back-end applications software** performs processing tasks in support of its client computers. For example, the server might accomplish those tasks associated with storage and maintenance of an enterprise customer database.

In a client/server database application (see Figure 6-17), users at client PCs run front-end software to *download* (server-to-client) parts of the database from the server for processing, perhaps updating customer sales. Upon receiving the requested data, perhaps sales data on customers in the mid-Atlantic region, the client user runs front-end software like Microsoft Access to work with the data. After local processing on the client is complete, the client computer may *upload* (client-to-server) updated data to the server's back-end software like Oracle (database software) for further processing. The server then updates the customer database.

FIGURE 6–17   A WALKTHROUGH OF A CLIENT/SERVER DATABASE APPLICATION

5.
The server receives the uploaded data and updates the server-based customer database.

Server computer

1.
A user at a client workstation requests customer data for the mid-Atlantic region from the server-based database.

2.
The server's back-end software downloads the requested data.

4.
The client uploads the results of processing.

Client PC

3.
The client's front-end software processes the downloaded data.

Communications Link

1.

4.

Client workstation

Client PC

Networking

- Network topologies
  - Star
  - Ring
  - Bus
  - Hybrid
- Types of networks
  - Personal area network (PAN)
  - Local area network (LAN or local net)
  - Metropolitan area network (MAN)
  - Wide area network (WAN)
- LAN access methods
  - Ethernet
  - Token
- LAN operating systems
  - Peer-to-peer
  - Client/server
- LAN applications software
  - Shared
  - Groupware for workgroup computing

Shared Applications Software

LANs enable the sharing of general-purpose software, such as CBT (computer-based training), word processing, spreadsheet, and so on. LAN-based applications software is licensed for sharing. The PCs on the LAN with a dedicated central server interact with a file server to load various applications programs. When a LAN-based PC is booted, software that enables the use of the network interface card, communication with the file server, and interaction with the operating system are loaded from the PC's hard disk to RAM. Depending on how the LAN system administrator configured the LAN, you may see a graphical user interface that lists software options or you may see a prompt from the operating system. When you select a software package, it is downloaded from the LAN's file server to your PC's RAM for processing. You can then work with shared files on the file server or with your own local files (those stored on your PC).

Groupware: Collaborative Tools

LANs have opened the door to applications that are not possible in the one-person, one-computer environment. For example, users linked together via a LAN can send electronic mail to one another. Scheduling meetings with other users on the LAN is a snap. This type of collaborative software designed to benefit a group of people is called **groupware**. Local area networks and groupware provide the foundation for *workgroup computing*. Three companies and their software dominate the groupware arena—Microsoft Exchange, IBM's Lotus software series, and Novell's GroupWise. Groupware is becoming increasingly important in the business world as knowledge workers become more mobile and information in all forms is converted to electronic format.

The breadth of workgroup computing encompasses any application that involves groups of people linked by a computer network. The following is a sampling of workgroup computing applications.

- *Electronic mail (e-mail).* E-mail enables people on a LAN to route messages to one another's electronic mailbox.

- *Instant messaging.* Instant messaging allows messages to be sent and displayed in real-time.

- *Calendar and scheduling.* People can keep online calendars and schedule meetings automatically. The scheduling software automatically checks appropriate users' electronic calendars for possible meeting times, schedules the meeting, and informs the participants via electronic mail.

- *Brainstorming and problem solving.* A LAN enables collaborative brainstorming and problem solving.

- *Shared whiteboarding.* Shared whiteboards permit a document or image to be viewed simultaneously by several people on the network. All people involved can draw or make text annotations directly on the shared whiteboard. The annotations appear in the color associated with a particular participant.

- *Setting priorities.* Groupware is available that enables LAN users to establish priorities for projects through collective reasoning.

- *Electronic conferencing.* Conferencing groupware lets LAN users meet electronically.

- *Electronic forms.* American businesses and government spend over $400 billion each year to distribute, store, and update paper forms. Electronic forms groupware lets LAN users create forms and then gather information from other LAN users.

The number and variety of workgroup computing applications can only increase. Already, notebook PC users are creating networks on the fly. That is, they bring their computers to the meeting and attach them to a common cable or activate their wireless transceivers to create a peer-to-peer LAN. In effect, we have progressed from the *portable computer* to the *portable network*. Once on a LAN, users can enjoy the advantages of networking and groupware. Many colleges now have classes in which students bring notebook PCs to class, then create a wireless LAN with each other and with the professor's PC.

1   Cat5 cabling and fiber optic cable are commonly used to connect nodes on a LAN via network interface cards. (T/F)

2   Client/server computing is possible with or without client computers. (T/F)

3   An endpoint in a network of computers is called a: (a) break point, (b) stop bit, (c) node, or (d) PC.

4   Which of the following doesn't fit: (a) WAN, (b) LAN, (c) DAN, or (d) MAN?

5   Which would not be a type of LAN server: (a) communications server, (b) file server, (c) print server, or (d) scan server?

6   The CSMA/CD protocol is associated with which access method: (a) token, (b) ring, (c) Ethernet, or (d) NIC?

6-5 HOME NETWORKING

A few years ago, it was unthinkable to maintain a local area network in a home. The cost of hardware, software, and professional technical support was simply prohibitive. Today, people routinely link their computers in a *home network* (see Figure 6-18). A **home network** is a small peer-to-peer LAN in the home—usually from two to six nodes.

Homes with one or more kids' PCs, a parent's PC, and perhaps a parent's notebook PC from the office are becoming more the norm than the exception in the United States. Most families subscribing to broadband Internet access are multiple PC homes and over 80% of them have opted to set up a home network. About 50 million American families have home networks. And, why not? They are inexpensive, easy to install, and provide tremendous value to the family. Broadband Internet access is made available to all PCs in the household. Plus, the home network permits the sharing of all kinds of resources, including files, printers, and modems. With a home network and a little cooperation between family members, you can easily share other peripheral resources, such as the scanner and CD/DVD burner. Not to be overlooked is the gaming aspect of home networking: at home, the whole family can join in a multiplayer game.

Why this section is important to you.

A growing number of multiple-PC families have their own home network. The material in this section will be very helpful when you decide to create or upgrade your own home network.

techtv
HOME NETWORKING
MADE EASY

HOME NETWORK TECHNOLOGIES

Setting up a home network is like buying a car—you'll have many options. Your basic choices are a wired network, wireless network, or a combination wired/wireless network.

Technologies commonly used for wired networks are Ethernet, HomePNA, and HomePlug. Ethernet home networking uses Cat5 cabling to achieve speeds of 10 M bps or 100 M bps (Fast Ethernet). Home phoneline networking, called **HomePNA (HPNA)**, allows the PCs on the network to communicate over the home's existing telephone wiring at speeds up to 10 M bps (HPNA 2.0) or 100 M bps (HPNA 3.0). **HomePlug** power-line networking is similar to HomePNA except that transmission is via the home's AC electrical power lines. Wi-Fi standards Wireless-B and Wireless-G have emerged as the most common wireless alternatives at 11 M bps and 54 M bps, respectively. These home networking options are summarized in Figure 6-19.

Ethernet, the most popular type of network in the corporate world, is enjoying a warm reception in the home, too. It helps that most modern PCs are configured with an Ethernet adapter, now the de facto standard for networking. When your PCs already have Ethernet capability, all you need to create an Ethernet network is a router and, possibly, an inexpensive Ethernet hub. As part of your subscription fee, your broadband

FIGURE 6–18

A WIRELESS HOME NETWORK

This notebook PC is linked to the Internet via a wireless home network.

Courtesy of International Business Machines Corporation. Unauthorized use not permitted.

FIGURE 6–19 POPULAR APPROACHES TO HOME NETWORKING

	Type of Home Network			
	Wired Networks			**Wireless Networks**
	Ethernet	**HomePNA**	**HomePlug**	**Wi-Fi**
Transmission Media	Cat-5 cabling with RJ-45 connectors	Standard telephone lines with RJ-11 connectors	AC electrical power lines	Wireless-B (802.11b) and Wireless-G (802.11g)
Speed (decreases as transmission distance increases)	10/100 M bps	10 M bps (HPNA 2.0); 128 M bps to 240 M bps (HPNA 3.0)	14 M bps	10 M bps for Wireless-B; 54 M bps for Wireless-G
Broadband router	All types of networks use a router for broadband Internet access. Cost: $40–$200, depending on features needed.			
Network adapters (NICs for USB, PCI and PC card)	A standard feature on most modern PCs; cost: about $20 per PC	Cost (HPNA 2.0): about $20–$40 per PC; cost (HPNA 3.0): about $40–$50 per PC	Cost: about $20 per PC	Cost: about $70 per PC
Other network hardware	Ethernet hub (half duplex) or Ethernet switch (full duplex); cost: about $40–$100			Access point Cost: $100–$150
Cost of hardware	Least expensive	Moderately priced	Moderately priced	Most expensive
Cost of media	Most expensive Cost: about $100 for Cat5 for a typical 3 PCs network	Minimal (if existing telephone lines used)	Minimal (if existing power lines used)	Least expensive (no wires)
Cost of media installation	Most expensive (new wiring)	Minimal (if existing telephone lines used)	Minimal (if existing power lines used)	Least expensive (no wires)
Advantages	High speed, low cost, reliable and proven technology; de facto standard in office LANs	Offers excellent balance between cost, ease of installation, and speed	Offers excellent balance between cost, ease of installation, and speed; multiple AC outlets in every room	Notebook PCs have network portability; easy to install; de facto standard in office wireless LANs
Disadvantages	Running cables between rooms/floors can be cumbersome		Security (vulnerable to unauthorized access from immediate neighbors)	Signal speed affected by location/obstructions; possible interference from devices on same frequency band (Bluetooth devices, portable phones, etc.); security (vulnerable to unauthorized access)
Effective range	328 feet	1000 feet	1000 feet	500–1600 feet

ISP often supplies the router. If this is not the case, you can purchase a router for as little as $50. If you need more Ethernet ports (some routers have only one), you can add an Ethernet hub to expand the number of available ports. The major challenge posed by an Ethernet network is not the hardware cost, it's the wiring. The cost for premade Cat5 cabling (with connectors) for a typical home with three PCs would be around $100. You may save some money by purchasing Cat5 in bulk, but you will need a special crimping tool and a little electrical savvy to attach the RJ-45 connectors. This cabling cost, however, may pale when you consider the costs associated with stringing the Cat5 through the walls and crawl spaces of your home.

Another popular wired alternative is the HomePNA networking standard developed by the Home Phoneline Networking Alliance (HPNA). HomePNA is an inviting option because it uses existing telephone wiring, people are familiar with phone line wiring and RJ-11 connectors, it does not need a hub, the network adapters are inexpensive, and it offers 10 M bps speed (HPNA 2.0). The new HPNA 3.0 standard offers 128 M bps speed with optional extensions up to 240 M bps, but with a higher price tag. A home's telephone lines can support voice/fax/data, broadband Internet access, and HPNA networking—simultaneously. This is possible because each service occupies a different frequency band. The principals of operation are the same for HomePlug, except that the existing wiring being used is the AC power lines that run throughout the house. One major advantage of HomePlug is that every room in the house will have at least one AC power outlet.

Most home networks use wire (Cat5, telephone line, or AC electrical wiring), but they can be set up as wireless LANs, as well. Wireless hardware (access points and wireless network adapters) is slightly more expensive; however, wireless offers the ultimate mobility to the notebook PC user. A Wireless-B (11 M bps) and/or Wireless-G (54 M bps) network lets you work as easily in the backyard under a shade tree as in the home office. The upside to wireless networking is its ease of installation and its PC portability. The downside is that wireless transmissions are vulnerable to obstructions and external electrical interference (a microwave oven or a 2.4 GHz portable telephone). Also, there is the security issue. Generally, wireless transmissions are intercepted more easily than transmissions over a controlled wired network. People have been known to obtain free broadband Internet access by tapping into a neighbor's wireless access point.

Each of these home networking options has its advantages and disadvantages (see Figure 6-19), but with advances in modern communications hardware, you no longer are forced to choose a single type of network. For a slightly larger investment, you can purchase a multifunction broadband router that provides a combination of these capabilities or all of them.

- Cable/DSL modem
- Ethernet hub or switch
- Wireless A, B, and/or G access point
- Ethernet to HomePNA bridge (bridge functionality enables two network types to work together in one network)
- Ethernet to HomePlug bridge

This means that you can have the reliability of Ethernet, the installation ease of HomePNA or HomePlug, and the flexibility of wireless, all in the same network (see Figure 6-20).

Before making a decision about which type(s) of home network to install, you should be aware of the following considerations.

- *Location and number of PCs.* Identify the location of all the PCs you want on the network, now and in the foreseeable future. If you plan to have one or more portable notebook PCs, then wireless access must be part of your planning.

FIGURE 6–20 **A NETWORKED HOME**

This home is set up for home networking, using both wired and wireless technologies. A multifunction broadband router with an embedded cable/DSL modem supports both Ethernet and HomePNA wired networking. The router also has a built-in access point for Wireless-B and Wireless-G support.

PC with HomePNA
adapter (NIC)

Printer

HomePNA

Notebook with
wireless B and G PC card

Wireless B and G
radio waves

PCs with **Ethernet** adapters **(NICs)**

Printer

Scanner

Cat5 cabling with
RJ-45 connectors

Notebook with
wireless B and G PC card

HomePNA
(phoneline wiring
with RJ-11
connectors)

Cat5 cabling

Ethernet hub
(used to link other
PCs and Ethernet
devices for gaming)

Broadband Internet
Access

Broadband Multifunction Router
Cable/DSL modem
Ethernet (4 ports)
Wireless B and G Access Point
Ethernet to HomePNA or HomePlug Bridge

- *Amount of budget.* Home networking solutions are relatively inexpensive, but each increment in speed and flexibility has a cost.

- *Level of personal networking expertise.* The hardware/software installation of any type of home network is relatively straightforward. However, solutions that require the implementation of multiple types of networks demand more expertise. Carpentry and electrician skills are handy if you choose to string your own wiring through the walls and crawl spaces of your home.

- *Expected growth.* Every network seems to have a life of its own and will eventually grow. Think ahead to what you might envision for the network in two or three years (more or different types of PCs, integration with home entertainment systems, and so on).

- *Applications.* All modern home networking solutions enable sharing of broadband Internet access, the primary reason people set up home networks. If streaming DVD-quality video across the network and/or the routine sharing of large files are priorities, then you will need a network capable of handling at least 30 M bps.

After assessing your needs, you are ready to select a type of network, usually Ethernet, HomePNA, HomePlug, or wireless. Or, you can choose to have it all and enjoy pieces of all of these in your home network (see Figure 6-20).

STEPS TO INSTALLING A HOME NETWORK

Follow these steps to create a home network.

- *Install network interface cards*. Purchase and install the appropriate network adapters in any empty expansion slot in the PCs or insert PC card slots in notebook PCs, as needed.
- *Set up communications hardware*. Install the broadband router and other communications hardware, as needed (Ethernet hubs/switches, wireless access points, and so on).
- *Link PCs to router/hub/switch*. For wired networks, install network cabling that links each PC via the network adapter to the router/hub/switch, as needed.
- *Set up network software*. Modern operating systems, such as Windows, make it easy for users to become part of a peer-to-peer local area network. For example, when you turn on a networked PC for the first time, the Windows network wizard leads you through the setup procedure.
- *Identify files and printer(s) to be shared*. During setup, you will be asked to identify the files and/or printer(s) you wish to share with others on the network.
- *Set up Internet connection sharing*. Although Internet connection sharing can be achieved by designating one of the PCs as a "gateway" to the Internet, most new home networks rely on a broadband router. The router, which usually serves as the broadband modem, too, is the gateway to the Internet and Internet access sharing. The router handles processing duties, so any PC on the network can be turned off or on without affecting Net sharing or the network.

For the price of an average printer and a little effort, you can set up an efficient, time saving, and money saving LAN in your home. If you already have one, you might wish to consider upgrading to a higher speed and/or one with wireless capabilities. Over the next decade, our home networks will grow in scope and functionality. For example, our telephones, PDAs, MP3 players, automobile PCs, entertainment systems, and many other devices will ultimately fall under the home networking umbrella. This is just the ground floor of home networking.

Home Networking
- Common home network types
  - Wired
    - Ethernet
    - HomePNA (phone line)
    - HomePlug (AC power line)
  - Wireless
- Capabilities
  - Peripheral and file sharing
  - Internet connection sharing
  - Multiplayer gaming

1 The Cat5 connector is the RJ-45. (T/F)
2 The maximum line speed for any home network is 14 M bps. (T/F)
3 Which of these is not a wired approach to home networking: (a) HomePlug, (b) Ethernet, (c) HomePNA, or (d) 802.11b?
4 Which of these capabilities would not be found in a multifunction router: (a) broadband modem, (b) Ethernet to HomePNA bridge, (c) Wireless-Q access point, or (d) Ethernet to HomePlug bridge?
5 Which of the following devices would be an unlikely component in a home network: (a) router, (b) notebook PC, (c) dedicated Internet server, or (d) network adapter?

SECTION

Chapter Review

6-1 OUR WIRED WORLD

We rely on computer networks to retrieve and share information quickly. Connectivity facilitates the electronic communication between companies and the free flow of information within an enterprise.

This is the era of cooperative processing. To obtain meaningful, accurate, and timely information, businesses have decided that they must cooperate internally and externally to take full advantage of available information. To promote internal cooperation, businesses are promoting both intracompany and intercompany networking. To do this, they use extranets and intranets. An extranet is an extension of an intranet, which is a closed or private version of the Internet.

A virtual private network uses tunneling technology to enable a private network over the Internet. A VPN employs encryption and other security measures to ensure that communications are not intercepted.

6-2 DATA COMMUNICATIONS HARDWARE

Data communications (also called telecommunications) is the electronic collection and distribution of information from and to remote facilities. Data communications hardware is used to transmit digital information between terminals and computers or between computers.

The essential elements in any network are the server computers and client computers. In client/server computing, a server computer supports many client computers. The proxy server computer sits between the client PC and a normal server, and handles many client requests.

Voice/data/fax modems, both internal and external, modulate and demodulate signals so that data can be transmitted over telephone lines. The cable modem, a DSL modem, or a satellite modem enables broadband Internet access. The DSLAM (Digital Subscriber Line Access Multiplexor) routes DSL signals to telephone companies for processing.

A network interface card (NIC) that enables and controls the exchange of data between PCs in a LAN. The primary hardware/software technologies used to link networks and facilitate the routing of information among networks are the router and the gateway. The router establishes the link between the source and destination in a process called handshaking, then sends the message to a network address. A backbone is composed of one or more routers and/or gateways and the associated transmission media.

Terminals enable interaction with a remote computer system. The general-purpose terminals are the video display terminal (VDT) and the telephone. Terminals come in all shapes and sizes and have a variety of input/output capabilities. A thin client is a smart terminal; that is, it has some processing capabilities and RAM.

Telephony is the integration of computers and telephones.

An assortment of special-function terminals, such as automatic teller machines (ATMs) and point-of-sale (POS) terminals, are designed for a specific application.

6-3 THE DATA COMMUNICATIONS CHANNEL

A communications channel is the facility through which digital information must pass to get from one location in a computer network to the next.

A channel may be composed of one or more of the following transmission media: telephone lines or Cat5 cabling of copper twisted-pair wire, coaxial cable, fiber optic cable, microwave signals, radio-frequency signals, and wireless transceivers. Communications satellites are essentially microwave repeater stations that maintain a geosynchronous orbit around the earth. Two services are made available over twisted-pair wire: POTS (plain old telephone services) and Digital Subscriber Line (DSL). Some cable television systems offer high-speed Internet access over coaxial cable (cable modem).

The two most popular communications standards used for enabling devices and PCs to talk to one another are Wi-Fi (Wireless-B, Wireless-A, and Wireless-G) and Bluetooth. Wi-Fi is a "longwire" replacement technology in LANs. Bluetooth is a "shortwire" replacement technology. A new wireless standard, 802.16, will permit 70 M bps over a 30-mile range.

WAP, the Wireless Application Protocol, enables the creation of Web applications for mobile devices.

Line-of-sight wireless technologies MMDS (Multichannel Multipoint Distribution Service) and LMDS (Local Multipoint Distribution Service) provide for network access at fiber optic-level speeds.

Communications common carriers provide communications channels to the public, and lines can be arranged to suit the application. A private or leased line provides a dedicated communications channel. A switched or dialup line is available on a time-and-distance charge basis.

Communications protocols are rules established to govern the way data are transmitted in a computer network. Protocols fall into two general classifications: asynchronous and synchronous.

6-4 NETWORKS

Computer systems are linked together to form a computer network. In a computer network, the node can be a terminal, a computer, or any other destination/source device. The basic physical topologies for configuring computer systems within a computer network are star topology, ring topology, and bus topology. The bus topology permits the connection of nodes along a network bus. In practice, most networks are actually hybrids of these network topologies.

The personal area network (PAN) is a short-range, low-cost, low-speed wireless technology. The local area network (LAN), or local net, connects nodes in close proximity and does not need a common carrier. A WAN, or wide area network, connects nodes, usually LANs, in widely dispersed geographic areas. The MAN, or metropolitan area network, is a network designed for a city.

The physical transfer of data and programs between LAN nodes is controlled by the access method embedded in the network interface card's ROM, usually the Ethernet or token access method. The three most popular servers are the file server, the print server, and the communications server. These server functions may reside in a dedicated LAN server.

The network operating system (NOS) is actually several pieces of software, a part of which resides in each LAN component's RAM. In a peer-to-peer LAN, all PCs are equals. Any PC can share its resources with its peers. In LANs with dedicated servers, the controlling software resides in the file server's RAM.

In client/server computing, both client and server computers perform processing to maximize system efficiency. Client computers run front-end applications software and server computers run back-end applications software.

LANs and groupware provide the foundation for workgroup computing. The breadth of workgroup computing encompasses any application that involves groups of people linked by a computer network. Workgroup computing applications, called groupware, include electronic mail, instant messaging, calendar and scheduling, brainstorming and problem solving, shared whiteboarding, and others.

6-5 HOME NETWORKING

The home network is a term coined to refer to small LANs in the home. Home networks enable Internet connection sharing, peripherals sharing, and multiplayer gaming. Common home wired networking technologies include Ethernet, HomePNA (uses telephone lines), and HomePlug (uses AC power lines). Most wireless home networks are built around Wireless-B and Wireless-G technologies. Any or all of these technologies can coexist in a single home network. The implementation and set up of a home network is relatively inexpensive and straightforward.

KEY TERMS

MATCHING

_____ **1.** VPN

_____ **2.** node

_____ **3.** WAN

_____ **4.** intranet

_____ **5.** fiber optic cable

_____ **6.** twisted-pair wire

_____ **7.** Ethernet

_____ **8.** MAN

_____ **9.** asynchronous transmission

_____ **10.** DSLAM

a combines DSL signals

b network access method

c transmitted at irregular intervals

d tunnels on Net

e PC in a home network

f network in metropolitan area

g POTS media

h more encompassing than a LAN

i pulses of light

j internal Internet

CHAPTER SELF-CHECK

TRUE/FALSE

1. Either a company has connectivity or it does not, with no in-between. (T/F)

2. An intranet uses the TCP/IP protocol. (T/F)

3. In client/server computing, a client computer supports many server computers. (T/F)

4. The typical telephone-link modem is a voice/data/fax modem. (T/F)

5. The DSLAM facilitates satellite broadband communications. (T/F)

6. Special-function terminals can be found in most department stores. (T/F)

7. ATMs are now available in some areas of the country that will let you order and receive Internal Revenue Service (IRS) forms and airline tickets. (T/F)

8. The telephone can be a terminal. (T/F)

9. The two basic types of service offered by common carriers are a private line and a switched line. (T/F)

10. Microwave relay stations are located approximately 500 miles apart. (T/F)

11. The channel capacity for DSL service is about 10 times that of cable TV digital service. (T/F)

12. Communications protocols describe how data are transmitted in a computer network. (T/F)

13. In a LAN with a dedicated server, the network operating system for the entire LAN resides in the server processor's RAM. (T/F)

14. In a peer-to-peer LAN, the less powerful PCs are clients to the more powerful PCs. (T/F)

15. A LAN is designed for "long-haul" data communications. (T/F)

16. A router facilitates Internet sharing in home networks. (T/F)

17. HomePNA and HomePlug use existing wiring for the home network. (T/F)

MULTIPLE CHOICE

1. Connectivity is implemented: (a) all at once, (b) after the Internet option has failed, (c) in degrees, or (d) to thwart B2B.

2. VPN stands for: (a) virtual private network, (b) very personal network, (c) virtual POTS net, or (d) vat pat nat.

3. A closed or private version of the Internet is called: (a) a fishnet, (b) an intranet, (c) an overnet, or (d) an addnet.

4. A communications device establishes the link between the source and destination in a process called: (a) handshaking, (b) greeting, (c) hello good-bye, or (d) messaging.

5. What device converts digital signals into analog signals for transmission over telephone lines: (a) router, (b) brouter, (c) modem, or (d) client/server?

6. Which of these is not used for broadband communications: (a) cable modem, (b) DSL modem, (c) wrapped-pair modem, or (d) satellite modem?

7. Which terminal permits system interaction via a GUI: (a) a dumb terminal, (b) a thin client, (c) a text-based terminal, or (d) a traditional VDT?

8. The primary input/output on the VDT is: (a) the mouse and microphone, (b) the keyboard and speaker, (c) a hard disk and monitor, or (d) the keyboard and monitor.

9. The unit of measure for the capacity of a data communications channel is: (a) bps, (b) bytes per second, (c) RAM units, or (d) megabits.

10. Which of these terms is not used to refer to a communications channel: (a) link, (b) pipe, (c) passageway, or (d) line?

11. DSL service is delivered into homes over what kind of line: (a) POTS, (b) satellite, (c) cable, or (d) fiber?

12. Which transmission media offers the greatest capacity: (a) fiber optic cable, (b) Cat5, (c) coax, or (d) radio wave?

13. Which of these communications standards is not Wi-Fi: (a) IEEE 802.11a, (b) IEEE 806.11q, (c) IEEE 802.11b, or (d) IEEE 802.11g?

14. The Bluetooth range is: (a) 30 feet, (b) 3000 feet, (c) 3 miles, or (d) 30 miles.

15. The central cable called a network bus is most closely associated with which network topology: (a) ring, (b) star, (c) bus, or (d) train.

16. Which LAN access method passes a token from node to node: (a) token, (b) Ethernet, (c) contention, or (d) parity checking?

17. Which of these applications permits a document or image to be viewed simultaneously by several people on the network: (a) scheduling, (b) whiteboarding, (c) electronic forms, or (d) brainstorming?

18. Which of these is not a type of home network: (a) PDair, (b) HomePNA, (c) Wi-Fi, or (d) Ethernet?

19. A portable phone would be most likely to interfere with which type of home network: (a) HomePlug, (b) HomePNA, (c) Ethernet, or (d) Wireless-G?

20. Home networks are set up as what type of LAN: (a) peer to peer, (b) peer to server, (c) client/server, or (d) WAN-LAN?

IT ETHICS AND ISSUES

1. MONITORING OF PERSONAL COMMUNICATIONS

Many organizations have monitored the telephone conversations of their employees for decades; now networking has made it possible to monitor written communications, too. These organizations cite productivity and quality control as justification. People who used to chat at the water cooler or snack counter do so now over office e-mail or instant messaging. Monitored e-mail is just as likely to surface "meet you at the gym after work" as "meet you in the conference room."

Realistically, e-mail is monitored to discourage non-business messages and to keep employees focused on job-related activities. We now know that e-mail and instant messaging, when used responsibly, can boost productivity. We also know that, if abused, it can be counter-productive.

Once an organization decides to monitor personal communications, it can do so in several ways. Individuals can scan e-mail archives for inappropriate transmissions, often a time-consuming process. In large organizations, computers scan e-mail archives for keywords (baseball, party, boss, and so on) and kick out messages with questionable content. Already many employees have been fired or disciplined for abusing e-mail.

Employees feel that monitoring of personal communications is an invasion of privacy. Many workers view e-mail and instant messaging as tools, such as a telephone, and that they should be allowed some reasonable personal use. The issue is being argued in the courts.

Discussion: Does an employer's right to know outweigh the employee's right to privacy?

Discussion: What statements do you feel should be included in a corporate policy on e-mail usage?

Discussion: Which do you feel is more invasive, the monitoring of voice mail and inspection of lockers or the monitoring of e-mail? Why?

Discussion: The use of instant messaging is growing in the corporate world, but companies that monitor e-mail seldom monitor instant messaging. To be consistent, should they monitor instant messaging, too? Why or why not?

2. TERM-PAPER FRAUD

Plagiarism, more specifically term-paper fraud, has been a problem in higher education throughout this century. However, only during the past few years have for-sale term papers on every common subject been showcased to the world, made readily available over the Internet, and spread over campus networks. Students purchase these papers hoping to pass them off as originals. Typically, they will use a variety of software tools to add a personal touch to these recycled papers.

Many sites on the Internet offer "term-paper assistance" in a variety of topic areas. One site has both off-the-shelf and custom term-paper services, inviting students to "Get a brand-new paper written from scratch according to your exact specifications. Click here." Some states have passed laws prohibiting the sale of prefabricated term papers. However, term-paper mills circumvent these laws by stating that the intended purpose of their term papers is that they be used as models that students can use during the preparation of their own term papers.

Discussion: Is plagiarism a problem on your campus? If so, how big a problem?

Discussion: What can students do to help deter plagiarism and encourage academic honesty? What can college administrators do? What can professors do? What can government do?

Discussion: Do students who plagiarize the work of others rob themselves of the knowledge and experience they gain from writing a well-developed paper? Explain.

3. ACCESSIBILITY TO E-MAIL ARCHIVES

Corporate networks have prompted a mountain of stored e-mails. E-mail may be the corporate Achilles heel when it comes to lawsuits. Attorneys can subpoena e-mail archives on disk or tape relative to pending lawsuits. Among the thousands of e-mail messages sent each day in a typical medium-sized company, attorneys are likely to find statements that support their cause. People tend to be conversational when writing e-mail messages. People don't write e-mail with the thought that it might be shown as evidence in a court of law. To avoid the potential for litigation, many companies routinely purge e-mail archives. Had the people at Microsoft Corporation been more diligent about purging their e-mail, U.S. government prosecutors would not have been able to subpoena the company's e-mail. The e-mail they eventually found was critical to the government's antitrust suit against Microsoft.

Discussion: Should companies save e-mail? If so, for how long?

Discussion: Should attorneys be allowed to subpoena e-mail archives? Why or why not?

4. THE INTERNET'S IMPACT ON THE FAMILY UNIT

According to the results of an Internet usage survey at Stanford University's Institute for the Quantitative Study in Society, Americans report they spend less time with friends and family, shopping in stores, and watching television. Also, Americans spend more time working for their employers at home—without cutting back their hours in the office. Another result indicated that time on the Internet increased with Internet experience (number of years using the Internet).

Discussion: Is the Internet having a negative impact on the family unit? Explain.

Discussion: The survey showed that regular Internet users (those who spend 5 or more hours per week) choose to work more at home than others in the general population. Why do you think they do this?

Discussion: A key finding of the study was that "the more hours people use the Internet, the less time they spend in contact with real human beings." Should society make an effort to educate people to this trend? Why or why not?

5. SHARING INTERNET ACCESS VIA WIRELESS

The price structure for broadband Internet service, such as cable modem and DSL, is based on the statistical reality that the average consumer will use less than 1% of the line's potential capacity to carry information. Many consumers have picked up on the fact that they have a lot of excess capacity and are willing to share this capacity through wireless "home networking," which, in fact, may involve PCs in a dozen apartments and a dozen families. Broadband providers claim that their fee structure is designed for single-family usage. Broadband consumers claim that they are paying for always-on Internet access and how they use it is up to them.

Discussion: Businesses pay significantly more for broadband capacity, primarily because businesses can be expected to use a significantly higher percentage of the line's capacity than a family would. Should individuals be allowed to share Internet capacity, even if they do it for free?

Discussion: In many cases, a broadband line is installed and billed to a particular address, but users in nearby apartments on a wireless LAN share the Internet and the bill. Discuss the legal ramifications of this arrangement from the account owner's perspective. From the perspective of those who share the line. From the Internet provider's perspective.

DISCUSSION AND PROBLEM SOLVING

1. Discuss ways that the trend toward greater connectivity has changed your life over the last two years. Speculate on ways that it might change your life during the next five years.

2. Select a type of company and give an example of what information the company might make available over its Internet, its intranet, and its extranet.

3. Explain why you must use a modem to send data over a plain old telephone line.

4. A bank is assessing whether to replace its aging PCs, which are linked in a LAN, with new PCs or thin clients. Present an argument for new PCs or for thin clients.

5. It's getting crowded in space with so many companies and countries launching communications satellites into geosynchronous orbit. Is there a danger of having too many satellites hovering above the earth? If so, what can be done about it?

6. The cost of a normal 56 K bps dialup connection with unlimited access to the Internet costs anywhere from $15 to $25. How much more would you pay to get Internet access via cable TV, satellite, or DSL that is 10 to 50 times faster than that provided by a 56 K modem? Explain.

7. Speculate on the different types of transmission media that might be used to transmit data for a one-hour Internet session.

8. Identify the type and location of at least five different types of nodes in your college's network.

9. A variety of communications hardware, including a router, is needed to link local area networks that use different communications protocols. Why are LANs not designed to use the same standards for communication so that communications hardware tasks can be simplified?

10. Describe how information can be made readily accessible to many people in a company, but only on a need-to-know basis.

11. The five PCs in the purchasing department of a large consumer goods manufacturer are used primarily for word processing and database applications. What would be the benefits associated with connecting the PCs in a local area network?

12. The mere fact that PCs on a LAN are networked poses a threat to security. Why?

13. Some metropolitan area networks are completely private; that is, communications common carrier services are not used. Network nodes can be distributed throughout large cities. How do companies link the nodes on the network without common carrier data communications facilities?

14. Describe at least one situation in academia or the business world where creating a portable network would be inappropriate. That is, a situation where people with notebook PCs link them in a network by attaching them to a common cable or by using wireless transceivers. Briefly describe what the network might do.

15. Do you have a home network? If so, describe it in detail, listing all related communications hardware and software. If not, speculate on when and why you might consider installing a home network.

FOCUS ON PERSONAL COMPUTING

1. *Help for Home Networking.* On your Windows desktop, click *Start* on the taskbar, then choose *Help and Support.* Enter "home networking" and then open appropriate descriptions in the results list. Read these to learn more about home networking in the Windows environment. Click on hypertext links to expand your knowledge of the topic, as needed. Now, do the same for "HPNA," one of the technologies used in home networks, and "ICS," the type of software that enables Internet connection sharing. Briefly describe at least one newfound piece of knowledge for each topic that you feel will help you in the creation of a home network.

2. *Designing a Home Network.* Do the preliminary design for either an Ethernet, HomePNA, HomePlug, or wireless home or small office network, preferably for one with which you are familiar. Draw a diagram of the house or office including the location of each PC, shared resource (printer, scanner, DVD burner, and so on), each jack for connectors, the router/gateway, any hubs/switches, and other network hardware, as need. Make a list of all the communications hardware and cabling you will need to create the network.

Go online and price out the hardware and cabling (at least one source for each item). Compute a total network cost.

3. *Tracing Internet Paths.* The Windows trace-route utility, "tracert," traces the path of a packet as it travels through a network, out onto the Internet, into a destination network, then back. Trace route logs a packet's intermediate hops as it travels through network/Internet routers/servers. The hops begin with your home/office network and your ISP. The next hops are over the Internet backbone and eventually to the destination. For each hop, Tracert shows timing (in milliseconds) and routing information (IP addresses and URLs). Typically, the greater the number of hops, the longer it takes for a packet to reach its destination. In Windows, click *Start, All Programs,* then select *MS-DOS,* or click *Start, Run,* then enter "*command*". At the command prompt (>), enter "*tracert www.yourdomain. com*", except enter an actual domain of your choosing. Trace the paths for several domains and compare the results. Enter "exit" to close the MS-DOS window.

1. The Online Study Guide (multiple choice, true/false, matching, and essay questions)
2. Internet Learning Activities
   - Online Books
   - Transmission Media
   - Terminals
   - Networks
3. Serendipitous Activities
   - Government

IT ETHICS, CRIME, AND PRIVACY

LEARNING OBJECTIVES

Once you have read and studied this chapter, you will be able to:

- Appreciate the information technology code of ethics and the importance of IT ethics in our information society (Section 7-1).

- Understand the scope of workplace ethics along with key ergonomic and environmental considerations in the design of your workplace (Section 7-2).

- Answer important questions about the privacy of personal information (Section 7-3).

- Identify types and the scope of computer and IT crime (Section 7-4).

How we fare as a society depends on how we cope with a continuous stream of information technology issues. Just about any IT issue is fuzzy, and there are few historical individual, corporate, or national perspectives from which to derive a solution. Frequently, we must address these issues as they surface to determine what course of action to take. This chapter should make you more sensitive to IT ethics and help you make better decisions on the critical information technology issues of the day, such as the privacy of personal information.

Most of us spend much of our day an arm's length from a PC. Reading this chapter will give you a better understanding of the importance of workplace ethics and the ergonomics (human–machine interaction) of computing.

You and the organizations with which you are associated are vulnerable to computer and information technology crime. Cybercrime is on the rise and this chapter will provide you with a foundation of understanding that will help you avoid and prevent technology-based crime.

7-1 ETHICS IN INFORMATION TECHNOLOGY

Why this section is important to you.

People who conscientiously apply the principles of IT ethics are more likely to protect personal privacy, honor copyright laws, report unethical activity, and generally do what is right when confronted with controversial situations relating to technology. The material in this section will prepare you to make good decisions regarding IT ethics and issues.

Generally, information technology is applied for the good of humanity; however, it also can be abused and used as a tool for crime. As a result, the computer revolution has generated intense controversy and raised serious issues about IT ethics. An ethical person accepts and lives by a set of moral principles and values. These principles define what is socially accepted as "good" and, by implication, what is "bad." An ethical person has an obligation to take morally appropriate action when confronted with an ethical dilemma (Figure 7-1).

Society continues to raise questions about what is and is not ethical in the information technology arena. These ethics issues are so important to our society that IT ethics are being integrated into college curricula. Educators believe that if people are made aware of the consequences of their actions, then fewer people will be motivated to plant dangerous computer viruses, contaminate information systems with false information, post pornographic material to the Internet, or abuse the sanctity of intellectual property. Educators warn us of dire consequences should we fail to instill a sense of ethics in future generations. If ethical abuses are left unabated, all roads on the information superhighway will be toll roads for encrypted data; that is, only those who pay for the key to the encrypted information can view it. If this were to happen, we would become a more secretive society, far less willing to share accumulated knowledge.

AN IT CODE OF ETHICS

Most major IT professional societies have adopted a code of ethics. Their codes warn members, who are mostly professionals in the information technology fields, that they can be expelled or censured if they violate them. Rarely, however, has any action been taken against delinquent members. Does this mean there are no violations? Of course not. A carefully drafted IT code of ethics provides some guidelines for conduct, but professional

FIGURE 7-1 PRACTICING IT ETHICS

HONORING SENSITIVE INFORMATION

This crew member on-board the "Radiance of the Seas" is also a knowledge worker and must be ever-conscious of IT ethics. She has in-cabin access to the Internet and CrewNection, the service which links the ship's crew and permits access to sensitive information on the ship's database.

Courtesy of International Business Machines Corporation. Unauthorized use not permitted.

PROTECTING CORPORATE SECRETS

We all have an obligation to adopt a code of ethics when working with computers. The focus of this CAD designer's work is a closely held corporate secret until the first newly designed automobile hits the showroom.

Courtesy of Sun Microsystems, Inc.

societies cannot be expected to police the misdeeds of their members. We are bound by the same laws in cyberspace as we are in the physical world, so, in some instances, a code violation is also a violation of a local, state, or federal law.

An IT code of ethics provides direction for knowledge workers so that they can act responsibly in their creation and application of information technology. The Association for Computing Machinery (ACM) Code of Conduct is summarized in Figure 7-2. ACM is the largest professional society for computing and IT professionals. The ACM Code of Conduct provides excellent guidelines for both knowledge workers and IT professionals. The ACM ethical considerations, which are derived from more general ethical principles, are expressed as imperatives which apply to IT ethics.

If you adopt the principles in the ACM code shown in Figure 7-2, it is unlikely that anyone will question your IT ethics. Unfortunately, well-meaning people routinely violate this simple code because they are unaware of the tremendous detrimental impact of their actions. With the speed and power of computers, a minor code infraction can be magnified to a costly catastrophe. For this reason, we must be aware of the important ethical questions of our electronic age.

IT ETHICS AND ISSUES

If we all lived within the boundaries of the ACM Code of Conduct described in Figure 7-2, any discussion of IT ethics would be irrelevant. Unfortunately, most PC users have violated one or more of these ethical principles. For example, how many people do you know who have downloaded copyright material from the Internet, then played, viewed, or used it without permission to do so? IT ethics is presented in each chapter of this book as it relates to chapter

PERSONAL COMPUTING
Spyware

Even though you use antivirus software and keep a "clean" computer, cyberspies may be lurking around your computer in the form of spyware. Spyware is a program that is installed on your PC without your consent to gather information about you. Over 1000 spyware programs are floating around the Internet. They push pop-up ads your way, sending your preferences back to a central site. They enable a grid network to use your PC's spare computing capacity. Another reports your Web-surfing tendencies. Search for "remove spyware" in your Internet browser for instructions on how to remove spyware.

FIGURE 7–2   **A CODE OF CONDUCT FOR KNOWLEDGE WORKERS AND IT PROFESSIONALS**

The first two sections of the Association for Computing Machinery (ACM) Code of Conduct (shown here in the left column) are applicable to all knowledge workers and IT professionals. The full code and detailed explanations can be found at the ACM Web site at <http://acm.org>.

1. GENERAL MORAL IMPERATIVES

1.1 Contribute to society and human well-being	This principle is an affirmation of an obligation to use and apply information technology for the common good.
1.2 Avoid harm to others	This principle prohibits the use of IT in any way that results in injury or negative consequences to anyone. Implied is an obligation to report violations of this principle.
1.3 Be honest and trustworthy	Honesty is an essential component of trust, without which an organization cannot function effectively.
1.4 Be fair and take action not to discriminate	This imperative is founded on the values of equality, tolerance, respect for others, and the principles of equal justice.
1.5 Honor property rights including copyrights and patents	IT ethics adhere to the laws of our land, which strictly prohibit violations of copyrights, patents, trade secrets, and the terms of license agreements.
1.6 Give proper credit for intellectual property	This principle demands that those practicing IT ethics must protect the integrity of intellectual property and, by implication, not take credit for the ideas or work of others.
1.7 Respect the privacy of others	This principle demands that those practicing IT ethics must protect the integrity of data describing individuals. This includes ensuring the integrity of data and protecting it from unauthorized access or accidental disclosure. The implication of this imperative is that only the personal information required for an application is collected and that this information is used only for the purposes intended.
1.8 Honor confidentiality	This ethical concern tells us to respect our obligations of confidentiality.

2. MORE SPECIFIC PROFESSIONAL RESPONSIBILITIES

2.1 Strive to achieve the highest quality, effectiveness, and dignity in both the process and products of professional work	Excellence in performance of duties should be an objective for every professional.
2.2 Acquire and maintain professional competence	Information technology is in constant motion and those dealing with IT must commit themselves to keeping pace with the technology.
2.3 Know and respect existing laws pertaining to professional work	Those who create and use IT must be aware of all applicable local, state, province, national, and international laws. The implication is that the immoral or inappropriate laws must be challenged.
2.4 Accept and provide appropriate professional review	This imperative invites professionals who create and use IT to review and critique one another's work in an effort to seek the highest level of quality.
2.5 Give comprehensive and thorough evaluations of computer systems and their impacts, including analysis of possible risks	Because those who deal with information technology are in a position of special trust, they must strive to be perceptive, thorough, and objective when evaluating, recommending, and presenting system descriptions and alternatives.
2.6 Honor contracts, agreements, and assigned responsibilities	Honoring one's commitments is a matter of integrity and honesty. IT professionals are obligated to ensure that a system performs as intended.
2.7 Improve public understanding of computing and its consequences	Anyone working with IT is charged with sharing technical knowledge with the public and encouraging understanding of IT, including its impact and limitations.
2.8 Access computing and communication resources only when authorized to so	This imperative prohibits trespassing and the unauthorized use of a computer or communications system. Trespassing includes accessing communication networks and computer systems without explicit authorization. No one should enter or use another's computer system, software, or data files without permission.

material. The "IT Ethics and Issues" scenarios at the end of each chapter pose common ethical dilemmas for debate and discussion. These are summarized, chapter by chapter, in Figure 7-3.

The IT ethics scenarios listed in Figure 7-3 represent of a broad range of IT ethical concerns. These and the discussions of real-world ethical dilemmas that follow should give you pause for reflection on the importance that we should give to ethics that relate to or involve information technology.

- *Abuse of PC privileges at work.* According to a study by the University of Maryland, employees spend an average of 3.7 hours a week on nonbusiness activity on the Internet. Ironically, the same study revealed that employees spend an average of 5.9 hours a week at home catching up on their work. Should employers explicitly ban personal use of the Internet while at work or should employees be allowed a "reasonable" amount of personal Net time?

- *Technology in clinical health care.* Relatively few physicians take advantage of the information-producing potential of IT to improve patient care. There are expert systems that can help them diagnose diseases, drug-interaction databases that can help them prescribe the right drug, and computer-assisted searches that can call up literature pertinent to a particular patient's illness. Are medical schools failing in their duty to train doctors to give the best possible care?

- *Exposing trade secrets—legally.* Most of us simply accept the volatility and unpredictability of airline ticket prices. Prices, however, are set by sophisticated computer-based models and if you know how the model works, price variations become predictable. A professor used data collected over a long period of time from Internet-based ticketing Web sites to create an algorithm which mirrored that of the airlines. Would it be ethical to sell this legally obtained trade secret-type information?

- *Software with bugs.* A study by the National Institute of Standards and Technology revealed that software errors embedded in commercial software products costs the United States economy about $60 billion a year. We expect baby carriages, DVD players, and tennis rackets to work. Shouldn't we expect the same of software products?

- *Cell phone spam.* By law, telemarketers cannot call cell phones, but no law prohibits them from sending text messages to cellular telephones. Already, computer-based systems route spam to cell phones in the form of text messages, the cost of which is paid by the cell phone owner. Is there any ethical justification for this approach to marketing?

- *Smart homes.* We have the technology to create smart homes that feature computer-controlled lighting, temperature, and security systems. This technology pays for itself in a few years on energy saving alone. Why do people in the construction industry not promote energy-saving smart houses that offer tremendous benefits to the owners and to society?

- *File swapping and pornography.* We hear music and movie executives complain about the money they are losing from file swapping and now we are beginning to hear from executives of one of the most lucrative areas of e-commerce—pornography. It is estimated that close to 50% of all file swapping activity involves blue images and movies. Is it ethical for those who share pornographic files to dilute the profits of those companies that create them?

- *Writing computer viruses—a college course.* At least one university offers a course in which students can learn to write computer viruses and "malware" (bad software). Can such a course be justified within the realm of modern IT ethics?

- *Spam out of control.* Approximately half of all e-mail is bulk unsolicited e-mail—spam. AOL's 35 million customers receive 2 billion spam messages a day. Spam is responsible for $10 billion worth of lost productivity in the United States alone. The big problem is that spam is an effective marketing tool. In most states, spam is legal, but is it ethical?

FIGURE 7–3 **IT ETHICS AND ISSUES: CHAPTER BY CHAPTER**

Information technology ethics and issues are covered throughout this book in context with content. This table shows the chapter and page number of IT ethics and issues scenarios and their accompanying discussion questions.

CHAPTER	END-OF-CHAPTER IT ETHICS AND ISSUES	OVERVIEW
Chapter 1 Computers and IT	Should PC Ownership be an Entrance Requirement for Colleges? (p. 54)	Is it ethical for colleges to require students to pay tuition *and* purchase a PC?
	Hate Sites on the Internet (p. 55)	Should hate Web sites be protected under the umbrella of free speech?
Chapter 2 Software	The Quality of Software (p. 111)	Is it ethical for software vendors to rush their products to market, bugs and all, in an effort to beat the competition?
	Counterfeit Software (p. 111)	Is it ethical to violate software copyright laws since "Everybody does it?"
Chapter 3 Going Online	E-Mail Etiquette (p. 151)	Is it ethical to enforce strict rules of e-mail etiquette even if the rules have a negative impact on the free flow of electronic communication?
	The Unwanted Chat Room Guest (p. 151)	Is it ethical to close popular chat rooms because a few visitors choose to abuse their privilege of participation?
	Ads in Personal E-mail (p. 151)	Is it ethical for ISPs to allow advertisers to wrap commercial messages around personal e-mail?
Chapter 4 Inside the Computer	Is What We See and Hear Real or Not? (p. 182)	Is it ethical to present digitally altered images, music, advertisements, as if they are real?
	The Digital Divide: Is It Racial or Economic? (p. 182)	Is it ethical to passively accept the growing digital divide between the computer/IT haves and have nots?
	Recycling Old Computers (p. 182)	Is it ethical for companies and individuals to be forced by law to pay for the proper disposal of computer hardware, which contains hazardous materials?
Chapter 5 Storage and I/O Devices	Assistive Technology in the IT Workplace (p. 235)	Is it ethical for employers to provide opportunities for people without disabilities and not do the same for people with disabilities?
	File Sharing (p. 235)	With millions of files containing intellectual property (music, movies and so on) being swapped on the Internet each day, is it ethical to become one of the participants?
	The Spycam (p. 236)	Is it ethical to use tiny remote video cameras in private or public places without disclosure of their presence?
Chapter 6 Networks and Networking	Monitoring of Personal Communications (p. 267)	Is it ethical for employers to monitor personal communications, such as e-mail and instant messages?
	Term-Paper Fraud (p. 267)	Is it ethical to provide or use, in any way, pre-written term papers distributed via the Internet?
	Accessibility to E-mail Archives (p. 268)	Is it ethical for government prosecutors to have access to corporate e-mail archives?
	The Internet's Impact on the Family Unit (p. 268)	Does the Internet have a negative impact on the family unit?
	Sharing Internet Access via Wireless (p. 268)	Is it ethical to tap into broadband Internet access intended for use by one account?

FIGURE 7–3 continued

CHAPTER	END-OF-CHAPTER IT ETHICS AND ISSUES	OVERVIEW
Chapter 7 **IT Ethics, Privacy,** **and Crime**	Violating the Copyright of Intellectual Property (p. 308)	How does society instill respect for the copyrights on itellectual property?
	Scanning for Shoplifters (p. 308)	Is it ethical to identify individuals via face-recognition technology who might consider such passive identification an invasion of privacy?
	Moral Filtering of Internet Content (p. 308)	Is it ethical to established Internet policy that may result in the moral filtering of Web site content and applications?
	Prescreening of Online Communications (p. 309)	Is it ethical for businesses, ISPs, and others to invoke electronic filters that prescreen online communications based on the presence of offensive language?
	Inappropriate Usage Use of the Internet at Work (p. 310)	Is it ethical for knowledge workers to abuse their Internet privileges at work or for employers to fire those who do non-job-related activities on the Net?
Chapter 8 **E-Commerce, Databases,** **and Security**	The Internet Sales Tax (p. 359)	Is it morally and economically appropriate to impose taxes on Internet sales?
	Addicition to the Internet (p. 359)	Is the Internet addictive?
	Cybersquatting (p. 359)	Is it ethical for a Web site to lock you into their Web site by disabling the "Back" button?
	Mouse Trapping (p. 359)	Is it ethical for individuals to register domain names of popular trademarks or names that imply affiliation to well-known individuals or companies?
Chapter 9 **Information Systems and** **Engineering Technology**	E-Commerce and Profiling (p. 394)	Is it ethical for companies involved in e-commerce to gather information and build user profiles, without customer knowledge, so they can better target their marketing efforts?
	Does the Internet Really Change Everything? (p. 395)	To what extent has the Internet changed our society?
Chapter 10 **Business Information** **Systems**	Cooperative Development of Information Systems (p. 429)	Is it ethical for competing companies, such as airline companies, to collaborate on Internet-based systems?
	Locational Computing (p. 429)	Is it ethical for an organization to use GPS technology to track an individual's location then use this information to promote a product or agenda?

GREEN COMPUTING

The dawning of the age of green computing is upon us. **Green computing** is merely environmentally sensible computing, an increasingly important topic in both individual and corporate IT ethics. Computers drain critical resources such as electricity and paper. They also produce unwanted electrical, chemical, and bulk-waste side effects. As a society, we finally are adopting a more environmentally sound position with respect to the use, manufacture, and disposal of computing hardware.

Saving Energy and Trees

United States government agencies and many businesses have adopted policies that require all new PCs, monitors, and printers to comply with the Environmental Protection Agency's *Energy Star* guidelines. To comply with Energy Star requirements, monitors and processors in standby mode (not in use) can consume no more than 30 watts of power. Printers are permitted a range of 30 to 45 watts. Computer manufacturers have been moving toward more energy-efficient products in hopes of reducing manufacturing costs and increasing product competitiveness.

It costs about $250 a year to keep a PC and laser page printer running 24 hours a day. We could save a lot of money and fossil fuel if we turn off our PCs and peripheral devices or place them in energy-saving standby mode when not in use. Judicious computing can even save trees—why print a letter or send a fax when e-mail is faster and better for the environment? Green computing means printing only what needs to be printed, saving the paper for more meaningful applications.

Other recommendations by green computing proponents include buying equipment from vendors who are manufacturing environmentally safe products, purchasing recycled paper, recycling paper and toner printer cartridges (which would probably end up in landfills), buying reconditioned components rather than new ones, recycling old PCs and printers, shopping electronically to save gas, and telecommuting at least once or twice a week.

What to Do with Old PCs?

Eventually every PC wears out or simply becomes obsolete. No level of maintenance, upgrading, or troubleshooting can save them. Within the next year, over 300 million computers will outlive their usefulness and have no market value. If these PCs were simply thrown out with the trash, they would contribute over 8 million tons of very unfriendly waste to landfills. A typical PC and its peripherals will contain mercury, cadmium, lead, and other toxic and bioaccumulative compounds. Any environmentalist can tell you that these elements and compounds can have a dramatic impact on ground, water, and air quality.

The average useful life is about three years for a business PC and about four years for a home PC. Currently, only about 20% of PCs and peripherals are recycled, compared to 70% for major appliances, such as dishwashers and refrigerators. Clearly, we need to act more responsibly with PCs at the end of their lives.

At present, there is little or no economic incentive to recycle hardware. For most companies, it is less expensive and easier to throw old hardware in the dumpster (but only where it is legal to do so). Companies that practice IT ethics are adopting a *product stewardship policy* that encourages responsible consideration of products, during and after their useful life. This policy often is the difference between practicing environmentally responsible recycling and having a dumpster full of potentially harmful electrical components. Consider this: a CRT monitor contains 2-plus pounds of lead to protect users from radiation.

The throwaway option, however, may disappear over the next few years as more states place PCs and their peripheral devices on their lists of hazardous materials. In some states, dumping old hardware already is illegal. Many states are requiring or will be requiring consumers to pay a disposal fee in advance when they purchase their PC systems. It is only a matter of time before each of us will have "cradle-to-grave" responsibility for PCs and computer hardware.

If you feel your system still has some useful life, consider giving it to an individual or to an organization, such as a preschool, that needs it. However, keep this in mind: about 70% of all hardware donations are discarded. Literally millions of people are looking for individuals and organizations that might want their old PCs and peripherals, so

FIGURE 7-4

RECYCLING OBSOLETE PCS

Most of the components in obsolete PCs and peripherals can be recycled. This shredder/granulator at Hewlett-Packard Company shreds computers such that the granulated results (see inset) can be separated into piles of steel, plastic, lead, and other materials.

Photo courtesy of Hewlett-Packard Company

only give away systems that are no more than four or five years off the technology, fully functional, have a good mix of software, and are Internet ready. Realistically, the rest have little or no value.

A number of recycling companies and several major computer vendors, such as Hewlett-Packard (see Figure 7-4), Intel, and IBM, provide PC recycling services both to consumers and to businesses of all sizes. If your old PC system is a candidate for recycling, send your old system away for proper disposal. Expect to pay between $30 and $40 (including shipping) for this service.

SELF-CHECK

SECTION

1   Hardware manufacturers that comply with the Environmental Protection Agency's Energy Star guidelines sell only recycled PCs. (T/F)

2   Most PC users have violated one or more of the ethical principles in the ACM Code of Conduct. (T/F)

3   Environmentally sensible computing is called: (a) blue computing, (b) green computing, (c) yellow computing, or (d) red computing.

4   A typical PC contains all but which of the following: (a) potassium hydroxide, (b) cadmium, (c) mercury, or (d) lead?

7-2   WORKPLACE ETHICS: HEALTHY COMPUTING

Each era defines new responsibilities for employers. Miners, steel workers, and others working in hazardous conditions fought for decades to enjoy safety in the workplace. Eventually, employers created a safe working environment, but some did so reluctantly. Only after costly labor strikes, which threatened the existence of many companies, did these companies decide to do the right thing for their workers.

> ## Why this section is important to you.
>
> The material in this section highlights the importance of workplace ethics and provides information that will help you to be comfortable in and to remain healthy at your workplace.

Today, corporate executives are more sensitive to *workplace ethics*. Of course, strict government safety regulations provide extra incentive for them to create a safe working environment. Knowledge workers do not work in mines or steel plants and, unless they leave their offices, they rarely are exposed to life-threatening situations. Nevertheless, workplace safety is a serious concern for knowledge workers.

Because safety regulators have focused their attention on cleanup of the Industrial Revolution, relatively few regulations govern health and safety in the knowledge worker's workplace. Because relatively few government regulations apply to our information revolution, some employers have chosen to ignore health concerns at the white-collar worker's workplace, which normally is office space with a networked computer. Workplace ethics is about employers doing the right thing to protect the health of their IT and knowledge workers. Our workplace is changing and it is important that you and your employer be attuned to considerations involving human safety and comfort.

ERGONOMICS AND THE WORKPLACE

For close to a hundred years, the design of automobiles was driven by two basic considerations: appearance and functionality. Engineers were asked to design cars that were visually appealing and could go from point A to point B. Surprisingly, little attention was given to the human factor. That is, no one considered the connection between the driver and passengers and the automobile. About 30 years ago, automobile executives discovered that they could boost sales and enhance functionality by improving this human connection. Thus began the era of ergonomically designed automobiles. Today, human factors engineers apply the principles of ergonomic design to ensure that the interface between people and cars is *safe, comfortable, effective,* and *efficient*.

Ergonomics is the study of the relationships between people and the things they use. The emergence of ergonomics is beginning to have an impact on the relationship between knowledge workers and their workplaces. Only recently has ergonomics, the genesis of workplace ethics, emerged as an important consideration in fitting computers into workplace design (see Figure 7-5).

REASONS FOR CONCERN

During the 1980s, the knowledge worker's workplace gained attention when workers began to blame headaches, depression, anxiety, nausea, fatigue, and irritability on prolonged interaction with a terminal or PC. These and other problems often associated with extended use of a terminal or PC are called **video operator's distress syndrome, or VODS.** Although there was little evidence to link these problems directly with using terminals or PCs (the same problems occurred in other work environments), VODS caused people to take a closer look at the workplace and the types of injuries being reported. As the number of *repetitive-stress injuries* (RSIs) increased for knowledge workers, workstation ergonomics became an increasingly important issue for corporate productivity.

A poorly designed workplace has the potential to cause **cumulative trauma disorder (CTD)**, a condition that can lead to a permanent disability of motor skills. CTD now accounts for more than half of all work-related problems. It typically occurs when workers ignore human factors considerations while spending significant time at the keyboard. Other workstation-related injuries include mental stress, eyestrain, headaches, muscular injuries, and skeletal injuries. Hand and wrist problems associated with keyboarding have always been the main complaint, with the repetitive-stress injury called **carpal tunnel syndrome (CTS)** being the most common. A few years ago, the options for reducing keystrokes were few. Today, we speak to our computers via speech-recognition software with accuracy rates in excess of 95%, thus substantially reducing keystrokes and, in some situations, eliminating keystrokes altogether.

Talk about the radiation emitted by CRT-type monitors has unduly frightened office workers. A controversial, and apparently flawed, study in the late 1980s concluded that women who are exposed to the radiation emitted from terminals and PCs may have a higher rate of miscarriage than those who are not. A comprehensive four-year federal government study concluded that women who work with terminals and PCs and those who do not have the same rate of miscarriage. The controversy may be moot as workers move to space-saving flat-panel screens.

WORKPLACE DESIGN

Practicing workplace ethics and ensuring that workers enjoy the benefits of proper workplace design is good business. Good managers know that a healthy, happy worker is a more productive worker. They also know that the leading causes of lost work time are back/shoulder/neck pain and CTD.

The key to designing a proper workplace for the knowledge worker is *flexibility*. Those companies providing one-size-fits-all workplaces are not in step with the spirit of workplace ethics. The knowledge worker's workplace should be designed with enough flexibility to be custom fitted to its worker. Figure 7-6 highlights important considerations in workplace design. The figure provides hints that relate to the hardware, the chair, the desk, the room, and other equipment. Although progress is slow, ergonomic problems in the workplace are being addressed in legislation and in proposed regulations from the Occupational Safety and Health Administration (OSHA).

It's important for those companies in violation of workplace ethics to know that attention to the overall environment can increase worker performance. For example, indirect lighting can reduce glare. Proper ventilation eliminates health concerns caused by the ozone emitted by laser printers. Excessive exposure to ozone can cause headaches and nausea.

WORKING SMART

One of the most important elements of workplace ethics is employee training. Workers should be shown how to analyze their workstations and make necessary adjustments (such as lowering monitor contrast and brightness or increasing chair lumbar support). Each

FIGURE 7–5 HARDWARE FOR THE ERGONOMICALLY DESIGNED WORKPLACE

HANDS-FREE MOUSE

The NaturalPoint™ Smart-Nav™ mouse alternative gives you hands-free control of a computer cursor. The ergonomic Smart-Nav™ provides precise cursor control through simple head movement allowing your hands to remain on your keyboard, or at your side. The user positions a reflective dot on his/her forehead, glasses, or microphone and an infrared camera tracks its motion to move the cursor.

Courtesy of Natural Point

USING THE FEET FOR INPUT

Give your hands a rest with a programmable Foot Switch. This Foot Switch adds input versatility with a three-button keyboard for your feet.

Courtesy of Kinesis Corporation

FULLY ADJUSTABLE KEYBOARD

This innovative keyboard is ergonomically designed to fit the shape and movements of the human body. The design puts less stress and strain on muscles, reducing the user's risk for fatigue in hands, wrists, and arms.

Courtesy of Kinesis Corporation

STRESS RELIEVER

The repetitive-stress injuries (RSIs) associated with the keyboard may eventually be eliminated as more people move to speech-recognition technology to interact with their PCs.

Courtesy of International Business Machines Corporation. Unauthorized use not permitted.

FACTORY MICE

This ITAC Systems Mouse-Track is a mouse alternative, ergonomically designed for use in extremely harsh environments. The dust-resistant dome encoder lets you point with your index finger and is designed to reduce the risk of carpal tunnel syndrome.

Courtesy of ITAC Systems, Inc.

knowledge worker can then contribute to the quality of his or her workplace by following a couple of simple rules. For example, make the adjustments necessary to custom -fit your workplace. Also, take periodic minibreaks. These minibreaks should involve looking away from your monitor and/or generally altering your body orientation for a few seconds (make a fist, turn your head from side to side, roll your shoulders, walk around your desk, wiggle your toes, wrinkle your nose, twirl your arms, and so on).

FIGURE 7-6 **ERGONOMIC CONSIDERATIONS IN WORKPLACE DESIGN**
Knowledge workers often spend 4 or more hours each day at a PC or terminal. Today workers are more sensitive to the impact of workplace design on their health and effectiveness, so they are paying more attention to the ergonomics (efficiency of the person–machine interface) of the hardware, including chairs and desks.

The Hardware
Monitor location (A). The monitor should be located directly in front of you at arm's length with the top at forehand level. Outside windows should be to the side of the monitor to reduce glare. *Monitor features.* The monitor should be high-resolution with anti-glare screens. *Monitor maintenance.* The monitor should be free from smudges or dust buildup. *Keyboard location (B).* The keyboard should be located such that the upper arm and forearms are at a 90-degree angle. *Keyboard features.* The keyboard should be ergonomically designed to accommodate better the movements of the fingers, hands, and arms.

The Chair
The chair should be fully adjustable to the size and contour of the body. Features should include: *Pneumatic seat height adjustment (C); Seat and back angle adjustment (D); Back-rest height adjustment (E); Recessed armrests with height adjustment (F); Lumbar support adjustment (for lower back support) (G); Five-leg pedestal on casters (H).*

The Desk
The swing space. Use wraparound workspace to keep the PC, important office materials, and files within 18 inches of the chair. *Adjustable tray for keyboard and mouse (I):* The tray should have height and swivel adjustments.

The Room
Freedom of movement. The work area should permit freedom of movement and ample leg room. *Lighting.* Lighting should be positioned to minimize glare on the monitor and printed materials.

Other Equipment
Wrist rest (J). The wrist rest is used in conjunction with adjustable armrests to keep arms in a neutral straight position at the keyboard. *Footrest (K).* The adjustable footrest takes pressure off the lower back while encouraging proper posture.

Information technology has proven many times over that it can play a role in improving personal productivity and overall office efficiency. If abused, however, information technology, especially relating to the PC and the Internet, can have the opposite effect. A good workplace ethics training program would include discussions of common abuses, each of which violates the IT code of conduct outlined in Figure 7-2.

- *Sending and receiving frivolous e-mail.* Most organizations tolerate an appropriate amount of personal e-mail, just as they do personal telephone calls. But, there is a limit. Nonessential e-mail, live chat, and instant messaging cause breaks in work momentum resulting in reductions in efficiency of as much as 50%. Of course, knowledge workers should resist the urge to subscribe to nonbusiness-related mailing lists (joke of the day, bizarre news, and so on).

- *Engaging in nonbusiness Internet browsing.* With all the resources of the Internet at our fingertips it is easy to seek out reviews of the latest movies, determine the book value of your old car, or check out the statistics from last night's game. Some companies have adopted zero-tolerance policies while others are struggling with ways to control nonbusiness cybersurfing.

- *Gaming on company time.* Personal computing offers plenty of opportunities to play games. Operating systems are even distributed with games. Hundreds of games are available for download. It is easy to join a multiplayer game on the Internet. Corporations frown on employees doing gaming on company time.

- *Toying with the technology.* The typical user exploits less than 20% of a software package's features. Some people view software as a toy and are carried away with all of the interesting features. They learn about and integrate sophisticated features into their projects even though all of the extra effort does little or nothing to enhance the end result. This type of technological overkill wastes time.

The PC can be an invaluable tool in the workplace or it can be a serious diversion. People who adhere to the ethical code of conduct enjoy greater efficiency and, ultimately, make greater contributions to their companies. In the end, the ethical IT worker tends to realize his/her career goals more quickly.

1 Attention to the overall workplace design can reduce stress and increase worker performance. (T/F)

2 Problems associated with extended use of a PC are collectively called: (a) VODS, (b) CTS, (c) CTD, or (d) SOV.

3 The typical user exploits less than what percent of a software package's features: (a) 1%, (b) 5%, (c) 10%, or (d) 20%?

SECTION

7-3 THE PRIVACY OF PERSONAL INFORMATION

The issue with the greatest IT ethical overtones is the privacy of personal information. How is it collected? Is it accurate and up-to-date? Who is responsible for the integrity of this information? Who has access to this information? How is it used? Is the information for sale? Are procedures in place for correcting erroneous information? The questions are many and the answers often are in conflict with IT ethics. Some people fear that computer-based databases offers too much of an opportunity for the invasion of an individual's privacy.

Why this section is important to you.

The more you know about how your personal information is collected, maintained, and used, the better prepared you will be to protect the privacy and integrity of this important information. This section will help you understand the scope and risks associated with computer-based databases that contain personal information about you.

WHO KNOWS WHAT ABOUT YOU?

Each day your name and personal information are passed from computer to computer. Depending on your level of activity, this could happen 100 or more times a day. Thousands of public- and private-sector organizations maintain data on individuals (see Figure 7-7). The data collection begins before you are born and continues throughout your life. Much of this personal data is collected without your consent and then is passed freely between organizations, again, without your consent.

Prentice Hall
**train &
assess**
generation

SECURITY AND PRIVACY

 Tax data. The Internal Revenue Service maintains the most visible stockpile of personal information. It, of course, keeps records of our whereabouts, earnings, taxes, deductions, employment, and so on. Now the IRS is supplementing basic tax information with external information to create personal profiles to tell if a person's tax return is consistent with his or her lifestyle. By law, all IRS data must be made available to about 40 different government agencies.

Education data. What you have accomplished during your years in school, such as grades and awards, is recorded in databases. Included in these databases is a variety of information such as your scores on college entrance exams, data on loan applications that include details of your family's financial status, roommate preferences, disciplinary actions, and so on.

Medical data. Medical files contain a mountain of sensitive personal data. Your medical records list all your visits to clinics and hospitals, your medical history (and often that of your family), allergies, and diseases you (and often members of your extended family) have or have had. They also may include assessments of your mental and physical health.

Driver and crime data. State motor vehicle bureaus maintain detailed records on over 150 million licensed drivers. This information includes personal descriptive data

FIGURE 7-7

PERSONAL INFORMATION

Many times each day, even as you sleep, businesses, government agencies, or other institutions are creating or updating your personal information on their databases. Here, the Municipal Services Department uses image processing to maintain records on parking violations.

Courtesy of Lockheed Martin Corporation

(sex, age, height, weight, color of eyes and hair) as well as records of arrests, fines, traffic offenses, and whether your license has been revoked. Some states sell descriptive information to retailers on the open market. The FBI's National Crime Information Center (NCIC) and local police forces maintain databases that contain rap sheet information on 20 million people. This information is readily available to hundreds of thousands of law-enforcement personnel.

Census data. With the 2000 census still fresh in our minds, we are reminded that the U.S. Bureau of the Census maintains some very personal data: names, racial heritage, income, the number of bathrooms in our home, and persons of the opposite sex who share our living quarters. Individual files are confidential. Statistics, however, are released without names.

Insurance data. Insurance companies have formed a cooperative to maintain a single database containing medical information on millions of people. This revealing database includes claims, doctors' reports, whether you have been refused insurance, how risky you would be as an insuree, and so on.

Lifestyle data. A number of cities are installing two-way cable TV that allows the accumulation of information on people's personal viewing habits. When you watch an X-rated movie, or any type of movie, your choice is recorded in the family's viewing database. As interactive cable TV matures, you will be able to use it to pay bills, respond to opinion polls, and make dinner reservations. This, of course, will add a greater variety of information to your personal file.

Credit data. Credit bureaus routinely release intimate details of our financial well-being. About one third of those who ask to review their records (you have the right to do this at any time) challenge their accuracy. Credit bureaus are bound by law to correct inaccuracies within two weeks of being notified of them.

World Wide Web data. When you visit a Web site, your e-mail address may be recorded in a user database on the Web site's server computer. If you interact with a site, your selections and preferences may be noted and placed on the database. Any personal information you enter goes in the database, too. Some Web sites share information for the same e-mail address enabling them to build a more comprehensive personal profile of their visitors/customers. Frequent cybersurfers may have records in hundreds or even thousands of Web site databases.

Employment data. Even before you report to work, your employer has gathered a significant body of data on you. Job-related information is maintained at current and past employers, including the results of performance reports, disciplinary actions, and other sensitive data.

Financial institutions. Banks and various financial institutions not only keep track of your money, they also monitor the volume and type of transactions you make. Their records include how much money you have or owe and how you choose to invest your money.

Miscellaneous data. The few organizations discussed here represent the tip of the personal information iceberg. For example, local and state governments maintain records of property transactions that involve homes, automobiles, boats, guns, and so on. Political organizations, magazines, telemarketers, charities, and hundreds of other organizations maintain and often share personal information.

We, of course, hope that the information about us is up-to-date and accurate. However, this is not always the case. You can't just write to the federal government and ask to see your files. To be completely sure you examine all your federal records for completeness and accuracy, you would have to write and probably visit more than 5,000 agencies, each of which maintains databases on individuals. The same is true of personal data maintained in the private sector. For the most part, these and thousands of other organizations are making a genuine attempt to handle personal data in a responsible manner. However, instances of abuse are widespread and give us cause for concern.

The social security number, now assigned to all U.S. citizens, is the link that ties all our personal information together. It doubles as a military serial number, and in many states, it serves as your driver's license number. It is the one item, along with your name, that appears on almost all personal forms. For example, your social security number is a permanent entry in hospital, tax, insurance, bank, employment, school, and scores of other types of records.

Information technology is now the basis for processing and storing personal information. However, it's not IT or computers that abuse the privacy of our personal information; it's the people who manage them. We as a society must be prepared to meet the challenge with a system of laws that deals realistically with the problem. At present, federal laws give individuals little protection. We are not told when data are being gathered about us. We are not allowed to choose who sees this information. In most cases, we are not allowed to view, remove, or correct personal information contained on some database. The good news is that laws are being put in place that will, though slowly, provide better protection for our personal information. For example, a new law limits what data-gathering companies can do with "personally identifiable financial information." The law dictates that these companies must get your permission before they can sell your credit report data, including your name, address, telephone number, and social security number. This means that those in the data gathering business and direct marketers will need to work harder and spend more money to get targeted personal information.

Computer experts feel that, whatever the source, the integrity of personal data can be more secure in computer databases than it is in file cabinets. They contend that we can continue to be masters and not victims if we implement proper safeguards for the maintenance and release of this information and enact effective legislation to cope with the abuse of it.

PROFILING

There is indeed reason for concern regarding the privacy of personal information. For example, credit card users unknowingly leave a "trail" of activities and interests when making purchases with various companies. In a process called **profiling**, these companies examine and evaluate the data to create a surprisingly comprehensive personal profile.

The date and location of all credit card transactions are recorded. In effect, when you charge lunch, gasoline, or clothing, you are creating a chronological record of where you have been and your spending habits. A computer-based expert system uses rules and guidelines to analyze this information and compile an accurate profile of your lifestyle. For example, the system could predict how you dress by knowing the type of clothing stores you patronize. On a more personal level, records are kept that detail the duration, time, and numbers of all your telephone calls. With computers, these numbers easily can be matched to people, businesses, institutions, and telephone services. So each time you make a phone call, you also leave a record of whom or where you call. The IRS, colleges, employers, creditors, hospitals, insurance companies, brokers, and so on maintain enormous amounts of personal data on everyone. A person (or a computer) with access to this and other personal information from a variety of sources (colleges, employers, brokers, hospitals, and so on) could create quite a detailed profile of almost anyone, including you. The profile could be fine-tuned further by examining your Internet activity, such as what messages you posted to the Internet, what sites you visited, and the kinds of software you downloaded.

The IRS gathers descriptive personal data, such as neighborhood and automobile type, then uses sophisticated models to create lifestyle profiles. These profiles are matched against reported income on tax returns to predict whether people seem to be underpaying taxes. When the income and projected lifestyle do not match, the return is audited.

THE CRYSTAL BALL
Centralized Online Placement Services for College Graduates

For decades, face-to-face on-campus interviews have defined the student recruitment process. Many students still find jobs through this traditional approach to placement services; however, within a few years we can expect a single, mature one-stop Web site to emerge that will be sensitive to the privacy of student information. Today, students may send hundreds of printed resumes only to be filtered by employers with a one-criterion glance. The one-stop site offers a more efficient approach. It will allow students to post comprehensive resumes that would allow interested employers to drill down for more information. Employers would have a new level of filter options.

VIOLATING THE PRIVACY OF PERSONAL INFORMATION

Now you know that a lot of your personal information exists on computers, but is this information being misused? Some say yes, and most will agree that the potential exists for abuse. Consider the states that sell lists of the addresses and data on their licensed drivers. At the request of a manager of several petite women's clothing stores, a state provided the manager with a list of all its licensed drivers who were women between the ages of 21 and 40, less than 5 feet 3 inches tall, and under 120 pounds. Is the sale of such a list an abuse of personal information? Does the state cross the line of what is considered ethical practice? You be the judge.

When you visit a Web site, the server may gather and store information about you, both on its system and on your system. Frequently, Web sites will leave a cookie on your hard disk. The **cookie** is a message given to your Web browser by the Web server being accessed (see Figure 7-8). The information in the cookie, which is in the form of a text file, then is sent back to the server each time the browser requests a page from the server. The cookie may contain information about you, including your name, e-mail address, interests, and personal preferences. Anytime you enter personal information at a Web site, chances are your browser is storing it in a cookie. The main purpose of the cookie is to personalize your interaction with the Web site and to enable the server to present you with a customized Web page, perhaps with your name at the top of the page. A cookie is not necessarily bad because it contains your personal preferences and basic personal information. A good cookie can make your interaction with an often-visited Web site more efficient and effective.

A recent study found that none of the 100 most popular shopping Web sites was in compliance with Fair Information Practices, a set of principles that provides basic privacy protection. Personal information has become the product of a growing industry. Companies have been formed that do nothing but sell information about people, including their e-mail addresses. Not only are the people involved not asked for permission to use their data, they seldom are told that their personal information is being sold! A great deal of personal data can be extracted from public records, both manual and computer-based. For example, one company sends people to county courthouses all over the United States to gather publicly accessible data about people who have recently filed papers to purchase a home. Computer-based databases then are sold to insurance companies, landscape companies, members of Congress seeking new votes, lawyers seeking new clients, and so on. Such information even is sold and distributed over the Net. Those placed on these electronic databases eventually become targets of commerce and special-interest groups.

The use of personal information for profit and other purposes is growing so rapidly that the government has not been able to keep up with abuses. Antiquated laws, combined with judicial unfamiliarity with information technology, make policing and prosecuting abuses of the privacy of personal information difficult and, in many cases, impossible.

FIGURE 7-8

THE COOKIE

When you visit a Web site, a cookie (a text file) containing information about you and your interaction with the Web site may be stored on your computer. Responsible Web sites use this information for only one purpose—to personalize your experience with their Web site.

Photo courtesy of Intel Corporation

COMPUTER MONITORING

One of the most controversial applications of information technology involving the privacy of personal information is **computer monitoring.** Computers monitor the activities and job performance of millions of workers worldwide (see Figure 7-9). Companies can monitor employee e-mails, instant messages, Internet activity, and telephone activity, and sometimes they monitor the content of computer files. Management does

FIGURE 7-9 COMPUTER MONITORING

MONITORING MOBILE WORKERS

With a portable terminal, this trucker is expected to communicate with headquarters. He can send sales information, transaction records, and progress reports quickly, accurately, and wirelessly to the host computer. The host computer can also dispatch instructions, updates, and work orders back out to its workforce.

Courtesy of Symbol Technologies, Inc.

MONITORING OFFICE KNOWLEDGE WORKERS

The scope and extent of computer monitoring is on the rise in companies throughout the world, especially among knowledge workers who perform transactions.

Courtesy of Sun Microsystems, Inc.

this to encourage employees to focus on their work and to avoid nonbusiness activity. Most knowledge workers are online and routinely interact with a server computer system via a terminal or PC. Others work with electronic or mechanical equipment linked to a computer system.

Many clerical workers are evaluated by the number of documents they process per unit of time. At insurance companies, computer-monitoring systems provide supervisors with information on the rate at which clerks process claims. Supervisors can request other information, such as time spent at the PC or terminal and the keying-error rate.

Computers also monitor the activities of many jobs that demand frequent use of the telephone. A computer logs the number of inquiries handled by directory-assistance operators. Some companies employ computers to monitor the use of telephones by all employees.

Although most computer monitoring involving job performance is done at the clerical level, it also is being applied to persons in higher-level positions, such as commodities brokers, programmers, loan officers, and plant managers. For example, CIM (computer-integrated manufacturing) enables corporate executives to monitor the effectiveness of a plant manager on a real-time basis. At any given time, executives can tap the system for productivity information, such as the rate of production for a particular assembly.

Most U.S. companies monitor employee e-mail and/or Internet browsing activities. Companies would prefer that their employees not view pornography, play games, gamble, or engage in nonwork browsing while at work. In fact, one in every four companies has fired at least one employee based on the results of Web monitoring information.

Many organizations encourage management scrutiny of employee electronic mail. In this form of monitoring, a robotic scanner "reads" employee e-mail searching for key words and phrases ("party," "skiing," "have a drink," and so on). Questionable e-mail messages are sent to management for review. The purpose of this type of monitoring is to ensure that internal communications are work-related and of a certain level of quality.

Companies justify e-mail monitoring by citing their need to protect intellectual property and to provide documentation that can protect the company in case of litigation. Many organized worker groups have complained that this form of monitoring is an unnecessary invasion of privacy and can actually be counterproductive.

Workers complain that being constantly observed and analyzed by a computer adds unnecessary stress to their jobs. However, management is reluctant to give up computer monitoring because it has proved itself to be a tool for increasing worker productivity. In general, affected workers are opposing any further intrusion into their professional privacy. Conversely, management is equally vigilant in its quest for better information on worker performance and Internet activities.

NO EASY ANSWERS TO THE PRIVACY QUESTION

The ethical questions surrounding the privacy of personal information are complex and difficult to resolve. For example, consider the position of the American Civil Liberties Union. On one hand, the ACLU is fighting to curb abuses of personal information, and on the other, it is lobbying the government for greater access to government information, which may include personal information. Are these goals in conflict?

On one side of the fence, consumer organizations and privacy advocates are lobbying for privacy legislation that can protect the interests and rights of online users. The e-commerce sector is pulling legislatures in the other direction. Online businesses want voluntary controls and industry self-regulation instead of new privacy legislation. New laws probably will reflect a compromise between the two views on the privacy of personal information.

As automation continues to enrich our lives, it also opens the door for abuses of personal information. Research is currently being done that may show that people with certain genetic and/or personality makeups have a statistical predisposition to a physical problem or a mental disorder, such as early heart failure or depression. Will employers use such information to screen potential employees?

By now, it should be apparent to you that we may never resolve all of the ethical questions associated with the privacy of personal information. Just as the answer to one question becomes clearer, a growing number of applications that deal with personal information raises another.

CREATING NEW APPLICATIONS FOR PERSONAL INFORMATION

The mere fact that personal information is so readily available creates opportunities for many new IT applications. Some people will praise their merits and others will adamantly oppose them. For example, one federal proposal is to have computer-based background checks done on all airline passengers. The results of the checks would be used to identify which passengers' luggage to search. The proposed system would examine names, addresses, telephone numbers, travel histories, and billing records to search for irregularities that might indicate possible terrorist or smuggler activity. This application, like many others that involve the use of personal information, has the potential to have a positive impact on society. Protectors of the rights of individuals will argue that the benefits derived may not be great enough to offset this invasion into personal information.

Each new application involving the use of personal information will be scrutinized carefully; but it is inevitable that our personal information will be used for a variety of applications. These may include systems that locate compatible mates, assign schoolchildren to classes, track sex offenders, identify employees who do not meet company character standards, target sales to likely customers, and so on.

1   Personal information has become the product of a growing industry. (T/F)
2   Your personal data cannot be passed from one organization to another without your consent. (T/F)
3   A message given to your Web browser by the Web server being accessed is a: (a) cake, (b) pie, (c) cookie, or (d) tart.
4   The term used to describe the computer-based collection of data on worker activities is called: (a) computer matching, (b) computer monitoring, (c) footprinting, or (d) pilferage.

7-4 COMPUTER AND IT CRIME

The ethical spectrum for computer issues runs from that which is ethical, to that which is unethical, to that which is against the law—a **computer crime**. There are many types of computer and IT crimes, sometimes called **cybercrimes**, ranging from the use of an unauthorized password by a student in a college computer lab to a billion-dollar insurance fraud. Most of us associate computer crime with the theft of bits and bytes—sensitive data, copyright software, a patented algorithm, a movie, and so on. This type of crime is unique in that the owner still has possession of whatever was stolen. Of course, some computer crimes result in significant physical loss, as well—money, inventory, hardware, and more.

The first case of computer crime was reported in 1958. Since then, all types of computer-related crimes have been reported: fraud, theft, larceny, embezzlement, burglary, sabotage, espionage, and forgery. We know computer crime is a serious problem, but we don't know how serious. Some studies estimate that each year the total money lost from computer crime is greater than the sum total of that taken in all other robberies. In fact, no one really knows the extent of computer crime because much of it is either undetected or unreported. In those cases involving banks, bank officers may elect to write off the loss rather than announce the crime and risk losing the goodwill of their customers. Computer crimes involving the greatest amount of money have to do with banking, insurance, product inventories, and securities.

Even though a record number of computer crime cases are being reported each year, the federal government is opting not to prosecute many of them. The increase in computer crime combined with the reluctance to prosecute gives us some insight into the progress of the government's war on computer crime. In recent years, prosecutors filed charges in only 25% of the hundreds of computer crime cases given to federal prosecutors. This percentage of referrals being prosecuted is considerably lower than the average of all referrals. The FBI has noted that computer crime is very difficult to prove. Also, prosecutors may be ill-prepared from a technical perspective to prosecute such cases. Most of those who are convicted receive relatively light sentences or are released on probation with no jail time.

Fortunately, only a small percentage of the people with an inclination toward crime are capable of committing high-tech crimes. Unfortunately, the criminal element in our society, like everyone else, is moving toward information technology competency. Thanks to the improved controls made possible through automation, though, business-related crime, in general, is decreasing. Computers have simply made it more difficult for people to commit business crimes. For the most part, stereotypical criminals and undesirables do not commit computer crimes. The typical computer criminal is a trusted employee with authorized access to sensitive information.

COMPUTERS AND THE LAW

Companies try to employ information technology within the boundaries of any applicable laws. Unfortunately, the laws are not always clear because many legal questions involving the use of information technology are being debated for the first time. For example, is e-mail like a letter or a memo, subject to freedom-of-information laws? Or, is it private, like a telephone call? This question is yet to be resolved. To no one's surprise, IT law is the fastest growing type of law practice.

Laws governing information technology are beginning to take shape (see Figure 7-10). Prior to 1994, federal laws that addressed computer crime were limited because they

THE CRYSTAL BALL
Online Voting on the Horizon

After the Florida election debacle, we are acutely aware that United States voting machines are antiquated. Similar punched-card technology was used in 1890 for taking the national census. It is now apparent that U.S. cities, counties, states, and the nation need a better way to elect candidates that is not subject to voting fraud. Several major companies and consortiums claim that the U.S. could implement a standardized, federally supported online voting system that would be easier to use, more accessible, more accurate, far more reliable, verifiable, and more secure. Plus, the results would be posted internationally in real time. Other countries, including Brazil, and even states, including Arizona, have conducted online elections. You should be able to vote from your PC within this decade.

FIGURE 7-10   IT LEGISLATION

Information technology-related legislation is being revised in the House of Representatives as quickly as it is being proposed. The background screen shows the most recent version of a proposed bill—the *Networking and Information Technology Research Advancement Act*. The House and Senate Web sites make the full text of proposed legislation and other pertinent information available online, including pages dedicated to providing current information for the press (see inset).

applied only to those computer systems that in some way reflected a "federal interest." The *Computer Abuse Amendments Act of 1994* expanded the scope of computer crimes to computers "used in interstate commerce." Effectively, this applies to any computer, including home PCs, with a link to the Internet. These laws make it a felony to gain unauthorized access to a computer system with the intent to obtain anything of value, to defraud the system, or to cause more than $1,000 in damage. Although most states have adopted computer crime laws, current laws are only the skeleton of what is needed to direct an orderly and controlled growth of information technology applications.

The *Children's Online Privacy Protection Act* (COPPA) went into effect in 2000. COPPA is the first law governing online privacy. The law requires that Internet Web sites obtain verifiable consent from parents before collecting, using, or disclosing personal information from children under the age of 13. The law offers a variety of methods for parental consent, including e-mail, snail mail, fax, and so on. Parents are overwhelmingly in favor of this law; however, critics say that it may limit the variety of activities that children will have on the Internet.

Existing federal and state laws concerning the privacy of personal information are being updated every year. At the same time, new laws are being written. Current federal laws outline the handling of credit information, restrict what information the IRS can obtain, restrict government access to financial information, permit individuals to view records maintained by federal agencies, restrict the use of education-related data, and regulate the matching of computer files. States have or are considering laws to deal with the handling of social security numbers, criminal records, telephone numbers, financial information, medical records, and other sensitive personal information.

Spam accounts for about half of all global e-mail traffic, about 2,500 unsolicited and mostly unwanted messages per e-mail address per year. New anti-spam laws are desperately needed because spammers simply view the current civil fines as the cost of doing business. Anti-spam laws are being proposed in the federal government and by most state governments. The gist of these proposals is that the new laws would make it illegal for any person or company to use fraudulent or deceptive return e-mail addresses, false e-mail headers, or false and misleading subject lines. These characteristics, of course, describe spam. It is likely that any new law will require that e-mail marketing messages be properly labeled as advertisements, that the sender's physical address and other contact information be included with all messages, and that the sender offer an easy way for recipients to "opt out" of receiving any further marketing e-mail messages.

Computer crime is a relatively recent phenomenon. As a result, legislation, the criminal justice system, and industry are not yet adequately prepared to cope with it. Relatively few police and FBI agents have been trained to handle cases involving computer crime. And when a case comes to court, few judges and even fewer jurors have the background necessary to understand the testimony.

AREAS OF COMPUTER AND IT CRIMINAL ACTIVITY

Computer and IT crimes can be grouped into several categories. Each is described in the following sections.

Crimes That Create Havoc Inside a Computer

Computers can get sick just like people. A variety of highly contagious viruses can spread from computer to computer, much the way biological viruses do among human beings. Just as a virus can infect human organs, a computer virus can infect programs, documents, and databases. It can also hide duplicates of itself within legitimate programs, such as an operating system or a word processing program. A **computer virus** is a man-made program or portion of a program that causes an unexpected event, usually a negative one, to occur. Viruses take control of the victim's system, with results that range from exasperating (the display of a harmless political message) to tragic (the loss of all programs and data). Viruses flow freely throughout the Internet, often as attachments to e-mail, and they reside on and are passed between magnetic disks. They copy themselves from system to system via the Internet or when unsuspecting users exchange infected disks.

It is estimated that computer viruses cost businesses and individuals worldwide up to $20 billion a year. There are many viruses—over 50,000, to date. Some act quickly by erasing user programs and files on disk. Others grow like a cancer, destroying small parts of a file each day. Some act like a time bomb. They lay dormant for days or months but eventually are activated and wreak havoc on any software on the system. Several **denial of service** viruses cause the Internet to be flooded with e-mail, each with an attached program that causes more infected e-mail to be sent. These viruses place such heavy demands on e-mail server computer resources that they are unable to handle the volume, thus the denial of service. Some viruses attack hardware and have been known to throw the mechanical components of a computer system, such as disk-access arms, into costly spasms. Many companies warn their PC users to back up all software prior to every Friday the thirteenth, a favorite date of those who write virus programs. For example, a disgruntled employee might plant a logic bomb to be "exploded" on the first Friday the thirteenth after his or her record is deleted from the personnel database. A **logic bomb** is a set of instructions that is executed when a set of conditions are met.

Some viruses are relatively benign, but can be annoying. For example, an error message might pop up that says, "This one's for you, Bosco." Another might insert the word "WAZZU" in the middle of your text. The Cookie Monster virus displays "I want a cookie" then locks up the system until you key in "Fig Newton."

Types of Computer Viruses

Two types of viruses—macro viruses and worms—have become alarmingly popular during the last few years. A **macro virus** is a program or portion of a program that is written in the macro language of a particular application. A **macro language** is a programming language whose instructions relate specifically to the functionality of the parent application, such as Microsoft Word or Microsoft Outlook. One well-publicized and hugely destructive macro virus was *Melissa,* which was distributed as an e-mail attachment. When opened, the macro program caused the virus to be sent to the first 50 people in the Outlook contact list. Melissa so overwhelmed millions of e-mail servers that they could no longer function (denial of service).

A **worm** is a computer program or portion of a program that makes copies of itself. Typically, the worm will interfere with the normal operation of a program or a computer. Worms exist as separate entities and do not attach themselves to files, programs, or documents. One of the most devastating incarnations of the worm was *SQL Slammer*. At its peak, three minutes after it was released, Slammer was scanning 55 million Internet

PERSONAL COMPUTING
Virus Protection

Don't leave home without protection from viruses and crackers. There is too much at stake, possibly your almost-completed term paper, your family photo album, the use of your PC for days or weeks, and so on. Typically, a new computer will have one of the popular virus protection programs installed; however, for continued protection from new viruses you will need to subscribe to the software vendor's online update service. Having antivirus software provides only partial protection (legacy viruses), so it is important to update the virus definitions database continually.

servers per second and infecting hundreds of thousands of computers. With 10 minutes, Slammer had infected computers through the world, making it the fastest spreading virus to date.

Though not officially a virus because it does not replicate itself, the Trojan horse can be equally damaging. A **Trojan horse** is any seemingly useful program that hides a computer virus or a logic bomb. Named after the wooden horse the Greeks used to capture Troy, the Trojan horse needs someone to e-mail it to you for it does not e-mail itself. Fortunately, most Trojan horses take the form of a practical joke, but some can be harmful. In a classic Trojan horse scenario, one claims to rid your PC of viruses but, instead, plants viruses in your system.

The profile of a virus writer looks something like this: a computer-obsessed male between 14 and 34 years old who is a social outcast with few, if any, female friends. These people, who fall into two groups, write and circulate an estimated 1,000 viruses a month. The first group creates viruses to impress each other with their cleverness. They view viruses as electronic graffiti. The second, and far more dangerous group, creates viruses with malicious intent. Some do not know the harm they do, but some do. These people are just plain mean and want their viruses to result in property damage and cause human suffering. Sadly, terrorists have embraced the virus as a weapon of war.

Sources of Computer Viruses

In the PC environment, there are three primary sources of computer viruses (see Figure 7-11).

- *The Internet.* The most common source of viral infection is the very public Internet, on which people download and exchange software and send e-mail. All too often, a user logs on to the Internet and downloads a game, a utility program, or some other enticing piece of freeware from an unsecured site, but gets the software with an embedded virus instead. Sometimes viruses are attached to e-mails. A good rule is to know the sender before opening anything sent with an e-mail.

- *Diskettes and DVDs/CD-ROMs.* Viruses also are spread from one system to another via common interchangeable disks. For example, a student with an infected application program on a floppy disk or CD-ROM might unknowingly infect several other laboratory computers with a virus, which, in turn, infects the applications software of other students. Software companies have unknowingly distributed viruses with their proprietary software products. Ouch!

- *Computer networks.* Viruses can spread from one computer network to another.

How serious a problem are viruses? They have the potential of affecting an individual's career and even destroying companies. For example, a financial adviser who inadvertently forwards a virus to his clients may lose credibility and clients. A company that loses its accounts receivable records—records of what the company is owed—could be a candidate for bankruptcy.

Virus Protection

The software package distributed with new PCs usually includes an antivirus program and a limited subscription to a virus update service. An **antivirus program** is a utility program that periodically checks a PC's hard disk for computer viruses then removes any that are found. It also can check ingoing and outgoing e-mail for viruses. The best way to cope with viruses is to recognize their existence and use an antivirus program. Your chances of living virus free are greatly improved if you use this program to check for viruses and are careful about what you load to your system's hard disk. Computer viruses are introduced continuously into the cyberworld, so antivirus vendors, such as Symantec and McAfee, offer a subscription service that lets you download protection for new viruses.

Here are some tips that will help minimize your vulnerability to viruses.

- Delete e-mails from unknown, suspicious, or untrustworthy sources, especially those with files attached to an e-mail.

- Never open a file attachment to an e-mail unless you know what it is, even if it appears to come from a friend.

FIGURE 7–11 HOW VIRUSES ARE SPREAD

A. Virus is distributed via the Internet.

1. Virus is intentionally uploaded to an Internet server or distributed via e-mail.

2. The Internet server hard disk is infected with the virus or the server facilitates distribution of the virus.

3. The virus is in some way downloaded to an unsuspecting user—BOOM.

BOOM!

B. Virus is distributed via common diskettes.

1. Virus-infected diskette is loaded to a microcomputer system and the hard disk is infected.

2. A clean diskette is loaded to an infected system.

3. When removed the previously clean diskette is infected with the virus.

C. Virus is distributed via networks.

1. Virus is planted in legitimate program code.

2. Virus is transmitted via data communications to another node on the network.

3. Virus propagates itself to other nodes on the network.

- Download files from the Internet only from legitimate and reputable sources.
- Update your antivirus software frequently as over 200 new viruses are discovered each week.
- Back up your files periodically. If you catch a virus, your chances of surviving are pretty good if you maintain current backups of important data and programs.

Traditionally, virus protection has been at the PC or client level. However, this may change as companies look to network and Internet service providers for more services. New tools are being developed that can check for viruses at the server level before files reach the PC. An ISP's prescan of all files will protect subscribers from all known viruses at the time. This service is inviting for companies concerned about keeping current with protection from the never-ending stream of viruses circulating the Internet.

Crimes That Involve Fraud and Embezzlement

Most computer crimes fall under the umbrella of fraud and embezzlement. *Fraud* involves intentional deception for the purpose of personal gain.

- Over 400 men sent about $3,000 each to a Net-based organization that promised each of them the hand of a beautiful Russian bride.
- Visitors to a pornography Web site were given a "free" tour of explicit content, but only if they would validate they are adults by providing credit card information. The Web site charged their visitors up to $90 a month on their credit cards.

A common street thug does not have the knowledge or the opportunity to be successful at this type of computer crime. Over 50% of all computer frauds are internal, that is, employees of the organization being defrauded commit them. About 30% of those defrauding employees are IT specialists.

Embezzlement concerns the misappropriation of funds or theft.

- A 17-year-old high school student tapped into an AT&T computer and stole more than $1 million worth of software.
- One person hacked his way into a system and illegally transferred $10,200,000 from a U.S. bank to a Swiss bank. He probably would have gotten away with this electronic heist if he had not felt compelled to brag about it.
- A U.S. Customs official modified a program to print $160,000 worth of unauthorized federal payroll checks payable to himself and his co-conspirators.
- Three data entry clerks in a large metropolitan city conspired with welfare recipients to write over $2 million of fraudulent checks.

The **salami technique** for embezzlement requires that a Trojan horse be planted in the program code of a financial system that processes a large number of accounts. These covert instructions cause a small amount of money, usually less than a penny, to be debited periodically from each account and credited to one or more dummy accounts. A number of less sophisticated computer-manipulation crimes are the result of data diddling. *Data diddling* is changing the data, perhaps the "ship to" address, on manually prepared source documents or during online entry to the system.

One of the methods used by law enforcement personnel to uncover IT embezzlement and fraud is computer matching. In **computer matching,** separate databases are examined and individuals common to both are identified. In one computer-matching case, a $30-million fraud was uncovered when questionable financial transactions were traced to common participants. Having so much personal information in databases opens the door for many types of computer matching applications. For example, federal employees are being matched with those having delinquent student loans. When a match is found, the government garnishes wages until the loan is paid. Proponents of computer matching cite the potential to reduce criminal activity. Opponents of computer matching consider it an unethical invasion of privacy.

Crimes That Involve Negligence or Incompetence

Not all computer crime is premeditated. *Negligence* or *incompetence* can be just as bad for an organization as a carefully planned crime. Such crimes usually are a result of poor input/output control. For example, after she paid in full, a woman was sent follow-up notices continually and was visited by collection agencies for not making payments on her automobile. Although the records and procedures were in error, the company forcibly repossessed the automobile without thoroughly checking its procedures and the legal implications. The woman had to sue the company for the return of her automobile. The court ordered the automobile returned and the company to pay her a substantial sum as a penalty.

Companies that employ computers to process data must do so in a responsible manner. Irresponsible actions that result in the deletion of a bank account or the premature discontinuation of electrical service would fall into this category. Lax controls and the availability of sensitive information invite scavenging. **Scavenging** is searching for discarded information that may be of some value on the black market, such as a printout containing credit card numbers.

Crimes That Involve Unauthorized Access to the Internet and Networking

The omnipresence of hackers and crackers (both discussed in Chapter 3) has made security on the Internet and computer networks an ongoing problem. *Hackers* are benign computer enthusiasts who enjoy stretching the limits of personal computing. *Crackers*, however, are "electronic vandals," who often leave evidence of unlawful entry, perhaps a revised record or access during nonoperating hours, called a **footprint.** These footprints tell us that Internet-related intrusions number in the thousands each month.

Many of the millions of Internet sites are vulnerable to attacks by crackers. This vulnerability has resulted in a rapid growth in the number of attacks. Vandals substitute images and words on home pages with ones that are embarrassing to the organization. Almost 90% of existing Web sites have been victims of *Web site defacement*. Crackers break into systems and steal personal information that can be used for identity theft. College students gain access to campus computers to charge books, food, and services to the accounts of other students. The range of reasons for unlawful entry is as varied as the Internet's Web sites.

One of the major motivators for unauthorized access is **industrial espionage,** the theft of proprietary business information. Companies representing most of the world's countries have attempted a shortcut to success by stealing product design specifications, product development schedules, trade secrets, software code, strategic plans, sales strategies, customer information, or anything else that would give them a competitive advantage. The typical corporate computer has everything corporate spies would want, so their objective is to gain access to a target company's system, look around, and extract whatever pertinent information they can.

The *Computer Abuse Amendments Act of 1994* changed the standard for criminal prosecution from "intent" to "reckless disregard," thus increasing the chances of successful prosecution of crackers. Two computer crackers were sentenced to federal prison for their roles in defrauding long-distance carriers of more than $28 million. The crackers stole credit card numbers from MCI. The cracker who worked at MCI was sentenced to three years and two months, and the other cracker was sentenced to a one-year prison term. Countries throughout the world are struggling to define just punishment for cybercrimes. Some countries have adopted a zero tolerance policy in their cyberlaws. For example, two brothers in China were executed for a $30,000 electronic heist. There is a concern that the media glorifies criminally oriented crackers, creating heroes for a new generation of computer criminals. This glorification may begin to fade as we read about more and more crackers serving hard time.

The Internet's cybercops, the **CERT Coordination Center (CERT/CC)**, often work around the clock to thwart electronic vandalism and crime on the Internet. Until recently, CERT/CC was the Computer Emergency Response Team. CERT/CC concentrates its efforts on battling major threats to the global Internet. Lesser problems are left to the Internet service providers and to police. CERT/CC, which is a federally funded research and development center operated by Carnegie Mellon University, provides technical advice, coordinates responses to Net security incidents, identifies solutions to security problems, spreads information on security, and provides security training.

A decade ago, the CERT/CC cybercops were being tested by hackers who were out to prove their ingenuity by breaking into systems just to prove they could. These hackers were mostly harmless, more out to prove their hacking abilities than to act maliciously. Now cyberthiefs are after more than self-esteem: They want to steal something. They intercept credit card numbers, reroute valuable inventory, download copyrighted software, or make illegal monetary transactions. Fortunately, CERT/CC has found that hacking incidents generally are decreasing relative to the size of the Internet. Unfortunately, as soon as CERT/CC people plug a hole in the Internet, another is found. The problem will not go away and may become more difficult to cope with as perpetrators gain sophistication.

Unauthorized entry to a computer network is achieved in a variety of ways. The most common approach is **masquerading.** People acquire passwords and personal information that will enable them to masquerade as an authorized user. Company outsiders use the **tailgating** technique to gain access to sensitive information. The perpetrator simply begins using the terminal or computer of an authorized user who has left the room without terminating his or her session. The more sophisticated user might prefer building a trap door, scanning, or superzapping. A **trap door** is a Trojan horse that permits unauthorized and undetected access to a computer system. Insiders, usually programmers, implement trap doors during system development. **Scanning** involves the use of a computer to test different combinations of access information until access is permitted (for example, by stepping through a four-digit access code from 0000 to 9999). **Superzapping** involves using a program that enables someone to bypass the security controls.

Crimes in Which the Internet Becomes a Tool for Crime

To thousands of con artists, the Internet offers a quicker, more efficient vehicle for dozens of old-fashioned scams: pyramid schemes, chain letters, offers of free government money, debt-elimination schemes, rip and tear (the big prize—for a fee), and a wealth of get-rich-quick rip-offs. Most people with an e-mail address have received the "Nigerian letter" from a downtrodden African prince. The note contains a plea for money to help bribe Government officials so both you and the prince can get a large sum of money held illegally by the Government of Nigeria. The Internet, also, has opened the door for more sophisticated, technology-based scams, such as **pumping and dumping,** which is illegal. In this scam, seemingly legitimate sources flood the Internet with bogus information about the successes of a particular company. The Internet blitz travels via e-mail, newsgroups, instant messaging, and other means of Internet communication. If the fraud works, the net effect is to artificially "pump" up the price of the company's stock. The con artists then "dump" their stock at peak value to realize big gains. A student at the University of California at Los Angeles (UCLA) played the pump-and-dump game to enjoy big profits until he was caught and fined over $500,000.

Online auction sites, such as eBay, expand the con artist's reach to millions of people. Scammers are delighted to have this opportunity to sell things they do not have and will never deliver. With over 100,000 bids being posted every hour on millions of items up for auction, this type of fraud is difficult to prevent. Auction sites also have served as distribution vehicles for items that are illegal. Opium poppy pods, with their golf-ball sized pods, were listed as decorations. The auction sites are vigilant about removing illegal or illicit items, but the cybercriminals seem to stay a few bids ahead of the delete button.

Cyberstalking has emerged as one of the fastest-growing areas of Internet crime. **Cyberstalking** is technology-based stalking where the Internet becomes a vehicle by which the stalker directs threatening behavior and unwanted advances to another netizen (citizen of the Internet). Cyberstalkers find their victims in chat rooms, newsgroups, discussion forums, via instant messaging, and through e-mail. Most cyberstalkers are men and target women and children. However, an increasing number of people, both male and female, become cyberstalkers when a cyber relationship goes bad. Cyberstalking can be in the form of a threatening or obscene communication (real-time or e-mail), flaming (verbal abuse), mountains of junk e-mail, sexually explicit images, inappropriate messages left at various online locations, viruses, and identity theft. When cyberstalking goes offline, it can become a terrifying experience that elevates electronic harassment to the potential for physical harm.

The Net has become a new venue for sexual predators. At any give time 2,000-plus sexual predator adults, mostly males, are combing chat rooms attempting to lure females, especially vulnerable teenagers, into abusive relationships. It is now commonplace to hear about teenage girls running off with these predators.

Crimes That Involve the Abuse of Personal Information

Identity theft occurs when someone is able to gather enough personal information on you (without your knowledge) to assume your identity. With so much personal information floating around cyberspace, identity theft has emerged as one of the fastest growing criminal activities. The U.S. Justice Department estimates that 700,000 people are victimized by identity theft each year. The objective of identity theft is fraud or theft. Identity thieves open new credit card accounts using your name, address, date of birth, and social security numbers. Then, they spend away, sticking you with the bill. Identity thieves have become very imaginative, setting up cellular phone accounts and bank accounts in your name. Usually, an insider provides the personal information used for identity theft.

A man known as the Buffalo spammer (from Buffalo, New York) sent almost a billion spam messages over ISP giant EarthLink's network. The spammer and his accomplices were able to do this by opening over 300 EarthLink accounts, all with stolen identities and credit cards. A federal judge awarded EarthLink $16.4 million in damages. EarthLink, however, should wait before spending the money as the company is still waiting on payment for an earlier $25 million award.

Any willful release or distribution of inaccurate personal information would fall into this category, as well. For example, it is a crime to post false information about an individual to the Internet with intent to defame.

Crimes That Support Criminal Enterprises

Money laundering and databases that support drug distribution would fall into this category. Technology has tremendous potential to improve the plight of humanity. Sadly, it has just as much potential for evil. The criminal elements of our society have ingeniously used information technology to support hundreds of criminal ventures from illegal gambling to complex multicountry money laundering schemes.

Crimes That Involve the Theft of Software or Intellectual Property

Federal copyright law automatically protects software from the moment of its creation. This law is the same one that protects other intellectual property (books, audio recordings, films, and so on). The *Copyright Law of 1974* gives the owner of the copyright "the exclusive rights" to "reproduce the copyrighted word." Unless specifically stated in the license agreement, the purchasers can install the software to only one computer. The general rule is: one software package per computer. Any other duplication, whether for sale or for the owner's personal use, is an infringement of copyright law.

It is copyright infringement to allow simultaneous use of a single-user version of software on a LAN by more than one person. LAN versions of software packages are sold with a **site license** that permits use by a specific number of users. Also, the *Software Rental Amendments Act of 1990* prohibits the rental, leasing, or lending of copyright software.

The unlawful duplication of proprietary software, called **software piracy**, is making companies vulnerable to legal action by the affected vendors (see Figure 7-12). The term **pilferage** is used to describe the situation in which a company purchases a software product without a site-usage license agreement, then copies and distributes the software throughout the company. If such piracy is done "willfully and for the purpose of commercial advantage or private financial gain," perpetrators are subject to fines up to $250,000 and 5 years in jail. Two pirates in Canada were forced to walk the plank with a $22,500 fine. This and similar rulings have sent the message loud and clear: Software piracy doesn't pay and will not be tolerated.

Vendors of software for personal computers estimate that for every software product sold, two more are copied illegally. Software piracy is a serious problem, and software vendors are acting vigorously to prosecute people and companies who violate their copyrights. Worldwide, the software industry loses an estimated $15 billion a year to software piracy. Recently, Thai officials arrested a Ukrainian man who is accused of selling $1 billion worth of counterfeit software. According to figures compiled by the Business Software Alliance (BSA), virtually all of the software in Vietnam (95%) is illegal (without a license). China is close behind at 92%, followed by Indonesia (89%) and Russia (89%). The good news is that software piracy in these countries is down by about 2% over the previous year.

Besides the software companies, the paying customers also are victims of software piracy. In order for software vendors to maintain product quality and a certain level of customer service, legitimate customers must pay inflated prices for their products.

Some company managers confront the issue head-on and state bluntly that software piracy is a crime and offenders will be dismissed. This method has proven effective. Some,

FIGURE 7-12 PROTECTION FOR INTELLECTUAL PROPERTY

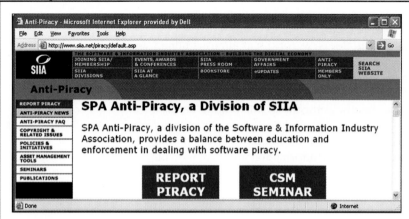

SOFTWARE PIRACY

The Software & Information Industry Association (SIIA) sponsors a vigorous ongoing anti-piracy campaign to protect copyrighted software. Anti-piracy information and support are available from its Web site at http://www.siia.net. The site makes it easy for people to report copyright abuses.

COPYRIGHT LAW

Copyright laws protect literature, music, software, and the design of a silicon chip, such as Intel's innovative bumpless technology chip design shown here.

Photo courtesy of Intel Corporation

who are actually accomplices, look the other way as subordinates copy software for office and personal use.

Intellectual property rights issues have been front-page news since recording companies began actively suing file sharing enterprises to get them to stop promoting the sharing of copyrighted MP3 songs. The sharing of songs has been attractive to netizens. With the rapid expansion of broadband access and the proliferation of CD/DVD burners, netizens are beginning to share pirated versions of feature length movie files, too. Industry analysts are estimating that up to a half million first-run movies are downloaded illegally each day. Films on DVD-ROM are copied and posted to the Net. Digital camcorders are taken to movie theaters where they are used to capture films illegally for Net distribution. The abuse of intellectual property rights in the film industry is nowhere near that of the music recording industry; however, we can look for aggressive litigation as movie moguls take action to protect their intellectual property rights.

The abuse of intellectual property rights is having a serious impact on the worldwide economy. Over 100,000 IT professional jobs are lost because of the revenues lost due to software piracy alone. The governments of software producing countries lose billions in taxes. The balance of trade is tipped unfairly to those countries that permit abuses of another country's copyright products.

The penalties being handed down for copyright infringements are becoming increasingly severe. Four college students who were charged with using their campus network to distribute illegal copies of music agreed to settle a Recording Industry Association of America lawsuit by paying from $12,000 to $17,000 each. The creation of counterfeit intellectual material, such as software, music, and books, can result in prison sentences up to 16 months, no matter what the motivation of the perpetrator. The greater the market value of the counterfeit copies, the stiffer the punishment.

Crimes That Involve the Theft of Hardware

There is a growing black market for PCs and computer parts. A high-end notebook PC can fetch up to $1,000 and a computer chip can be worth its weight in gold. Notebook PCs are the most stolen item in the world, almost 2,000 a day in the United States alone. According to the Federal Bureau of Investigation, one of every 14 notebooks is reported stolen. The Los Angeles School District had to cut back on their computer curriculum because so many of the district's PCs have been stolen. Ironically, only 5% to 15% of PC/hardware theft is due to forcible entry, indicating that most hardware theft is by insiders and employees. In these circumstances, alarms and traditional theft deterrence are ineffective. Three IBM employees stole $20 million worth of parts, mostly RAM, from the company's Poughkeepsie, New York plant.

Crimes That Involve the Theft of Data and Information

It is estimated that the value of data and information stolen is roughly equivalent to that of hardware and software theft combined. The electronic theft of the contents of a $200 disk or theft of the disk itself could, in effect, be a $100 million crime. Several such disks containing Social Security numbers, credit card numbers, and other personal information have been stolen and the information used for widespread identity theft. A PC stolen from a major credit card company's information technology center contained information on 300,000 plus card holders.

Information that may be of little value to one person or group may be of great value to others. For example, files showing the layout of the World Trade Center's high-tech security system were stolen. To most people, these files are of little value, but they are of significant value to terrorist organizations who would plot the destruction of the buildings. A notebook PC containing the entire Desert Storm war plan was stolen from the British Defense Ministry in the early 1990s. Fortunately, the information never was used.

SECTION

1 A computer virus is a computer-generated program that causes an unpleasant event on a computer. (T/F)

2 Many legal questions involving computers and information processing are yet to be incorporated into the federal laws. (T/F)

3 In computer matching, separate databases are examined and individuals common to both are identified. (T/F)

4 The number of computer viruses is in which range: (a) 25–50, (b) 100–500, (c) 20,000–30,000, or (d) 50,000 and up?

5 A denial of service virus places high demands on: (a) backup capabilities, (b) hackers, (c) server resources, or (d) vaccine research.

6 What law is violated when an organization duplicates proprietary software without permission: (a) civil rights, (b) antitrust, (c) copyright, or (d) patent?

7 The first law governing online privacy is: (a) COPPA, (b) Cabana, (c) adult-oriented, or (d) temporary.

Chapter Review

7-1 ETHICS IN INFORMATION TECHNOLOGY

Society continues to raise questions about what is and is not ethical in the information technology arena. A code of ethics provides direction for IT professionals and users so they can apply computer technology responsibly.

Green computing, an important IT ethics topic, adopts a more environmentally sound position with respect to the use, manufacture, and disposal of computing hardware. The EPA's *Energy Star* guidelines are being used to standardize energy usage for hardware. Good green computing includes sending e-mail (rather than paper), purchasing recycled paper, buying reconditioned components, and telecommuting once or twice a week.

Individuals and companies should adopt a product stewardship policy that encourages recycling and the proper handling of obsolete PCs and computer hardware.

7-2 WORKPLACE ETHICS: HEALTHY COMPUTING

Today, corporate executives are more sensitive to workplace ethics. Human factors engineers are applying the principles of ergonomic design to ensure that the interface between knowledge worker and workplace is safe, comfortable, effective, and efficient. The knowledge worker's workplace should be designed with enough flexibility to enable it to be custom-fitted to its worker. Attention to the overall environment (lighting, noise, and ventilation) can reduce stress and increase worker performance.

Problems associated with extended use of a terminal or PC are referred to as video operator's distress syndrome, or VODS. As the number of repetitive-stress injuries (RSIs) increased for knowledge workers, workstation ergonomics became an increasingly important issue for corporate productivity. A poorly designed workplace has the potential to cause cumulative trauma disorder (CTD), a condition that can lead to a permanent disability of motor skills.

The PC can be an invaluable tool in the workplace or it can be a serious diversion. These diversions may include sending and receiving frivolous e-mail, engaging in non-business Internet browsing, gaming on company time, and toying with the technology.

7-3 THE PRIVACY OF PERSONAL INFORMATION

Thousands of public- and private-sector organizations maintain data on individuals, including tax, education, medical, driver and crime, census, insurance, lifestyle, credit, Web, employment, financial, and other data.

The dominant ethical issue is the privacy of personal information. As automation continues to enrich our lives, it also opens the door for abuses of personal information. Personal information has become the product of a growing industry. Not only are the people involved not asked for permission to use their data, they seldom are told that their personal information is being sold. The mere fact that personal information is so readily available has opened the door for many new applications of information technology. For example, companies examine and evaluate personal data to create a surprisingly comprehensive personal profile. This process is called profiling. Cookies containing personal information are passed freely around the Internet. Computer monitoring enables the ongoing monitoring of worker activities and the measurement of worker performance.

The ethical questions surrounding the privacy of personal information are complex and difficult to resolve.

7-4 COMPUTER AND IT CRIME

Computer and IT crime, called cybercrime, is a relatively recent phenomenon. Therefore, laws governing information technology are few, and those that do exist are subject to a variety of interpretations.

Crimes that create havoc inside a computer include computer viruses, such as those that result in denial of service. A Trojan horse is any seemingly useful program that hides a computer virus or a logic bomb, which is a set of instructions that is executed when a set of conditions are met. The primary sources of computer viruses are the Internet (e-mail and downloads), common interchangeable disks, and computer networks. Antivirus programs exist to help fight viruses.

Most computer crimes fall under the umbrella of fraud and embezzlement. *Fraud* involves intentional deception for the purpose of personal gain. *Embezzlement* concerns the misappropriation of funds or theft. The salami technique and data diddling are used for fraud and embezzlement.

In computer matching, separate databases are examined and individuals common to both are identified

Negligence or incompetence can be just as bad for an organization as a premeditated crime. Such crimes usually are a result of poor input/output control.

Many computer and IT crimes involve unauthorized access to the Internet and networking. Overzealous hackers and crackers often leave evidence of unlawful entry called a footprint. One of the major motivators for unauthorized access is industrial espionage. The Internet's cybercops, the CERT/CC are ever vigilant in the fight against Internet crimes. Unauthorized entry to a computer network is achieved in several ways, including masquerading, tailgating, a trap door, scanning, and superzapping.

The Internet has become a tool for crime where con artists have updated traditional scams for use in the cyberworld and have created new technology-based crimes such as pumping and dumping and cyberstalking.

Identity theft, one of the fastest growing criminal activities, is a crime that involves the abuse of personal information.

Computers and IT are used in support of many criminal enterprises, including money laundering.

Crimes that involve the theft of software or intellectual property often leave evidence of the unlawful duplication of proprietary software, called software piracy, and pilferage. The sharing of copyrighted MP3 and movie files over the Internet is a crime.

There is a growing black market for PCs and computer parts and for data and information, especially that which can be used for identity theft.

KEY TERMS

antivirus program (p. 298)
carpal tunnel syndrome (CTS) (p. 286)
CERT Coordination Center (CERT/CC) (p. 301)
computer crime (p. 295)
computer matching (p. 300)
computer monitoring (p. 292)
computer virus (p. 297)
cookie (p. 292)
cumulative trauma disorder (CTD) (p. 286)
cybercrime (p. 295)

cyberstalking (p. 302)
denial of service (p. 297)
ergonomics (p. 285)
footprint (p. 301)
green computing (p. 283)
identity theft (p. 302)
industrial espionage (p. 301)
logic bomb (p. 297)
macro language (p. 297)
macro virus (p. 297)
masquerading (p. 302)
pilferage (p. 303)
profiling (p. 291)

pumping and dumping (p. 302)
salami technique (p. 300)
scanning (p. 302)
scavenging (p. 301)
site license (p. 303)
software piracy (p. 303)
superzapping (p. 302)
tailgating (p. 302)
trap door (p. 302)
Trojan horse (p. 298)
video operator's distress syndrome (VODS) (p. 286)
worm (p. 297)

MATCHING

_____ **1.** pilferage

_____ **2.** green computing

_____ **3.** ergonomics

_____ **4.** logic bomb

_____ **5.** cracker

_____ **6.** computer monitoring

_____ **7.** CTD

_____ **8.** cookie

_____ **9.** pumping and dumping

_____**10.** COPPA

a contains information sent to a Web site

b can result in motor skill disability

c overzealous hacker

d stock scam

e causes damage to computers

f measurement of worker performance

g engineering for humans

h environmentally sensible computing

i corporate theft of copyright software

j online privacy law

CHAPTER SELF-CHECK

TRUE/FALSE

1. The ACM Code of Conduct was adopted recently by the U.S. Senate and is now the law of the land. (T/F)

2. All states now require that PCs be recycled. (T/F)

3. According to the Energy Star requirements, monitors in standby mode can consume no more than 30 watts of power. (T/F)

4. A CRT monitor emits radiation. (T/F)

5. Personal e-mail never is tolerated in a business environment. (T/F)

6. Credit bureaus are bound by law to correct inaccuracies in their personal data. (T/F)

7. All Internet Web sites must be in compliance with Fair Information Practices. (T/F)

MULTIPLE CHOICE

1. What is the approximate cost of running a PC and a laser printer 24 hours a day for a year: (a) $10, (b) $50, (c) $250, or (d) $2,250?

2. Which of these is not an emphasis in medical school curricula: (a) the use of IT, (b) internal medicine, (c) SDTs, or (d) human anatomy?

3. Errors embedded in commercial software products cost the United States economy: (a) $100 million, (b) $500 million, (c) $6 billion, or (d) $60 billion.

4. The study of the relationships between people and their machines is called: (a) humanology, (b) human economics, (c) ergology, or (d) ergonomics.

5. Hand and wrist problems are associated with: (a) ACL, (b) carpal tunnel syndrome, (c) CLA, or (d) SC syndrome.

6. Laser printers can emit: (a) lead, (b) a harmless water-based compound, (c) sulfur dioxin, or (d) ozone.

7. About what percentage of all U.S. companies monitor e-mail and/or employee Internet browsing activities: (a) 1%, (b) 5%, (c) 25%, or (d) more than 50%?

8. The number of federal government agencies that maintain computer-based files on individuals is at least: (a) 50, (b) 500, (c) 5,000, or (d) 50,000.

9. A set of instructions that is executed when a certain set of conditions are met is called a: (a) logic virus, (b) scavenger, (c) data diddler, or (d) logic bomb.

10. One way to fight computer viruses is to use what type of software: (a) antibug, (b) antivirus, (c) redo, or (d) backup?

11. The unlawful duplication of proprietary software is called: (a) copyright crime, (b) software bootlegging, (c) software piracy, or (d) software thievery.

12. When separate databases are examined and individuals common to both are identified, this is: (a) computer matching, (b) footprinting, (c) computer monitoring, or (d) pilferage.

13. In the United States, gaining unauthorized access to any computer system with the intent of defrauding the system is a: (a) violation of public ethics, (b) misdemeanor, (c) high crime, or (d) felony.

14. Which term is used to describe the situation in which a company copies and distributes software without a site-usage license agreement: (a) pilferage, (b) thieving, (c) pinching, or (d) filching?

15. The evidence of unlawful entry to a computer system is called a: (a) bitprint, (b) footprint, (c) handprint, or (d) fingerprint.

16. What name is given to a program intended to damage the computer system of an unsuspecting victim: (a) virus, (b) bug, (c) germ, or (d) fever?

IT ETHICS AND ISSUES

1. VIOLATING THE COPYRIGHT OF INTELLECTUAL PROPERTY

Educators report that they are having difficulty instilling respect for the copyrights on intellectual property. The statistics confirm their concerns. It is estimated that for every legitimate copy of a software package there are two pirated versions installed on other PCs. In some countries, virtually all software is counterfeit. The original developers receive no royalties for sales and legitimate customers must pay artificially high prices.

Discussion: The capabilities for copying CDs, CD-ROMs, and DVDs are now commonplace in the home and office. People routinely use these capabilities to duplicate copyrighted music and software for friends and, occasionally, for corporate use. If you knew of someone who routinely violated copyright laws, would you report him or her? Why or why not?

Discussion: Your boss asked you to install your graphics program on three other PCs in the office. The license permits only one installation. What would be your response to your boss's request?

Discussion: A neighbor of yours who lives paycheck to paycheck has asked if he can borrow your copy of Quicken (financial management software). He installs the software on his computer and returns the Quicken CD-ROM to you within an hour. Was anyone guilty of violating copyright laws? Explain.

Discussion: How would you respond to a teenager arrested for shoplifting who downplayed the crime saying, "Everybody does it and nobody ever gets caught"? How would you respond to a manager charged with duplicating copyrighted software who downplayed the incident saying, "Everybody does it and nobody ever gets caught"?

Discussion: What can each of us do to help guard against the pirating of copyrighted software?

2. SCANNING FOR SHOPLIFTERS

A high-tech surveillance technology that has been used in the past to trap pedophiles, terrorists, and, at European soccer games, hooligans, is being employed by some retailers to identify shoplifters. The face-recognition technology matches a digital facial scan against a database of known shoplifters. The technology can scan people's faces within a crowd using 80 facial features and identify people with 99% accuracy. There are, of course, concerns about invasion of personal privacy; however, individual scans are deleted after they had been matched against the database. Also, this technology offers great promise for apprehending criminals; the governments of many countries are using it or evaluating it.

Discussion: Do you consider this application of face-recognition technology an invasion of privacy? If so, do the benefits justify the means?

Discussion: Identify and describe at least two other applications (not mentioned above) for face-recognition technology.

3. MORAL FILTERING OF INTERNET CONTENT

There has been considerable debate in the cyber community among organizations that set policy for the Internet about whether these organizations should provide some level of moral filtering of Web site content and applications. For example, one site published the names of British Intelligence agents, thus putting their lives at risk. Another lists doctors who perform abortions, then crosses them off as they are killed. Then, of course, there is the issue of easily accessible pornography, which currently comprises 1.5% of Internet content.

Discussion: What role, if any, should be played by Internet policy-making organizations regarding the assessment of the Internet content and applications?

Discussion: If possible, should cooperative international legislation be enacted to better control access to pornographic content on the Internet?

4. PRESCREENING OF ONLINE COMMUNICATIONS

Millions of people have access to and participate in newsgroups, chat rooms, and online forums. Some sponsors and information services feel obligated to give their subscribers an environment that is free of offensive language. These organizations use an electronic scanner to "read" each message before it is posted to a newsgroup or forum. In a split second, the scanner flags those words and phrases that do not comply with the information service's guidelines. The scanner even catches words or phrases that may be disguised with asterisks and so on. Generally, the guidelines are compatible with accepted norms in a moral society. These include the use of grossly repugnant material, obscene material, solicitations, and threats. The scanner also scans for text that may be inappropriate for a public discussion, such as the use of pseudonyms, attempts at trading, presentation of illegal material, and even speaking in foreign languages. Messages that do not pass the prescreening process are returned automatically to the sender.

Some might cry that their rights to freedom of expression are violated. This, of course, is a matter that may ultimately be decided in a court of law. In the meantime, those who wish a more open discussion have plenty of opportunities. On most international newsgroups and information services, anything goes.

Discussion: Is prescreening of electronic communications a violation of freedom of expression?

Discussion: What are the advantages and disadvantages of prescreening online communications from the user's perspective? From the perspective of the organization doing the prescreening?

5. INAPPROPRIATE USE OF THE INTERNET AT WORK

Internet usage monitoring at the workplace has revealed what many workers already know, at least some of the Internet surfing is not job related (more than half at the U.S. Internal Revenue Service). Most of this surfing is treated much like nonbusiness telephone calls, such as a call home or to confirm a doctor's appointment. However, management is getting involved when abuse is extensive or "inappropriate" material is viewed or downloaded on company PCs. Although corporate policy on such actions may be nonexistent or unclear, some people are losing their jobs.

Discussion: What would be appropriate punishment, if any, for an employee who, against company policy, downloaded and kept "inappropriate" material on his or her PC?

Discussion: What punishment is appropriate for an employee who abuses his or her Internet connection by doing non-job-related surfing at least one hour per day?

DISCUSSION AND PROBLEM SOLVING

1. Two lawyers used the Internet to broadcast thousands of e-mail messages advertising their services. They were subsequently flamed (sent angry e-mail messages) and vilified by Internet users for what they believed to be an inappropriate use of the Net. The attorneys broke no laws. Was the reaction of the Internet users within the IT code of ethics? Explain.

2. Why is green computing important to society?

3. What can you do, that you are not doing now, that would be a move toward green computing?

4. Expand these abbreviations and briefly describe what they mean: VODS, RSI, and CTD.

5. Evaluate your workplace at home, school, or work from an ergonomic perspective. Consider the concepts presented in Section 7-2 and the guidelines illustrated in Figure 7-6.

6. Give an example of how computer monitoring might be applied at the clerical level of activity. Give another example for the management level.

7. The Internal Revenue Service also uses computer matching to identify those who might be underpaying

taxes. Is this an invasion of privacy or a legitimate approach to tax collection?

8. In the past, bank officers have been reluctant to report computer crimes. If you were a customer of a bank that made such a decision, how would you react?

9. Who knows what about you? List as many nongovernment organizations (specific names or generic) as you can that collect and maintain personal information about you. Do the same for government organizations.

10. Discuss the kinds of personal information that can be obtained by analyzing a person's credit card transactions during the past year.

11. Why would a judge sentence one person to 10 years in jail for an unarmed robbery of $25 from a convenience store and another to 18 months for computer fraud involving millions of dollars?

12. Discuss what you can do at your college or place of employment to minimize the possibility of computer crime.

13. Generally, society has an erroneous perception of hackers. What is this perception and why is it erroneous?

14. Internet cybercops at CERT/CC are no longer concerned with minor intrusions to Net security. Why is this?

FOCUS ON PERSONAL COMPUTING

1. *Practicing Green Computing.* With green computing now a societal imperative, if not law, we have cradle-to-grave responsibility for our PCs. Survey five people who have discarded obsolete PCs. Assess each with regard to proper product stewardship. Find an organization that will accept and probably dispose of computer hardware. Describe the process by which you transfer your obsolete hardware to the organization and note the cost to you.

2. *Personal Computing Code of Ethics.* Write a personal computing code of ethics that relates to your specific computing environment and can serve as your guide during personal computing activities, including your interaction with the cyberworld.

3. *Workplace Assessment.* Assess your workplace. Describe what you can do to make it more ergonomically compatible with personal computing, that is, minimize health concerns and maximize effective interaction.

ONLINE EXERCISES @ www.prenhall.com/long

1. The Online Study Guide (multiple choice, true/false, matching, and essay questions)

2. Internet Learning Activities
  • Ethics in Computing
  • Ergonomics

3. Serendipitous Internet Activities
  • Music

IT ILLUSTRATED

Prentice Hall
train &
assess **it**
generation

**BUYING
A PC**

Personal Computing Buyer's Guide

From the time you purchase and plug in your first PC, you are committed to a lifetime of buying newer and better PCs, PC upgrades, PC peripherals, and PC software. Also, you subscribe to PC services and are caught up in an endless loop of PC supplies and accessories. The personal computing adventure is great fun, but it isn't cheap. But neither is Disneyworld.

The emphasis in this buyer's guide is on the actual buying and decision processes. Other sections of the book cover hardware, software, and Internet concepts.

BEFORE YOU BUY: ANSWER THESE QUESTIONS

A sleek new PC is like a shiny new car; it invites impulse buying. Resist this urge and get a system that fits your budget and meets your personal computing needs. Before you purchase anything, answer these important questions.

How Much to Spend?

You can purchase a new personal computer for under $500. However, if you choose an array of performance features and opt for the latest technology in peripheral and storage devices, the cost of a personal computer could easily exceed $5000. Ultimately, the amount you spend on a personal computer depends on your financial circumstances and your spending priorities. If personal computing is one of your priorities, here is a good rule to follow: *purchase as much power and functionality in a personal computer system as your budget will permit.* You'll need it more quickly than you think.

Desktop PC or Notebook PC?

The choice between a *desktop PC* and a *notebook PC* (see Figure 7-13) usually hinges on two considerations: need for *portability* and *cost*.

- **Portability.** If your lifestyle demands portability in personal computing and you are willing to pay considerably more for approximately the same computing capability as a comparable desktop PC, then you should seriously consider a notebook PC.
- **Cost.** If cost is a concern and portability isn't, the desktop PC is for you.

Notebook PC owners sacrifice some conveniences to achieve portability. For instance, input devices, such as the keyboard and point-and-draw devices, are given less space in portable PCs and may be more cumbersome to use. These inconveniences, however, are offset by the convenience of having your PC and its capabilities with you wherever you are.

Notebook PCs outsold desktop PCs for the first time in 2003. This trend should continue with notebook PCs comprising an increasingly larger share of the PC market.

Which Platform?

The Wintel PC (Windows operating system, Intel or equivalent processor) represents the dominant PC platform with over 90% of the PC pie. The Apple Computer Company line of personal computers represents about 5% of the PC market, and the remainder of the market is composed mostly of Linux-based systems and those with legacy Microsoft operating systems.

When making the platform decision, consider compatibility with the other PCs in your life: your existing PC (if you have one), the one at work/home, and/or the one in your college lab. Also, consider your career interests. Apple computers have it all and do it all; some would argue that they do it better than

Figure 7-13 **DESKTOP OR NOTEBOOK PC?**
The desktop PC offers more power for your personal computing dollar, but the notebook PC offers portability.

1) Courtesy of International Business Machines Corporation. Unauthorized use not permitted. 2) Courtesy of Microsoft Corporation

Wintel machines. Nevertheless, Apple computers, especially at the high end, have been tabbed as niche machines because they are so pervasive in certain types of industries, including publishing, video/film editing, graphics, animation, illustration, and music.

Companies, whether software or automobile, tend to build products for the largest markets. In the case of software—Wintel. Therefore, Wintel PCs have a substantial advantage in the range of available software and, because of volume sales, software prices. Apple computer users also have access to a wide range of software; however, the Apple selection pales when you compare it to available Wintel software.

Who Will Use the PC and How Will It Be Used?

Plan not only for yourself but also for others in your home that might use the system. Get their input and consider their needs along with yours. The typical off-the-shelf entry-level notebook or desktop personal computer has amazing capabilities and will do most anything within the boundaries of the digital world. Nevertheless, depending on how you plan to use the system (for example, video editing, gaming, multimedia viewing), you may need to supplement the basic system with additional hardware and software.

What Input/Output Peripheral Devices Do You Need?

A good mix of input/output peripheral devices can spice up your computing experience. I/O devices come in a variety of speeds, capacities, and qualities. Generally, the more you pay, the more you get. However, there is no reason to pay for extra speed, capacity, or quality if you do not need it.

Several suggestions for I/O devices are listed below for the "typical" user. *Priority suggestions are listed first.* Of course, priorities will vary, but these should give you a benchmark for decision making. Normally, the printer (or possibly an all-in-one peripheral: print, scan, fax, and copy) is the only additional peripheral input/output device that you would get at or near the time of purchase; however, you should consider upgrading the monitor, mouse, and keyboard. All other optional I/O devices you might want can be purchased as the need arises and at the best prices.

1. PRINTER OR ALL-IN-ONE PERIPHERAL

No PC system is complete without access to a printer. The key word here is "access." If you already have a PC system in your home with an acceptable printer, you probably don't need two printers. This resource is easily shared via walk-net or a home network. Walk-net is just transferring print files via interchangeable discs or diskettes.

The ink-jet printer has emerged as the overwhelming choice of budget-minded people buying home/home office PC

systems. The quality of any of today's mainline ink-jet printers is remarkable, so your decision boils down to how much you are willing to pay for additional print quality, faster print speeds, and special features (for example, printing on both sides of the paper).

You might wish to consider getting an all-in-one multi-function peripheral, that is, a device that prints, faxes, scans, and copies (duplicates). The considerable overlap in the technologies used in these machines has enabled manufacturers to create a reasonably priced machine that does it all.

2. PC HEADSET

Desktop PCs are sold with a basic microphone and speakers. You'll need to purchase a quality headset with a mike (from $25 to $50) if you wish to take advantage of the speech recognition capability made available with the newer Microsoft Office suites (see Figure 7-14). If you purchase speech recognition software separately, the headset comes with the product.

Figure 7-14 THE PC HEADSET
If you plan to use speech recognition technology, you will need a high-quality headset with a directional microphone that picks up the user's voice but not the ever-present noises around the office and home.

Courtesy of International Business Machines Corporation.
Unauthorized use not permitted.

3. SCANNER

If you choose an all-in-one peripheral (see priority peripheral #1), you will not need a stand-alone scanner. The scanner is a good investment in your personal computing adventure. With a scanner, you can convert any color hardcopy document and even small 3D images (jewelry, heirlooms, and so on) to an electronic image that can be integrated into anything from a newsletter to a greeting card. The scanner can read text and speak the words with the help of text-to-speech software. The scanner doubles as a copy machine for small volume copying (scanner to printer) and as a fax machine (used in conjunction with the fax software that comes with all PCs and a dial-up modem). Any name-brand flatbed scanner with an 8.5-inch by 11.7-inch scanning area that scans at 1200 × 2400 dpi (dots per inch) or better should be all you need unless you are doing professional image editing.

4. INTERNET OR WEB CAMERA

The Internet or Web camera certainly is not a PC system necessity, but for as little as $50, it can add some serious spice to your personal computing experience. These versatile little cameras, which can capture both still and video images, plug into your computer like any other peripheral. You can use them for many tasks, including videophone conversations, setting up a Webcam (streaming images over the Internet), maintaining security, or for monitoring your baby.

5. GAME CONTROLLERS

If you have gamers in the house, game controllers are must-have items. The game controller is very much a matter of personal preference, so be sure and invite input from your gamers before buying. Many computer games are multiplayer games, so you may wish to purchase two of these relatively inexpensive devices.

6. DIGITAL CAMERA/DIGITAL CAMCORDER

If you enjoy taking and sharing pictures, then you will want to consider owning a digital camera. With a digital camera, the cost of photography plummets because the costly, time-consuming developing processing is eliminated. With digital cameras, you can take all the photos you want and just keep the good ones. Once the images are downloaded to your PC, you can enhance, edit, send, or view them at your leisure.

If you are in the market for a *digital camcorder*, you may not need to spend the extra money for a separate digital camera for still photography. Most modern digital camcorders let you take excellent megapixel still images, as well as digital video.

7. USB MULTIPORT HUB

The most popular way to connect input/output devices to a PC is via a USB port. Typically, a personal computer will have two or six USB ports. Those ports, however, can be filled quickly. Fortunately, USB technology allows you to daisy-chain multiple devices to a single port. It's quite possible that you'll need more ports than are made available on the system unit, and, if you do, you will need to purchase a USB 2.0 multiport hub.

Entry Level, Sweet Spot, and Performance Personal Computers

New desktop or notebook PCs can be grouped into three general categories based on cost and performance—*entry-level systems, sweet spot systems,* and *performance systems.* Soon after their introduction, these systems begin their slow slide into a lower category or obsolescence—for example, the performance system moves into the sweet spot category and, eventually, into the entry-level category.

Technological innovation continues its relentless march toward defining a new level of across-the-board performance each year. This means that what was a performance system a couple of years ago can look very much like today's entry-level system.

Buying an Entry-Level Personal Computer

If your financial circumstances and spending priorities dictate that you purchase an entry-level system, you have no choice but to go with a minimal system or, perhaps, a used PC system. In most circumstances, this system will do the job. Today's entry-level PCs can be five times as fast as a performance PC that was purchased five years ago for $5000. All modern PCs are amazingly capable machines.

Entry-level or "affordable" personal computers offer good value, but, typically, they do not give the buyer as much flexibility to customize the PC at the time of the sale. For example, you may have only one or two choices for the monitor. Often, affordable personal computers are sold off-the-shelf, as is.

Generally, *fewer, slower, less,* and *older* are terms used to describe the system components for entry-level PCs. For example, an affordable PC system might have fewer USB ports, a slower CD-RW disc drive, less RAM, and a processor with older technology. But you have to put these descriptors into perspective. An affordable PC may have a processor that is 40% slower than a performance machine processor, but it still is very, very fast.

The downside of purchasing an entry-level system is that a new affordable PC may be at least one year, and as much as two years, closer to technological obsolescence than one of the more expensive intermediate or high-end PCs. To be sure, if you purchase an entry-level PC you will lose out on technology bragging rights, but you can always brag about saving enough money to purchase a big-screen TV.

Hitting the Sweet Spot PC

In sports, the "sweet spot" is the area on a baseball bat, a tennis racket, or head of a golf club that is the most effective part with which to hit a ball. Every consumer market has a sweet spot, too. The PC market's sweet spot offers the greatest value. When you purchase a sweet spot PC, you're not paying a premium for state-of-the-art technology, but you still are getting near leading-edge performance. Most people looking to buy their first PC or another PC will want a good, solid PC that will run virtually all current and future applications over the next two or three years. For these people, a good place to look is the sweet spot in the personal computing market.

Typically, the PC sweet spot is a desktop PC that is about 6 to 12 months off the technology; that is, the major components in the system, such as the processor and hard disk, were introduced up to a year earlier. State-of-the-art performance systems might be 30% faster and capable of storing twice the information, but they may cost twice, even three times, as much as a sweet spot PC.

FINDING THE SWEET SPOT PC

Generally, the sweet spot is relatively easy to find. To find it, go to the Web site for any major PC vendor that markets directly to the public (for example, Dell, Hewlett Packard, IBM, or Gateway), then navigate to the page that features their home/small office desktop PC options. The system in the middle represents the current "sweet spot." Once you have perused the system specifications at several vendor Web sites, you should have a good read on the current PC sweet spot. Be advised, however, that the sweet spot is continuously changing, and what you see today as the high-end system may be featured as a sweet spot system in a few days.

If you don't have access to the Internet, the sweet spot is fairly obvious at any major PC retailer, such as Best Buy, Office Depot, and so on. The sweet spot is represented by those similarly priced PC systems in the middle price range.

CUSTOMIZING THE PC SWEET SPOT SYSTEM

You may not have the flexibility to customize a sweet spot system. Those sold in retail outlets and, sometimes, online via direct marketers may be offered as a package deal—what you see is what you get. However, most vendors that market directly to customers, via the Internet or telephone sales, give the consumer plenty of flexibility to customize their orders.

It is likely that the come-on price of a sweet spot system will not include some needed and important upgrades. Depending on your budget and personal computing needs, consider the following recommendations. *The recommendations are listed by value, with the biggest payout for your PC dollar listed first.*

- **Buy a surge suppressor.** Inexpensive surge protectors provide essential protection from lightning hits and other electrical aberrations. An uninterruptible power source (UPS) offers protection superior to a surge suppressor's but adds $60 to $80 to the system price.

- **Upgrade memory.** The easiest and most effective way to improve performance of a personal computer is to increase RAM. Modern PCs operate reasonably well at 256 MB; however, increasing RAM to 512 MB or more has a tremendous impact on overall performance, as much as 50%, depending on your mix of applications.

- **Buy the three-year warranty.** This is the best deal of all the manufacturers' options at the time of purchase,

especially for notebooks. It gives you piece of mind that you have somewhere to go when something goes wrong or you need some answers—and, there is a good chance that it will and you will.

- **Upgrade the size/type of the monitor.** The standard off-the-shelf PC system normally comes with a manufacturer-grade CRT monitor (15 to 17 inches). These are of acceptable quality for home use and should outlast the other PC components. However, with so much of what we do being presented as multimedia, a 19-inch or bigger monitor will enhance your personal computing adventure. Expect to pay about $100 per extra inch for a CRT-style monitor. An alternative to the CRT monitor is the space-saving, flat-panel LCD monitor. Although the price of flat-panel LCD monitors is dropping, you can expect to pay a premium for LCD monitors—especially the larger ones (19 inches and up).

- **Upgrade the speaker system.** For $30 to $90 extra, you can have a speaker system with surround sound and a floor-shaking subwoofer that will make those DVD movies, MP3 downloads, and games come alive with sound. If you choose top-of-the-line speakers, you may need to upgrade the *sound card,* as well.

- **Upgrade the keyboard and mouse.** For about $30 to $60 extra, you can get an enhanced keyboard and an ergonomically designed mouse that will last the useful life of the system (which may not be the case with the standard devices). Wireless versions of these devices let you interact with your computer from anywhere near the PC.

- **Upgrade the hard disk capacity.** You can never have enough hard disk space, especially if you have gamers in the house and/or you plan to store digital images and videos on the PC. Generally, choose a hard disk that is at least one step above the hard disk bundled with the standard sweet spot system.

- **Choose the de facto standard office suite.** Given a choice between Microsoft Office and some other office suite, choose the home or small business version of Microsoft Office. The applications in the Microsoft Office suite are taught in virtually all schools at all levels and this suite is the de facto standard in business and government. If you work at home, consider the professional version.

- **Upgrade the CD-ROM/DVD option.** If the sweet spot system is not configured with a rewritable option, CD-RW and/or DVD±RW, you should consider choosing a combination drive (DVD/CD-RW) or choosing one of the rewritable options for the second drive bay, which is normally empty. If you plan on creating and copying custom CDs, having a CD-ROM drive and a separate drive for rewritable media is handy. Also, having a rewritable disc drive facilitates important backup duties.

- **Upgrade the video card.** The interface between the processor and the monitor is the video card. Any modern video card will handle the display tasks for a typical user; however, if you expect to be involved with sophisticated multimedia applications and/or serious gaming, you should consider upgrading to a high-quality video card with at least 64 MB of VRAM.

- **All-in-one multifunction peripheral: print, scan, fax, and copy.** An all-in-one multifunction peripheral (see Figure 7-15) capable of handling all print, scan, fax, and copy functions rounds out any PC system. Purchasing individual devices to achieve this level of functionality could cost up to $1000. A quality multifunction peripheral can be purchased for 25% of that amount. You can live a long and healthy life without sending/receiving another fax, but we now live in a multimedia world where printing and scanning high-resolution images is commonplace. Plus, the duplication capability comes in handy.

Figure 7-15 **THE ALL-IN-ONE MULTIFUNCTION PERIPHERAL**
This telecommuter configured his tower PC with a multifunction peripheral that is a printer, fax machine, a copier, and a scanner—an all-in-one device. Multifunction printers are ideal for the home or small offices where volume for any single function is low.

Photo courtesy of Hewlett-Packard Company

- **Home networking adapter.** For an extra $20 or so, you can add a home networking adapter PCI card (HomePNA or HomePlug) to your system. This relatively inexpensive upgrade makes your new PC ready for phoneline or power-line home networking if and when you need it. A wireless adapter will cost a little more.

These are the essential upgrades and/or choices you might wish to consider. Everything else, such as game pads, digital cameras, extra USB ports, software, and so on can be purchased later as your personal computing needs come into focus.

The Performance PC

If you are in the market for a performance PC, you are flushed with a surplus of discretionary funds or you are a power user with special processing needs. Those special needs might include, but are not limited to, video editing, computer-aided design (CAD), Web design, software development, IT writing/publishing, and graphics/illustration.

The performance PC represents leading-edge technology and, in contrast to the entry-level system, the key descriptors are *more, faster, greater,* and *newer.* The performance PC will have every kind of port, and plenty of them. It will have a DVD±RW drive and, perhaps, 1 to 2 GB of RAM. It will have at least one state-of-the-art processor. The performance PC is feature rich, with high-end video and sound cards that could add as much as $700 to the price of the system. The system might be configured with a video editing package that would include a video capture card and related software. The system unit would include an enhanced power unit and extra fans for cooling the many heat-producing components.

People who buy performance PCs are veteran PC users who have collaborated on the purchase of many PCs in the past. They already are aware of the considerations presented in this buyer's guide.

WHAT SPECIAL HARDWARE DO YOU NEED FOR INTERNET ACCESS AND HOME NETWORKING?

Your personal computer can be linked to the rest of the world through the Internet or to the other PCs at your house via home networking.

Internet Access

Internet access falls into two categories, *dialup access* and *broadband access.* You pay a little more for broadband, which can be up to 50 times faster than the traditional dialup access.

DIALUP INTERNET ACCESS

The dialup, 56 K bps data/voice/fax modem is installed in virtually all new PCs. Keep this relatively inexpensive (about $20) option because, eventually, you may need it for data, voice, or fax communications.

BROADBAND INTERNET ACCESS

The difference between dialup and broadband access is stark: Dialup is a lot of click and wait, whereas broadband displays Web pages in seconds or fractions of seconds. *Cable* (via cable modems), *DSL,* and *satellite* are the leading broadband technologies for home Internet access.

Depending on which service you choose, you will need a cable modem, a DSL modem, or a satellite modem, but, normally, you purchase the broadband modem when you subscribe to the service, not when you purchase your PC. Sometimes the modem is included with the subscription fee and sometimes you must buy it. In any case, it's always a good idea to use the modem suggested by the broadband service provider.

Home Networking

The spread of PCs throughout the house has prompted the growth of home networking (see Figure 7-16). Wired and wireless network adapters (network interface cards or NICs) allow families to link all their PCs using ordinary phone lines, AC power lines, or wireless communications for simultaneous Internet access, printer and file sharing, and multiplayer gaming.

***Figure 7-16* HOME NETWORKING**
These two teenagers' PCs are on a phone-line home network with mom's PC, which has the printer, and dad's PC, which has the scanner. The router (on top of the system unit in the inset) enables sharing of the DSL broadband signal via the phone-line network. All PCs have HPNA phone-line adapters, two external (to the left of the monitor) and two internal.

To set up a home network, you need the software, which is built into all Windows operating systems, and you need a home networking NIC, a *network adapter,* installed on each PC on the network (about $20 each for wired and double that for wireless). The adapter can be installed internally or can be connected via USB externally. Network adapters can be

selected as an option at the time you purchase your PC or they can be purchased and easily installed at a later date.

FACTORS TO CONSIDER WHEN BUYING A PC

It's easy to overlook important considerations that could influence your decisions. This summary offers insight that can help you avoid some of the problems incurred by other PC buyers.

What Software Is Preinstalled on the PC?

Arguably, the most challenging aspect of choosing between alternative PCs is appraising the worth of the software preinstalled with the system and integrating that assessment into the overall evaluation of the PC system. And, that's the way PC vendors meant it to be. They want the quality or variety of their software bundle(s) to either confuse the buyer or be the difference maker, depending on the quality of their offerings.

If the PC purchase decision were based solely on hardware, we could compare oranges with oranges—but it's not. When you bundle software into the PC purchase price, and all vendors do this, it's more like comparing oranges to grapefruit.

The bundled software frequently is the biggest variable in the PC purchase decision process. What software PC vendors choose to offer with their systems can be substantially different between competitors and even within their own line of PCs.

The Operating System

Every new PC is sold with an operating system, typically the latest version of *Microsoft Windows,* either the *Home Edition* or the *Professional Edition.* The Home Edition is sufficient for 95% of the home computers. The Professional Edition has a few security and networking features that might be reason enough for the telecommuter to pay extra for this advanced version of Windows.

The Software Suite

A software suite is bundled with all but the very low-end PCs and some promotional PCs. Most new personal computers are bundled with *Microsoft Office XP Standard* (also called *Office XP Small Business*), *Microsoft Office XP Professional,* or *Microsoft Works Suite.* Occasionally, a vendor will offer an alternative suite, such as the *WordPerfect Suite,* which continues to be popular in the legal field.

If Microsoft Works is the default software bundle for a particular system, you can expect to pay about $100 to upgrade to the industry standard Microsoft Office suite. If you are buying an off-the-shelf PC with Works already installed, the upgrade to Office XP may not be an option.

These software suites may or may not be accompanied by other software or service incentives. For example, additional software preinstalled with Microsoft Office XP might include antivirus software, a personal finance package, or perhaps an online encyclopedia.

Optional Software Bundles

When you purchase a PC online or via mail order, major direct marketer manufacturers will give you an opportunity to order additional software. These offerings are in two main categories: *individual software packages* and *optional bundles* (topical groups of three or four software packages).

Generally, any of the individual software packages can be purchased online or at retail outlets at the PC vendor's offering price or for a few dollars less. Don't feel as if you need to make a decision now on these individual software packages, unless antivirus software is not included with the price of the PC. If this is the case and the vendor offers a quality antivirus package, you should purchase it with the system.

Quality of Hardware/Software Support Services

PC hardware is very reliable and routinely operates continuously without incident for years. Even with a history of reliability, the possibility does exist that one or several of the components eventually will fail and have to be repaired. Most retailers or direct-marketer vendors will offer a variety of hardware service contracts from same-day, on-site repairs that cover all parts and service to a carry-in (or mail-in) service that does not include parts and can take several weeks.

Since hardware support services vary within and between vendors, you should look over the options carefully and choose the one right for your circumstances. It's important that you understand *exactly* what you must do to get your system repaired. As a rule of thumb, choose at least some level of repair service for the effective life of your system (about 3 years).

WHERE TO BUY HARDWARE/SOFTWARE?

PCs and associated hardware and software can be purchased at thousands of convenient bricks-and-mortar locations and from hundreds of retail sites on the Internet.

Bricks-and-Mortar Computer Retailers with Authorized Service Centers

Several national retail chains and many regional chains specialize in the sale of PC hardware and/or software. Also, there are thousands of computer stores with no chain affiliation.

Most market and service a variety of PC systems. Some make their own line of computers and are happy to custom-build one for you. Find these dealers under "Computer and Equipment Dealers" in the Yellow Pages.

Bricks-and-Mortar Computer Retailers Without Authorized Service Centers

Computer/electronics departments of most department stores, discount warehouse stores, and office supply stores sell PCs and PC software. For the most part, these stores treat computers as they would any consumer item. When you walk out the door, you are covered by the manufacturer's warranty. For this category of retailers, what you see on the shelf is what you get. Any further technical support comes from the hardware and software manufacturers within the limits of their warranties. These are prepackaged systems and the retailer has relatively little flexibility in system configuration because they do not have a service center.

Direct Marketers

Most major manufacturers of PC hardware (Dell, Gateway, Hewlett-Packard, IBM, and so on) and most major software companies (Microsoft, Symantec, Broderbund, and so on) are direct marketers; that is, they sell directly to the customer. The direct marketer's "store window" is a site on the Internet (see Figure 7-17). Orders can be entered via the Internet, telephone,

Figure 7-17 BUYING DIRECT
Dell Computer Corporation is a direct marketer with a Web site that provides detailed information about any available system. The customer can go to the Dell Web site to customize and purchase a system entirely online.

fax, or mail. The trend is toward entering orders interactively via the Internet. The direct marketer makes and sends the requested product(s) to the customer within a few days. Direct marketers offer an array of popular PC software and accessories.

The strength of the direct marketer's sales program is online sales via the Internet. Once you decide which PC system you want, you can *customize,* or *configure,* it to pick exactly the options you want on your PC system.

Buying directly from the manufacturer via the Internet has many advantages. The manufacturers' Web sites are comprehensive in that they present all available options, plus they provide enough information to answer any questions you might have.

Retailers of Preowned and Refurbished Computers

The used-computer retailer was as inevitable as the used-car dealer was. A computer that is no longer powerful enough for one user may have more than enough power for another. Used-computer retailers are easy to find: just look under "Computer and Equipment Dealers—Used" in the Yellow Pages.

Most major computer manufacturers also sell used computers, called *refurbished* or *remanufactured computers.* Typically, such systems are current models and were used only for a few days or weeks. For whatever reason, these systems were returned to the manufacturer. The problem components were replaced, probably with refurbished components, and the system was offered for sale via the company's Web site at a 10 to 15% discount off the price of the new system. The warranty remains the same.

Online Auctions

A great source for anything used is an online auction. PCs and electronics are among the most popular items up for auction on the Internet. Online auctions go on 24 hours a day with people all over the world registering bids on millions of items. The typical PC system put up for auction on eBay at www.ebay.com is 3 to 5 years off the technology and goes for $50 to $250. Avoid bidding on any system that is deinstalled because it offers no software.

WHICH PC MANUFACTURER IS BEST FOR YOU?

All big-name manufacturers, such as Dell, Hewlett-Packard, Compaq (now part of Hewlett-Packard), Gateway, IBM, and Apple, produce quality personal computers that can be expected to last well beyond their useful life. Surprisingly, however, these big-name manufacturers account for a less than half of personal computer sales.

The bulk of PC sales are by small "white box" PC vendors. Many small PC companies have emerged that custom-build and sell "no-name" PCs to school districts, city governments, small companies, and individuals. Some of these small players are excellent and have a solid record of providing good service, price, and flexibility. White box vendors typically sell for less than mainstream manufacturers. To do so, however, they may use components of lesser quality, reduced motherboard features, and/or components that may be off the technology.

Ultimately, the answer to the question "Which PC manufacturer is best for you?" is the manufacturer that offers systems that provide the best match for your personal computing needs and your personal bank account.

THE TOTAL COST OF OWNERSHIP

The spending on personal computing continues once you have paid for and installed the hardware and software. As soon as you get your PC system, you will want to stock up on supplies, subscribe to vital services, and purchase important accessories. Invariably, you will want to build your software portfolio (see Figure 7-18). Most personal computing consumables are associated with the printer and interchangeable disk drives (Zip disks, CD-R, DVD+RW discs, and other storage media). These considerations bring us to an important concept in personal computing—*the total cost of ownership.*

The amount shown on the price tag for a PC system does not completely represent what you must pay to get into the personal computing business. That price tag doesn't include a printer. The cost of a printer seldom includes a cable, another expense. Of course, you will want paper on which to print, probably two or three different qualities and in several shades. Printer cartridges can cost $40 or more.

It's easy for a teenager to spend $500 a year on gaming hardware and software. You'll need a place to put the PC and a comfortable chair. Access to the Internet will cost you from $20 to $60 a month. And the costs go on and on. If you have a spending limit, consider the estimated incidental costs shown in Figure 7-19.

Figure 7-18
THE SOFTWARE PORTFOLIO
This mix of software, which includes a smattering of utility, applications, and games software, might be considered typical for a home office software portfolio. The retail cost of the software shown here is over $2000.

	One-Time Cost	Annual Cost
Software	$100–$1500	$100–$500
Cables	$0–$50	
Supplies (printer cartridges, plain paper, photo paper, diskettes, Zip disks, CD-RW and/or DVD±RW discs, and DVD/CD-R blanks, and so on)	$100–$200	$100–$500
Internet service provider (ISP) and/or Information service	$0–$500 (one-time ISP costs are setup and installation fees plus equipment cost [modem, router, satellite dish, and so on] for broadband service)	$250–$800 (includes basic Internet service; the high-side expense is for broadband service)
Subscriptions (technology magazines, virus protection service, online databases, and so on)		$0–$200
UPS (uninterruptible power source) or Surge Protector	$40–$300	$0–$100 (UPS battery replacement)
Additional data telephone line (optional)	$0–$50	$0–$350
Furniture and Accessories (desk, chair, lights, mouse pad, and so on)	$30–$500	$50–$150
System Maintenance (this amount is nothing until the warranty runs out)		$0–$300
Insurance		$0–$100
Miscellaneous, including accessories (USB 2.0 hub, new game pad, and so on)		$0–$300
TOTAL ESTIMATED INCIDENTAL EXPENSES	$270–$3100	$500–$3600

Figure 7-19 ONE-TIME AND ANNUAL INCIDENTAL EXPENSES FOR PERSONAL COMPUTING
The personal computing cost ranges listed are for a first-time user. The low end of the ranges is representative for casual home users, and the high end of the ranges is applicable to sophisticated users with home offices.

IT ILLUSTRATED SELF-CHECK

1 As a rule, you should purchase as much power and functionality in a PC system as your budget will permit. (T/F)

2 The choice between a desktop PC and a notebook PC usually hinges between the need for portability and styling. (T/F)

3 An entry-level PC has components that are no more than six months off the technology. (T/F)

4 The surge protector is designed to provide protection from lightning hits. (T/F)

5 Hardware upgrades are not advised for sweet spot PC systems. (T/F)

6 As a rule of thumb, choose at least some level of repair service for the effective life of your new PC system. (T/F)

7 The all-in-one peripheral device does all but which of the following document tasks: (a) fax, (b) print, (c) scan, or (d) shred?

8 Which device would you expect to be the most costly: (a) game pad, (b) scanner, (c) Web camera, or (d) headset with a mike?

9 Which of these devices is required for phoneline home networking: (a) multifunction peripheral device, (b) 1394 ports, (c) surge protector, or (d) HomePNA adapters?

10 Although direct marketers offer customers a variety of ways to enter their PC orders, the trend is toward entering orders via: (a) telephone, (b) the Internet, (c) fax, or (d) snail mail.

11 The total cost of ownership of a PC encompasses all but which of the following: (a) opportunity costs, (b) PC purchase price, (c) ISP charges, or (d) printer supplies?

E-COMMERCE, DATABASES, AND SECURITY

8

CHAPTER

LEARNING OBJECTIVES

Once you have read and studied this chapter, you will be able to:

- Understand the scope of and concepts associated with e-commerce (Section 8-1).

- Describe database concepts, features, and applications (Section 8-2).

- Identify points of security vulnerability and how to address security concerns for a computer center, an information system, the Internet, e-commerce, and a PC (Section 8-3).

Life at school, at home, and at work is easier if you understand the directions in which our information society is headed. Clearly, one of those trends is electronic commerce (e-commerce)—e-tailing, e-money, business-to-business, consumer-to-consumer applications, electronic publishing, Web marketing, and much more. Electronic commerce has emerged as a major strategic priority in most corporations. Consumers are embracing its potential, as well.

The database is integral to all levels of information technology activity and, especially, to e-commerce applications. Understanding the principles of data management can help you to create your own databases and to be a more effective user of existing databases.

E-commerce and databases are magnets for people who will attempt unauthorized access for personal gain. For this reason, we must build an envelope of security around them. The material in this chapter identifies points of vulnerability and presents specific approaches you can employ at home and at work in order to enjoy a secure computing environment.

8-1   E-COMMERCE

Why this section is important to you.

As businesses and educational institutions strive for the competitive advantage and government organizations strive for improved service, implementation of electronic commerce (e-commerce) has emerged as a strategic planning priority. This section will give you the understanding you need to become a full partner in the inevitable shift to e-commerce.

THE CRYSTAL BALL

Internet-Based Personal Communications

The telephone has been the foundation of remote personal communication for almost 100 years and it remains so today. Over the next few years, however, we can expect costly electronic telephone switching networks and their limited audio communications capability to give way to a new area of e-commerce—sophisticated Internet telephony. Although at its embryonic stage of development, Internet telephony is on target to provide a wide range of communications capabilities, including videoconferencing, for considerably less cost. Each year a greater percentage of our personal communications will shift to the Internet, and the telephone as we know it will begin to fade away.

You do not have to look much further than the campus mailroom to see the future of commerce. For the past few years, college mailrooms have been deluged with packages containing items purchased via the Internet. With some campus mailroom's handling 100,000 packages a month, campus mailrooms throughout the land are being expanded and redesigned for a new era of economics—electronic commerce. **E-commerce** is simply business conducted online or via some form of data communications.

This on-campus parcel activity tells us much about what we can expect in the new economy. These indicators tell us that the next generation of shoppers will be comfortable purchasing goods and services online and that the trend toward e-commerce will accelerate as today's students begin careers. To accommodate this trend, whatever can go online probably will go online—in business, in academia, and in government. E-commerce is a relatively small percentage of the bricks and mortar economy, but that percentage will grow rapidly as the computer/Internet generation comes of age.

The consensus in the industrial world is that e-commerce eventually will account for trillions of dollars, perhaps within a few years. Every company would like a piece of the action; however, successful e-commerce sites are the exception rather than the rule. It is not unusual for a company to spend millions of dollars in anticipation of tremendous returns only to find out that it was too late or used the wrong approach. Nevertheless, the corporate world has no option but to make a commitment to e-commerce, as there is too much at stake to be left behind.

FIGURE 8-1 E-COMMERCE ON THE ROAD

HIGH-SPEED TOLL BOOTHS

Electronic commerce takes on many forms. For example, scanners along many toll roads read driver information sent from windshield-mounted transponders (see inset) as cars pass through at highway speeds. The electronic tollbooths transmit the data directly to a central computer system, often over the Internet, and the toll is deducted from the driver's account.

Courtesy of Lockheed Martin Corporation

GAMING IS BIG BUSINESS

Rather than purchase gaming software, some gamers pay a monthly fee to a gaming service, then download and play any of hundreds of games. This young man is on vacation in a car, enjoying the scenery, and playing a video game with a friend back home via a wireless Internet link.

Photo courtesy of Microvision Incorporated

THE SCOPE OF E-COMMERCE

The scope of electronic commerce includes a variety of activities related to the buying and selling of goods or services over the Internet (see Figure 8-1). Some of the major activities often associated with e-commerce include the following.

- Virtual marketplaces that provide **e-tailing** (online retailing)
- **Business-to-business** (or **B2B**), the computer-to-computer exchange of data and information between businesses (for example, between Wal-Mart and its suppliers)
- **Business-to-consumer** (**B2C**), the electronic interactions between businesses and consumers via Internet server computers (for example, online retailer Amazon.com)
- **Consumer-to-consumer** (**C2C**), the electronic interactions between consumers via Internet server computers (for example, online auctions on eBay.com)

- Internet-based marketing or advertising
- Online market research and surveys designed to gather product use, demographic, and other appropriate market research data
- Those technologies aiding interactions among businesses and between businesses and consumers (e-mail, fax, intranets, extranets, Internet telephony, and so on)

The scope of e-commerce is illustrated in Figure 8-2. Customers can go online to obtain information, an approach that is much less expensive than having to mail expensive brochures, newsletters, or manuals. Also, customers/patrons can complete transactions and submit information online. For example, a growing number of taxpayers file their tax returns online, which are checked and processed electronically.

Customers can shop online. E-tailers can sell and process orders entirely online, and then ship goods directly from the manufacturer/supplier, thus eliminating the need for hand processing and for bricks-and-mortar storefronts. Businesses can communicate computer to computer via business-to-business (B2B) on many applications, such as payment and billing, eliminating the need for time-consuming paper transaction processing and the delays associated with postal delivery.

Now that you're familiar with the scope of e-commerce some of the ways it is used, let's explore its impact on the business world.

ELECTRONIC COMMERCE LEVELS THE PLAYING FIELD

The business model of the twentieth century made it very difficult for small companies to go head-to-head with larger companies. E-commerce, which appears to be emerging as the business model for the twenty-first century, has helped to level the playing field among large and small companies. Of course, large companies with name recognition and an existing customer base still have an advantage, but each company, no matter how big or small can have a presence on the Internet and a worldwide audience.

Companies no longer need large, geographically dispersed sales staffs or experienced international trade specialists to operate on a global scale. Judicious use of e-commerce enables people to reach potential customers without dedicating huge amounts of money to sales staff, advertising, and public relations campaigns. In the e-commerce world, small and large businesses compete side-by-side. The same is true for start-up and established businesses. Once a business gets a customer's attention, it can establish a close relationship with the consumer by offering a variety of real-time Net-based services, such as online buying, online training sessions, access to databases, continuously updated product catalogs, and so on.

E-COMMERCE AND E-MONEY

Over the past few millennia, people have used many different types of personal assets to make busi-

FIGURE 8–2 **SCOPE OF E-COMMERCE**

The Internet's servers, databases, and communications facilities enable a wide array of e-commerce applications

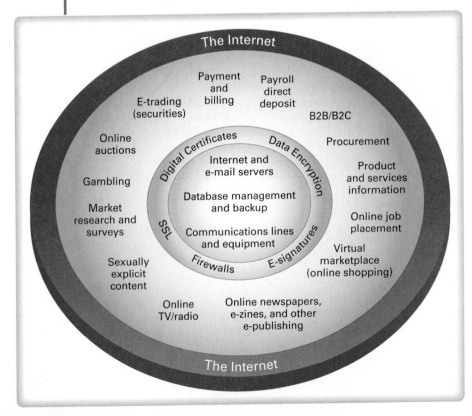

ness transactions. We've bartered (traded) with animals, goods (precious stones, corn, and so on), and personal services. In modern times, we've used money (paper and coin) and written checks. We've used charge cards, debit cards, and various electronic banking systems, such as automatic withdrawal. We are drawing closer to a cashless society, and because e-commerce revolves around systems where money changes hands over the Internet or through other electronic means, it is giving us a push to move even closer (see Figure 8-2).

E-commerce deals in **e-money,** digital money, where withdrawals and deposits of any size and complexity are done at the speed of light. Standards for the manner in which money is exchanged are continuing to evolve. For example, several companies offer online purchasing systems that enable consumers to create and use an **electronic wallet** that stores their billing and shipping information in controlled server facilities. Credit card numbers are encrypted in a database that is not connected to the Internet. The consumer simply clicks on a "Pay" button to send all billing and shipping information already stored in the electronic wallet to the merchant and makes a credit card transaction via a secure Internet server.

BUSINESS-TO-BUSINESS APPLICATIONS

As mentioned, *business-to-business* (B2B) applications are the computer-to-computer exchange of data and information between businesses. Wal-Mart, the world's largest corporation, has implemented a sophisticated B2B application that cuts costs for both Wal-Mart and its suppliers while expediting the product distribution process. Energy companies cooperate via B2B to share electrical resources and optimize the use of available power (see Figure 8-3). Business-to-business applications have the potential to save companies substantial amounts of money. For example, companies are estimating that B2B can reduce purchasing costs by up to 20%. Companies are buying direct and using just-in-time strategies to minimize third-party involvement and reduce inventories.

The most popular and easily implemented B2B applications involve buying and selling between companies. However, the applications for B2B are limitless, so we can expect increasing electronic cooperation between companies. At present, those industries enjoying the greatest growth in business-to-business e-commerce are in hardware and software, automobile parts, health care, electronics, chemicals, and transportation.

Until recently, B2B was conducted over communications channels leased from a common carrier; however, the trend in B2B e-commerce is to use the Internet, an extranet, or a virtual private network (extranets and VPNs are discussed in Chapter 6). Figure 8-4 contrasts the traditional interactions between a customer and supplier company with interactions via B2B and extranets. Business-to-business commerce is expected to grow to a whopping $1.6 trillion by 2005, almost 10% of all U.S. business trade!

B2B also is being explored in many other areas, including the matching of unused patents to companies that might benefit from them, thus slashing R&D expenses. Now, almost everything is on the Internet auction block. That is, any excess in services (extra seats at a seminar or a Broadway musical) or in production (too many perishable apples or too much electricity) that might otherwise be wasted can be made available to the highest bidder.

FIGURE 8-3   **BUSINESS-TO-BUSINESS IN THE ENERGY INDUSTRY**

APX (shown here) offers Internet B2B services to energy companies that facilitates the trading of green power (solar, wind, geothermal) and/or brown power (natural gas, hydroelectricity, coal, nuclear power).

FIGURE 8-4 **BUSINESS-TO-BUSINESS E-COMMERCE**

In the figure, the traditional interaction between a customer company and a supplier company are contrasted with similar interactions via business-to-business (B2B) e-commerce. Enabling technologies for B2B include extranets and VPNs.

BUSINESS-TO-CONSUMER APPLICATIONS

Whenever businesses can reach and interact with consumers more efficiently via the Internet, they turn that opportunity into a *business-to-consumer* (B2C) application. Government agencies, places of learning, and companies are encouraging each other and us to do more business online. It simply costs less money when activities are moved online and paper, people, and other expenses are minimized.

One of the revolutionary developments emerging from the new economy is **disintermediation,** essentially the removal of the middleman. Disintermediation is the dominant force behind the B2C revolution. In the new economy, online retailers sell directly to their customers. By eliminating an intermediate step—a wholesaler and/or a storefront retailer in the old economy—companies are able to sell products for less and get them to their customers more quickly.

Some people will argue that the level of service for B2C applications may be better, too. For example, why do people in the United States who file their taxes electronically via PC receive a tax credit? It's both economics and service. The cost of manually handling a return is much higher than the cost of the $10 tax credit. Because the return is processed faster, the taxpayer receives his or her refund more quickly. The IRS is on target to get 80% participation by 2007.

The number and variety of B2C applications continues to expand (see Figure 8-5). For example, you can do a week's worth of grocery shopping in 10 minutes, check out job openings in your area of the country, do your banking transactions from home, or send flowers to someone special (virtual and real).

In a few years, according to projections, e-commerce in cyberspace will be just as significant as in-person, mail, and telephone sales. Any business that hopes to stay in business in this new millennium is offering or planning to offer its products and/or services online. These few examples should give you some insight into the current realities and the future possibilities of B2C e-commerce.

FIGURE 8-5 BUSINESS-TO-CONSUMER (B2C) APPLICATIONS

VIRTUAL GROCERY STORE

The Peapod system lets subscribers point and click their way around a virtual supermarket. Selected groceries are hand picked and delivered.

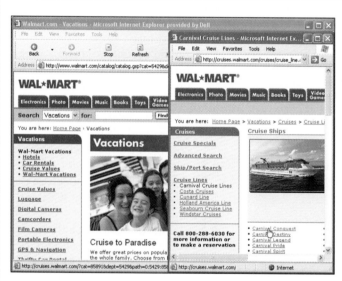

E-TAILING

The world's largest retailer may someday be the world's largest e-tailer. Forecasters are predicting that Internet shopping will comprise an increasing share of all retail dollars spent, eventually passing that of storefront sales.

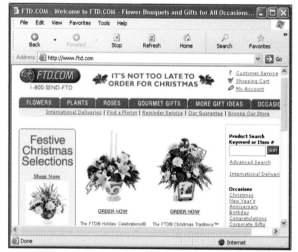

FLOWERS FAST

One of the most frequently purchased items on the Net is flowers. At this FTD site, click on the type of occasion, select a floral arrangement, then enter the desired delivery date, a gift card message, billing information, and a send-to address.

E-Tailing: Internet Retailing

Online shopping via e-tailers that sell consumer goods remains the foundation of B2C. Online shoppers can purchase toys, electronics, greeting cards, automobiles, securities, houses, U.S. stamps, and a lot more. Currently, the most popular consumer items purchased over the Internet are books, CDs, and all computer products. However, action is rapidly increasing on everything from groceries to pickup trucks.

If you've traveled in the World Wide Web at all, you've probably run across Amazon.com and Barnes&Noble.com, two of the best-known online stores (see Figure 8-6). Named after the world's largest river to depict a grand adventure into merchandising, Amazon.com is purely a virtual store. In less than a decade, Amazon.com emerged to offer more book and CD titles for sale that any *bricks and mortar* store. Barnes and Noble is *click and brick;* that is, it is an e-tailer (Barnes&Noble.com) and a storefront retailer with a chain of Barnes and Noble bookstores. Both of these e-tailing pioneers offer thousands of books, CDs, audiobooks, DVDs, computer games, toys, and more, including customer reviews, personal recommendations, free courses, best-seller lists, musical chart toppers, and gift suggestions. From Alternative to Zydeco, Hip-hop to Bebop, their online customers will find everything from the latest releases to hard-to-find gems in nearly 300 musical genres.

People go online to shop for many reasons. The reason cited most often is that the stores are always open. People love the convenience of shopping anytime—day or night—and in whatever they happen to be wearing. People also go online to save time. They avoid traffic, crowds, lines, and the never-ending search for a parking space. Another reason is product availability. You may need to go to a dozen different shoe stores to find a particular style and size of sneaker. In contrast, an e-tailer would offer every style in every size for one-stop shopping (see Figure 8-7). Increasingly, shoppers are noting price and service as reasons to shop electronically. Many e-tailers can sell for less, sometimes a lot less. They can keep a low inventory or, when items are shipped directly from the manufacturer, no inventory. Plus, they avoid the real estate and personnel expenses associated with a traditional storefront. E-tailers can offer a variety of services that might not be available in a traditional store. For example, online e-tailers make detailed product information readily available to consumers. Online shoppers can configure customizable products, such as personal computers, and see how changes to the configuration affect the price. Also, online shoppers can create three-dimensional models of themselves for when they wish to "try on" clothes.

In the traditional economy you had to call or visit retail stores to compare prices. In the virtual marketplace, **shop bots** scan the Internet to help you find e-tailers for a particular product and then give you prices for comparison. Shop bots, such as mySimon, DealTime, and PriceGrabber.com, are easy to use and provide valuable shopping information within seconds. In the Figure 8-8 example, "GPS" was entered and mySimon.com returned 21 global positioning system products. When "Garmin eTrex Vista" is selected, a chart displays this

FIGURE 8-6   **BARNES&NOBLE.COM**

Amazon.com and Barnes&Noble.com (shown here) have sold billions of dollars in books and CDs. Both have expanded their retail offerings to include software, toys, electronic greeting cards, DVD and video, magazine subscriptions, electronic books, gifts, and more. Plus they offer a variety of services, including free online courses (see inset) and are publishing original e-books.

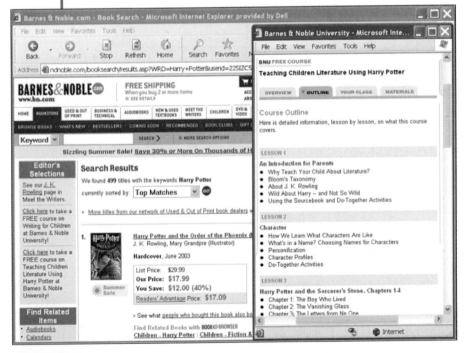

FIGURE 8–7   BUYING ONLINE FROM AN E-TAILER

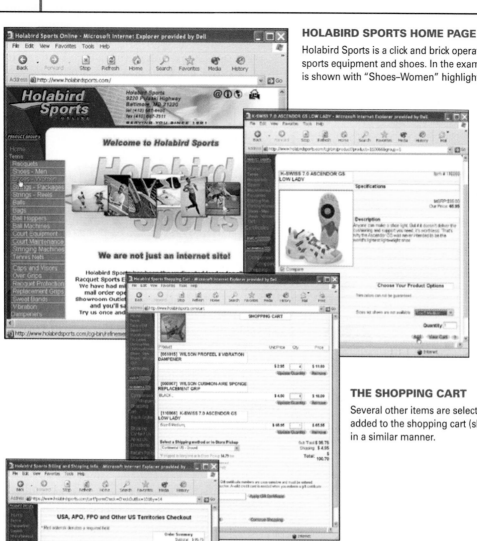

HOLABIRD SPORTS HOME PAGE

Holabird Sports is a click and brick operation that specializes in racquet sports equipment and shoes. In the example, the pop-up menu for tennis is shown with "Shoes–Women" highlight.

SELECT PRODUCT AND ADD TO SHOPPING CART

K-Swiss was selected from a list of all shoe manufacturers and a pictured list of all available K-Swiss shoe styles is displayed. The K-Swiss 7.0 Ascendor GS Low Lady (shown here) is chosen and added to the virtual shopping cart.

THE SHOPPING CART

Several other items are selected and added to the shopping cart (shown here) in a similar manner.

CHECKOUT

When you're finished shopping, click "proceed to checkout" and enter your billing information into a secure Web page.

THE ORDER ARRIVES TWO DAYS LATER

E-MAIL CONFIRMATION

Within seconds after you submit your order, you receive an e-mail confirmation and an order number that can be used to track the progress of your package within Holabird Sports and en route through the shipper.

FIGURE 8-8 SHOP BOTS

Shop bots, such as mySimon, help online shoppers find and buy products at the best available prices. This display shows the results of a search on "GPS" and comparison information for the first item on the list (inset).

information for each shopping site that handles this product: a hyperlink to the e-tailer's Web page containing the requested item, a store rating, the price, the shipping cost, the telephone number, and whether or not the item is in stock.

The one big advantage that the traditional storefront has over cyberbusinesses is *fulfillment*; that is, the process of actually delivering the product or service to the customer. Rather than walking out of a store with your purchase, the cyberworld requires that you exchange your money, receive a shipping order via e-mail, and wait for your purchase to arrive. Most online stores shoot for fulfillment within five business days. Still, fulfillment has been the biggest problem for the so-called "dot.com" businesses. Many that have failed to deliver in a timely manner have folded. We can expect to see a variety of imaginative solutions to the fulfillment problem over the next few years.

The future of online retailing and selling is very bright, but what about traditional approaches to sales? What will become of our department stores, specialty stores, bookstores, and so on? It is unlikely that any of these would disappear anytime soon; however, it is apparent that as time goes on, people are shopping and buying more at the virtual store and less at the bricks-and-mortar store. For the foreseeable future, however, it looks like we'll still have the option to shop downtown or online: whichever you prefer.

FIGURE 8-9 ONLINE TRADING

E-Trade is one of several dot.com's that provide online discount brokerage services. These services include automated order placement for securities, personal portfolio tracking, real-time stock quotes (IBM in the inset example) and market status, plus stock market news around the clock.

E-Trading: Internet Brokerage Services

A growing number of investors are opting for e-trading. **E-trading** is using an Internet-based brokerage service to make investments (see Figure 8-9). Why would you want to make online investments electronically through an online brokerage service instead of through a full-service broker? Those who do, cite price and the ability to make their own trading decisions as the main reasons they go online. Generally, an e-trading charge is less than that of a traditional broker. Frequent users of online brokerage services enjoy the autonomy of having the information resources they need to do their own research on a particular investment opportunity.

Online trading companies, such as E-Trade Group Inc., Charles Schwab & Co. Inc., and Datek Online Brokerage Services Corporation, are providing online discount brokerage services, including automated order placement, portfolio tracking and related market information, news, and other information services 24 hours a day, 7 days a week. Online services offer essentially the same order options as their full-service cousins, including limit, stop, and stop limit orders for all securities trading on U.S. exchanges.

Currently, less than 10% of U.S. households are involved in online finance, including securities trading and online banking. However, online trading companies are experiencing tremendous growth in trading volume as more and more investors switch to online trading.

Big Business B2C

Businesses not associated with selling consumer products are moving toward B2C as well. For example, most major airlines are committed to **electronic ticketing** (e-ticketing) and have begun to phase out traditional paper tickets. Several online ticketing companies, such as Orbitz.com and Travelocity.com, provide com-

prehensive, up-to-the-minute schedules and pricing (see Figure 8-10). Once you have selected your flight(s), your e-ticket confirmation is e-mailed, faxed, or mailed directly to you. The e-ticket offers a number of advantages, one of which is reduced cost to airlines and passengers. E-tickets cannot be lost; they make it easy to change your flight itinerary; they offer same-day ticketing; and they offer faster refunds. Also, most major airports offer time-saving self-service check-in kiosks that let you check in, obtain a boarding pass, check your luggage, and, if you wish, change your seat assignment. The boarding pass, along with a picture ID, is shown at the departure gate, resulting in one less line on your trip.

General Motors executives are hoping that B2C will enable them to offer what customers say they want most—efficiently delivered, customized vehicles. They expect that the majority of all vehicles will be customized in the near future. GM has hundreds of e-commerce experts dedicated to creating B2C applications. Already over a million customers subscribe to GM's OnStar, a wireless emergency communications service that provides security services and navigation guides, among other conveniences. GM and other automakers are developing a B2B and B2C system that will enable large-scale online trading of auto parts among automotive businesses and between businesses and consumers.

CONSUMER-TO-CONSUMER APPLICATIONS

The most visible areas of *consumer-to-consumer* (C2C) e-commerce are the *online auction* and the *online dating service*. You can be part of a live auction 24 hours a day when you visit the eBay (see Figure 8-11) or ONSALE site. Just enter "online auctions" into an Internet search engine and you will be amazed at what can be traded, bought, and sold via C2C. match.com, Yahoo! Personals, and eHarmony, and other online dating services bring people together for dates. Each has a database with profiles for millions of people. Matches are based on user criteria such as location, age, and gender.

Every day you can experience a new set of auctions where you will find thousands of items on which to bid. eBay boasts itself as the world's largest personal online trading community with millions of registered users. Individuals can use eBay to buy and sell items in more than 1000 categories, including collectibles, antiques, sports memorabilia, computers, toys, Beanie Babies, dolls, figures, coins, stamps, books, magazines, music, pottery, glass, photography, electronics, jewelry, gemstones, and much more. Users can find the unique and the interesting on eBay—everything from china to chintz chairs, teddy bears to trains, and furniture to figurines. Even Universal Studios has online auctions of exclusive celebrity memorabilia and collectibles direct from popular movies and television shows.

FIGURE 8-11

CONSUMER-TO-CONSUMER: ONLINE AUCTIONS

Online auction Web sites, such as eBay Motors, let you bid on automobiles, trucks, and other vehicles that people from all over the world are willing to put up for auction. In the example, "Porsche 911" was selected and 1935 related items were being auctioned off, including many Porsche 911 cars.

To make a bid, registered users simply select the item they want and enter the amount they wish to bid. At the end of the bidding period, which can be hours, a week, or more, the highest bid wins. Buyer and seller communicate directly to complete the deal.

ELECTRONIC PUBLISHING

For centuries, the words and images of the world were written, published, and viewed on paper. But today, much of what used to be printed is now in electronic format. A few years ago, we wrote and sent letters and memos, but today e-mail outnumbers print correspondence 300 to 1.

An alternative to producing hard copy documents is electronic publishing. In **electronic publishing** (**e-publishing**), *electronic documents* are created that can be retrieved from disk storage—locally on a PC, on a public kiosk, on a portable device, or from a remote server computer (see Figure 8-12). Electronic publishing is one of the driving forces behind the e-commerce revolution, especially for B2B and B2C, because it is redefining the way we enter, retrieve, send, maintain, and view information.

Electronic documents, also called *online documents,* are normally stored on a hard disk or in flash memory on a portable device. All such documents are designed to be viewed on a monitor and most are interactive with hyperlinks to other parts of the same document or to other local or Net-based documents. Restaurant menus, college textbooks, magazines, romance novels, corporate sales manuals, civic club newsletters, annual reports, travel brochures, IRS forms, and many more traditional print documents are being published electronically.

The Advantages of E-publishing

When compared to print publishing, the advantages of e-publishing become overwhelming. First, electronic publishing is good for the environment. Digitally published material has eliminated the need to use trees to produce billions of printed pages. The availability of electronic publishing raises an important question: Can the fossil fuel, as well as the human effort, required to distribute millions of pounds of personnel manuals, reports, policy statements, newsletters, and many other types of printed material be put to better use?

From a user's perspective, an electronic format provides a much richer form of communication by enabling the integration of audio clips, video clips, and even animation, within the traditional text and graphics of print documents. Electronic travel advertisements frequently include video clips that take you on visual tours of the local sites.

PERSONAL COMPUTING

Shifting to Electronic Documents

You may never take full advantage of your PC until you adopt an attitude that emphasizes electronic documents over printed hard copy. Even though we work with electronic documents and we surf the Internet's Web pages, many of us still feel compelled to print them, often for no reason. The next time you prepare to print a document, ask yourself if you really need a hard copy. You may be surprised to find that in many cases, a hard copy is not needed and the best approach would be simply to recall the electronic document as needed. The shift to e-documents requires a shift in attitude, too. If you organize your folders to enable ready access to your electronic documents, you can save a lot of paper.

FIGURE 8-12 READING THE ELECTRONIC DOCUMENT

EARLY CHILDHOOD LEARNING STATION

For these preschool children using IBM's KidSmart Early Learning Program, it is likely that interactive electronic documents, from e-books to quizzes, will be the norm throughout their years of formal and continued education.

Courtesy of International Business Machines Corporation. Unauthorized use not permitted.

THE ELECTRONIC BOOK

The main advantage of a traditional paper book over an electronic book is that you can take it anywhere and read it anywhere. That advantage is disappearing as people move to small, mobile notebook PCs, handheld PCs, and special-function e-books, such as this eBook.

Photo courtesy of RCA

DISPLAYING E-DOCUMENTS IN A SQUARE INCH

An entire set of user manuals and corporate procedures can be placed on a memory card in a wearable PC. This knowledge worker can view any of thousands of "pages" of electronic documents on his high resolution miniature display.

Courtesy of Kopin Corporation

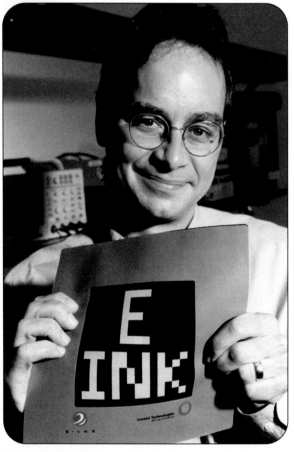

ELECTRONIC INK

E Ink has created a technology that will enable us to read electronic documents, even books, that have the same look and feel as paper. A special type of electronic ink is applied to flexible paper or almost any surface. The company expects that e-books using this technology will be possible in a few years.

Courtesy of E Ink Corporation

Electronic documents also are interactive and facilitate navigation. In the electronic environment, it is easy to move between areas of the documents by using hyperlinks. In the print world, documents stand alone. In the electronic world, documents are "networked." A viewer has only to click on a hyperlink to navigate to and view related material. These hyperlinks enable a single electronic document to reach far beyond what you see on the screen.

Electronic documents are also electronically searchable. An automobile parts sales representative can use the *find* feature to locate all references to a particular part in an online sales manual.

E-publishing is also advantageous from a business perspective. Consider those glossy brochures you get in your mailbox almost daily. These could cost the sender as much as five dollars or more. Already, most colleges in the United States now provide electronic catalogs and virtual tours of their campuses for prospective students.

In addition, electronic documents can be easily updated. A company may print thousands of sales manuals. But when the company changes product prices, the printed sales manuals become out of date. In contrast, companies, the government, and anyone else can produce online documents that can be updated quickly to reflect current circumstances. There is only one copy of an electronic document to change, and it is available electronically on demand.

Creating Electronic Documents

The three most popular formats for electronic documents are *word processing, HTML,* and *portable document.* Figure 8-13 shows how the material can be presented in portable and HTML format.

Word Processing Documents

During the early 1990s, word processing was used extensively to create both print and online documents. This type of online document works well as long as all users have the same word processing program.

HTML Documents

The most popular format for electronic documents is *HTML.* All Internet browsers can retrieve HTML documents from their servers and display them for viewing. Companies and individuals who wish to make publications available via Internet servers must create HTML-compliant documents. A number of Web design programs are available; however, one of the easiest ways to create HTML documents is to use a word processing program to create a document, then simply save it as an HTML document (with the file extension *htm* or *html*). The result is an HTML folder, which contains the elements that make up the Web page and is ready to be posted to the Internet.

Portable Documents

You can pass a **portable document** around the electronic world as you would a print document in the physical world. It can be embedded in HTML-based Web pages on the Internet, attached to e-mail messages, distributed on a CD-ROM, and generally made available in any computing environment. The most popular format is the *portable document format,* or **PDF file** (created by Adobe Corporation). The PDF file has emerged as the de facto standard for portable documents, including contracts, financial reports, advertising brochures, personnel forms, and many other publishing needs. Millions of Internet users have downloaded the Adobe Acrobat Reader (for free), the software needed to view PDF documents. PDF documents are created with a variety of proprietary products from Adobe Corporation, including Acrobat and Acrobat Capture. These Adobe software products can automatically convert anything that can be printed to a PDF file.

The PDF format is ideal for Internet publishing because the PDF files can be highly compressed, thereby reducing the time required to send them to the end user. Also, a PDF file looks the same on all platforms.

FIGURE 8-13 ELECTRONIC DOCUMENTS

CATALOGS IN PDF FORMAT

Most colleges and universities post their catalogs to the Internet as a PDF file (shown here) and/or in HTML format. The entire 502-page University of Oklahoma catalog can be downloaded from the university's Web site and viewed with Adobe Acrobat Reader.

E-ZINES IN HTML FORMAT

Shown here is *Slate,* an interactive magazine of politics and culture. *Slate,* an electronic magazine, or e-zine, is presented in HTML format. You can find many e-zines on the Internet, all of which can be continuously updated to reflect breaking events and news.

The Trend toward Electronic Publishing

During this transition from print to electronic publishing, the debate continues as to when, if ever, traditional print publishing will fade away. Already, one-third of the population cites the Internet as their primary source of news. Every important newspaper, magazine, and television network maintains a major presence on the Internet, often offering a significant amount of content for free. Some **e-zines** (electronic magazines) and other publishers require a paid subscription.

Both publishers and readers are continually evaluating the benefits of electronic publishing. For example, many new and established professional journals, which publish scholarly findings, are going electronic to enable these time-sensitive journals to be made available to the academic and scientific communities more quickly and at a reduced cost. It will be many years before we know whether the transition will ever be complete. But for now, the trend toward e-publishing continues.

WEB MARKETING

No discussion of commerce is complete without mentioning marketing and advertising. The emergence of the Internet as a tool for commerce has opened up new opportunities for those who sell goods and provide services to reach their customers. For example, *banner ads* (thin horizontal ads) or *skyscraper ads* (thin vertical ads) on portals and other Web pages entice us to click on the hyperlink and travel to a totally unrelated site. With increasing frequency, Net surfers are experiencing *pop-under ads* (ads that open in a separate browser window under the requested page) and *floating ads* (ads that float over the requested pages for a few seconds). These ads often are context sensitive based on your preferences stored in cookies during previous visits. For example, if you indicated an interest in skiing, a pop-under ad might present you with a special promotion package for a skiing vacation. Sometimes the ads appear based on your menu selection or search item. If you choose "skiing," up pops a related ad in a separate browser window.

Some of the approaches employed in Web marketing and advertising are controversial. For example, some Web sites use a technique called mouse trapping where the *Back* button is disabled, thus locking you into their site. When you visit some sites, you are automatically placed on their e-mail distribution list so they can target you with promotional information for their products and services. Although helpful, always be aware that search engines are advertising and promotion vehicles. They sell the priority rights to keywords. If you enter "cars," you can expect the first few items in the response to be paid "sponsors," "partners," or "alliances." In fact, part of the alliance is to give competitor organizations low-priority presentation.

The Internet is a relatively new medium and advertisers are continuing to explore new methods to improve the **click through rate,** the percentage of people who click on the hyperlink advertisement to view the full ad or Web site. In that regard, advertisers are doing what they can to focus readers' attention on their ads (for example, blinking links, animation, and/or music). Frequently, banner and skyscraper ads are displayed for several seconds before the remainder of the Web page content is downloaded to complete a Web page.

BUILDING A WEB SITE FOR E-COMMERCE

The system design and programming work that go into creating an e-commerce Web site to support a worldwide online auction site, such as eBay, or a large commercial e-tail site, such as Wal-Mart online, could take many millions of dollars and even a year or more to complete. However, a small company can get into the e-commerce business within a week for as little as $100 a month.

A number of **e-commerce hosting services** are available that enable customers with little or no experience in e-commerce to build their own e-commerce site. The e-commerce hosting service offers a customer everything needed to create an e-commerce site that will let customers shop and then place products in an *online shopping cart* (see Figure 8-7). Customers simply click *check out* and the e-commerce hosting service processes the orders, all for a small monthly fee. Since the construction of e-commerce sites is relatively quick, easy, and inexpensive, we are seeing an explosion of B2C applications as small businesses come online to sell their goods and services. Entrepreneurial success, however, is related to the quality of the Web site. Figure 8-14 contains tips for authoring a Web site.

1 In commerce, the removal of the middleman is called disintermediation. (T/F)

2 B2B is the computer-to-computer exchange of data and information between businesses. (T/F)

3 The electronic interaction between consumers via Internet server computers is: (a) B2C, (b) C2C, (c) B2B, or (d) C2B.

4 What stores individual billing and shipping information to facilitate consumer e-commerce: (a) e-billfold, (b) handheld purse, (c) digital folder, or (d) electronic wallet?

5 This feature enables an electronic link between different sections of an electronic document: (a) hypolink, (b) HTML, (c) hyperlink, or (d) hydralink.

6 PDF stands for: (a) portable data format, (b) personal data format, (c) portable document file, or (d) portable document format.

8-2 DATABASES: INFORMATION STORAGE AND RETRIEVAL

Getting the data necessary to generate meaningful information is always one of the more challenging tasks in information processing. Data have many sources. They can be compiled as a result of a telephone call (telephone orders); received in the form of letters and turnaround documents (for example, utility bills with returnable stubs); and collected on

FIGURE 8-14 WEB AUTHORING TIPS

Authoring Tips for E-Commerce Web Sites	
Have a purpose for the Web site	People on the Net tend to navigate to and view Web sites that have a clear and meaningful reason to exist.
Know the audience	Talk to those who will be visiting your site in the language and imagery they will appreciate and understand.
Keep it simple	The most effective Web pages are clean, carefully-planned presentations that can be visually comprehended with ease.
Minimize download time	People on the Net tend to click through slow-building pages. Present thumbnail image hyperlinks to larger versions of the images.
Make the Web site an electronic ambassador for the organization	A Web site should reflect an organization's integrity.
Maintain the Web site	Web site content is dynamic, ever-changing, so keep content current.
Invite feedback	People on the Net expect Web sites to provide them with contact information.

remote workstations, perhaps as part of a point-of-sale transaction at a department store. Some data are generated outside the company, for example, when a customer submits an order specifying type and quantity of products. Most data, however, are generated internally, such as expenses, inventory activity, hours worked, and so on.

Data can come from strange places. For example, metal sensors in the streets relay data to a central computer that controls traffic. Long-distance telephone calls generate destination and duration data for billing purposes. The digitizing of an image, perhaps an X-ray, creates data. Even hardware errors provide a source of data. A GPS system working with navigation satellites creates locational data (see Figure 8-15).

The data that we need are not always readily available. Existing data are usually not in the proper format, or they are not complete or up to date. Once consistent and reliable sources of data have been identified for a particular application, procedures must be established to obtain these data. To do this, users and MIS professionals work together to establish a scheme for collecting and organizing the data and a method by which to manage the data. The material in this chapter will provide some insight into how this is done.

MANAGING DATA

Just as you need to learn sentence structure and grammar to be an effective user of word processing software, you need to learn fundamental data management principles to be an effective user of PCs. Many types of software, including popular *spreadsheet* and *database* software, let you assemble random pieces of data in a structured and useful manner. The principles of data management, which are new to most people taking this course, include the terms and concepts associated with the *hierarchy of data organization*.

The Hierarchy of Data Organization

This hierarchy of data organization is the basis for most information processing. Figure 8-16 illustrates the six levels

Why this section is important to you.

Data are the fuel for all information technology applications. Understanding these fundamental data management concepts will enable you to grasp the critical relationship between data, information, and computers.

PERSONAL COMPUTING
Getting the Job Done—at Home
One of the primary reasons people go to the office is to have access to their company's database. Now, knowledge workers can have total and rapid access their enterprise's systems and databases while working at home. If you are self-motivated and feel you can cope with the routine distractions of home (the kids, the goodies in the refrigerator, the telephone, ever-present domestic chores, and so on), working at home can be personally rewarding. Working at home can save time, money, and the environment as well.

FIGURE 8-15

THE ONBOARD MAPPING DATABASE

Many travelers are beginning to depend on their onboard navigation systems. The systems, such as the Hertz's NeverLost® system, integrate location data provided by a GPS (global positioning system) receiver with a mapping database that contains the information for every road in the United States. The system gives drivers turn-by-turn driving directions to almost any destination via an in-car video screen and/or voice prompts.

©2000 Hertz Systems, Inc. Hertz is a registered service mark and trademark of Hertz Systems, Inc.

of the hierarchy: bit, character, field, record, file, and database. Each succeeding level in the hierarchy is the result of combining the elements of the preceding level. Data are combined logically in this fashion until a database is achieved. The following paragraphs explain each level of the hierarchy and how it relates to the succeeding level.

- *Bits and characters.* In a computer system, a character (A, B, C, 1, 2, and so on) is represented by a group of bits (1s and 0s) that are configured according to an encoding system, such as ASCII. The combination of bits used to represent a character is called a byte. In ASCII, a C is represented inside a computer as 01000011 (see Chapter 4, Inside the Computer, for more on encoding systems). Audio, video, graphics, and all other types of data and information are stored as combinations of bits, as well.

- *Fields.* The field is the lowest level in the data hierarchy at which we can derive any meaning from the data. For example, a single character (such as A) has little meaning out of context. But when characters are combined to form a name (for example, Alicia or Alvin), they form a logical unit. A field is best described by example: name, employee ID, street address, job classification, and marital status. These are all fields, the basic subdivisions of a record. In the spreadsheet in Figure 8-16, note that an address is represented as four fields: street address, city, state, and ZIP code. Because name-and-address files often are sorted by city, state, and/or ZIP code, it is a good idea to store these data as separate fields.

- *Records: describing events, items, or persons.* A record is a description of an event (for example, a sale, a hotel reservation), an item (a part or product), a person (an employee or customer), and so on. Related fields describing an event or an item are logically grouped to form a record. The spreadsheet in Figure 8-16 shows some of the fields that might be found in a typical employee record, as well as their values for Alvin Adams and other employees.

- *Files: related records.* A file is a collection of related records. For example, the employee file in Figure 8-16 contains a record for each employee. An inventory file contains a record for each inventory item. Files are sorted, merged, and processed by a key field. For example, in an employee file, the key might be last name/first name or ID, and in an inventory file, the key might be part number. File is a common term in information technology and has a broader meaning. A file refers to any named area in a computer's permanent storage that may contain an image, a letter, a song, data, a report, and so on.

- *The database: integrated data resource.* The database is the integrated data resource for an information system. In essence, a database is a collection of files that are in some way logically related to one another. That is, one file might contain logical links that identify one or more files containing related information.

The two most visible productivity software tools for data management are spreadsheet and database. Each deals with organizing, storing, and manipulating data within the hier-

FIGURE 8-16 **THE HIERARCHY OF DATA ORGANIZATION**

Illustrated here is the hierarchy of data organization and its relationship to a typical employee record. An employee record might include these ten fields as well as a variety of other information (benefits, job evaluations, milestone dates, vacation tracking, and so on).

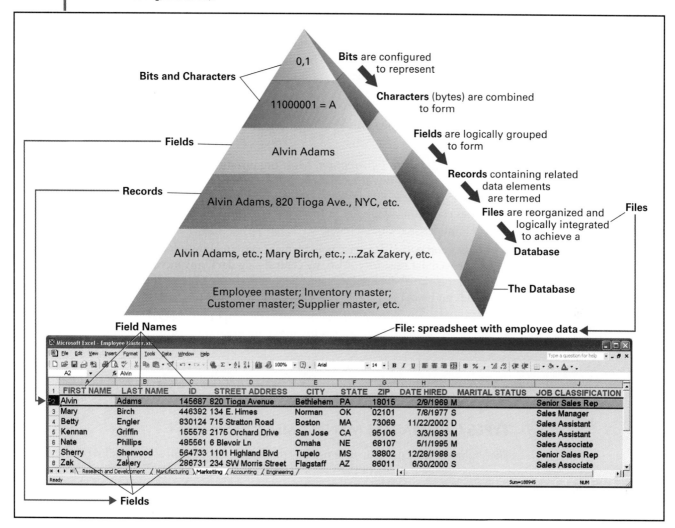

archy of data organization, but they do it in very different ways. The spreadsheet, illustrated in Figure 8-16, is conceptual and straightforward. Database software is more involved and is discussed later. After you enter data into this "Employee Master" Excel spreadsheet file in Figure 8-16, the file can be easily sorted, searched, and revised (fields edited, records added and deleted, and so on), copied, sent via the Internet, and manipulated to produce information and graphs. In the example, records are sorted by last name. This spreadsheet could just as easily be sorted by ID, zip code, job classification, or any other field (in either ascending or descending order). Note that the "Marital Status" field is coded for ease of data entry and to save storage space.

Data Integration

Through the early 1980s, most installed information systems were implemented with a single functional objective in mind—accounting, human resources, inventory, marketing, and so on. These systems were built around **flat files,** files that did not point to or physically link with another file. A flat file was designed to meet the specific information and data processing requirements of a particular functional-area department, such as accounting, sales, or purchasing. Many of the data elements on each of these flat files are common. For example, each of these functional areas has a need to maintain customer data, such as customer name, address, and the contact person at the customer location. When the name of the contact person changes in a flat file environment, each file must be updated separately.

During that time, the integration of information systems was not a priority. In addition, IT specialists didn't have the data management tools they do today. With all of these flat files, organizations were saddled with massive system, procedural, and data redundancies. These redundancies promote inefficiencies and result in unnecessary expenses. Today, organizations are using **database management systems (DBMSs)**, a software tool that integrates data management and information flow within an organization. Data redundancy can be minimized by designing an integrated database to serve the organization as a whole, not just one specific department. The tool for creating an integrated database is database management system software.

Benefits of an Integrated Database

There are many reasons why a company would begin with or convert to an integrated database.

- *Greater access to information.* Most organizations have accumulated a wealth of data, but translating these data to meaningful information has, at times, proven difficult, especially with unlinked flat files. The structure of an integrated database provides enormous flexibility in the types of reports that can be generated and the types of inquiries that can be made.

- *Better control.* A database management system allows data to be centralized for improved data security. Also, by centralizing data, advanced data structures can be used to control data redundancy. *Data structures* refer to the manner in which the fields and records are related to each other.

- *More efficient software development.* The programming task is simplified with a database management system because data are more readily available. Also, in a database, data are independent of the applications programs. That is, data elements can be added, changed, and deleted from the database, and this does not affect existing programs. Adding a field to a record of a traditional flat file may require the modification and testing of dozens, and sometimes hundreds, of programs.

TYPES OF DATABASE MANAGEMENT SYSTEMS

The sophisticated data structures used by database management systems allow the DBMS to overcome the limitations of flat files and to enable integrated database. The data structures vary considerably among commercially available DBMS software packages. There are several approaches to the design of DBMS software. Three popular approaches are introduced in this section: the *network DBMS*, the *relational DBMS*, and *the object-oriented DBMS*.

The Network DBMS

The **network DBMS** is a database management system whose data structures established relationships between its records. The best way to describe a network DBMS is by example. Consider the following situation. A library currently maintains a flat file with these fields on book: title, ISBN number, publication year, publisher, publisher's address, author(s). The head librarian wants more flexibility in obtaining decision-making information. Many of the librarian's requests would be impractical with the existing flat file (see Figure 8-17). A database administrator (an IT specialist who designs and maintains the database) recommends restructuring the file for a network DBMS.

The library's existing flat file has certain data redundancies. Since each book or title has a separate record, the *name* of an author who has written several books is repeated for each book written. A given publisher may have hundreds, even thousands, of books in the library,

FIGURE 8-17 RECORD LAYOUT

This book inventory record layout is for a traditional flat file in a library.

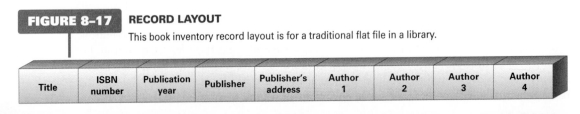

| Title | ISBN number | Publication year | Publisher | Publisher's address | Author 1 | Author 2 | Author 3 | Author 4 |

but in the current flat file, the *publisher* and *publisher's address* are repeated for each title. To eliminate these data redundancies, the database administrator suggests the *records* or *segments* shown in Figure 8-18.

Next, the database administrator establishes the relationships between the records. There is a *one-to-many* relationship between the publisher and title records. That is, one publisher may publish any number of titles. The publisher-title relationship is represented in Figure 8-18 by a connecting line between the two records. A double arrow toward the title record represents the possibility of more than one title per publisher. The publisher-title combination is called a **set**. Other sets defined by the database administrator are title-author and author-title. Figure 8-18 is a graphic representation of the logical structure of the database, called a **schema** (pronounced *SKEE-muh*). Figure 8-19 shows an occurrence of the database structure.

In the database schema of Figure 8-18, a particular author's name appears only once. The author's name then is linked to the title records of those books that he or she has authored. The publisher record is linked to all the titles that it publishes. When accessing a record in a program, you simply request the record of a particular title, author, or publisher. Once you have the author's record, you can use the links between records to retrieve the titles of the books written by that author. Similarly, if you request the record of a particular publisher, you can obtain a list of all titles published by that publisher.

This database design eliminates, or at least minimizes, data redundancy and permits the head librarian to make a wide range of inquiries, such as, "What titles were written by Mark Twain?" Or, "List those titles published in 1986 by Prentice Hall (alphabetically by title)." While responses to these inquiries can be cumbersome to the library's existing traditional flat file (Figure 8-17), similar inquiries are relatively easy to obtain with a database management system.

The Relational DBMS

In contrast to the network DBMS, the **relational DBMS (RDBMS)** accesses data by *content* rather than by *address*. That is, the relational approach uses the computer to search the database for the desired data rather than accessing data through a series of

---

FIGURE 8-18 **A NETWORK OR CODASYL DATA BASE SCHEMA**

The book inventory flat file (Figure 8-17) is reorganized into database records and integrated into a database schema to minimize data

---

FIGURE 8-19 AN OCCURRENCE OF THE NETWORK DATA BASE STRUCTURE OF FIGURE 8-18.

Notice that publishers can be linked to authors via the title record, and vice versa.

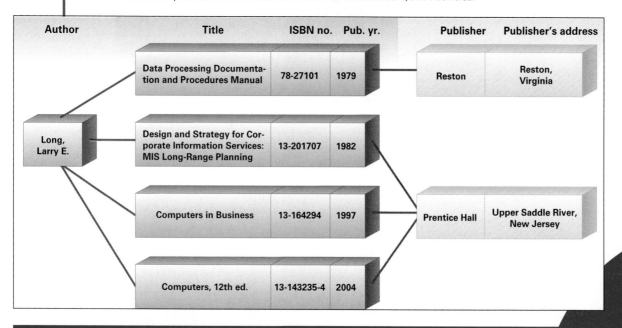

indices and physical hard disk addresses, as with network DBMSs. In relational DBMSs, the data structures, or relationships between data, are defined in *logical,* rather than *physical,* terms. That is, the relational database has no predetermined relationship between the data, such as the one-to-many sets in the network schemas (see Figure 8-18). In this way, data can be accessed at the *field* level. In network structures, the entire database record must be retrieved to examine a single field.

The relational DBMS had a slow start but has been gaining momentum for 30 years and is now the DBMS of choice for most enterprises. All PC-based database packages, such as Microsoft Access and Paradox, use the *relational* approach to database management. All enterprise-level RDBMSs are **distributed DBMSs;** that is, they permit the interfacing of databases located in various places throughout a computer network. For example, an enterprise DBMS might be distributed among server computers at several plants and at company headquarters. However, the distributed DBMS functions as if it was centralized. The fact that it is distributed is transparent to the end user. That is, a user making an inquiry would not be concerned about the source of the data or how the data are retrieved.

Creating a Relational Database with Microsoft Access

Relational DBMSs organize data into *tables* in which a *row* is equivalent to a *record* that contains *fields* (set apart by columns). The database *table* is conceptually the same as a *file.* One or more tables comprise a relational database, which refers to all of the tables in the database and the relationships between them.

Again, the best way to explain the concepts of relational database software is by example. The chairperson of the Computer Information Systems (CIS) department uses Microsoft Access to help with record-keeping tasks and to provide valuable information. She has created an education database with two tables: COURSE and STUDENT (see Figure 8-20). The COURSE table contains a record for each course offered in the CIS Department. Each record (row) in the COURSE table contains the following fields: *course ID, course title, type* of course (lecture, lab, or lecture/lab), *instructor* name, and *credit* hours awarded for completion of course.

The STUDENT table contains a record for each student who is enrolled in or has taken a CIS course. The table has only a few students to enable ease of demonstration of concepts, but it works just the same with hundreds of students. Each record contains the following fields: *student* (name of student, last name first), *course ID* (provides a link to the course table), *major, date enrolled,* and *status* (course status: incomplete [I], withdrew [W], or a grade [A, B, C, D, E, or F]).

No single field in the STUDENT table uniquely identifies each record. However, the combined *student* and *course ID* fields do identify each record. Therefore, to access a particular record in the STUDENT table, the chairperson must specify both the *student* and *course ID* (for example, Targa, Phil, CIS 330). The COURSE and STUDENT tables can be linked because they have the *course ID* field in common.

The first thing you do to set up a database table is to specify its structure by identifying the characteristics of each field in it. This structuring is done interactively, with the system prompting you to enter the field name, the field type, and so on. For example, in the first row of

FIGURE 8–20 **EDUCATION DATABASE: COURSE TABLE AND STUDENT TABLE**

The Microsoft Access Education database has two tables. The COURSE table contains a record for each course offered by the Computer Information Systems Department. The STUDENT table contains a record for each student who is enrolled in or has taken a course. The *course ID* field links the two tables.

COURSE : Table

COURSE ID	COURSE TITLE	TYPE	INSTRUCTOR	CREDIT
CIS 100	Telecommunications	lecture	Babbage	3
CIS 101	Database Management	lecture/lab	Babbage	2
CIS 110	Intranets and Extranets	lab	Gates	3
CIS 150	Mgt. Info. Systems	lecture	Eckert	3
CIS 202	Visual Basic Programming	lecture/lab	Wang	4
CIS 310	Network Administration	lecture	Gates	4
CIS 320	Desktop Publishing	lab	Eckert	3
CIS 330	Information Retrieval	lecture/lab	Wang	3
CIS 350	Web Site Design	lab	Gates	1
CIS 401	Local Area Networks	lecture/lab	Wang	3

Record: I◄ ◄ 1 ► ►I ►* of 10

STUDENT	COURSE ID	MAJOR	DATE ENROLLED	STATUS
Adler, Phyllis	CIS 401	Marketing	2/10/2004	W
Austin, Jill	CIS 330	Finance	1/12/2003	I
Austin, Jill	CIS 401	Finance	1/12/2004	C
Bell, Jim	CIS 330	Marketing	1/12/2004	A
Day, Elizabeth	CIS 310	Accounting	3/18/2003	B
Fitz, Paula	CIS 310	Finance	4/4/2003	A
Johnson, Charles	CIS 100	Marketing	1/10/2003	W
Klein, Ellen	CIS 100	Accounting	1/10/2003	C
Massey, Rose	CIS 101	Management	2/14/2003	I
Mendez, Carlos	CIS 310	Accounting	1/20/2004	A
Mendez, Carlos	CIS 150	Accounting	1/15/2003	I
Targa, Phil	CIS 330	Finance	1/12/2004	B
Targa, Phil	CIS 100	Finance	1/4/2003	B

Record: I◄ ◄ 1 ► ►I ►* of 13

Figure 8-21, the *field name* is *course ID*, the *data type* is "text," and the *field size*, or field length, is seven positions. The field names for the COURSE and STUDENT tables are listed at the top of each table in Figure 8-20 (*course ID, course title, type,* and so on). Content for a text field can be a single word or any alphanumeric phrase. For number field types, you can specify the number of decimal positions that you wish to have displayed (none in the example because credit hours are whole numbers).

Once you have defined the structure of the database table, you are ready to enter the data. The best way to enter data is to create a *screen format* that allows convenient data entry. The data entry screen format is analogous to a hard-copy form that contains labels and blank lines for you to fill in (for example, a medical questionnaire). Data are entered and edited (added, deleted, or revised) one record at a time with database software, just as they are on hard-copy forms. Figure 8-22 shows the data entry screen format for the COURSE table.

FIGURE 8-21   **STRUCTURE OF THE EDUCATION DATABASE**

This display shows the structure of the COURSE and STUDENT tables of the education database of Figure 8-20. The COURSE record (left) has four text fields and one number field. The STUDENT record has four text fields and one date/time field.

Query by Example

Database software also lets you retrieve, view, and print records based on query by example. In **query by example** (QBE), you set conditions for the selection of records by composing one or more example *relational expressions*. A relational expression normally compares one or more field names to numbers or character strings using the **relational operators** (= [equal to], > [greater than], < [less than], and combinations of these operators). Several conditions can be combined with **logical operators** (*AND, OR,* and *NOT*). Figure 8-23 demonstrates three types of query by example—one condition, using logical operators, and two conditions.

SQL: The Relational DBMS Query Language

In query by example, you point and click within dialog boxes to set criteria (see Figure 8-23); however, the actual information retrieval is done with a query language program. A **query language** is a user-friendly programming language for requesting information from a database. When you enter criteria for a query, Microsoft Access generates a **SQL** (**Structured Query Language**) program which is executed to retrieve the requested information. The SQL, pronounced "sequel," programs in Figure 8-24 show the sequel code generated for the queries of Figure 8-23. SQL is the standard query language for relational databases and is supported by all commercial RDBMSs. This broad support means that SQL can be used to permit the sharing of data between dissimilar software packages and DBMSs, such as you might find in intercompany and intracompany networking.

Sorting: Rearranging Records

The records in a database table also can be sorted for display in a variety of formats. For example, the COURSE table in Figure 8-20 has been sorted and is displayed in ascending order by *course ID*. To obtain this sequencing of the database records, the department chairperson selected *course ID* as the key field and "ascending" (versus descending) as the sort order. To get a presentation of the COURSE table sorted by *course ID* within *instructor,* she needs to identify a *primary sort field* and a *secondary sort field*. Secondary sort fields are helpful when duplicates exist in the primary sort field (for example, there are three records for *instructor*=Gates). She selects *instructor* as the primary sort field, but she wants the courses offered by each *instructor* to be listed in ascending order by *course ID* (see Figure 8-25).

Generating Reports

A *report* is the presentation of information derived from one or more databases. The simple listings of selected and ordered records in Figure 8-23 are "quick and

FIGURE 8-22

DATA ENTRY SCREEN FORMAT

The screen format for entering, editing, and adding records to the COURSE table is illustrated.

FIGURE 8-23 QUERY BY EXAMPLE

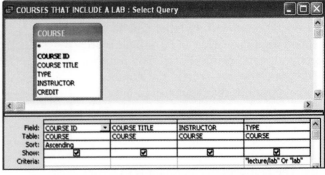

QBE: ONE CONDITION

To get a listing of all students taking courses from Professor Wang, the department chairperson requested a list of all courses that meet the condition *instructor=Wang* (see Figure 8-20). All records that meet this condition (see criteria query box shown here) are displayed in the answer window in ascending alphabetical order by student name. She selected only three fields to be included in the results display (checked boxes in figure). Notice that the query needed information from both tables.

QBE: USING LOGICAL OPERATORS

To produce the results shown here, the department chairperson set up her query by example to select only those courses that include a lab; that is, the criteria is (course) *type=lab* OR *lecture/lab*. The OR operator can be applied between fields (see example) or within fields. Only the COURSE table is needed for the query.

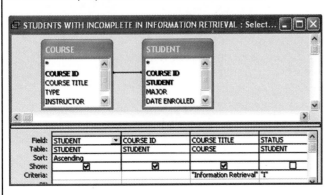

QBE: TWO CONDITIONS

The query in this example is set up to list those students who have an incomplete *(status)=I* in the course entitled Information Retrieval *(course ID=Information Retrieval)*. The query requires the use of both tables in the database.

dirty" reports. Such reports are the bread and butter of database capabilities and can be easily copied or imported into word processing or desktop publishing documents.

Database software allows you to create customized reports and to design their *layout*. This design capability allows you to change spacing and to include titles, subtitles, column headings, separation lines, and other elements that make a report more readable. Managers often use this capability to generate periodic reports, such as the Course Status Summary report shown in Figure 8-26.

The Object-Oriented DBMS

The data structures for traditional database management systems are limited mostly to text and numbers, with a few variations such as date and currency. The demands of modern Web-based information systems extend to audio, video, images, and to complex relationships between objects. Loosely, an **object** is any item that can be individually selected

FIGURE 8-24   **SQL PROGRAMS RESULTING FROM QUERY BY EXAMPLE INQUIRIES**

These SQL programs were generated by Microsoft Access as a result of the QBE inquiries in Figure 8-23.

SQL QUERY: One Condition
List all students taking courses from Professor Wang.

SELECT STUDENT.STUDENT, STUDENT.[COURSE ID], COURSE.[COURSE TITLE]
FROM COURSE INNER JOIN STUDENT ON COURSE.[COURSE ID] = STUDENT.[COURSE ID]
WHERE (((COURSE.INSTRUCTOR)="Wang"))
ORDER BY STUDENT.STUDENT;

SQL QUERY: Using Logical Operators
List only those courses that include a lab.

SELECT COURSE.[COURSE ID], COURSE.[COURSE TITLE], COURSE.INSTRUCTOR, COURSE.TYPE
FROM COURSE
WHERE (((COURSE.TYPE)="lecture/lab" Or (COURSE.TYPE)="lab"))
ORDER BY COURSE.[COURSE ID];

SQL QUERY: Two Conditions
List those students who have an incomplete in the course entitled Information Retrieval.

SELECT STUDENT.STUDENT, STUDENT.[COURSE ID], COURSE.[COURSE TITLE]
FROM COURSE INNER JOIN STUDENT ON COURSE.[COURSE ID] = STUDENT.[COURSE ID]
WHERE (((COURSE.[COURSE TITLE])="Information Retrieval") AND ((STUDENT.STATUS)="I"))
ORDER BY STUDENT.STUDENT;

and manipulated. The object can be a block of text, numbers, all or part of a graphic image, a sound or video clip, an animation, or a procedure for manipulating data. The **object-oriented database management system (OODBMS)** may be the wave of the future because it is able to handle the complex data structures needed in our increasingly multi-media world. For example, the object-oriented database at MapQuest, the Web site (see Figure 8-27), is set up to provide comprehensive trip planner information. To give you point-to-point driving directions, the database includes many complex data structures, including street maps, aerial photographs, street addresses, detailed information on every road (type of road, name, and so on), methods for determining the best route, sponsor information (hotels, real estate, and so on), and much more. The MapQuest OODBMS ties these objects together in a way that gives Web surfers the flexibility to do comprehensive trip planning.

Information technology is in transition from traditional database methods to those that involve the storage and manipulation of objects. An interim step on the journey to OODBMSs is the **object/relational DBMS,** which combines the best features of RDBMS and OODBMS. The future, however, appears to be the OODBMS with its ability to keep pace with increasingly complex data storage and retrieval demands of information technology.

DATA WAREHOUSING AND DATA MINING

Two of the most important concepts in data management are data warehousing and data mining, both made possible with the emergence of sophisticated DBMSs. **Data warehousing** involves moving existing

FIGURE 8-25   **COURSE TABLE SORTED BY *COURSE ID* WITHIN *INSTRUCTOR***

This display is the result of a sort operation on the COURSE table with the *instructor* field as the primary sort field and the *course ID* field as the secondary sort field. Notice that the *course ID* field entries are in alphabetical order by instructor; that is, the three "Gates" records are in sequence by *course ID* (CIS 110, CIS 310, and CIS 350).

INSTRUCTOR	COURSE ID	COURSE TITLE	TYPE	CREDIT
Babbage	CIS 100	Telecommunications	lecture	3
Babbage	CIS 101	Database Management	lecture/lab	2
Eckert	CIS 150	Mgt. Info. Systems	lecture	3
Eckert	CIS 320	Desktop Publishing	lab	3
Gates	CIS 110	Intranets and Extranets	lab	3
Gates	CIS 310	Network Administration	lecture	4
Gates	CIS 350	Web Site Design	lab	1
Wang	CIS 202	Visual Basic Programming	lecture/lab	4
Wang	CIS 330	Information Retrieval	lecture/lab	3
Wang	CIS 401	Local Area Networks	lecture/lab	3

COURSE BY ID WITHIN INSTRUCTOR : Select Query

Record: 1 of 10

FIGURE 8-26 CUSTOMIZED REPORT

To obtain this Course Status Summary report, the CIS Department chairperson needed both the COURSE and STUDENT tables of Figure 8-20 from the education database.

FIGURE 8-27 MAPQUEST OBJECT-ORIENTED DATABASE

MapQuest uses an OODBMS to provide comprehensive online trip planning information, including road maps and aerial photographs (downtown Atlanta shown here).

operational files and integrated databases to a **data warehouse.** The data warehouse is a relational database created specifically to help managers get the information they need to make informed decisions.

In many organizations, mountains of mission-critical data are compiled during routine transaction processing, but may be spread among various data resources. Modern DBMSs enable scattered data from existing files and databases to be collected and copied to a data warehouse. The data in the data warehouse are reorganized into a format that gives decision makers ready access to valuable, time-sensitive information. The operational files and databases may include data about customer buying patterns, inventory supply, seasonal manufacturing trends, and so on, and they must be updated constantly. This constant change of the operational data means that the data warehouse must be reconstructed periodically, perhaps each day or each week, depending on the volatility of the data.

Once data are consolidated in a data warehouse, managers can make complex queries and do analysis not possible with data spread all over the organization. For example, data mining, one of many analytical techniques, involves the analysis of large databases, such as data warehouses. **Data mining** essentially is searching for answers to unasked questions and detecting unanticipated trends from databases. Data mining software is composed of very sophisticated algorithms that examine large amounts of data for elusive relationships or correlations. Data mining has resulted in information that has led to increased sales per customer, getting new customers, reducing marketing expenses, identifying cross-selling opportunities, creating customer loyalty, and reducing exposure to fraud. At Coca-Cola, data mining revealed that Diet Coke drinkers buy seven or more books a year, whereas Classic Coke drinkers buy only one or two. This unexpected piece of information resulted in changes to Coca-Cola's marketing campaigns. Telecommunications companies such as MCI use data mining to detect fraud as early as possible. For example, data mining might highlight an account whose pattern of calls has changed dramatically, such as infrequent calls to Colorado becoming frequent calls to Colombia.

1. The lowest level in the data hierarchy at which we can derive any meaning from the data is the file. (T/F)

2. In relational DBMSs, the data structures are defined in physical, rather than logical, terms. (T/F)

3. If the COURSE database table in Figure 8-20 is sorted in descending order by course ID, the third course record would be Local Area Networks. (T/F)

4. A technique used to search large databases for unanticipated trends is called: (a) data extraction, (b) data migration, (c) data mining, or (d) data warehousing.

5. Which of these is not a type of DBMS: (a) object-oriented, (b) object-phased, (c) relational, or (d) network?

6. The relational DBMS query language is: (a) Sequel, (b) 4GL, (c) Access, or (d) SQL.

7. Database files are sorted, merged, and processed by: (a) a key field, (b) an ISBN, (c) columnar index, or (d) a lock entry.

8-3 COMPUTER, INTERNET, AND SYSTEM SECURITY

In Chapter 7, "IT Ethics, Privacy, and Crime," we identified 10 areas of computer crime, each of which continues to grow. Computer security has been breached and financial losses incurred (often millions of dollars) in four out of five organizations with an Internet presence. Over five million Americans are victims of identity theft. To minimize unethical abuses of information technology and computer crime, individuals and organizations must build an envelope of security around hardware and embed safeguards into databases and information systems. Security concerns take on added importance now that millions of businesses are actively involved in e-commerce. Their link to the Net is just one of many points of vulnerability, and too much is at stake to overlook the threats to the security of any computer system. These threats take many forms—white-collar crime, computer viruses, natural disasters (such as earthquakes and floods), vandalism, and carelessness.

In this section, we discuss commonly applied measures that can help to neutralize security threats to a computer center, Web sites, an information system, and a PC.

> ## *Why this section is important to you.*
>
> Four of every five business computer systems have been violated in some way, resulting in loss of critical information, property, or data integrity. Read on to see what can be done to minimize IT vulnerability at work and at home.

Prentice Hall **train & assess** **it** generation

SECURITY AND PRIVACY

COMPUTER-CENTER SECURITY

If a business computer system were, for whatever reason, rendered inoperable, there is a good chance that the company would cease to exist within a few days. It is estimated that a large bank would be out of business in two days if its computer systems went down. A distribution company would last three days, a manufacturing company would last five days, and an insurance company would last six days. Recognizing their dependence on computers, most companies have made computer-center security a high priority.

Enterprise-wide information systems provide information and processing capabilities to workers throughout a given organization. Some systems involve extranets that extend to customers, suppliers, and others outside the organization. Generally, network server computers located in centralized computer centers handle such systems. Whether a room or a building, the computer center has a number of points of vulnerability: *hardware, software, files/databases, personnel, the Internet,* and *e-commerce.* We discuss each separately in this section and illustrate them in Figure 8-28.

> ### *THE CRYSTAL BALL*
> #### Cyber War
>
> We now live in a world in which we must be ever vigilant—there are those who want to harm us because of the color of our skin, our religious beliefs, our nationality, or for no particular reason at all. Traditionally, the efforts of terrorists have focused on the destruction of property and physical harm; however, terrorists now are researching ways to destroy one of our most valuable personal and commercial assets—the contents of our disks. They do this by seeking points of vulnerability in PCs and servers and by planting destructive viruses. Terrorists will also continue their denial-of-service attacks in an attempt to cripple server computers worldwide. Sadly, cyber terror is now part of the terrorist's arsenal of evil.

FIGURE 8-28   **SECURITY PRECAUTIONS**

Some or all of the security measures noted in the figure are in force in most organizations. Each precaution helps minimize the risk of a computer center, an information system, or a PC being vulnerable to crime, disasters, and failure.

Hardware

If the hardware fails, the information system fails. The threat of failure can be minimized by implementing security precautions that prevent access by unauthorized personnel and by taking steps to keep all hardware operational.

Common approaches to securing the premises from unauthorized entry include the use of closed-circuit TV and monitors, alarm systems, as well as computer-controlled devices that check employee badges (see Figure 8-29), fingerprints, or voice prints before unlocking doors at access points. Computer centers also should be isolated from pedestrian traffic. Computer-room fires should be extinguished by a special chemical that douses the fire but does not destroy the files or equipment.

Any complex system is subject to failure. However, for many organizations, network failure is simply unacceptable. For example, if the network supporting the Hilton Hotel reservation system went down for a couple of hours, thousands of reservations and, perhaps, millions of dollars would be lost. Such systems must be made fault-tolerant. **Fault-tolerant** systems are designed to permit continuous operation even if important components fail. To accomplish this goal, parts of the system, such as the server computer or hard disks, must be duplicated. For example, a LAN might have an alternate LAN server in a different physical location. Of course, no network can be made totally fault-tolerant. The degree to which a network is made fault-tolerant depends on the amount of money an organization is willing to spend.

Computers must have a "clean," continuous source of power. "Dirty" power, with sags and surges in power output or brownouts (low power), causes data transmission errors and program execution errors, and power outages can cause loss of function as well as critical data. To minimize the effects of "dirty" power or power outages, each critical computer should draw its power from an uninterruptible power source. An **uninterruptible power source (UPS)** system is a buffer between the external power source and the computer system. In a UPS system, batteries deliver clean power to the computer and are regenerated continuously by an external power source. If the external power source fails, the UPS system permits operation to continue for a period of time after an outage. This time cushion allows operators to either "power down" normally or switch to a backup power source, usually a diesel-powered generator. UPS systems are considered essential equipment in the business world where server computers must be operational 24/7. Each year, the UPS system is becoming more widely accepted as a critical component of a home or small office PC.

Software

Unless properly controlled, the software for an information system can either be modified for personal gain or vandalized and rendered useless. Close control of software development and the documentation of an information system are needed to minimize the opportunity for computer crime and vandalism.

Unlawful Modification of Software

Bank programmers certainly have opportunities to modify software for personal gain. In one case, a couple of programmers used the salami embezzlement technique and modified a savings system to make small deposits from other accounts to their own accounts. Programs were modified to round down all interest calculations and put the "extra" penny in one of the programmers' savings accounts. Even auditors had difficulty detecting this crime because the total interest paid on all accounts was correct. However, the culprits got greedy and were apprehended when someone noticed that they repeatedly withdrew inordinately large sums of money from their own accounts. Unfortunately, other enterprising programmers in other industries have been equally imaginative.

Operational control procedures built into the design of an information system will constantly monitor processing accuracy. Unfortunately, cagey programmers have been known to get around some of them. Perhaps the best way to safeguard programs from unlawful tampering is to use rigorous change-control procedures. Such procedures require programmers to obtain authorization before modifying an operational program. Change-control procedures make it difficult to modify a program for purposes of personal gain.

Viruses

Slammer, Melissa, Chernobyl, Michelangelo, Friday the 13th, Stoned, Jerusalem, and *Love Bug* are phrases that strike fear in PC users. They are names of computer viruses. Left undetected, a virus can result in loss of data and/or programs and even physical damage to the hardware. The average recovery cost from a virus disaster (at least 25 infected PCs) is over $80,000. Virus prevention measures are discussed in Chapter 7.

Files/Databases

At one time or another, just about every organization and every PC user loses data or work for which there is no backup. Because of this, the first commandment in computing security, at any level, is *back up your files!*

The backup process serves two important functions. First, backing up protects against loss of valuable files. If a disk on which you've stored important documents or spreadsheets is in some way destroyed (hard disk crash, demagnetized, burned, and so on), stolen, or lost, your files

---

PERSONAL COMPUTING
The Importance of UPS

One of the best personal computing investments you can make is the purchase of an uninterruptible power source (UPS). A UPS unit can provide clean, uninterruptible power and can protect your PC's valuable components from damaging power surges, power outages, and lightning strikes. A UPS unit is installed between the AC power and the PC, and between the Internet connection and the modem/router. A UPS unit can be purchased for $60 and up. The unit's battery must be replaced every few years.

are gone unless you have a backup. Second, backing up serves the purpose of archiving files. Important files no longer needed for active processing can be archived to a backup medium. For example, banks archive old transactions (checks and deposits) for a number of years. PC users periodically archive their e-mail.

Backup for Home/Small Office PCs

PC users employ a variety of backup media, including CD-RW, DVD±RW, Zip disks, and portable hard disks as discussed in Chapter 5. With the growth of home/small office networks, many people are choosing to back up their files to the hard disks on other networked PCs. You can choose from three common backup methods.

- *Full backup*. A full backup copies all files on a hard disk to backup media.
- *Selective backup*. Only user-selected files are backed up.
- *Incremental backup*. Only those files that have been modified since the last backup are backed up.

The frequency with which files are backed up depends on their *volatility* or how often you update the files on the disk. If you spend time every day working with files, you should back them up each day. Others should be backed up no more often than they are used. Figure 8-30 illustrates a six-CD-RW or DVD±RW backup rotation.

Backup for Internet and Network Servers

Often the files/databases of a company are its lifeblood. For example, how many companies can afford to lose their accounts receivable data, which documents who owes what, or their customer information? To minimize the impact of catastrophic disk failure, companies use **RAID (Redundant Array of Independent Disks)** to provide fault-tolerant backup of disk systems. RAID spreads data across several integrated disk drives so that a duplicate copy is maintained on a separate disk system at all times. When an online transaction is completed and logged on one disk, an exact entry is made to a duplicate disk. The disk system is considered fault-tolerant because it is highly unlikely that two disks will fail at the same time.

Businesses keep several generations of backups (backups to backups, too) on hard disk, optical media, or tape backup units. **Tape backup units (TBUs)** use a 1/4-inch cartridge (QIC), also called a **data cartridge**. The self-contained data cartridge is inserted into and removed from the tape drive in much the same way you would load or remove a videotape from a VCR. Some businesses use automatic retrieval tape storage (see Figure 8-31). The

FIGURE 8-30 **BACKUP ROTATION: SIX CD-RW OR DVD±RW DISCS**

This six-CD-RW disc or six-DVD±RW disc backup rotation is common in small businesses and with individuals whose files have high volatility. Two total backups are done every Monday, one of which is taken to an offsite location. Only incremental backups (files that are modified on a given day) are made for each of the other weekdays. If all files are lost on Friday, the total backup from Monday is restored to the hard disk, then incremental backups are restored for Tuesday through Thursday.

Total backup (keep off-site)

off-site

Monday   Tuesday   Wednesday   Thursday   Friday

Monday   Tuesday   Wednesday   Thursday   Friday

Full backup   Back up modified files on each day to CD/RW or DVD±RD backup media are stored in fireproof safes in separate rooms, preferably in separate buildings.

Personnel

A major threat to a company's security system is the dishonesty and/or negligence of its own employees. Managers should pay close attention to who is hired for positions with access to computer-based information systems and sensitive data. Many companies flash a message on each networked PC or terminal such as: "All information on this system is confidential and proprietary." It's not very user-friendly, but it gets the message across to employees that they may be fired if they abuse the system. An employee who is grossly negligent can cause just as much harm as one who is dishonest.

INTERNET AND E-COMMERCE SECURITY

The fact that computers are linked via data communications and the Internet poses a threat to security. A knowledgeable criminal can tap into the system from a remote location and use it for personal gain. In a well-designed system, such hacking is not an easy task. The typical company experiences over 30 hacker attacks each week, but rarely is an attack successful. But it can be and has been done! When one criminal broke a company's security code and tapped into the computer network, he was able to order certain products without being billed. He filled a warehouse before he was caught. Another tapped into an international banking exchange system to reroute funds to his own account in a Swiss bank. In another case, an oil company consistently was able to outbid a competitor by "listening in" on the latter's data transmissions. On several occasions, overzealous hackers have tapped into sensitive defense computer systems. Fortunately, no harm was done.

FIGURE 8–31

TAPE BACKUP SYSTEM

This robotic tape storage and retrieval unit holds hundreds of high-density tape cartridges (25 GB) used to backup production files and databases. The tape cartridges are automatically loaded and unloaded to a tape drive as they are needed to backup processing.

Courtesy of International Business Machines Corporation. Unauthorized use not permitted.

Encryption of Digital Communications

How do companies protect themselves from these criminal activities? Most companies use encryption to scramble sensitive communications sent over computer networks or the Internet. **Cryptography** is a crime prevention technology that uses a key in conjunction with **encryption** techniques to scramble messages sent over communication channels. Modern cryptography works much like the code book used by intelligence people during the cloak-and-dagger days of the post-World War II era. However, a mathematical algorithm and a key now replace the code book. Before a message is sent, it is *encrypted* such that the bit structure of the message is rearranged according to some mathematical algorithm. Once encrypted according to an algorithm and its key, the message becomes a meaningless string of bits to anyone who might unlawfully intercept it. The receiver, a person or a computer, uses a key to decrypt and read the message.

The most popular encryption systems uses public-key encryption. **Public-key encryption** requires both a private key, known only to the sender person/computer, and a public key. To enable secure transmissions, a secure Web server site sends a public key to the destination. The client software, a browser, is used in conjunction with an algorithm and the public key to encrypt sensitive data, such as name, Social Security number, and credit card numbers. The encrypted message is returned to the secure Web site and the server software uses its private key to decrypt it. Now here is the good news: The encryption process is transparent to the end user; that is, it happens automatically without any action on the part of the person interacting with a secure Web site.

The public-key encryption approach is inefficient in that several transmissions must take place before an encrypted message can be sent. A new encryption technology called **identity-based encryption** converts the recipient's e-mail address into a number, which feeds a mathematical algorithm that completes the encryption process. Time will tell whether this or another approach to encryption will replace the widely used public-key encryption technology.

FIGURE 8–32

OBTAINING A DIGITAL CERTIFICATE

Anyone can purchase a digital certificate (digital ID) from a certifying authority, such as VeriSign (shown here), that can ensure security for e-mail messages and attachments.

With the rapid growth of e-commerce, Internet security is beginning to mature. In just a few years, people have become much more comfortable using credit cards to make purchases on the Internet. The difference between then and now is that Web site security has been beefed up with protocols for transmitting data securely over the World Wide Web. One protocol, **Secure Sockets Layer (SSL)**, uses public-key encryption technology to encrypt data that are transferred over the SSL link. Many Web sites use this protocol to transmit sensitive information, such as credit card numbers, between Web client and Web server. There are a couple of ways to tell if you are using a secure Internet protocol. The "http" in the browser's URL bar becomes "https" and/or a padlock icon appears in the status bar at the bottom of the browser (see the e-tail billing information example in Figure 8-7).

Most personal transmissions over the Internet are e-mail. A **digital certificate**, also called a **digital ID**, is an attachment to an electronic message which verifies that the sender is who he or she claims to be. Such devices minimize the possibility that a credit card number, a legal document, financial information, or a private communication can be intercepted or passed off as something that it is not. The digital certificate serves as an electronic substitute for a sealed envelope. Some who send sensitive information are opting to use a digital ID. A digital ID can be purchased from a *certifying authority,* such as VeriSign and GlobalSign (see Figure 8-32). The digital ID becomes part of the browser or e-mail software and allows you to encrypt your e-mail. The digital ID ensures that messages and attachments are protected from tampering, impersonation, and eavesdropping.

Firewalls

E-commerce means the electronic transfer of money, which provides plenty of opportunity for fraud and theft. It is estimated that one in every 20 transactions on the Net is fraudulent or is an attempt at theft. Because of this, organizations have been forced to return to the days of walled forts and castles and take precautions to protect themselves from cyberthieves. Their electronic wall is a firewall. A **firewall** is software that sets up a protective "wall" between a particular network, the private side, and the rest of cyberspace, the public side.

Internet server computers are protected by firewalls. Firewalls can be set up to screen electronic traffic in both directions; that is, they can restrict unwanted access to an organization's network and they can block certain types of communications from traveling outside the private side. Most firewalls are set up to automatically block any unsolicited attempts at communication from the public side of the wall (mostly crackers attempting unauthorized entry to the system). Firewall software lets you set restrictions on what information is allowed through the wall. The screening process can be adjusted to various levels of security. For example, an organization can set restrictions on the size, type, and/or number of e-mail attachments permitted to enter the system. Many corporate firewalls are set to block any e-mail with an executable attachment, which could be a virus.

Always-on broadband Internet access via DSL, cable modem, and satellite poses greater risks of unauthorized access for home networks and individual computers. Fortunately, firewalls are available for home networks and individual PCs, as well, through either the *operating system,* such as Windows, or a *router,* which is often provided by the broadband Internet service provider.

INFORMATION SYSTEMS SECURITY

Information systems security is classified as physical or logical. **Physical security** refers to hardware, facilities, magnetic disks, and other items that could be illegally accessed, stolen, or destroyed. For example, restricted access to the server computer room is a form of physical security.

Logical security is built into the software by permitting only authorized persons to access and use the system. Logical security for online systems, including Internet-based systems, is achieved primarily by utilizing *user IDs* and *passwords*. Only those people with a need to know are given user IDs and told the password. The user ID is your electronic identifier and may be known by your friends and colleagues. The password, however, is yours alone to protect and use.

- Never tell anyone your password.
- Never write down your password.
- Change your password frequently.

Keeping user IDs and passwords from the computer criminal is not easy. One approach companies use is to educate employees about techniques used to obtain user IDs and passwords, such as **tailgating.** The tailgater simply continues a session begun by an authorized user when the user leaves the room. Some companies have added another layer of security with digital signature. The digital signature, which is built into hardware or software, can be a number or even a digitized version of an individual's signature. The host or server computer checks the digital signature against an approved list before permitting access to the system. This measure thwarts the tailgater who attempts to use illegally obtained passwords on unauthorized PCs or software.

Once considered revolutionary, biometric identification systems are now in common use all around us and may someday replace the password logon procedure. **Biometric identification systems** detect unique personal characteristics that can be matched against a database containing the characteristics of authorized users. Several biometric methods are illustrated in Figure 8-33, including fingerprint, palm print (hand geometry), iris scans, and facial recognition. The voiceprint is another common means of biometric identification. Biometric devices are considered superior to traditional methods because they detect personal characteristics that can't be duplicated. All of these biometric technologies are being used for IT security and for other types of security, as well.

In the aftermath of the September 11, 2001 terrorist attack on America, it has become apparent that Americans may be willing to make greater personal privacy sacrifices than in the past in return for safety. **Face recognition technology,** which has been implemented at a number of major airports, enables the identification of known criminals and terrorists. The system creates a digital map of a person's face, called a *faceprint,* which is matched against a database of digital maps to see if there is a match. In all likelihood, your face will be matched against a database of criminals and terrorists at some time in the future at airports and other public venues that might be vulnerable to attack.

PC SECURITY

PCs more powerful than the mainframes of 25 years ago pepper the corporate landscape. We even carry them with us. For these reasons, physical security is no longer enough to protect our PCs. In order to use the advantages of mobile computing safely, IT professionals have been forced to take more complex security measures to protect their equipment and data.

The conscientious PC user has several physical and logical security measures that can be used to safeguard valuable and/or sensitive information. The most frequently used physical tools include the *lock and key* and the *badge reader* (see Figure 8-34). The lock and key, which is installed easily on any PCs, work like an automobile ignition switch. That is, the PC functions only when the lock is turned to the enable position. The badge reader is an optional peripheral device that reads magnetic stripes on badges, such as credit cards. The PC is disabled until an authorized card is inserted and read by the badge reader.

Often the content of your PC's screen bares your soul or perhaps sensitive corporate data. Some people place a special filter over the screen that permits only straight-on viewing. People use it in the office, airplane, or wherever they need to feel secure about their display.

Individual files on a PC can be secured by assigning them unique passwords. For example, if you were using a word processing package to prepare personnel performance evaluations, you could secure these files by assigning each a password. To recall a file at a

techtv
FIREFIGHTERS TURN
TO BIOMETRICS

FIGURE 8–33

BIOMETRIC ACCESS METHODS

Shown here are four biometrics techniques. Your fingerprint, palm print, retina, or face can be used to verify your identity. The security industry has looked to biometric identification technologies to help consumers protect themselves against theft and fraud.

FULL HAND PALM SCANNER

The full hand palm scanner captures a digital image of the entire hand from the carpal crease to the fingertips. Over 30% of the latent prints at a crime scene are from the palm, not the fingers, so forensic examiners have more information they can use to find criminals.

Courtesy of Identix Corporation

FINGERPRINT SCANNER

In a fraction of a second, this biometric sensor can verify, compare, and store a user's fingerprint template. This fingerprint recognition system can be used to secure a computer system from unauthorized use and/or limit access to specific data or files.

Courtesy of Identix Corporation

IRIS SCANNER

Biometric iris scanning technology, which scans the eye's retina through the pupil, provides a quick security access system in businesses and public facilities around the world.

Courtesy of International Business Machines Corporation. Unauthorized use not permitted.

FACE RECOGNITION SYSTEM

Face recognition software (left) uses a neural-based pattern-recognition technology that can extract local features unique to each face to eliminate the need for passwords or user IDs. Although face recognition systems do their job automatically, security control room operators have the flexibility to home in on specific subjects and do manual scans, as well (right).

Courtesy of Identix Corporation

FIGURE 8–34 COMPUTER AND IT SECURITY

LOCK IT UP

The Kensington MemoryLock™ effectively blocks access to the inside of your computer. The hard drive, memory, and all your important information are protected when you lock it up.

Courtesy of Kensington Technology Group

THE PC ID CARD

This Secure ID Document System uses a tamperproof identification card to permit access to sensitive information for such applications as border monitoring, health care, and voter registration.

Courtesy of E-Systems, Inc.

later session, you or any other user would have to enter the name of the file and the associated password to gain access.

SECURITY AND LEVEL OF ACCEPTABLE RISK

No combination of security measures will completely remove the vulnerability of a computer center, an information system, a PC, or a file. An information system can be made marginally secure or very secure, but never totally secure. Each company must determine the level of risk that it is willing to accept and implement their security systems accordingly.

1 Public-key encryption requires both a private key and a public key. (T/F)
2 The frequency with which work files are backed up depends on their volatility. (T/F)
3 Logical security for online systems is achieved primarily by user IDs and: (a) passwords, (b) secret codes, (c) numerical IDs, or (d) social security numbers.
4 What letter is added to "http" in the URL bar to indicate a secure Internet protocol: (a) i, (b) p, (c) s, or (d) t?
5 Data can be transmitted securely over the World Wide Web with which protocol: (a) Secure Sockets Layer, (b) ATM, (c) ASCII, or (d) security sheet protocol?
6 In the full backup method: (a) only user-selected files are backed up, (b) only those files that have been modified since the last backup are backed up, (c) only volatile files are backed up, or (d) all files are backed up.

SELF-CHECK

SECTION

Chapter Review

8-1 E-COMMERCE

E-commerce is simply business conducted online or via some form of data communications. Activities often associated with e-commerce include virtual marketplaces that provide e-tailing (online retailing), e-trading (online brokerage services), Internet-based marketing or advertising, online market research and surveys, business-to-business (B2B), business-to-consumer (B2C), consumer-to-consumer (C2C), and other technology-based approaches to doing business.

E-commerce makes good economic sense and appears to be emerging as the business model for the twenty-first century. Standards for the way in which e-money is exchanged continue to evolve. Several companies offer online purchasing systems that enable consumers to create and use an electronic wallet that stores their billing and shipping information in controlled server facilities.

There are many applications for business-to-business e-commerce, but the most popular and easily implemented B2B applications involve buying and selling between companies. Whenever businesses can reach and interact with consumers more efficiently online, they turn that opportunity into a B2C application. One element of B2C is disintermediation, removal of the middleman. For example, airlines are committed to letting customers purchase their e-tickets directly from the airline. Other B2C applications include buying groceries, books, and CDs; online investment management; e-tailing; and much more. Shop bots scan the Internet to give you the best prices on a product.

The most visible areas of consumer-to-consumer e-commerce are the online auction and the online dating service. Each day millions of items go on the auction block and people scan databases containing profiles for millions of people.

The ability to make stored information available through the Internet and networking has resulted in a greater and more varied use of electronic publishing (e-publishing). Electronically published documents, such as e-zines, have many advantages: Paper is eliminated (no sacrificing of trees); they provide a richer form of communication; they more readily permit interactivity and navigation; they are easily searchable; they can be tied together by hyperlinks; and they are updated easily.

The three most popular formats for electronic documents are word processing, HTML, and portable document. The PDF file has emerged as the standard for portable documents.

Creating an e-commerce Web site can be done by the businesses themselves or through an e-commerce hosting service that offers a customer everything needed to create an e-commerce site.

Follow these Web site design principles: have a purpose for the Web site, know the audience, keep it simple, minimize download time, be an ambassador for the organization, maintain the Web site, and invite feedback.

8-2 DATABASES: INFORMATION STORAGE AND RETRIEVAL

The six levels of the hierarchy of data organization are bit, character, field, record, file, and database. Traditional flat files did not point to or physically link with another file. Integrated database management systems (DBMSs) overcame the limitations of flat files to integrate data management and information flow within an organization. The benefits of an integrated database include greater access to information, better control, and more efficient software development.

Three popular DBMSs include the network DBMS, relational DBMS, and the object-oriented DBMS. In the network DBMS, the data structures establish relationships between the records (for example, one-to-one, one-to-many). The schema is a graphic representation of the logical structure of a network database.

In the relational DBMS (RDBMS) approach to data management, databases are organized in tables in which a row is a record and a column is a field. The user-defined structure of a database table identifies the characteristics of each field in it. Related fields are grouped to form records.

Relational database software also permits you to retrieve, view, and print records based on query by example. To make a query by example, users set conditions for the selection of records by composing a relational expression containing relational operators that reflects the desired conditions. Several expressions can be combined into a single condition with logical operators. When you enter criteria for a query, the RDBMS software generates a SQL (Structured Query Language) program which is executed to retrieve the requested information.

Records in a database can be sorted for display in a variety of formats. To sort the records in a database, select a primary sort field and, if needed, a secondary sort field. Database software can create customized, or formatted, reports.

The object-oriented database management system (OODBMS) is able to handle the complex data structures needed in our increasingly multimedia world. They do this by manipulating objects, which can be a graphic image, a video clip, or a procedure for manipulating data.

Data warehousing involves moving existing operational files and databases from multiple applications to a data warehouse. The data warehouse is a relational database created specifically to help managers get the information they need to make informed decisions. Data mining in data warehouses is used to identify unanticipated trends and problems.

8-3 COMPUTER, INTERNET, AND SYSTEM SECURITY

The threats to the security of computer centers and information systems call for precautionary measures. A computer center can be vulnerable in its hardware, software, files/databases, personnel, the Internet, and e-commerce.

Organizations use a variety of approaches to secure the computer center, including the installation of an uninterruptible power source (UPS) and fault-tolerant systems.

The files/database backup process provides protection against loss of valuable files and enables archiving of files. Three common backup methods are full backup, selective backup of files, and incremental backup.

Popular PC backup media includes rewritable optical media, Zip disks, and portable hard disks. Businesses keep several generations of backups (backups to backups), on hard disk, optical media, or tape backup units. The use of RAID (Redundant Array of Independent Disks) minimizes the impact of catastrophic disk failure by spreading data across several integrated disk drives.

Another security measure for the Internet and e-commerce is the use of cryptography to scramble messages sent over communications channels. A key is used in conjunction with encryption techniques to scramble the message. The most widely used technology is public-key encryption; however, the new identity-based encryption or another more efficient technology may evolve in the next few years.

The Secure Sockets Layer (SSL) protocol enables the transmission of data securely over the World Wide Web. The digital certificate (digital ID) is the equivalent of a sealed envelope for our e-mail.

Firewall software sets up a protective "wall" between a particular network, the private side, and the rest of cyberspace, the public side.

To protect your work, maintain several generations of backups, storing them in fireproof safes in separate rooms or buildings.

Information systems security is classified as physical security or logical security. Logical security for online systems is achieved primarily by utilizing user IDs and passwords. Another security measure is the digital signature. For an extra layer of security, some organizations incorporate biometric security methods, such as fingerprint, palm print, iris scans, and facial recognition.

In the PC environment, people use several methods to control accessibility, including the lock and key and the badge reader.

Security systems are implemented in degrees, and no computer center, LAN server, PC, or system can be made totally secure.

KEY TERMS

1. firewall
2. shop bot
3. disintermediation
4. fault-tolerant system
5. eBay
6. SQL
7. HTML
8. PDF file
9. object-oriented database
10. business-to-consumer

a online auction site
b elimination of middleman
c query language
d B2C
e OODBMS
f e-tail pricing information
g permits continuous server operation
h online document
i portable document
j restricts unwanted access

CHAPTER SELF-CHECK

TRUE/FALSE

1. An Internet server computer is an integral part of B2C. (T/F)
2. E-money and debit cards are the same. (T/F)
3. E-tailing would be considered e-commerce. (T/F)
4. A disadvantage of electronic documents is that they are not electronically searchable. (T/F)
5. A record is a collection of files that are in some way logically related to one another. (T/F)
6. Database objects can only be text and numbers. (T/F)
7. AND and OR are relational operators. (T/F)
8. Fields are grouped to form records. (T/F)
9. Although expensive, some companies implement the security measures needed to be totally secure. (T/F)
10. Normal ceiling-mounted water sprays are installed in all computer centers for fire protection. (T/F)
11. A firewall provides unrestricted access from the public side to an organization's intranet. (T/F)
12. The backup process serves two important functions—protection against loss of valuable files and archiving of files. (T/F)

MULTIPLE CHOICE

1. An electronic magazine is an: (a) e-periodical, (b) e-zine, (c) e-mag, or (d) e-pub.
2. Virtual marketplaces: (a) are oriented to C2B, (b) offer reference services, (c) are oriented to B2C, or (d) are ISPs.
3. Which of the following does not fall under the e-commerce umbrella: (a) B2B, (b) online dating service, (c) B2C, or (d) Net etiquette?
4. Which of these would not be considered among the more popular consumer items purchased over the Internet: (a) shop tools, (b) computer products, (c) CDs, or (d) books?
5. Which corporation created the PDF format: (a) Adobe, (b) IBM, (c) Apple, or (d) Microsoft?

6. Electronic documents are stored permanently in all but which of the following: (a) CD-ROM, (b) cache memory, (c) flash memory, or (d) hard disk?
7. The combination of bits used to represent a character is the: (a) nibble, (b) byte, (c) code, or (d) field?
8. The software tool that integrates data management and information flow within an organization is the: (a) DBMS, (b) DBSM, (c) OLTP, or (d) OOMS.
9. A relationship between two records in a networked DBMS is a: (a) group, (b) set, (c) cluster, or (d) combo.
10. Which record(s) would be selected from the COURSE table in Figure 8-20 for the condition type=lecture/lab: (a) 100, 330, 110, 401, (b) 101, 202, 330, 401, (c) 202, 150, 320, 350, or (d) 110, 150, 320, 350?
11. The definition of the structure of a relational database table would not include which of the following: (a) field names, (b) field sizes, (c) data types, or (d) pointer cell?
12. The relational operator for greater than or equal to is: (a) > OR =, (b) < AND = , (c) < NOT = , or (d) < OR =.
13. Which record(s) would be selected from the STUDENT table in Figure 8-20 for the condition status=complete AND MAJOR=marketing: (a) Targa, Phil/330, (b) Targa, Phil/100, (c) Johnson, Charles/100, (d) Bell, Jim/330?
14. Which of these is normally not associated specifically with database terminology: (a) table, (b) query by example, (c) relational, (d) audio clip?
15. When network downtime is unacceptable, the network must be made: (a) earthquake ready, (b) faultless, (c) uptime tolerant, or (d) fault-tolerant.
16. What can be used to scramble messages sent over data communications channels: (a) community keys, (b) encoding, (c) cryptography, or (d) ASCII plus?
17. Which of these would not be considered a backup medium: (a) DVD±RW, (b) Zip disk, (c) DVD-ROM, or (d) portable hard disk?

18. Which of the following is not true of Secure Sockets Layer: (a) provides a secure connection to a particular Internet server, (b) is abbreviated as SSL, (c) is a communications protocol, or (d) secures all peripheral cables to a PC's system unit?

IT ETHICS AND ISSUES

1. THE INTERNET SALES TAX

One moment, we read in the news that an Internet sales tax is imminent, and then we read that a ban on Internet taxes is gaining support in Congress. This hotly debated issue rages on in the public and political arenas. Tax wise, e-commerce is treated the same as out-of-state catalog and telephone sales; therefore, states cannot collect taxes from e-tailers outside their borders. Also, The Internet Tax Freedom Act bans over 7500 U.S. tax jurisdictions from creating taxes unique to the Internet. However, the Internet tax landscape is changing. Recently, an agreement among the majority of states would allow the sales tax on Internet transactions where the e-tailer has a presence in the customer's state. Support is strong in the U.S. congress to keep e-commerce sales free from taxes. Senators and congresspersons cite the importance of fostering the continued growth of e-commerce. Of course, consumers would like to keep taxes out of Internet sales as well. On the other side, bricks and mortar businesses complain that e-businesses have an unfair advantage, especially on high-dollar items.

Discussion: Argue for or against Internet sales taxes.

Discussion: Describe alternative ways to tax e-commerce (other than sales tax). Would you be for or against such taxes? Explain.

2. ADDICTION TO THE INTERNET

The Internet, with everything from e-commerce to gaming, has emerged as the centerpiece in the lives of many people; but is it addictive? People who study this issue believe that Internet addiction is as real as alcoholism. People will spend time on anything that is fun to do, but many in the medical community have observed that some people have moved past fun to clinical addiction.

These people are said to have Internet addiction disorder (IAD). People with this disorder often lose control and crave surfing the Internet, much as a smoker craves a cigarette. Numerous cases have been reported where the Internet was blamed for broken marriages, students dropping out of school, and even illnesses that result in hospital stays. Although most are addicted to the Internet in general, many are addicted to a particular facet of the Net, such as C2C auctions, multiplayer gaming, pornography, or instant messaging.

It's ironic, but people with IAD often use the Internet to help them cope with their disorder. Some seek out online IAD support groups. Addicts routinely confess their addiction on the Internet.

Discussion: Have you seen any evidence of Internet addiction disorder (IAD)? If so, describe what you perceive to be the symptoms.

Discussion: Is it possible for someone to become addicted to the Internet in a clinical sense? If so, what, if anything, can you do to help someone who has IAD? How can a college help? An employer?

3. CYBERSQUATTING

Legislation has been passed that is aimed at curtailing "cybersquatting." Cybersquatters register Internet domain names that are similar to well-known trademarks, such as Ford, Sony, or Microsoft. In the past, many companies pursuing e-commerce have had to purchase registered domain names from someone who had the foresight to register enticing names that imply affiliation with an organization and/or include a company or product's name within the domain name (for example, Microsoft-technology.com). The practice of cybersquatting has made many people millionaires.

Discussion: Some would argue that cybersquatting plays on a company's trademark name or that it is unethical. Others say that cybersquatters are simply imaginative entrepreneurs taking full advantage of business opportunities. Where do you stand on this issue and why?

Discussion: Most common words in the dictionary are registered as Internet domain names. Cybersquatters are not interested in creating Web sites with these names. They simply register the names, then hope that someday, some company will pay them for the right to use its name. Discuss the ethics of wholesale domain name registration of common words.

4. MOUSE TRAPPING

Have you ever been surfing the Web and suddenly your *Back* button is dimmed, thus locking you into the current page? This is called mouse trapping. Some Web sites automatically add scripts to pages that cause the display of more of their pages when you click the *Back* or *Close* buttons. When this happens, you're in their "mousetrap" and are kept from leaving the Web site. A couple of years ago this mouse trapping practice was limited to the sleazy sites on the Web. Now, many mainstream sites use this practice.

Discussion: Should laws be passed to stop Web sites' attempts to control a visitor's online behavior? Why or why not?

Discussion: Have you been a victim of mouse trapping? Did the "trap" change your attitude toward the organization supporting the Web site? If so, in what way?

1. Many traditional bricks-and-mortar companies have failed to turn a profit with B2C e-commerce solutions. Why do think this occurs? What do you think are the keys to successful implementation of e-commerce?

2. Why would buying online be less risky than buying face-to-face in a regular storefront? Via telephone mail order?

3. Name two types of companies that might benefit from B2B. Describe the B2B interactions between the two companies.

4. Identify and describe at least three B2C applications that you have used or with which you are familiar.

5. Identify and describe at least one C2C application that you have used or with which you are familiar.

6. Discuss the advantages, if any, of buying online. What are some advantages of selling online?

7. Given your current computing situation, how convenient would it be to check the daily news online versus that of a daily newspaper or television? Explain.

8. What types of electronic publishing documents have you used in the last month? Relate your experiences.

9. Many of our federal tax documents (forms and instructions) are online. What types of problems do you think officials must consider when deciding to put these documents online?

10. Speculate on what year, if ever, the sale of e-books will surpass the sale of print books.

11. Describe circumstances for which a company might create a Web site for an extranet.

12. Give examples and descriptions of at least two other fields that might be added to the record for the STUDENT table (Figure 8-20).

13. Name two possible key fields for an employee file. Name two for an inventory file.

14. For the database in Figure 8-20 use appropriate relational and logical operators to set conditions for displaying STUDENT, COURSE TITLE, and MAJOR for all courses completed by marketing or accounting majors that include a lecture. Illustrate the results showing column headings and the appropriate entries sorted by student.

15. What could be done at your college to improve computer security?

16. What could be done at your place of work to improve computer security?

17. Which scenario offers the greatest security for your credit card: paying for a meal at a restaurant, buying a pair of shoes over the Internet, or purchasing a PC via telephone mail order? Explain.

18. What precautions can be taken to minimize the effects of hardware failure?

19. The use of a digital ID provides secure passage for your e-mail and its attachments. How much would you pay annually for the use of a digital ID?

20. Describe a backup method, including backup medium, that might be used in a small company with a local area network serving 28 users.

21. Every Friday night a small company makes backup copies of all databases and programs (over 60 GB). Why is this necessary? The company has a TBU (50-GB cartridges), a DVD±RW drive, and two 120-MB portable hard disk drives. Which storage medium would you suggest for the backup? Why?

FOCUS ON PERSONAL COMPUTING

1. *Exploring e-commerce.* Visit at least three e-commerce Web sites (for example, online shopping, e-trading, and travel). You may be asked to register as a user. Familiarize yourself with the services provided at each site and work through an e-commerce process but do not complete the transaction (for example, scheduling a flight between Chicago and Seattle). Briefly, contrast these e-commerce transactions with traditional off-line transactions.

2. *Electronic documents.* Go online and find at least three electronic documents (at least one PDF document and at least one HTML document) that relate to your personal circumstances (for example, a college catalog or the user's manual for your cellular phone). List and indicate the format for each document.

3. *Backing up files.* Set up a backup procedure within the context of available hardware that meets your ongoing backup needs. Label all interchangeable media, if applicable, and write up the backup procedure, including diagrams as needed. Backup your user files.

ONLINE EXERCISES @ www.prenhall.com/long

1. The Online Study Guide (multiple choice, true/false, matching, and essay questions)

2. Internet Learning Activities
   • E-commerce

3. Serendipitous Internet Activities
   • Online Shopping
   • Politics
   • Jobs

INFORMATION SYSTEMS AND EMERGING TECHNOLOGIES

LEARNING OBJECTIVES

Once you have read and studied this chapter, you will be able to:

- Explain how the use of computers and information technology can result in a competitive business advantage (Section 9-1).

- Describe the qualities of information and how information needs and decision making vary at each level of an organization (Section 9-2).

- Identify the function and characteristics of a data processing system and a management information system (MIS) (Section 9-3).

- Categorize the tools and capabilities of a decision support system (DSS) (Section 9-4).

- Grasp artificial intelligence (AI) concepts and applications, including expert systems, intelligent agents, and robotics (Section 9-5).

- Appreciate the concepts and long-term potential of virtual reality (VR) (Section 9-6).

In the world of computers, systems are everywhere. There are enterprise systems, real-time systems, information systems, expert systems, computer systems, operating systems, and these are just the beginning. Many computer terms and concepts begin with the word *system(s)*. There's a *system this* or a *system that* in just about every office conversation. We've got the *system operator,* the *system board,* the *system administrator,* the *system check,* the *system life cycle,* and on and on. At times, you'll be convinced that everything is some kind of system. Generally, that's true in information technology (IT).

Most systems involve and/or affect people; and that's where you come in. Every day of your life you will be a part of a system, a direct or indirect target of a system, or a user of a system. On most days, we are all of these.

The material in this chapter will help you sort out common systems terminology so you can understand your role within a system better, be more effective as a target of a system, and know when and what kind of system to use.

This chapter also delves into the future of information technology—artificial intelligence. Computers can be partners who offer wise council; they can see and hear; they can serve as cyber butlers; and they can pick, place, move, assemble, paint, weld, and much, much more. Through virtual reality, they can create a virtual world in which you literally are immersed in an ocean floor adventure, an electronic book, or a building yet to be built. Sound interesting? Read on.

9-1 LEVERAGE INFORMATION TECHNOLOGY AS A COMPETITIVE STRATEGY

Why this section is important to you.

Managers and knowledge workers are seeking strategies that can give their companies the competitive advantage, especially in the area of computers and information technology. Often, having effective IT strategies can mean the difference between profitability and failure.

The days are gone when good management and hard work were considered competitive advantages that would invariably result in success and profits. Today, these corporate qualities are the standard for mere survival. Managers are seeking any strategies that can give their companies the competitive advantage. Improved profitability can be achieved in many ways, such as expanding the product line, workforce reduction, and adjusting pricing. But in a world that is going digital, the most important profitability strategy is leveraging information technology.

Information technology can give a company ready access to a world market, improve product and service quality, reduce costs, increase productivity, aid communication between employees, and even improve company morale. What's more, new and innovative uses of information technology are being discovered and implemented every day. We know now that money invested in IT yields tremendous returns, sometimes 50% or more.

Not only are computers and information technology changing the way we do things, they are changing the function and purpose of major companies. We can expect companies to merge and provide vertical integration of information technology-based products and services. For example, look for banks, brokerage firms, insurance companies, and other financial services companies to begin offering similar products and services. In this B2B/B2C era, companies are looking to use IT to leverage their information resources into better decision making and higher profitability (see Figure 9-1).

Corporate performance

Computer and information technology

Increased sales
Increased productivity and reduced cost
Improved customer service
Better resource management

The obvious question becomes, "If information technology is so clearly the solution to establishing a competitive advantage, why isn't everybody doing it?" There are three primary reasons.

- *IT solutions often are expensive and time consuming.* The implementation of IT solutions is a perfect example of a situation in which you have to spend money to make money.

- *IT solutions can be risky.* Managers often opt to maintain the status quo rather than risk failure.

- *IT solutions involve change.* People inherently resist change.

Those enterprises that challenge their managers and executives to tap the potential of IT are gaining the competitive advantage.

INCREASING SALES

IT technology can be leveraged to increase sales in a number of ways, including increasing market share and creating new business. For example, even junkyards have gone high tech. Traditionally, dealers in recycled auto parts have been local businesses that catered to customers in the immediate vicinity of the yard. If they did not have what the customer needed, they would call a competitor at the other end of town or in a nearby city. If none of them had the part, the customer would be out of luck. Today, hundreds of "local" auto salvage dealers have banded together via an Internet database of recycled parts to create a national market for their products. The net effect of this system is to increase each of the participating salvage dealer's share of the recycled auto parts market. Without the system, a dealer is limited to selling what he or she has in stock or to what he or she can find by making a few telephone calls. With the system, the online salvage dealer has a distinct competitive advantage over other nonnetworked dealers.

Another way to increase sales is to be there first with information about a product. The key to the successful implementation of this strategy is knowing when to arrive with the information and when to return with more information. For example, several manufacturers that specialize in baby products have used this strategy to establish a competitive advantage. One manufacturer gives sampler kits to hospitals to be distributed to expectant mothers. The kits include a return card that requests critical marketing information, such as name, address, and expected date of birth. This information is entered into a database and an information system automatically triggers the delivery of prenatal promotional literature, samples, and a monthly newsletter (both hard copy and via e-mail) on caring for newborns. The company provides a valuable service to potential consumers while keeping its name and products in the forefront of the consumer's mind.

INCREASING PRODUCTIVITY AND REDUCING COST

Increased productivity and cost reduction go hand in hand (see Figure 9-2). For example, overcapacity and the emergence of for-profit hospitals have forced hospital administrators to become more competitive, usually via implementation of information technology. A

FIGURE 9-2 LEVERAGING IT IN INDUSTRY

USING IT IN THE INSURANCE INDUSTRY

The USAA insurance company has a high-tech relationship with USAA members. The company does not have field agents, so members interact with the company via the member services Web site and, if needed, by telephone. *Consumer Reports* consistently ranks USAA at or near the top of all insurance companies in customer satisfaction.

TECHNOLOGY AS A COMPETITIVE TOOL

In today's competitive environment, there is no such thing as business as usual. This man at a bicycle manufacturing company enjoys increased productivity by using an arm-mounted PC along with a scanner to select assembly components and update inventory.

Courtesy of Symbol Technologies, Inc.

study at one hospital revealed that nurses devoted over 40% of their time to recording what they do. For example, nurses must log every prescription that they deliver and every time they respond to a patient call. At that hospital, a computer-based data collection system was developed and installed that enables data to be captured in machine-readable format (for example, bar codes) from bedside terminals at the point of care. The system reduces the time that nurses spend recording data from 40% down to 5%, thus freeing up time that can be devoted to direct patient care.

IMPROVING CUSTOMER SERVICE

techtv

VISITING THE
BATTLEFIELD—BEFORE
THE BATTLE BEGINS

All things being equal, customers tend to take their business to the companies that can provide the best service. For example, financial institutions, especially banks, have been among the most progressive users of IT. Deregulation of the banking industry has sent bank executives scurrying for strategic advantages, especially in the area of customer convenience. Today, most banks offer 24-hour ATMs, so they must implement some other IT strategy. Many now offer the next level of banking convenience—*home banking*. The bank that gives their customers the freedom to go online and view their accounts, open an account, apply for a loan, get a credit/debit card, pay bills, and transfer funds has a distinct advantage over the bank that does not offer this service. IT has become such a strategic weapon in the banking industry that second-tier banks are merging to be able to justify expensive technological solutions to gain the advantage in competitive situations.

SECTION

1 Managers are seeking the competitive advantage through IT strategies. (T/F)

2 IT solutions are inviting to organizations because they have little or no risk. (T/F)

3 Which of these is not a way to improve corporate profitability: (a) adjusting prices, (b) workforce reduction, (c) expanding the product line, or (d) limiting the use of IT?

9-2 ALL ABOUT INFORMATION AND DECISION MAKING

To be successful, managers and knowledge workers must fully understand and use the four major resources: money, materials, people, and information. Managers have become skilled at taking full advantage of the resources of *money*, *materials*, and *people*; but only recently have they begun to tap the potential of the *information* resource.

> **Why this section is important to you.**
>
> Your success at work, and possibly in life, mirrors the quality of your decisions. You'll make better decisions if you understand information and decision-making concepts.

QUALITIES OF INFORMATION

Too often, managers at all levels are quick to accept computer-generated information as gospel. This can be a mistake. Information is only as good as the data from which it is derived. As the saying goes, "garbage in, garbage out" or **GIGO** (pronounced "*GUY go*"). For this reason, evaluating the quality of computer-generated information is often just as important as the information itself. Just as we describe automobiles in terms of features, color, and size, we describe information in terms of its *accuracy, verifiability, completeness, timeliness, relevance,* and *accessibility*.

Accuracy and Verifiability of Information

The *accuracy* quality of information refers to the degree to which information is free from error. Information usually is assumed to be accurate. Sometimes, however, it is not feasible to collect information that is 100% accurate. For example, a market analyst may poll only a fraction of the potential consumers for a proposed product, and then extrapolate the results to all potential consumers. Also, the possibility of a data entry error is ever present.

Accuracy and *verifiability* go hand in hand. A decision maker is reluctant to assume that information is accurate unless it is verifiable. For example, managers usually are comfortable with the accuracy of financial information because it is verified by auditors. Unverifiable information must be viewed with skepticism.

Completeness of Information

Information can be totally accurate and verifiable, but it may not tell the whole story. The *completeness* quality of information refers to the degree to which it is free from omissions. There is, of course, no relationship between the amount of information supplied to a decision maker and its completeness. Benefit/cost analysis offers a good example of the importance of considering the completeness of information in the decision-making process. If the benefit information is complete and the cost information is incomplete, the omission of the rest of the costs may result in an unprofitable project being approved.

Timeliness of Information

The *timeliness* quality of information refers to the time sensitivity of information. Up-to-the-minute information on today's market trends may be of significant value to an executive. The same information will have less value in a month and probably no value in six months. IT has made it possible for managers and knowledge workers to have not only the right information, but also the *right information* at the *right time* (see Figure 9-3).

Relevance of Information

The *relevance* quality of information refers to the appropriateness of the information as input for a particular decision. *Information overload* continues to be a problem for decision makers. Information overload occurs when the volume of available information is so great that the decision maker can't determine which information is relevant and which is not. One of the primary causes of information overload is the accumulation of information that is not relevant to a particular decision.

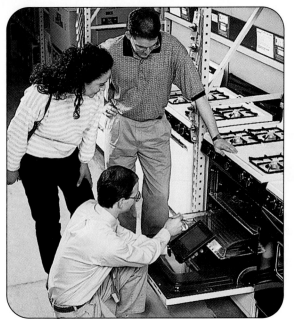

FIGURE 9-3

ACCESS TO QUALITY INFORMATION

A sales assistant is helping this couple make an informed decision about which appliance to put into their new kitchen. With his wireless handheld PC and access to a database, he can respond in a timely manner to customer inquiries relating to the product, stock status, and delivery schedules.

Courtesy of International Business Machines Corporation. Unauthorized use not permitted.

Accessibility of Information

Information technology has redefined the *accessibility* quality of information. Information in a well-organized database can be made easily accessible via the Internet and computer networks to all with a need to know. A considerable body of information remains untapped because it is poorly organized and buried in manual file cabinets or poorly designed flat files. For all practical purposes, this information is inaccessible.

MAKING DECISIONS TO PRODUCE PRODUCTS AND SERVICES

Now that you understand the qualities of information, let's move on to discuss how this information is used to make decisions. There are four levels of information activity within a company: *strategic, tactical, operational,* and *clerical.* IT-based information systems *process data* at the clerical level. In contrast, information systems *provide information* for managerial decision making at the strategic, tactical, and operational levels.

- *Strategic.* Strategic-level managers determine long-term strategies and set corporate objectives and policies to be consistent with these objectives. The information available for a strategic-level decision is almost never conclusive. To be sure, information is critical to strategic-level decision making, but virtually all decision makers at this level rely heavily on personal judgment and intuition.

- *Tactical.* Tactical-level managers must implement the objectives and policies made at the strategic level of management by identifying specific tasks that need to be accomplished. The information available for a tactical-level decision is seldom conclusive. That is, the most acceptable alternative cannot be identified from information alone. At this level, personal judgment and intuition used in conjunction with available information provide the foundation for most decisions.

- *Operational.* Operational-level managers complete the specific tasks as directed by tactical-level managers. The information available for an operational-level decision is often conclusive. That is, the most acceptable alternative can be clearly identified based on information available to the decision maker. At this level, personal judgment and intuition play a reduced role in the decision-making process.

The business system model shown in Figure 9-4 helps place the decision-making environment in its proper perspective. Managers (the top three levels) must use all the resources at their disposal to meet corporate objectives and perform the management functions of *planning, organizing, leading,* and *controlling.*

Figure 9-4 also illustrates how the corporate resources of *money, materials* (including facilities and equipment), *people,* and *information* become "input" to the various functional units, such as operations, sales, and accounting. Employees use their talent and knowledge, together with these resources, to produce products and services.

The business system acts together with several *entities,* such as employees, customers, and suppliers (see Figure 9-4). An entity is the source or destination of information flow. An entity also can be the source or destination of materials or product flow. For example, suppliers are a source of both information and materials. They are also the destination of payments for materials. The customer entity is the destination of products and the source of orders.

FILTERING INFORMATION

Different employees in a company need different types of information to do their jobs. The information requirements of an administrative assistant are very different from the needs

FIGURE 9-4 **A BUSINESS SYSTEM MODEL**

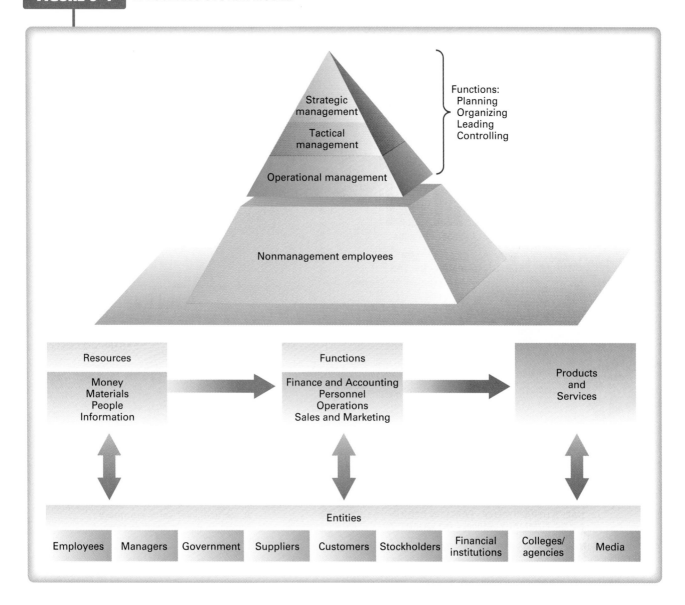

of the company's president. The key to using information effectively is to *filter* it. This way, employees receive just the information they need to accomplish their job functions—no more, no less. Well designed information systems can **filter** information such that the *right information* reaches the *right decision maker* at the *right time* in the *right form*. There are four basic levels of knowledge workers in every company, and each level has its own information needs.

Clerical Level

Clerical-level personnel, those involved in repetitive tasks, are concerned primarily with *transaction handling*. For example, a sales clerk might key in customer orders on his or her terminal, and an airline ticket agent might confirm and make flight reservations.

Operational Level

Personnel at the operational level have well-defined short-term tasks that might span as long as three months. Their information requirements often consist of *operational feedback*. For example, the manager of the Eastern Regional Sales Department for Bravo International, a small high-tech firm, might want an end-of-quarter sales summary report (see Figure 9-5).

FIGURE 9–5 FILTERING OF INFORMATION

FOUR-YEAR SALES TREND BY PRODUCT

A strategic-level sales-trend-by-product report shown in graphic format.

CORPORATE SALES REGIONAL SUMMARY

A tactical-level sales summary report shown in graphic format.

SALES DEPARTMENT - EASTERN REGION
SALES SUMMARY ($1000) - 1ST QUARTER

An operational-level sales summary in tabular format (high/low salespersons highlighted).

SALESPERSON	ALPHAS	BETAS	GAMMAS	DELTAS	TOTAL
BAKER	70	10	14	65	159
COOK	60	40	37	77	214
JONES	55	28	40	57	180
LUCAS	20	50	48	68	186
MILLER	45	34	28	48	155
OTT	39	47	29	42	157
RITTER	32	24	28	10	94
TOTALS	321	233	224	367	1145

Managers and knowledge workers at the operational, tactical, and strategic levels often request **exception reports** that highlight critical information. They can make such inquiries directly to the system (see the example in Figure 9-5).

Tactical Level

At the tactical level, managers and knowledge workers concentrate on achieving a series of goals required to meet the objectives set at the strategic level. The information requirements at this level are usually *periodic,* but on occasion workers require one-time and what-if reports. *What-if reports* are generated in response to inquiries that depict what-if scenarios ("What if sales increase by 15% next quarter?"). Tactical-level personnel are concerned primarily with operations and budgets from year to year. In the sales information system, the national sales manager, who is at the tactical level, might want the "Corporate Sales" report shown in Figure 9-5.

Strategic Level

Strategic-level managers are objective-oriented. Their information system requirements are often *one-time reports*, *what-if reports*, and *trend analyses*. For example, the president of the company might ask for a report that shows the four-year sales trend for each of the company's four products (see Figure 9-5).

FIGURE 9–6 TYPES OF DECISIONS

Decision Characteristic	Programmed Decisions	Nonprogrammed Decisions (information-based decisions)
Difficulty	Easy	Tough
Horizon	Short-term	Long-term
Decision-maker level	Clerical	All management levels
Decision problem	Well-defined and structured	Ill-defined and unstructured
Confidence in making the right decision	High	Low to medium
Information requirement	Primarily applicable policies, standards, or procedures	Relevant information in meaningful format

TYPES OF DECISIONS

Two basic types of decisions are the relatively easy programmed decisions and the tough information-based decisions (see Figure 9-6). IT supports both types of decisions. Purely **programmed decisions** address well-defined problems (see Figure 9-7). For example, the decision required to restock inventory levels of raw materials is often a programmed decision. When the inventory level of a particular item drops below the reorder point, perhaps a two-months' supply, a decision to replenish the inventory by submitting an order to the supplier can be automatic.

With **information-based decisions,** the decision maker needs information to make a rational decision. Such decisions involve unstructured problems; that is, the problems are hard-to-define and the rules are unclear. The information requirement implies the need for managers to use judgment and intuition in the decision-making process.

FIGURE 9–7 JOHN GLENN'S RETURN TO SPACE

Shown here is the liftoff for John Glenn's historic flight to space to investigate the effects of weightlessness on senior citizens. NASA's computer systems at the space flight center and onboard the space shuttle make routine programmed decisions, leaving the operators and astronauts more time to make the more difficult information-based decisions.

NASA

1 GIGO stands for garbage in, garbage out. (T/F)

2 What-if reports usually are associated with knowledge workers at the operational level. (T/F)

3 Which of these is not one of the four levels of information activity within a company: (a) managerial, (b) strategic, (c) operational, or (d) tactical?

9-3 ALL ABOUT INFORMATION SYSTEMS

Why this section is important to you.

During a typical day, you will probably interact with several information systems, perhaps a retailer's POS system, a bank's customer service system (at an ATM), or a Web-based system with a music lyrics database. This section gives you the information system basics you need to understand all this activity.

Every day, most of us are directly or indirectly affected by several information systems. There are the ones we're aware of, such as eBay and your college's online registration system. Also, you may be unaware of the many information systems processing your personal information, perhaps the system at your state's revenue office, the system at your cellular phone company, or a system evaluating you as a candidate for employment. This section describes an information system and what it can do.

WHAT IS AN INFORMATION SYSTEM AND WHAT CAN IT DO?

Before answering these questions, we need to define *system*. A **system** is any group of components (functions, people, activities, events, and so on) that interface with and complement one another to achieve one or more predefined goals. An **information system** is a generic reference to a technology-based system that does two things:

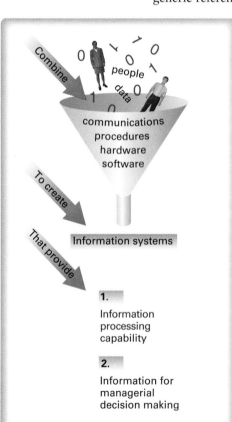

FIGURE 9-8

CREATING AN INFORMATION SYSTEM

- Provides *information processing capabilities* for an individual or, perhaps, an entire company. The processing capability refers to the system's ability to handle and process information (for example, order processing).

- Provides *information people need to make better, more informed decisions*. Information systems provide decision makers with on-demand reports and inquiry capabilities as well as routine periodic reports (daily, weekly, and so on) and feedback. Information systems routinely make programmed decisions without people being involved.

Hardware, software, procedures, and *communications* combine *people* and *data* to create an *information system* (see Figure 9-8).

Not surprisingly, an information system has the same four capabilities as a computer system: *input, processing, storage,* and *output* (see Figure 9-9). The information system has the capability to accept various forms of input, to perform various types of processing, to store *data, text, images* (graphs, pictures), and *other digital information* (voice messages) for recall or further processing, and to produce output in a variety of formats.

An information system (see Figure 9-10) can service a portion of an organization (perhaps a department), an entire organization (perhaps a company), the extended organization (perhaps a company and all business-to-business partners), or the world (an Internet-based e-commerce system).

GETTING DATA INTO AN INFORMATION SYSTEM

In a computer system, the input, output, and data storage components receive data from and transmit data to RAM and, eventually, the processor. These hardware components are said to be *online* to the processor. Hardware devices that are not accessible to a processor are said to be

FIGURE 9–9 INFORMATION SYSTEM CAPABILITIES

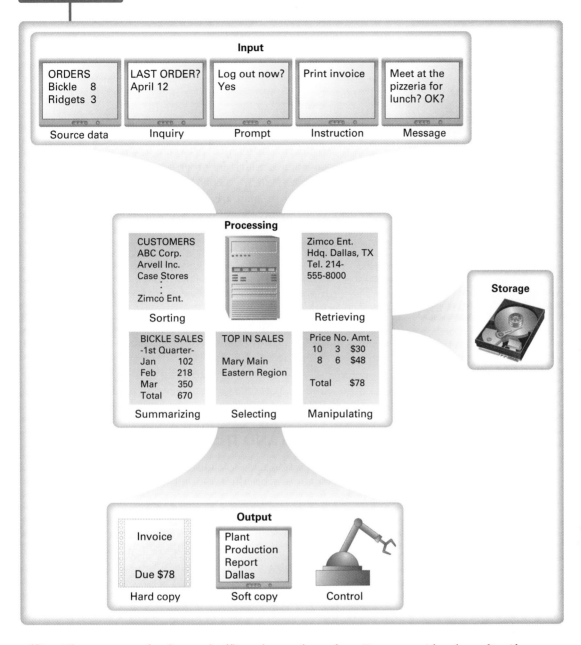

Input

ORDERS Bickle 8 Ridgets 3	LAST ORDER? April 12	Log out now? Yes	Print invoice	Meet at the pizzeria for lunch? OK?
Source data	Inquiry	Prompt	Instruction	Message

Processing

CUSTOMERS ABC Corp. Arvell Inc. Case Stores ⋮ Zimco Ent.		Zimco Ent. Hdq. Dallas, TX Tel. 214- 555-8000
Sorting		Retrieving

BICKLE SALES -1st Quarter- Jan 102 Feb 218 Mar 350 Total 670	TOP IN SALES Mary Main Eastern Region	Price No. Amt. 10 3 $30 8 6 $48 Total $78
Summarizing	Selecting	Manipulating

Storage

Output

Invoice Due $78	Plant Production Report Dallas	
Hard copy	Soft copy	Control

offline. The concepts of online and offline also apply to data. Data are said to be *online* if they can be accessed and manipulated by the processor. All other data are considered *offline.*

Often, data do not exist in a form that can be "read" by the computer. For example, supervisors may record manually the hours worked by the staff on a time sheet. Before the payroll checks can be computed and printed, the data on these time sheets must be entered to the computer. Someone does this in an online operation at a PC or terminal. The time sheet is the **source document,** and, as you might expect, the data on the time sheet are the **source data.** Whenever possible, data are entered via source data automation, such as with point-of-sale UPC scanners in grocery stores.

Data entry is the process of entering data into an information system. Information systems are designed to provide users with display-screen prompts to make online data entry easier. The display on the user's screen, for example, may be the image of the source document (such as a time sheet). A **prompt** is a brief message to the user that describes what should be entered (for example, "Enter hours worked"). Data entry generally falls into one of these categories.

- *Batch processing.* In **batch processing,** transactions are grouped, or batched, and entered consecutively, one after the other.
- *Online transaction processing.* In **online transaction processing (OLTP),** transactions are entered directly to the system as they occur.

To illustrate the difference between batch and transaction-oriented processing, consider the order processing system illustrated in Figure 9-11. The system accepts orders by both mail and phone. The orders received by mail are accumulated, or batched, for data entry—usually at night. Phone orders do not need to accumulate. People taking the phone orders interact with the company information system via PCs or terminals and enter the order data online while talking with the customer. Batch processing is appropriate mainly when information on source documents needs to be transcribed.

The primary advantage of online transaction processing data entry is that records on the database are updated immediately, as the transaction occurs. With batch data entry, records are batched periodically. In an OLTP environment, the database remains continuously up-to-date and can be queried at any time. Most data entry into enterprise-wide systems or into local area network-based systems is done online, regardless of whether the processing being done is batch or OLTP.

THE DP SYSTEM AND THE MIS

Information technology is constantly redefining itself, and so it is with information systems. This section describes the evolution of information systems.

Data Processing System

Early information systems were **data processing systems,** or **DP systems,** which are concerned with *transaction handling* and *record keeping,* usually for a particular functional area. Data are entered and stored in a flat file format. Periodic outputs include *action documents* (invoices) and *scheduled reports,* primarily for clerical personnel and operational-level managers. The major drawback of data processing systems is that they are inflexible and cannot accommodate data processing or information needs that are not already built into the system. Most companies have moved beyond the scope of DP systems and now have systems with the flexibility of providing management with information in support of an ever-changing decision-making environment.

Management Information Systems

In the not-too-distant past, most payroll systems were data processing systems that did little more than process time sheets, print payroll checks, and keep running totals of annual wages and deductions. As managers began to demand more and better information about their personnel, payroll *data processing systems* evolved into human resource management information systems. A human resource management information system is capable of predicting the average number of worker sick days, monitoring salary equality between minority groups, making more effective use of available personnel skills, and providing other information needed at all three levels of management—operational, tactical, and strategic.

If you were to ask any five executives or IT professionals to define a management information system, or MIS, the only agreement you would find in their responses is that there is no agreement on its definition. An MIS has been called a method, a function, an approach, a process, an organization, a system, and a subsystem. The following definition is a mouthful, but it captures the essence of the MIS: A **management information system**, or **MIS**, is a computer-based system that optimizes the collection, transfer, and presentation of information throughout an organization by using an integrated structure of databases and information flow (see Figure 9-12).

The following are the *desirable* characteristics of an MIS:

- An MIS supports transaction handling and record keeping.

- An MIS uses an integrated database and supports a variety of functional areas.

- An MIS provides operational-, tactical-, and strategic-level managers with easy access to timely but, for the most part, *structured information* (for example, a weekly inventory status report with predefined content and format).

FIGURE 9-11 **BATCH AND TRANSACTION-ORIENTED PROCESSING**
This typical order entry system accepts orders by mail, by phone, and online via the Internet.

Mail orders are processed in batch mode usually at night

Phone orders are processed in transaction mode, as they occur

Customer master file

Server computer

Mail and phone orders are entered via a LAN PC

Customer orders entered on an Internet-linked PC are processed via online transaction processing (OLTP)

- An MIS is somewhat flexible and can be adapted to meet the changing information needs of the organization.

- An MIS can boost system security by limiting access to authorized personnel.

The MIS in Action

All major airlines rely on management information systems to assist in day-to-day operations and provide valuable information for short- and long-term planning. At the core of such an MIS is the airline reservation subsystem. Airline reservation agents and individuals scheduling their own flights interact with the MIS's integrated database via computer networks and/or the Internet to update the database the moment a seat on any flight is filled or becomes available.

An airline MIS does much more than keep track of flight reservations. It also closely monitors departure and arrival times so that ground crew activities can be coordinated. Systems provide passengers with flight status information via e-mail, telephone, or cell phone text messaging. The system compiles and produces many kinds of information needed by management: the number of passenger miles flown, profit per passenger on a particular flight, percentage of arrivals on time, average number of empty seats on each flight for each day of the week, and so on.

The influence of the MIS is just as pervasive in hospitals (patient accounting, point-of-care processing, and so on), insurance (claims-processing systems, policy administration, actuarial statistics, and so on), colleges (student registration, placement, and so on), and other organizations that use computers both for information processing and to gather information for decision making.

FIGURE 9-12 MANAGEMENT INFORMATION SYSTEMS

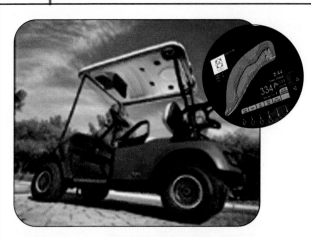

GOLF COURSE MANAGEMENT SYSTEM

Golf courses throughout the world use the ProLink golf course management system to facilitate play on the golf course and course administration in the office. The system is driven by a GPS (global positioning system) navigation system to deliver a real-time information flow to golfers on the course and to course managers.

Courtesy of ProLink

THE FEDEX INFORMATION SYSTEM

Federal Express has one of the world's most sophisticated information systems, providing up-to-the-minute information for its 150,000 employees. The system uses advanced telecommunications to monitor the status of millions of shipments as they move through key handling points in the system. The FedEx system handles more than 60 million online data transmissions each day.

Courtesy of Federal Express Corporation. All rights reserved.

SELF-CHECK

SECTION

1 An information system can provide information processing capabilities for an individual or an entire company. (T/F)

2 The DP system is considered the most sophisticated information system. (T/F)

3 The summarizing activity would be associated with which capability of an information system: (a) input, (b) output, (c) processing, or (d) storage?

4 In which type of processing are transactions grouped together for processing: (a) transaction-oriented, (b) bin, (c) batch, or (d) group-driven?

5 Which type of information system integrates the information flow between functional areas: (a) DP system, (b) MIS, (c) DSS, or (d) intelligent agent?

The decision support system and its many tools enable managers and knowledge workers to make better and timelier decisions. This section describes the decision support system and compares it to the MIS.

Why this section is important to you.

Knowing what kinds of decision support systems and tools are available will ultimately make you a better decision maker.

WHAT IS A DECISION SUPPORT SYSTEM?

Decision support systems (DSS) are *interactive* information systems that rely on an integrated set of user-friendly decision support tools (both hardware and software) to produce and present information to support management in the decision-making process. Mostly, managers and knowledge workers rely on their experience and the information available from the MIS to guide them in decision making. However, decision makers, especially at the tactical and strategic levels, are sometimes confronted with complex decisions whose factors are beyond their human abilities to synthesize properly. These types of decisions are "made to order" for decision support systems.

Generally, the DSS helps decision makers choose between alternatives. Some DSSs can even automatically rank alternatives based on the decision maker's criteria. Decision support systems help remove the tedium of gathering and analyzing data and of presenting information. Also, with the availability of a variety of user-oriented DSS tools, managers and knowledge workers can get the information they need without having to depend on direct technical assistance from an IT professional.

A decision support system can help close the gap between available information and the information needed to make quality decisions. For example, at Johns Hopkins University, a decision support system helps administrators predict enrollment. The admissions officers are adapting various DSS techniques to predict which accepted applicants will ultimately select Johns Hopkins. The system examines trends and patterns in student data, past and present, looking for common personal characteristics among university enrollees. This system has proven to be twice as accurate as traditional decision models. This type of system is extremely important to universities that limit admissions in that small errors can have a dramatic impact on the university. For example, accepting too many students can result in some students not having university-guaranteed housing. Accepting too few might cause budget problems.

Management information systems are best at supporting decisions that involve *structured* problems, such as when to replenish raw materials inventory and how much of an inventory item to order. In contrast, the DSS is designed to support decision-making processes involving *semistructured* and *unstructured* problems. A semistructured problem might be the need to improve the delivery performance of suppliers. The problem is structured partially in that information comparing the on-time delivery performance of suppliers can be obtained directly from the integrated database supporting the MIS. The unstructured facets of the problem, such as extenuating circumstances, rush-order policy and pricing, and so on, make this problem a candidate for a DSS.

CHARACTERISTICS OF DECISION SUPPORT SYSTEMS

The following are the *desirable* characteristics of a DSS:

- A DSS helps the decision makers, especially those at the tactical and strategic levels, in the decision-making process.
- A DSS is designed to address semistructured and unstructured problems.
- A DSS is an interactive, user-friendly system that can be used by the decision maker with little or no assistance from an IT professional.
- A DSS makes general-purpose models, simulation capabilities, and other analytical tools available to the decision maker.

- A DSS can be readily adapted to meet the information requirements of any decision environment.
- A DSS can interact with the corporate database.

THE DSS TOOL BOX

A DSS consists of a set of decision support tools that can be adapted to any decision environment (see Figure 9-13). Together, these tools help managers address decision-making tasks in specific application areas (the evaluation and promotion of personnel, the acquisition of companies, and so on). DSS includes the following tools.

- *Applications Development.* Some decision support systems provide users with the ability to develop computer-based systems that support the decision-making process. The ease with which DSS applications can be created has spawned a new term—*throwaway systems.*

- *Data Management.* DSS software packages have many approaches to database management—that is, the software mechanisms for the storage, maintenance, and retrieval of data. These include *data warehousing* and *data mining,* both discussed in Chapter 8, "E-Commerce, Databases, and Security."

- *Modeling.* Decision support systems enable managers to use mathematical modeling techniques to re-create the functional aspects of a system within the confines of a computer. For example, simulation models often are used when uncertainty and risk are introduced, when several decision makers are involved, and when multiple outcomes are anticipated. In manufacturing, for instance, managers use modeling DSS software to simulate sales, production, and demand.

- *Statistical Analysis.* The DSS statistical analysis capability can handle everything from simple statistics to complex procedures. Risk analysis and trend analysis are common applications of DSS statistical tools.

- *Planning.* Managers often are faced with making decisions that will be implemented at some time in the future. To help get a glimpse into the future, they rely on DSS software that permits forecasting, what-if analysis, and goal seeking. In what-if analysis, managers make inquiries such as "What would be the impact on sales if we boosted the advertising budget by 30%?" In goal seeking, managers make inquiries such as "How much do we need to increase the advertising budget to achieve a goal of $120 million in sales for next year?"

- *Inquiry.* DSS software helps managers to make online inquiries to the DSS database using English-like commands.

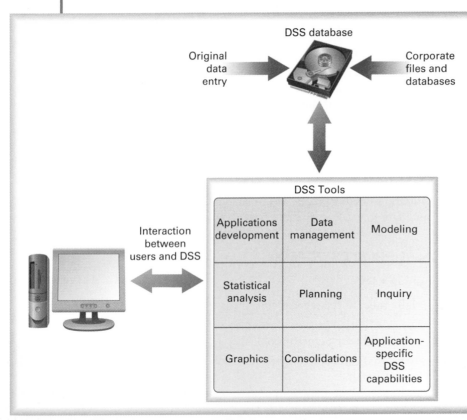

FIGURE 9-13 **THE DECISION SUPPORT SYSTEM**

A decision support system is a set of software and hardware tools that can be adapted to any decision environment.

DSS database

Original data entry

Corporate files and databases

Interaction between users and DSS

DSS Tools

Applications development	Data management	Modeling
Statistical analysis	Planning	Inquiry
Graphics	Consolidations	Application-specific DSS capabilities

For example, a personnel manager may enter this request: "What percentage of employee compensation goes to retirement benefits?"

- *Graphics*. With the graphics DSS tool, managers can create a variety of presentation graphics based on data in the DSS database, including bar graphs, pie graphs, and line graphs. The graphics tool allows you to "drill down" into a graph to uncover additional information. For example, a user viewing a monthly sales bar graph can "drill down" and display a weekly sales bar graph for any given month.

- *Consolidations*. DSS tools are available that enable the consolidation of like data from different sources. A sample use of this DSS tool is the consolidation of financial statements from subsidiary companies into a single corporate financial statement.

- *Application-Specific DSS Capabilities*. DSS tools that support a particular decision environment, such as financial analysis and quality control, are being introduced routinely into the marketplace.

EXECUTIVE INFORMATION SYSTEMS

Just when we start to get used to decision support systems, the IT community introduces us to an even more intricate information system: the **executive information system.** The **EIS** offers the same decision support tools as the DSS, but each tool is designed specifically to support decision making at the executive levels of management, primarily the tactical and strategic levels. The EIS is easy to use, yet offers powerful information gathering and presentation tools. Like the MIS and the DSS, the EIS may eventually gain an identity of its own, but today's commercially available executive information systems look suspiciously like what most managers know as decision support systems.

1 Decision support systems are designed to support decision-making processes involving totally structured problems. (T/F)
2 Forecasting and goal seeking are addressed with the DSS planning tool. (T/F)
3 Which of the following types of information systems is designed specifically for decision support at the tactical and strategic levels of management: (a) expert systems, (b) executive information systems, (c) DP systems, or (d) management information systems?

SECTION

9-5 ARTIFICIAL INTELLIGENCE

The kinds of problems that can be solved by computers extend well past those usually associated with computation and information retrieval. Today's computers can simulate many human capabilities, such as reaching, grasping, calculating, speaking, remembering, comparing numbers, and drawing. Researchers are working to expand these capabilities and, therefore, the power of computers, by developing hardware and software that can imitate intelligent human behavior. This area of research, known as **artificial intelligence (AI),** involves the creation of systems that have the ability to reason, to learn or accumulate knowledge, to strive for self-improvement, and to simulate human sensory and mechanical capabilities. AI is broad in scope and has many definitions. AI pioneer Marvin Minsky offers a time-honored definition: "Artificial intelligence is the science of making machines do things that would require intelligence if done by man."

> **Why this section is important to you.**
>
> Terms like *neural network, expert system, artificial life,* and *virtual reality* sound futuristic and, to some, a bit threatening to humanity. After reading this section you will be able to sort out myth from reality.

To some, the mere mention of artificial intelligence creates visions of electromechanical automatons replacing human beings. Computers will never be capable of simulating the distinctly human qualities of creativity, humor, and emotions. However, computers can drive machines that mimic human movements (such as picking up objects and placing them at a prescribed location), enable us to talk to our computers, and provide the "brains" for systems that simulate the human thought process within the domain of a particular area of expertise (tax preparation, medical diagnosis, and so on). For example, computers have proven to be effective marriage counselors and wise corporate colleagues. **Artificial life (ALife),** which is the study of and creation of computer-based systems that behave like biological systems, falls under the AI umbrella.

This AI overview will introduce you to several of the more visible areas of AI, including the simulation of human sensory capabilities, expert systems, neural networks, intelligent agents, and robotics.

SIMULATION OF HUMAN SENSORY CAPABILITIES

One area of AI research involves computer simulation of human capabilities. The focus of this area is on equipping computer systems with the capabilities of hearing, speaking, smelling, feeling (touching), and seeing. To varying degrees, these artificial intelligence capabilities are possible with current technology. Speech recognition (hearing) and speech synthesis (speaking), which are among the more mature AI applications, are discussed in Chapter 6, "Storage and Input/Output Devices." Systems that smell are used in a variety of applications, including quality control at perfume factories. The research on feeling capabilities is still in the laboratory. Vision systems are now in common usage.

Some data are best entered and processed visually. However, the simulation of human senses, especially vision, is extremely complex. A computer does not actually see and interpret an image the way a human being does. Computers need cameras for their "eyesight." To create a visual database, a **pattern recognition system,** via a camera, digitizes the images of all objects to be identified, and then stores the digitized form of each image in the database. The system compares the digitized image to be interpreted with the prerecorded digitized images in the computer's database; much like a speech-recognition system does with speech input. The computer identifies the image by matching the structure of the input image with those images in the database. This process is illustrated by the digital vision-inspection system in Figure 9-14.

Pattern recognition systems are best suited to specialized tasks in which only a few images will be encountered. These tasks are usually simple, monotonous ones, such as inspection. For example, in Figure 9-14, a digital vision-inspection system on an assembly line rejects those parts that do not meet certain quality control specifications. The vision system performs rudimentary gauging inspections, and then signals the computer to take appropriate action. Security using biometric identification is another popular application for pattern recognition (see Figure 9-15).

AI offers great promise for the future. For example, several automobile manufacturers have made prototype cars

FIGURE 9-14 **DIGITAL VISION-INSPECTION SYSTEM**

In this digital vision-inspection system, the system examines parts for defects. If the digitized image of the part does not match a standard digital image, the defective part is placed in a reject bin.

Digitized image compared to standard

Standardized image

Conveyor movement

Reject bin

that can "see" and can drive themselves. In time, cars will be able to talk, listen, and even smell the roses.

EXPERT SYSTEMS

An **expert system** is an interactive system that responds to questions, asks for clarification, makes recommendations, and generally helps the user in the decision-making process (see Figure 9-16). In effect, expert systems simulate the human thought process. To varying degrees, they can *reason, draw inferences,* and *make judgments.* Except for the personal interaction, working with an expert system is much like working directly with a human expert to solve a problem. In many ways, expert systems re-create the decision process better than humans do. We tend to miss important considerations or alternatives; expert systems don't.

An expert system applies IF–THEN rules to solve a particular problem, such as determining a patient's illness. An expert system relies on factual knowledge from a database and on *heuristic knowledge* such as intuition, judgment, and inferences. Both the factual knowledge and the heuristic rules of thumb used in an expert system are acquired from one or more real live *domain experts,* human experts in a particular field, such as jet engine repair, life insurance, oceanography, or property assessment. The expert system uses this human-supplied knowledge to

PATTERN RECOGNITION APPLICATIONS

Security is an emerging application for pattern recognition, including fingerprint and facial identification.

FIGURE 9–16   **EXPERT SYSTEMS IN PRACTICE**

EXPERT SYSTEMS IN THE OIL BUSINESS

Phillips Petroleum Company was one of the first companies to create and employ widespread use of expert systems. As many as 75 expert systems have given knowledge workers guidance in the oil refinery (shown here), research and development, administration, and other areas throughout the company.

Photo courtesy of Phillips Petroleum Company

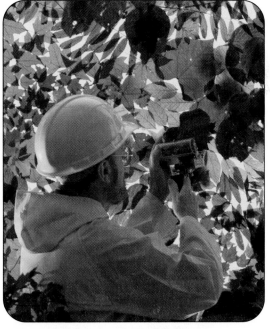

EXPERT SYSTEMS IN ECOSYSTEMS

Here, an Oak Ridge National Laboratory scientist gathers data on the effect of greenhouse gases on a forested ecosystem. The data go into a knowledge base for an expert system that provides insight into how changes in climate affect plant photosynthesis and, by extension, food production.

Courtesy of Lockheed Martin Corporation

model the human thought process within a particular area of expertise. Once completed, an expert system can approximate the logic of a well-informed human decision maker.

Technically speaking, an expert system is the highest form of a **knowledge-based system.** The less sophisticated knowledge-based systems are called **assistant systems.** An assistant system helps users make relatively straightforward decisions. They usually are implemented to reduce the possibility that the end user will make an error in judgment rather than to resolve a particular problem. For example, assistant systems are used to help people make online charge-card approvals and quote rates for life insurance.

Expert System in Practice

Let's use medical diagnosis expert systems, which have proven themselves remarkably accurate, as an example. Upon examining a patient, a physician might use an expert diagnosis system to get help in diagnosing the patient's illness or, perhaps, to get a second opinion. First, the doctor would relate the symptoms to the expert system: male, age 10, temperature of 103°, and swollen glands about the neck. Needing more information, the expert system might ask the doctor to examine the parotid gland for swelling. Upon receiving an affirmative answer, the system might ask a few more questions and even ask for lab reports before giving a diagnosis. A final question for the physician might be whether the patient had been previously afflicted with or immunized for parotitis. Based on the information, the expert system would diagnose the illness as parotitis, otherwise known as mumps. Online medical expert systems are available for consumers, too (see Figure 9-17).

FIGURE 9-17   **MEDICAL EXPERT SYSTEM**

The EasyDiagnosis Web site includes expert systems for a variety of symptoms, such as chest pain (shown here), headache, and lower back pain and for a variety of conditions, including depression and hearing loss. The results, based on interactive questioning, show possible diagnoses with their estimated probability.

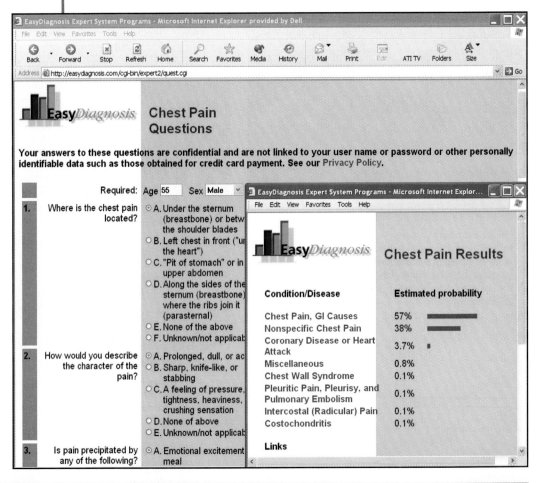

In recent years, expert systems have been developed to support decision makers in a broad range of disciplines, including medical diagnosis, oil exploration, financial planning, tax preparation, chemical analysis, surgery, locomotive repair, weather prediction, computer repair, troubleshooting satellites, computer systems configuration, nuclear power plant operation, newspaper layout, interpreting government regulations, and many others.

Are Expert Systems in Your Future?

The number and variety of expert system applications have increased dramatically in the past decade. Expert systems advise financial analysts on the best mix of investments; help taxpayers interpret the tax laws; help computer repairpersons diagnose the problems of a malfunctioning computer; and help independent insurance agents select the best overall coverage for their clients. Expert systems have operated impressively, and decision makers in every environment are developing or contemplating developing an expert system.

Expert systems augment the capabilities of humans and make them more productive, but they will never replace people. Expert systems and humans complement one another. The computer-based expert system can handle routine situations with great accuracy. However, humans have that ability to combine the insight of an expert system with their flexible intuitive abilities to resolve complex problems.

THE CRYSTAL BALL
Expert System in Your Future

The potential of expert systems is virtually untapped, but the time is ripe for the acceptance of and applications for expert systems to explode. Within a few years, expert systems will be conceived and implemented in every situation that calls for IF–THEN logic and consistent decision making. Expert systems will be a part of our everyday life: They will diagnose our illnesses and advise treatment; they will help us troubleshoot PC problems; they will provide assistance at tax time; they will help us choose a college or an employer; and they will provide counseling to people in need.

NEURAL NETWORKS: WAVE OF THE FUTURE?

Digital computers are great at solving structured problems involving computations and logic operations. However, most of the challenges we face from day to day can't be solved with these capabilities. For example, several times each year we are confronted with this problem: finding a pair of shoes that fits. This is a very human problem, better suited to the workings of the human brain than for digital computers. Such problems involve unstructured input and outcomes that are unclear, so we use the best available processor—our brain. AI scientists are studying the way the human brain works and are attempting to build computers that mimic the incredible human mind. The base technology for these computers is **neural networks.**

The neural network computer employs hundreds, even thousands, of small, interconnected processors, called *processing units.* The neural network functions by creating connections and maintaining relationships between these processing units, the computer equivalent of neurons in the brain. Working within a specific sphere of knowledge (for example, worldwide agriculture strategies), the neural network computer can draw from its human-supplied knowledge base, learn through experience, and make informed decisions in an unstructured environment. Here are just a few of an increasing number of neural network applications: playing chess, improving automobile engine efficiency, enabling improved vision technology, planning crop rotation strategies, and forecasting financial market fluctuations.

The primary difference between traditional digital computers and neural networks is that digital computers process *structured data sequentially* whereas neural networks process *unstructured information simultaneously.* Digital computers will always be able to outperform neural networked computers and the human brain when it comes to fast, accurate numeric computation. However, if neural networks live up to their potential, they will be able to handle tasks that are currently very time consuming or impossible for conventional computers, such as recognizing a face in the crowd.

INTELLIGENT AGENTS AND BOTS

In days of yore, well-to-do people had butlers and maids to do their bidding, day and night (and some still do). A recent innovation in information technology may enable a return to the days of yore—sort of. In cyberland, **intelligent agents** will "live" in our computer systems and assist us with the chores of life, both at home and at work. Intelligent agents, also called **bots** (short for software robots), are a type of artificial intelligence.

Intelligent agents provide information that can help us make decisions, but they do it in a very different way. An intelligent agent has the authority to act on our behalf, just as a human agent does. We set the information or processing goals for our agents, and the agents act to reach those goals. The agent reacts to meet the demands of a specified goal in several different ways.

● The agent may remain in continuous motion working toward an ongoing goal.

● The agent performs an action when a specified event occurs.

● The agent performs actions needed to accomplish a one-time goal.

For example, you might ask an agent to alert you one week prior to birthdays of selected friends and relatives (an ongoing goal). A week before a birthday, the agent will alert you (an action triggered by an event):

Linda's 25th birthday is Monday, June 3. Last year you sent a humorous Internet birthday greeting and two dozen red roses from Higdon Floral.

The agent can then be set up to send an e-mail or postal greeting, send flowers (you specify price range), or arrange a party and send out announcements, whatever you tell it to do. If you wish, you can instruct the agent to purchase and deliver a present to Linda (a one-time goal). The agent's response is based on the information contained in Linda's profile (friends, preferences, and so on).

The number and variety of intelligent agents is growing steadily, especially those focusing on the Internet or intranets. Today, uses for intelligent agents include the following:

● Intelligent agents can sort through e-mail. The agent scans each message and routes junk e-mail to the electronic equivalent of the trash can. E-mail from designated correspondents is given priority treatment (see Figure 9-18).

● Intelligent agents scan online newspapers and magazines for articles in our interest areas (for example, your favorite college basketball team, folk music, environmental issues).

● Intelligent agents, called *shop bots*, can search the Internet for the best price on specified products.

● Intelligent agents can scan the Internet for jobs that meet your criteria and alert you to applicable job openings.

● In a few years, intelligent agents will be helping us do many more jobs.

● A sailor might instruct an intelligent agent to alert her to favorable wind conditions at the local lake. To achieve this goal, the agent must tap weather information on a regular basis.

● We can tell the intelligent agent the type of vacation we want to take, and it will comb through online databases, looking for the best combination of price and luxury. When the bot reports back, we can make our selection, and the bot will make the reservations.

It won't be long before our computers and we are online 24 hours a day to our office, home, college, and the information superhighway. As we evolve to an environment in which we are always online, look for intelligent agents and other artificial intelligence applications to take on an ever-increasing workload. Unlike butlers and maids who have a few days off, intelligent agents never stop working for us.

FIGURE 9-18 **SPAM BOT**

Spam Blocker software is a spam bot that is continually on the lookout for spam and other unwanted e-mail. The spam bot filters e-mail based according to user preferences.

ROBOTS AND ROBOTICS

To date, the area of artificial intelligence having the greatest impact on our society and experiencing the greatest commercial success is robotics. **Robotics** is the field of study that deals with creating **robots,** which are computer-controlled mechanical devices capable of doing human-like tasks with machine-like precision.

R2D2 and the Terminator can do amazing things, but these Hollywood creations are a lifetime away from reality. As you read this section, you will see that today's robots can do amazing things, too, including working tirelessly to make appliances, clothes, automobiles and a thousand other useful products. Most applications of robotics are in manufacturing and the use of *industrial robots*. Industrial robots are quite good at repetitive tasks and tasks that require precision movements, moving heavy loads, and working in hazardous areas. However, robots are emerging as major players not only in manufacturing but also in nonmanufacturing industries, such as health care and other service industries. Already we can give robots crude human sensory capabilities and some degree of artificial intelligence. As these capabilities mature over the next decade, look for robots in other areas of the workplace, in our homes, and even on stage and in museums.

Robotics offers the potential for increased productivity and better service. These benefits have not been overlooked by the manufacturing and service industries. Progressive organizations are rushing to install more and more applications of robotics as a means of staying competitive in the global economy. Industries throughout the world are looking to robots to help them control costs, respond more quickly to market needs, and reduce labor-related costs.

Rudimentary Robotics

The "steel-collar" workforce is made up of hundreds of thousands of industrial robots (see Figure 9-19). The most common industrial robot is a single mechanical arm controlled by a computer. The arm, called a *manipulator,* has a shoulder, forearm, and wrist and is capable of performing the motions of a human arm. The manipulator is fitted with a hand designed to accomplish a specific task, such as painting, welding, picking and placing, and so on.

The automotive industry is the largest user of robots (for painting and welding) and the electronics industry (for circuit testing and connecting chips to circuit boards) is second. General Motors, for example, now has a robot base of over 20,000. Many of these robots perform operations that are difficult or impossible for human workers to perform. For example, robots are used to install sharp windshield glass on cars and trucks. This requires the application of adhesive beads in a precise and uniform manner—something a robot can perform quickly with high repeatability.

Teaching Robots to Do Their Job

A computer program is written to control the robot just as one is written to print payroll checks. It includes such commands as when to reach, in which direction to reach, how far to reach, which tool to use, and when to grasp, weld, paint, and so on. Many robots are programmed to reach to a particular location, find a particular item, and then place it somewhere else. This simple application of robotics is called *pick and place*. Instead of a grasping mechanism, other robots are equipped with a variety of industrial tools such as drills, paint guns, welding torches, and so on. Once programmed, robots do not need much attention. One plant manufactures vacuum cleaners 24 hours a day, 7 days a week!

Robots Come to Their Senses

With the recent innovations in sensor technology, roboticists are outfitting robots with artificial intelligence and human sensory capabilities. A robot with the added dimension of vision can be given some intelligence. Robots without intelligence simply repeat preprogrammed motions. Even though the technology for the vision systems is primitive, a robot can be "taught" to distinguish between dissimilar objects under controlled conditions (see Figure 9-14). With this sensory subsystem, the robot has the capability of making crude but important decisions. For example, a robot equipped with a vision subsystem can dis-

MEMORY BITS

Artificial Intelligence
- Knowledge-based systems
  - Expert system
  - Assistant system
- Simulation of human sensory capabilities
- Neural networks (for unstructured information)
- Intelligent agents (bots)
  - Has the authority to act on our behalf
  - Performs a variety of tasks
- Robots and robotics
  - Stationary robots
  - Mobile robots

FIGURE 9-19 THE STEEL COLLAR WORKFORCE

FLEXING MUSCLES

The typical industrial robot has a manipulator arm with a shoulder, forearm, wrist, and hand that is designed for a specific task. Here, this precision industrial robot tirelessly paints automobiles during manufacturing.

Courtesy of FANUC Robotics North America, Inc.

PICK AND PLACE

Computer-controlled industrial robots help ensure the flow of work during production. Here a robot transfers boxes between conveyors in a pick-and-place application. This robot can handle 45 boxes up to 130 pounds each per minute.

Courtesy of FANUC Robotics North America, Inc.

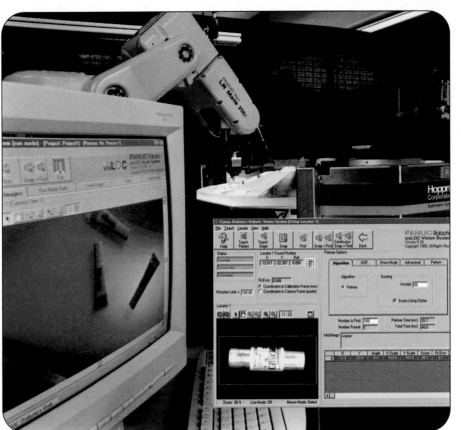

MACHINE VISION

This robotic vision system is used for determining an object's location and orientation. It provides advanced robot guidance capabilities for machine loading/unloading, material handling, packaging, and assembly applications. The robot simplifies the integration of machine vision, as no programming is required to calibrate, train, and run the system (see inset). The system performs visual tasks at a speed and precision unattainable with the human eye.

Courtesy of FANUC Robotics North America, Inc.

FIGURE 9-19 continued

THE ROBOT TEAM

The precise, untiring movement of computer-controlled industrial robots helps assure quality in the assembly of everything from electrical components to automobiles. Here in this DaimlerChrysler Corporation plant, 66 industrial robots apply spot welds. About 300 robots weld, seal, train, paint, clean, and handle material at this plant.

DaimlerChrysler Corporation

tinguish between boxes of differing sizes and shapes as they approach on the conveyor. It can be programmed to place a box of particular dimensions on an adjacent conveyer and let all other boxes pass.

As vision system technology continues to improve, more and more robots will have the ability to move—*navigational capabilities* (see Figure 9-20). Now, most robots are stationary; those that are not can only detect the presence of an object in their path or are programmed to operate within a well-defined work area where the positions of all obstacles are known. Service industries using mobile-robot technology applications include hospitals, security and patrol, commercial floor care, hazardous waste handling, bomb disposal, nuclear plant cleanup, janitorial services, rehabilitation programs, and the military.

Autonomous robots can make functional decisions without being guided or remotely piloted by a human operator. These robots can react intuitively to real-world stimuli by using the developing technology of image pattern recognition, mobility, agility, and perceptual cognition. Military self-guided cruise missiles are able to make automatic navigational adjustments in response to changing conditions while constantly reviewing their onboard flight maps. Other potential applications for

FIGURE 9-20 ROBOTS WITH NAVIGATIONAL CAPABILITIES

ROBOMOW® AT WORK

This dual-mode (automatic and manual) hands-free lawn mower is one smart little robot. Robomow mows in uniformly straight lines to produce a striped, manicured lawn.

Courtesy of Friendly Machines

MOTORING AROUND MARS

The Mars Pathfinder delivered a stationary lander and a surface rover to the Red Planet on July 4, 1997. The rover vehicle, a mobile robot, was manipulated by controllers some 120,000,000 miles away! The six-wheel rover, named Sojourner, explored the area near the lander, testing the soil and sending back pictures of Mars.

Courtesy NASA

MOBILE ROBOTS CAN DELIVER

The 575-pound trackless robotic courier is designed to perform material transport tasks for health-care facilities. It can deliver mail, medication, supplies, and meal trays to the nursing units throughout the hospital. Vision and ultrasonic proximity sensors are used to understand the environment and avoid obstacles. It can even use the elevator!

Courtesy of HelpMate Robotics, Inc.

autonomous robots, especially in situations where human workers would be exposed to great risk, include deep underwater exploration (robots helped in the exploration of the *Titanic*), interior surveillance of nuclear reactors (robots helped clean up after the Chernobyl nuclear incident), and surface navigation of other planets (the Sojourner robot scooted around Mars gathering data).

Opportunities for Robots Are Growing

Each day, engineers and entrepreneurs find new ways to use robots (see Figure 9-21). Even surgeons are using robots to help in brain surgery. Robots can be set up to manipulate the surgical drill and biopsy needle with great accuracy, thereby making brain surgery faster,

FIGURE 9–21   INNOVATIVE ROBOTICS APPLICATIONS

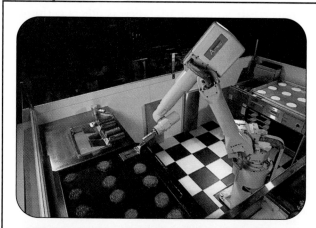

FLIPPER THE ROBOT

"Flipper," a typical industrial robot, was programmed to prepare hamburgers and pancakes on two griddles simultaneously. This hamburger-flipping robot was designed originally as a promotional gimmick, but restaurateurs have been so impressed with the speed at which it makes consistently perfect hamburgers and pancakes that we may someday see Flipper in commercial kitchens.

Courtesy of AccuTemp Products, Inc.

FULL-SERVICE SERVICE STATIONS

Shell Oil Company's automated SMART Pump may give us a glimpse at the future of artificial intelligence-based robotics and information systems. The SMART pump being tested at a site in Sacramento, California, will offer consumers the ability to refuel their car without leaving the driver's seat. All transactions are recorded automatically, as well.

Courtesy of Shell Oil Company

AIBO ENTERTAINMENT ROBOT

AIBO is an entertainment robot. AIBO, which means "pal" in Japanese, has 20 motors that enable it to walk, play soccer, sit, lie down, and right itself. AIBO uses its eyes, tail, ears, and lights to express a wide variety of emotions. With its Wireless LAN capability, you can communicate with it and control it from remote locations.

Courtesy of Sony Electronic, Inc.

more accurate, and safer. Other surgical applications of robotics include help with hip replacements, knee replacements, and pelvic and spinal surgeries.

Autonomous kinetic sculpture is a new class of robotics and is found in art galleries and in the performing arts. Some robots create works of art, whereas others perform by themselves or with humans. How a performance or robotic sculpture will turn out is often unique because the robots are designed to react in real-time situations and adapt to their environment through their own creative behaviors.

The future of robotics offers exciting opportunities in manufacturing, health care, art, and many other areas of endeavor. Who knows, we may someday have robots as helpers around the home and as workmates at the office.

1 Artificial intelligence refers to an area of research that trains humans to have computer-like capabilities. (T/F)

2 An assistant system is the highest form of a knowledge-based system. (T/F)

3 Intelligent agent software has the authority to act on our behalf. (T/F)

4 Pattern recognition systems are best suited to generalized tasks in which a wide variety of images will be encountered. (T/F)

5 Which of these is not a part of a manipulator on an industrial robot: (a) arm, (b) forearm, (c) knuckle, or (d) wrist?

6 Neural networks process unstructured information: (a) intermittently, (b) sequentially, (c) simultaneously, or (d) as time permits.

9-6   VIRTUAL REALITY

Why this section is important to you.

With increasing frequency, people are entering virtual worlds that simulate the real world. It's important that you understand virtual reality concepts so you are aware of how this amazing technology is expanding our options in life.

Imagine that your job is to monitor the operation of a vast telecommunications network. Cables snake underground and underwater. Data flow between communications satellites and Earth and across wiring inside building walls. Now imagine that a graphic image of this vast grid and its data flows could be laid out below you, as you float above, an "infonaut" looking for the kink that is blocking service to millions of customers. Far below, you see a pulsing light. There's the problem. With a gestured command, you fix it—without leaving your office. That's the promise of virtual reality, and it's moving from computer fantasy to computer fact. In fact, telecommunications firms are already experimenting with such systems.

Virtual reality (VR) combines computer graphics with special hardware to immerse users in an artificial three-dimensional world, sometimes called a **virtual world.** Instead of passively viewing data or graphics on a screen, users can move about, handle "virtual" representations of data and objects, and get visual, aural, and tactile feedback. The audio, visual, and other stimuli for the virtual world vary, depending on what you do. In the world of computers, the term *virtual* refers to an environment that is *simulated by hardware and software* (for example, virtual memory, virtual department store).

In contrast to AI, which is best at leading users to a solution through exploration and discovery, VR is a visualization tool that lets users actually see and comprehend complex relationships. Often, artificial intelligence techniques are used in concert with virtual reality to create an *intelligent environment.*

VR Applications

Virtual reality was born in the late 1960s when the U.S. Air Force began experimenting with flight simulators. From there, NASA picked up the technology. Today, NASA and a number of universities and corporations are either developing or using virtual reality systems for a variety of applications (see Figure 9-22).

- *Tele-immersion.* **Tele-immersion** is a VR concept that enables people in remote locations to interact with one another as if they were sharing the same space. This approach is different from conventional teleconferencing in that the user's view of the remote location changes depending upon where the person is looking.

FIGURE 9–22 VIRTUAL REALITY IN OUR LIVES

FLIGHT SIMULATORS

This pilot is training in a flight simulator, one of the more mature applications of virtual reality. In the simulator, a pilot can be exposed to many challenging flying situations in a relatively short period of time.

DESIGNING AUTOMOBILES

For this engineer, showing up for work can be as much fun as going to the video arcade. But she's not playing games. She is experimenting with the use of virtual reality to help design cars for the future. This engineer wears a helmet and goggles equipped with two small screens (see inset of the 3D image). A special glove fitted with sensors covers her right hand and allows her to manipulate objects during the design process.

Courtesy of Ford Motor Company

THRILLS WITHOUT SPILLS

Virtual reality enables this hang glider to fly among the skyscrapers of Los Angeles. Virtual hang gliders ride in an actual hang glider harness positioned in front of a box that contains an image generator displaying pictures of a futuristic Los Angeles.

Courtesy of Evans and Sutherland Computer Corporation

FIGURE 9–22 continued

3-D IMAGES THAT INCLUDE YOU

Virtual reality may be the ultimate multimedia experience. The virtual reality (VR) theater at Iowa State University lets you interact with 3D images, including a tornado. The VR theater presents computer-generated images on the walls, floor, and ceiling, and the view changes based on the viewer's perspective.

Courtesy of Iowa State University Photo Service

Researchers tell us that someday tele-immersion will let us literally walk into electronic books and movies such that we become part of the scene.

- *Architecture and computer-aided design.* Architects already have access to a number of commercial VR systems that let them conduct electronic "walkthroughs" of proposed buildings.

- *Visualization of data.* NASA has created a virtual wind tunnel that lets a user climb inside an airstream. By gesturing with a data glove, the user can change the airflow and then walk around to experience it from different angles.

- *Exploration of hostile environments.* NASA is using raw data to create a VR version of an Antarctic lake bottom that will let researchers study life forms beneath the frigid waters without risk.

- *Sales.* A Japanese department store uses a "virtual kitchen" for planning custom-designed remodeling projects. After store personnel input a kitchen's existing layout and measurements using CAD software, customers don the VR gear and play around with different appliances, open drawers, turn on faucets, and visualize different arrangements.

- *Exercise.* Exercise bikes and massage chairs are finding a place in the virtual world. With the new lighter headgear, you can add adventure to your exercise as you cycle through virtual towns.

- *Training.* Flight training is one of the most sophisticated and oldest applications of VR. This virtual world is almost as realistic as the real world. Pilots can take the controls of a fully loaded passenger plane for their first flight because of the training they received in the simulator. It's only a matter of time before high school drivers' training classes will be conducted in virtual reality.

- *Education.* The learning experience through VR is truly active (versus passive). It allows students to experience first hand such things as life in a medieval village or walking among dinosaurs.

- *Psychology.* A California psychologist is experimenting with VR therapy for acrophobics (those who fear heights). Wearing a VR headset, a patient walks a plank, crosses a bridge, which spans water and hills, and accomplishes other acts that would instill fear. Over 90% of the patients now feel confident enough to climb ladders and cross the Golden Gate Bridge.

- *Virtual weddings.* A bride and groom can join their minister in a virtual world and say their vows amid a virtual re-creation of a significant historical venue, such as the lost city of Atlantis with its palaces, chariots, carousels, and even doves.

Dressing for Cyberspace

To enter the virtual world, users don special hardware for the feeling of total immersion in a three-dimensional world (see Figure 9-22).

- *Headpiece.* The goggles-like head-mounted display (HMD) blocks out visual sensations from the real world and substitutes images presented on *two small video screens*—one for each eye, creating a three-dimensional effect. The headpiece also contains *motion,* or *balance, sensors*—move your head and the computer will shift the view presented on the video screens. Just flip up the visor on your headpiece to see what is going on in the real world. Or, flip it down to enter the virtual world.

- *Headphones.* Headphones block out room noise and substitute three-dimensional *holophononic* sounds. Generally, the headphones are built into the helmet.

- *Data glove.* A data glove outlined with fiber optic sensors and cables completes the ensemble. The glove can be used, like a floating mouse, to "gesture" a command or to grasp and move virtual objects about.

Each piece of hardware is tethered to a computer via wireless or cable links to record the user's movements and provide real-time feedback.

The Future of VR

Virtual reality is still in its infancy, but the breadth and success of existing VR applications have shown us that VR will play an important role in the future. Although some VR applications can be run on PCs, the most realistic experiences are created with complex and expensive computer systems. However, with hardware costs decreasing and software sophistication increasing, virtual reality may emerge as the user interface of the future.

1 Tele-immersion is a virtual reality concept. (T/F)

2 Typical VR hardware includes all but which of the following: (a) information vest, (b) data glove, (c) headpiece, or (d) headphones?

3 What is the VR concept that enables people in remote locations to interact with one another: (a) teleconferencing, (b) tele-immersion, (c) virtual interaction, or (d) fantasy-talk?

Chapter Review

CHAPTER SUMMARY

9-1 LEVERAGING INFORMATION TECHNOLOGY AS A COMPETITIVE STRATEGY

New and innovative uses of information technology are being implemented every day. Each company has a seemingly endless number of opportunities to use technology to achieve a competitive edge. Money spent on information technology yields tremendous returns.

The increased competition of the world market is pressuring corporate managers and knowledge workers into leveraging computer and information technology to gain a competitive advantage. IT technology can be leveraged to increase sales, increase productivity, reduce cost, and improve customer service.

9-2 ALL ABOUT INFORMATION AND DECISION MAKING

Information is only as good as the data from which it is derived ("garbage in, garbage out," or GIGO). The quality of information can be described in terms of its accuracy, verifiability, completeness, timeliness, relevance, and accessibility.

Traditionally, managers and knowledge workers have been adept at taking full advantage of the resources of money, materials, and people, but only recently have they begun to make effective use of information. By filtering information, the right information reaches the right decision maker at the right time in the right form.

Information systems help process data at the clerical level and provide information for managerial decision making at the operational, tactical, and strategic levels. Managers at the operational, tactical, and strategic levels often request exception reports that highlight critical information.

The two basic types of decisions are programmed decisions and information-based decisions. Purely programmed decisions address well-defined problems. Information-based decisions involve ill-defined and unstructured problems.

9-3 ALL ABOUT INFORMATION SYSTEMS

A system is any group of components that interface with and complement one another to achieve one or more predefined goals. An information system provides companies with data processing capabilities and the company's people with information. Hardware, software, procedures, and communications combine people and data to create an information system

An information system has the same four capabilities as a computer system: input, processing, storage, and output. The processing capabilities include sorting; retrieving, recording, and updating data in storage; summarizing; selecting; and manipulating.

Source data on source documents must be transcribed into a machine-readable format before a computer can interpret them. Data entry describes the process of entering data into an information system.

When transactions are grouped together for processing, it is called batch processing. In online transaction processing (OLTP), transactions are entered as they occur.

Data processing (DP) systems are flat file systems that focus on transaction handling and record keeping and provide periodic output aimed primarily at operational-level management.

A management information system, or MIS, is a computer-based system that optimizes the collection, transfer, and presentation of information throughout an organization by using an integrated structure of databases and information flow. An MIS not only supports the traditional data processing functions but also relies on an integrated database to provide managers at all levels with easy access to timely but structured information.

9-4 THE DECISION SUPPORT SYSTEM AND THE EXECUTIVE INFORMATION SYSTEM

Decision support systems are interactive information systems that rely on an integrated set of user-friendly hardware and software tools to produce and present information targeted to support management in the decision-making process.

A DSS supports decision making at all levels by making general-purpose models, simulation capabilities, and other analytical tools available to the decision maker. In contrast to the MIS, decision support systems are designed to support decision-making processes involving semistructured and unstructured problems.

The categories of DSS tools include applications development (frequently resulting in throwaway systems), data management, modeling, statistical analysis, planning, inquiry, graphics, consolidations, and application-specific DSS capabilities.

The executive information system (EIS) is designed specifically to support decision making at the tactical and strategic levels of management.

9-5 ARTIFICIAL INTELLIGENCE

Artificial intelligence (AI) is an area of research concerned with giving computer systems an ability to reason, to learn or accumulate knowledge, to strive for self-improvement, and to simulate human sensory and mechanical capabilities. To varying degrees, hearing, speaking, smelling, feeling, and seeing are possible with current AI technology. Expert systems, an area of AI, help managers resolve problems and make better decisions. These interactive systems respond to questions, ask for clarification, make recommendations, and generally help in the decision-making process. An expert system is the highest form of a knowledge-based system, but in practice, the two terms are used interchangeably. The less sophisticated knowledge-based systems are called assistant systems.

Neural networks mimic the way the human brain works. The neural network computer uses many small, interconnected processors to address problems that involve unstructured information.

Intelligent agents have the authority to act on our behalf, just as human agents do. We set the goals for our intelligent agents, also called bots, and they act to reach those goals.

The area of artificial intelligence having the greatest impact on our society is robotics, the field of study that deals with creating robots. Most applications of robotics are in manufacturing and the use of industrial robots. Industrial robots are quite good at repetitive tasks and tasks that require precision movements, moving heavy loads, and working in hazardous areas.

The most common industrial robot has a single mechanical arm, called a manipulator, which can be fitted with a variety of hands for painting, welding, and so on. Roboticists are outfitting robots with artificial intelligence and human sensory capabilities, such as vision, that enable them to simulate human behavior. Some robots have navigational capabilities.

9-6 VIRTUAL REALITY

Virtual reality (VR) combines computer graphics with special hardware to immerse users in an artificial three-dimensional world, sometimes called a virtual world. In IT parlance, the term "virtual" refers to an environment that is simulated by hardware and software. To enter the three-dimensional virtual world, users don special hardware, including a headpiece, headphones, and a data glove.

KEY TERMS

artificial intelligence (AI) (p. 377)
artificial life (ALife) (p. 378)
assistant system (p. 380)
batch processing (p. 372)
data entry (p. 371)
data processing system (DP system) (p. 372)
decision support system (DSS) (p. 375)
exception report (p. 368)
executive information system (EIS) (p. 377)

expert system (p. 379)
filter (p. 367)
GIGO (p. 365)
information system (p. 370)
information-based decision (p. 369)
intelligent agent (bot) (p. 381, 382)
knowledge-based system (p. 380)
management information system (MIS) (p. 373)
neural network (p. 381)
online transaction processing (OLTP) (p. 372)

pattern recognition system (p. 378)
programmed decision (p. 369)
prompt (p. 372)
robot (p. 383)
robotics (p. 383)
source data (p. 371)
source document (p. 371)
system (p. 370)
tele-immersion (p. 388)
virtual reality (VR) (p. 388)
virtual world (p. 388)

MATCHING

1. decision support system
2. robotics
3. artificial life
4. exception report
5. filtering
6. expert system
7. GIGO
8. programmed decision
9. VR
10. intelligent agent

a highlights critical information
b ALife
c has the authority to act on our behalf
d the right information at the right time
e artificial three-dimensional world
f relies on heuristic knowledge
g garbage in, garbage out
h analytical tools for managers
i addresses well-defined problems
j industrial robots

TRUE/FALSE

1. The traditional shotgun approach to creating new business is still more effective than IT-based targeting. (T/F)

2. Money spent on information technology yields positive returns. (T/F)

3. It is easier for a manager to detect trends presented in a tabular format than in a graphic format. (T/F)

4. Exception reports highlight critical information. (T/F)

5. Source data result from the recording of a transaction or an event. (T/F)

6. An MIS is a subset of an EIS. (T/F)

7. Industrial robots excel at repetitive tasks. (T/F)

MULTIPLE CHOICE

1. Which of these would not be considered a quality of information: (a) verifiability, (b) relevance, (c) weight, or (d) timeliness?

2. Common corporate resources would include all but which of the following: (a) prestige, (b) money, (c) materials, or (d) information?

3. A CD-ROM sitting on a shelf is said to be: (a) offline, (b) online, (c) system-oriented, or (d) sealed.

4. Which of these is not an information system processing capability: (a) selecting, (b) manipulating, (c) soft copying, or (d) sorting?

5. The focus of data processing systems is: (a) transaction handling only, (b) record keeping only, (c) transaction handling and record keeping, or (d) strategic reporting.

6. Which of these is not a characteristic of an MIS: (a) is flexible, (b) provides security, (c) uses an integrated database, or (d) does not support transaction handling?

7. DSS applications that are discarded after providing information support for a one-time decision are called: (a) throwaway systems, (b) toss-out programs, (c) junk systems, or (d) legacy systems.

8. Which type of information system has the greatest potential to reduce dependencies on critical personnel: (a) MIS, (b) expert system, (c) DP system, or (d) EIS?

9. An intelligent agent reacts to meet the demands of a: (a) working relationship, (b) personal wish, (c) system intention, or (d) specified goal.

10. Intelligent agents fall under which of these software umbrellas: (a) operating systems, (b) IT, (c) artificial intelligence, or (d) data management?

11. The base technology for computers that mimic the human mind is called: (a) HAL, (b) neural network, (c) human brain focus, or (d) interconnected processing.

12. The application where robots find a particular item and then place it somewhere else is called: (a) select and set, (b) move and put, (c) choose and locate, or (d) pick and place.

13. Industrial robots are equipped with a variety of industrial tools that include all of these except: (a) drills, (b) paint guns, (c) welding torches, or (d) pagers.

14. An artificial environment made possible by hardware and software is known as: (a) virtual planet, (b) near reality, (c) virtual reality, or (d) cyberrealism.

IT ETHICS AND ISSUES

1. E-COMMERCE AND PROFILING

Many companies involved in e-commerce build and maintain user profiles so they can use their information systems to better target their marketing efforts. They gather information about you through your interaction with their site and, often, from other sources. A recent report concluded that profiling is becoming more extensive and marketing techniques are becoming more intrusive. Most major Web sites post their "Privacy Policy" but if you read it closely, it doesn't necessarily mean that your personal information is safe; it just means that they have a policy.

Discussion: Enter "privacy policy" on any search engine to find sites with written privacy policies. Read one of these policies in detail. Evaluate the policy relative to what you perceive to be good policy regarding the privacy of personal information.

Discussion: Generally, these privacy policy statements place no limit on the amount of information that can be gathered and maintained on you or anyone else. Should there be limitations? If so, describe these limitations.

Discussion: Some sites gather and sell information about you. If you have surfed pornography sites, done some online gambling, spent time at the Alcoholics Anonymous site, or requested information on HIV, then that interest may have been added to someone's profile on you. Someone might even sell that information to others. Discuss the ethical considerations of selling personal information gathered over the Internet.

Discussion: The potential exists for profiles to be leaked or subpoenaed for custody or divorce cases, employment decisions, insurance coverage, and so on. Is this ethical? If not, what can be done about it?

2. DOES THE INTERNET REALLY CHANGE EVERYTHING?

It has been said many times in the media, the home, and in small group conversations at work that "the Internet changes everything." To be sure, it has changed the way we communicate with one another. Internet-based information systems are changing the way we plan vacations and the way we buy and sell merchandise. It is emerging as the source of preference for news and other information for the majority of Americans.

Discussion: The Internet has changed much of what we do, but is it an exaggeration to say "the Internet has changed everything"? If so, what is unaffected by the Internet? If there are elements of our society untouched by the Internet, will they remain so in the future?

Discussion: Are we developing a healthy or unhealthy dependency on the Internet? Explain.

DISCUSSION AND PROBLEM SOLVING

1. What is meant when someone says that a company is on the bleeding edge of technology?

2. What is the major difference between improving profitability through traditional approaches and through those that involve computer and information technology?

3. Describe IT strategies that any specific federal agency or body (FBI, CIA, the Senate, IRS, White House, and so on) could employ to reduce the burden on the taxpayer and/or provide better service.

4. Describe IT strategies that universities could employ to achieve a competitive advantage in their efforts to attract the better students.

5. The insurance company featured Figure 9-2 has no field insurance agents, yet it is ranked consistently at or near the top of all insurance companies in customer satisfaction. How can this be?

6. It is often said that "time is money." Would you say that "information is money"? Discuss.

7. In general, top executives have always treated money, materials, and people as valuable resources, but only in the last decade have they recognized that information is also a valuable resource. Why do you think they waited so long?

8. Pick a type of business (for example, automobile manufacturing, hotels, or city government) and give an example of how information may be filtered for use by management.

9. Select an article in the newspaper on a current event and evaluate the information relative to its accuracy, verifiability, completeness, timeliness, relevance, and accessibility.

10. For each of the three levels of management illustrated in the business system model in Figure 9-4, what would the horizon (time span) be for planning decisions? Explain.

11. Give examples within the context of a corporate information system for these information system processing capabilities: retrieving, summarizing, and manipulating.

12. Reflect on your activities of the past week and identify those activities that generated source data for information systems.

13. Describe transactions that might be processed by an insurance company's MIS.

14. Describe reports that might be requested by an operational-level manager at a large bank. By a tactical-level manager. By a strategic-level manager.

15. Suppose the company you work for batches all sales data for data entry each night. You have been asked to present a convincing argument to top management about why funds should be allocated to convert the current system to an MIS with OLTP data entry. What would you say?

16. Give examples of what-if inquiries that the mayor of a large city might make to a DSS.

17. The IT community regularly introduces buzzwords, especially for tools designed to provide information for management. Frequently, these terms are not clearly defined when introduced (for example, DSS and EIS). Would having definitions that are more concrete help or hinder IT progress? Explain.

18. Describe at least three ways in which artificial intelligence applications can help disabled persons cope with the routine of everyday living.

19. AI researchers have spent more time creating a chess-playing computer than on any other project. Why?

20. To varying degrees, computers can see, hear, speak, feel, and smell. Some people think we should continue to pursue this area of AI research with vigor. Some feel that machines should not be given human qualities. Where do you stand and why?

21. Describe a specific decision environment that would be appropriate for the implementation of an expert system. An assistant system.

22. Compare today's pattern recognition systems with the vision capability portrayed in such films as 2001 and 2010. Do you believe we will have a comparable vision technology by the year 2010?

23. Give an example of how an intelligent agent might be able to help you at home. At work.

24. Industrial robots are performing tasks formerly done by hundreds of thousands of human beings. Should something be done to curtail this worldwide loss of jobs? Explain.

25. Robots with navigational capabilities are used routinely in health care and warehousing. In what other industry do you envision the use of mobile robots? What will they be doing?

26. Virtual reality enables us to roam around an artificial world. Discuss the upside and the downside of VR.

27. Speculate on possible applications for virtual reality in education. In retail. In the government.

FOCUS ON PERSONAL COMPUTING

1. *Exploring Information Systems.* A decade ago, the only people interacting with information systems were knowledge workers logged on to their company's computer network. Today, individuals (customers, citizens, and so on) have access to a variety of Internet-based information systems. Go online, and then seek out and explore at least one such system (for example, the student system at your college, the state license tag renewal system, an employee system, an employment system, and so on). You may need to become a registered user. Describe your experience.

2. *Using Bots.* The Internet is filled with intelligent agents—bots. Enter "intelligent agents" or "Bots" into any search engine. You will find search bots, shopping bots, stock bots, chatterbots, weather bots, and many more. Select one of interest that offers a free program or a demo program. Experiment with it and describe your experience.

ONLINE EXERCISES @ www.prenhall.com/long

1. The Online Study Guide (multiple choice, true/false, matching, and essay questions)

2. Internet Learning Activities
   - Internet Issues MIS/DSS/EIS
   - Artificial Intelligence
   - Virtual Reality

3. Serendipitous Internet Activities
   - Distance Learning

INFORMATION SYSTEMS DEVELOPMENT AND PROGRAMMING

10

CHAPTER

LEARNING OBJECTIVES

Once you have read and studied this chapter, you will be able to:

- Describe the four stages of the system life cycle (Section 10-1).

- List the basic system development techniques and the concepts associated with these techniques (Section 10-2).

- Understand the scope and capabilities of CASE (Computer-Aided Software Engineering) tools (Section 10-3).

- Explain the concepts and phases of prototyping, including the general activities that take place during system analysis and design (Section 10-4).

- Discuss approaches to converting an existing information system to a new one (Section 10-5).

- Describe basic programming concepts and techniques, as well as the types of programming languages (Section 10-6).

Everywhere we go, we run into an information system—at the point-of-sale terminal in a department store, when making an online airline reservation, or while enrolling at college. But information systems don't just happen. They might be purchased, leased, or developed from scratch. In any case, those who will use the system frequently are involved in the development and/or implementation process. If you are part of the system, and there is a good chance you will be, it is to your advantage to provide input into the development process. Ultimately, the quality of an information system depends on the input and ongoing feedback from you and other users. Too often, life at work is a joy or a pain depending on the quality and effectiveness of the information system being used.

Information systems are ever changing, and must be constantly upgraded to meet the changing information and processing needs of your organization. It is likely that you will be part of this dynamic process, either as a knowledge worker or an IT professional. Knowledge workers are users of information systems and it is their responsibility to provide input into the system design process and ongoing feedback on system effectiveness. IT professionals are intimately involved with every aspect of system development, including analysis, design, programming, and implementation. This chapter acquaints you with the system life cycle, giving you the background you need to be an effective contributor to any system development project.

10-1 THE SYSTEM LIFE CYCLE

Why this section is important to you.

There is a very good chance that you, as a knowledge worker, will provide feedback to or be directly involved in the information systems development process. Knowing the stages of the system life cycle and related software options will help you to make better decisions regarding the development of information systems.

During the early years of automation, information systems were built to handle the basic flow of information within an organization: general accounting data and reports, inventory management, and human resource applications. Typically, these systems were custom built by in-house IT employees to meet specific organization needs. Most were batch systems where transactions were accumulated or batched prior to processing. Data entry, reporting, and computation were done in or near a central computer center.

After a couple of decades in this mode, technology specialists began to seek out ways to improve existing information systems. First, they integrated separate function-based information systems via an enterprise-wide database, thus eliminating many system redundancies. Second, they began to incorporate wide area and local area networks into system design, thus moving information processing activities closer to the action (for example, into the accounting office or on the shop floor).

Today, corporate executives, users, and IT specialists are continually seeking new ways to employ technology to improve productivity and product quality. For example, throughout most of the twentieth century, trucking companies knew when their trucks departed and arrived only if the driver telephoned the dispatcher. Today, modern trucking companies use global positioning systems (GPS) to track trucks wherever they go. This GPS information system constantly feeds dispatchers the exact geographic location (and speed) of company trucks. This and all other information systems have a well-defined system life cycle.

STAGES OF THE SYSTEM LIFE CYCLE

Information systems, like human beings, have life cycles. Information systems are born from an idea and grow to become ready-to-use systems, complete with hardware, software, communications capabilities, procedures, and data. Once operational, information systems contribute to organizations by processing data, providing information, or providing Internet-based services. As in life, information systems grow old and pass on. This life cycle for information systems is called the **system life cycle**. The four stages of this life cycle (birth, development, production, and end-of-life) are illustrated in Figure 10-1. The emphasis in this chapter is on the *development stage* of the life cycle.

- *Birth stage.* In the birth stage of the system life cycle, someone has an idea about how the computer can help provide better and timelier information.
- *Development stage.* The idea becomes a reality during the development stage of the system life cycle. In this stage, IT professionals and users work together to analyze an organization's information processing needs and design an information system. Then, the design specifications are translated into programs and the system is implemented.
- *Production stage.* Upon implementation, the information system enters the production stage and becomes operational, serving the information needs of an organization. This stage normally will last from four to seven years. During this stage, an information system is continuously modified to keep up with the changing needs of the organization.
- *End-of-life stage.* The accumulation of system modifications to a dynamic information system eventually takes its toll on system efficiency. The end-of-life stage arrives when an information system becomes so cumbersome to maintain that it is no longer economically or operationally effective. At this time, it is discarded and the system life cycle is repeated.

INFORMATION SYSTEM DEVELOPMENT OPTIONS

An organization can progress through the development stage of the system life cycle in three basic ways. Organizations can *buy, rent,* or *make* an information system.

Purchase an Information System

An organization can purchase and install a proprietary software package. A **proprietary information system** is developed by a vendor to sell to a specific audience, perhaps large universities. The proprietary information system industry thrives because similar types of

---

| FIGURE 10-1 | THE SYSTEM LIFE CYCLE |

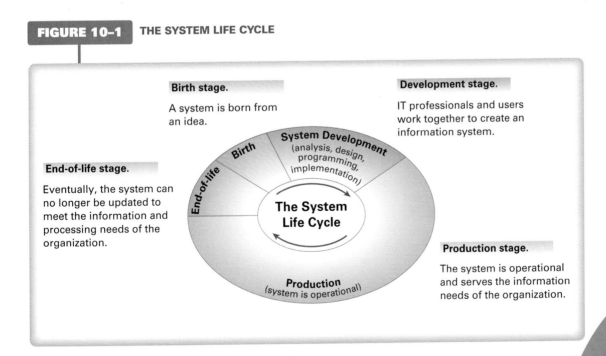

Birth stage.

A system is born from an idea.

Development stage.

IT professionals and users work together to create an information system.

End-of-life stage.

Eventually, the system can no longer be updated to meet the information and processing needs of the organization.

System Development
(analysis, design, programming, implementation)

Birth

End-of-life

The System Life Cycle

Production
(system is operational)

Production stage.

The system is operational and serves the information needs of the organization.

organizations have similar information processing needs. Software vendors have created thousands of proprietary information systems that can fit in millions of organizations, from billing systems for veterinarians to general-ledger accounting systems for billion-dollar multinational companies. There are proprietary systems to handle the processing and information needs for small public accounting firms, for Rotary clubs, for small and large cities, for banks, for dermatology clinics, for department stores, for Boy Scout troops, and for hundreds of other types of organizations.

Outsourcing to an Application Service Provider

There is a growing trend to outsource support for all or part of an organization's information services needs to an **applications service provider (ASP)**. An ASP is a company that provides software-based services and solutions from a central server computer to customers through either a wide area network (WAN) or the Internet (see Figure 10-2). Companies pay the third-party ASP to use its applications software, server computer, and storage capabilities. By "renting" a system from an ASP, a company can have information systems without having to maintain hardware, software, or an in-house staff. ASPs are thriving because they help organizations overcome some of today's serious challenges, such as hiring and retaining qualified information technology professionals. Another challenge is the need to continually upgrade personnel skills, software, and hardware to keep pace with the technology.

Although ASPs are frequently thought of as solutions for small to medium-sized businesses that might not be able to afford the full range of information technology services, ASPs are beginning to provide enterprise-wide systems for large companies as well. For example, many large school districts are opting to use ASP services via the Internet. ASPs offer a full range of information services to a growing number of organization types, including health care, manufacturing, universities, state governments, and many others.

The downside of outsourcing IT development and/or systems to an ASP is that an organization becomes dependent on the expertise, experience, and services of an ASP. Organizations that outsource to an ASP accept reduced control of IT activities and, generally, have less flexibility to respond to their changing information technology needs.

FIGURE 10-2   APPLICATIONS SOFTWARE DEVELOPMENT OPTIONS

APPLICATIONS SERVICE PROVIDER

This ASP partners with customers to provide systems integration, IT training and outsourcing services to clients, including data center operations.

Courtesy of Lockheed Martin Corporation

CUSTOM INFORMATION SYSTEM

Hertz's Instant Return information system was developed in-house by Hertz and offers credit card customers a speedy return service. Using handheld computer with a wireless link to a server, a Hertz representative processes a return and issues an itemized receipt for the rental in under a minute.

©2000 Hertz System, Inc. Hertz is a registered service mark and trademark of Hertz Systems, Inc.

Develop a Custom Information System

Most organizations employ IT professionals who can develop custom information systems, sometimes referred to simply as *applications*. The various careers for IT professionals and their responsibilities in system development are described in the Appendix, "Information Technology and Careers." Often outside consultants are retained to augment the in-house IT staff during development projects. In some cases, the entire project is outsourced to a consulting firm that delivers a **turnkey system;** that is, a system that is created and implemented, ready to use, by outside consultants. As a rule of thumb, organizations choose custom development when the operational characteristics of the proposed system are unique to that particular organization (see Figure 10-2). In these cases, there is no proprietary software available for the task anyway.

These three options pose the classic "make-versus-buy" decision. Managers acknowledge that each approach has its pros and cons. Given the choice, corporate management typically will opt for proprietary software or an ASP over in-house development. The best *application portfolios* (an organization's applications software) contain an optimal mix of these.

1   The best corporate application portfolios contain only proprietary software packages. (T/F)

2   The information system becomes operational in the birth stage of the system life cycle. (T/F)

3   Systems are implemented during which stage of the information system life cycle: (a) birth, (b) development, (c) production, or (d) end-of-life?

10-2 SYSTEM DEVELOPMENT TECHNIQUES AND CONCEPTS

There is no one best analytical technique. In fact, there are dozens of system development and design techniques. The techniques, however, are just tools. It's your understanding of these techniques, in combination with your skill and imagination, that will enable you to help make an information system or program a reality.

Before we launch into discussions on approaches to applications development, we need to discuss several common development techniques, including *structured system design*, *data flow diagrams*, and *entity relationship diagrams*.

> **Why this section is important to you.**
>
> System development is an ongoing part of a knowledge worker's life, as systems you might use are continuously being created and updated. Part of the development process demands that you, the user, provide input to and feedback on the system design.

STRUCTURED SYSTEM DESIGN

Information systems, even small ones, can be complex to analyze, design, and implement. It is easier to address the design of a complex information system in small, manageable modules than as one big task. For these reasons, information systems are designed using the principles of **structured system design.** The structured approach to system design encourages the top-down design technique. That is, the project team divides the system into independent modules for ease of understanding and design. The **structure chart** in Figure 10-3 illustrates how a payroll system can be conceptualized as a hierarchy of modules. Eventually the logic for the modules is represented in detail in step-by-step diagrams that illustrate the interactions among input, processing, output, and storage activities for a particular module.

DATA FLOW DIAGRAMS

Data flow diagrams enable systems analysts to design and document systems using the structured approach to system development. Only four symbols are needed for data flow diagrams: entity, process, flow line, and data storage. The symbols are identified in Figure 10-4 and their use is illustrated in Figure 10-5.

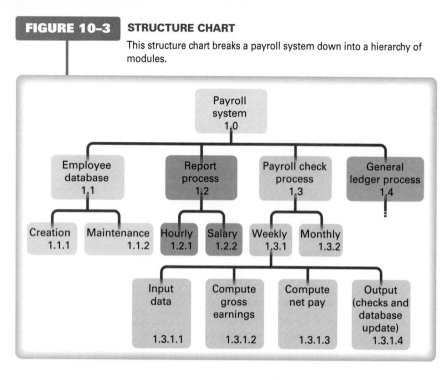

FIGURE 10-3 | STRUCTURE CHART

This structure chart breaks a payroll system down into a hierarchy of modules.

- *Entity symbol.* The entity symbol is the source or destination of data or information flow. An entity can be a person, a group of people (for example, customers or employees), a department, or even a place (such as a warehouse).

- *Process symbol.* Each process symbol contains a description of a function to be performed. Process symbols can also be depicted as circles. Typical processes include enter data, calculate, store, create, produce, and verify. Process-symbol identification numbers are assigned in levels (for example, Processes 1.1 and 1.2 are subordinate to Process 1).

- *Flow line.* The flow lines indicate the flow and direction of data or information.

- *Data storage.* Data storage symbols identify storage locations for data, which could be a file drawer, a shelf, a database or file on magnetic disk, and so on.

The data flow diagram shown in Figure 10-5 is for an enterprise-wide MIS at BrassCo, a manufacturing company with about 1,200 employees at its corporate headquarters and four plant sites. The data flow diagram in Figure 10-5 provides an overview of BrassCo's MIS, showing information flow between its functional components and the integrated database. The functional components of BrassCo's MIS are

Process 1   Finance and Accounting

Process 2   Human Resources

Process 3   Operations

Process 4   Sales and Marketing

All the MIS component systems share a common database. Any company that manufactures and sells products would have a similar overview data flow diagram, because all companies, whether large or small, have these four fundamental processes.

In Figure 10-6, the Human Resources Process (2) of the BrassCo MIS (Figure 10-5) is *exploded* to show greater detail. The Human Resources Process (2) is essentially a personnel accounting system that maintains pertinent data on employees. The major processes within this human resources component are Recruiting (2.1), Pay and Benefits Administration (2.2), and Training and Education (2.3). Process 2.1 could be exploded to a third level of processes to show even greater detail (for example, 2.1.1, 2.1.2, and so on).

ENTITY RELATIONSHIP DIAGRAMS

Another similar business modeling tool, the **entity relationship diagram,** is widely used for defining the information needs of a business. Like the data flow diagrams, the entity relationship diagram involves identifying the entities. The focus of the entity relationship diagram is the *attributes* (a

FIGURE 10-4 | DATA FLOW DIAGRAM SYMBOLS

An entity that is source or destination of data/information

ID
Description
Process

Direction of flow of data/information

Data storage

FIGURE 10-5

MIS OVERVIEW FOR BRASSCO ENTERPRISES

This MIS overview data flow diagram shows the general flow of information within BrassCo. The database symbol and several entities are repeated (indicated by a diagonal line) to simplify the presentation.

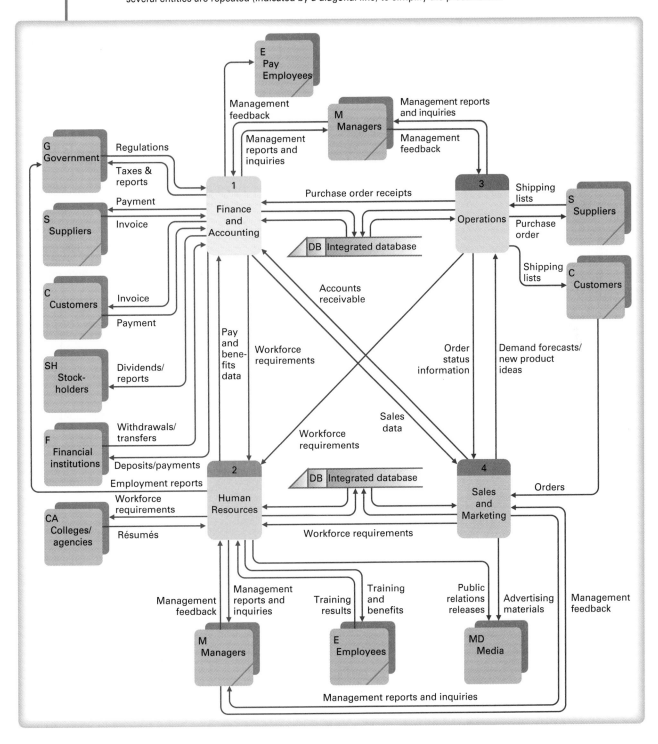

FIGURE 10–6 **BRASSCO'S HUMAN RESOURCES SYSTEM**

This data flow diagram is the explosion of Process 2 (Human Resources) of the MIS overview data flow diagram in Figure 10-5.

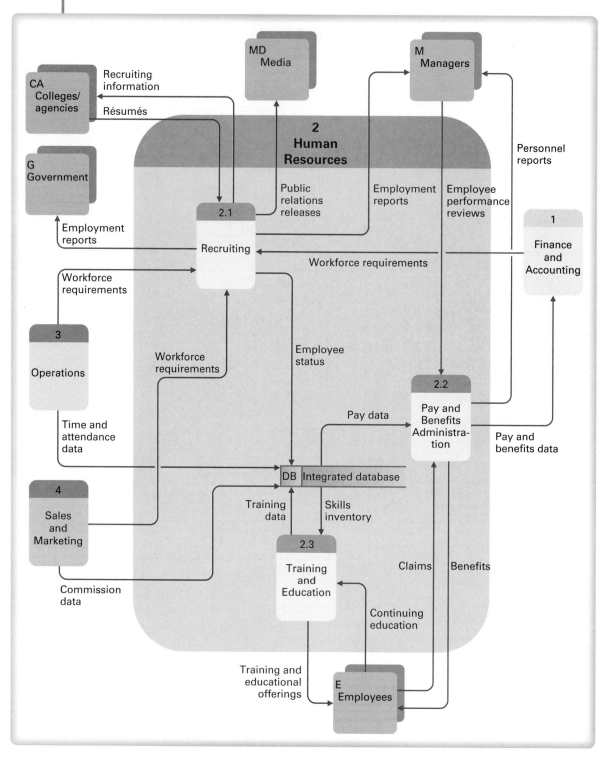

description) of the entities and the *relationship* between them. On the other hand, the focus of the data flow diagram is *information flow*, which may also define the relationship between both entities and processes. Also in contrast to data flow diagrams, the resulting entity relationship model is independent of any data storage or access method.

10-3 COMPUTER-AIDED SOFTWARE ENGINEERING

The system development process is a cooperative effort of users and IT professionals. On one hand, IT professionals are familiar with the technology and how it can be applied to meet a business's information processing needs. On the other, users have in-depth familiarity with their respective functional areas (marketing, manufacturing, human resources, nursing, construction management, and so on) and the information processing needs of the organization. The methods and tools used to create information systems have changed dramatically over the past decade. Modern methods take full advantage of technology to coordinate and automate the applications development process.

For years, IT innovators thought the best way to improve productivity in system development was to make it easier for programmers to create programs. Very high-level programming languages are an outgrowth of this quest for better programmer productivity. In essence, these languages were designed to let the computer do much of the programming. However, in the early 1980s people began asking, "Why can't the power of the computer be applied to analysis and design work as well?" Now we know that it can. Many of the time-consuming manual tasks, such as creating a database and documenting information flow, can be automated. This general family of software development productivity tools falls under the umbrella of **computer-aided software engineering,** or **CASE,** tools.

The term **software engineering** was coined to emphasize an approach to software development that combines automation with the rigors of the engineering discipline. CASE tools have made it possible to automate much of the coordination and work associated with system development. The use of CASE tools can result in higher-quality information systems, reduced cost and time to create information systems, and the elimination of much of the laborious work associated with system development.

CASE tools provide automated support throughout the entire system life cycle. Several companies market CASE tools. The different proprietary CASE tools use different nomenclature and techniques for the elements of the system development process. Figure 10-7 shows the interface for a popular CASE tool from Oracle Corporation.

Software engineers are developing software products to bridge the gap between design and executable program code, the software that makes the system run. In a two-step process, these CASE tool kits enable project teams to use automated software packages to help them complete the logic design (information flow, input/output) and the database organization; then the CASE software translates the logical design into the physical implementation of the system (the software). Some CASE-developed applications emerge ready to implement with little or no actual programming required. CASE tools, however,

FIGURE 10-7

CASE TOOLS EXAMPLES

This figure shows one of Oracle Corporation's CASE tools, Oracle9i JDeveloper, which provides end-to-end support for developing, debugging, and implementing business applications and Web services. Systems analysts, programmers, users, and others use a variety of system modeling tools to capture business and user needs. A shared repository makes up-to-date documentation, from entity relationship diagrams to screen layouts, readily available to those working on the project.

are seldom that efficient. An operational information system may require anywhere from a little to a considerable amount of **custom programming** (the writing of original programs) to achieve full implementation.

The CASE tool kit continues to grow with the technology, encompassing tools for a variety of applications development tasks. The basic tool kit, however, includes the following:

- Design tools
- Information repository tools
- Program development tools

Each tool is discussed in the following sections. Note that there is some overlap in the functions of the various CASE tools.

DESIGN TOOLS

Prior to the introduction of CASE technologies, systems analysts and programmers used plastic flowcharting and data flow diagram templates, rulers, scissors, glue, pencils, pens, and plenty of erasers and "whiteout." The CASE *design tools* provide an automated alternative. They help analysts and programmers prepare schematics that graphically depict the logic of a system or program (for example, data flow diagrams, entity relationship diagrams, and/or structure charts). These automated design tools are to a systems analyst as word processing software is to a writer.

Automated design tools enable an analyst or programmer to select and position symbols, such as the data flow diagram process and entity symbols, and to connect these symbols with flow lines. Both symbols and flow lines can be labeled. Because all the design techniques supported by CASE products are structured design techniques, systems ultimately are depicted in several levels of generality.

CASE design tools also help designers prepare the user interface and generate screen and report layouts. The *user interface* capability enables the project team to design and create the system's user interface. The *screen generator* capability provides systems analysts with the capability of generating a mockup, or layout, of a screen while in direct consultation with the user. The **layout** is a detailed output and/or input specification that graphically illustrates exactly where information should be placed, or entered, on a screen or on printer output. The *report generator* permits the calculation of summary totals by criteria and overall, the creation of graphs and charts, and the editing of output. For example, a report generator can produce a sales report that includes summary totals for each sales region, plus a bar graph of the information.

INFORMATION REPOSITORY TOOLS

The **information repository** is a central computer-based storage facility for all design information. For example, in an information repository, each field in a database is cross-referenced to all other components in the system. That is, the field *customer number* would be cross-referenced to every screen, report, graph, record/file, database, program, or any other design element in which it occurred. Processes in data flow diagrams and entity relationship diagrams are also cross-referenced with this information. Cross-references can be extended between information systems, too. In addition, the information repository permits all system documentation to be packaged electronically. That is, any part of the system—layouts, database design, notes, project schedules, and so on—can be recalled and displayed for review or modification. In effect, the information repository is the "database" for the system development project.

PROGRAM DEVELOPMENT TOOLS

Program development tools focus on the programming aspect of the system development effort. Of the CASE program development tools, the **application generators** make the biggest contribution to productivity. Instead of actually coding programs, programmers use application generators in conjunction with the design specifications and the structure of a database to generate software for a particular application. Another program development tool helps the project team with the generation of test data, one of the more laborious tasks associated with applications development.

THE FUTURE OF CASE

The creation of an information system is a cooperative effort between those who use it and IT professionals, with the latter handling most of the technical aspects of systems development. This, however, is changing. Each year, CASE technology makes it possible for us to assign more of the hard-core programming and design work to computers. The next generation of CASE technology may be for the user, giving the user a new level of technical independence. User-friendly CASE software will allow users to describe, in general terms, what they want the system to accomplish. The CASE software will then create a prototype system that can be refined by the user. Once refined, the *user-oriented* CASE software will generate the necessary programs and install the system.

Most of us depend on the expertise of IT professionals to accomplish our jobs. Ultimately, it may be CASE technology that frees us from this dependence, making us masters of our information processing destiny.

1 Many of the manual tasks in system development, such as creating a database and documenting information flow, can be automated. (T/F)

2 The creation of an information system is a cooperative effort between those who use it and IT professionals. (T/F)

3 Which CASE tool is a central computer-based storage facility for all design information: (a) design tool, (b) information repository tool, (c) program development tool, or (d) prototype tool?

10-4 PROTOTYPING

Why this section is important to you.

In prototyping, you, the user, become an integral part of an interactive computer-assisted process that results in an information system. The better you understand the prototyping process the more effective you can be.

The CASE tool kit enables the system development project team to work with users to develop a **prototype system,** a model of a full-scale system. This approach to applications development is called **prototyping.** In effect, a prototype system permits users a sneak preview of the completed system. A typical prototype system:

● Handles the main transaction-oriented procedures

● Produces common reports

● Permits typical interactions (data entry and inquiries) to the database

Throughout the twentieth century, manufacturers have built prototypes of everything from toasters to airplanes to integrated circuits (see Figure 10-8). Automobile manufacturers routinely build prototypes according to design specifications. Scaled-down clay models are made to evaluate aesthetics and aerodynamics. Ultimately, a full-size, fully functional prototype is created that enables the driver and passengers to test all aspects of the car's functionality. If engineers see possibilities for improvement, the prototypes are modified and retested until they meet or exceed all specifications. Today, building *scalable* prototype systems is standard procedure in software development. A **scalable system** is one whose design

---

FIGURE 10–8 **PROTOTYPING IN CHIP MANUFACTURING**

For years, manufacturers have built physical prototypes, such as this chip, to test product functionality. Now most new information systems emerge from prototype systems.

Courtesy of Micron Technology

Photo courtesy of National Semiconductor Corporation

can handle any size database or any number of users. Scalable systems are desirable because they can be implemented at one level, and then expanded to keep up with corporate growth by simply adding more hardware (server, PCs, and so on). With additional hardware, a well-designed scalable system can easily handle a new branch bank, another Wal-Mart Supercenter, a new line of PCs, and so on.

THE EMERGENCE OF PROTOTYPING

Prior to the emergence of CASE and information system prototyping, project teams would progress through the sequential phases of the traditional **system development life cycle** (**SDLC**): *review of current system, systems analysis and design, system development, conversion, and implementation*. This approach has one serious shortcoming—most managers have a *good idea* of what they want in an information system, but they do not know *exactly* what they want. The traditional SDLC requires users to commit themselves to **system specifications** long before they are comfortable with the specifications. These *specs* include everything from the functionality of the system to the format of the system's output screens and reports. The specifications also describe the logic of the system (input/output, work, and information flow) from the *user's perspective*. Once the specs are set in the traditional SDLC, users have relatively little input until the system is implemented.

Realistically, though, users cannot know exactly what they want, nor can they recognize the potential of a system, until they have had an opportunity to work with it. In the traditional approach to system development, user familiarity comes after the fact and too late for quick fixes and inexpensive modifications. After system implementation, even small changes to an information system can be time-consuming and expensive.

Today, project team members are able to use CASE tools to create prototype systems that, to the user at a terminal or PC, appear and act very much like the finished product.

THE PROTOTYPE SYSTEM

The three objectives of prototyping are

- To analyze the current situation
- To identify information needs
- To develop a model of the proposed system, often called the **target system**

The prototype system gives users an actual opportunity to work with the functional aspects of the proposed system long before the system is implemented. Once users gain hands-on familiarity with the prototype system, they can relate more precise information processing needs to the project team.

A prototype system can be anything from a nonfunctional demonstration of the input/output of a proposed information system to a full-scale operational system. These models are tested and refined until the users are confident that the resulting system will meet their needs. In some cases, the prototype is a scalable system that can be expanded to become a fully operational information system. However, in most cases, the prototype system provides a vehicle for compiling the design specifications.

RAPID APPLICATION DEVELOPMENT

Rapid application development (**RAD**) has emerged to be a generic reference to using software tools (CASE) to design, develop, and implement information systems. Implementing RAD results in information systems of varying degrees of sophistication. At the low end, there is the "quick and dirty" RAD prototype, which gives users an opportunity to experiment with the look and feel of a system. This resulting system is just for show and doesn't permit interaction with a database. At this level, RAD focuses on three aspects of the design: the user interface, data entry displays, and system outputs.

THE CRYSTAL BALL
Streamlining Interaction with the Customer

Competition and the economy demand that companies seek IT solutions to improve customer service and reduce costs. For example, airlines are in the process of eliminating paper tickets. Information systems in virtually every industry are being retrofitted to interact electronically with customers. Shortly, your quarterly stock report, insurance policy, credit card bill, college class schedule, and much more will be available for your perusal via a secure Internet site. If you want a hardcopy, you will have to pay for it. Printing, packaging, stamping, and mailing an invoice is becoming an unaffordable luxury.

At the other end of the RAD spectrum is the fully functional prototype system. This kind of prototype system enables users to try out the features of the target system during interactive practice sessions. The prototype is modified and refined based on user feedback. Some fully functional systems are for design only and provide specifications for the system development process. In contrast, some prototype systems are scalable systems and can be implemented directly at the enterprise level when complete. For example, Wal-Mart information systems are scalable such that all they do is add more computing capacity as new stores are opened.

THE PROTOTYPING PROCESS

Both the prototyping and the traditional approaches to system development depend on the efforts of a project team. The composition of the project team is essentially the same for both approaches. The team consists of *systems analysts, programmers,* perhaps the *database administrator,* users who will eventually use the system, and perhaps one or more managers. All work together to develop the system design specifications. The database administrator assists the team in designing and creating the database.

The development of an information system via prototyping is done in four phases (see Figure 10-9).

- Phase I—Define System Specifications
- Phase II—Create Prototype System
- Phase III—Refine Prototype System
- Phase IV—Develop Operational System

Phase I—Define System Specifications

In the traditional approach to system development, system specifications are "frozen" early in the project. In other words, no more changes can be made to the specs. In prototyping, the specs do not need to be frozen because the prototype system is easily modified to meet changing needs. It is during this phase (see Figure 10-9) that the current system is analyzed (system analysis) and the target system is designed (system design). Typically,

FIGURE 10-9 THE FOUR PHASES OF THE PROTOTYPING PROCESS

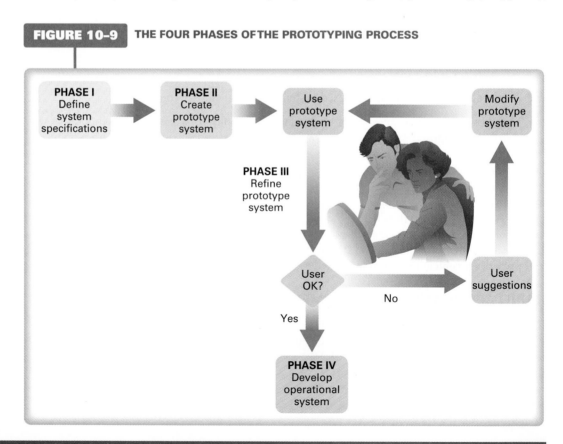

specifications are determined during interactive sessions with users. During the sessions, the team will define system specifications for graphical user interfaces, menus, reports, various input/output screens, and the database. The results are the specifications (database structure, input/output layouts, and so on) needed to develop the prototype system.

System Analysis: Understanding the System

System analysis produces the following results.

- *Existing system review.* Before designing a new or enhanced information system, the members of the project team examine existing work and information flow, be it manual or computer-based. Here the team documents the work and information flow of the system by reducing it to its basic components—input, processing, and output.

- *System objectives.* Once the existing system is documented, the project team can begin to identify the problem areas (for example, procedural bottlenecks, duplication of effort, and so on). This knowledge is formalized as system objectives.

- *Design constraints.* The purpose of this activity is to detail any costs, hardware, schedule, procedural, software, database, and operating constraints that may limit the definition and design of the target system.

- *Requirements definition.* In order to define the information and information processing requirements for the target system, the project team completes a needs analysis.

System Design: Putting It All Together

During system design, the project team takes information from the system analysis and develops a design for the target system. The design of an information system is more of a challenge to the human intellect than it is a procedural challenge. Just as an author begins with a blank page and an idea, the members of the project team begin with empty RAM and the information requirements definitions. From here they must create what sometimes can be a very complex information system.

The system design process involves continuous communication between members of the project team and all affected users. After evaluating several alternative approaches, the project team translates the specifications into a system design. The documentation completed in the system design stage might include the following:

- A graphic illustration that depicts the fundamental operation of the target system (for example, overview and detailed data flow diagrams)

- A written explanation of the graphic illustration

- Descriptions of the outputs to be produced by the system, including display screens and hard-copy reports and documents

Eventually the system design documentation depicts the relationship among *all processing activities* and the *input/output associated with them.*

The database must be defined during system design as well. The database is the common denominator of any system. It contains the raw material (data) necessary to produce the output (information). In manufacturing, for example, you would first decide what you are going to make, then order the raw material. In the process of developing an information system, you decide what your output requirements are, and then determine which data are needed to produce the output. In a sense, output requirements can be thought of as input to database design.

The system design is the cornerstone of the system development process. It is here that the relationships among the various components of the system are defined. As a result, the system design is the *blueprint* for all project team activities that follow. The project team uses their imagination and skill to transform the system specifications into an information system.

Phase II—Create Prototype System

To create a prototype system, project team members first rough out the logic of the system and how the elements fit together, and then they work with the user to define the I/O interfaces (the system interaction with the user). The next challenge is to translate the system design and specifications into instructions that can be interpreted and executed by the computer. This, of course, involves software development.

During this phase (see Figure 10-9), the creation of software becomes the dominant activity. Project team members use CASE tools to create screen images (menus, reports, inquiries, and so on), to create a database, and to generate much of the programming code (software). Typically, programmers will need to write custom programs to complement automatically generated programs. The custom programming task, in which programmers write, or *code*, the necessary programs, is made easier with the well-documented specifications from the design stage. The subsequent programs result in a physical representation of a target system.

Phase III—Refine Prototype System

In this phase (see Figure 10-9), users actually sit down at a terminal or PC and evaluate portions, and eventually all, of the prototype system. Invariably, users have suggestions for improving the user interfaces and/or the format of the I/O. And, without fail, their examination reveals new needs for information. In effect, the original prototype system is the beginning. From here, the system is expanded (if needed) and refined to meet the users' total information needs. The use-and-modify cycle depicted in Figure 10-9 is repeated until users are satisfied with the prototype system.

Phase IV—Develop Operational System

At this point in the prototyping process (see Figure 10-9), users have a system that looks and feels like what they want. If the system is a fully functional scalable prototype, or working model of the target information system, it can be scaled to meet the organization's information processing needs and implemented directly. If the system is other than a fully functional scalable prototype, it must be enhanced; or another system, based on the prototype system, must be developed. In the latter case, the prototype system is discarded once the specs have been determined. From these specs, the software for an operational information system capable of handling the required volume of work is developed.

SECTION

1 A fully functional prototype system is essentially a complete information system, but without the capability to access a database. (T/F)

2 Which results are realized during the system design: (a) description of outputs, (b) existing system review, (c) design constraints, or (d) final system approval?

3 The target system's specifications are done in which of the four phases of prototyping: (a) Phase I, (b) Phase II, (c) Phase III, or (d) Phase IV?

4 The system specifications describe the logic of a target system from whose perspective: (a) systems analyst, (b) CIO, (c) programmer, or (d) user?

10-5 SYSTEM CONVERSION AND IMPLEMENTATION

Why this section is important to you.

Every knowledge worker will be involved in many system conversions and/or system implementations at one time or another. When it's your turn, you will know the key options and considerations.

Once an information system has been developed and approved by those who will use it, it is implemented within the organization. This section will examine the process from testing to conversion to actual interaction with an operational system.

SYSTEMS AND ACCEPTANCE TESTING

The first step of the system conversion and implementation process is systems testing. This testing encompasses everything that makes up the information system—the hardware, software, end users, data and procedures (for example, effectiveness of online help documents). If needed, the interfaces between the system and other systems are tested as well.

During Phase II, Create Prototype System, programs are written according to system specifications and are individually tested. Although the programs that make up the software for the system have undergone **unit testing** (individual testing) and have been debugged, they also must be tested together. Integrated **systems testing** is needed to ensure that all software works together to enable an operational information system.

To conduct the system test, the project team compiles and thoroughly tests the system with *test data*. In this first stage, tests are run for each subsystem (one of the functional aspects of the system) or cycle (weekly or monthly activities). The test data are compiled so all program and system options and all error and validation routines are tested. The tests are repeated and modifications are made until all subsystems or cycles function properly. At this point, the entire system is tested as a unit. Testing and modifications continue until the components of the system work as they should and all input/output is validated.

Several of the people who will eventually use the system do the second stage of systems testing with *live data*. Live data have already been processed through the existing system. Testing with live data provides an extra level of assurance that the system will work properly when implemented.

APPROACHES TO SYSTEM CONVERSION

Once systems testing is complete, the project team trains the users, creates the database, and then integrates hardware, software, procedures, and communications into an operational information system. This normally involves a conversion from the existing system to the new one. An organization's approach to system conversion depends on its *willingness to accept risk* and the *amount of time available* for the conversion. The four common approaches are illustrated in Figure 10-10.

Parallel Conversion

In **parallel conversion,** the existing system and the new system operate simultaneously, or in parallel, until the project team is confident the new system is working properly. Parallel conversion has two important advantages. First, the existing system serves as a backup if the new system fails to operate as expected. Second, the results of the new system can be compared to the results of the existing system to ensure that the new system is processing the information correctly.

Although there is less risk with this strategy (because the present system provides backup), the downside is that it doubles the workload of personnel and hardware resources during the conversion. Parallel conversion usually takes one month or a major system cycle. For a public utility company, this might be one complete billing cycle.

Direct Conversion

Some companies forego parallel conversion in favor of a **direct conversion,** whereby the old system is terminated when the new system goes online. Direct conversion involves a greater risk because there is no backup if the system fails. Companies select this "cold-turkey" approach when there is no existing system or when the existing system is substantially different.

Phased Conversion

In **phased conversion,** an information system is implemented one module at a time by either parallel or direct conversion. For example, in a point-of-sale system, the first phase might be to convert the sales-accounting module. The second phase could involve the inventory-management module, followed by the credit-check module, and so on.

Phased conversion has the advantage of spreading the demand for resources over time to avoid an intense demand of shorter duration. The disadvantages are that the conversion takes longer and an interface must be developed between the existing system and the new one.

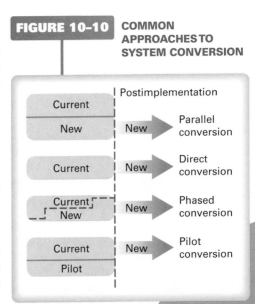

FIGURE 10–10 COMMON APPROACHES TO SYSTEM CONVERSION

Pilot Conversion

In **pilot conversion,** the new system is implemented by parallel, direct, or phased conversion as a pilot system in only one of the areas for which it is targeted. Suppose a company wants to implement a manufacturing resources planning system in its eight plants. One plant would be selected as a pilot, and the new information system would be implemented there first.

The advantage of pilot conversion is that the inevitable bugs in a system can be removed before the system is implemented at the other locations. The disadvantage is that the implementation time for the total system takes longer than if the entire system were implemented at once.

THE SYSTEM BECOMES OPERATIONAL

Once the conversion has been completed, the information system enters the production stage of the system life cycle. During the production stage, the system becomes operational and is turned over to the users. Once an information system is implemented and goes online, the emphasis switches from *development* to *operations*. In a payroll system, supervisors begin to enter hours worked on their PCs or terminals, and the computer center produces and issues payroll checks. Once operational, an information system becomes a cooperative effort between users and IT professionals.

Just as a new automobile will need some screws tightened after a few hundred miles, an information system will need some fine-tuning just after implementation. Thereafter, and throughout the production stage of the system life cycle, the system will be modified many times. An information system is dynamic and must be responsive to the changing needs of the company and those who use it (see Figure 10-11). The process of modifying an information system to meet changing needs is known as **system maintenance.**

Prior to the emergence of CASE technology, making modifications, called **patches,** to operational systems was time-consuming and expensive. CASE tools, however, permit flexibility in system design. For example, when fields are added to the database or screen formats are modified, affected programs are automatically updated to reflect the changes.

Though an information system can be modified to change and grow, it cannot live forever. The accumulation of modifications and enhancements eventually will make any information system cumbersome and inefficient. Toward the end of the useful life of an information system, it is more trouble to continue patching the system than it is to redesign the system completely. Depending on the number of patches and enhancements, an information system will remain operational—that is, be in the production stage of the system life cycle (see Figure 10-1)—an average of four to seven years. The end of the production stage signals the end-of-life stage of the system life cycle. A new system is then born of need, and the system development process is repeated.

SECTION

1 Greater risk is associated with direct conversion than with phased conversion. (T/F)

2 In pilot conversion, the new system is always implemented by parallel conversion. (T/F)

3 Once an information system is implemented, the emphasis is switched from development to: (a) testing, (b) operations, (c) training, or (d) programming.

10-6 PROGRAMMING

Why this section is important to you.

The foundation of all computing is software, which is created through programming. This section will help you understand the various programming options and show you how programming fits into the systems development process.

Before the newly designed system can go online, the software must be created. Some, and sometimes all, of the programs are created as a by-product of the CASE prototyping process. However, most systems require considerable amounts of *custom programming* by *programmers*, people who write programs. Perhaps no other element of computing changes as much or as often as the way we program computers (see Figure 10-12).

FIGURE 10–11 FEDEX INFORMATION SYSTEMS

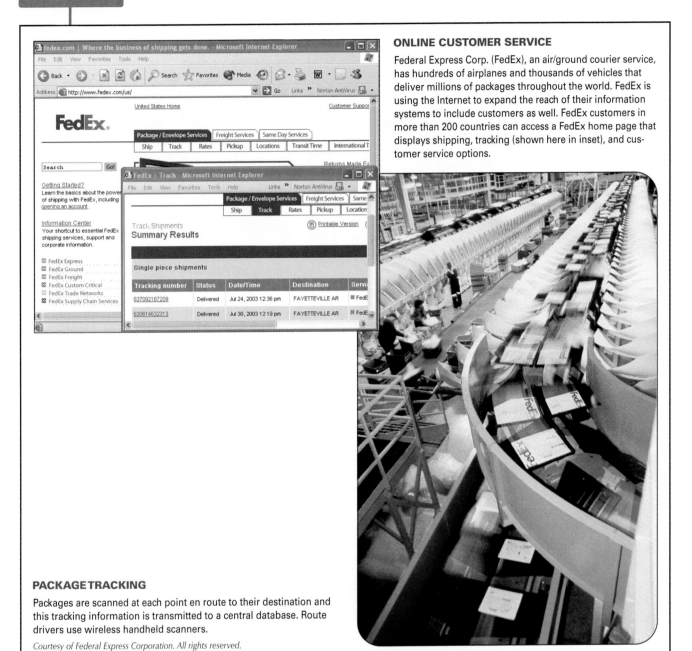

ONLINE CUSTOMER SERVICE

Federal Express Corp. (FedEx), an air/ground courier service, has hundreds of airplanes and thousands of vehicles that deliver millions of packages throughout the world. FedEx is using the Internet to expand the reach of their information systems to include customers as well. FedEx customers in more than 200 countries can access a FedEx home page that displays shipping, tracking (shown here in inset), and customer service options.

PACKAGE TRACKING

Packages are scanned at each point en route to their destination and this tracking information is transmitted to a central database. Route drivers use wireless handheld scanners.

Courtesy of Federal Express Corporation. All rights reserved.

Programs are made up of instructions that are logically sequenced and assembled through the act of programming. Programmers use a variety of **programming languages,** such as C++, Visual BASIC, Perl, COBOL, and Java, to communicate instructions to the computer. Twenty years ago, virtually all programmers were IT specialists. Today, office managers, management consultants, engineers, politicians, and people in all walks of life write programs to meet business and domestic needs. Unless you plan to become an IT professional, it is unlikely that you will write programs in support of an enterprise-wide information system. You may, however, write programs to perform many personal tasks, such as preparing graphs from spreadsheet data and sequencing displays for multimedia presentations. As you develop expertise and confidence you may tackle more challenging programming tasks.

Many spoken languages have emerged over thousands of years of oral communication. Although computers have existed for only a short while, there are already as many pro-

FIGURE 10-12 PROGRAMMING THEN AND NOW

If you ever feel intimidated by the idea of programming a computer, just remember how much easier it is today than in the computer's early days.

PROGRAMMING ELECTROMECHANICAL ACCOUNTING MACHINES

Prior to the invention of the electronic digital computer, companies relied on electro-mechanical accounting machines (EAM) for automated data processing. Early program-mers literally created the circuitry for the devices by inserting wires into interchange-able removable control panels.

Courtesy of International Business Machines Corporation

PROGRAMMING THE FIRST ELECTRONIC DIGITAL COMPUTERS

The quantum leap in technology brought about by the invention of the ENIAC (1946), the first large-scale fully operational electronic digital computer, was offset by the cumbersome method of programming the machine. For each program to be run, switches had to be set manually and wires inserted into a series of panels.

Courtesy of UNISYS Corporation

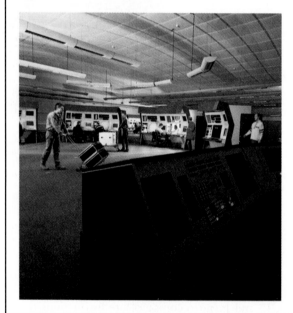

PROGRAMMING MODERN COMPUTERS

Today CASE tools are able to generate much of the software for an information system. For custom programming, pro-grammers choose the best programming language for the job, then use high-level instructions to interactively create and debug the program. In this example, Amsterdam's Schiphol Airport in the Netherlands uses software designed to help meet the growing demands of air traffic control.

Courtesy of Raytheon Company

gramming languages as there are spoken languages. In this section, we will sort out these languages and explain what they mean to you. But first, let's put software into perspective.

SOFTWARE IN PERSPECTIVE

Suppose you are sick in bed and you ask a friend to get you a glass of ice water. Your friend then instinctively goes to the kitchen, opens the cabinet door and selects a glass, opens the freezer, gets some ice, turns on the tap, fills the glass with water, returns to your bedside, and hands you the water. Now imagine making the same request to a computer. You would have to tell the computer not only where to get the water but also how to get there, which end of the glass to fill, when to shut off the water, how to grasp the ice, and much, much, more.

A single program addresses a particular problem—to compute grades, to monitor a patient's heart rate, and so on. In effect, when you write a program, you are solving a *problem*, which requires you to use your powers of *logic* to develop a procedure for solving the problem. Creating a program is like constructing a building. Much of the brainwork involved in the construction goes into the blueprint. The location, appearance, and function of a building are determined long before the first brick is laid. With programming, the design of a program, or its *programming logic* (the blueprint), is completed before the program is written.

Each programming language has an instruction set with a variety of instructions. For example, *input/output instructions* direct the computer to "read from" or "write to" a peripheral device. *Computation instructions* direct the computer to perform arithmetic operations. *Control instructions* can alter the sequence of the program's execution. With these and a few other types of instructions, you can create software to model almost any business or scientific procedure, whether it is sales forecasting or guiding rockets to the moon.

TYPES OF PROGRAMMING LANGUAGES

We "talk" to computers within the framework of a particular programming language, and the selection of a programming language depends on who is doing the talking and the nature of the "conversation." There are many different types of programming languages in use today. Several representative programming languages are discussed in this section.

Machine Language: Native Tongue

In Chapter 4, we learned that all programs ultimately are executed in *machine language,* the computer's native language. Creating programs in the *low-level* machine language is a cumbersome process, so we write programs in more programmer-friendly *high-level* languages. However, our resulting programs must be translated into machine language before they can be executed. This conversion of high-level instructions to machine-level instructions is done by system software programs called *compilers* and *interpreters*. The **compiler** program translates the **source program,** the actual high-level programming-language instructions, into a machine-language program called an **object program.** The object program is the output of the compilation process. High-level programming languages are simply a programmer convenience; they cannot be executed in their source, or original, form. The source program instructions (for example, in COBOL or C++) are translated, or *compiled*, into machine-language instructions by a compiler.

An **interpreter** performs the same function as a compiler—but in a different manner. Instead of translating the entire source program in a single pass, an interpreter translates *and* executes each source program instruction before translating and executing the next. The obvious advantage of interpreters over compilers is that an error in *instruction syntax* (for example, an invalid instruction format) is brought to the attention of the programmer immediately, thereby prompting the programmer to make corrections during interactive program development.

Programmers often develop and debug their programs using an interpreter. Then they compile the finished program to create a more efficient object program that can be used for routine processing. A separate compiler or an interpreter is required for each programming language intended for use on a particular computer system.

Procedure-Oriented Languages

The introduction of more user-friendly programming languages (in 1955) resulted in a quantum leap in programmer convenience. Programmers could write a single instruction instead of several cumbersome machine language instructions. These early languages were **procedure-oriented languages,** which require programmers to solve programming problems using traditional programming logic. Instructions are **coded,** or written, sequentially and processed according to program specifications. Procedure-oriented languages are classified as *business*, *scientific*, or *multipurpose*. **COBOL,** shown in Figure 10-13, is a good example of a procedure-oriented language designed for use in creating business systems. **FORTRAN** (*Formula Tran*slator), the first procedure-oriented language, was developed in 1955 and remains a popular scientific language. Multipurpose languages, such as **Pascal,** are equally effective for both business and scientific applications.

OOP and Object-Oriented Languages

In procedure-oriented languages, the emphasis is on *what* is done (the procedure). In **object-oriented languages,** the emphasis is on the *object* of the action. The structure of **object-oriented programming** (**OOP**) makes programs easier to design and understand. Also, OOP (rhymes with "*hoop*") handles images, videos, and sound better than procedure-oriented languages. Programming languages based on OOP have experienced phenomenal growth in numbers, acceptance, and use during the last two decades. Examples of object-oriented languages include **Smalltalk,** one of the first OOP languages, **C++,** a popular languages for developing graphical applications (for example, Windows applications), and **Java,** which is similar to C++.

A program that adheres to OOP is a collection of objects. An **object** is a self-contained module that *encapsulates*, or describes, *data* and the *methods* for manipulating the data. The module includes programming code, as well. Objects are grouped hierarchically into *classes* and *subclasses*. For example, an object class (see Figure 10-14) might be Personal Computer with subclass objects called Notebook PC and Desktop PC. Subclasses, by definition, have the same *attributes* and *methods* of the object class. This OOP principle is call *inheritance*. The attributes are facts that describe the object and the methods that describe possible behaviors or operations for the object (see Figure 10-14). The hierarchy can be extended to specific notebook and desktop computers. For example, a Dell notebook PC, an IBM notebook PC, and an HP notebook PC might be objects under the subclass, Notebook PC. These objects would inherit the attributes and methods of both the object class, Personal Computer, and the Notebook PC subclass.

FIGURE 10-13 **A COBOL PROGRAM**

This COBOL program accepts the number of hours worked and the pay rate for an hourly wage earner, then computes and displays the gross pay amount. The interactive session below the program listing shows the input prompt, the values entered by the user, and the result.

```
0100    IDENTIFICATION DIVISION.
0200    PROGRAM-ID.              PAYPROG.
0300    REMARKS.          PROGRAM TO COMPUTE GROSS PAY.
0400    ENVIRONMENT DIVISION.
0500    DATA DIVISION.
0600    WORKING-STORAGE SECTION.
0700    01 PAY DATA.
0800          05 HOURSPIC 99V99.
0900          05 RATE PIC 99V99.
1000          05 PAY       PIC 9999V99.
1100    01 LINE-1.
1200          03 FILLER      PIC X(5).      VALUE SPACES.
1300          03 FILLER      PIC X(12).     VALUE "GROSS PAY IS."
1400          03 GROSS-PAY   PIC $$$9.99.
1500    01 PRINT-LINE.       PIC X(27).
1600    PROCEDURE DIVISION.
1700    MAINLINE-PROCEDURE.
1800          PERFORM ENTER-PAY.
1900    PERFORM COMPUTE-PAY.
2000    PERFORM PRINT-PAY.
2100    STOP RUN.
2200    ENTER-PAY.
2300          DISPLAY "ENTER HOURS AND RATE OF PAY."
2400          ACCEPT HOURS, RATE.
2500    COMPUTE-PAY.
2600          MULTIPLY HOURS BY RATE GIVING PAY ROUNDED.
2700    PRINT PAY.
2800          MOVE PAY TO GROSS-PAY.
2900          MOVE LINE-1 TO PRINT-LINE.
3000          DISPLAY PRINT-LINE.
```

Enter hours and rate of pay
43, 8.25

Gross pay is $354.75

OOP techniques and languages offer an advantage of procedure-oriented languages in that programs are more easily created and modified to meet changing system requirements. Programmers using OOP languages, such as C++, often create programs from existing objects. Once an object is created, it can be recycled into many different applications. For example, e-tailer Web sites often are created through the careful selection and integration of objects. These reusable objects might enable logon to secure sites, handle the customer database, maintain the product/inventory database, keep track of the "shopping cart," and complete the checkout procedure. The objects send *messages* to each other to trigger the procedures described within the object. For example, a message from the "check out" object alerts to the order processing object. When this happens, the methods for order processing embedded in the program instructions are performed.

Objects libraries, both free and commercial, contains thousands of ready-to-use objects that can be

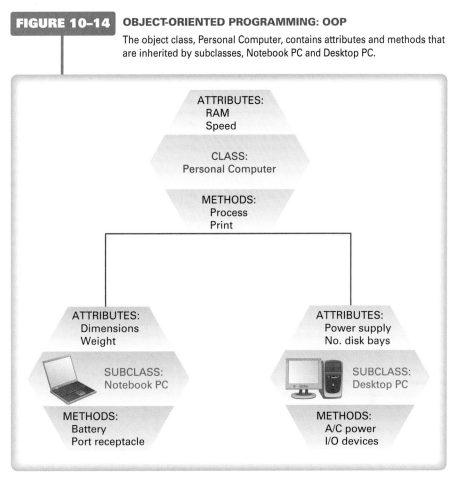

FIGURE 10-14 OBJECT-ORIENTED PROGRAMMING: OOP

The object class, Personal Computer, contains attributes and methods that are inherited by subclasses, Notebook PC and Desktop PC.

applied to a wide variety of data management and programming problems. OOP techniques make it possible to add new objects easily because they inherit the properties of an existing class of objects. With OOP, the programmer no longer is required to start from scratch to create a program; instead, programmers have the option to choose from available objects that are applicable to the programming problem.

Because Java supports OOP and is platform-independent (can run on just about any computer), Java has emerged as an important language for Web-based applications (see Figure 10-15). Java and OOP languages, such as Microsoft's **C#** (pronounced, C sharp), have enabled Web developers to create dynamic content that enables us to trade stocks, purchase almost anything, get online news based on our preferences, and take virtual tours of historic places throughout the world. The object-oriented nature of Java and C# fits well with Web-based programming in that small programs in the form of objects, called *applets*, can be downloaded as they are needed. **Perl,** a popular language with Web developers, enables, but does not require, object-oriented programming.

The Fourth Generation: 4GLs

Most of the programming in procedure- and object-oriented languages is done by IT specialists. Programming in user-friendly fourth-generation languages is done by IT specialists and also a growing legion of end users. **Fourth-generation languages** (4GLs) use high-level English-like instructions to retrieve and format data for inquiries and reporting. In 4GLs, the programmer specifies what to do, *not* how to do it. A few simple 4GL instructions are all that is necessary to respond to the following typical management requests:

- Which employees have accumulated more than 20 sick days since May 1?
- Which deluxe single hospital rooms, if any, will be vacated by the end of the day?
- List departments that have exceeded their budgets alphabetically by the department head's name.

FIGURE 10-15 PROGRAM SEGMENT FOR A JAVA APPLET

These are a few of the 400 lines of Java programming code written to create this bouncing ball applet. An applet is a Java program that is run within a Web browser. The applet lets you move and resize a rectangle to manipulate the bouncing balls. Note the hierarchical structure of this program segment.

```
{
        if (collide)
        {
                double xvect=coll_x-getCenterX0;
                double yvect=coll_y-getCenterY0;
                if((xinc>0 && xvect>0) || (xinc<0 && xvect<0))
                        xinc=-xinc;
                if((yinc>0 && yvect>0) || (yinc<0 && yvect<0))
                        yinc=-yinc;
                collide=false;
        }
        x+=xinc;
y+=yinc;
        //when the ball bumps
        against a boundary, it
        bounces off
if(x<6 || x>width-diameter)
{
```

Query languages, a subset of 4GLs, allow users to request information directly from a database. *SQL* (pronounced like *sequel*) is the de facto standard for query languages. The following SQL instructions tap the CIA World Factbook database. The first SQL instruction determines the population of the world—6,080,153,149. The second instruction creates a table listing all countries with their region and population.

SELECT SUM FROM cia

SELECT name, region, population
FROM cia

SQL is introduced and illustrated in more detail in Chapter 8 in the database discussion.

Visual Languages: Icons for Words

As they say, a picture is worth a thousand words, and so it is in programming. **Visual programming** takes object-oriented programming to the next level, replacing text-based instructions with symbolic icons, each of which represents an object or a common programming function (see Figure 10-16). Microsoft's **Visual BASIC** is one of the most popular visual languages for both the casual user and the professional software developer. Visual BASIC, which permits object-oriented programming, allows programmers to drag and drop objects onto a screen and make links between these objects within the context of a visual interface. Because it is easy to learn and use, novice programmers are creating sophisticated Windows-based programs. **Visual C#** is gaining popularity for Internet-based applications.

Macro Languages: The User Language

As end users, we issue commands and initiate operations by selecting items from a hierarchy of menus. When we choose an item on a menu, that operation is performed and the applications software causes the system to wait for further commands. We select operations (menu items) one at a time until we have accomplished what we wish to do. This one-at-a-time approach to system interaction is fine for one-time jobs, such as preparing and printing a sales summary bar chart. But what if you prepare the same charts from an updated spreadsheet at the end of each week? Then, you might wish to consider creating a macro to do the job automatically. A **macro** is a sequence of frequently used operations or keystrokes that can be recalled as needed. A macro is actually a short program, containing a sequence of instructions to be performed.

The original macro concept grew from a need to automate repetitive interactions with applications software. The first macros (for spreadsheet and word processing software) simply recorded command interactions for replay at a later time. *Record-and-play macros* are handy for performing interactions that are done over and over. Straightforward macros can be created easily by recording operations as they are entered, then storing their sequence as a named macro for later recall. Once a macro is created, you simply run it whenever you wish to "play" the keystroke sequence.

PERSONAL COMPUTING
Writing Macros

If you are like most managers and knowledge workers, you can expect to spend most of your working day within arm's length of a PC. Most of us, even at the highest levels, perform repetitive tasks. These tasks can range from recording sales data to capturing weekly production data in a bar chart. Any repetitive actions you do at the PC are candidates for a record-and-play macro or a macro program. The few minutes you spend learning to create keystroke macros and the few hours you spend learning to program in Visual BASIC (the macro language of Microsoft Office) can save you countless hours at work.

Record-and-play macros work for most situations. Occasionally, however, you will need to create more complex macros, in which case, you would use a **macro language.** For example, spreadsheet users often create powerful macros to facilitate data entry and the creation of business charts and graphs. The more complex macros use macro languages that enable flow control (decisions and loops), the use of variables, and interaction with users. Most of today's office software (word processing, spreadsheet, database, and so on) have their own powerful macro language (Visual BASIC for Microsoft Office applications). Users can use these languages to write macros to do simple tasks or to create comprehensive office information systems.

WRITING THE PROGRAM

The programmer's challenge is to translate the system design and specifications created during the prototyping process into instructions that can be interpreted and executed by the computer. To do so, they follow these steps.

VISUAL PROGRAMMING

Macromedia Director "movies," which are interactive multimedia images, are the result of a scripting program. A variety of Director visual programming objects are selected, linked, and described to enable the creation of the program (see center of example). When played, the resulting "Using Keyboard Input" (lower right) demonstrates interactively, with sound and motion, the use of a keyboard. The Score window (top left) graphically illustrates the sequencing and play attributes of the elements in the Director "movie." The Internal Cast window (bottom left) shows the member of the cast (elements under program control).

System Specifications Review

The system specifications completed during the systems analysis and design are all that is necessary for programmers to write, or *code,* the programs to implement the target information system. But before getting started, programmers should review and study the system specifications (layouts, design, Web-based interfaces, and so on) until they thoroughly understand what needs to be accomplished.

techtv™
USING PHP

Program Identification and Description

An information system needs an array of programs and program modules (programs within programs) to create and update the database, print reports, enable Internet-based inquiry, and so on. Depending on the scope of the system and how many programs can be generated using applications development tools, as few as three or four or as many as several thousand programs may need to be written before the system can be implemented. At this point, all programs necessary to make the system operational are identified and described (tasks to be performed, input, output, interactivity, and so on).

Program Design, Coding, Testing, and Documentation

Armed with system specifications and program descriptions, programmers can begin the actual design and coding of programs. The development of a program is actually a project within a project. Just as there are certain steps the project team takes to develop an information system, there are certain steps a programmer takes to write a program. These seven steps are summarized in Figure 10-17. Programmers use a variety of techniques to help

FIGURE 10-17 STEPS IN WRITING A PROGRAM

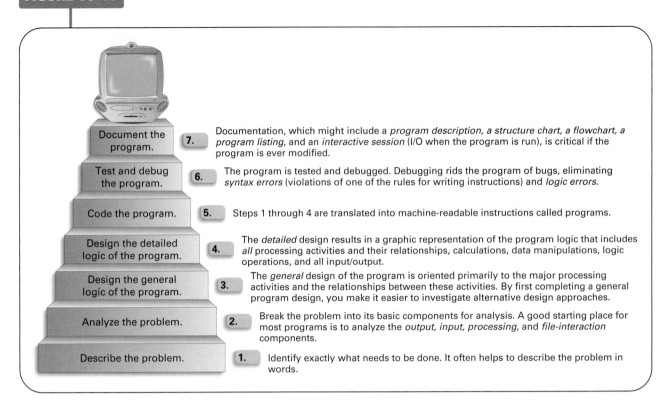

7. Documentation, which might include a *program description, a structure chart, a flowchart, a program listing,* and an *interactive session* (I/O when the program is run), is critical if the program is ever modified.

6. The program is tested and debugged. Debugging rids the program of bugs, eliminating *syntax errors* (violations of one of the rules for writing instructions) and *logic errors.*

5. Steps 1 through 4 are translated into machine-readable instructions called programs.

4. The *detailed* design results in a graphic representation of the program logic that includes *all* processing activities and their relationships, calculations, data manipulations, logic operations, and all input/output.

3. The *general* design of the program is oriented primarily to the major processing activities and the relationships between these activities. By first completing a general program design, you make it easier to investigate alternative design approaches.

2. Break the problem into its basic components for analysis. A good starting place for most programs is to analyze the *output, input, processing,* and *file-interaction* components.

1. Identify exactly what needs to be done. It often helps to describe the problem in words.

them analyze a problem and design the program. These include traditional approaches, such as *flowcharting* and *pseudocode,* and new wave approaches, such as *extreme programming.*

Flowcharting

In **flowcharting,** flowcharts are used to illustrate data, information, and work flow by the interconnection of *specialized symbols* with *flow lines.* The combination of symbols and flow lines portrays the logic of the program or system. The more commonly used flowchart symbols are shown in Figure 10-18. Although flowcharting was initially a program design tool, it is also a common business tool for analyzing and documenting work flow, procedures, and decision processes.

Through the 1970s, many programmers unknowingly wrote what is now referred to as "spaghetti code." It was so named because their program flowcharts appeared more like a plate of spaghetti than like logical analyses of programming problems. The unnecessary branching (jumps from one portion of the program to another) of a spaghetti-style program resulted in confusing logic, even to the person who wrote it.

IT specialists overcame this dead-end approach to developing program logic by identifying three basic *control structures* into which any program or subroutine can be segmented. By conceptualizing the logic of a program in these three structures—*sequence, selection,* and *loop*—programmers can produce programs that are easy to understand and maintain. Figure 10-19 illustrates these control structures.

- *Sequence control structure.* In the sequence structure, the processing steps are performed in sequence, one after another.

- *Selection control structure.* In the selection structure, a decision, or *test-on-condition,* is made as to which sequence of instructions is to be executed next. The two option selection in Figure 10-19 is an IF-THEN-ELSE structure: IF a condition is met THEN one process is performed, ELSE (condition not met) another process is performed. In the other example, any one of four of processing options can be performed depending on which condition is met.

- *Loop control structure.* The loop structure is used to represent the program logic when a portion of the program is to be executed repeatedly until a particular condition is met. There are two variations of the loop structure. When the decision is placed at the beginning of the statement sequence, it becomes a *DOWHILE loop*. When the decision is placed at the end, it becomes a *DOUNTIL loop* (pronounced *doo while* and *doo until*).

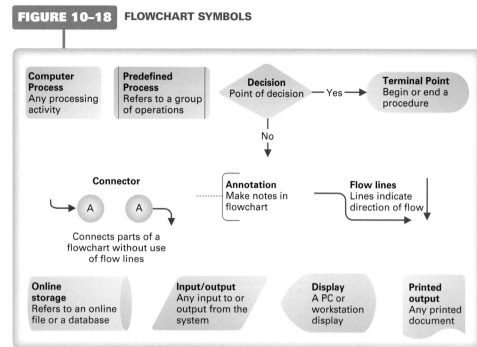

FIGURE 10–18 FLOWCHART SYMBOLS

Computer Process Any processing activity

Predefined Process Refers to a group of operations

Decision Point of decision — Yes →

Terminal Point Begin or end a procedure

No

Connector

A   A

Connects parts of a flowchart without use of flow lines

Annotation Make notes in flowchart

Flow lines Lines indicate direction of flow

Online storage Refers to an online file or a database

Input/output Any input to or output from the system

Display A PC or workstation display

Printed output Any printed document

In structured programming, each program has a **driver module,** sometimes called the **main program,** which causes other program modules to be executed as they are needed. The driver module in the payroll program of Figure 10-20 is a loop that "calls" each of the subordinate modules, or **subroutines,** as needed for the processing of each employee. The program is designed so that when the payroll program is initiated, the Input Data Module (1.1) is executed first. That portion of the Input Data Module (1.1) that reads an employee record is illustrated in a DOUNTIL loop. That is, *do the loop until* the end of the file is reached. After execution of Module 1.1, control is returned to the driver module unless there are no more employees to be processed, in which case execution is terminated (the "Finish" terminal point). For each hourly or commission employee, Modules 1.2, 1.3, and 1.4 are performed (a sequence control structure embedded in a loop), and at the completion of each subroutine, control is passed back to the driver module.

Pseudocode

Another program design technique is **pseudocode.** While the other techniques graphically represent the logic of the program, pseudocode represents the logic in program-like statements written in plain English. Because pseudocode does not have any syntax guidelines (rules for formulating instructions), you can concentrate solely on developing the logic of your program. Once you feel that the logic is sound, the pseudocode is easily translated into a procedure-oriented language such as COBOL or BASIC that can be run on a computer. The following pseudocode program depicts the logic of a program to compile a list of students who have qualified for the dean's honor roll.

```
Print heading of report "Dean's Honor Roll"
DOUNTIL end-of-file is detected
    read a student's record
    compute semester grade average
    IF average > or = 3.0
        THEN print name and grade average
        ELSE continue
    ENDIF
ENDDO
```

FIGURE 10-19 PROGRAMMING CONTROL STRUCTURES

Sequence Control Structure

Loop Control Structures

DOWHILE

DOUNTIL

Selection Control Structures

2 Options (IF-THEN-ELSE)

4 Options

Extreme Programming

Extreme programming (XP) is a collaborative team approach in which the programming team works together to write programs in iterative cycles, beginning with the design and coding of the smallest useful feature of the system. Each iteration introduces another feature and gets the team that much closer to an operational system. XP, as much a culture of programming as it is a technique, is based on a group of time-honored core programming practices. For example, extreme programming begins with *users stories* written out on 4 by 6 cards that describe desired features. XP employs the *simplest possible design* to get the job done. *Pair programming* is an XP practice; that is, two programmers sit at one workstation so that each program is reviewed as it is written. The *team "owns" the code,* not a particular programmer; therefore, any programmer can work on any part of the code at any time. And, one the most important XP principles is that the *40-hour work week* is in force—programmers go home on time.

FIGURE 10–20

PROGRAM FLOWCHART

This flowchart presents the logic of a payroll program to compute and print payroll checks for hourly and commission employees. The logic is designed so that a driver module calls subroutines as they are needed to process each employee. Only the "Input Data" subroutine is shown here.

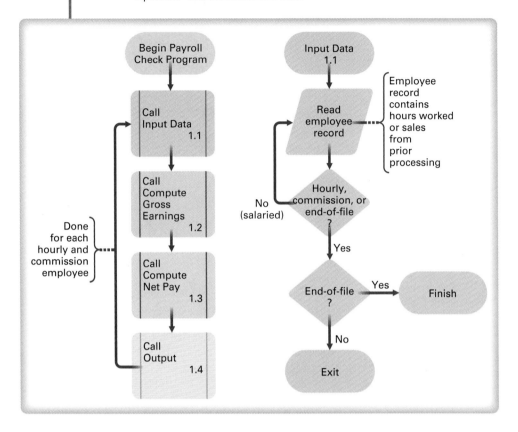

PROGRAMMING AND YOU

As you continue to gain experience with PCs and PC software, you, like so many before you, will probably begin to seek greater speed, power, and efficiency from your PC and its software. To gain speed and power, you will need to upgrade your hardware with the latest technology. To improve efficiency, you might wish to consider learning to write programs—yes, programs. You do not have to be a professional programmer—most people who program are not. They are users who write programs to accomplish personal processing objectives, often freeing up valuable time that can be used for other important tasks.

1 C++, Visual BASIC, and Java are programming languages. (T/F)

2 Record-and-play macros are now obsolete. (T/F)

3 When you write a program, you solve a problem using your powers of: (a) visual interpretation, (b) personality, (c) common sense, or (d) logic.

4 Which of these programming languages is a query language: (a) Visual BASIC, (b) assembler, (c) COBOL, or (d) SQL?

5 Another term for writing a program is: (a) coding, (b) logicizing, (c) converting, or (d) implementing.

6 In a structured program, subordinate modules that are called as needed are termed: (a) subroutines, (b) sub par routines, (c) program pieces, or (d) instruction slices.

Chapter Review

CHAPTER SUMMARY

10-1 THE SYSTEM LIFE CYCLE

The four stages of a computer-based information system comprise the system life cycle. These stages are birth, development, production, and end-of-life.

There are three basic approaches to satisfying a company's information processing needs. The first is to purchase and install a proprietary software package. Some companies obtain information services support from an applications service provider (ASP), a company that provides services and solutions via a wide area network or the Internet. An alternative is to use company employees and/or outside consultants to create an information system customized to meet user specifications.

10-2 SYSTEM DEVELOPMENT TECHNIQUES AND CONCEPTS

The system's design includes all processing activities and the input/output associated with them. When adhering to structured system design, designers divide the system into independent modules for ease of understanding and design. The structure chart enables system designers to conceptualize a system in a hierarchy of modules.

Data flow diagrams enable analysts to design and document systems using the structured approach to system development. The four symbols used in data flow diagrams are entity, process, flow line, and data storage. The focus of the data flow diagram is information flow. Another similar business modeling tool is the entity relationship diagram, which focuses on the attributes of the entities and the relationship among them.

10-3 COMPUTER-AIDED SOFTWARE ENGINEERING

The family of automated software development productivity tools falls under the umbrella of computer-aided software engineering, or CASE, tools. The term software engineering was coined to emphasize an approach to software development that combines automation and the rigors of the engineering discipline. The basic CASE tool kit includes design tools, information repository tools, and program development tools.

CASE design tools help analysts, programmers, and other project team members prepare schematics that graphically depict the logic of a system, as well as a physical representation of a target information system. CASE design tools also help designers prepare the user interface and generate screen and report layouts. The information repository is a central computer-based storage facility for all design information. In an information repository, each piece of system documentation is cross-referenced to all other components in the system. The CASE program development tools, which include application generators, use the system design to generate the software for the sys-

tem. Occasionally, custom programming is required to complete the system. Software engineers develop software products to bridge the gap between design and executable program code.

10-4 PROTOTYPING

The CASE tool kit enables the system development project team to work with users to develop a prototype system. This approach to applications development is called prototyping. Modern prototyping tools enable the development of a scalable system, one whose design can handle any size database or any number of users.

Before CASE and prototyping, project teams would progress through the phases of the traditional system development life cycle (SDLC): *review of current system, systems analysis and design, system development, conversion, and implementation.* In this approach the system specifications are "frozen" early in the development cycle, often before the users know exactly what they want.

The three objectives of prototyping are to analyze the current situation, to identify information needs, and to develop a scaled-down model of the target system. The prototyping process enables users to relate accurate information processing needs to the project team throughout the project.

Rapid application development (RAD) is a generic reference to using software tools (CASE) to design, develop, and implement information systems. Implementation of RAD results in information systems of varying degrees of sophistication.

The prototyping process consists of four phases. During Phase I, Define System Specifications, the current system is analyzed (system analysis) and the target system is designed (system design). During system analysis, the team does the existing system review in which it documents the work and information flow of the system. Team members also formalize the system objectives, identify design constraints, and complete a needs analysis that results in a requirements definition. During system design, the project team takes information from the system analysis and develops a system design and a database design for the target system.

During Phase II, Create Prototype System, the project team translates the system design and specs into instructions that can be interpreted and executed by the computer. During this phase, the creation of CASE-generated and custom software becomes the dominant activity.

During Phase III, Refine Prototype System, a use-and-modify cycle is repeated until users are satisfied with the prototype system.

During Phase IV, Develop Operational System, programmers develop software capable of handling the required volume of work for an operational information system.

10-5 SYSTEM CONVERSION AND IMPLEMENTATION

Once an information system has been developed, it must be implemented within the organization. Although the programs that make up the software for an information system have been debugged on an individual basis (unit testing), they must be combined and subjected to integrated systems testing prior to implementation.

The four common approaches to system conversion are parallel conversion, direct conversion, phased conversion, and pilot conversion. The approach that an organization selects depends on its willingness to accept risk and the amount of time available for the conversion.

An information system is dynamic and must be responsive to the changing needs of the company and those who use it. The process of modifying, or patching, an information system to meet changing needs is known as system maintenance.

10-6 PROGRAMMING

Programmers use a variety of programming languages to communicate instructions to the computer. The design of a program, or its programming logic, is completed before the program is written. Each language uses several types of instructions.

All programming languages ultimately are translated into machine language in order to be executed. Compilers and interpreters translate high-level programming-language instructions (the source code) into a machine-language programs called an object programs. In procedure-oriented languages, such as COBOL and FORTRAN, programmers code the instructions in the sequence in which they must be executed to solve the problem.

Object-oriented languages, such as Smalltalk, C++, C#, and Java, emphasize the *object* of the action. An object is a self-contained is a module that *encapsulates*, or describes, *data* and the *methods* for manipulating the data. Objects are grouped hierarchically into *classes* and *subclasses*. The objects send *messages* to each other to trigger the procedures described within the object. The hierarchical structure of object-oriented programming (OOP) makes programs easier to design and understand.

In fourth-generation languages (4GLs), the programmer need only specify *what* to do, not *how* to do it. One feature of 4GLs is the use of English-like instructions. Query languages, such as SQL, let users request information directly from a database.

In visual programming, text-based instructions are replaced with symbolic icons, each of which represents a common programming function. Examples include Visual BASIC and Visual C#.

A macro is a sequence of frequently used operations or keystrokes that can be recalled as needed. The more complex macros use macro languages that enable flow control, the use of variables, and interaction with users.

Programmers translate the system design and specifications created during the prototyping process into instructions for programs. First, they do a system specifications review. Then they describe all programs necessary to make the system operational. Finally, they design and write the programs, test them, and document them.

Flowcharting is a popular technique for portraying system and programming logic. Flowcharts illustrate data, information, and work flow by the interconnection of specialized symbols with flow lines. IT specialists often conceptualize the logic of a program in three basic control structures—*sequence, selection,* and *loop.* In structured programming, each program is designed with a driver module, or main program, that calls subroutines as they are needed.

Another program design technique is pseudocode, where programmers represent the logic of the program in programlike statements written in plain English.

Extreme programming (XP) is a collaborative team approach to programming in which the programming team works together to write programs in iterative cycles while adhering to time-honored programming practices.

KEY TERMS

application generator (p. 407)
applications service provider (ASP) (p. 400)
C# (p. 419)
C++ (p. 418)
COBOL (p. 418)
code (p. 418)
compiler (p. 417)
computer-aided software engineering (CASE) (p. 405)

custom programming (p. 406)
data flow diagram (p. 401)
direct conversion (p. 413)
driver module (p. 423)
entity relationship diagram (p. 402)
extreme programming (XP) (p. 424)
flowcharting (p. 422)
FORTRAN (p. 418)
fourth-generation languages (4GLs) (p. 419)

information repository (p. 407)
interpreter (p. 417)
Java (p. 418)
layout (p. 407)
macro (p. 420)
macro language (p. 421)
main program (p. 423)
object (p. 418)
object program (p. 417)
object-oriented language (p. 418)

object-oriented programming (OOP)
(p. 418)
parallel conversion (p. 413)
Pascal (p. 418)
patch (p. 414)
Perl (p. 000)
phased conversion (p. 413)
pilot conversion (p. 414)
procedure-oriented language (p. 418)
programming language (p. 415)
proprietary information system
(p. 399)
prototype system (p. 408)

prototyping (p. 408)
pseudocode (p. 423)
rapid application development (RAD)
(p. 409)
scalable system (p. 408)
Smalltalk (p. 418)
software engineer (p. 405)
software engineering (p. 405)
source program (p. 417)
structure chart (p. 401)
structured system design (p. 401)
subroutine (p. 423)

system development life cycle (SDLC)
(p. 409)
system life cycle (p. 399)
system maintenance (p. 414)
system specifications (p. 409)
systems testing (p. 413)
target system (p. 409)
turnkey system (p. 401)
unit testing (p. 413)
Visual BASIC (p. 420)
Visual C# (p. 420)
visual programming (p. 420)

MATCHING

1. macro
2. C++
3. computer-aided software engineering
4. object-oriented programming
5. data flow diagram
6. loop
7. scalable system
8. information repository
9. prototype
10. parallel conversion

a automation of system development
b sequence of instructions to be performed
c repeated until a condition is met
d entity, process, flow line, and storage
e OOP
f f. old and new system working together
g model of system
h central facility for design information
i language used for developing Windows
   applications
j can expand with information needs

CHAPTER SELF-CHECK

TRUE/FALSE

1. System software, such as operating systems, normally is proprietary software. (T/F)

2. The use of applications service providers (ASPs) is on the downswing. (T/F)

3. The application generator is one of the CASE program development tools. (T/F)

4. Custom programming involves the writing of original programs. (T/F)

5. Modern prototyping tools enable the development of a scalable system that can be used by any number of users. (T/F)

6. A needs analysis results in a definition of the information and information processing requirements for the target system. (T/F)

7. Systems testing is always completed prior to unit testing. (T/F)

8. Companies may select the direct conversion approach when there is no existing system. (T/F)

9. Flowcharts can be used to illustrate both information and work flow. (T/F)

10. There are only five programming languages. (T/F)

11. Object-oriented programming handles images, videos, and sound better than does COBOL, a procedure-oriented language. (T/F)

12. In machine language, the programmer specifies what to do, not how to do it. (T/F)

MULTIPLE CHOICE

1. In which stage of the information system life cycle are systems maintained: (a) birth, (b) development, (c) production, or (d) end-of-life?

2. An organization can progress through the development stage of the system life cycle in all but which of

these ways: (a) purchasing proprietary software, (b) using an ASP, (c) relying on government consultants, or (d) creating custom software?

3. Which of the following is not a design technique: (a) flowcharting, (b) data flow diagrams, (c) RE charts, or (d) entity relationship diagrams?

4. Which of these is not one of the four symbols used in data flow diagrams: (a) entity, (b) process, (c) data storage, or (d) decision?

5. Which CASE tool provides systems analysts with the capability of generating a mockup of a screen: (a) design tool, (b) information repository tool, (c) program development tool, or (d) prototype tool?

6. A detailed output and/or input specification is: (a) a layout, (b) an I/O outline, (c) a screen image spec, or (d) a GUI.

7. A model of a full-scale information system is: (a) an archetype, (b) a prototype, (c) a system instance, or (d) a blueprint.

8. System specifications include requirements for system input, output, and: (a) timing, (b) processing, (c) benefits, or (d) feedback.

9. Which of these includes all processing activities and the input/output associated with them for a target information system: (a) driver module flowchart, (b) blueprint, (c) system design documentation, or (d) system review results?

10. Individual program testing is known as: (a) unit testing, (b) module testing, (c) hierarchical testing, or (d) bullet testing.

11. In which approach to system conversion do both the full existing system and the full new system operate simultaneously: (a) direct, (b) parallel, (c) pilot, or (d) phased?

12. What kind of program instructions alter the sequence of the program's execution: (a) control, (b) computation, (c) input/output, or (d) format?

13. Which of these programming languages is a procedure-oriented language: (a) Visual BASIC, (b) assembler, (c) COBOL, or (d) SQL?

14. Because Java can run on just about any computer it is said to be: (a) platform-free, (b) platform-independent, (c) platform-dependent, or (d) platformless.

15. Objects may contain all but which of the following: (a) methods, (b) attributes, (c) pseudocode, or (d) programming code.

16. The seventh and last step in writing a program is: (a) problem description, (b) testing, (c) documentation, or (d) detailed design.

IT ETHICS AND ISSUES

1. COOPERATIVE DEVELOPMENT OF INFORMATION SYSTEMS

A few years ago, cooperative development of information systems was unheard of. Today, competing companies are cooperating to create shared Internet-based systems and services. For example, several major airlines (American Airlines, Continental Airlines, Delta Air Lines, Northwest Airlines, and United Airlines) have joined together to create a super-site (Orbitz.com) where travelers can go to obtain airline tickets and make other travel arrangements. Many other airlines have asked to post fares and schedules to the site, also. The airlines supersite has the potential, in time, to eliminate the need for travel agents, who take a percentage of the value of each ticket they write. Currently, airline tickets, most of which are now e-tickets, can be conveniently purchased online. However, this joint venture is being viewed by some as a deliberate attempt to eliminate the middleman.

Discussion: Is this cooperative processing venture in violation of any law? If so, which law?

Discussion: The American Society of Travel Agents attempted to block development of the Orbitz supersite, citing the possibility of price fixing. Is this a valid argument? Explain.

Discussion: If the middleman is eliminated, should the money saved be passed on to the consumer? Explain.

2. LOCATIONAL COMPUTING

Wireless connections via telephone and computer are enabling us to become increasingly mobile in our computing. The wireless world creates opportunities for a variety of new applications and information systems, one of which is *locational computing*. A global positioning system (GPS) gives your geographic position anywhere in the world. Integrate GPS with a cell phone, notebook computer, or handheld computer and you have some very interesting and controversial systems. Being geographically connected has obvious advantages, but it has its downside, mainly the threat to personal privacy. If you are equipped with an integrated GPS and wireless Internet connection and you access a Web site, that Web site has information on who you are and where you are. This opens up many possibilities. For example, your cell phone might beep you when you are near a particular restaurant and offer you a free dessert with any entrée. If you volunteer your whereabouts, you could create a locational "buddy list" such that each person on the list would know the whereabouts of the others. You could even ask the system to notify you if two or more of your friends are gathered at your favorite pub.

Discussion: Would you give up your locational privacy for the prospects of geographically targeted promotions, such as retail coupons or unsolicited information that might be applicable to a person with your interests?

Discussion: Discuss the advantages and disadvantages of a locational buddy list.

Discussion: Speculate on other applications of locational computing and discuss their impact on personal privacy.

DISCUSSION AND PROBLEM SOLVING

1. Would it be possible for a company with 600 employees to maintain a skeleton information services division of about five IT professionals and use commercially available packaged software for all its computer application needs? Explain.

2. In general, is it better to change internal procedures to fit a particular proprietary software package or to modify the software to fit existing procedures? Discuss.

3. Name one way in which data flow diagrams and entity relationship diagrams are alike and one way in which they are not.

4. Discuss the rationale for the "divide and conquer" approach to system analysis and design.

5. Break down the registration system at your college into a simple structure chart. Discuss each box in the chart.

6. Put yourself in the role of a systems analyst. Draw a first-level data flow diagram depicting your college's student registration system.

7. Expand on the above question and explode one of the processes in the data flow diagram to show detail.

8. Twenty years ago, IT professionals didn't have CASE. Discuss how CASE has changed the traditional approach to system development.

9. Explain how using a CASE information repository during the system development process can have a positive impact on target system quality.

10. Much of the programming code for an information system can be generated with CASE tools. Nevertheless, the demand for programmers remains strong. Explain.

11. One of the objectives of prototyping is to develop a scaled-down model of the target system. However, some prototype systems are fully functional. Describe how a functional prototype system is scaled down.

12. Design a screen layout for an online hospital admittance system. Design only that screen with which the

hospital clerk would interact to enter basic patient data. Distinguish between input and output by underlining the input.

13. Although software tools are available for rapid application development (RAD), many companies continue to use traditional approaches to system development despite greater costs and longer project times. Why do these companies stay with traditional techniques?

14. Why do information systems need patches? What is accomplished when we patch an information system?

15. What is the downside of testing a system only with test data and not with live data, too?

16. What advantage does direct conversion have over parallel conversion? Parallel over direct?

17. During the last fifty years, hundreds of programming languages have been developed, with over a hundred used widely throughout the world. Why do we need so many programming languages?

18. Discuss the steps you must take to turn on your TV and select the ESPN channel. Be very specific as you would in a computer program.

19. Give a system-oriented example, perhaps relating to the registration system at your college, of when you might use each of the flowcharting symbols in Figure 10-18.

20. Discuss the difference between a procedure-oriented language and a fourth-generation language.

21. Complete a flowchart to illustrate the programming logic for a program that accepts three quiz grades from each of any number of students. The program should compute and display the average for each student. Include a driver module in your logic.

22. For the object class, boats, identify at least two subclass objects. Identify attributes and methods for all objects.

23. Do you believe that you may eventually write computer programs in your chosen profession? If so, what kind of programs? If not, why?

1. *Using keystroke macros.* Every productivity software program has built-in keystroke macros in the form of shortcut key combinations. Open Microsoft Word and list these shortcuts. In the *Tools* menu, point to *Macro,* and then click *Macros.* In the *Macros in* box, choose *Word commands.* In the *Macro name* box, choose *ListCommands.* Click *Run,* choose *Current menu and keyboard settings,* and then click *OK* to display a table containing all of the Word shortcut key combinations. Identify at least a dozen (and no more than 30) shortcuts that you feel might be helpful and delete the others. Save and print the table. These shortcut keys can be real time savers when you work with Word documents.

2. *Creating macros.* Open any software suite productivity tool, such as Word, PowerPoint, or Excel. Tap the F1 key for Help and then enter "macros." Choose the option which tells you how to create or set up a macro. Read about macros, then create a record-and-play macro of your own. The macro can be of any repetitive process (for example, setting up a homework document in accordance with instructor specifications). Describe the macro and, if applicable, print a document that illustrates the use of the macro.

ONLINE EXERCISES @ www.prenhall.com/long

1. The Online Study Guide (multiple choice, true/false, matching, and essay questions)
2. Internet Learning Activitiess
   - System Development
   - Computers at Work
   - Web Page Development
3. Serendipitous Internet Activities
   - Business
   - Telecommuting

Whether you are seeking employment or a promotion as a teacher, an accountant, a writer, a fashion designer, a lawyer, or in any of hundreds of other jobs, someone is sure to ask, "What do you know about computers?" Today, information technology applications are part of the daily routine for millions of knowledge workers and are increasingly common for blue-collar workers. No matter which career you choose, it is likely that computers and information technology will be intertwined with your career path.

CAREER OPPORTUNITIES FOR THE IT-COMPETENT MINORITY

Upon completion of this course, you will be part of the IT-competent minority, and you will be able to respond with confidence to any inquiry about your knowledge of computers. This knowledge gives you a career advantage over that 80% of our society that is not computer competent.

JOBS AND THE TREND TOWARD IT DEPENDENCE

Today, most professional jobs come with a telephone, a desk, a PC, and Internet access, making IT competency a prerequisite for people pursuing almost any career (see Figure A-1). This trend toward greater dependence on technology in the workplace has had a dramatic effect on how we do our jobs.

- The terminal or networked PC has become standard equipment at hospital nursing stations and often is found in operating rooms.
- Draftspeople have traded drawing tables for computer-aided design (CAD) workstations.
- Teachers are integrating the power of computers into their instruction and the students' learning experience.
- Economists would be lost without the predictive capabilities of their decision support systems (DSS).
- Truck dispatchers query their information systems, which may include the exact location of fleet trucks (via onboard global positioning systems), before scheduling deliveries.
- Construction contractors keep track of on-site inventory with notebook PCs.
- The PC is the administrative assistant's constant companion for everything from word processing to conference scheduling.
- Stockbrokers often have terminals on both sides of their desks and an Internet-enabled cell phone.
- An attorney's law library is no longer on the shelf behind the desk, but on CD-ROM, DVD-ROM, and/or the Internet.
- Professional football coaches rely on their play databases to give them insight into what offense or defense to run for given situations.
- Politicians frequently tap Internet-based polls before casting their votes.

Career mobility is intertwined with an individual's current and future knowledge of computers and information technology. Of course, career advancement ultimately depends on your abilities, imagination, and performance, but understanding computers and IT can open doors to opportunities that might otherwise be shut. All things being equal, the per-

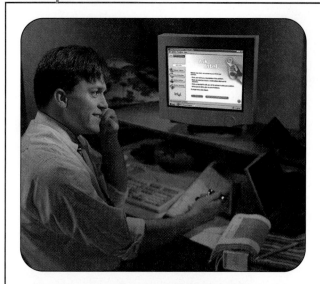

THE KNOWLEDGE WORKER'S TOOLS

In the business world, PCs are networked to enable the sharing of information and ideas. Here a knowledge worker joins another worker in two ways, via telephone and via a network link.

Photo courtesy of Intel Corporation

IT IN HEALTH CARE

Hospital and home health care can be easier and more effective when nurses have a patient's complete medical records with them. This nurse reviews a patient's records and updates them on the spot as circumstances change, such as the results of the bone densitometry test (shown here).

Courtesy of Merck & Co., Inc.

IT IN EDUCATION

This instructor spends much of his workday interacting with students and computers.

Courtesy of International Business Machines Corporation.
Unauthorized use not permitted.

son who has the knowledge of and the will to work with computers and IT will have a clear career advantage over those who do not.

INTERNET JOBS FOR NONTECHNOLOGY PEOPLE

Contrary to what you might imagine, the glamour and high potential of the high-tech industries has room for people who may not consider themselves techies. Millions of workers have asked these questions: What do I need to do to get a technology-related job? How can I get that job without returning to entry-level work?

To be sure, all job functions in the technology industries require IT-competent people. Many people, however, have the misconception that jobs in technology companies require programming knowledge. In fact, many positions require relatively little technical knowledge or experience. For example, many jobs deal exclusively with Internet content (from creating artistic Web pages to collection and analysis of online surveys). Other jobs focus more on project management than on the specifics of technology.

Most of the projects in the high-tech industries involve teams with all types of skills, both technical and nontechnical. A Web site that exhibits state-of-the-art technological features may be of little value to the organization if it is not presented artistically and does not contain well-written content.

If you consider yourself a nontechnical IT-competent person and want to become a part of the Internet and high-tech industries, be aware that job titles and descriptions vary enormously between companies. Positions in high-tech companies are evolving at the same pace as the Internet with new types of jobs and titles coming into existence each month. If you are looking for this type of job, pay close attention to the job description and how it relates to your range of experience and salary history.

WORKING AT HOME

For most people, the workday involves dressing for work, then spending from 30 minutes to 2 hours a day driving to and from the office in rush hour traffic. Information technology is rapidly changing this traditional approach to corporate employment. IT has made it possible for a growing number of people to telecommute to work from their homes. Powerful PCs, broadband Internet access, home networks, and corporate VPNs can make the home office look and feel very much like the corporate office. Today's telecommuters have immediate access to company data and information, plus they have many ways to communicate with their colleagues, including everything from instant messaging to videoconferencing.

THE TREND TOWARD TELECOMMUTING

The most significant workplace trend, especially for IT-competent people, is toward more telecommuting (see Figure A-2); that is, "commuting" to work via data communications. Forecasters are predicting that most knowledge workers will telecommute to work at least one day a week by the end of this decade.

Through the early 1990s, telecommuting was discouraged. Managers were concerned that workers would give priority to personal, not business, objectives. A number of studies have shown that, on average, telecommuters put in more hours and, actually, are more productive at home than at the office.

- The United States Department of Transportation (DOT) has announced a pilot program with significant incentives to encourage "e-commuting" to reduce traffic and pollution. Pilot cities include Los Angeles, Houston, Philadelphia, Denver, and Washington.

- AT&T is encouraging its employees to telecommute on Tuesdays. Among other reasons, AT&T management is trying to support the lifestyle people think is desirable.

- The Canadian government hopes to save taxpayers hundreds of millions of dollars by encouraging telecommuting for public servants. Those who participated in a government-sponsored telecommuting pilot project reported a 73% increase in productivity.

- Telecommuters at American Express handled 26% more calls and produced 43% more business than their office-based counterparts.

- Blue Cross and Blue Shield of South Carolina reported 50% gains in productivity for telecommuters.

TOOLS OF TELECOMMUTING

The typical PC-ready, Internet-connected home can be easily set up for telecommuting. These are the essential elements of a telecommuter's office.

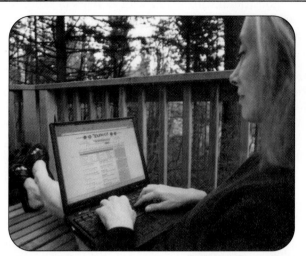

TELECOMMUTING OFFERS FLEXIBILITY

Because of her wireless link to a home network and broadband Internet access, this telecommuter is able to stay online no matter where she is around the house. The familiar surroundings of home inspire some people to do their best work. Others, however, are more comfortable working in a traditional office setting.

Photo courtesy of Intel Corporation

TELECOMMUTING FOR THOSE WITH DISABILITIES

Telecommuting may be a solution for people who are blind, deaf, or have other disabilities that impede their mobility. John Gardner (shown here), a professor of physics at Oregon State University, is working to improve the Internet interface to make Net access easier for these groups of people.

Copyright 2001 Oregon State University

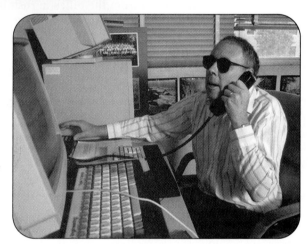

- Ergonomically designed workspace, preferably isolated from the main corridors of the home.
- A PC with Internet access (preferably broadband).
- All-in-one multifunction peripheral (print, scan, fax, and copy) or these peripherals as separate devices.
- Backup storage device and media (for example, DVD ± RW).
- Other peripheral devices to meet application needs, such as a digital video camera.
- Uninterruptible power supply (UPS).
- Software to meet application needs.
- Dedicated voice telephone line.

Even telecommuters like to know that they can go to their company's office building on occasion and have a place to work. Companies recognize this need and are implementing an office space management concept called hoteling. In **hoteling,** a pool of fully equipped offices is designated for telecommuters and mobile workers who reserve offices by the day as they would a room in a hotel.

THE PROS AND CONS OF WORKING AT HOME

Telecommuting has its proponents and opponents. Many managers see telecommuting as a win-win situation in which both employee and company benefit. Others feel that telecommuting causes resentment among office-bound colleagues and weakens corporate loyalty.

Why Work at Home?

Everyone has a different reason for wanting to telecommute. These are the most frequently cited reasons for working at home.

- *Increased productivity*. Telecommuters get more done at home than at the office.
- *Better retention of employees*. Having the telecommuting option attracts and helps to retain top talent.
- *Improve employee morale*. Telecommuters cite improved morale and job satisfaction.
- *Greater flexibility*. Telecommuters can optimize the scheduling of their personal and work activities.
- *Money savings on office space*. Companies need less office space.
- *Money savings on commuting expenses*. Employees can save from $25 to $250 a week in fares, tolls, parking, gasoline, and automobile wear-and-tear costs.
- *Improved relations with family*. Telecommuters spend more time with or around their family.
- *No commute*. The average commuter in a major metropolitan area spends the equivalent of one working day a week traveling to and from work.
- *More comfortable and less expensive clothes*. Men willingly trade ties for T-shirts and women prefer sneakers to heels.
- *Reduction of sick time*. Telecommuters miss fewer days of work as a result of sickness, thus lowering overall health-care-related costs.

One very inviting benefit of full-time telecommuting is that you can live wherever you want. Now, literally millions of telecommuters are migrating to wherever their lifestyle criteria takes them—to smaller towns, warmer weather, their roots, nearer water, or the Rocky Mountains. Urban sprawl used to be constrained by commuting distance. Now the "sprawl" has no limits and this mass migration is actually changing the face of the United States and of other countries, too.

Arguments Against Working at Home

Working at home is not the answer for all workers or companies. Some people are easily distracted and need the ready access to management and the routine of the office to maintain a business focus. The culture, function, and/or tradition at some companies may be incompatible with telecommuting. Telecommuting is not possible when job requirements demand daily face-to-face meetings (for example, bank tellers and elementary school teachers). Those arguing against telecommuting say that electronic interaction does not permit "pressing of the flesh" and the transmittal of the nonverbal cues that are essential to personal interaction.

A Silicon Valley dot.com executive says, "We're creating new things and building new solutions and we need people working side by side, in the office, sharing ideas." A CEO of a consulting firm is concerned that "You just miss out on the value of hallway conversations and the quickly scheduled five-minute meetings." These views, though valid, have done little to hamper the emergence of telecommuting as a mainstream business strategy.

OPPORTUNITIES FOR IT SPECIALISTS

People with computer and information technology education always are at or near the top of the "most wanted" list (see Figure A-3), even when the economy is down. With millions (yes, millions!) of new computers being purchased and linked to the Internet each year, it is likely that this trend will continue. Of course, the number of people attracted to the booming IT field and IT-related fields is also increasing. One of the many reasons for this migration to the IT field is that IT careers are consistently ranked among the most desirable jobs. A recent *Money* magazine article ranked 100 jobs in terms of earnings, long- and short-term job growth, job security, prestige rating, and "stress and strain" rating. The magazine called computer systems analyst the best job in America, with physician, physical therapist, electrical engineer, and civil engineer rounding out the top five. The systems analyst is but

FIGURE A-3 IT SPECIALIST CAREER OPPORTUNITIES

ROBOTICS ENGINEERS AND PROGRAMMERS
Industrial robots now perform many repetitive tasks, such as those on this automobile assembly line. Although the emergence of industrial robots has eliminated some jobs, they have created thousands of jobs for IT specialists who build and program them.

Courtesy of Sun Microsystems, Inc.

NETWORK ADMINISTRATOR AND WEBMASTER
These IT specialists, a network administrator and a Webmaster, develop and maintain a network and a corporate Internet presence. All of these people need a solid foundation of computer knowledge to accomplish their jobs effectively.

Courtesy of Novell

DESIGN ENGINEERS
Computer-aided design (CAD) has revolutionized the way in which engineers and scientists design, draft, and document a product. With CAD, most of the "bugs" can be worked out of a design before a product or plant (in the example) is built.

Courtesy of Intergraph Corporation

one of dozens of IT specialist careers. These are some of the more visible information technology jobs.

- *Chief information officer*. The director of information services within an organization often is called the **chief information officer (CIO)**. This person is responsible for all the information services activity in the company. The CIO, often a vice president, must be somewhat futuristic, predicting which information technologies will become reality so the company can position itself to use them as they become available.

- *Systems analyst*. **Systems analysts** analyze, design, and implement information systems. They work closely with people user groups to design information systems that meet their information processing needs. These "problem solvers" are assigned a variety of support tasks, including feasibility studies, system reviews, security assessments, long-range planning, and hardware/software selection.

- *Programmer*. **Applications programmers** translate analyst-prepared system and input/output specifications into programs. Programmers design the logic, then code, debug, test, and document the programs. A person holding a **programmer/analyst** position performs the functions of both a programmer and a systems analyst.

- *Network administrator*. **Network administrators** design and maintain networks: LANs, MANs, and WANs. This work involves selecting and installing appropriate system software and appropriate hardware, such as modems and routers, and selecting the transmission media.

- *Systems programmer*. **Systems programmers** design, develop, maintain, and implement system software. System software, such as the operating system and system performance management software, is fundamental to the general operation of the computer; that is, it does not address a specific business or scientific problem.

- *Database administrator*. The **database administrator (DBA)** designs, creates, and maintains the integrated database. The DBA coordinates discussions between user groups to determine the content and format of the database so that data redundancy is kept to a minimum. The integrity and the security of the database are also responsibilities of the database administrator.

- *Web application developer*. The **Web application developer** is responsible for creating and maintaining one or more Internet sites. This specialist uses Internet development tools and source material from throughout the organization to create and maintain World Wide Web sites and pages. Occasionally, people in this job function also are responsible for the hardware required at the server site.

- *Webmaster*. The **Webmaster** is an Internet specialist who, depending on the size of the organization, may have a range of responsibilities. Typically, the Web server and its software are the responsibility of the Webmaster. The Webmaster monitors Internet traffic on the server computer and responds to external inquiries regarding Web site operations. Some Webmasters are actively involved in the design and update of Web site pages.

- *Computer operator*. The **computer operator** performs those hardware-based activities needed to keep enterprise-wide systems operational. The operator is in constant communication with the computer(s) while monitoring the progress of online systems, a number of simultaneous production runs, initiating one-time jobs, and troubleshooting.

- *User liaison*. Computer and information processing activity is very intense in companies that seek to exploit the full potential of information technology. In this environment, someone who is working in a particular functional area (perhaps the marketing department) is told to seek ways to take advantage of available IT resources. More often than not, this person is the user liaison. The **user liaison** is a "live-in" IT specialist who coordinates all computer-related activities within a particular functional area.

The trend toward client/server computing has resulted in the distribution of both hardware and IT specialists throughout the organization. As a result, IT-related jobs can be found in a centralized information services department or they can be found in marketing, plant operations, or any department throughout the organization.

The variety and types of IT specialist jobs are ever changing. For example, there's the *information detective*. Companies and individuals call on these high-tech detectives to help them answer such questions as: Has my child's sitter had any driving accidents? Has my materials supplier ever filed for bankruptcy? Did this applicant for the sales manager position really earn an MBA at Harvard? Another related job is the professional *Internet researcher*. Someone who really knows his or her way around the Internet can do in minutes what might take a Net newbie several days to do. Some artistic careers, such as *animator* and *video production editor,* have become so heavily steeped in technology, that they, too, are considered IT specialists careers.

THE GROWING IT SPECIALIST FIELDS

Almost every company, no matter how small or large, employs or contracts with IT specialists, and most of these companies are looking for qualified information technology people. IT specialists have many doors open to them. If they accept employment in an organization's information services department, they often are given the option of working in a traditional office environment or telecommuting to work at least part of the time. Those who prefer working in a variety of environments are working for consulting firms or working as independent contractors. If the trend toward outsourcing (contracting with external personnel to do in-house work) continues, look for the number of consultants and contractors to surpass the number of traditional in-house IT personnel in the near future.

IT workers are in demand not just for their skills but also for what they contribute to the organization. The findings in a United States Department of Commerce report indicated that information technology workers were more than twice as productive as workers in other areas were during the 1990s.

Of course, employment opportunities in any profession are tied to the economy. The better the economy, the greater the demand for IT specialists. Fortunately for IT specialists, the number of computers and applications continues to grow, even in a down economy, so the job outlook for IT specialists continues to be bright. The salary table in Figure A-4 should give you a feel for the salaries that can be expected in familiar IT positions for the year 2004.

WOMEN IN INFORMATION TECHNOLOGY

The Internet explosion has created a new business culture in which women can more easily climb the corporate ladder. In the IT career field, the number of women in senior management positions is approximately that of men. Factors contributing to this shift away from a male-dominated business world include the enormous demand by Internet companies for knowledgeable, talented employees. Also, the hierarchical structure of Internet and high-tech businesses is more loosely defined and ever changing, enabling significant promotions both laterally and into management. Web companies, especially the smaller ones, are under great pressure to achieve quick success, and they face stiff competition in finding the people who will make that happen. The Internet has made IT employment a new game in which traditional patterns of employment no longer apply.

LICENSING AND CERTIFICATION

If you are an IT specialist or your chosen career overlaps with information technology, you may be in constant contact with sensitive data. Also, it is likely that you may have the power to control important, even life threatening, events. In either case, it is your responsibility to maintain the integrity of the system and its data. Failure to do so could have a disastrous effect on the lives of individuals and even on the stability of the organization. Trillions of dollars are handled each day by computer-based systems that are created and

PROJECTED AVERAGE SALARY AND INDUSTRY SALARY RANGE FOR 2004 (IN $1,000s)

The table shows estimated average salaries (plus bonuses) and salary range for familiar information technology positions. The range is the range of the average salaries by industry. Some industries (for example, high-tech and consulting services) pay higher salaries to IT people than do other industries (for example, education, government, and retail). Actual salaries could be lower or higher. Salaries are projected from year 2002 salary surveys based on historical cost-of-living increases for IT workers and general economic conditions.

TOP MANAGEMENT

Position	Average Salary Range
Chief information officer (CIO)/vice president	$160 ($100–$300)
Chief technology officer	$150 ($95–$180)
Director of systems development	$135 ($90–$172)
Director of IT operations	$115 ($75–$150)
Internet technology strategist	$120 ($60–$140)
Webmaster	$90 ($53–$140)
Director of networks	$120 ($90–$180)

MIDDLE MANAGEMENT

Position	Average Salary Range
Manager of voice and data communications	$85 ($60–$150)
Network manager	$80 ($55–$105)
Manager of Internet/intranet technology	$92 ($55–$134)
Project manager	$96 ($82–$120)
Database manager	$102 ($75–$120)
Computer operations manager	$85 ($67–$125)
Help desk/technical support manager	$82 ($65–$100)

STAFF (INCLUDING ENTRY LEVEL)

Position	Average Salary Range
Network administrator	$70 ($61–$91)
Network engineer	$72 ($55–$85)
Web application developer	$58 ($50–$75)
Senior systems analyst	$85 ($74–$95)
Systems administrator	$71 ($60–$80)
Senior systems programmer	$80 ($69–$95)
Senior programmer	$70 ($55–$90)
Senior programmer/analyst	$80 ($70–$95)
Programmer/analyst	$69 ($60–$82)
Software engineer	$80 ($63–$95)
Database analyst/administrator	$80 ($60–$92)
User liaison	$75 ($60–$90)
Information security specialist	$75 ($49–$90)
Lead computer operator	$55 ($42–$65)
Computer operator	$46 ($38–$55)
PC technical specialist	$60 ($40–$77)
Help desk/technical support specialist	$50 ($40–$60)

controlled by IT specialists. The lives of millions of air travelers depend on the responsiveness of air traffic controllers and their systems. Life sustaining systems in hospitals are designed, programmed, and maintained by IT specialists.

At present, licensing or certification is usually not a requirement for any IT professional; nor is it required for users of computers. Licensing and certification are hotly debated issues. Many professions require demonstration of performance at a certain level of competence before permission is granted to practice. Through examination, the engineer becomes a registered professional engineer, the attorney becomes a member of the bar, and the accountant becomes a certified public accountant. Many people in the trades, including hairdressers, plumbers, and electricians, must be licensed to practice.

Within the computer community, there are a number of certifications. Several professional organizations provide certification options, including the Institute for Certification of Computer Professionals (ICCP), which awards the *Certified Computing Professional (CCP)* and the *Associate Computing Professional (ACP)*. The CCP and ACP are general certifications in the area of computers and information technology. A growing number of companies whose products have become de facto standards offer certifications. For example, IT giants Microsoft, Novell, Sun, and Cisco sponsor a range of widely accepted certifications. Microsoft awards these certificates to information technology professionals who have completed a series of rigorous tests (see Figure A-5).

- *Microsoft Certified Professional.* The MCP credential is for professionals who have the skills to implement successfully a Microsoft product or technology as part of a business solution in an organization.

- *Microsoft Certified Systems Administrators.* MCSAs administer network and systems environments based on the Microsoft Windows platforms.

- *Microsoft Certified Systems Engineer.* The MCSE analyzes business requirements to design and implement an infrastructure solution based on the Windows platform and Microsoft Servers software.

- *Microsoft Certified Database Administrator.* MCDBAs design, implement, and administer Microsoft SQL Server™ databases.

- *Microsoft Certified Trainers.* MCTs are certified by Microsoft to deliver Microsoft training courses to IT professionals and developers.

FIGURE A-5 **EXAMS FOR PROFESSIONAL CERTIFICATION**

This is an example question for the Windows XP Professional Exam, which is part of several Microsoft certification programs, including the MCP, the MCSE, and the MCSA. The actual exam has 215 questions. Example questions to all Microsoft exams can be found at the Microsoft Web site.

- *Microsoft Certified Application Developers.* The MCAD uses Microsoft technologies to develop and maintain department-level applications, components, Web or desktop clients, or back-end data services.

- *Microsoft Certified Solution Developer.* MCSDs design and develop business solutions with Microsoft technologies.

- *Microsoft Office Specialist.* Office Specialists are recognized globally for demonstrating advanced skills with Microsoft Office desktop software, such as PowerPoint or Word.

- *Microsoft Office Specialist Master Instructor.* Office Specialist Master Instructors are certified as trainers for Microsoft Office desktop programs.

Novell, a company that specializes in networking products, offers several levels of certification for people who work with its widely used network products.

- *Certified Novell Administrator.* CNAs provide network support for Novell networking products, NetWare and GroupWise.

- *Certified Novell Engineer.* The CNE can provide advanced company-wide networking support, including planning, installation, configuration, troubleshooting, and upgrade.

- *Master CNE.* A Master CNE is a multivendor, multisolution specialist of the network industry.

The *Certified Novell Instructor* and *Novell Authorized Instructor* certifications are available to people who provide training on Novell networking products. Novell also awards other IT specialist certificates in such areas as Internet security and database integration.

Sun Microsystems offers several certifications for Java, the "write once, run anywhere" programming language that is so popular with Web-based applications. Certifications are awarded at different skill levels and for Web or enterprise applications. These include the *Sun Certified Programmer for the Java 2 Platform*, the *Sun Certified Developer for the Java 2 Platform*, the *Sun Certified Web Component Developer for the Java 2 Platform (Enterprise Edition)*, and the *Sun Certified Enterprise Architect for J2EE Technology*.

Cisco Systems, the world leader in Internet networking equipment, offers a range of certifications. The top level Cisco Career Certification is the *Cisco Certified Internetwork Expert*. Other professional certifications include the *Cisco Certified Design Professional*, *Cisco Certified Internetwork Professional*, *Cisco Certified Network Professional*, and *Cisco Certified Security Professional*. Cisco offers a group of specialist certifications in such areas as IP, virtual private networks, and wireless LAN design.

People seeking any of these certifications must pass an array of tests. Generally, recruiters and employers view certifications favorably. Often, being certified results in a higher salary. However, certifications are seldom a requirement for employment.

GETTING A JOB

Whether you are entering the job market for the first time or seeking alternative employment, resources on the Internet can help you land the position you want.

- *Comprehensive career/employment Web sites.* The Internet now has a number of comprehensive career/employment Web sites designed to help employer and candidate find one another. These include sites like Monster.com and CareerMosaic.com, which offer a wide variety of career services.

- *Industry-specific or professional career/employment Web sites.* These sites offer similar services to the comprehensive sites, but their orientation is to a specific industry, such as health care, oil and gas, or airlines. Or, their orientation is to specific professionals, such as accountants, lawyers, engineers, or physicians.

- *Company job opening pages.* Most company Web sites now have a page called something like "career opportunities" or "job seekers." This page and its links will contain detailed information about available openings, often by geographical location, division, or job function (see Figure A-6).

The career/employment Web sites offer these types of resources and services.

- *Jobs database.* Potential employers post job openings to a searchable job-openings database.

- *Candidates database.* You can post a résumé to the site's candidates database. This database is made available to potential employers.

- *Job search.* A comprehensive site may have hundreds of thousands of job openings in its database. You can search the job-openings database

| FIGURE A-6 | **FIND A JOB AT A SPECIFIC COMPANY** |

IBM's "Jobs at IBM" Web site offers a continuously updated listing of available jobs at IBM. The site invites applicants to submit a résumé, as well.

by keyword, industry type, job type, and geographic locale to get a listing of jobs that meet your criteria.

- *Candidate search*. Employers continuously search the candidates database, which contains the résumés of those seeking jobs, to find candidates who can fill their job openings.

- *Career resources*. Major career sites have extensive resources for those people who are contemplating a job or career change or are seeking employment for the first time. These could include interactive tools that help people prepare a résumé and cover letter templates, tips on preparing for an interview, relocation information (including comparisons between cities), compensation statistics, tips on salary negotiation, information on employers, and much more.

The online jobs search has revolutionized the manner in which those seeking employment find jobs and those companies seeking employees find candidates. The tradition of sending a snail mail résumé in response to a help-wanted ad in a newspaper or magazine may have lost its effectiveness in our connected information society. In this new era, the jobs search process is made easier for both employer and candidate. Also, some say that the online process results in a better match for both employee and employer.

OUR JOBS ARE CHANGING

Automation is causing the elimination of some jobs. For example, the revenue accounting staff at a major U.S. airline was reduced from 650 to 350 with the implementation of a new computer-based system. Those remaining had to be retrained to work with the new system. Those displaced had to be retrained for other work opportunities in an increasingly automated society.

IT solutions have caused all or at least part of many job functions to be replaced with automated systems (see Figure A-7). Automated telephone systems have eliminated the need for many receptionists. The presence of ATMs means fewer bank tellers are needed. The emergence of e-trading reduces the demand for stockbrokers. E-tailing, much of which is completely automated, affects a variety of retail jobs. Some people get loans from banks online, whereby an expert "loan" system makes the decisions. The explosion of online classes hasn't eliminated the need for professors, but, for some professors, their job function has changed dramatically from in-class instruction to online course development and delivery.

Fortunately, information technology is responsible for the creation of many other jobs. The explosion of information technology has resulted in thousands of new companies that provide a variety of previously unknown products and services. Dot.com giant America Online was founded in 1985. Yahoo! and Netscape were founded in 1994. Many other high-tech companies didn't exist a decade ago. Now they employ hundreds, even tens of thousands, of people in high-paying jobs. Ten years ago, relatively few companies had Web sites. Today, every company desiring to stay in business has a Web site and a site support staff.

As information technology continues to move to the forefront in our society, jobs in every discipline are being redefined. For example, ten years ago sales representatives carried manuals and products to the customer site. Today, they still knock on doors, but to a much lesser extent because much of what used to be personal interaction is now electronic interaction. When they do make sales calls, they bring their notebook PCs, not heavy manuals. Thanks to technology, the sales rep is no longer the sole source of product/service information. Customers can get up-to-

FIGURE A-7

KEEPING SCORE THE ELECTRONIC WAY

The way tennis is played hasn't changed much, but the way players train and the way it is tracked and reported have changed. Every point is documented during the Olympics (shown here), during all professional tennis matches, and during many juniors matches, too. The data are analyzed by players and coaches and reported by broadcasters and reporters.

Courtesy of International Business Machines Corporation.

Unauthorized use not permitted.

date information directly from the vendor via its extranet (an extension of a company's private intranet). Many customers don't deal with sales reps at all. They obtain needed information by browsing the Internet or an extranet, and then they place their orders electronically.

Radical changes in the way we do our jobs are not limited to the business community. Poets, the clergy, politicians, music composers, and others are continually evaluating what they do and how they do it within the context of emerging technology.

APPENDIX SELF-CHECK

1 At present, less than half of the companies in the United States employ or contract with IT specialists. (T/F)

2 Because of privacy concerns, companies rarely post their job opportunities to their Internet Web sites. (T/F)

3 In general, IT workers are more productive than workers in other areas. (T/F)

4 Automation does not eliminate jobs. (T/F)

5 At present, certification is not a requirement to become an IT professional. (T/F)

6 Telecommuting has shown increases in productivity between 2 and 5% per telecommuter. (T/F)

7 Telecommuters cite improved morale and job satisfaction as justification for telecommuting. (T/F)

8 The culture, function, and/or tradition at some companies may be incompatible with telecommuting. (T/F)

9 Which of these is not a Microsoft certification: (a) MCP, (b) CNE, (c) MCAD, or (d) MCSA?

10 The director of information services within an organization is called the: (a) DBA, (b) Webmaster, (c) network administrator, or (d) CIO.

11 The "live-in" IT specialist who coordinates computer-related activities within a particular functional area is called a: (a) user liaison, (b) computer operator, (c) CIO, or (d) Web application developer.

12 Which certification recognizes advanced skills with Microsoft Office desktop software: (a) MCDBA, (b) CDE, (c) Novell Authorized Instructor, or (d) Microsoft Office Specialist?

13 The focus of certification programs from Sun Microsystems is what programming language: (a) Visual Basic, (b) Java, (c) Perl, or (d) COBOL?

14 The career/employment Web sites offer all but which of these types of resources and services: (a) jobs database, (b) job search capability, (c) career resources, or (d) college degree programs?

15 Which of these is not an argument in favor of telecommuting: (a) increased productivity, (b) increased sick time off from work, (c) less on-site office space required, or (d) reduced clothing expense?

16 An office space management concept intended to provide on-site office space for telecommuters and mobile workers is: (a) hosteling, (b) internetting, (c) intranetting, or (d) hoteling.

Getting Started

Page 18
1. B
2. A
3. B
4. B
5. A
6. C
7. B
8. A
9. B
10. D
11. A
12. B
13. B
14. C
15. B
16. D
17. A
18. C
19. B
20. D
21. C
22. B
23. A
24. D

CHAPTER 1
Section Self-Check
Page 21
1. F
2. B
3. B
Page 24
1. F
2. T
3. B
Page 35
1. C
2. C

3. C
4. A
5. C
Page 39
1. B
2. A
3. C
Page 48
1. T
2. F
3. B
4. D
5. B
6. B
Page 51
1. B
2. D
3. C
Matching
1. i
2. c
3. d
4. b
5. e
6. h
7. j
8. f
9. g
10. a
Chapter Self-Check
True/False
1. F
2. F
3. F
4. F
5. F
6. F
7. F
8. F

9. T
10. T
Multiple Choice
1. A
2. C
3. C
4. D
5. D
6. A
7. A
8. D
9. A
10. A
11. D
12. C
13. B
14. C
15. C
16. A
17. D
18. B
19. B
20. D
IT Illustrated
1. T
2. T
3. F
4. T
5. T
6. B
7. C
8. A
9. B
10. D

CHAPTER 2
Section Self-Check
Page 77
1. T
2. B

3. D
4. A
5. B
6. T
7. B
Page 89
1. F
2. F
3. T
4. A
5. D
6. C
7. B
Page 92
1. T
2. T
3. C
4. F
5. B
Page 99
1. T
2. T
3. C
4. A
Page 107
1. C
2. B
3. B
4. C
Matching
1. d
2. f
3. e
4. c
5. i
6. a
7. b
8. h
9. g
10. j

Chapter Self-Check

True/False

1. F
2. F
3. F
4. F
5. T
6. F
7. F
8. T
9. F
10. T
11. F
12. T
13. F
14. T

Multiple Choice

1. B
2. C
3. B
4. D
5. C
6. D
7. C
8. A
9. C
10. B
11. C
12. B
13. D
14. A
15. A
16. A
17. C
18. A

CHAPTER 3

Section Self-Check

Page 123

1. F
2. T
3. A
4. A
5. B
6. D
7. B

Page 128

1. T
2. F
3. B
4. A

Page 142

1. T
2. F
3. C
4. D
5. B
6. C

Page 147

1. F
2. F
3. C
4. A

Matching

1. b
2. j
3. d
4. e
5. c
6. f
7. h
8. i
9. a
10. g

Chapter Self-Check

True/False

1. T
2. F
3. F
4. F
5. F
6. F
7. F
8. T
9. T
10. T
11. F
12. T

Multiple Choice

1. A
2. C
3. B
4. A
5. B
6. A
7. B
8. B
9. B
10. D
11. C
12. B
13. D
14. D
15. B
16. C
17. C
18. B
19. D
20. B
21. B
22. B

CHAPTER 4

Section Self-Check

Page 160

1. T
2. T
3. A
4. D
5. B

Page 172

1. F
2. T
3. B
4. A
5. B

Page 177

1. T
2. F
3. B
4. A
5. B

Page 179

1. T
2. F

Matching

1. i
2. j
3. g
4. a
5. h
6. c
7. e
8. d
9. f
10. b

Chapter Self-Check

True/False

1. F
2. F
3. F
4. T
5. T
6. T
7. F
8. F
9. T
10. F
11. F
12. F

Multiple Choice

1. A
2. B
3. C
4. A
5. D
6. A
7. C
8. B
9. A
10. D
11. A
12. C
13. C
14. C

IT Illustrated

1. T
2. F
3. T
4. C
5. A
6. D

CHAPTER 5

Section Self-Check

Page 202

1. F
2. F
3. B
4. A
5. C

Page 206

1. T
2. F
3. A
4. D
5. A

Page 222

1. T
2. F

3. A
4. A
5. B
6. C

Page 231

1. T
2. F
3. A
4. C
5. A

Matching

1. b
2. f
3. d
4. a
5. h
6. i
7. g
8. c
9. j
10. e

Chapter Self-Check

True/False

1. F
2. T
3. T
4. F
5. F
6. T
7. T
8. T
9. T
10. T
11. F
12. F
13. T
14. F
15. T
16. F
17. F

Multiple Choice

1. C
2. B
3. A
4. D
5. C
6. B
7. C
8. A
9. A
10. C
11. A
12. B
13. C
14. C
15. D
16. A
17. A
18. D
19. A
20. C
21. C
22. B
23. C
24. B

CHAPTER 6

Section Self-Check

Page 237

1. T
2. F
3. B
4. B

Page 242

1. T
2. A
3. D
4. A
5. B

Page 249

1. F
2. F
3. B
4. B

Page 259

1. F
2. F
3. C
4. C
5. D
6. C

Page 263

1. T
2. F
3. D
4. C
5. C

Matching

1. d
2. e
3. h
4. j
5. i
6. g
7. b
8. f
9. c
10. a

Chapter Self-Check

True/False

1. F
2. T
3. F
4. T
5. F
6. T
7. T
8. T
9. T

10. F
11. F
12. T
13. F
14. F
15. F
16. T
17. T

Multiple Choice

1. C
2. A
3. B
4. A
5. C
6. C
7. A
8. D
9. A
10. C
11. A
12. A
13. C
14. A
15. C
16. A
17. B
18. A
19. D
20. A

CHAPTER 7

Section Self-Check

Page 285

1. F
2. T
3. B
4. A

Page 289

1. T
2. A
3. D

Page 294

1. T
2. F
3. C
4. B

Page 305

1. F
2. T
3. T
4. D
5. C
6. C
7. A

Matching

1. i
2. h
3. g
4. e
5. c
6. f
7. b
8. a
9. d
10. j

Chapter Self-Check

True/False

1. F
2. F
3. T
4. T
5. F
6. F
7. F

Multiple Choice

1. C
2. A
3. D
4. D
5. B
6. D

7. D
8. C
9. D
10. B
11. C
12. A
13. D
14. A
15. B
16. A

IT Illustrated

1. T
2. F
3. F
4. T
5. F
6. T
7. D
8. B
9. D
10. B
11. A

CHAPTER 8

Section Self-Check

Page 336

1. T
2. T
3. B
4. D
5. C
6. D

Page 347

1. F
2. F
3. F
4. C
5. B
6. D
7. A

Page 335

1. T
2. T
3. A
4. C
5. A
6. D

Matching

1. j
2. f
3. b
4. g
5. a
6. c
7. h
8. i
9. e
10. d

Chapter Self-Check

True/False

1. T
2. F
3. T
4. F
5. T
6. F
7. F
8. T
9. F
10. F
11. F
12. T

Multiple Choice

1. B
2. C
3. D
4. A
5. A
6. B
7. B

8. A
9. B
10. B
11. D
12. A
13. D
14. D
15. D
16. C
17. C
18. D

CHAPTER 9

Section Self-Check

Page 364

1. T
2. F
3. D

Page 370

1. T
2. F
3. A

Page 374

1. T
2. F
3. C
4. C
5. B

Page 377

1. F
2. T
3. B

Page 388

1. F
2. F
3. T
4. F
5. C
6. C

Page 391

1. T
2. A
3. B

Matching

1. h
2. j
3. b
4. a
5. d
6. f
7. g
8. i
9. e
10. c

Chapter Self-Check

True/False

1. F
2. T
3. F
4. T
5. T
6. F
7. T

Multiple Choice

1. C
2. A
3. A
4. C
5. C
6. D
7. A
8. B
9. D
10. C
11. B
12. D
13. D
14. C

CHAPTER 10

Section Self-Check

Page 401

1. F
2. F
3. B

Page 405

1. T
2. F
3. B
4. D

Page 408

1. T
2. T
3. B

Page 412

1. F
2. A
3. A
4. D

Page 414

1. T
2. F
3. B

Page 425

1. T
2. F
3. D
4. D
5. A

6. A

Matching

1. b
2. i
3. a
4. e
5. d
6. c
7. j
8. h
9. g
10. f

Chapter Self-Check

True/False

1. T
2. F
3. T
4. T
5. T
6. T
7. F
8. T
9. T
10. F
11. T
12. F

Multiple Choice

1. C
2. C
3. C

4. D
5. A
6. A
7. A
8. B
9. C
10. A
11. B
12. A
13. C
14. B
15. C
16. C

Appendix

1. F
2. F
3. T
4. F
5. T
6. F
7. T
8. T
9. B
10. D
11. A
12. D
13. B
14. D
15. B
16. D

1394 bus A bus standard that supports data transfer rates of up to 800 M bps. (Also called *FireWire*.)

1394 port Enables connection to the 1394 (FireWire) bus.

A

Access arm The disk drive mechanism used to position the read/write heads over the appropriate track.

Access point A communications hub that enables a link to a LAN via short-range radio waves.

Access time The time between the instant a computer makes a request for a transfer of data from disk storage and the instant this operation is completed.

Accumulator The computer register in which the result of an arithmetic or logic operation is formed. (Related to *arithmetic and logic unit*.)

ActiveX controls A program that uses Microsoft's ActiveX technology that can be downloaded and executed by a browser to enable multimedia in Web pages. (See also *applet*.)

Address (1) A name, numeral, or label that designates a particular location in RAM or disk storage. (2) A location identifier for nodes in a computer network.

Address bus Pathway through which source and destination addresses are transmitted between RAM, cache memory, and the processor. (See also *data bus*.)

AGP (Accelerated Graphics Port) board A graphics adapter that permits interfacing with video monitors.

AGP bus A special-function bus designed to handle high-resolution 3-D graphics.

All-in-one multifunction device A multifunction machine that can handle the paper-related tasks of printing, facsimile, scanning, and copying.

Alpha A reference to the letters of the alphabet. (Compare with *numeric* and *alphanumeric*.)

Alphanumeric Pertaining to a character set that contains letters, digits, punctuation, and special symbols. (Related to *alpha* and *numeric*.)

Analog signal A continuous waveform signal that can be used to represent such things as sound, temperature, and velocity. (See also *digital signal*.)

Animation software Software that facilitates animation, the rapid repositioning of objects on a display to create the illusion of movement.

Anonymous FTP site An Internet site that permits FTP (file transfer protocol) file transfers without prior permission.

ANSI The American National Standards Institute is a nongovernmental standards-setting organization that develops and publishes standards for "voluntary" use in the United States.

Antivirus program A utility program that periodically checks a PC's hard disk for computer viruses then removes any that are found.

Applet A small program sent over the Internet or an intranet that is interpreted and executed by Internet browser software. (See also *ActiveX controls*.)

Application generator A system development tool used to actually generate the system programming code based on design specifications.

Application icon A miniature visual representation of a software application on a display.

Application window A rectangular window containing an open, or running, application in Microsoft Windows.

Applications programmer A programmer who translates analyst-prepared system and input/output specifications into programs. Programmers design the logic, then code, debug, test, and document the programs.

Applications service provider (ASP) An ASP is a company that provides software-based services and solutions to customers via the Internet from a central server computer.

Applications software Software designed and written to address a specific personal, business, or processing task.

Arithmetic and logic unit That portion of the computer that performs arithmetic and logic operations. (Related to *accumulator*.)

Arithmetic operators Mathematical operators (add [+], subtract [−], multiply [*], divide [/], and exponentiation [^]) used in programming and in spreadsheet and database software for computations.

Artificial intelligence (AI) The ability of a computer to reason, to learn, to strive for self-improvement, and to simulate human sensory capabilities.

Artificial life (ALife) The study of and creation of computer-based systems that behave like biological systems.

ASCII [American Standard Code for Information Interchange) A 7-bit or 8-bit encoding system.

ASCII file A generic text file that is stripped of program-specific control characters.

Assembler language A programming language that uses easily recognized symbols, called mnemonics, to represent instructions.

Assistant system This knowledge-based system helps users make relatively straightforward decisions. (See also *expert system*.)

Assistive technology Enabling input/output peripherals and software for people with disabilities.

Asynchronous transmission A protocol in which data are transmitted at irregular intervals on an as-needed basis. (See also *synchronous transmission*.)

Attached file A file that is attached and sent with an e-mail message.

Audio file   A file that contains digitized sound.

Authoring software   Software that lets you create multimedia applications that integrate sound, motion, text, animation, and images.

Automatic teller machine (ATM)   An automated deposit/withdrawal device used in banking.

B

B2B (business-to-business)   An e-commerce concept that encourages intercompany processing and data exchange via computer networks and the Internet. (Contrast with *B2C*.)

B2C (business-to-consumer)   An e-commerce concept that encourages electronic interactions between businesses and consumers via Internet-server computers. (Contrast with *B2B*.)

Backbone   A system of routers and the associated transmission media that facilitates the interconnection of computer networks.

Back-end applications software   This software on the server computer performs processing tasks in support of its clients, such as tasks associated with storage and maintenance of a centralized corporate database. (See also *front-end applications software*.)

Background   (1) That part of RAM that contains the lowest priority programs. (2) In Windows, the area of the display over which the foreground is superimposed. (Contrast with *foreground*.)

Backup   Pertaining to equipment, procedures, or databases that can be used to restart the system in the event of system failure.

Backup file   Duplicate of an existing file.

Badge reader   An input device that reads data on badges and cards.

Bandwidth   Generally the range of frequencies in a communications channel or, specifically, the number of bits the channel can transmit per second.

Bar code   A graphic encoding technique in which printed vertical bars of varying widths are used to represent data.

Bar graph   A graph that contains bars that represent specified numeric values.

Batch processing   A technique in which transactions and/or jobs are collected into groups (batched) and processed together.

Binary   A base-2 numbering system.

Biometric identification system   Systems that detect unique personal characteristics that can be matched against a database containing the characteristics of authorized users.

BIOS (Basic Input Output System)   Flash memory-based software that contains the instructions needed to boot a PC and load the operating system.

Bit   A *binary digit* (0 or 1).

Bit-mapped graphics   Referring to an image that has been projected, or mapped, to a screen based on binary bits. (See also *raster graphics*.)

Bits per second (bps)   The number of bits that can be transmitted per second over a communications channel.

Bluetooth   A short-range wireless communications technology. (Contrast with *Wi-Fi*.)

BMP   A popular format for bit-mapped files.

Boilerplate   Existing text in a word processing file that can in some way be customized for use in a variety of word processing applications.

Boot   The procedure for loading the operating system to RAM and readying a computer system for use.

Bots   See *intelligent agent*.

Broadband   Typically, a reference to a high-speed Internet link via cable, satellite, or DSL.

Broadband access   Generic term for high-speed Internet access.

Browsers   Programs that let you navigate to and view the various Internet resources.

Bug   A logic or syntax error in a program, a logic error in the design of a computer system, or a hardware fault. (See also *debug*.)

Bus topology   A computer network that permits the connection of terminals, peripheral devices, and microcomputers along an open-ended central cable.

Business-to-business   See *B2B*.

Business-to-consumer   See *B2C*.

Button bar   A software option that contains a group of pictographs that represent a menu option or a command.

Byte   A group of adjacent bits configured to represent a character or symbol.

C

C   A transportable programming language that can be used to develop software.

C++   An object-oriented version of the C programming language.

C#   A Microsoft object-oriented programming language aimed at Web development.

Cache memory   High-speed solid-state memory for program instructions and data.

CAD   See *computer-aided design*.

Cascading menu   A pop-up menu that is displayed when a command from the active menu is chosen.

Cascading windows   Two or more windows that are displayed on a computer screen in an overlapping manner.

Cat5 cabling   One hundred M bps LAN cabling that uses twisted pair wire with RJ-45 connectors.

Cat5e cabling   One G bps LAN cabling that uses twisted pair wire with RJ-45 connectors.

Cathode-ray tube   See *CRT monitor*.

CBT   See *computer-based training*.

CD-R (compact disc-recordable) The medium on which CD writers create CDs and CD-ROMs.

CD-ReWritable (CD-RW) This technology allows users to rewrite to the same CD media.

CD-ROM disc (compactdisk read-only memory disc) A type of optical laser storage media.

CD-ROM drive A storage device into which an interchangeable CD-ROM disc is inserted for processing.

CD-RW See *CD-ReWritable*.

Celeron® A line of Intel®microprocessors designed for low-cost PCs.

Cell The intersection of a particular row and column in a spreadsheet.

Cell address The location—column and row—of a cell in a spreadsheet.

Central processing unit (CPU) See *processor*.

CERT Coordination Center (CERT/CC) An agency that works to thwart electronic vandalism and crime on the Internet.

CGM A popular vector graphics file format.

Channel The facility by which data are transmitted between locations in a computer network (e.g., terminal to host, host to printer).

Channel capacity The number of bits that can be transmitted over a communications channel per second.

Chat An Internet application that allows people on the Internet to converse in real time via text or audio.

Chief information officer (CIO) The individual responsible for all the information services activity in a company.

Chip See *integrated circuit*.

Chipset A motherboard's intelligence that controls the flow of information between system components connected to the board.

CISC (complex instruction set computer) A computer design architecture that offers machine language programmers a wide variety of instructions. (Contrast with *RISC*.)

Click through rate The percentage of people who click on the hyperlink advertisement.

Client application (1) An application running on a networked workstation or PC that works in tandem with a server application. (See also *server application*.) (2) In object linking and embedding, the application containing the destination document. (See also *OLE*.)

Client computer Typically a PC or a workstation that requests processing support or another type of service from one or more server computers. (See also *server computer*.)

Client program A software program that runs on a PC and works in conjunction with a companion server program that runs on a server computer. (See also *server program*.)

Client/server computing A computing environment in which processing capabilities are distributed throughout a network such that a client computer requests processing or some other type of service from a server computer.

Clip art Prepackaged electronic images that are stored on disk to be used as needed in computer-based documents.

Clipboard An intermediate holding area in internal storage for information en route to another application.

Clone A hardware device or a software package that emulates a product with an established reputation and market acceptance.

Cluster The smallest unit of disk space that can be allocated to a file.

Coaxial cable A shielded wire used as a medium to transmit data between computers and between computers and peripheral devices.

COBOL (Common Business Oriented Language) A third-generation programming language designed to handle business problems.

Code (1) The rules used to translate a bit configuration into alphanumeric characters and symbols. (2) The process of compiling computer instructions into the form of a computer program. (3) The actual computer program.

Color depth The number of bits used to display each pixel on a display.

Command An instruction to a computer that invokes the execution of a preprogrammed sequence of instructions.

Common carrier A company that provides channels for data transmission.

Communications channel The facility by which data are transmitted between locations in a computer network.

Communications protocols Rules established to govern the way data in a computer network are transmitted.

Communications satellite A repeater station for microwave signals set in a geosynchronous orbit about the earth to facilitate data communications.

Communications server The LAN component that provides external communications links.

Communications software (1) Software that enables a microcomputer to emulate a terminal and to transfer files between a micro and another computer. (2) Software that enables communication between remote devices in a computer network.

Compact disc-recordable See *CD-R*.

Compatibility Pertaining to the ability of computers and computer components (hardware and software) to work together.

Compile To translate a high-level programming language into machine language in preparation for execution.

Compiler A program that translates the instructions of a high-level language to machine language instructions that the computer can interpret and execute. (Contrast with *interpreter*.)

Computer An electronic device capable of interpreting and executing programmed commands for input, output, computation, and logic operations.

Computer-aided design (CAD) Use of computer graphics in design, drafting, and documentation in product and manufacturing engineering.

Computer-aided software engineering (CASE) An approach to software development that combines automation and the rigors of the engineering discipline.

Computer-based training (CBT) Using computer technologies for training and education.

Computer literacy See *information technology competency*.

Computer matching The procedure whereby separate databases are examined and individuals common to both are identified.

Computer monitoring Observing and regulating employee activities and job performance through the use of computers.

Computer network An integration of computer systems, terminals, and communications links.

Computer operator One who performs those hardware-based activities needed to keep production information systems operational in the server computer environment.

Computer system A collective reference to all interconnected computing hardware, including processors, storage devices, input/output devices, and communications equipment.

Computer virus A man-made program or portion of a program that causes an unexpected event, usually a negative one, to occur within a computer system.

Configuration The computer and its peripheral devices.

Connectivity Pertains to the degree to which hardware devices, software, and databases can be functionally linked to one another.

Control unit The portion of the processor that interprets program instructions, directs internal operations, and directs the flow of input/output to or from RAM.

Cookie A message given to your Web browser by the Web server being accessed. The cookie is a text file containing user preference information.

Cooperative processing An environment in which organizations cooperate internally and externally to take full advantage of available information and to obtain meaningful, accurate, and timely information. (See also *intracompany networking*.)

CPU See *processor*.

Cracker An overzealous hacker who "cracks" through network security to gain unauthorized access to the network. (Contrast with *hacker*.)

Cross-platform technologies Enabling technologies that allow communication and the sharing of resources between different platforms.

CRT monitor A video monitor based on cathode-ray tube technology.

Cryptography A communications crime-prevention technology that uses methods of data encryption and decryption to scramble codes sent over communications channels.

CSMA/CD protocol A network access method in which nodes on the LAN must contend for the right to send a message.

Cumulative trauma disorder (CTD) Repetitive motion disorders of the musculoskeletal and nervous systems that, often, are a result of poor workplace design.

Cursor, graphics Typically an arrow or a crosshair that can be moved about a monitor's screen by a point-and-draw device to create a graphic image or select an item from a menu. (See also *cursor, text*.)

Cursor, text A blinking character that indicates the location of the next keyed-in character on the display screen. (See also *cursor, graphics*.)

Custom programming Program development to create software for situations unique to a particular processing environment.

Cybercrime A generic reference to criminal activities that involve computers, communications, and/or information technology.

Cyberphobia The irrational fear of, and aversion to, computers.

Cyberstalking Technology-based stalking where the Internet becomes a vehicle by which the stalker directs threatening behavior and unwanted advances to another person.

Cylinder A disk-storage concept. A cylinder is that portion of the disk that can be read in any given position of the access arm. (Contrast with *sector*.)

D

Data Representations of facts. Raw material for information. (Plural of *datum*.)

Database The integrated data resource for a computer-based information system.

Database administrator (DBA) The individual responsible for the physical and logical maintenance of the database.

Database software Software that permits users to create and maintain a database and to extract information from the database.

Data bus A common pathway between RAM, cache memory, and the processor through which data and instructions are transferred. (See also *address bus*.)

Data cartridge Magnetic tape storage in cassette format.

Data communications The collection and distribution of the electronic representation of information between two locations.

Data compression A method of reducing disk-storage requirements for computer files.

Data entry The transcription of source data into a machine-readable format.

Data file This file contains data organized into records.

Data flow diagram A design technique that permits documentation of a system or program at several levels of generality.

Data mining An analytical technique that involves the analysis of large databases, such as data warehouses, to identify possible trends and problems.

Data path The electronic channel through which data flows within a computer system.

Data processing (DP) system Systems concerned with transaction handling and record-keeping, usually for a particular functional area.

Data transfer rate The rate at which data are read/written from/to disk storage to RAM.

Data/voice/fax/modem A modem that permits data communication with remote computers via a telephone-line link and enables telephone calls and fax machine simulation via a PC.

Data warehouse A relational database created from existing operational files and databases specifically to help managers get the information they need to make informed decisions.

Data warehousing An approach to database management that involves moving existing operational files and databases from multiple applications to a data warehouse.

DDR SDRAM A "double data rate" SDRAM. (See also *SDRAM*.)

Debug To eliminate bugs in a program or system. (See also *bug*.)

Decision support system (DSS) An interactive information system that relies on an integrated set of user-friendly hardware and software tools to produce and present information targeted to support management in the decision-making process. (Contrast with *management information system* and *executive information system*.)

Decode To reverse the encoding process. (Contrast with *encode*.)

Decoder That portion of a processor's control unit that interprets instructions.

Default options Preset software options that are assumed valid unless specified otherwise by the user.

Defragmentation Using utility software to reorganize files on a hard disk such that files are stored in contiguous clusters.

Denial of service virus A computer virus that places such heavy demands on e-mail server resources that they are unable to handle the volume.

Density The number of bytes per linear length or unit area of a recording medium.

Desktop The screen in Windows upon which icons, windows, a background, and so on are displayed.

Desktop PC A nonportable personal computer that is designed to rest on the top of a desk. (Contrast with *laptop PC* and *tower PC*.)

Desktop publishing software (DTP) Software that allows users to produce near-typeset-quality copy for newsletters, advertisements, and many other printing needs, all from the confines of a desktop.

Detailed system design That portion of the systems development process in which the target system is defined in detail.

Device controller Microprocessors that control the operation of peripheral devices.

Device driver software Software that contains instructions needed by the operating system to communicate with the peripheral device.

Dialog box A window that is displayed when the user must choose parameters or enter further information before the chosen menu option can be executed.

Dialup connection Temporary modem-based communications link with another computer.

Dialup line See *switched line*.

Digicam See *digital camera*.

Digital A reference to any system based on discrete data, such as the binary nature of computers.

Digital camcorder Portable digital video camera.

Digital camera A camera that records images digitally rather than on film.

Digital certificate An attachment to an electronic message that verifies that the sender is who he or she claims to be.

Digital convergence The integration of computers, communications, and consumer electronics, with all having digital compatibility.

Digital ID A digital code that can be attached to an electronic message that uniquely identifies the sender.

Digital jukebox An Internet-based software application that enables the selection, management, and playing of Internet-based music.

Digital signal Electronic signals that are transmitted as in strings of 1s and 0s. (See also *analog signal*.)

Digital Subscriber Line See *DSL*.

Digital video camera A camera that enables the capture of motion video directly into a PC system (used for Webcam applications).

Digital video disc See *DVD*.

Digitize To translate data or an image into a discrete format that can be interpreted by computers.

Digitizer tablet and pen A pressure-sensitive tablet with the same *x-y* coordinates as a computer-generated screen. The outline of an image drawn on a tablet with a stylus (pen) or puck is reproduced on the display.

DIMM (dual in-line memory module) A small circuit board, capable of holding several memory chips, that has a 64-bit data path and can be easily connected to a PC's motherboard. (Contrast with *SIMM*.)

Dimmed A menu option, which is usually gray, that is disabled or unavailable.

Direct access See *random access*.

Direct-access storage device (DASD) A random-access disk storage device.

Direct conversion An approach to system conversion whereby operational support by the new system is begun when the existing system is terminated.

Disc, optical laser A storage medium which uses lasers for the data read/write operations.

Disintermediation A reference to the removal of the middleman.

Disk address The physical location of a particular set of data or a program on a magnetic disk.

Disk caching A hardware/software technique in which frequently referenced disk-based data are placed in an area of RAM that simulates disk storage. (See also *RAM disk*.)

Disk defragmenter A utility program that consolidates files into contiguous clusters on a hard disk.

Disk density The number of bits that can be stored per unit of area on the disk-face surface.

Disk drive, magnetic A magnetic storage device that records data on flat rotating disks. (Compare with *tape drive, magnetic*.)

Diskette A thin interchangeable disk for secondary random-access data storage (same as *floppy disk*).

Disk, magnetic A storage medium for random-access data storage available in permanently installed or interchangeable formats.

Distributed DBMS An approach to database management that permits the interfacing of databases located in various places throughout a computer network.

Docking station A device into which a notebook PC is inserted to give the notebook PC expanded capabilities, such as a high-capacity disk, interchangeable disk options, a tape backup unit, a large monitor, and so on.

Document A generic reference to whatever is currently displayed in a software package's work area or to a permanent file containing document contents.

Document window Window within an application window that is used to display a separate document created or used by that application.

Domain expert An expert in a particular field who provides the factual knowledge and the heuristic rules for input to a knowledge base.

Domain name That portion of the Internet URL following the double forward slashes (//) that identifies an Internet host site.

DOS (Disk Operating System) See *MS-DOS*.

Dot-matrix printer A printer that arranges printed dots to form characters and images.

Dot pitch The distance between the centers of adjacent pixels on a display.

Download The transmission of data from a remote computer to a local computer.

Downsizing Used to describe the trend toward increased reliance on smaller computers for personal as well as enterprise-wide processing tasks.

Downstream rate The data communications rate from server computer to client computer.

Downtime The time during which a computer system is not operational.

Drag A point-and-draw device procedure by which an object is moved or a contiguous area on the display is marked for processing.

Drag-and-drop software Software that lets users drag ready-made shapes from application-specific stencils to the desired position on the drawing area to do drawings for flowcharting, landscaping, business graphics, and other applications.

Draw software Software that enables users to create electronic images. Resultant images are stored as vector graphics images.

Driver The software that enables interaction between the operating system and a specific peripheral device.

Driver module The program module that calls other subordinate program modules to be executed as they are needed (also called a *main program*).

DSL (Digital Subscriber Line) A digital telecommunications standard for data delivery over twisted-pair lines with downstream transmission speeds up to 9 M bps.

DSLAM (Digital Subscriber Line Access Multiplexor) A device that communications companies use to multiplex DSL signals to/from the Internet.

DTP See *desktop publishing software*.

Dual in-line memory module See *DIMM*.

DVD (digital video disc) The successor technology to the CD-ROM that can store up to about 8.5 gigabytes per side.

DVD-R, DVD+R The capability to record data to a DVD disc. (Contrast with *CD-R*.)

DVD-ROM High-density read-only optical laser storage media.

DVD+RW, DVD-RW Rewritable standards for high-capacity DVD, often available on the same unit. (Contrast with *CD-RW.*)

DVD-Video DVD format for playing movies.

Dynamic IP address A temporary Internet address assigned to a user by an ISP.

E

EBCDIC (Extended Binary Coded Decimal Interchange Code) An 8-bit encoding system.

E-book An electronic version of a book.

E-commerce (electronic commerce) Business conducted online, primarily over the Internet.

E-commerce hosting services A service that helps customers build and maintain their own e-commerce site.

EDI See *electronic data interchange.*

Edutainment software Software that combines *edu*cation and enter*tainment.*

Electronic commerce See *e-commerce.*

Electronic data interchange (EDI) The use of computers and data communications to transmit data electronically between companies.

Electronic dictionary A disk-based dictionary used in conjunction with a spelling-checker program to verify the spelling of words in a word processing document.

Electronic document See *online document.*

Electronic mail (e-mail) A computer application whereby messages are transmitted via data communications to "electronic mailboxes." (Contrast with *voice message switching.*)

Electronic messaging A workgroup computing application that enables electronic mail to be associated with other workgroup applications.

Electronic money (e-money) A payment system in which all monetary transactions are handled electronically.

Electronic publishing (e-publishing) The creation of electronic documents that are designed to be retrieved from disk storage and viewed.

Electronic ticket (e-ticket) An electronic alternative to the traditional paper ticket for airlines, movies, and so on.

Electronic trading (e-trading) Making online investments electronically through an online brokerage service.

Electronic wallet An electronic version of a wallet/purse, which can be used to make online purchases.

E-mail See *electronic mail.*

E-mail server A host or network that services e-mail.

E-money See *electronic money.*

Emoticons Keyboard emotion icons used to speed written interaction and convey emotions in online communications.

Encode To apply the rules of a code. (Contrast with *decode.*)

Encoding system A system that permits alphanumeric characters and symbols to be coded in terms of bits.

Encryption The encoding of data for security purposes. Encoded data must be decoded or deciphered to be used.

Enhanced television A TV presentation combining video and general programming from broadcast, satellite, and cable networks.

Enterprise computing Comprises all computing activities designed to support any type of organization.

Enterprise system Information system that provides information and processing capabilities to workers throughout a given organization.

Entity relationship diagram A business modeling tool used for defining the information needs of a business, including the attributes of the entities and the relationship between them.

EPS (*Encapsulated PostScript*) A vector graphics file format used by the PostScript language.

Ergonomics The study of the relationships between people and machines.

E-signature An electronic method of placing a legal signature on an electronic document.

E-tailing Online retailing.

Ethernet A local-area-net protocol in which the nodes must contend for the right to send a message. (See also *token access method.*)

Ethernet card An Ethernet-standard network interface card.

E-ticket See *electronic ticket.*

E-time See *execution time.*

E-trading See *electronic trading.*

Exception report A report that has been filtered to highlight critical information.

Execution time (e-time) The elapsed time it takes to execute a computer instruction and store the results.

Executive information system (EIS) A system designed specifically to support decision making at the executive levels of management, primarily the tactical and strategic levels.

Exit routine A software procedure that returns you to a GUI, an operating system prompt, or a higher-level applications program.

Expansion board These add-on circuit boards contain the electronic circuitry for many supplemental capabilities, such as a fax modem, and are made to fit a particular type of bus (also called *expansion cards*).

Expansion bus An extension of the common electrical bus that accepts the expansion boards that control the video display, disks, and other peripherals. (See also *bus.*)

Expansion card See *expansion board.*

Expansion slots Slots within the processing component of a microcomputer into which optional add-on circuit boards may be inserted.

Expert system An interactive knowledge-based system that responds to questions, asks for clarification, makes recommendations, and generally helps users make complex decisions. (See also *assistant system.*)

Explorer Windows software that enables the user to do file management tasks.

Export The process of converting a file in the format of the current program to a format that can be used by another program. (Contrast with *import.*)

Extranet An extension of an intranet such that it is partially accessible to authorized outsiders, such as customers and suppliers. (See also *intranet.*)

Extreme programming (XP) A collaborative team approach to programming in which the team works together to write programs in iterative cycles.

E-zine An online magazine.

F

Face recognition technology A biometric technology that enables personal identification via a faceprint.

Facsimile (fax) The transferring of images, usually of hard-copy documents, via telephone lines to another device that can receive and interpret the images.

FAQ A frequently asked question.

Fault-tolerant Referring to a computer system or network that is resistant to software errors and hardware problems.

Fax See *facsimile.*

Fax modem A modem that enables a PC to emulate a facsimile machine. (See also *modem.*)

Feedback loop A closed loop in which a computer-controlled process generates data that become input to the computer.

Fiber optic cable A data transmission medium that carries data in the form of light in very thin transparent fibers.

Field The smallest logical unit of data. Examples are employee number, first name, and price.

File (1) A collection of related records. (2) A named area on a disk-storage device that contains a program or digitized information (text, image, sound, and so on).

File allocation table (FAT) Method of storing and keeping track of files on a disk.

File compression A technique by which file size can be reduced. Compressed files are decompressed for use.

File format The manner in which a file is stored on disk storage.

File server A dedicated computer system with high-capacity disk for storing the data and programs shared by the users on a local area network.

File Transfer Protocol (FTP) A communications protocol that is used to transmit files over the Internet.

Filtering The process of selecting and presenting only that information appropriate to support a particular decision.

Filtering program A program that denies Internet access to specified content.

Firewall Software that is designed to restrict access to an organization's network or its Intranet.

FireWire The Apple Computer Company name for the 1394 bus standard.

Fixed disk See *hard disk.*

Flaming A barrage of scathing messages from irate Internet users sent to someone who posts messages out of phase with the societal norms.

Flash memory A type of nonvolatile memory that can be altered easily by the user.

Flat files A file that does not point to or physically link with another file.

Flat-panel monitor A monitor, thin from front to back, that uses liquid crystal and gas plasma technology.

Floating menu A special-function menu that can be positioned anywhere on the work area until you no longer need it.

Floppy disk See *diskette.*

Floppy disk drive A disk drive that accepts either the 3.5-inch or 5.25-inch diskette.

FLOPS (floating point operations per second) A measure of computer speed.

Flowchart A diagram that illustrates data, information, and work flow via specialized symbols which, when connected by flow lines, portray the logic of a system or program.

Flowcharting The act of creating a flowchart.

Folder An object in a Windows® graphical user interface that contains a logical grouping of related files and subordinate folders.

Font A typeface that is described by its letter style, its height in points, and its presentation attribute.

Footprint (1) The evidence of unlawful entry or use of a computer system. (2) The floor or desktop space required for a hardware component.

Foreground (1) That part of RAM that contains the highest priority program. (2) In Windows, the area of the display containing the active window. (Contrast with *background.*)

Formatted Reference to a disk that has been initialized with the recording format for a specific operating system.

Form factor Refers to a computer's physical shape and size.

FORTRAN (Formula Translator) A high-level programming language designed primarily for scientific applications.

Fourth-generation language (4GL) A programming language that uses high-level English-like instructions to retrieve and format data for inquiries and reporting.

Frame A rectangular area in a desktop publishing-produced document into which elements, such as text and images, are placed.

Frames (Web page) The display of more than one independently controllable sections on a single Web page.

Freeware Copyright software that can be downloaded and used free of charge.

Front-end applications software Client software that performs processing associated with the user interface and applications processing that can be done locally. (See also *back-end applications software*.)

Full-duplex line A communications channel that transmits data in both directions at the same time. (Contrast with *half-duplex line*.)

Function key A special-function key on the keyboard that can be used to instruct the computer to perform a specific operation.

Functional specifications Specifications that describe the logic of an information system from the user's perspective.

G

Gb See *gigabit*.

GB See *gigabyte*.

General system design That portion of the system development process in which the target system is defined in general.

Geosynchronous orbit An orbit that permits a communications satellite to maintain a fixed position relative to the surface of the earth.

GFLOPS A billion FLOPS. (See *FLOPS*.)

GIF A popular format for bit-mapped files.

Gigabit (Gb) One billion bits.

Gigabyte (GB) One billion bytes.

Gigahertz (GHz) Billions of clock cycles per second.

GIGO Garbage in, garbage out.

GPS (global positioning system) A system that uses satellites to provide location information.

Graphical user interface (GUI) A user-friendly interface that lets users interact with the system by pointing to processing options with a point-and-draw device.

Graphics adapter A device controller that provides the electronic link between the motherboard and the monitor.

Graphics software Software that enables you to create digital line drawings, art, and presentation graphics.

Gray scales The number of shades of a color that can be presented on a monochrome monitor's screen or on a monochrome printer's output.

Green computing Environmentally sensible computing.

Grid computing Using available computing resources more effectively by tapping the unused processing capabilities of many PCs via a network and/or the Internet.

Groupware Software whose application is designed to benefit a group of people. (Related to *workgroup computing*.)

H

Hacker A computer enthusiast who uses the computer as a source of mischievous recreation. (Contrast with *cracker*.)

Half-duplex line A communications channel that transmits data in one direction at the same time. (Contrast with *full-duplex line*.)

Handheld computer Any personal computer than can be held comfortably in a person's hand (usually weighs less than a pound). (Also called *pocket PC*, *palmtop PC*, and *personal digital assistant*.)

Handshaking The process by which both sending and receiving devices in a computer network maintain and coordinate data communications.

Hard copy A readable printed copy of computer output. (Contrast with *soft copy*.)

Hard disk A permanently installed, continuously spinning magnetic storage medium made up of one or more rigid disk platters. (Same as *fixed disk*; contrast with *interchangeable disk*.).

Hard disk drive See *hard disk*.

Hardware The physical devices that comprise a computer system. (Contrast with *software*.)

Help desk A centralized location (either within an organization or outside of it) where computer-related questions about product usage, installation, problems, or services are answered.

Hexadecimal A base-16 numbering system.

High-level language A language with instructions that combine several machine-level instructions into one instruction. (Compare with *machine language* or *low-level language*.)

Hit When a Web page is retrieved for viewing or is listed in results of a search.

Home network A network of PCs in a home.

Home page The Web page that is the starting point for accessing information at a site or in a particular area.

HomePlug A HomePlug standard that allows the elements of the network to communicate over a home's existing AC electrical power lines.

HomePNA (HPNA) A Home Phone-line Networking Alliance standard that allows the elements of the network to communicate over a home's existing telephone wiring or via wireless links.

Host computer A computer system that is accessible to multiple users at remote locations.

Hot plug A feature that allows peripheral devices to be connected to or removed from a port while the PC is running.

Hoteling Providing on-site office space that is a shared by mobile workers.

Hotkey A seldom used key combination that, when activated, causes the computer to perform the function associated with the key combination.

HTML (HyperText Markup Language) The language used to compose and format most of the content found on the Internet.

http (HyperText Transfer Protocol) The primary access method for interacting with the Internet.

Hub A common point of connection for computers and devices in a network.

Hyperlink Clickable image or text phrase that lets you link to other parts of a document or to different documents together within a computer system or on the Internet.

I

I/O (input/output) Input or output or both.

IBM Personal Computer (IBM PC) IBM's first personal computer (1981). This PC was the basis for PC-compatible computers.

Icons Pictographs used in place of words or phrases on screen displays.

Identity theft When a person gathers personal information to assume the identity of another person for illicit reasons.

Identity-based encryption An encryption technology that converts the recipient's e-mail address into a number, which feeds a mathematical algorithm that completes the encryption process.

IEEE 802.11a A Wi-Fi wireless communications standard capable of 11 M bps up to about 300 feet from an access point.

IEEE 802.11b A Wi-Fi wireless communications standard capable of 54 M bps up to about 50 feet from an access point.

IEEE 802.11g A Wi-Fi wireless communications standard capable of 54 M bps up to about 300 feet from an access point.

Image processing A reference to computer applications in which digitized images are retrieved, displayed, altered, merged with text, stored, and sent via data communications to one or several remote locations.

Image scanner A device that can scan and digitize an image so that it can be stored on a disk and manipulated by a computer.

Import The process of converting data in one format to a format that is compatible with the calling program. (Contrast with *export*.)

Industrial espionage Theft of proprietary business information.

Industrial robot Computer-controlled robots used in industrial applications.

Information Data that have been collected and processed into a meaningful form.

Information-based decision A decision that involves an ill-defined and unstructured problem.

Information repository A central computer-based database for all system design information.

Information service A commercial network that provides remote users with access to a variety of information services.

Information society A society in which the generation and dissemination of information becomes the central focus of commerce.

Information superhighway A metaphor for a network of high-speed data communication links that will eventually connect virtually every facet of our society.

Information system A computer-based system that provides both data processing capability and information for managerial decision making.

Information technology (IT) A collective reference to the integration of computing technology and information processing.

Information technology competency (IT competency) Being able to interact with and use computers and having an understanding of IT issues.

Infrared port See *IrDA port*.

Ink-jet printer A nonimpact printer in which the print head contains independently controlled injection chambers that squirt ink droplets on the paper to form letters and images.

Input Data entered to a computer system for processing.

Input/output (I/O) A generic reference to input and/or output to a computer.

Input/output-bound application An IT application in which the amount of work that can be performed by the computer system is limited primarily by the speeds of the I/O devices.

Instant messaging Internet application in which personal communications are sent and displayed in real-time.

Instruction A programming language statement that specifies a particular computer operation to be performed.

Instruction cycle Defines the process by which computer instructions are interpreted and executed.

Instruction time The elapsed time it takes to fetch and decode a computer instruction (also called *I-time*).

Integrated circuit (IC) Thousands of electronic components that are etched into a tiny silicon chip in the form of a special-function electronic circuit.

Intelligent agent Artificial intelligence-based software that has the authority to act on a person or thing's behalf. (Also called *bots;* see also *shop bot.*)

Interactive Pertaining to online and immediate communication between the user and the computer.

Interchangeable disk A disk that can be stored offline and loaded to the computer system as needed. (Contrast with *hard disk* or *fixed disk.*)

Intercompany networking Companies cooperating with customers and other companies via electronic data interchange and extranets. (Contrast with *intracompany networking.*)

Internet (the Net) A global network that connects more than tens of thousands of networks, millions of large multiuser computers, and tens of millions of users in more than one hundred countries.

Internet appliance An inexpensive communications device for Internet applications.

Internet backbone The major communications lines and nodes to which thousands of Internet host computers are connected.

Internet Protocol address See *IP address.*

Internet Relay Chat (IRC) An Internet protocol that allows users to join and participate in group chat sessions.

Internet service provider (ISP) Any company that provides individuals and organizations with access to or presence on the Internet.

Interoperability The ability to run software and exchange information in a multiplatform environment.

Interpreter A program that translates source program instructions, one at a time, to a form that can be executed by a computer. Contrast with *compiler.*)

Intracompany networking Computer networking within an organization. (See also *cooperative processing;* contrast with *intercompany networking.*)

Intranet An Internet-like network whose scope is restricted to the networks within a particular organization. (See also *extranet.*)

Invoke Execute a command or a macro.

IP address (Internet protocol address) A four-number point-of-presence (POP) Internet address (for example, 206.28.104.10).

IRC See *Internet Relay Chat.*

IrDA port Enables wireless transmission of data via infrared light waves between PCs, printers, and other devices (also called *infrared port*).

ISP See *Internet service provider.*

Itanium® High-end Intel processor.

IT competency See *information technology competency.*

I-time See *instruction time.*

J

Java Platform-independent language used for Web-based applications.

Joystick A vertical stick that moves the mouse pointer on a screen in the direction in which the stick is pushed.

JPEG, JPG A bit-mapped file format that compresses image size.

Jukebox A storage device for multiple sets of CD-ROMs, tape cartridges, or disk modules enabling ready access to vast amounts of online data.

K

Kb See *kilobit.*

KB See *kilobyte.*

Kernel An operating system program that loads other operating system programs and applications programs to RAM as they are needed.

Keyboard A device used for key data entry.

Key field The field in a record that is used as an identifier for accessing, sorting, and collating records.

Keypad That portion of a keyboard that permits rapid numeric data entry.

Kilobit (Kb) 1024, or about 1000, bits.

Kilobyte (KB) 1024, or about 1000, bytes.

Knowledge base The foundation of a knowledge-based system that contains facts, rules, inferences, and procedures.

Knowledge-based system A computer-based system, often associated with artificial intelligence, that helps users make decisions by enabling them to interact with a knowledge base.

Knowledge worker Someone whose job function revolves around the use, manipulation, and dissemination of information.

L

Landscape Referring to the orientation of the print on the page. Printed lines run parallel to the longer side of the page. (Contrast with *portrait.*)

LAN operating system The operating system for a local area network.

LAN server A high-end PC on a local area network whose resources are shared by other users on the LAN.

Laptop PC Portable PC that can operate without an external power source. (Contrast with *desktop PC* and *tower PC;* see also *pocket PC.*)

Laser printer A page printer that uses laser technology to produce the image.

Layout A reference to the positioning of the visual elements on a display or page.

LCD projector An output peripheral device that can project the screen image (display) onto a large screen for group viewing.

Leased line See *private line*.

LindowsOS A commercial Linux-based operating system for PCs that has a Windows-like interface.

Linux An open source spinoff of the UNIX operating system that runs on a number of hardware platforms and is made available for free over the Internet.

Listserv A reference to an Internet mailing list.

LMDS A fixed line-of-sight wireless technology designed to enable high-bandwidth "last mile" connectivity.

Load To transfer programs or data from disk to RAM.

Local area network (LAN or local net) A system of hardware, software, and communications channels that connects devices on the local premises. (Contrast with *wide area network*.)

Local bus A bus that links expansion boards directly to the computer system's common bus.

Local net See *local area network*.

Logic bomb A harmful set of instructions that are executed when a certain set of conditions is met.

Logical operators AND, OR, and NOT operators can be used to combine relational expressions logically in spreadsheet, database, and other programs. (See also *relational operators*.)

Logical security That aspect of computer-center security that deals with user access to systems and data.

Log off The procedure by which a user terminates a communications link with a remote computer. (Contrast with *logon*.)

Logon The procedure by which a user establishes a communications link with a remote computer. (Contrast with *log off*.)

Loop A sequence of program instructions executed repeatedly until a particular condition is met.

Low-level language A language comprising the fundamental instruction set of a particular computer. (Compare with *high-level language*.)

M

Machine cycle The cycle of operations performed by the processor to process a single program instruction: fetch, decode, execute, and place result in memory.

Machine language The programming language that is interpreted and executed directly by the computer.

Mac OS X The operating system for the Apple family of micro-computers.

Macro A sequence of frequently used operations or keystrokes that can be invoked to help speed user interaction with microcomputer productivity software.

Macro language Programming languages whose instructions relate specifically to the functionality of the parent software.

Macro virus A program written in the macro language of a particular application.

Magnetic disk See *disk, magnetic*.

Magnetic disk drive See *disk drive, magnetic*.

Magnetic-ink character recognition (MICR) A data entry technique used primarily in banking. Magnetic characters are imprinted on checks and deposits, then scanned to retrieve the data.

Magnetic stripe A magnetic storage medium for low-volume storage of data on badges and cards. (Related to *badge reader*.)

Magnetic tape See *tape, magnetic*.

Magnetic tape cartridge Cartridge-based magnetic tape storage media.

Magnetic tape drive See *tape drive, magnetic*.

Mailing list An Internet-based capability that lets people discuss issues of common interest via common e-mail.

Mail merge A computer application in which text generated by word processing is merged with data from a database (e.g., a form letter with an address).

Mainframe computer A large computer that can service many users simultaneously in support of enterprise-wide applications.

Main program See *driver module*.

MAN See *Metropolitan Area Network*.

Management information system (MIS) A computer-based system that optimizes the collection, transfer, and presentation of information throughout an organization, through an integrated structure of databases and information flow. (Contrast with *decision support system* and *executive information system*.)

Markup language A language such as HTML that uses codes within the context of text processing to describe what is to be done with a block of text or a named file.

Masquerading An approach to unauthorized entry to a computer network where people acquire passwords and personal information that will enable them to masquerade as an authorized user.

Massively parallel processing (MPP) An approach to the design of computer systems that involves the integration of thousands of microprocessors within a single computer.

Mass storage Various techniques and devices used to hold and retain electronic data.

Master file The permanent source of data for a particular computer application area.

Mb See *megabit*.

MB See *megabyte*.

Megabit (Mb) 1,048,576, or about one million, bits.

Megabyte (MB) 1,048,576, or about one million, bytes.

Megahertz (MHz) One million hertz (cycles per second).

Memory See *RAM*.

Menu A display with a list of processing choices from which a user may select.

Message A series of bits sent from a terminal to a computer, or vice versa.

Metafile (WMF) A class of graphics that combines the components of raster and vector graphics formats.

Metropolitan area network (MAN) A data network designed for use within the confines of a town or city.

MHz See *megahertz*.

MICR See *magnetic-ink character recognition*.

MICR reader-sorter A scanning device that reads and sorts MICR documents.

Microcomputer (or micro) A small computer. (See also *PC*.)

Micropayment Electronic payment for goods and services in very small amounts.

Microprocessor A computer on a single chip. The processing component of a microcomputer.

Microsecond One millionth of a second.

Microsoft Network (MSN) An information service provider sponsored by Microsoft Corporation.

Microwave signal A high-frequency line-of-sight electromagnetic wave used in wireless communications.

MIDI (Musical Instrument Digital Interface) An interface between PCs and electronic musical instruments, like the synthesizer.

MIDI file A nonwaveform file result for MIDI applications.

Millisecond One thousandth of a second.

MIPS Millions of instructions per second.

MMDS A fixed line-of-sight wireless technology designed to deliver network access at fiber-optic speeds.

Modem (modulator-demodulator) A device used to convert computer-compatible signals to signals that can be transmitted over the telephone lines, then back again to computer signals at the other end of the line.

Monitor A television-like display for soft-copy output in a computer system.

Moore's Law The density of transistors on a chip doubles every 18 months.

Morphing Using graphics software to transform one image into an entirely different image. The term is derived from the word *metamorphosis*.

Motherboard A microcomputer circuit board that contains the microprocessor, electronic circuitry for handling such tasks as input/output signals from peripheral devices, and memory chips.

Mouse A point-and-draw device that, when moved across a desktop a particular distance and direction, causes the same movement of the pointer on a screen. Mouse buttons are "clicked" to enable interaction with the system.

MP3 A sound file format that enables CD-quality music to be compressed to about 8% of its original size while retaining CD sound quality.

MPEG A video file format with the extension MPG or MPEG.

MPP See *massively parallel processing*.

MS-DOS (Microsoft Disk Operating System) The pre-Windows PC operating system.

Multimedia Computer application that involves the integration of text, sound, graphics, motion video, and animation.

Multiplatform environment A computing environment that supports more than one platform. (See also *platform*.)

Multiplexor A communications device that collects data from a number of low-speed devices, then transmits the combined data over a single communications channel. At the destination, it separates the signals for processing.

Multitasking The concurrent execution of more than one program at a time.

Multiuser PC A microcomputer that can serve more than one user at any given time.

N

Nanosecond One billionth of a second.

National database A central repository for all personal data for citizens.

National Information Infrastructure (NII) Refers to a futuristic network of high-speed data communications links that eventually will connect virtually every facet of our society. (See also *information superhighway*.)

Native file format The file format normally associated with a particular application.

Natural language A programming language in which the programmer writes specifications without regard to the computer's instruction format or syntax[md]essentially, using everyday human language to program.

Netiquette Etiquette on the Internet.

NET platform A reference to a Microsoft computing environment that encompasses the operating system plus a suite of software tools and services that facilitates interaction between people, networked computers, applications, and the Internet.

Network access method The set of rules by which networks determine usage priorities for a shared medium.

Network address An electronic identifier assigned to each computer system and terminal/PC in a computer network.

Network administrator A data communications specialist who designs and maintains local area networks (LANs) and wide area networks (WANs).

Network bus A common cable in a bus topology that permits the connection of terminals, peripheral devices, and microcomputers to create a computer network.

Network, computer See *computer network*.

Network DBMS A database management system whose data structures established relationships between its records.

Network interface card (NIC) A PC expansion card or PCMCIA card that facilitates and controls the exchange of data between the PC and its network.

Network topology The configuration of the interconnections between the nodes in a communications network.

Neural network A field of artificial intelligence in which millions of chips (processing elements) are interconnected to enable computers to imitate the way the human brain works.

Newsgroup The electronic counterpart of a wall-mounted bulletin board that enables Internet users to exchange ideas and information via a centralized message database.

Node An endpoint in a computer network.

Nonvolatile memory Solid-state RAM that retains its contents after an electrical interruption. (Contrast with *volatile memory*.)

Notebook PC A notebook-size portable PC (also called *laptop PC*).

Numeric A reference to any of the digits 0–9. (Compare with *alpha* and *alphanumeric*.)

O

Object (1) In Windows: any item that can be individually selected and manipulated. (2) In OOP: a self-contained module that encapsulates data and the methods for manipulating the data.

Object linking and embedding See *OLE*.

Object-oriented database management system (OODBMS) This system is able to handle the complex data structures needed in our increasingly multimedia world.

Object-oriented language A programming language structured to enable the interaction between user-defined concepts that contain data and operations to be performed on the data.

Object-oriented programming (OOP) A form of software development in which programs are built with entities called objects, which model any physical or conceptual item. Objects are linked together in a top-down hierarchy.

Object program A machine-level program that results from the compilation of a source program. (Compare with *source program*.)

Object/relational DBMS An approach to database management which combines the best features of RDBMS and OODBMS.

OCR See *optical character recognition*.

Offline Pertaining to data that are not accessible by, or hardware devices that are not connected to, a computer system. (Contrast with *online*.)

OLE (object linking and embedding) The software capability that enables the creation of a compound document that contains one or more objects from other applications. Objects can be linked or embedded.

Online Pertaining to data and/or hardware devices accessible to and under the control of a computer system. (Contrast with *offline*.)

Online document Documents that are designed to be retrieved from disk storage (locally or over a network) and viewed on a monitor. (Same as *electronic document*.)

Online transaction processing (OLTP) An approach to processing where online transactions are recorded and entered as they occur.

Open application A running application.

Open source software Referring to software for which the actual source programming code is made available to users for review and modification.

Operating system The software that controls the execution of all applications and system software programs.

Optical character recognition (OCR) A data entry technique that permits original source data entry. Coded symbols or characters are scanned to retrieve the data.

Optical laser disc See *disc, optical laser*.

Optical scanner A peripheral device that can read written text and hardcopy images, then translate the information into an electronic format that can be interpreted by and stored on computers.

Option buttons Circle bullets in front of user options that when selected include a dot in the middle of the circle.

Output The presentation of the results of processing.

P

Packet Strings of bits that contain information and a network address that are routed over different paths on the Internet according to a specific communications protocol.

Page (Web) The area in which information is presented on the World Wide Web.

Paint software Software that enables users to "paint" electronic images. Resultant images are stored as raster graphics images.

Parallel conversion An approach to system conversion whereby the existing system and the new system operate simultaneously prior to conversion.

Parallel port A direct link with the microcomputer's bus that facilitates the parallel transmission of data, usually one byte at a time.

Parallel processing A processing procedure in which one main processor examines the programming problem and determines what portions, if any, of the problem can be solved in pieces by other subordinate processors.

Parallel transmission Pertaining to the transmission of data in groups of bits versus one bit at a time. (Contrast with *serial transmission*.)

Parameter A descriptor that can take on different values.

Parity checking A built-in checking procedure in a computer system to help ensure that the transmission of data is complete and accurate. (Related to *parity error*.)

Parity error Occurs when a bit is dropped in the transmission of data from one hardware device to another. (Related to *parity checking*.)

Password A word or phrase known only to the user. When entered, it permits the user to gain access to the system.

Patch A modification of a program or an information system.

Path The hierarchy of folders that lead to the location of a particular file.

Pattern recognition system A device that enables limited visual input to a computer system.

PC (personal computer) A small computer designed for use by an individual. (See also *microcomputer*.)

PC card Same as *PCMCIA card*.

PCI local bus (Peripheral Component Interconnect) Intel's local bus. (See also *local bus*.)

PCMCIA card A credit-card-sized module that is inserted into a PCMCIA-compliant interface to offer add-on capabilities such as expanded memory, fax modem, and so on (also called *PC card*).

PC specialist A person trained in the function and operation of PCs and related hardware and software.

PCX A bit-mapped file format.

PDF See *portable document format*.

Peer-to-peer LAN A local area network in which all PCs on the network are functionally equal.

Pen-based computing Computer applications that rely on the pen-based PCs for processing capability.

Pen-based PC A portable personal computer that enables input via an electronic pen in conjunction with a pressure-sensitive monitor/drawing surface.

Pentium® An Intel microprocessor.

Pentium® II Successor to the Intel® Pentium Pro microprocessor.

Pentium® III Successor to the Intel® Pentium II microprocessor.

Pentium® 4 Successor to the Intel® Pentium III microprocessor.

Pentium® Pro Successor to the Intel® Pentium microprocessor.

Peripheral device Any hardware device other than the processor.

Perl A popular programming language for Web development.

Personal area network (PAN) A connectivity concept that employs short-range, low-speed wireless technology to link an individual's personal world of electronics.

Personal computer (PC) See *PC*.

Personal computing A computing environment in which individuals use personal computers for domestic and/or business applications.

Personal digital assistant (PDA) A handheld computer.

Personal home page A Web site for an individual.

Personal identification number (PIN) A code or number that is used in conjunction with a password to permit the user to gain access to a computer system.

Personal information management (PIM) system Software application designed to help users organize random bits of information and to provide communications capabilities, such as e-mail and fax.

Phased conversion An approach to system conversion whereby an information system is implemented one module at a time.

Photo illustration software Software that enables the creation of original images and the modification of existing digitized images.

Physical security That aspect of computer-center security that deals with access to computers and peripheral devices.

Picosecond One trillionth of a second.

Picture element See *pixel*.

Pilferage A special case of software piracy whereby a company purchases a software product without a site-usage license agreement, then copies and distributes it throughout the company.

Pilot conversion An approach to system conversion whereby the new system is implemented first in only one of the several areas for which it is targeted.

Pipelining When a processor begins executing another instruction before the current instruction is completed, thus improving the system throughput.

Pixel (picture element) An addressable point on a display screen to which light can be directed under program control.

Platform A definition of the standards by which software is developed and hardware is designed.

Plotter A device that produces high-precision hard-copy graphic output.

Plug-and-play Refers to making a peripheral device or an expansion board immediately operational by simply plugging it into a port or an expansion slot.

Plugin A complementary application to an Internet browser.

PNG A license-free bit-mapped file format, similar to GIF.

Pocket PC A handheld computer.

Point-and-draw device An input device, such as a mouse or track-pad, used to *point* to and select a particular user option and to *draw*.

Polling A line-control procedure in which each terminal is "polled" in rotation to determine whether a message is ready to be sent.

POP (point-of-presence) An access point to the Internet.

Pop-up menu A menu that is super-imposed in a window over whatever is currently being displayed on the monitor.

Port An access point in a computer system that permits communication between the computer and a peripheral device.

Portable document An electronic document that can be passed around the electronic world as you would a print document in the physical world.

Portable document format (PDF) A standard, created by Adobe Corporation, creating portable documents.

Portable hard disk External hard disk device that is easily connected to any PC.

Portal A Web site or service that offers a broad array of Internet-based resources and services.

Portrait Referring to the orientation of the print on the page. Printed lines run parallel to the shorter side of the page. (Contrast with *landscape*.)

Port replicator A device to which a notebook PC can be readily connected to give the PC access to whatever external peripheral

devices are connected to its common ports (keyboard, monitor, mouse, network, printer, and so on).

POTS Short for *plain old telephone service*, the standard voice-grade telephone service common in homes and business.

PowerPC processor A RISC-based processor used in Apple computers and other computers.

PPP (point-to-point protocol) A method by which a dialup link is connected to an ISP's local POP.

Presentation software Software used to prepare information for multimedia presentations in meetings, reports, and oral presentations.

Printer A device used to prepare hard-copy output.

Print server A LAN-based PC that handles LAN user print jobs and controls at least one printer.

Private line A dedicated communications channel provided by a common carrier between any two points in a computer network. (Same as *leased line*.)

Procedure-oriented language A high-level language whose general-purpose instruction set can be used to produce a sequence of instructions to model scientific and business procedures.

Processor The logical component of a computer system that interprets and executes program instructions.

Processor-bound application The amount of work that can be performed by the computer system is limited primarily by the speed of the computer.

Profiling The examination and evaluation of personal data for the purpose of creating a personal profile.

Program (1) Computer instructions structured and ordered in a manner that, when executed, causes a computer to perform a particular function. (2) The act of producing computer software. (Related to *software*.)

Programmed decision Decisions that address well-defined problems with easily identifiable solutions.

Programmer One who writes computer programs.

Programmer/analyst The title of one who performs both the programming and systems analysis function.

Programming The act of writing a computer program.

Programming language A language programmers use to communicate instructions to a computer.

Program register The register that contains the address of the next instruction to be executed.

PROM (programmable read-only memory) ROM in which the user can load read-only programs and data.

Prompt A program-generated message describing what should be entered.

Proprietary software package Vendor-developed software that is marketed to the public.

Protocols See *communications protocols*.

Prototype system A model of a full-scale system.

Prototyping An approach to systems development that results in a proto-type system.

Proxy server computer A computer between the client PC and a actual server that handles many client requests before they reach the actual server.

Pseudocode Nonexecutable program code used as an aid to develop and document structured programs.

Public-domain software Software that is not copyrighted and can be used without restriction.

Public-key encryption Communications-based encryption that requires a private key and a public key.

Pull technology Technology where data are requested from another program or computer, such as with an Internet browser. (Contrast with *push technology*.)

Pumping and dumping A scam where someone floods the Internet with bogus information about a particular company.

Push technology Technology where data are sent automatically to an Internet user. (Contrast with *pull technology*.)

Q

Query by example A method of database inquiry in which the user sets conditions for the selection of records by composing one or more example relational expressions.

Query language A user-friendly programming language for requesting information from a database.

QuickTime® Software that lets you view videos, listen to music, and view panoramas.

R

Radio frequency (RF) signals Line-of-sight wireless data communications between radio transmitters and receivers.

RAID (Redundant Array of Independent Disks) An integrated system of disks that enables fault-tolerant hard disk operation.

RAM (Random-Access Memory) The memory area in which all programs and data must reside before programs can be executed or data manipulated.

RAM disk That area of RAM that facilitates disk caching. (See also *disk caching*.)

Random access Direct access to records, regardless of their physical location on the storage medium. (Contrast with *sequential access*.)

Random-access memory See *RAM*.

Random processing Processing data and records randomly. (Contrast with *sequential processing*.)

Rapid application development (RAD) Using sophisticated development tools to create a prototype or a functional information system.

Raster graphics A method for maintaining a screen image as patterns of dots. (See also *bit-mapped graphics*.)

Read The process by which a record or a portion of a record is accessed from the disk storage medium and transferred to RAM for processing. (Contrast with *write*.)

Read-only memory (ROM) A memory chip with contents permanently loaded by the manufacturer for read-only applications.

Read/write head That component of a disk drive or tape drive that reads from and writes to its respective storage medium.

Record A collection of related fields (such as an employee record) describing an event or an item.

Register A small high-speed storage area in which data pertaining to the execution of a particular instruction are stored.

Relational DBMS (RDBMS) A database, made up of logically linked tables, in which data are accessed by content rather than by address.

Relational operators Used in formulas to show the equality relationship between two expressions (= [equal to], < [less than], > [greater than], <= [less than or equal to], >= [greater than or equal to], <> [not equal to]). (See also *logical operators*.)

Resolution Referring to the number of addressable points on a monitor's screen or the number of dots per unit area on printed output.

RGB monitor Color monitors that mix red, green, and blue to achieve a spectrum of colors.

Ring topology A computer network that involves computer systems connected in a closed loop, with no one computer system the focal point of the network.

RISC (reduced instruction set computer) A computer design architecture based on a limited instruction set machine language. (Contrast with *CISC*.)

Robot Computer-controlled mechanical devices capable of doing human-like tasks with machine-like precision.

Robotics The field of study that deals with creating robots.

ROM (read-only memory) RAM that can be read only, not written to.

Root directory The directory at the highest level of a hierarchy of directories.

Router Communications hardware that enables communications links between networks by performing the necessary protocol conversions.

Run To open and execute a program.

S

Salami technique An approach to electronic embezzlement that involves stealing very small amounts of money from a large number of legitimate accounts.

Scalable system A system whose design permits expansion to handle any size database or any number of users.

Scalable typeface An outline-based typeface from which fonts of any point size can be created. (See also *typeface*.)

ScanDisk A Windows utility program that enables the repair of lost clusters on a hard disk.

Scanner A device that scans hard copy and digitizes the text and/or images to a format that can be interpreted by a computer.

Scavenging Searching for discarded information that may be of some value on the black market.

Schema A graphic representation of the logical structure of a network database.

Screen name Another name for user ID at logon.

Screen saver A utility program used to change static screens on idle monitors to interesting dynamic displays.

Script A small scripting language program downloaded with a Web page and run on the client PC.

Scripting language A programming language for creating scripts.

Scrolling Using the cursor keys to view parts of a document that extend past the bottom or top or sides of the screen.

SCSI bus A device interface to which up to 15 peripheral devices can be daisy-chained to a single SCSI port.

SDRAM (synchronous dynamic RAM) RAM that is able to synchronize itself with the processor enabling high-speed transfer of data to/from the processor.

Search engine An Internet resource discovery tool that lets people find information by keyword(s) searches.

Sector A disk-storage concept of a pie-shaped portion of a disk or diskette in which records are stored and subsequently retrieved. (Contrast with *cylinder*.)

Sector organization Magnetic disk organization in which the recording surface is divided into pie-shaped sectors.

Secure Sockets Layer (SSL) A protocol developed by Netscape for transmitting private documents via the Internet.

Sequential access Accessing records in the order in which they are stored. (Contrast with *random access*.)

Sequential processing Processing of files that are ordered numerically or alphabetically by a key field. (Contrast with *random processing*.)

Serial port A direct link with the microcomputer's bus that facilitates the serial transmission of data.

Serial representation The storing of bits, one after another, on a storage medium.

Serial transmission Pertaining to processing data one bit at a time. (Contrast with *parallel transmission*.)

Server application (1) An application running on a network server that works in tandem with a client workstation or PC application. (See also *client application*.) (2) In object linking and embedding, the application in which the linked object originates.

Server computer Any type of computer, from a PC to a supercomputer, that performs a variety of functions for its client computers, including the storage of data and applications software. (See also *client computer*.)

Server program A software program on the server computer that manages resources and can work in conjunction with a client program. (See also *client program*.)

Set A relationship between records in a network database schema.

Shareware Copyrighted software that can be downloaded for free, with its use based on an honor pay system.

Shop bot An intelligent agent that automatically scans Internet e-tailers for the best prices for a desired product.

Shortcut key A key combination that chooses a menu option without the need to display a menu.

SIMM (single in-line memory module) A small circuit board, capable of holding several memory chips, that has a 32-bit data path and can be easily connected to a PC's motherboard. (Contrast with *DIMM*.)

Site license A legal agreement that permits use a software package by a specific number of users.

Smalltalk An object-oriented language.

Smart card A card or badge with an embedded microprocessor.

Soft copy Temporary output that can be interpreted visually, as on a monitor. (Contrast with *hard copy*.)

Soft keyboard A keyboard displayed on a touch-sensitive screen such that when a displayed key is touched with a finger or stylus, the character or command is sent to memory for processing.

Software The programs used to direct the functions of a computer system. (Contrast with *hardware;* related to *program*.)

Software engineer A person who develops software products to bridge the gap between design and executable program code.

Software engineering A term coined to emphasize an approach to software development that embodies the rigors of the engineering discipline.

Software package One or more programs designed to perform a particular processing task.

Software piracy The unlawful duplication of proprietary software. (Related to *pilferage*.)

Software portfolio The mix of software on a PC.

Software suite An integrated collection of software tools that may include a variety of business applications packages.

Sort The rearrangement of fields or records in an ordered sequence by a key field.

Source data Original data that usually involve the recording of a transaction or the documenting of an event or an item.

Source-data automation Entering data directly to a computer system at the source without the need for key entry transcription.

Source document The original hard copy from which data are entered.

Source program The code of the original program (also called *source code*). (Compare with *object program*.)

Spam Unsolicited junk e-mail.

Speech-recognition technology A combination of hardware and software technology that enables voice input to a computer system.

Speech synthesis system A system that converts raw data into electronically produced speech.

Spreadsheet software Refers to software that permits users to work with rows and columns of data.

SQL A type of query language.

Star topology A computer network that involves a centralized host computer connected to a number of smaller computer systems.

Stop bits A data communications parameter that refers to the number of bits in the character or byte.

Streaming audio Internet-based audio that is received and played in a steady, continuous stream.

Streaming video Internet-based video that is received and played in a steady, continuous stream.

Structure chart A chart that graphically illustrates the conceptualization of an information system as a hierarchy of modules.

Structured system design A systems design technique that encourages top-down design.

Stylus A pen-like point-and-draw device.

Subroutine A group or sequence of instructions for a specific programming task that is called by another program.

Supercomputer The category that includes the largest and most powerful computers.

SuperDisk A disk-storage technology that supports very high-density diskettes.

Switched line A telephone line used as a regular data communications channel (also called *dialup line*).

Synchronous dynamic RAM (SDRAM) See *SDRAM*.

Synchronous transmission A communications protocol in which the source and destination points operate in timed alignment to enable

high-speed data transfer. (See also *asynchronous transmission*.)

Syntax The rules that govern the formulation of the instructions in a computer program.

System Any group of components (functions, people, activities, events, and so on) that interface with and complement one another to achieve one or more predefined goals.

System bus An electrical pathway through which the processor sends data and commands to RAM and all peripheral devices.

System development life cycle (SDLC) An approach to system development in which the project team works sequentially through these phases until project completion: review of current system, systems analysis and design, system development, conversion, and implementation.

System life cycle A reference to the four stages of a computer-based information system—birth, development, production, and end-of-life.

System maintenance The process of modifying an information system to meet changing needs.

System programmer A programmer who develops and maintains system programs and software.

System prompt A visual prompt to the user to enter a system command.

Systems analysis The examination of an existing system to determine input, processing, and output requirements for the target system.

Systems analyst A person who does systems analysis.

System software Software that is independent of any specific applications area.

System specifications (specs) Information system details that include everything from the functionality of the system to the format of the system's output screens and reports.

Systems testing A phase of testing where all programs in a system are tested together.

System unit An enclosure containing the computer system's electronic circuitry and various storage devices.

T

T-1 line A high-speed digital link to the Internet (1.544 M bps).

T-3 line A high-speed digital link to the Internet (44.736 M bps).

Tape backup unit (TBU) A magnetic tape drive designed to provide backup for data and programs.

Tape drive, magnetic The hardware device that contains the read/write mechanism for the magnetic tape storage medium. (Compare with *disk drive, magnetic*.)

Tape, magnetic A storage medium for sequential data storage and backup.

Target system A proposed information system that is the object of a systems development effort.

Task The basic unit of work for a processor.

Taskbar In a Windows session, the bar shows what programs are running and available for use.

TCP/IP (Transmission Control Protocol/Internet Protocol) A set of communications protocols developed by the Department of Defense to link dissimilar computers across many kinds of networks.

Telecommunications The collection and distribution of the electronic representation of information between two points.

Telecommuting "Commuting" via a communications link between home and office.

Tele-immersion A virtual reality concept that enables people in remote locations to interact with one another as if they were sharing the same space.

Telemedicine Describes any type of health care administered remotely over communication links.

Telephony The integration of computers and telephones.

Template A model for a particular microcomputer software application.

Terabyte (TB) About one trillion bytes.

Terminal Any device capable of sending and receiving data over a communications channel.

Terminal emulation mode The software transformation of a PC so that its keyboard, monitor, and data interface emulate that of a terminal.

Text cursor A symbol controlled by the arrow keys that shows the location of where the next keyed-in character will appear on the screen.

Text-to-speech software Software that reads text and produces speech.

Thin client A networked workstation that depends on a server computer for much of its processing and for permanent storage.

Thread (newsgroup) An original Internet newsgroup message and any posted replies to that message.

Throughput A measure of computer system efficiency; the rate at which work can be performed by a computer system.

Throwaway system An information system developed to support information for a one-time decision, then discarded.

Thumbnail A miniature display of an image or a page to be viewed or printed.

TIF, TIFF A bit-mapped file format often used in print publishing.

Tiled windows Two or more windows displayed on the screen in a nonoverlapping manner.

Toggle The action of pressing a single key on a keyboard to switch between two or more modes of operation, such as insert and replace.

Token access method A local-area-net protocol in which an electronic token travels around a network giv-ing priority transmission rights to nodes. (See also *Ethernet*.)

Toolbar A group of rectangular graphics in a software packages user interface that represent a frequently used menu option or a command.

Top-level domain (TLD) The highest level in the Internet URL (com, org, edu, and so on).

Touch-screen monitors Monitors with touch-sensitive screens that enable users to choose from available options simply by touching the desired icon or menu item with their finger.

Tower PC A PC that includes a system unit that is designed to rest vertically. (Contrast with *laptop PC* and *desktop PC*.)

Trackball A ball mounted in a box that, when moved, results in a similar movement of the mouse pointer on a display screen.

Track, disk That portion of a magnetic disk-face surface that can be accessed in any given setting of a single read/write head. Tracks are configured in concentric circles.

Trackpad A point-and-draw device with no moving parts that includes a touch-sensitive pad to move the mouse pointer or cursor.

Trackpoint A point-and-draw device that functions like a miniature joystick, but is operated with the tip of the finger.

Tracks per inch (TPI) A measure of the recording density, or spacing, of tracks on a magnetic disk.

Transaction A procedural event in a system that prompts manual or computer-based activity.

Transaction file A file containing records of data activity (transactions); used to update the master file.

Transmission medium The central cable along which terminals, peripheral devices, and microcomputers are connected in a bus topology.

Transparent A reference to a procedure or activity that occurs automatically and does not have to be considered by the user.

Trap door A Trojan horse that permits unauthorized and undetected access to a computer system.

Trojan horse A virus that masquerades as a legitimate program.

TSR (terminate-and-stay-resident) Programs that remain in memory so they can be instantly popped up over the current application by pressing a hotkey.

Tunneling The technology where one network uses the channels of another network to send its data.

Turnaround document A computer-produced output that is ultimately returned to a computer system as a machine-readable input.

Twisted-pair wire A pair of insulated copper wires twisted around each other for use in transmission of telephone conversations and for cabling in local area networks.

Typeface A set of characters that are of the same type style.

U

Unicode A 16-bit encoding system.

Uniform Resource Locator (URL) An Internet address for locating Internet elements, such as server sites, documents, files, bulletin boards (newsgroups), and so on.

Uninterruptible power source (UPS) A buffer between an external power source and a computer system that supplies clean, continuous power.

Unit testing That phase of testing in which the programs that make up an information system are tested individually.

Universal product code (UPC) A 10-digit machine-readable bar code placed on consumer products.

Universal Serial Bus (USB) A bus standard that permits up to 127 peripheral devices to be connected to an external bus.

UNIX A multiuser operating system.

Upload The transmission of data from a local computer to a remote computer.

Upstream rate The data communications rate from client computer to server computer.

Uptime That time when the computer system is in operation.

URL See *uniform resource locator*.

USB 2.0 A second generation USB standard that is 40 times faster than the original.

USB hub A device that expands the number of available USB ports.

USB port (Universal Serial Bus port) A high-speed device interface to which up to 127 peripheral devices can be daisy-chained to a single USB port.

USENET A worldwide network of servers, often hosting newsgroups that can be accessed over the Internet.

User The individual providing input to the computer or using computer output.

User ID A unique character string that is entered at logon to a network to identify the user during personal communications and to the server computer. (See also *screen name*.)

User interface A reference to the software, method, or displays that enable interaction between the user and the software being used.

User liaison A person who serves as the technical interface between the information services department and the user group.

User name Same as *user ID*.

Utility program System software program that can assist with the day-to-day chores associated with computing and maintaining a computer system.

V

Vaccine An antiviral program.

VDT (video display terminal) A terminal on which printed and graphic information are displayed on a television-like monitor and into which data are entered on a typewriter-like keyboard.

Vector graphics A method for maintaining a screen image as patterns of lines, points, and other geometric shapes.

VGA (video graphics array) A circuit board that enables the interfacing of very high-resolution monitors to microcomputers.

Video capture card An expansion card that enables full-motion color video with audio to be captured and played on a monitor or stored on disk.

Video display terminal See *VDT*.

Video editing software Software that facilitates the manipulation of video images.

Video file This file contains digitized video frames that when played rapidly produce motion video.

Video operator's distress syndrome (VODS) Headaches, depression, anxiety, nausea, fatigue, and irritability that result from prolonged interaction with a terminal or PC.

Video RAM (VRAM) RAM on the graphics adapter.

Videophone An Internet-based capability that permits two parties to both see and hear one another during a conversation.

Virtual file allocation table (VFAT) Windows® method for storing and keeping track of files on a disk.

Virtual machine The processing capabilities of one computer system created through software (and sometimes hardware) in a different computer system.

Virtual marketplace A generic reference to the whole of Internet-based retailing.

Virtual memory The effective expansion of the capacity of RAM through the use of software and hard disk storage.

Virtual private network (VPN) A private network over the Internet.

Virtual reality (VR) An artificial environment made possible by hardware and software.

Virtual world An environment that is simulated by hardware and software.

Visual Basic A visual programming language.

Visual C # A visual programming language based on C.

Visual programming An approach to program development that relies more on visual association with tools and menus than with syntax-based instructions.

Voice message switching Using computers, the telephone system, and other electronic means to store and forward voice messages. (Contrast with *electronic mail*.)

Voice-response system A device that enables output from a computer system in the form of user-recorded words, phrases, music, alarms, and so on.

Volatile memory Solid-state semiconductor RAM in which the data are lost when the electrical current is turned off or interrupted. (Contrast with *nonvolatile memory*.)

VPN See *virtual private network*.

W

WAN See *wide area network*.

Wand scanner A handheld OCR scanner.

Wave file A Windows sound file.

Wearable display A display that is worn on a wireless headset.

Wearable PC A small personal computer that is worn.

Web See *World Wide Web*.

Web application developer A person responsible for creating and maintaining one or more Internet sites.

Webcam A digital video camera that sends still and video imagery over the Internet.

Webcast The broadcasting of real-time audio and/or video streams over the Internet.

Web hosting company A company that hosts individual and corporate Web sites on their Internet servers for a fee.

Webmaster An individual who manages a Web site.

Web page A document on the Web that is identified by a unique URL.

Web page design software A Web site authoring system.

Whiteboarding An area on a display screen that permits a document or image to be viewed and worked on simultaneously by several users on the network.

Wide area network (WAN) A computer network that connects nodes in widely dispersed geographic areas. (Contrast with *local area network*.)

Wi-Fi A generic reference to the any IEEE 802.11 communications standard.

Window A rectangular section of a display screen that is dedicated to a specific document, activity, or application.

Windows® A generic reference to all Microsoft Windows operating system products.

Windows® application An application that conforms to the Windows standards for software and operates under the Microsoft Windows platform.

Windows CE .NET A Microsoft operating system that is designed for handheld, pocket PCs, and other small-footprint devices

Windows® 95 An operating system by Microsoft Corporation.

Windows® 98 An operating system by Microsoft Corporation (the successor to Windows 95).

Windows® 2000 A 32-bit operating system by Microsoft Corporation (successor to Windows NT).

Windows® 2003 Server The server-side portion of the Windows XP operating system.

Windows® Me (Millennium Edition) A consumer-oriented operating system by Microsoft Corporation (the successor to Windows 98).

Windows® NT A 32-bit operating system by Microsoft Corporation.

Windows® terminal An intelligent terminal that can run Windows operating systems, but is not designed for stand-alone operation.

Windows® XP An 32-bit operating system by Microsoft Corporation (successor to Windows 2000).

Windows® XP 64-Bit Edition A 64-bit version of Windows XP.

Windows® XP Home Edition The client-side operating system for home and small business.

Windows® XP Professional Edition The client-side operating system for businesses.

Wintel PC A personal computer using a Microsoft Windows® operating system in conjunction with an Intel® or Intel-compatible processor.

Wireless LAN PC card A device to enable a wireless link between a PC and a LAN.

Wireless transceiver Short for *transmitter-receiver,* a device that both transmits and receives data via high-frequency radio waves.

Wizard A utility within an application that helps you use the application to perform a particular task.

WMF (Windows metafile) A popular format for metafiles.

Word (1) For a given computer, an established number of bits that are handled as a unit (bus width). (2) Word processing component of Microsoft Office.

Word processing software Software that uses the computer to enter, store, manipulate, and print text.

Workgroup computing Computer applications that involve cooperation among people linked by a computer network. (Related to *groupware*.)

Workspace The area in a window below the title bar or menu bar containing everything that relates to the application noted in the title bar.

Workstation A high-performance single-user computer system with sophisticated input/output devices that can be easily networked with other workstations or computers.

World Wide Web (the Web, WWW, W3) An Internet server that offers multimedia and hypertext links.

Worm A virus that invades computers via e-mail and IRC.

WORM disk (write-once read-many disk) An optical laser disc that can be read many times after the data are written to it, but the data cannot be changed or erased.

Write To record data on the output medium of a particular I/O device (tape, hard copy, PC display). (Contrast with *read*.)

WYSIWYG (what you see is what you get) A software package in which what is displayed on the screen is very similar in appearance to what you get when the document is printed.

X

XHTML The new standard for Web page development, replacing HTML.

Y

Yahoo! An Internet portal.

Year 2000 problem (Y2K) An information systems problem brought on by the fact that many legacy information systems still treat the year field as two digits (98) rather than four (1998).

Z

Zip® disk The storage medium for Zip drives. (Contrast with *SuperDisk*.)

Zip® drive A storage device that uses optical technology together with magnetic technology to read and write to an interchangeable floppy-size 100, 250, or 750 MB Zip disks.

Zip file A popular file compression format.

Zoned recording Disk recording scheme where zones contain a greater number of sectors per track as you move from the innermost zone to the outermost zone.

Zoom An integrated software command that expands a window to fill the entire screen.

Index

TCP (*see* Transmission Control Protocol)